MCA
Modern Desktop Administrator
Complete Study Guide
Exam MD-100 and Exam MD-101

MCA
Modern Desktop Administrator
Complete Study Guide
Exam MD-100 and Exam MD-101

William Panek

SYBEX®
A Wiley Brand

This book is dedicated to the three ladies of my life: Crystal, Alexandria, and Paige.

Acknowledgments

I would like to thank my wife and best friend, Crystal. She is always the light at the end of my tunnel. I want to thank my two daughters, Alexandria and Paige, for all of their love and support during the writing of all my books. The three of them are my support system and I couldn't do any of this without them.

I want to thank my family, and especially my brothers, Rick, Gary, and Rob. They have always been there for me. I want to thank my father, Richard, who helped me become the man I am today, and my mother, Maggie, for all of her love and support.

I would like to thank all of my friends and co-workers at StormWind Studios (www.stormwindstudios.com). Thanks to all of you for everything that you do. I would not have been able to complete this book without all of your help and support.

I want to thank everyone on my Sybex team, especially my development editor, Mary Ellen Schutz, who helped me make this the best book possible, and Jon Buhagiar, who is the technical editor of this book and an outstanding resource on this book. It's always good to have the very best technical guy backing you up. I want to thank Katie Wisor, who was my production editor, and Judy Flynn for being the copyeditor.

I want to also thank Jon Buhagiar who is my technical proofreader. Special thanks to my acquisitions editor, Kenyon Brown, who was the lead for the entire book. Finally, I want to thank everyone else behind the scenes that helped make this book possible. It's truly an amazing thing to have so many people work on my books to help make them the very best. I can't thank you all enough for your hard work.

About the Author

 **William Panek** holds the following certifications: MCP, MCP+I, MCSA, MCSA+ Security and Messaging, MCSE-NT (3.51 and 4.0), MCSE (2000, 2003, 2012/2012 R2), MCSE+Security and Messaging, MCDBA, MCT, MCTS, MCITP, CCNA, CCDA, and CHFI. Will is also a five-time and current Microsoft MVP winner.

After many successful years in the computer industry, Will decided that he could better use his talents and his personality as an instructor. He began teaching for schools such as Boston University and the University of Maryland, just to name a few. He has done consulting and training for some of the biggest government and corporate companies in the world, including the United States Secret Service, Cisco, United States Air Force, and United States Army.

In 2015, Will became a Sr. Microsoft Instructor for StormWind Studios (www.stormwindstudios.com). He currently lives in New Hampshire with his wife and two daughters. Will was also a Representative in the New Hampshire House of Representatives from 2010 to 2012. In his spare time, he likes to do blacksmithing, shooting (trap and skeet), snowmobiling, playing racquetball, and riding his Harley. Will is also a commercially rated helicopter pilot.

Contents at a Glance

Contents

configure removable devices and how to create and configure storage spaces. Finally, I will show you how to troubleshoot storage and removable devices issues.

Chapter 4: Managing the Windows 10 Environment   This chapter takes you through the different ways to configure the Windows 10 environment, including performing post-installation configuration, configuring Edge and Internet Explorer, configuring mobility settings, configuring sign-in options, and customizing the Windows desktop.

Chapter 5: Configuring Security and Devices   This chapter takes you through the different ways to configure Windows 10 devices, including configuring Windows Defender Firewall and implementing encryption.

Chapter 6: Configuring Network Connectivity   This chapter will show you how to implement and configure Windows networking, including workgroups and domains. I will also talk about HomeGroups and how to configure TCP/IP.

Chapter 7: Configuring Recovery   This chapter will explain to you how to implement and configure Windows backups and recovery points. I will show you how to use cloud -based backups and how to recover the Windows 10 system using advanced boot options.

Part II: MD-101

Chapter 8: Installing and Updating Windows 10   In the first chapter, I explain the requirements and steps to install and configure Windows 10. I will also show you the different versions of Windows 10. This chapter also shows you how to configure automated installation of Windows 10.

Chapter 9: Managing Authentication   This chapter shows you how to configure user authorization and authentication. Understanding how users authenticate onto your network and Azure is one of the most important tasks that administrators must perform. I will also teach you how to manage user profiles.

Chapter 10: Managing Devices   I show you how to implement conditional access and compliance policies for devices. I will show you how to configure device profiles and also how to plan and implement co-management between your on-site network with your Azure based network.

Chapter 11: Planning and Managing Microsoft Intune   This chapter takes you through the different ways to manage Intune device enrollment and inventory. I will also show you how to deploy and update your applications. Finally, I will talk about implanting Mobile Application Management.

Chapter 12: Managing Security   This chapter teaches you how to configure and manage Windows Defender. I will show you how to use Windows Defender Credential Guard, Windows Defender Exploit Guard, Windows Defender Advanced Threat Protection, Windows Defender Application Guard, and Windows Defender Antivirus.

Chapter 13: Configuring Auditing   This chapter will show you how to monitor your different devices. I will also talk about how to monitor the health of your devices using Windows Analytics and cloud-based tools.

What's Included with the Book

There are many helpful items intended to prepare you for the Microsoft 365 Certified: Modern Desktop Administrator Associate certification included in this book:

Assessment Test There is an Assessment Test at the conclusion of the introduction that can be used to quickly evaluate where you are with Windows 10. This test should be taken prior to beginning your work in this book and should help you identify areas in which you are either strong or weak. Note that these questions are purposely more simple than the types of questions you may see on the exams.

Opening List of Objectives Each chapter includes a list of the exam objectives that are covered in that chapter.

Helpful Exercises Throughout the book, I have included step-by-step exercises of some of the more important tasks you should be able to perform. Some of these exercises have corresponding videos that can be downloaded from the book's website. Also, later in this introduction you'll find a recommended home lab setup that will be helpful in completing these tasks.

Video Resources After each chapter summary, if the chapter includes exercises with corresponding videos, a list or description of the exercises with video resources will be provided. The videos can be accessed at www.wiley.com/go/Sybextestprep.

Exam Essentials The end of each chapter also includes a listing of exam essentials. These are essentially repeats of the objectives, but remember that any objective on the exam blueprint could show up on the exam.

Chapter Review Questions Each chapter includes review questions. These are used to assess your understanding of the chapter and are taken directly from the chapter. These questions are based on of the exam objectives and are similar in difficulty to items you might actually receive on the MCA: Windows 10 exams.

 The Sybex Interactive Online Test Bank, flashcards, videos, and glossary can be accessed at www.wiley.com/go/Sybextestprep.

Interactive Online Learning Environment and Test Bank

The interactive online learning environment that accompanies the MCA Modern Desktop Administrator Study Guide, Exam MD-101 study guide provides a test bank with study tools to help you prepare for the certification exams and increase your chances of passing the exam the very first time! The test bank includes the following elements:

Sample Tests   All of the questions in this book are provided, including the assessment test, which you'll find at the end of this introduction, and the chapter tests that include the review questions at the end of each chapter. In addition, there are four practice exams. Use these questions to test your knowledge of the study guide material. The online test bank runs on multiple devices.

Electronic Flashcards   The flashcards are included for quick reference and are great tools for learning quick facts. You can even consider these as additional simple practice questions, which is essentially what they are.

Videos   Some of the exercises include corresponding videos. These videos show you how the author does the exercises. There is also a video that shows you how to set up virtualization so that you can complete the exercises within a virtualized environment. I also have videos to help you on the Microsoft exams at www.youtube.com/c/williampanek.

PDF of Glossary of Terms   There is a glossary included that covers the key terms used in this book.

Recommended Home Lab Setup

To get the most out of this book, you will want to make sure that you complete the exercises throughout the chapters. To complete the exercises, you will need one of two setups. First, you can set up a machine with Windows 10 and complete the labs using a regular Windows 10 machine.

The second way to set up Windows 10 is by using virtualization. I set up Windows 10 as a virtual hard disk (VHD) and I did all the labs this way. The advantages of using virtualization are that you can always just wipe out the system and start over without losing a real server. Plus, you can set up multiple virtual servers and create a full lab environment on one machine.

I created a video for this book showing you how to set up a virtual machine and how to install Windows 10 onto that virtual machine. This video can be seen at www.youtube .com/c/williampanek.

How to Contact Sybex or the Author

Sybex strives to keep you supplied with the latest tools and information you need for your work. Please check the website at www.wiley.com/go/Sybextestprep, where I'll post additional content and updates that supplement this book should the need arise.

You can contact Will Panek by going to his website at www.willpanek.com. Will Panek also has videos and test prep information located at www.youtube.com/c/williampanek. Will also has a Windows 10 Facebook page and a Twitter account @AuthorWillPanek.

Objective Mapping

Table I.1 contains an objective map to show you at-a-glance where you can find each objective covered.

TABLE I.1   MD-100 Objective Map

Objective	Chapter
Deploy Windows (15–20%)	
Deploy Windows 10.	Chapter 1
■ Configure language packs; migrate user data; perform a clean installation; perform an in-place upgrade (using tools such as MDT, WDS, ADK, etc.); select the appropriate Windows edition; troubleshoot activation issues.	Chapter 1
Perform post-installation configuration.	Chapter 4
■ Configure Edge and Internet Explorer; configure mobility settings; configure sign-in options; customize the Windows desktop.	Chapter 4
Manage Devices and Data (35–40%)	
Manage local users, local groups, and devices.	Chapter 2
■ Manage devices in directories; manage local groups; manage local users.	Chapter 2
Configure data access and protection.	Chapter 3
■ Configure NTFS permissions; configure shared permissions.	Chapter 3
Configure devices by using local policies.	Chapter 2
■ Configure local registry; implement local policy; troubleshoot group policies on devices.	Chapter 2

TABLE I.1   MD-100 Objective Map *(continued)*

Objective	Chapter
Manage Windows security.	Chapter 5
■ Configure user account control (UAC); configure Windows Defender Firewall; implement encryption.	Chapter 5
Configure Connectivity (15–20%)	
Configure networking.	Chapter 6
■ Configure client IP settings; configure mobile networking; configure VPN client; troubleshoot networking; configure Wi-Fi profiles.	Chapter 6
Configure remote connectivity.	Chapter 2
■ Configure remote management; enable PowerShell Remoting; configure remote desktop access.	Chapter 2
Maintain Windows (25–30%)	
Configure system and data recovery.	Chapter 7
■ Perform file recovery (including OneDrive); recover Windows 10; troubleshoot startup/boot process.	Chapter 7
Manage updates.	Chapter 1
■ Check for updates; troubleshoot updates; validate and test updates; select the appropriate servicing channel; configure Windows update options.	Chapter 1
Monitor and manage Windows.	Chapter 7
■ Configure and analyze event logs; manage performance; manage Windows 10 environment.	Chapter 7

TABLE I.2   MD-101 Objective Map

Objective	Chapter
Deploy and update operating systems (35-40%)	
Plan and implement Windows 10 by using dynamic deployment	**Chapter 8**
<ul><li>evaluate and select an appropriate deployment options</li><li>pilot deployment</li><li>manage and troubleshoot provisioning packages</li></ul>	Chapter 8
Plan and implement Windows 10 by using Windows Autopilot	**Chapter 8**
<ul><li>evaluate and select an appropriate deployment options</li><li>pilot deployment</li><li>create, validate, and assign deployment profile</li><li>extract device HW information to CSV file</li><li>import device HW information to cloud service</li><li>troubleshoot deployment</li></ul>	Chapter 8
Upgrade devices to Windows 10	**Chapter 8**
<ul><li>identify upgrade and downgrade paths</li><li>manage in-place upgrades</li><li>configure a Windows analytics environment</li><li>perform Upgrade Readiness assessment</li><li>migrate user profiles</li></ul>	Chapter 8
Manage updates	**Chapter 8**
<ul><li>configure Windows 10 delivery optimization</li><li>configure Windows Update for Business</li><li>deploy Windows updates</li><li>implement feature updates</li><li>monitor Windows 10 updates</li></ul>	Chapter 8
Manage device authentication	**Chapter 9**
<ul><li>manage authentication policies</li><li>manage sign-on options</li><li>perform Azure AD join</li></ul>	Chapter 9

TABLE I.2   MD-101 Objective Map *(continued)*

Objective	Chapter
Manage Intune device enrollment and inventory	**Chapter 11**
<ul><li>configure enrollment settings</li><li>configure Intune automatic enrollment</li><li>enable device enrollment</li><li>enroll non-Windows devices</li><li>enroll Windows devices</li><li>generate custom device inventory reports' Review device inventory</li></ul>	Chapter 11
Monitor devices	**Chapter 13**
<ul><li>monitor device health (e.g., log analytics, Windows Analytics, or other cloud-based tools, etc.)</li><li>monitor device security</li></ul>	Chapter 13
Manage apps and data (10-15%)	
Deploy and update applications	**Chapter 11**
<ul><li>assign apps to groups</li><li>deploy apps by using Intune</li><li>deploy apps by using Microsoft Store for Business</li><li>deploy O365 ProPlus</li><li>enable sideloading of apps into images</li><li>gather Office readiness data</li><li>configure and implement kiosk (assigned access) or public devices</li></ul>	Chapter 11
Implement Mobile Application Management (MAM)	**Chapter 11**
<ul><li>implement MAM policies</li><li>manage MAM policies</li><li>plan MAM</li><li>configure Windows Information Protection</li><li>implement Azure Information Protection templates</li><li>securing data by using Intune</li></ul>	Chapter 11

Assessment Tests

MD-100

1. You want to create roaming profiles for users in the Sales department. They frequently log on at computers in a central area. The profiles should be configured as mandatory and roaming profiles. Which users are able to manage mandatory profiles on Windows 10 computers?

   A. The user who uses the profile

   B. Server operators

   C. Power users

   D. Administrators

2. What filename extension is applied by default to custom consoles that are created for the MMC?

   A. .mmc

   B. .msc

   C. .con

   D. .mcn

3. You are the IT administrator for a large computer-training company that uses laptops for all its employees. Currently the users have to connect to the wireless network through the wireless network adapter. Windows 10 now includes this built in as which feature?

   A. Available Network Finder (ANF)

   B. View Networks (VN)

   C. Network Availability Viewer (NAV)

   D. View Available Networks (VAN)

4. If you wanted to require that a user enter an administrator password to perform administrative tasks, what type of user account should you create for the user?

   A. Administrator user account

   B. Standard user account

   C. Power user account

   D. Authenticated user account

5. You have installed a clean installation of Windows 10 on your computer. You want to create an image of the new installation to use as a basis for remote installs. What Windows 10 utility should you use to accomplish this?

   A. WDS

   B. Windows SIM

   C. ImageX

   D. Sysprep

6. You are the administrator in charge of a computer that runs both Windows 7 and Windows 10. Windows 10 is installed on a different partition from Windows 7. You have to make sure that the computer always starts Windows 7 by default. What action should you perform?

    A. Run bcdedit.exe and the /default parameter.

    B. Run bcdedit.exe and the /bootcd parameter.

    C. Create a boot.ini file in the root of the Windows 10 partition.

    D. Create a boot.ini file in the root of the Windows 7 partition.

7. You have a user with limited vision. Which accessibility utility is used to read aloud screen text, such as the text in dialog boxes, menus, and buttons?

    A. Read-Aloud

    B. Orator

    C. Dialog Manager

    D. Narrator

8. You have just purchased a new computer that has Windows 10 preinstalled. You want to migrate existing users from a previous computer that was running Windows XP Professional. Which two files would you use to manage this process through the User State Migration Tool? (Choose two.)

    A. usmt.exe

    B. scanState.exe

    C. loadState.exe

    D. windows7migrate.exe

9. You are using Windows 10 Home and you want to update your video drivers. How do you accomplish this?

    A. Install new drivers using Driver Manager.

    B. Upgrade the drivers using Device Manager.

    C. Upgrade the drivers using Driver Manager.

    D. Install new drivers using Device Manager.

10. You are the network administrator for a large organization. You have a Windows 10 machine that is working fine, but you downloaded and installed a newer version of the network adapter driver. After you load the driver, the network device stops working properly. Which tool should you use to help you fix the problem?

    A. Driver rollback

    B. Driver Repair utility

    C. Reverse Driver application

    D. Windows 10 Driver Compatibility tool

11. You are the network administrator for your organization. Your organization has been using Windows 10 Enterprise. You need to run the Print Management tools from the command prompt. What command do you run?

A. printmgmt.exe

B. printMig.exe

C. prtmgmt.exe

D. printbrm.exe

12. You are configuring power settings on your laptop. You configure the laptop to enter sleep mode after a specified period of inactivity. Which of the following will occur when the computer enters sleep mode?

A. The computer will be shut down gracefully.

B. Data will be saved to the hard disk.

C. The monitor and hard disk will be turned off, but the computer will remain in a fully active state.

D. The user session will not be available when you resume activity on the computer.

13. You are the administrator for a large organization that is moving to Windows 10. You need to set up a way that you can run multiple storage commands from a scripting tool. How can you set this up?

A. Use SCCM for scripting.

B. Use PowerShell for scripting.

C. Use AD FS for scripting.

D. Use Disk Administrator scripting.

14. What is the CIDR equivalent for 255.255.255.224?

A. /24

B. /25

C. /26

D. /27

15. You have compressed a 4 MB file into 2 MB. You are copying the file to another computer that has a FAT32 partition. How can you ensure that the file will remain compressed?

A. When you copy the file, use the XCOPY command with the /Comp switch.

B. When you copy the file, use the Windows Explorer utility and specify the option Keep Existing Attributes.

C. On the destination folder, make sure that you set the option Compress Contents To Save Disk Space in the folder's properties.

D. You can't maintain disk compression on a non-NTFS partition.

16. You are the network administrator for Stellacon. Your network consists of 200 Windows 10 computers, and you want to assign static IP addresses rather than use a DHCP server. You want to configure the computers to reside on the 192.168.10.0 network. What subnet mask should you use with this network address?

    A. 255.0.0.0

    B. 255.255.0.0

    C. 255.255.255.0

    D. 255.255.255.255

17. You are using a laptop running Windows 10 Home. You want to synchronize files between your laptop and a network folder. Which of the following actions must you perform first in order to enable synchronization to occur between your laptop and the network folder?

    A. Upgrade your laptop to Windows 10 Enterprise.

    B. Enable one-way synchronization between the laptop and the network folder.

    C. Enable two-way synchronization between the laptop and the network folder.

    D. Configure the files on your laptop as read-only.

18. You have a DNS server that contains corrupt information. You fix the problem with the DNS server, but one of your users is complaining that they are still unable to access Internet resources. You verify that everything works on another computer on the same subnet. Which command can you use to fix the problem?

    A. `ipconfig /flush`

    B. `ipconfig /flushdns`

    C. `ping /flush`

    D. `DNS /flushdns`

19. You are the network administrator for a medium-sized company. Rick was the head of HR and recently resigned. John has been hired to replace Rick and has been given Rick's laptop. You want John to have access to all of the resources to which Rick had access. What is the easiest way to manage the transition?

    A. Rename Rick's account to John.

    B. Copy Rick's account and call the copied account John.

    C. Go into the Registry and do a search and replace to replace all of Rick's entries with John's name.

    D. Take ownership of all of Rick's resources and assign John Full Control to the resources.

20. Which of the following statements are true regarding the creation of a group in Windows 10? (Choose two.)

    A. Only members of the Administrators group can create users on a Windows 10 computer.

    B. Group names can be up to 64 characters.

    C. Group names can contain spaces.

    D. Group names can be the same as usernames but not the same as other group names on the computer.

21. You need to expand the disk space on your Windows 10 computer. You are considering using spanned volumes. Which of the following statements are true concerning spanned volumes? (Choose all that apply.)

A. Spanned volumes can contain space from 2 to 32 physical drives.

B. Spanned volumes can contain space from 2 to 24 physical drives.

C. Spanned volumes can be formatted as FAT32 or NTFS partitions.

D. Spanned volumes can be formatted only as NTFS partitions.

22. You have a network folder that resides on an NTFS partition on a Windows 10 computer. NTFS permissions and share permissions have been applied. Which of the following statements best describes how share permissions and NTFS permissions work together if they have been applied to the same folder?

A. The NTFS permissions will always take precedence.

B. The share permissions will always take precedence.

C. The system will look at the cumulative share permissions and the cumulative NTFS permissions. Whichever set is less restrictive will be applied.

D. The system will look at the cumulative share permissions and the cumulative NTFS permissions. Whichever set is more restrictive will be applied.

23. Your home computer network is protected by a firewall. You have configured your Windows 10 home computer to use Windows Mail. After you configure your email accounts, you discover that you are unable to send email messages from Windows Mail. Your email provider uses POP3 and SMTP. What should you do on the firewall?

A. Open the Pop3 and SMTP Ports.

B. Turn off the firewall for Pop3 and SMTP.

C. Use an application that is accepted on the firewall.

D. Disable the firewall.

24. You need Windows 10 to be the primary operating system on a dual-boot machine. Which file do you configure for this?

A. boot.ini

B. bcdedit

C. bcboot.ini

D. bcdboot

25. Which of the following versions of Windows 10 can be upgraded to Windows 10 Enterprise edition? (Choose all that apply.)

A. Windows 8 Home

B. Windows 8 Professional

C. Windows 8 Home Premium

D. Windows 8 Enterprise

26. You are configuring a Windows 10 computer that is going to be used by your children. You are configuring access restrictions using the Parental Controls feature of Windows 10. Which of the following can be configured by setting Parental Controls? (Choose all that apply.)

   A. When your children can access the computer

   B. Which websites your children can view

   C. Which programs your children can access

   D. Which other computers on your home network your children can access

27. How do you access the Advanced Boot Options menu in Windows 10 during the boot process?

   A. Hold the Shift key down and choose the Restart option.

   B. Press F6.

   C. Press F8.

   D. Press F10.

28. You have a computer that runs Windows 10. Your computer has two volumes, C: and D:. Both volumes are formatted by using the NTFS filesystem. You need to disable previous versions on the D: volume. What should you do?

   A. From System Properties, modify the System Protection settings.

   B. From the properties of the D: volume, modify the Quota settings.

   C. From the properties of the D: volume, modify the Sharing settings.

   D. From the Disk Management Snap-in, convert the hard disk drive that contains the D: volume to Dynamic.

29. Which utility is used to upgrade a FAT32 partition to NTFS?

   A. UPFS

   B. UPGRADE

   C. Disk Manager

   D. Convert

30. If you want to use Device Health Attestation on your network or in the cloud, what port should you open on the firewall?

   A. 25

   B. 110

   C. 443

   D. 995

MD-101

31. You need to automatically register all the existing computers to the Azure AD network and also enroll all of the computers in Intune. What should you use?

A. Use a DNS Autodiscover address record.

B. Use a Windows Autopilot deployment profile.

C. Use an Autodiscover service connection point (SCP).

D. Set up a Group Policy Object (GPO).

32. You have a Windows 10 Windows Image (WIM) that is mounted. You need to view the list of third-party drivers installed on the WIM. What should you do?

A. Run DISM and specify the /get-drivers parameter.

B. Run Driverquery.exe and use the /si parameter.

C. From Device Manager, view all hidden drivers.

D. From Windows Explorer, open the mount folder.

33. You have a computer that runs Windows 10 Pro. The computer is joined to Azure Active Directory (Azure AD) and enrolled in Microsoft Intune. You need to upgrade the computer to Windows 10 Enterprise for another user. What should you configure in Intune?

A. Windows Autopilot device profile

B. A device enrollment policy

C. A device cleanup rule

D. A device compliance policy

34. You decide to install Windows Deployment Services (WDS). You are using a Windows Server 2019 domain and have verified that your network meets the requirements for using WDS. What command-line utility can you use to configure the WDS server?

A. dism.exe

B. wdsutil.exe

C. setup.exe

D. The WDS icon in Control Panel

35. You have installed a clean installation of Windows 10 on your computer. You want to create an image of the new installation to use as a basis for remote installs. What Windows 10 utility should you use to accomplish this?

A. WDS

B. Windows SIM

C. DISM

D. Sysprep

36. You are the administrator in charge of a computer that runs both Windows 7 and Windows 10. Windows 10 is installed on a different partition from Windows 7. You have to make sure that the computer always starts Windows 7 by default. What action should you perform?

   A. Run bcdedit.exe and the /default parameter.

   B. Run bcdedit.exe and the /bootcd parameter.

   C. Create a boot.ini file in the root of the Windows 10 partition.

   D. Create a boot.ini file in the root of the Windows 7 partition.

37. An administrator wants to look at an Azure Active Directory application policy for your user's applications. What PowerShell command would you use to accomplish this task?

   A. Add-AzureADPolicy

   B. Add-AzureADApplicationPolicy

   C. Create-AzurePolicy

   D. Install-AzureADPolicy

38. Your boss has asked you about Azure security and making sure that user logins are secure. What feature can you explain to your boss to ease their concerns?

   A. Azure AD User Security

   B. Azure AD Identity Protection

   C. Azure AD Security add-on

   D. Azure Identity Protection

39. An administrator wants to change an Azure Active Directory policy for one of their users. What PowerShell command would you use to accomplish this task?

   A. New-AzureADPolicy

   B. Edit-AzureADPolicy

   C. New-AzurePolicy

   D. Set-AzureADPolicy

40. An administrator wants to view their Azure AD directory settings for the company's Azure AD subscription. What PowerShell command would you use to accomplish this task?

   A. View-AzureADDirectorySetting

   B. Get-AzureADDirectorySetting

   C. Add-AzureADDirectorySetting

   D. Set-AzureADDirectorySetting

41. You need to upgrade 100 Windows 10 Pro computers to Windows 10 Enterprise. What should you configure in Intune?

   A. A device enrollment policy

   B. A device cleanup rule

   C. A device compliance policy

   D. A device configuration profile

42. An administrator needs to create a device configuration profile in Microsoft Intune. You need to implement an ADMX-backed policy. Which profile type should you use?

   A. Identity protection

   B. Custom

   C. Device restrictions

   D. System restrictions

43. You need to set up a Windows 10 system in a break room where all employees can use it. Which device configuration profile type should you use?

   A. Kiosk

   B. Endpoint protection

   C. Identity protection

   D. Device restrictions

44. You have compressed a 4 MB file into 2 MB. You are copying the file to another computer that has a FAT32 partition. How can you ensure that the file will remain compressed?

   A. When you copy the file, use the `xcopy.exe` command with the `/comp` switch.

   B. When you copy the file, use the Windows Explorer utility and specify the option Keep Existing Attributes.

   C. On the destination folder, make sure that you set the option Compress Contents To Save Disk Space in the folder's properties.

   D. You can't maintain disk compression on a non-NTFS partition.

45. An administrator suspects that a problem in Windows 10 is related to the files being spread over the disk. What utility can be used to store the files contiguously on the disk?

   A. Disk Defragmenter

   B. Disk Manager

   C. Disk Administrator

   D. Disk Cleanup

46. When your users get added to Intune and get licensed, how many devices can each user use by default?

   A. 14

   B. 15

   C. 16

   D. 17

47. How do you allow your tablets to connect to your cell phones for Internet access?

   A. Configure the broadband connection as a metered network.

   B. Turn on cellular tethering.

   C. Enable tablet tethering.

   D. Enable tablet metering in the tablets settings.

48. An administrator needs to secure some of the Microsoft operating system's loopholes that hackers use. What type of updates would you need to install to help solve this problem?

  A. Security Updates

  B. Definition Updates

  C. Critical Updates

  D. Software Updates

49. You want to enable self-service password reset on the sign-in screen. Which settings should you configure from the Microsoft Intune blade?

  A. Device configuration

  B. Device compliance

  C. Device enrollment

  D. Conditional access

50. What do you need to do to be sure that all iOS devices can be managed by the Intune Administrators?

  A. Add an Employee Portal app from the Apple App Store.

  B. Create a device enrollment manager account.

  C. Configure an Intune Service Connector for Exchange.

  D. Import an Apple Push Notification service (APNs) certificate.

51. Your work computer network is protected by a firewall. You have configured your Windows 10 computer to use HTTPS. What port should you open on the firewall?

  A. 25

  B. 110

  C. 443

  D. 995

52. Your home computer network is protected by a firewall. You have configured your Windows 10 home computer to use Windows Mail. After you configure your email accounts, you discover that you are unable to send email messages from Windows Mail. Your email provider uses POP3 and SMTP. What port should you open on the firewall?

  A. 25

  B. 110

  C. 443

  D. 995

53. Your company is using Microsoft Azure Active Directory and all computers are enrolled in Microsoft Intune with EMS. The administrator needs to make sure that only approved applications are allowed to run on all of these computers. What should you implement to ensure this?

   A. Windows Defender Credential Guard

   B. Windows Defender Exploit Guard

   C. Windows Defender Application Control

   D. Windows Defender Antivirus

54. What two ports use FTP?

   A. Ports 12 and 15

   B. Ports 20 and 21

   C. Ports 80 and 443

   D. Ports 80 and 110

55. You have a Windows 10 machine that has a virus that was caused by a malicious font. You need to stop this type of threat from affecting your corporate computers in the future. What should you use?

   A. Windows Defender Exploit Guard

   B. Windows Defender Application Guard

   C. Windows Defender Credential Guard

   D. Windows Defender System Guard

56. What port does DNS use?

   A. Port 20

   B. Ports 25

   C. Ports 53

   D. Ports 80

57. The IT manager wants CPU utilization, disk utilization, and memory utilization all included in the data collected. How should you accomplish this?

   A. Create a User Defined Data Collector set.

   B. Create a custom performance set.

   C. Create a Trace event.

   D. Create a session Data Collector set.

58. You need to use a Microsoft Azure monitoring tool to monitor devices and change settings. Which of the following tools can you use?

   A. Performance Monitor

   B. Microsoft Azure IoT Central Application

   C. Azure Performance Center

   D. Intune Performance Center

59. You need to stop an application from running in Task Manager. Which tab would you use to stop an application from running?

   A. Performance

   B. Users

   C. Options

   D. Details

60. You have a computer named Portable1. You need to view the events collected from Portable1. Which query would an administrator run in Log Analytics?

   A. Eventview | where SourceSystem = = "Portable1"

   B. Eventview | where Computer = = "Portable1"

   C. Event | where SourceSystem = = "Portable1"

   D. Event | where Computer = = "Portable1"

23. A. Port 25 should be opened on the firewall. SMTP is used for outbound mail and uses port 25. POP3, which is used for receiving inbound mail, uses port 110. You need to configure your firewall to allow these ports to be opened. See Chapter 5 for more information.

24. B. You should configure the bcdedit utility to configure your boot order. See Chapter 1 for more information.

25. B, D. You can upgrade Windows 8 Professional and Windows 8 Enterprise to Windows 10 Enterprise edition. See Chapter 1 for more information.

26. A, B, C. Using Parental Controls, you can configure which websites your children can access, when they can use the computer, which games they can play, and which programs they can run, and you can view reports regarding their activity. See Chapter 2 for more information.

27. A. Hold the Shift key down and choose the Restart option to access the Advanced Boot Options menu. You can do this within the Windows 10 operating system or at the sign-in screen. See Chapter 7 for more information.

28. A. If you need to disable previous versions on the D: volume, this needs to be done from the System Protection settings from the computer system properties. See Chapter 4 for more information.

29. D. The Convert utility is used to convert a FAT32 partition to NTFS. See Chapter 5 for more information.

30. C. Internet communication needs to be established between your Configuration Manager Client agent and has.spserv.microsoft.com (port 443) Health Attestation service. See Chapter 2 for more information.

MD-101

31. B. Windows Autopilot profiles allow an administrator to choose how the Windows 10 system will be set up and configured on Azure AD and Intune. See Chapter 1 for more information.

32. A. The DISM utility with the /get-drivers switch allows you to find out which drivers are installed on the WIM. See Chapter 1 for more information.

33. A. Windows Autopilot profiles allow an administrator to choose how the Windows 10 system will be set up and configured on Azure AD and Intune. See Chapter 1 for more information.

34. B. wdsutil.exe is a command-line utility that can be used to configure the WDS server. Several other configuration options need to be specified on the WDS server, and you can set them using wdsutil.exe. See Chapter 1 for more information.

35. C. You can use the DISM utility to create an image of a Windows 10 installation. After the image has been created, you can prepare the image with a utility such as the System Preparation Tool (Sysprep). The image can then be used for remote installations of Windows 10. See Chapter 1 for more information.

36. A. The Boot Configuration Data (BCD) store contains boot information parameters that were previously found in boot.ini in older versions of Windows. To edit the boot options in the BCD store, use the bcdedit utility, which can be launched only from a command prompt. See Chapter 1 for more information.

37. B. Administrators can use the Add-AzureADApplicationPolicy command to add an application policy. See Chapter 2 for more information.

38. B. Azure AD Identity Protection allows an Azure administrator to use the same type of protection that Microsoft uses to protect and secure users' identities. See Chapter 2 for more information.

39. D. Administrators can use the Set-AzureADPolicy command to update an Azure AD policy. See Chapter 2 for more information.

40. B. Administrators can use the Get-AzureADDirectorySetting command to view their directory settings. See Chapter 2 for more information.

41. D. You can upgrade your devices by using a device configuration profile. The option that you want to configure is Edition Upgrade. Edition Upgrade allows you to upgrade Windows 10 (and later) devices to a newer version of Windows. See Chapter 3 for more information.

42. B. One of the options you have in device configuration profiles is the ability to set up custom profiles. Custom profile settings allow an Intune administrator to configure options that are not automatically included with Intune. See Chapter 3 for more information.

43. A. Kiosk systems are normally designed in a location where many people can use the same device and that device will only run limited applications. See Chapter 3 for more information.

44. D. Windows 10 data compression is supported only on NTFS partitions. If you move the file to a FAT32 partition, then it will be stored as uncompressed. See Chapter 3 for more information.

45. A. The Disk Defragmenter utility is used to rearrange files so that they are stored contiguously on the disk. This optimizes access to those files. You can also defragment disks through the command-line utility Defrag. See Chapter 3 for more information.

46. B. By default, licensed users can add up to 15 devices to their accounts. Device Administrators have the ability to add devices to Intune, but users do have the ability to enroll 15 devices on their own. See Chapter 4 for more information.

47. B. Tethering means that users can connect one device to another for Internet services. See Chapter 4 for more information.

48. A. Security updates are updates that need to be applied to fix a security issue. These security issues are used by hackers to either hack into a device or software. See Chapter 4 for more information.

49. A. You will want to configure device configuration settings. To do this, sign in to the Azure portal and click Intune. Create a new device configuration profile by going to Device Configuration ➤ Profiles ➤ Create Profile. See Chapter 4 for more information.

50. D. An Apple Push Notification service (APNs) certificate must be imported from Apple so that the company can manage iOS devices. See Chapter 4 for more information.

51. C. Port 443 should be opened on the firewall. Simple Mail Transfer Protocol (SMTP) is used for outbound mail and uses port 25. Post Office Protocol (POP3), which is used for receiving inbound mail, uses port 110. See Chapter 5 for more information.

52. A. Port 25 should be opened on the firewall. Simple Mail Transfer Protocol (SMTP) is used for outbound mail and uses port 25. Post Office Protocol (POP3), which is used for receiving inbound mail, uses port 110. See Chapter 5 for more information.

53. C. Administrators can use Windows Defender Application Control to ensure that only applications that you explicitly allow can run on the Windows 10 computers. See Chapter 5 for more information.

54. B. File Transfer Protocol (FTP) servers use port 20 and port 21. See Chapter 5 for more information.

55. A. Windows Defender Exploit Guard helps protect your system from common malware hacks that use executable files and scripts to attack applications like Microsoft Office. See Chapter 5 for more information.

56. C. Domain Name System (DNS) servers use Port 53. See Chapter 5 for more information.

57. A. Data Collector Sets are used to collect data into a log so that the data can be reviewed. You can view the log files with Performance Monitor. See Chapter 6 for more information.

58. B. Use Microsoft Azure Internet of Things (IoT) Central Application to monitor devices and change settings. Azure IoT Central Applications are hosted by Microsoft, which reduces the administration overhead of managing applications. See Chapter 6 for more information.

59. D. All of the applications that are running on the Windows 10 machine will show up under the Details tab. Right-click the application and end the process. See Chapter 6 for more information.

60. D. Administrator can view the events collected from a specific computer in Azure is to run a query in the Logs Analytics. See Chapter 6 for more information.

Exam MD-100

Chapter

1

Windows 10 Installation

MICROSOFT EXAM OBJECTIVES COVERED IN THIS CHAPTER:

✓ **Deploy Windows 10**

- Configure language packs; migrate user data; perform a clean installation; perform an in-place upgrade (using tools such as MDT, WDS, ADK, etc.); select the appropriate Windows edition; troubleshoot activation issues.

✓ **Manage updates**

- Check for updates; troubleshoot updates; validate and test updates; select the appropriate servicing channel; configure Windows update options.

This book is for exam MD-100, and this is the first of two Windows 10 exams (MD-100 and MD-101) for the Microsoft 365 Certified: Modern Desktop Administrator Associate. If you are using both of the Sybex books for the Microsoft 365 Certified: Modern Desktop Administrator Associate certification, you will notice that many of the topics in Chapter 1 are the same in both books. The reason for this is that no matter what test you take, the process for installing Windows 10 is the same. Let me be the first to welcome you to Windows 10 and the beginning of a new journey.

But as with the start of any journey, we must take our first steps. The first step for this exam is to learn about the Windows 10 installation process. It is important that you understand the different versions of Windows 10 and which one is right for you and your organization.

In this chapter, I will show you the many different features of Windows 10, and then I will describe each edition. I will then show you how to install Windows 10 and also how to do an upgrade from a previous version.

Before you can install Windows 10, you must first be sure your hardware meets the minimum requirements and is supported by the operating system. After we install the Windows 10 operating system, I will show you how to get updates for the Windows 10 system.

Understanding the Basics

Microsoft Windows 10 is the latest version of Microsoft's client operating system software and, according to Microsoft, its last. Microsoft has announced that Windows 10 will be the last client operating system and it will just continue to do version updates. Windows 10 combines the best of Windows 7 and Windows 8, and it also makes it much easier to work within the cloud.

Microsoft has released many different versions of the Windows 10 operating system. The following list is just a few of the more popular versions:

- Windows 10 Home
- Windows 10 Pro
- Windows 10 Pro for Workstation
- Windows 10 Enterprise
- Windows 10 Enterprise E3
- Windows 10 Enterprise E5
- Windows 10 Education

Microsoft also offers some of these operating systems as slimmed down versions called "Windows 10 IoT Core." This version is one of the above Windows 10 versions that doesn't require a monitor or system. For example, you are building a toy robot and you want to load Windows 10 into your core computer. You can use the IoT versions to run the robot's functionality.

Windows 10 has been improved in many of the weak areas that plagued Windows 8. Windows 10 has a much faster boot time and shutdown compared to Windows 8. It also brings back the previous Start button that we are all so familiar with from previous editions.

The Windows 10 operating system functions are also faster than their previous counterparts. The processes for opening, moving, extracting, compressing, and installing files and folders are more efficient than they were in previous versions of Microsoft's client operating systems.

Let's take a look at some of the features of each Windows 10 edition (this is just an overview of some of the benefits to using Windows 10). Table 1.1 and Table 1.2 show each edition and what some of the features are for those editions.

 The information in Table 1.1 and Table 1.2 was taken directly from Microsoft's website and documentation.

TABLE 1.1   Windows 10 Security and Protection

Description	Home	Pro	Pro for Workstation	E3	E5
Integrity enforcement of operating system boot up process	▪	▪	▪	▪	▪
Integrity enforcement of sensitive operating system components	▪	▪	▪	▪	▪
Advanced vulnerability and zero-day exploit mitigations	▪	▪	▪	▪	▪
Reputation based network protection for Microsoft Edge, Internet Explorer, and Chrome	▪	▪	▪	▪	▪
Host based firewall	▪	▪	▪	▪	▪
Ransomware mitigations	▪	▪	▪	▪	▪
Pre-execution emulation executables and scripts	▪	▪	▪	▪	▪
Runtime behavior monitoring	▪	▪	▪	▪	▪

TABLE 1.1   Windows 10 Security and Protection *(continued)*

Description	Home	Pro	Pro for Workstation	E3	E5
In memory anomaly and behavior monitoring	▪	▪	▪	▪	▪
Machine learning and AI based protection from viruses and malware threats	▪	▪	▪	▪	▪
Cloud protection for fastest responses to new/unknown web-based threats	▪	▪	▪	▪	▪
Protection from fileless based attacks	▪	▪	▪	▪	▪
Industry standards based multifactor authentication	▪	▪	▪	▪	▪
Support for biometrics (Facial and Fingerprints)	▪	▪	▪	▪	▪
Support for Microsoft Authenticator	▪	▪	▪	▪	▪
Support for Microsoft compatible security devices	▪	▪	▪	▪	▪
Automatic encryption on capable devices	▪	▪	▪	▪	▪
Advanced encryption configuration options		▪	▪	▪	▪
Removable storage protection		▪	▪	▪	▪
Supports for Active Directory and Azure Active Directory		▪	▪	▪	▪
Hardware based isolation for Microsoft Edge		▪	▪	▪	▪
Application control powered by the Intelligent Security Graph		▪	▪	▪	▪
Device Control (e.g., USB)		▪	▪	▪	▪
Personal and business data separation		▪	▪	▪	▪
Application access control		▪	▪	▪	▪
Copy and paste protection		▪	▪	▪	▪

Description	Home	Pro	Pro for Workstation	E3	E5
Removable storage protection		▪	▪	▪	▪
Integration with Microsoft Information Protection		▪	▪	▪	▪
Network protection for web-based threats				▪	▪
Enterprise management of hardware-based isolation for Microsoft Edge				▪	▪
Hardware isolation of single sign-in tokens				▪	▪
Direct Access & Always On VPN device Tunnel				▪	▪
Centralized configuration mgmt, analytics, reporting, and security operations					▪
Centralized management, analytics, reporting, and operations					▪
Customizable network protection for web-based threats					▪
Host intrusion prevention rules					▪
Device-based conditional access					▪
Tamper protection of operating system					▪
Advanced monitoring, analytics, and reporting for attack surface					▪
Advanced machine learning and AI based protection for apex level viruses and malware threats					▪
Advanced cloud protection that includes deep inspection and detonation					▪
Emergency outbreak protection from the Intelligent Security Graph					▪
ISO 27001 compliance					▪

TABLE 1.1   Windows 10 Security and Protection *(continued)*

Description	Home	Pro	Pro for Workstation	E3	E5
Geolocation and sovereignty of sample data					▪
Sample data retention policy					▪
Monitoring, analytics, and reporting for Next Generation Protection capabilities					▪

TABLE 1.2   Windows 10 Updates

Description	Home	Pro	Pro for Workstation	E3	E5
In-place upgrades	▪	▪	▪	▪	▪
Express updates	▪	▪	▪	▪	▪
Delivery optimization	▪	▪	▪	▪	▪
Windows Analytics Upgrade Readiness		▪	▪	▪	▪
Windows Analytics Update Compliance		▪	▪	▪	▪
Windows Update for Business		▪	▪	▪	▪
Windows Analytics Device Health				▪	▪
30 months of support for September targeted releases				▪	▪
Windows 10 LTSC Access				▪	▪

Windows 10 Features

Now that you have seen which editions contain which features, let's take a look at some of the Windows 10 features in greater detail. This section describes only a few of these features, but all features will be explained throughout this book.

Cortana Integration   Windows 10 comes with Cortana integration. Cortana is your very own personal assistant. You can type in or ask Cortana a question and Cortana will seek out the best possible answer based on your question.

Secure Boot   Windows 10 provides the ability for securely booting the operating system. Secure boot validates all drivers and operating system components before they are loaded against the signature database.

Virtual Smart Cards   Windows 10 has started offering a new way to do two-factor authentication with virtual smart cards. Virtual smart cards help an IT department that doesn't want to invest in extra hardware and smart cards. Virtual smart cards use Trusted Platform Module (TPM) devices that allow for the same capabilities as physical smart cards with the physical hardware.

Miracast   Windows 10 allows you to project your Windows 10 laptop or mobile device to a projector or television. Miracast allows you to connect to an external device through the use of your mobile wireless display (WiDi) adapter.

Hyper-V   Windows 10 (except Home version) come with Hyper-V built into the operating system. Hyper-V is Microsoft's version of a Virtual Server.

Enterprise Data Protection   Windows 10 Enterprise Data Protection (EDP) helps protect corporate data in a world that is increasingly becoming a Bring Your Own Device (BYOD) environment. Since many organizations are allowing employees to connect their own devices to their network, the possibility of corporate data being compromised because of non-corporate programs running on these personnel devices is increasing. For example, many third-party apps may put corporate data at risk by accidently disclosing corporate information through the application.

Enterprise Data Protection helps protect information by separating corporate applications and corporate data from being disclosed by personal devices and personal applications.

Device Guard   Because employees can use multiple types of Windows 10 devices (Surface Pros, Windows Phones, and Windows 10 computer systems), Device Guard is a feature that helps guarantee that only trusted applications will run on any of these devices.

Device Guard uses both hardware and software security features to lock down a device so it can run only trusted and approved applications. This also helps protect against hackers from running malicious software on these devices.

Microsoft Passport / Windows Hello   Microsoft has introduced two security features for Windows 10 called Windows Hello and Microsoft Passport. Windows Hello is a biometrics' system integrated into Windows10 and it is a piece of the user's authentication experience. Microsoft Passport allows users to use a two-factor authentication system that combines a PIN or biometrics with an encrypted key from a user's device to provide two-factor authentication.

Start Menu   Windows 10 has brought back the Start Menu that users are familiar with. The Windows 10 Start Menu combines the best of both Windows 7 and Windows 8. So the Start Menu gives you a menu that we were familiar with in Windows 7 as well as the Live Tiles that users liked in Windows 8.

Microsoft Edge and Internet Explorer 11   Windows 10 has introduced a new way to surf the Internet with Microsoft Edge. But Windows 10 also still comes with Internet

Explorer 11 in the event that you need to run ActiveX controls or run backward-compatible web services or sites.

Microsoft Edge allows users to start using many new Microsoft features, including Web Note (allows you to annotate, highlight, and call things out directly on web pages), Reading View (allows you to print and save as a PDF for easy reading), and Cortana (personal assistant).

Domain Join and Group Policy   Depending on the version of Windows 10 that you are using, administrators have the ability to join Windows 10 clients to either a corporate version of Active Directory or a cloud-based version of Azure Active Directory.

Windows Store for Business   Microsoft Store has included many applications that allow users to get better functionality and productivity out of their Windows 10 devices. One advantage for corporations is that they can create their own applications and load them into the Microsoft Store for users to download (called *sideloading*).

Mobile Device Management   Mobile Device Management (MDM) allows administrators to set up Windows 10 policies that can integrate many corporate scenarios, including the ability to control users' access to the Windows Store and the ability to use the corporate VPN. MDM also allows administrators to manage multiple users who have accounts set up on Microsoft Azure Active Directory (Azure AD). Windows 10 MDM support is based on the Open Mobile Alliance (OMA) Device Management (DM) protocol 1.2.1 specification.

Windows 10 Architecture

Windows 10 has limited the number of files that load at system startup to help with the core performance of the operating system. Microsoft has also removed many of the fluff items that Windows Vista used, allowing for better performance.

Microsoft offers both a 32-bit version and a 64-bit version of Windows 10. The terms *32-bit* and *64-bit* refer to the CPU, or processor. The number represents how the data is processed. It is processed either as 2^{32} or 2^{64}. The larger the number, the larger the amount of data that can be processed at any one time.

To get an idea of how 32-bit and 64-bit processors operate, think of a large highway with 32 lanes. Vehicles can travel on those 32 lanes only, so when traffic gets backed up, the result is delays. Now think of how many more vehicles can travel on a 64-lane highway. The problem here is that a 32-lane highway can't handle the number of vehicles a 64-lane highway can. You need to have the infrastructure to allow for that volume of vehicles. The same is true for computers. Your computer has to be configured to allow you to run a 64-bit processor.

So what does all of this mean to the common user or administrator? It's all about random access memory, or RAM. A 32-bit operating system can handle up to 4 GB of RAM, and a 64-bit processor can handle up to 16 exabytes (EB) of RAM. None of this is new. Although 64-bit processors are just starting to get accepted with Windows systems, other operating systems, such as Apple, have been using 64-bit processors for many years.

Computer processors are typically rated by speed. The speed of the processor, or central processing unit (CPU), is rated by the number of clock
cycles that can be performed in 1 second. This measurement is typically
expressed in gigahertz (GHz). One GHz is one billion cycles per second.
Keep in mind that processor architecture must also be taken into account
when considering processor speed. A processor with a more efficient
pipeline will be faster than a processor with a less-efficient pipeline at the
same CPU speed.

Now that you have seen the new features of Windows 10, let's look at how to prepare
the machine to install Windows 10.

Preparing to Install Windows 10

Installing Windows 10 can be relatively simple because of the installation wizard. The
installation wizard will walk you through the entire installation of the operating system.

The most difficult part of installing Windows 10 is preparing and planning for the
installation. One thing I often say to IT pros is, "An hour of planning will save you days of
work." Planning a Windows 10 rollout is one of the hardest and most important tasks that
you will perform when installing Windows 10.

There are many decisions that should be made before you install Windows 10. The first
decision is which version of Windows 10 you want to install. As mentioned previously,
Microsoft has six different versions of the Windows 10 operating system. This allows an
administrator to custom-fit a user's hardware and job function to the appropriate version
of Windows 10. Many times, Microsoft releases multiple editions of the operating system
contained within the same Windows 10 media disk. You can choose to unlock the one you
want based on the product key you have. Let's take a closer look at the different versions of
Windows 10.

In this book, we will not talk much about Windows 10 Education.
Windows 10 Education is the counterpart to Windows 10 Enterprise, but
it is a volume-licensed version of Windows 10 that is specifically priced
for educational institutions. Educational institutions receive the same
Enterprise functionality, but they pay much less than a corporation.

Windows 10 Home

Windows 10 Home is the main operating system for home users. Windows 10 Home offers
many features, including these:

- Broad application and device compatibility with unlimited concurrent applications
- A safe, reliable, and supported operating system

- Microsoft Passport / Windows Hello
- HomeGroup, which allows a user to easily share media, documents, and printers across multiple PCs in homes or offices without the need of a domain
- Improved Taskbar and Jump Lists (Jump Lists is a feature in Windows 10 that allows you to quickly access files that you have been working on.)
- Live thumbnail previews and an enhanced visual experience
- Advanced networking support (ad hoc wireless networks and Internet connection sharing)
- View Available Networks (VAN) (Windows 10 by default has the ability, when you use a wireless network adapter, to choose the wireless network that you want to connect to by using the wireless network adapter properties.)
- Device Encryption
- Easy networking and sharing across all your PCs and devices
- Windows Update
- Multitouch
- Improved handwriting recognition

Windows 10 Pro

Windows 10 Pro is designed for small-business owners. Microsoft designed Windows 10 Pro for users to get more done and safeguard their data. Pro offers the following features:

- Broad application and device compatibility with unlimited concurrent applications
- A safe, reliable, and supported operating system
- Microsoft Passport / Windows Hello
- Domain Join
- Improved Taskbar and Jump Lists
- Enterprise Mode Internet Explorer (EMIE)
- Advanced networking support (ad hoc wireless networks and Internet connection sharing)
- View Available Networks (VAN) (Windows 10 by default has the ability, when you use a wireless network adapter, to choose the wireless network that you want to connect to by using the wireless network adapter properties.)
- Mobility Center
- Action Center, which makes it easier to resolve many IT issues yourself
- Easy networking and sharing across all your PCs and devices
- Group Policy Management
- Windows Update and Windows Update for Business

- Multitouch
- Improved handwriting recognition
- Domain Join, which enables simple and secure server networking
- BitLocker, which protects data on removable devices
- Device Encryption
- Encrypting File System, which protects data
- Client Hyper-V
- Location Aware Printing, which helps find the right printer when moving between the office and home
- Start Menu that includes Live Tiles

Windows 10 Enterprise

Windows 10 Enterprise is the version designed for midsize and large organizations. This operating system has the most features and security options of all Windows 10 versions. Here are some of the features:

- Broad application and device compatibility with unlimited concurrent applications
- A safe, reliable, and supported operating system
- Microsoft Passport / Windows Hello
- Enterprise Mode Internet Explorer (EMIE)
- Group Policy Management
- Windows Update and Windows Update for Business
- Advanced networking support (ad hoc wireless networks and Internet connection sharing)
- View Available Networks (VAN). Windows 10 by default has the ability, when you use a wireless network adapter, to choose the wireless network that you want to connect to by using the wireless network adapter properties.
- Mobility Center
- Easy networking and sharing across all your PCs and devices
- Multitouch
- Start menu that includes Live Tiles
- Improved handwriting recognition
- Domain Join, which enables simple and secure server networking
- Device Encryption
- Encrypting File System, which protects data
- Location Aware Printing, which helps find the right printer when you are moving between the office and home

- Client Hyper-V
- Credential Guard
- Device Guard
- BitLocker, which protects data on removable devices
- DirectAccess, which links users to corporate resources from the road without a virtual private network (VPN)
- BranchCache, which makes it faster to open files and web pages from a branch office
- AppLocker, which restricts unauthorized software and also enables greater security hardware requirements

Windows 10 Enterprise E3 and E5

Microsoft has released a new cloud based way to deploy Windows 10 Enterprise with the introduction of Windows 10 Enterprise E3 and E5. Windows 10 Enterprise E3 and E5 are subscription based versions of Windows 10 for organizations that like to work with Microsoft O365.

When Microsoft released Windows 10 version 1703, it included a Windows 10 Enterprise E3 and E5 benefit for Microsoft customers with either Enterprise Agreements (EA) or Microsoft Products & Services Agreements (MPSA).

One of the advantages of using the subscription-based service for Windows 10 E3 and E5 is that the users can activate the Windows 10 subscription on up to five (5) devices. Users can then download the corporate version of Windows 10 onto their work systems, personal systems, and other devices.

As you can see from Table 1.1 and Table 1.2, by purchasing the Windows 10 E3 and E5 subscriptions, you get many additional features, including enterprise-level security and control. Some of the E3 and E5 components are available if you would like to purchase them separately.

Windows 10 Requirements

Before you can install the operating system, you must make sure the machine's hardware can handle the Windows 10 operating system.

To install Windows 10 successfully, your system must meet or exceed certain hardware requirements. Table 1.3 lists the minimum requirements for a Windows 10–capable PC.

TABLE 1.3 Hardware requirements

Component	Requirements
CPU (processor)	1 GHz or faster processor or system-on-a-chip (SoC)
Memory (RAM)	1 GB for 32-bit or 2 GB for 64-bit

Component	Requirements
Hard disk	16 GB for 32-bit OS or 20 GB for 64-bit OS
Video adapter	DirectX 9 or later with WDDM 1.0 driver
Optional drive	DVD-R/W drive
Network device	Compatible network interface card

The hardware requirements listed in Table 1.3 are those specified at the time this book was written. Always check the Microsoft website for the most current information.

The Windows 10–capable PC must meet or exceed the basic requirements to deliver the core functionality of the Windows 10 operating system. These requirements are based on the assumption that you are installing only the operating system, without any premium functionality. For example, you may be able to get by with the minimum requirements if you are installing the operating system just to learn the basics of the software. Remember, the better the hardware, the better the performance.

 Real World Scenario

Deciding on Minimum Hardware Requirements

The company you work for has decided that everyone will have their own laptop running Windows 10. You need to decide on the new computers' specifications for processor, memory, and disk space.

The first step is to determine which applications will be used. Typically, most users will work with an email program, a word processor, a spreadsheet, presentation software, and maybe a drawing or graphics program. Additionally, an antivirus application will probably be used. Under these demands, a 1 GHz Celeron processor and 1 GB of RAM will make for a very slow-running machine. So for this usage, you can assume that the minimum baseline configuration would be higher than a 1 GHz processor with at least 2 GB of RAM.

Based on your choice of baseline configuration, you should then fit a test computer with the applications that will be used on it and test the configuration in a lab environment simulating normal use. This will give you an idea of whether the RAM and processor calculations you have made for your environment are going to provide a suitable response.

- Back up your data and configuration files. Before you make any major changes to your computer's configuration, you should back up your data and configuration files and then verify that you can successfully restore your backup. Chances are, if you have a valid backup, you won't have any problems. Likewise, if you don't have a valid backup, you will likely have problems.

- Delete any unnecessary files or applications, and clean up any program groups or program items you don't use. Theoretically, you want to delete all the junk on your computer before you upgrade. Think of this as the spring-cleaning step.

- Verify that there are no existing problems with your hard drive prior to the upgrade. Perform a disk scan, a current virus scan, and defragmentation. These too are spring-cleaning chores. This step just prepares your hard drive for the upgrade.

- Perform the upgrade. In this step, you upgrade from the Windows 7 or Windows 8/8.1 operating system to Windows 10.

- Verify your configuration. After Windows 10 has been installed, use the inventory to compare and test each element that was inventoried prior to the upgrade to verify that the upgrade was successful.

Handling an Upgrade Failure

Before you upgrade, you should have a contingency plan in place. Your plan should assume the worst-case scenario. For example, what happens if you upgrade and the computer doesn't work anymore? It is possible that, after checking your upgrade list and verifying that everything should work, your attempt at the actual upgrade may not work. If this happens, you may want to return your computer to the original, working configuration.

Indeed, I have made these plans, created my backups (two, just in case), verified them, and then had a failed upgrade anyway—only to discover that I had no clue where to find the original operating system CD. A day later, with the missing CD located, I was able to get up and running again. My problem was an older BIOS, and the manufacturer of my computer did not have an updated BIOS.

Disk Partitioning

Disk partitioning is the act of taking the physical hard drive and creating logical partitions. A logical drive is how space is allocated to the drive's primary and logical partitions. For example, if you have a 500 GB hard drive, you might partition it into three logical drives:

- C: drive, which might be 200 GB
- D: drive, which might be 150 GB
- E: drive, which might be 150 GB

The following items detail some of the major considerations for disk partitioning:

Partition Size   One important consideration in your disk-partitioning scheme is determining the partition size. You need to consider the amount of space taken up by your operating system, the applications that will be installed, and the amount of stored data. It is also important to consider the amount of space required in the future.

Microsoft recommends that you allocate at least 16 GB of disk space for Windows 10. This allows room for the operating system files and for future growth in terms of upgrades and installation files that are placed with the operating system files.

The System and Boot Partitions   When you install Windows 10, files will be stored in two locations: the system partition and the boot partition. The system partition and the boot partition can be the same partition.

The system partition contains the files needed to boot the Windows 10 operating system. The system partition contains the Master Boot Record (MBR) and boot sector of the active drive partition. It is often the first physical hard drive in the computer and normally contains the necessary files to boot the computer. The files stored on the system partition do not take any significant disk space. The active partition is the system partition that is used to start your computer. The C: drive is usually the active partition.

The boot partition contains the Windows 10 operating system files. By default, the Windows operating system files are located in a folder named Windows.

Disk Partition Configuration Utilities   If you are partitioning your disk prior to installation, you can use several utilities, such as the DiskPart utility or a third-party utility such as Partition Magic. You can also configure the disks during the installation of the Windows 10 operating system.

You might want to create only the first partition where Windows 10 will be installed. You can then use the Disk Management utility in Windows 10 to create any other partitions you need. The Windows 10 Disk Management utility is covered in Chapter 3, "Managing Data."

Language and Locale

Language and locale settings determine the language the computer will use. Windows 10 supports many languages for the operating system interface and utilities.

Locale settings are for configuring the format for items such as numbers, currencies, times, and dates. For example, English for the United States specifies a short date as mm/dd/yyyy (month/day/year), while English for South Africa specifies a short date as yyyy/mm/dd (year/month/day).

It is very important to only choose the locales that this machine will need to use. The reason for this is that your system will get updates for every locale you choose and set up.

Installing Windows 10

The first step to installing Windows 10 is to know what type of media you need to install the Windows 10 operating system. Windows 10 gives you multiple ways to do an install.

You can install Windows 10 either from the bootable DVD or through a network installation using files that have been copied to a network share point or USB device. You can also install Windows 10 by using a virtual hard drive (vhd). This option will be discussed in Chapter 2: "Configuring Users." You can also launch the setup.exe file from within the Windows 10 operating system to upgrade your operating system.

To start the installation, you simply restart your computer and boot to the DVD. The installation process will begin automatically. You will walk through the steps of performing a clean install of Windows 10 from the DVD in Exercise 1.1.

If you are installing Windows 10 from the network, you need a distribution server and a computer with a network connection. A distribution server is a server that has the Windows 10 distribution files copied to a shared folder. The following steps are used to install Windows 10 over the network:

1. Boot the target computer.

2. Attach to the distribution server and access the share that has the files copied to it.

3. Launch setup.exe.

4. Complete the Windows 10 installation using either the clean install method or the upgrade method. These methods are discussed in detail in the following sections.

Performing a Clean Install of Windows 10

On any installation of Windows 10, there are three stages.

Collecting Information   During the collection phase of the installation, Windows 10 gathers the information necessary to complete the installation. This is where Windows 10 gathers your local time, location, keyboard, license agreement, installation type, and installation disk partition information.

Installing Windows   This section of the installation is where your Windows 10 files are copied to the hard disk and the installation is completed. This phase takes the longest because the files are installed.

Setting Up Windows   In this phase, you set up a username, computer name, and password; enter the product key; configure the security settings; and review the date and time. Once this is finished, your installation will be complete.

As explained earlier, you can run the installation from the optical media, from a USB, or over a network. The only difference in the installation procedure is your starting point: from your optical drive or USB or a network share. The steps in Exercise 1.1 and Exercise 1.2 assume you are using the Windows 10 DVD to install Windows 10.

Setting Up Your Computer for Hands-On Exercises

Before beginning Exercise 1.1, verify that your computer meets the requirements for installing Windows 10, as listed earlier in Table 1.3. For Exercise 1.1, it is assumed you are not currently running a previous version of Windows that will be upgraded.

The exercises in this book are based on your computer being configured in a specific manner. Your computer should have at least a 50 GB hard drive (this exceeds the basic minimums) that is configured with the minimum space requirements and partitions.

When you boot to the Windows 10 installation media, the Setup program will automatically start the Windows 10 installation. In Exercise 1.1, you will perform a clean install of Windows 10. This exercise assumes that you have access to Windows 10 Enterprise; other editions may vary slightly. You can also download an evaluation version of Windows 10 from the Microsoft website.

Also, I may list steps that you may not see or I may not list steps that you see—this is because my version of Windows may be different. For example, I am installing an MSDN Windows 10 Enterprise edition. At this time, I am not required to enter a license number during install. A normal version bought from a vendor may ask for the license during the actual install.

 I am loading Windows 10 Enterprise into a VMware Workstation virtual machine. Again, this may make your installation a little different than the steps listed in Exercise 1.1. Plus, depending on your version and license model, not all screens may appear.

EXERCISE 1.1

Performing a Clean Install of Windows 10

1. Insert the Windows 10 DVD or .iso image in the machine or virtual machine with no operating system and start the computer.

2. If you are directed to "Hit any key" to start the DVD, press Enter.

3. The first screen will ask you to enter your language, time and currency format, and keyboard or input method (see Figure 1.1). After filling in these fields, click Next.

8. The next screen asks you to identify the disk to which you would like to install Windows 10. Choose an unformatted free space or a partition (partition will be erased) with at least 50 GB available. You can also click the Drive Options (Advanced) link to create and format your own partition, as shown in Figure 1.5. Click the New link and click Apply to create the new partition for Windows 10. A message will appear stating that Windows 10 will set some partitions for system files. Just click the OK button. After you choose your partition, click Next.

FIGURE 1.5 Windows disk setup screen

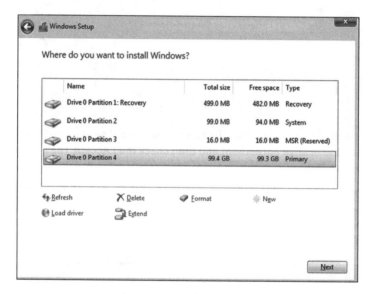

9. When your partition is set, the installation will start (as shown in Figure 1.6). You will see the progress of the installation during the entire process. When the installation is complete, the machine will reboot.

FIGURE 1.6 Windows installation status screen

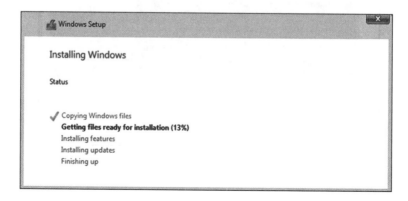

10. After the restart, a screen appears that asks you to choose your region. Select your region (see Figure 1.7), and then click the Yes button.

FIGURE 1.7   Choose your Region screen.

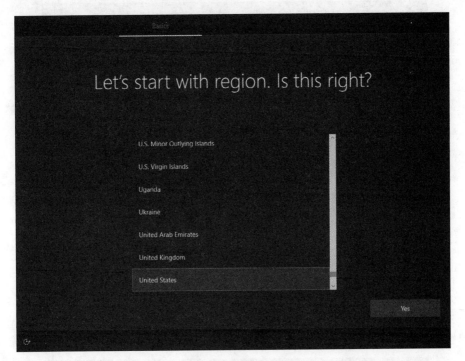

11. The next screen will ask you about your keyboard layout. Choose your keyboard layout (see Figure 1.8) and then click the Yes button.

12. The next screen will ask you if you have a second keyboard. If you do, click the Add Layout button. If not, click the Skip button (as seen in Figure 1.9).

13. At the sign in with Microsoft screen, choose the Domain Join Instead link. It will ask you who is going to use this PC. Enter your username and click the Next button.

FIGURE 1.8 Choosing your keyboard layout

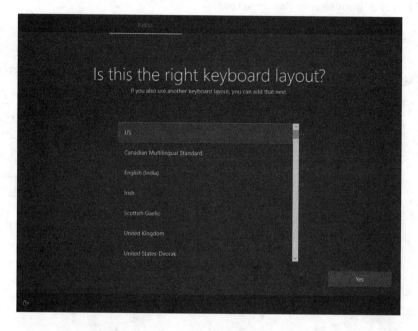

FIGURE 1.9 Adding a Second Keyboard

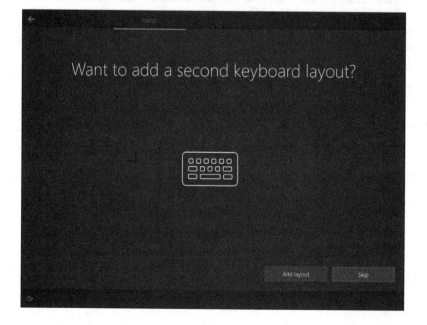

14. Next it's going to ask you to enter a super memorable password (as shown in Figure 1.10). Type in your password and click the Next button.

FIGURE 1.10   Windows 10 screen

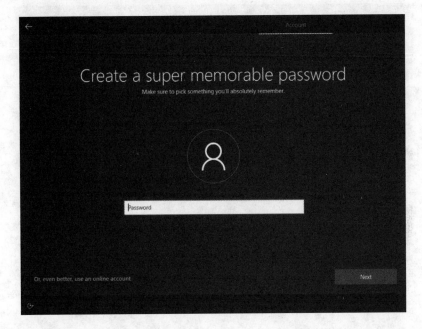

15. You will be asked to reenter your password. Enter your password again and click the Next button.

16. Depending on your version, you may be asked to create three security questions. If your edition asks this, put in your security questions and click the Next button for each security question. After the third question, click the Next button to move on.

17. The next screen will ask if you want to make Cortana your personal assistant. You can either accept or decline this. I am going to choose Decline.

18. The next screen will ask if you want Microsoft to save your activity history. If you accept this, you will send Microsoft information about all activities that you are doing. This allows you to continue to finish these activities from any other device. Since this is a corporate machine, I will choose not to send Microsoft my activity history by choosing the No button (see Figure 1.11).

FIGURE 1.11   Windows activity screen

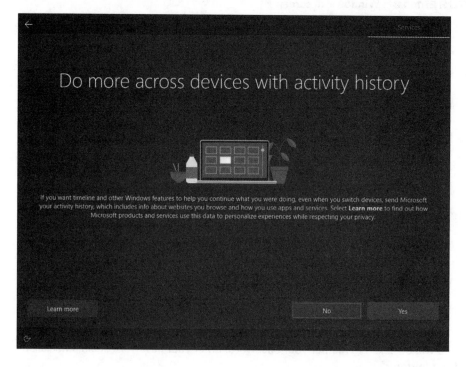

19. The next screen will be the privacy settings screen. Disable any of the privacy settings that you want disabled (all will be enabled by default). Once you're finished, click the Accept button.

20. A different screen will appear letting you know that the system is being set up. This may take a few minutes. Be sure not to turn off the machine during this process. Once this is all completed, the system may ask you to log in. Put in your password and click the right arrow next to the password box. Your installation is now complete.

Before we talk about the Windows 10 upgrade procedure, I want to quickly explain something that you saw during the Windows 10 install. In step 13, I had you choose "Domain Join Instead" instead of using a Microsoft password. We will explore both of the choices in greater detail, but I wanted to quickly explain why we chose one over the other.

Microsoft offers two main networks: workgroup-based or domain-based. *Workgroups* (also referred to as peer-to-peer networks) are when you just connect your computers together directly to each other. A perfect example for most of us is what you do in your home network. Most home users connect their machines together without the use of a main server.

Corporations normally do things a bit differently than that. *Domains* are networks that are controlled by servers called domain controllers. Domain controllers are Windows servers that have a copy of a database called Active Directory (AD). Recently Microsoft took domain-based networks a step further by allowing companies to set up a cloud-based version of an Active Directory domain (Azure AD). This means that companies no longer need to maintain and manage their own domain controllers. Since most people don't have a cloud-based version of Azure AD, I had you choose the option Join A Domain so that we could finish the Windows 10 install.

We will go over all of these options in greater detail throughout this book, but I wanted to introduce you to these two Windows 10 options.

Performing an Upgrade to Windows 10

This section describes how to perform an upgrade to Windows 10 from Windows 8.1. Similar to a clean install, you can run the installation from the installation DVD, from a USB, or over a network. The only difference in the installation procedure is your starting point: from your optical or USB drive or from a network share. For the steps in the following sections, it is assumed that you are using the Windows 10 DVD to install the Windows 10 operating system.

Upgrading a Windows 7 or Windows 8/8.1 system to Windows 10 will save you a lot of time and trouble. Because we are upgrading the system, all of the user's data and applications will remain installed and most likely still work the exact same way. Sometimes when we upgrade a system, we run into problems with applications. But many times that is caused by a driver or a needed software update that will most likely solve the issue.

The three main steps in the Windows 10 upgrade process are very similar to the ones for a clean install. The three steps of upgrading to Windows 10 are as follows:

1. Collecting information
2. Installing Windows
3. Setting up Windows

In Exercise 1.2, you will go through the process of installing Windows 10 by upgrading Windows 8.1. I have a Windows 8.1 Enterprise system that I will update to Windows 10 Enterprise.

EXERCISE 1.2

Upgrading Windows 8.1 to Windows 10

1. Insert the Windows 10 DVD. (We are upgrading Windows 8.1 Enterprise to Windows 10 Enterprise.)

2. If Autorun does not start, navigate to the DVD drive and click setup.exe. Once the setup starts (via either setup.exe or Autorun), click Run Setup.exe as shown in Figure 1.12.

FIGURE 1.12   DVD setup screen

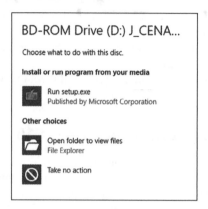

3. If a pop-up box appears for User Account Control, click the Yes button (see Figure 1.13).

FIGURE 1.13   User Account Control screen

You should then see a message appear stating that Windows is preparing the system, as shown in Figure 1.14.

FIGURE 1.14   Preparing screen

4. You may be prompted to Get Important Updates. You can choose to either download the updates or not do them at this time. Make a choice and click the Next button. (During my installation, I decided to download the updates.)

5. The Microsoft Windows 10 license terms appear. Read the terms and then click Accept. (The installation will not allow you to continue until you click Accept.)

6. At the Ready To Install screen (shown in Figure 1.15), you can change what files and/ or apps you want to keep by clicking the Change What To Keep link. Once you're ready, click the Install button.

FIGURE 1.15 Ready To Install screen

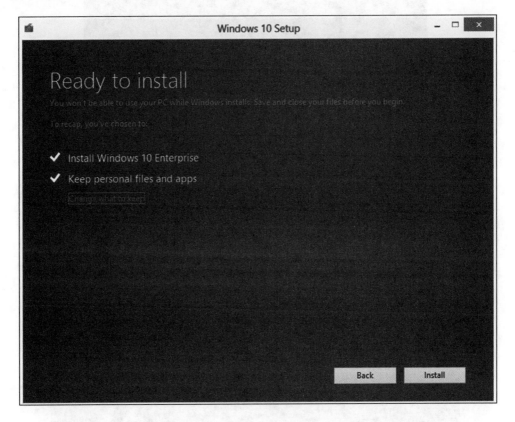

7. Windows 10 will begin to install (as shown in Figure 1.16). Your computer may restart multiple times. This is normal. As the upgrade status screen states, "Sit back and relax."

8. After the upgrade has completed, a welcome screen will be displayed, similar to the one shown in Figure 1.17. Click Next.

FIGURE 1.16   Installing Status screen

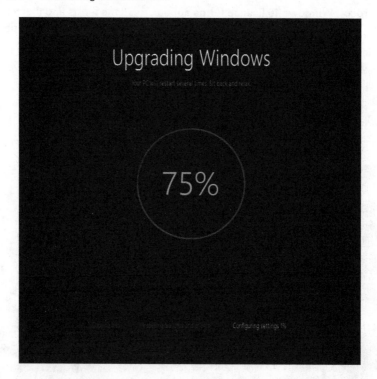

FIGURE 1.17   Welcome screen

9. At the Get Going Fast screen, click the Use Express Settings button.

10. At the New Apps screen, just click Next.

And that's it—Windows 10 is installed (see Figure 1.18). Congrats.

FIGURE 1.18   Windows 10 screen

Now that we have installed the Windows 10 operating system, let's take a look at how to change your system's locales. Earlier I explained that the locale settings help you with the system's language format, settings, and region-specific details.

In Exercise 1.3, I will show you how to change your current locale. This helps when you take your Windows 10 laptop, tablet, or phone to another part of the world.

EXERCISE 1.3

Configuring Locales

1. Click the Start button and choose Settings.

2. Once in the Settings screen, choose Time And Language.

3. This should place you on the Date & Time screen. Make sure your time zone is set correctly. If it's not, pull down the time zone options and choose your time zone.

4. Scroll down and make sure the date and time formats are set the way you want. If they are not, click the Change Date And Time Formats link. Change the formats to the way you want them set.

5. Click the Region And Language link on the left-hand side.

6. Make sure the country or region is set properly. If you want to add a second language to this Windows 10 system, click the Add A Language link. Choose the language you want.

7. Once completed, close the Settings screen.

Troubleshooting Installation Problems

The Windows 10 installation process is designed to be as simple as possible. The chances for installation errors are greatly minimized through the use of wizards and the step-by-step process. However, it is possible that errors will occur.

Identifying Common Installation Problems

As most of you are aware, errors sometimes do occur during installations. You might encounter some of the following installation errors:

Media Errors   Media errors are caused by defective or damaged DVDs. To check the disc, put it into another computer and see if you can read it. Also check your disc for scratches or dirt—it may just need to be cleaned.

Insufficient Disk Space   Windows 10 needs at least 16 GB for the 32-bit OS and 20 GB for the 64-bit OS to execute properly. If the Setup program cannot verify that this space exists, the program will not let you continue.

Not Enough Memory   Make sure your computer has the minimum amount of memory required by Windows 10 (1 GB for 32-bit or 2 GB for 64-bit). Having insufficient memory may cause the installation to fail or blue-screen errors to occur after installation.

Not Enough Processing Power   Make sure your computer has the minimum processing power required by Windows 10 (1 GHz or faster processor or SoC). Having insufficient processing power may cause the installation to fail or blue-screen errors to occur after installation.

Hardware That Is Not on the HCL   If your hardware is not listed on the hardware compatibility list (HCL), Windows 10 may not recognize the hardware or the device may not work properly.

Hardware with No Driver Support   Windows 10 will not recognize hardware without driver support.

Hardware That Is Not Configured Properly   If your hardware is Plug and Play (PnP)-compatible, Windows 10 should configure it automatically. If your hardware is not Plug and Play compatible, you will need to manually configure the hardware per the manufacturer's instructions.

Incorrect Product Key   Without a valid product key, the installation will not go past the Product Key screen. Make sure you have not typed in an incorrect key (check your Windows 10 installation folder or your computer case for this key).

Failure to Access TCP/IP Network Resources   If you install Windows 10 with typical settings, the computer is configured as a DHCP client. If there is no DHCP server to provide IP configuration information, the client will still generate an autoconfigured IP address but be unable to access network resources through TCP/IP if the other network clients are using DHCP addresses.

Installing Nonsupported Hard Drives   If your computer is using a hard disk that does not have a driver included on the Windows 10 media, you will receive an error message stating that the hard drive cannot be found. You should verify that the hard drive is properly connected and functional. You will need to obtain a disk driver for Windows 10 from the manufacturer and then specify the driver location by selecting the Load Driver option during partition selection.

Troubleshooting with Installation Log Files

When you install Windows 10, the Setup program creates several log files. You can view these logs to check for any problems during the installation process. Two log files are particularly useful for troubleshooting:

- The action log includes all of the actions that were performed during the setup process and a description of each action. These actions are listed in chronological order. The action log is stored as \Windows\setupact.log.

- The error log includes any errors that occurred during the installation. For each error, there is a description and an indication of the severity of the error. This error log is stored as \Windows\setuperr.log.

In Exercise 1.4, you will view the Windows 10 Setup logs to determine whether there were any problems with your Windows 10 installation.

EXERCISE 1.4

Troubleshooting Failed Installations with Setup Logs

1. Select Start ➢ Computer.

2. Double-click Local Disk (C:).

3. Double-click Windows.

4. In the Windows folder, double-click the Setupact.log file to view your action log in Notepad. When you are finished viewing this file, close Notepad.

5. Double-click the Setuperr.log file to view your error file in Notepad. If no errors occurred during installation, this file will be empty. When you are finished viewing this file, close Notepad.

6. Close the directory window.

Supporting Multiple-Boot Options

You may want to install Windows 10 but still be able to run other operating systems. *Dual-booting* or multibooting allows your computer to boot multiple operating systems. Your computer will be automatically configured for dual-booting if there was a dual-boot–supported operating system on your computer prior to the Windows 10 installation, you didn't upgrade from that operating system, and you installed Windows 10 into a different partition.

One reason for dual-booting is to test various systems. If you have a limited number of computers in your test lab and you want to be able to test multiple configurations, you should dual-boot. For example, you might configure one computer to dual-boot with Windows 7, Windows 8/8.1, and Windows 10.

Here are some keys to successful dual-boot configurations:

- Make sure you have plenty of disk space.

- Windows 10 must be installed on a separate partition in order to dual-boot with other operating systems.

- Install older operating systems before installing newer operating systems. If you want to support dual-booting with Windows 7 and Windows 10, Windows 7 must be installed first. If you install Windows 10 first, you cannot install Windows 7 without ruining your Windows 10 configuration.

- Do not install Windows 10 on a compressed volume unless the volume was compressed using NTFS compression.

Once you have installed each operating system, you can choose the operating system that you will boot to during the boot process. You will see a boot-selection screen that asks you to choose which operating system you want to boot.

The Boot Configuration Data (BCD) store contains boot information parameters that were previously found in boot.ini in older versions of Windows. To edit the boot options in the BCD store, use the bcdedit utility, which can be launched only from a command prompt. To open a command prompt window, you can do the following:

1. Launch \Windows\system32\cmd.exe.

2. Open the Run command by pressing the [Windows] key + R and then entering **cmd**.

3. Type **cmd.exe** in the Search Programs And Files box and press Enter.

Once the command-prompt window is open, type **bcdedit** to launch the bcdedit utility. You can also type **bcdedit/?** to see all the different bcdedit commands. A few bcdedit commands may be needed when dual-booting a machine. Table 1.5 shows some of the bcdedit commands that may be needed when dual-booting.

TABLE 1.5   bcdedit commands for dual-booting

Command	Explanation
/createstore	Creates a new empty Boot Configuration Data store
/default	Allows you to specify which operating system will start when the time-out expires
/deletevalue	Allows you to delete a specified element from a boot entry
/displayorder	Shows the display order that the boot manager uses when showing the display order to the user
/export	Allows you to export the contents of the system store into a file
/import	Restores the system store by using the data file previously generated by using the /export option
/set	Allows you to set an entry option value
/store	Specifies the store to be used
/timeout	Specifies the amount of time used before the system boots into the default operating system

Using Windows Activation

Windows Activation is Microsoft's way of reducing software piracy. Unless you have a corporate license for Windows 10, you will need to perform post installation activation. This can be done online or through a telephone call. Windows 10 will attempt automatic activation three days after you log on to it for the first time. There is a grace period when you will be able to use the operating system without activation. After the grace period expires, a permanent watermark is displayed. Until the activation key is entered certain personalization settings are not configurable until Windows 10 is activated. When the grace period runs out, the Windows Activation Wizard will automatically start; it will walk you through the activation process.

To access the Windows Activation screen, click on the Start button and choose settings (the spoke icon). Scroll down to Update and Security and click on that link. On the left side, you will see a link for Activation. When you click on Activation, you will see the Activation screen (shown in Figure 1.19). Scroll down to the Activate Windows Now section. You may need to click the Change Product Key button and put in the license number that came with your Windows 10 copy. Once Windows 10 is activated, it will show that you are activated.

FIGURE 1.19   The Windows Activation Wizard screen

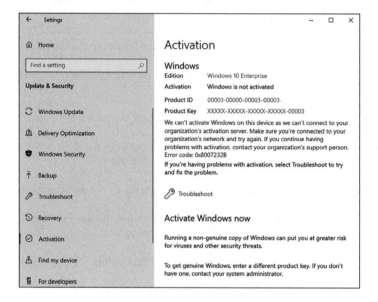

Understanding Automated Deployment Options

If you need to install Windows 10 on multiple computers, you could manually install the operating system on each computer. However, automating the deployment process will make your job easier, more efficient, and more cost effective if you have a large number of client computers on which to install Windows 10.

Windows 10 comes with several utilities that can be used for deploying and automating the Windows 10 installation. With access to multiple utilities with different functionality, administrators have increased flexibility in determining how to best deploy Windows 10 within a large corporate environment.

The following sections contain overviews of the automated deployment options, which will help you choose which solution is best for your requirements and environment. Each utility will then be covered in more detail throughout this chapter. The options for automated deployment of Windows 10 are as follows:

- Microsoft Deployment Toolkit (MDT)

- Unattended installation, or unattended setup, which uses Setup.exe

- Windows Automated Installation Kit (Windows AIK)

- Windows Assessment and Deployment Kit for Windows 10

- Windows Deployment Services (WDS) server, which requires Windows Server for deployment

- System Preparation Tool (Sysprep.exe), which is used to create images or clones

 Another option that you have to deploy Windows 10 is through System Center Configuration Manager (SCCM). Since SCCM is its own application, it is beyond the scope of this book. You can learn more about SCCM on the Microsoft website at www.microsoft.com.

An Overview of the Microsoft Deployment Toolkit

Microsoft released a deployment assistance toolset called the *Microsoft Deployment Toolkit (MDT)*. It is used to automate desktop and server deployment. The MDT provides an administrator with the following benefits:

- Administrative tools that allow for the deployment of desktops and servers through the use of a common console (see Figure 1.20)

FIGURE 1.20 Microsoft Deployment Toolkit console

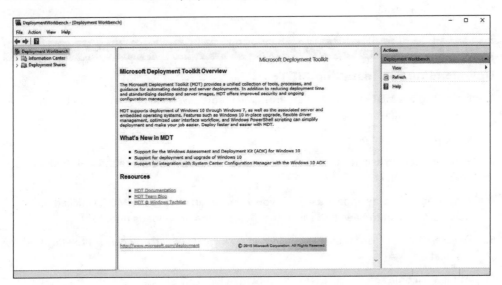

- Quicker deployments and the capabilities of having standardized desktop and server images and security
- Zero-touch deployments of Windows 10, Windows Server, and Windows 7 / 8 / 8.1.

To install the MDT package onto your computer (regardless of the operating system being deployed), you must first meet the minimum requirements of MDT. These components need to be installed only on the computer where MDT is being installed:

- Windows 10, Windows 7, Windows 8, Windows 8.1, or Windows Server.
- The Windows Assessment and Deployment Kit (ADK) for Windows 10 is required for all deployment scenarios.
- System Center 2012 R2 Configuration Manager Service Pack 1 with the Windows ADK for Windows 10 is required for zero-touch installation (ZTI) and user-driven installation (UDI) scenarios.
- If you are using ZTI and/or UDI, you are allowed to add the MDT SQL database to any version of System Center Configuration Manager with SQL Technology; if you are using LTI, you must use a separately licensed SQL Server product to host your MDT SQL database.

> You can install MDT without installing Windows (ADK) first, but you will not be able to use the package fully until Windows (ADK) is installed.

In Exercise 1.5, you will download and install MDT. You can install MDT on the Windows 10 operating system machine. If you decide to install the MDT onto a server or production machine, I recommend that you perform a full backup before completing Exercise 1.5. Installing MDT will replace any previous version of MDT that the machine may currently be using.

EXERCISE 1.5

Downloading and Installing MDT

1. Download the MDT Update 1 utility from Microsoft's website www.microsoft.com/en-us/download/details.aspx?id=54259).

2. Click the Download button.

3. You get a screen asking "Choose the download you want." Choose the x64 or x86 version. Click Next.

4. A message box may appear asking if you want to run or save the MDT. I clicked the down arrow next to Save and saved the files into the downloads directory.

5. Double-click MicrosoftDeploymentToolkit_xxx.exe, which you choose to start the installation.

6. At the Welcome screen, click Next as shown in Figure 1.21.

FIGURE 1.21   Microsoft Deployment Toolkit setup screen

7. At the License screen, click the I Accept The Terms In The License Agreement radio button and click Next.

8. At the Custom Setup screen, click the down arrow next to Microsoft Deployment Toolkit and choose Entire Feature Will Be Installed On Local Hard Drive. Click Next as shown on Figure 1.22.

FIGURE 1.22   Microsoft Deployment Toolkit Custom Setup screen

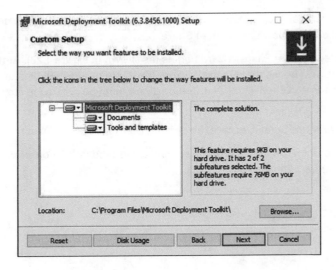

9. At the Customer Experience Improvement Program screen, choose if you want to participate or not and click Next.

10. At the Ready To Install screen, click the Install button.

11. If a User Account Control dialog box appears, click the Yes button.

12. When the installation completes, click the Finish button.

Now that you have installed MDT, you are going to configure the package. In Exercise 1.6, you will configure MDT and set up a distribution share and database. I am creating the MDT on a Windows Server machine so that we can distribute Windows 10. Make sure the Windows Assessment and Deployment Kit (ADK) for Windows 10 is installed because it is required for all deployment scenarios.

EXERCISE 1.6

Configuring MDT

1. Create a shared folder on your network called Distribution, and give the Everyone group Full Control to the folder for this exercise.

2. Open the MDT workbench by choosing Start ➢ Microsoft Development Toolkit ➢ Deployment Workbench.

3. If the User Account Control box appears, click Yes.

4. In the left-hand pane, click Deployment Shares, and then right-click the deployment shares and choose New Deployment Share.

5. The New Deployment Share Wizard begins (as shown in Figure 1.23). At the first screen, you will choose the directory where the deployments will be stored. Click the Browse button and choose the Distribution share that you created in step 1. Then click Next.

6. At the Share Name screen, accept the default, Distribution. Click Next.

7. At the Deployment Share Description screen, accept the default description name (as shown in Figure 1.24) and click Next.

FIGURE 1.23   New Deployment Share Wizard Path screen

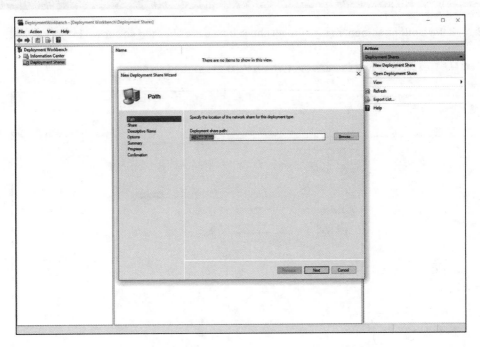

FIGURE 1.24   New Deployment Share Wizard Deployment Share Description screen

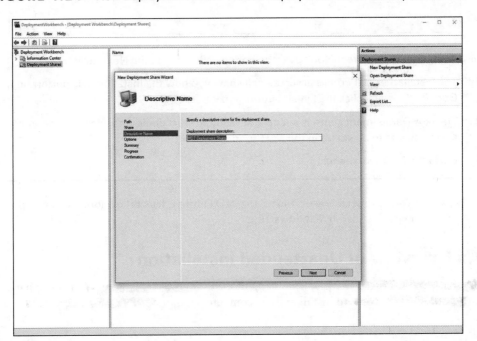

8. At the Options screen, make sure all check boxes are checked as shown in Figure 1.25.

FIGURE 1.25   New Deployment Share Wizard Options screen

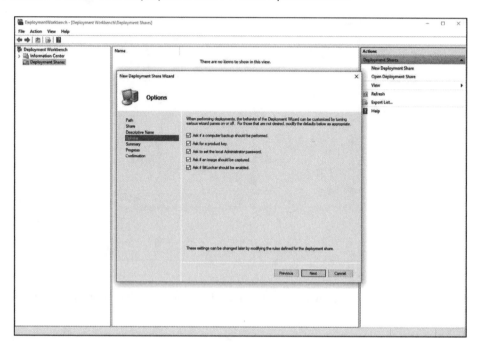

9. At the Summary screen, look over the options and choose the Next button.

10. The Installation Will Progress screen will show you how the installation is performing. Once it's finished, click the Finish button.

11. The new Deployment share is set up and ready to start deploying. Now an operating system needs to be set up in the MDT for deployment.

12. Close the MDT workbench.

Now that you have seen how to install the MDT utility, let's take a look at some other ways to automatically install Windows 10.

An Overview of Unattended Installation

Unattended installation is a practical method of automating deployments when you have a large number of clients to install and the computers require different hardware and software configurations. Unattended installations allow you to create customized installations that are specific to your environment. Custom installations can support custom hardware and software installations.

Unattended installations utilize an answer file called `Autounattend.xml` to provide configuration information during the installation process. Think about the Windows 10 installation from earlier in this chapter. You are asked for your locale, type of installation, and so on. The answer file allows these questions to be answered without user interaction. In addition to providing standard Windows 10 configuration information, the answer file can provide installation instructions for applications, additional language support, service packs, and device drivers.

With an unattended installation, you can use a distribution share to install Windows 10 on the target computers. You can also use a Windows 10 DVD with an answer file located on the root of the DVD, on a floppy disk, or on a universal flash device (UFD), such as an external USB flash drive.

Unattended installations allow you to create customized installations that are specific to your environment. Custom installations can support custom hardware and software installations. Since the answer file for Windows 10 is in XML format, all custom configuration information can be contained within the `Autounattend.xml` file. This is different from past versions of Windows, where creating automated installation routines for custom installations required multiple files to be used. In addition to providing standard Windows 10 configuration information, you can use the answer file to provide installation instructions for applications, additional language support, service packs, and device drivers.

If you use a distribution share, it should contain the Windows 10 operating system image and the answer file to respond to installation configuration queries. The target computer must be able to connect to the distribution share over the network. After the distribution share and target computers are connected, you can initiate the installation process. Figure 1.26 illustrates the unattended installation process.

FIGURE 1.26 Unattended installation with distribution share and a target computer

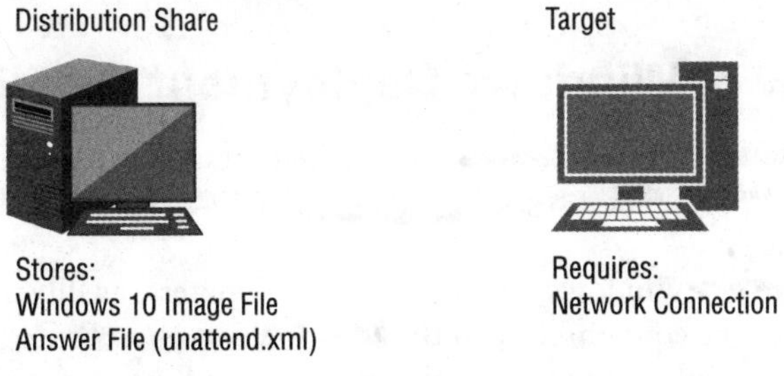

Distribution Share

Stores:
Windows 10 Image File
Answer File (unattend.xml)

Target

Requires:
Network Connection

Advantages of Unattended Installation

In a midsize or large organization, it just makes sense to use automated setups. As stated earlier, it is nearly impossible to install Windows 10 one at a time on hundreds of machines.

But there are many advantages to using unattended installations as a method for automating Windows 10:

- Unattended installation saves time and money because users do not have to interactively respond to each installation query.

- It can be configured to provide automated query responses while still selectively allowing users to provide specified input during installations.

- It can be used to install clean copies of Windows 10 or upgrade an existing operating system (providing it is on the list of permitted operating systems) to Windows 10.

- It can be expanded to include installation instructions for applications, additional language support, service packs, and device drivers.

- The physical media for Windows 10 does not need to be distributed to all computers on which it will be installed.

Disadvantages of Unattended Installation

As stated earlier, a manual installation is not practical for mass installations. But one of the biggest disadvantages to performing an unattended installation is that an administrator does not physically walk through the installation of Windows 10. A client operating system is one of the most important items that you will install onto a machine. As an IT manager and consultant, I have always felt better physically installing a client operating system. This way, if there are any glitches, I can see and deal with them immediately. If something happens during an unattended install, you may never know it, but the end user may experience small issues throughout the lifetime of the machine.

Two other disadvantages of using unattended installations as a method for automating Windows 10 installations are listed here:

- They require more initial setup than a standard installation of Windows 10.

- Someone must have access to each client computer and must initiate the unattended installation process on the client side.

An Overview of Windows Deployment Services

Windows Deployment Services (WDS) is an updated version of Remote Installation Services (RIS). WDS is a suite of components that allows you to remotely install Windows 10 on client computers.

A WDS server installs Windows 10 on the client computers, as illustrated in Figure 1.27. The WDS server must be configured with the Preboot Execution Environment (PXE) boot files, the images to be deployed to the client computers, and the answer file. WDS client computers must be PXE-capable. PXE is a technology that is used to boot to the network when no operating system or network configuration has been installed and configured on a client computer.

FIGURE 1.27   Windows Deployment Services (WDS) uses a WDS server and WDS clients.

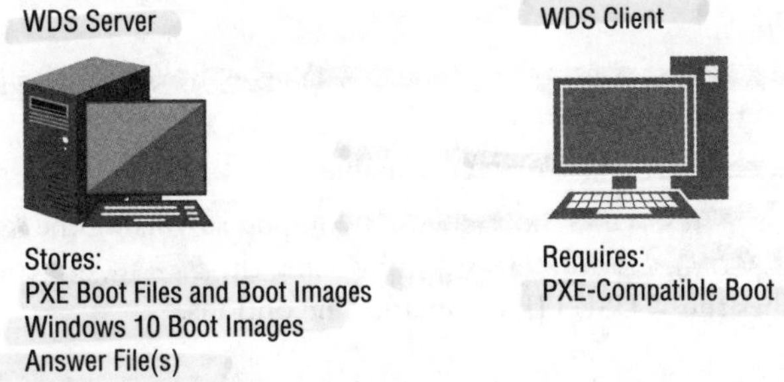

WDS Server

WDS Client

Stores:
PXE Boot Files and Boot Images
Windows 10 Boot Images
Answer File(s)

Requires:
PXE-Compatible Boot

The WDS clients access the network with the help of a Dynamic Host Configuration Protocol (DHCP) server. This allows the WDS client to remotely install the operating system from the WDS server. The network environment must be configured with a DHCP server, a Domain Name System (DNS) server, NTFS volumes, and Active Directory to connect to the WDS server. No other client software is required to connect to the WDS server. Remote installation is a good choice for automatic deployment when you need to deploy to large numbers of computers and the client computers are PXE-compliant.

Advantages of WDS

The advantages of using WDS as a method for automating Windows 10 installations are as follows:

- Allows an IT department to remotely install Windows operating systems through the network. This advantage helps reduce the difficulty and IT manpower cost compared to a manual installation.

- Allows an IT department to deploy multiple images for mixed environments, including Windows 7, Windows 8/8.1, Windows 10, and Windows Server

- Allows IT departments to use Windows setups including Windows Preinstallation Environment (Windows PE), .wim files, and image-based setups

- WDS uses multicasting to allow for the transmitting and image data to communicate with each other.

- An IT department can create reference images using the Image Capture Wizard, which is an alternative to the ImageX tool.

- Allows an IT administrator to install a driver package to the server and configure the drivers to be deployed to client computers at the same time the image is installed

- Allows IT departments to standardize Windows 10 installations throughout a group or organization

- The physical media for Windows 10 does not need to be distributed to all computers that will be installed.

- End-user installation deployment can be controlled through the Group Policy utility. For example, you can configure what choices a user can access or that are automatically specified through the end-user Setup Wizard.

Disadvantages of WDS

The disadvantages of using WDS as a method for automating Windows 10 installations include the following:

- WDS can be used only if your network is running Windows Server 2008 and above with Active Directory installed.
- The clients that use WDS must be PXE-capable.

You can configure WDS on a Windows Server computer by using the Windows Deployment Services Configuration Wizard or by using the WDSUTIL command-line utility. Table 1.6 describes the WDSUTIL command-line options.

TABLE 1.6   WDSUTIL command-line options

WDSUTIL Option	Description
/initialize-server	Initializes the configuration of the WDS server
/uninitialized-server	Undoes any changes made during the initialization of the WDS server
/add	Adds images and devices to the WDS server
/convert-ripimage	Converts Remote Installation Preparation (RIPrep) images to WIM images
/remove	Removes images from the server
/set	Sets information in images, image groups, WDS servers, and WDS devices
/get	Gets information from images, image groups, WDS servers, and WDS devices
/new	Creates new capture images or discover images
/copy-image	Copies images from the image store
/export-image	Exports to WIM files images contained within the image store
/start	Starts WDS services
/stop	Stops WDS services
/disable	Disables WDS services

WDSUTIL Option	Description
/enable	Enables WDS services
/approve-autoadddevices	Approves Auto-Add devices
/reject-autoadddevices	Rejects Auto-Add devices
/delete-autoadddevices	Deletes records from the Auto-Add database
/update	Uses a known-good resource to update a server resource

An Overview of the System Preparation Tool and Disk Imaging

The *System Preparation Tool*, or *Sysprep* (Sysprep.exe), is used to prepare a computer for disk imaging, and the disk image can then be captured using Image Capture Wizard (an imaging-management tool included with Windows 10) or third-party imaging software. Sysprep is a free utility that comes on all Windows operating systems. By default, the Sysprep utility can be found on Windows Server and Windows 10 operating systems in the \Windows\system32\sysprep directory.

Disk imaging is the process of taking a checkpoint of a computer and then using that checkpoints to create new computers, thus allowing for automated deployments. The reference, or source, computer has Windows 10 installed and is configured with the settings and applications that should be installed on the target computers. The image (checkpoints) is then created and can be transferred to other computers, thus installing the operating system, settings, and applications that were defined on the reference computer.

Using Imaging Software

Using the System Preparation Tool and disk imaging is a good choice (and the one most commonly used in the real world) for automatic deployment when you have a large number of computers with similar configuration requirements or machines that need to be rebuilt frequently.

For example, StormWind Studios, an online computer education company, reinstalls the same software every few week for new classes. Imaging is a fast and easy way to simplify the deployment process.

Most organizations use images to create new machines quickly and easily, but they also use them to reimage end users' machines that crash.

In most companies, end users will have space on a server (home folders) to allow them to store data. We give our end users space on the server because this way we need to back up only the servers at night and not the end users' machines. If your end users place all of their important documents on the server, that information gets backed up.

Now, if we are also using images in our company and an end user's machine crashes, we just reload the image and they are backed up and running in minutes. Since their documents are being saved on the server, they do not lose any of their information.

Many organizations use third-party imaging software (such as Ghost) instead of using Sysprep.exe and Image Capture Wizard. This is another good way of imaging your Windows 10 machines. Just make sure your third-party software supports the Windows 10 operating system.

To perform an unattended installation, the System Preparation Tool prepares the reference computer by stripping away any computer-specific data, such as the security identifier (SID), which is used to uniquely identify each computer on the network; any event logs; and any other unique system information. The System Preparation Tool also detects any Plug and Play devices that are installed and can adjust dynamically for any computers that have different hardware installed.

When the client computer starts an installation using a disk image, you can customize what is displayed on the Windows Welcome screen and the options that are displayed through the setup process. You can also fully automate when and how the Windows Welcome screen is displayed during the installation process by using the /oobe option with the System Preparation Tool and an answer file named Oobe.xml.

Sysprep is a utility that is good only for setting up a new machine. You do not use Sysprep to image a computer for upgrading a current machine. There are a few switches that you can use in conjunction with Sysprep to configure the Sysprep utility for your specific needs. Table 1.7 shows you the important Sysprep switches and what they will do for you when used.

TABLE 1.7 Sysprep switches

Switch	Explanation
/pnp	Forces a mini-setup wizard to start at reboot so that all Plug and Play devices can be recognized
/generalize	This allows Sysprep to remove all system-specific data from the Sysprep image. If you're running the GUI version of Sysprep, this is a check-box option.
/oobe	Initiates the Windows Welcome screen at the next reboot

Switch	Explanation
/audit	Initiates Sysprep in audit mode
/nosidgen	Sysprep does not generate a new SID on the computer restart. It forces a mini-setup on restart.
/reboot	Stops and restarts the computer system
/quiet	Runs without any confirmation dialog box messages being displayed
/mini	Tells Sysprep to run the mini-setup on the next reboot

 Real World Scenario

The SID Problem with Deployment Software

For many years, when you had to create many machines that each had a Microsoft operating system on it, you would have to use files to help deploy the multiple systems.

Then, multiple third-party companies came out with software that allowed you to take a picture of the Microsoft operating system, and you could deploy that picture to other machines. One advantage of this is that all the software that is installed on the system could also be part of that picture. This was a great way to copy all the software on a machine over to another machine.

There was one major problem for years—*security identifier (SID)* numbers. All computers get assigned a unique SID that represents them on a domain network. The problem for a long time was that when you copied a machine to another machine, the SID number was also copied.

Microsoft released Sysprep many years ago, and that helped solve this problem. Sysprep would allow you to remove the SID number so that a third-party software package could image it to another machine. Many third-party image software products now also remove the SID numbers, but Sysprep was one of the first utilities to help solve this problem.

When you decide to use Sysprep to set up your images, there are a few rules that you must follow for Sysprep to work properly:

- You can use images to restart the Windows activation clock. The Windows activation clock starts to decrease as soon as Windows starts for the first time. You can restart the Windows activation clock only three times using Sysprep.

- The computer on which you're running Sysprep has to be a member of a workgroup. The machine can't be part of a domain. If the computer is a member of the domain, when you run Sysprep, the computer will automatically be removed from the domain.

KMS ←
Server

- When installing the image, the system will prompt you for a product key. During the install, you can use an answer file, which in turn will have all the information needed for the install, and you will not be prompted for any information.

- A third-party utility or Image Capture Wizard is required to deploy the image that is created from Sysprep.

- If you are using Sysprep to capture an NTFS partition, any files or folders that are encrypted will become corrupt and unreadable.

One advantage to Sysprep and Windows 10 is that you can use Sysprep to prepare a new machine for duplication. You can use Sysprep to image a Windows 10 machine. The following steps are necessary to image a new machine:

1. Install the Windows 10 operating system.

2. Install all components on the OS.

3. Run Sysprep /generalize to create the image.

When you image a computer using the Windows Sysprep utility, a Windows image (.wim) file is created. Most third-party imaging software products can work with the Windows image file.

Advantages of the System Preparation Tool

The following are advantages of using the System Preparation Tool as a method for automating Windows 10 installations:

- For large numbers of computers with similar hardware, it greatly reduces deployment time by copying the operating system, applications, and Desktop settings from a reference computer to an image, which can then be deployed to multiple computers.

- Using disk imaging facilitates the standardization of Desktops, administrative policies, and restrictions throughout an organization.

- Reference images can be copied across a network connection or through DVDs that are physically distributed to client computers.

Disadvantages of the System Preparation Tool

There are some disadvantages of using the System Preparation Tool as a method for automating Windows 10 installations:

- Image Capture Wizard, third-party imaging software, or hardware disk-duplication devices must be used for an image-based setup.

- The version of the System Preparation Tool that shipped with Windows 10 must be used. An older version of Sysprep cannot be used on a Windows 10 image.

- The System Preparation Tool will not detect any hardware that is not Plug and Play compliant.

Overview of the Windows Assessment and Deployment Kit

Another way to install Windows 10 is to use the *Windows Assessment and Deployment Kit (ADK)*. The Windows (ADK) is a set of utilities and documentation that allows an administrator to configure and deploy Windows operating systems. An administrator can use the Windows (ADK) to do the following:

- Windows Configuration Designer

- Windows Assessment Toolkit

- Windows Performance Toolkit

The Windows (ADK) can be installed and configured on the following operating systems:

- Windows 10

- Windows 7 with SP1

- Windows 8 / 8.1

- Windows Server 2019

- Windows Server 2016

- Windows Server 2012 R2

- Windows Server 2012

- Windows Server 2008

- Windows Server 2008 R2

The Windows (ADK) is a good solution for organizations that need to customize the Windows deployment environments. The Windows (ADK) allows an administrator to have the flexibility needed for mass deployments of Windows operating systems. Since every organization's needs are different, the Windows (ADK) allows you to use all or just some of the deployment tools available. It allows you to manage deployments by using some additional tools.

Windows Configuration Designer   The tools included with this part of the Windows (ADK) will allow an administrator to easily deploy and configure Windows operating systems and images.

Windows Assessment Toolkit   When new Windows operating systems are installed, applications that ran on the previous version of Windows may not work properly. The Windows Assessment Toolkit allows an administrator to help solve these issues before they occur.

Windows Performance Toolkit   The Windows Performance Toolkit is a utility that will locate computers on a network and then perform a thorough inventory of them. This inventory can then be used to determine which machines can have Windows 10 installed.

Windows Configuration Designer

The Windows Configuration Designer allows an administrator to work with images. The Windows Configuration Designer allows an IT department to do the following;

- View and configure all of the settings and policies for a Windows 10 image or provisioning package.
- Create Windows provisioning answer files.
- Allow an answer file to add third-party drivers, apps, or other assets.
- Create variants and specify the settings that apply to each variant.
- Build and flash a Windows image.
- Build a provisioning package.

The Windows Configuration Designer gives an IT department many options on how to deploy and set up Windows 10 clients. Here are some of the following tools included with the Windows Configuration Designer:

- Configure and edit images by using the Deployment Image Servicing and Management (DISM) utility.
- Create Windows Preinstallation Environment (Windows PE) images.
- Migrate user data and profiles using the User State Migration Tool (USMT).
- Windows Configuration Designer (Windows Configuration Designer)

Summary of Windows 10 Deployment Options

Table 1.8 summarizes the installation tools and files that are used with unattended, automated installations of Windows 10, the associated installation method, and a description of each tool.

TABLE 1.8   Summary of Windows 10 unattended deployment utilities

Tool or File	Automated Installation Option	Description
Setup.exe	Unattended installation	Program used to initiate the installation process
Autounattend.xml	Unattended installation	Answer file used to customize installation queries

Tool or File	Automated Installation Option	Description
Windows System Image Manager	Unattended installation	Program used to create answer files to be used for unattended installations
DISM.exe	DISM	Command-line utility that works in conjunction with Sysprep to create and manage Windows 10 image files for deployment
Sysprep.exe	Sysprep	System Preparation Tool, which prepares a source reference computer that will be used in conjunction with a distribution share or with disk duplication through Image Capture Wizard, third-party software, or hardware disk-duplication devices

The Windows 10 installation utilities and resources relating to automated deployment are found in a variety of locations. Table 1.9 provides a quick reference for each utility or resource and its location.

TABLE 1.9   Location of Windows 10 deployment utilities and resources

Utility	Location
DISM.exe	Included with Windows 10; installed to %WINDIR%\system32\DISM
Sysprep.exe	Included with Windows 10; installed to %WINDIR%\system32\sysprep
Image Capture Wizard.exe	Installed with the WAIK; installed to C:\ProgramFiles\ Windows AIK\Tools\x86\Image Capture Wizard.exe
Windows System Image Manager	Installed with WAIK; installed to C:\ProgramFiles\Windows AIK\ Tools\Image Manager\ImgMgr.exe

Deploying Unattended Installations

You can deploy Windows 10 installations or upgrades through a Windows 10 distribution DVD or through a distribution server that contains Windows 10 images and associated files, such as Autounattend.xml for unattended installations. Using a DVD can be advantageous if the computer on which you want to install Windows 10 is not connected to the network or is connected via a low-bandwidth network. It is also typically faster to install a Windows 10 image from DVD than to use a network connection.

Unattended installations rely on options configured in an answer file that is deployed with the Windows 10 image. Answer files are XML files that contain the settings that are typically supplied by the installer during attended installations of Windows 10. Answer files can also contain instructions for how programs and applications should be run.

The Windows Setup program is run to install or upgrade to Windows 10 from computers that are running compatible versions of Windows. In fact, Windows Setup is the basis for the other types of installation procedures, including unattended installations, WDS, and image-based installations.

The Windows Setup program (Setup.exe) replaces Winnt32.exe and Winnt.exe, which are the setup programs used in versions of Windows prior to Windows 7. Although it's a graphical tool, Windows Setup can be run from the command line. For example, you can use the following command to initiate an unattended installation of Windows 10:

```
setup.exe /unattend:answerfile
```

The Windows Setup program has several command-line options that can be applied. Table 1.10 describes the Setup.exe command-line options.

TABLE 1.10   Setup.exe command-line options and descriptions

Setup.exe **Option**	**Description**
/1394debug: *channel* [baudrate: *baudrate*]	Enables kernel debugging over a FireWire (IEEE 1394) port for troubleshooting purposes. The [baudrate] optional parameter specifies the baud rate for data transfer during the debugging process.
/debug:*port* [*baudrate*:*baudrate*]	Enables kernel debugging over the specified port for troubleshooting purposes. The [baudrate] optional parameter specifies the baud rate for data transfer during the debugging process.
/DynamicUpdate {enable | disable}	Used to prevent a dynamic update from running during the installation process.
/emsport:{com1|com2| usebiossettings|off}[/ emsbaudrate:*baudrate*]	Configures EMS to be enabled or disabled. The [baudrate] optional parameter specifies the baud rate for data transfer during the debugging process.
/m: *folder_name*	Used with Setup to specify that replacement files should be copied from the specified location. If the files are not present, Setup will use the default location.

Setup.exe **Option**	**Description**
/noreboot	Normally, when the down-level phase of Setup.exe is complete, the computer restarts. This option specifies that the computer should not restart so that you can execute another command prior to the restart.
/tempdrive:*drive letter*	Specifies the location that will be used to store the temporary files for Windows 10 and the installation partition for Windows 10.
/unattend:[*answerfile*]	Specifies that you will be using an unattended installation for Windows 10. The answerfile variable points to the custom answer file you will use for installation.

Next we'll look at the System Preparation Tool (Sysprep); using it is one of many ways to install Windows 10 automatically.

Using the System Preparation Tool to Prepare an Installation for Imaging

You can use disk images to install Windows 10 on computers that have similar hardware configurations. Also, if a computer is having technical difficulties, you can use a disk image to quickly restore it to a baseline configuration.

To create a disk image, you install Windows 10 on the source computer with the configuration that you want to copy and use the System Preparation Tool to prepare the installation for imaging. The source computer's configuration should also include any applications that should be installed on target computers.

Once you have prepared the installation for imaging, you can use imaging software such as Image Capture Wizard to create an image of the installation.

The System Preparation Tool (Sysprep.exe) is included with Windows 10, in the %WINDIR%\system32\sysprep directory. When you run this utility on the source computer, it strips out information that is unique for each computer, such as the SID. Table 1.11 defines the command options that you can use to customize the Sysprep.exe operation.

TABLE 1.11   System Preparation Tool command-line options

Switch	Description
/audit	Configures the computer to restart into audit mode, which allows you to add drivers and applications to Windows or test the installation prior to deployment

TABLE 1.11   System Preparation Tool command-line options *(continued)*

Switch	Description
/generalize	Removes any unique system information from the image, including the SID and log information
/oobe	Specifies that the Windows Welcome screen should be displayed when the computer reboots
/quiet	Runs the installation with no user interaction
/quit	Specifies that the System Preparation Tool should quit after the specified operations have been completed
/reboot	Restarts the target computer after the System Preparation Tool completes
/shutdown	Specifies that the computer should shut down after the specified operations have been completed
/unattend	Indicates the name and location of the answer file to use

In the following sections, you will learn how to create a disk image and how to copy and install from it.

Preparing a Windows 10 Installation

To run the System Preparation Tool and prepare an installation for imaging, take the following steps:

1. Install Windows 10 on a source computer. The computer's hardware configuration should be similar to that of the destination computer(s). The source computer should not be a member of a domain.

2. Log on to the source computer as Administrator and, if desired, install and configure any applications, files (such as newer versions of Plug and Play drivers), or custom settings (for example, a custom Desktop) that will be applied to the target computer(s).

3. Verify that your image meets the specified configuration criteria and that all applications are properly installed and working.

4. Select Start ➤ Computer, and navigate to C:\%WINDIR%\System32\sysprep. Double-click the Sysprep application icon.

5. The Windows System Preparation Tool dialog box appears. Select the appropriate options for your configuration.

6. If configured to do so, Windows 10 will be rebooted into setup mode, and you will be prompted to enter the appropriate setup information.

7. You will now be able to use imaging software to create an image of the computer to deploy to other computers.

In Exercise 1.7, you will use the System Preparation Tool to prepare the computer for disk imaging. The Sysprep utility must be run on a machine with a clean version of Windows 10. If you upgraded a Windows 7 / 8 / 8.1 machine to Windows 10, you will not be able to run the Sysprep utility.

EXERCISE 1.7

Prepare a System for Imaging by Using the System Preparation Tool

1. Log on to the source computer as Administrator, and if desired, install and configure any applications that should also be installed on the target computer.

2. Select Start ➢ Computer, and navigate to `C:\%WINDIR%\System32\sysprep`. Double-click the Sysprep application icon.

3. In the System Preparation Tool dialog box, select Enter System Out-Of-Box Experience (OOBE) in the system cleanup action.

4. Under the shutdown options, depending on the options selected, the System Preparation Tool will quit, the computer will shut down, or the computer will be rebooted into setup mode, where you will need to configure the setup options. Choose the Reboot option. Click OK.

5. Configure the Sysprep utility and name the image **image.wim**.

After creating the Sysprep image, you need to use some type of third-party software to capture it. Windows includes a utility called Image Capture Wizard for just that purpose.

Using Windows Configuration Designer to Create a Disk Image

After you've run the System Preparation Tool on the source computer, you can create an image from the installation, and you can then install the image on target computers. To create an image, you can use Image Capture Wizard, which is a utility that can be used to create and manage Windows image (`.wim`) files.

To run the Image Capture Wizard utility to create a disk image of a Windows 10 installation, follow these steps:

1. Open Windows Configuration Designer.

2. Select your desired option on the Start page (see Figure 1.28).

FIGURE 1.28   Windows Configuration Designer Start Page

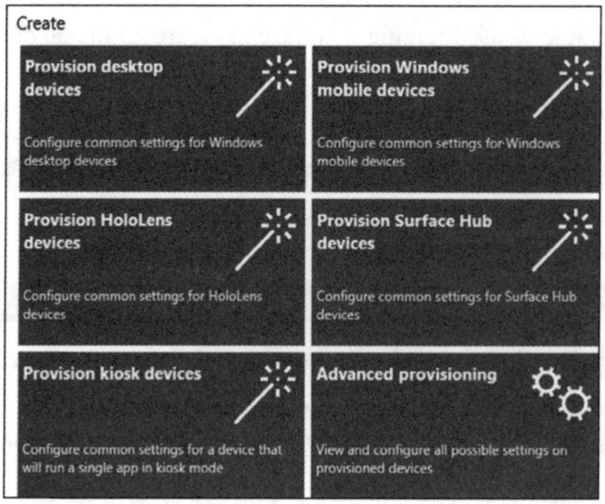

3. Name your project and click Finish. The pages for desktop provisioning will walk you through the following steps.

    1. Set up device (this includes device name and Product Key number).

    2. Set up network settings.

    3. Set up Account Management (this includes adding the machine to a domain or Azure domain and inputting the username and password).

    4. Adding applications

    5. Adding any needed certificates

    6. Finish configuration.

There is also a command line version of the Windows Configuration Designer tool that you can use called the Windows Configuration Designer command-line interface (CLI). The Microsoft exams have started using a lot of command line utilities on their tests. So let us take a look at the Windows Configuration Designer command line utility.

Table 1.12 shows you the Windows Configuration Designer command-line interface (CLI) Switches command and some of the switches that you can use to configure the images.

TABLE 1.12   Windows Configuration Designer command-line interface (CLI) switches

Switch	Description
/CustomizationXML	This command identifies the location of the Windows provisioning XML file. This file holds the information for customization assets and settings.

Switch	Description
/PackagePath	Identifies the location and the built provisioning package name where the package will be saved.
/StoreFile	This command allows IT administrators to use their own settings store instead of the default store used by Windows Configuration Designer. If an IT administrator does not determine their own store, then a default store that's common to all Windows editions will be loaded by Windows Configuration Designer.
/Variables	Identifies a macro pair that is separated by semicolon <name> and <value>.
Encrypted	Indicates if the provisioning package should be created with encryption or not. Windows Configuration Designer will then automatically generate a decryption password that is included with the output.
Overwrite	Indicates whether or not to overwrite the existing provisioning package.
/?	This command is used to access the Windows Configuration Designer help. The help lists the switches and their descriptions for the Windows Configuration Designer command-line tool.

Using the Deployment Image Servicing and Management Tool

Deployment Image Servicing and Management (DISM.exe) is a command-line utility that allows you to manipulate a Windows image. DISM also allows you to prepare a Windows PE image. DISM replaces multiple programs that were included with Windows 7 / 8 / 8.1. These programs include Package Manager (Pkgmgr.exe), PEimg, and Intlcfg. These tools have been consolidated into one tool (DISM.exe), and new functionality has been added to improve the experience for offline servicing.

When DISM was first released, it was primarily used for servicing and managing Windows images. But now DISM has become even more powerful, including capturing images and deploying images.

DISM provides additional functionality when used with Windows 10 and Windows Server. You can use DISM to do the following:

- Capture Windows images.
- Copy and move Windows images.
- Install Windows images.

- Add, remove, and enumerate packages.
- Add, remove, and enumerate drivers.
- Enable or disable Windows features.
- Apply changes to an Unattend.xml answer file.
- Configure international settings.
- Upgrade a Windows image to a different edition.
- Prepare a Windows PE 3.0 image.
- Work with all platforms (32-bit, 64-bit, and Itanium).
- Use of Package Manager scripts

Table 1.13 shows the different commands that can be used with DISM.exe.

TABLE 1.13 DISM.exe command-line commands

Command	Description
/Add-Driver	Adds third-party driver packages to an offline Windows image.
/Get-CurrentEdition	Displays the edition of the specified image.
/Get-Drivers	Displays basic information about driver packages in the online or offline image. By default, only third-party drivers will be listed.
/Get-DriverInfo	Displays detailed information about a specific driver package.
/Get-Help /?	Displays information about the option and the arguments.
/Get-TargetEditions	Displays a list of Windows editions that an image can be changed to.
/Remove-Driver	Removes third-party drivers from an offline image.
/Set-ProductKey:<productKey>	Can only be used to enter the product key for the current edition in an offline Windows image.
/Online /Enable-Feature /All /FeatureName:Microsoft-Hyper-V	This command allows you to install Hyper-V into a Windows image while it's an actual image.

Using Windows System Image Manager to Create Answer Files

Answer files are automated installation scripts used to answer the questions that appear during a normal Windows 10 installation. You can use answer files with Windows 10 unattended installations, disk image installations, or WDS installations. Setting up answer files allows you to easily deploy Windows 10 to computers that may not be configured in the same manner, with little or no user intervention. Because answer files are associated with image files, you can validate the settings within an answer file against the image file.

You can create answer files by using the Windows System Image Manager (Windows SIM) utility. There are several advantages to using Windows SIM to create answer files:

- You can easily create and edit answer files through a graphical interface, which reduces syntax errors.

- It simplifies the addition of user-specific or computer-specific configuration information.

- You can validate existing answer files against newly created images.

- You can include additional application and device drivers in the answer file.

In the following sections, you will learn about options that can be configured through Windows SIM, how to create answer files with Windows SIM, how to format an answer file, and how to manually edit answer files.

Configuring Components through Windows System Image Manager

You can use Windows SIM to configure a wide variety of installation options. The following list defines which components can be configured through Windows SIM and gives a short description of each component:

auditSystem   Adds additional device drivers, specifies firewall settings, and applies a name to the system when the image is booted into audit mode. Audit mode is initiated by using the sysprep/audit command.

auditUser   Executes RunSynchronous or RunAsynchronous commands when the image is booted into audit mode. Audit mode is initiated by using the sysprep/audit command.

generalize   Removes system-specific information from an image so that the image can be used as a reference image. The settings specified in the generalize component will be applied only if the sysprep/generalize command is used.

offlineServicing   Specifies the language packs and packages to apply to an image prior to the image being extracted to the hard disk.

oobeSystem   Specifies the settings to apply to the computer the first time the computer is booted into the Windows Welcome screen, which is also known as the Out-Of-Box

Experience (OOBE). To boot to the Welcome screen, the sysprep/oobe command should be used.

specialize Configures the specific settings for the target computer, such as network settings and domain information. This configuration pass is used in conjunction with the generalize configuration pass.

Windows PE Sets the Windows PE specific configuration settings as well as several Windows Setup settings, such as partitioning and formatting the hard disk, selecting an image, and applying a product key.

Windows Update

Windows Update is a utility that connects to the Microsoft website or to a local update server called a Windows Server Update Services (WSUS) server to ensure that the Windows 10 operating system (along with other Microsoft products) has the most up-to-date versions of Microsoft operating system files or software.

Some of the common update categories associated with Windows Update are as follows:

- Security updates
- Critical updates
- Service packs
- Drivers
- Product/software updates
- Windows Store

So let's begin by looking at how Windows 10 updates get created by Microsoft.

The Update Process

To truly understand updates, you need to understand how the update process works with Microsoft. Microsoft normally releases updates to their products on Tuesdays (this is why we use the term *Patch Tuesdays*). But before that update gets released to the public, it has already been tested at Microsoft.

It all starts with the Windows engineering team adding new features and functionality to Windows using product cycles. These product cycles are comprised from three phases; development, testing, and release.

After the new Windows 10 features or functionality are developed, Microsoft employees test these updates out themselves on their own Windows 10 machines. This is referred to as "selfhost testing."

After the updates get tested at Microsoft, they then get released to the public. With Windows 10, Microsoft has introduced new ways to service updates. Microsoft's new servicing options are referred to as Semi-Annual Channel, Long-Term Servicing Branch (LTSB), and Windows Insider. Table 1.14 (taken directly from Microsoft's website) shows the different servicing options and the benefits of those options.

TABLE 1.14 Servicing Options

From this channel	To this channel	You need to
Windows Insider Program	Semi-Annual Channel (Targeted)	Wait for the final Semi-Annual Channel release.
	Semi-Annual Channel	Not directly possible, because Windows Insider Program devices are automatically upgraded to the Semi-Annual Channel (Targeted) release at the end of the development cycle.
	Long-Term Servicing Channel	Not directly possible (requires wipe-and-load).
Semi-Annual Channel (Targeted)	Insider	Use the Settings app to enroll the device in the Windows Insider Program.
	Semi-Annual Channel	Select the **Defer upgrade** setting, or move the PC to a target group or flight that will not receive the next upgrade until it is business ready. Note that this change will not have any immediate impact; it only prevents the installation of the next Semi-Annual Channel release.
	Long-Term Servicing Channel	Not directly possible (requires wipe-and-load).
Semi-Annual Channel	Insider	Use the Settings app to enroll the device in the Windows Insider Program.
	Semi-Annual Channel (Targeted)	Disable the **Defer upgrade** setting, or move the device to a target group or flight that will receive the latest Current Semi-Annual Channel release.
	Long-Term Servicing Channel	Not directly possible (requires wipe-and-load).

TABLE 1.14   Servicing Options *(continued)*

From this channel	To this channel	You need to
Long-Term Servicing Channel	Insider	Use media to upgrade to the latest Windows Insider Program build.
	Semi-Annual Channel (Targeted)	Use media to upgrade. Note that the Semi-Annual Channel build must be a later build.
	Semi-Annual Channel	Use media to upgrade. Note that the Semi-Annual Channel build must be a later build.

Using Windows Update

There are two ways a user can receive updates: directly from Microsoft or using Microsoft Windows Server Update Services (WSUS). WSUS runs on a Windows server, and that server goes out to the Microsoft website and downloads the updates for your Windows clients. This allows client machines to receive their updates from a local server.

One advantage to using WSUS is that administrators can approve the updates before they get deployed to the client machines. Another advantage is that your clients only need to download updates locally, without using your Internet bandwidth.

WSUS is discussed in detail in *MCSA Windows Server 2016 Complete Study Guide: Exam 70-740, Exam 70-741, Exam 70-742, and Exam 70-743, 2nd Edition,* by William Panek (Wiley, 2018).

If you want the Windows 10 clients to access and get their own updates, they would follow these steps to configure Windows Update:

1.   Select Start ➢ Settings.

   ▪   From Settings, select Update And Security.

2.   Configure the options you want to use for Windows Update by clicking the Advanced Options link. You can access the following options from Windows Update:

   ▪   Give me updates for other Microsoft products

      ▪   This setting allows you to get updates for other Microsoft products like Microsoft Office.

   ▪   Choose when updates are installed

   ▪   Pause updates

- Delivery Optimization
    - Windows Update Delivery Optimization provides you with Windows and Store app updates and other Microsoft products quickly and reliably.
    - Allow updates from other PCs.
- Privacy settings
    - This option allows you to set all of your system's privacy settings.

Check For Updates

When you click Check For Updates, Windows Update will retrieve a list of available updates from the Internet. You can then click View Available Updates to see what updates are available. Updates are marked as Important, Recommended, or Optional. Figure 1.29 shows the Check for Updates button.

FIGURE 1.29   Check For Updates button

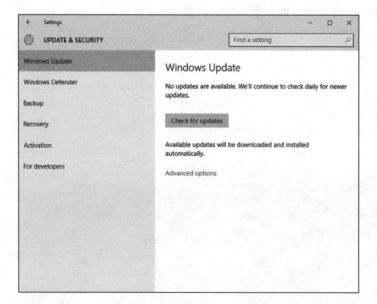

Using Command-Line Options

Command-line options are becoming more and more popular among administrators and users. Windows Update has a few command-line options that can be used to help configure and maintain it. First, to start Windows Update from a command prompt, you can type **wuapp.exe**. Another command-line option that works with Windows Update is called Windows Update Automatic Update Client (`wuauclt.exe`), which offers the following options:

Detectnow   When working with WSUS, waiting for detection to start can become very time-consuming. So Microsoft has added an option to allow you to initiate the process of detecting available updates right away. To run the detectnow option, type the following command at the command prompt: **`wuauclt.exe /detectnow`**.

Reportnow   This command allows you to send all queued reporting events to the server asynchronously. To execute this command, type **`wuauclt.exe /reportnow`** at the command prompt.

Resetauthorization   WSUS uses a cookie on Windows 10 client computers to store different types of information. By default, an hour after the cookie is created, it expires. If you need the cookie to expire now, you can use the resetauthorization option along with the detectnow option. Using these options will expire the cookie, initiate detection, and have WSUS update computer group membership. To execute this command, type **`wuauclt.exe /resetauthorization /detectnow`** at the command prompt.

Installing Windows Store Updates

Besides getting updates for the Windows 10 operating system and the different Microsoft products, you may also need to get updates for any of the applications, games, music, videos, and software that you downloaded from the Windows Store. To receive Windows Store updates, you need to go out to the Windows Store and then click on the three dots to the right of your Microsoft account (see Figure 1.30).

FIGURE 1.30   Windows Store button

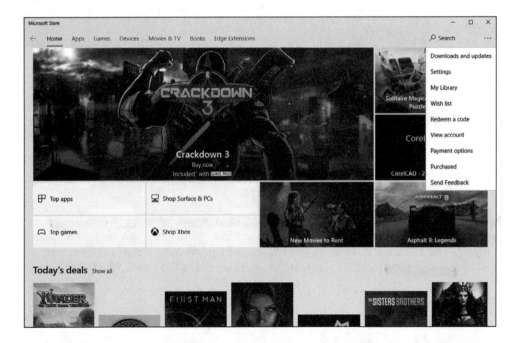

After you click on the three dots, you click on the Downloads And Updates option. That will take you to the Downloads and Updates page (see Figure 1.31). Once on this page, click the Get Updates button. This will allow you to download and install any Windows Store updates.

FIGURE 1.31   Check for updates button

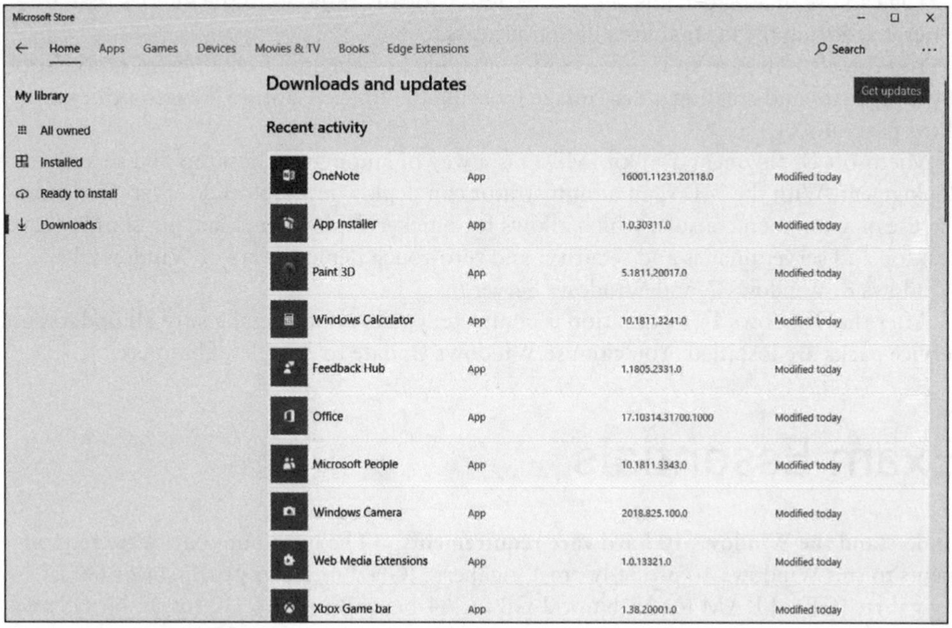

Summary

This chapter started with a discussion of the features included with Windows 10. We also took a look at the difference between 64-bit and 32-bit operating systems and showed some of the advantages that 64-bit entails, such as greater RAM and processor speed.

Then you learned about installing Windows 10. Installation is an easy process, but you must first make sure the machine is compatible with the Windows 10 operating system.

There are two main ways to install Windows 10: upgrade or clean install. You can upgrade a Windows 7 or Windows 8/8.1 machine to Windows 10. You can't upgrade Windows XP to Windows 10.

I discussed automated installation of Windows 10. Installing Windows 10 through an automated process is an effective way to install the Windows 10 operating system on multiple computers.

There are several methods for automated installation: unattended installations, Windows Deployment Services (WDS), Windows Assessment and Deployment Kit (ADK), third-party applications, unattended installations, and using the System Preparation Tool along with Image Capture Wizard.

Windows Deployment Services (WDS) is a suite of components that allows you to remotely install Windows 10 on client computers.

The Windows (ADK) is a set of utilities and documentation that allows an administrator to configure and deploy Windows operating systems.

You can use unattended answer files to automatically respond to the queries that are generated during the normal installation process.

You can also prepare an installation for imaging by using the System Preparation Tool (Sysprep.exe) and creating a disk image by using the Image Capture Wizard utility or a third-party utility.

Microsoft Deployment Toolkit (MDT) is a way of automating desktop and server deployment. With the MDT, an administrator can deploy desktops and servers through the use of a common console, which allows for quicker deployments; having standardized desktop and server images and security; and zero-touch deployments of Windows 10, Windows 8, Windows 7, and Windows Server.

After the Windows 10 installation is complete, you'll want to make sure all updates and service packs are installed. You can use Windows Update to complete that task.

Exam Essentials

Understand the Windows 10 hardware requirements.   The minimum hardware requirements to run Windows 10 properly are 1 gigahertz (GHz) or faster processor or SoC, 1 gigabyte (GB) of RAM for 32-bit or 2 GB for 64-bit of RAM, 16 GB for 32-bit OS and 20 GB for 64-bit OS of hard drive space, DirectX 9 or later with WDDM 1.0 video driver, and a DVD-R/W drive or compatible network interface card.

Understand how to complete a clean install.   If your machine meets the minimum hardware requirements, you can install Windows 10. There are a few different ways to install Windows 10 onto a computer. You can use the installation disk or USB, install it over a network, or install it from an image.

Understand how to complete an upgrade.   You can't upgrade a Windows Vista machine to Windows 10. To complete an upgrade on a Windows 7 or Windows 8 / 8.1 machine, insert the Windows 10 DVD into the Windows machine or connect to the Windows 10 files over the network and complete an upgrade on the computer.

You can't upgrade a Windows XP machine directly to Windows 10. If the machine is running Windows XP, you have to use a migration tool to migrate all the user data from Windows XP to a Windows 10 machine.

Know the difference between the various unattended installation methods.   Understand the various options available for unattended installations of Windows 10 and when it is appropriate to use each installation method.

Understand the features and uses of WDS.   Know when it is appropriate to use WDS to manage unattended installations. Be able to list the requirements for setting up WDS servers and WDS clients. Be able to complete an unattended installation using WDS.

Be able to use disk images for unattended installations.   Know how to perform unattended installations of Windows 10 using the System Preparation Tool and disk images.

Understand the Microsoft Deployment Toolkit (MDT).   Know that the MDT is a way of automating desktop and server deployment. Understand that the MDT allows an administrator to deploy desktops and servers through the use of a common console.

Understand how to receive updates.   You need to understand how to set up and receive Microsoft updates for Windows 10, Microsoft products, and the Windows Store. Make sure you know the different settings for configuring update advanced options.

Video Resources

There are videos available for the following exercises:

    1.1

    1.2

You can access the videos at http://www.wiley.com/go/sybextestprep.

Review Questions

1. You are the administrator in charge of a computer that runs both Windows 7 and Windows 10. Windows 10 is installed on a different partition from Windows 7. You have to make sure that the computer always starts Windows 7 by default. What action should you perform?

   A. Run Bcdedit.exe and the /default parameter.

   B. Run Bcdedit.exe and the /bootcd parameter.

   C. Create a Boot.ini file in the root of the Windows 10 partition.

   D. Create a Boot.ini file in the root of the Windows 7 partition.

2. You are the administrator for a Windows 10 computer. You have decided to use Windows Update, but you want to be able to change the settings manually. What should you do?

   A. Log on to Windows 10 as a member of the Administrators group.

   B. From the local Group Policy, modify the Windows Update settings.

   C. Right-click Windows Update and select Run As Administrator.

   D. Right-click the command prompt, select Run As Administrator, and then run Wuapp.exe.

3. You want to initiate a new installation of Windows 10 from the command line. You plan to accomplish this by using the Setup.exe command-line setup utility. You want to use an answer file with this command. Which command-line option should you use?

   A. /unattend

   B. /apply

   C. /noreboot

   D. /generalize

4. You are the network administrator for your organization. You have a reference computer that runs Windows 10. You need to create and deploy an image of the Windows 10 computer. You create an answer file named answer.xml. You have to make sure that the installation applies the answer file after you deploy the image. Which command should you run before you capture the image?

   A. DISM.exe /append answer.xml /check

   B. DISM.exe /mount answer.xml /verify

   C. Sysprep.exe /reboot /audit /unattend:answer.xml

   D. Sysprep.exe /generalize /oobe /unattend:answer.xml

5. You have a Windows 10 Windows Image (.wim) that is mounted. You need to view the list of third-party drivers installed on the WIM. What should you do?

   A. Run DISM and specify the /get-drivers parameter.

   B. Run Driverquery.exe and use the /si parameter.

C. From Device Manager, view all hidden drivers.

D. From Windows Explorer, open the mount folder.

6. You are planning on deploying 1,000 new Windows 10 computers throughout your company. Each new computer has the same configuration. You want to create a reference image that will then be applied to the remaining images. Which of the following utilities should you use?

   A. WDSUTIL

   B. Setup.exe

   C. Windows SIM

   D. DISM.exe

7. You are the network administrator for a large organization. You are in charge of developing a plan to install 200 Windows 10 computers in your company's data center. You decide to use WDS. You are using a Windows Server 2012 R2 domain and have verified that your network meets the requirements for using WDS. What command-line utility should you use to configure the WDS server?

   A. DISM

   B. WDSUTIL

   C. Setup.exe

   D. The WDS icon in Control Panel

8. Will is the network manager for a large company. He has been tasked with creating a deployment plan to automate installations for 100 computers that need to have Windows 10 installed. Will wants to use WDS for the installations. To fully automate the installations, he needs to create an answer file. Will does not want to create the answer files with a text editor. What other program can he use to create unattended answer files via a GUI interface?

   A. DISM

   B. Answer Manager

   C. Windows System Image Manager

   D. System Preparation Tool

9. You are using WDS to install 20 Windows 10 computers. When the clients attempt to use WDS, they are not able to complete the unattended installation. You suspect that the WDS server has not been configured to respond to client requests. Which one of the following utilities would you use to configure the WDS server to respond to client requests?

   A. Active Directory Users and Computers

   B. Active Directory Users and Groups

   C. WDS MMC Snap-in

   D. WDSMAN

10. You want to install a group of 25 computers using disk images created in conjunction with the System Preparation Tool. Your plan is to create an image from a reference computer and then copy the image to all the machines. You do not want to create an SID on the destination computer when you use the image. Which `Sysprep.exe` command-line option should you use to set this up?

   A. `/specialize`

   B. `/generalize`

   C. `/oobe`

   D. `/quiet`

Chapter

2

Configuring Users

MICROSOFT EXAM OBJECTIVES COVERED IN THIS CHAPTER:

✓ **Manage local users, local groups, and devices**

- Manage devices in directories; manage local groups; manage local users.

✓ **Configure remote connectivity**

- Configure remote management; enable PowerShell Remoting; configure remote desktop access.

✓ **Configure devices by using local policies**

- Configure local registry; implement local policy; troubleshoot group policies on devices.

Now that we have discussed installing Windows 10, we need to look at one of the most important topics to discuss, authorization and authentication.

Understanding how users authenticate onto your network and knowing some of the tricks on how to secure your network and users is one of the most important tasks that administrators must perform.

One administrative job that we need to perform is creating user and group accounts. Without a user account, a user cannot log on to a computer, server, or network. When users log on, they supply a username and password. Then their user accounts are validated by a security mechanism. In Windows 10, users can log on to a computer locally, or if the machine is a member of an Active Directory domain, the user can authenticate against a local copy of Active Directory or a cloud-based copy of Active Directory.

Groups are used to ease network administration by grouping users who have similar permission requirements. Groups are an important part of network management. Many administrators are able to accomplish the majority of their management tasks through the use of groups; they rarely assign permissions to individual users. Windows 10 includes built-in local groups, such as Administrators and Backup Operators.

You create and manage local groups through the Local Users and Groups utility. With this utility, you can add groups, change group membership, rename groups, and delete groups.

Windows 10 also offers a wide variety of security options. If the Windows 10 computer is a part of a domain, you can apply security through Group Policy Objects using the Group Policy Management Console. If the Windows 10 computer is not a part of a domain, then you can use Local Group Policy Objects to manage local security.

Understanding User Accounts

When you install Windows 10, several user accounts are created automatically. Additionally, you can create new user accounts. As you already know, user accounts allow a user to log on to machines and access resources.

You can create local user accounts, which reside locally on the Windows 10 machine. Such accounts cannot be utilized to gain access to any resources hosted on the network. If you have installed Active Directory either in the cloud (Azure Active Directory) or on a network that has a Windows Server domain controller, your network can have domain user accounts as well.

In the following sections, you will learn about the different account types: the default user accounts that are created by Windows 10 and the difference between local and domain user accounts.

Account Types

Windows 10 supports two basic types of user accounts: administrator and standard user (see Figure 2.1). Each of these accounts is used for specific reasons.

FIGURE 2.1   Choosing an account type

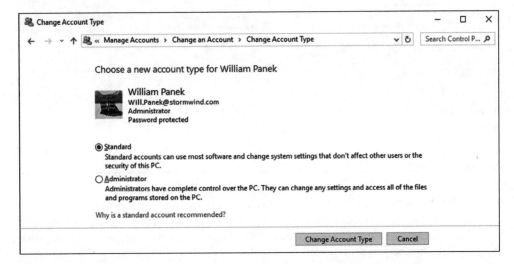

Administrator   The administrator account type provides unrestricted access for performing administrative tasks. As a result, administrator accounts should be used only for performing administrative tasks and should not be used for normal computing tasks.

Only administrator accounts can change the Registry. This is important to know because when most software is installed onto a Windows 10 machine, the Registry gets changed. This is why you need administrator rights to install most software.

Standard User   The standard user account type should be assigned to every user of the computer. Standard user accounts can perform most day-to-day tasks, such as running Microsoft Word, accessing email, using Internet Explorer, and so on. Running as a standard user increases security by limiting the possibility of a virus or other malicious code from infecting the computer. Standard user accounts are unable to make system-wide changes, which also helps to increase security.

When you install Windows 10, by default there are premade accounts called built-in accounts. Let's take a look at them.

Built-In Accounts

When installed into a workgroup environment, Windows 10 has four built-in accounts, which are created automatically at the time you install the operating system (see Figure 2.2). Figure 2.2 also shows the accounts that I created while writing this book.

FIGURE 2.2   The four built-in accounts

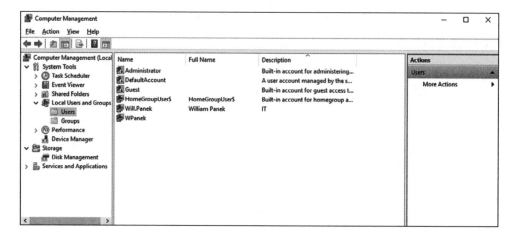

Administrator   The Administrator account is a special account that has Full Control over the computer. The Administrator account can perform all tasks, such as creating users and groups, managing the filesystem, installing applications, and setting up printing. Note that the Administrator account is disabled by default.

DefaultAccount   This is a user account created by the system and used by the system. This account is a member of the System Managed Accounts group.

Guest   The Guest account allows users to access the computer even if a person does not have a unique username and password. Because of the inherent security risks associated with this type of user, the Guest account is disabled by default. When this account is enabled, it is usually given very limited privileges.

Initial User   The Initial User account uses the name of the registered user. By default, the initial user is a member of the Administrators group.

By default, the name Administrator is given to a user account that is a member of the Administrators group. However, in Windows 10, this user account is disabled by default. You can increase the computer's security by leaving this account disabled and assigning other users to the Administrators group. This way, a malicious user will be unable to log on to the computer using the Administrator user account.

All four of these users are considered local users, and their permissions are contained to the Windows 10 machine. If the user's account needs to access resources on machines other than their own, you can have a user log in to the Windows 10 computer as a remote user (a user who is not in front of the machine they're logging on to), and this would be considered a domain user's account. Let's take a look at the difference between these account types.

Local and Domain User Accounts

Windows 10 supports two kinds of users: local users and domain users. Local users get set up on each Windows 10 client system. The Windows 10 system can be part of a workgroup or it can be a stand-alone system. A computer that is running Windows 10 has the ability to store its own user accounts database. The user accounts stored at the local computer are known as *local user accounts*.

Workgroups are networks that have user databases on each individual Windows 10 machine. However, you can share resources on the workgroup network.

Domains

Domains are networks where there is a centralized security database (Active Directory), and you can control all of your users and groups from one central location.

Active Directory is a directory service that stores information in a central database, which allows users to have a single user account for the network. The user accounts stored in Active Directory's central database are called *domain user accounts*. Active Directory is available in two different models. There is a cloud-based Active Directory called Azure Active Directory and a server-based version that runs on Windows Server platforms.

Workgroups

You can log on locally to a Windows 10 computer using a locally stored user account, or you can log on to a domain using an Active Directory account. When you install Windows 10 on a computer, you specify that the computer will be a part of a workgroup, which implies a local logon, or that it will be a part of a domain, which implies a domain logon.

On all Windows versions except domain controllers, you can create local users through the Local Users and Groups utility, as described in the section "Working with User Accounts" later in this chapter. On Windows Server domain controllers (Windows Server 2000 and above), you manage users with the Microsoft Active Directory Users and Computers MMC.

Active Directory is covered in detail in *MCSA Windows Server 2016 Complete Study Guide: Exam 70-740, Exam 70-741, Exam 70-742 and Composite Upgrade Exam 70-743 2nd Edition* by William Panek (Wiley, 2018).

Workplace Join

There may be times when you need someone to gain access to a domain resource but that person doesn't have a domain account. That's where Workplace Join can help. Workplace Join is a Windows tool that you can download and use on your domain.

Workplace Join allows an end user to use a corporate email address and password to connect a Windows system (Windows phone, tablet, or operating system) to a domain. The email address and password are then sent to an Active Directory server to be verified. The server can be set to then send a message to the device to confirm that the device should be given access to the domain. After the verification is done, Workplace Join creates a new device object in Active Directory and installs a certificate onto the Windows device.

Logging Off

No matter what type of network you have, you will eventually need to log off the Windows 10 system. When users are ready to stop working, they should either log off or shut down the system. A user can do either of these by right-clicking the Windows Start button and choosing Shut Down or Sign Out.

Working with User Accounts

To set up and manage your local user accounts, you use the Local Users and Groups utility or the User Accounts option in Control Panel. With either option, you can create, disable, delete, and rename user accounts as well as change user passwords.

Windows 10 includes User Account Control (UAC), which provides an additional level of security by limiting the level of access that users have when performing normal, everyday tasks. When needed, users can gain elevated access for specific administrative tasks.

Using the Local Users and Groups Utility

There are two common methods for accessing the Local Users and Groups utility:

- Load Local Users and Groups as a Microsoft Management Console (MMC) Snap-in.

- Access the Local Users and Groups utility through the Computer Management utility.

If your computer doesn't have a custom MMC configured, the quickest way to access the Local Users and Groups utility is through the Computer Management utility.

In Exercise 2.1, you will add the Local Users and Groups Snap-in MMC to the Desktop. You can also access the Local Users and Groups MMC by right-clicking Start and choosing Computer Management. This exercise needs to be completed in order to complete other exercises in this chapter.

EXERCISE 2.1

Adding the Local Users and Groups Snap-In

1. In the Search box, type **MMC** and press Enter.

2. If a warning box appears, click Yes.

3. Select File ➤ Add/Remove Snap-in.

4. Scroll down the list and highlight Local Users And Groups, and then click the Add button (shown in Figure 2.3).

FIGURE 2.3   MMC Snap-ins

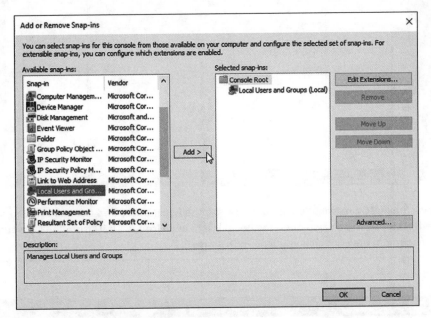

5. In the Choose Target Machine dialog box, click the Finish button to accept the default selection of Local Computer.

6. Click OK in the Add Or Remove Snap-Ins dialog box.

7. In the MMC window, right-click the Local Users And Groups folder and choose New Window From Here. You will see that Local Users and Groups is now the main window.

8. Click File ➤ Save As. Name the console **Local Users and Groups** and choose Desktop under the Save In pull-down box. Click the Save button. This is creating the shortcut shown in Figure 2.4 for you to use in exercises throughout this chapter.

FIGURE 2.4 Local Users and Groups MMC

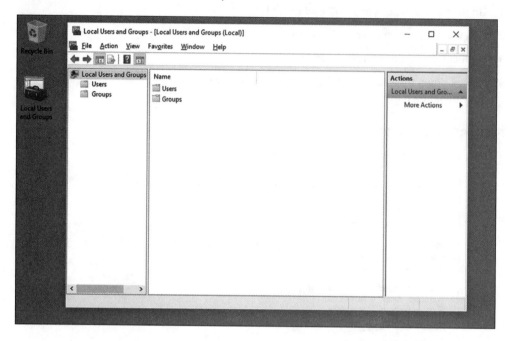

9. Close the MMC Snap-in. You should now see the Local Users and Groups Snap-in on the Desktop. You can also open the Local Users and Groups MMC from the Computer Management utility, which you'll do in Exercise 2.2.

EXERCISE 2.2

Accessing Local Users and Groups via the Computer Management Utility

1. Right-click the Start button and then choose Computer Management.

2. In the Computer Management window, expand the System Tools folder and then the Local Users and Groups folder.

Using the User Accounts Option in Control Panel

Now let's look at an alternative way to configure local users and groups, through the *User Accounts Control (UAC)* Control Panel option, which provides the ability to manage user accounts in addition to configuring parental controls. To access the User Accounts Control

Panel option, click Start ➤ Windows Systems ➤ Control Panel ➤ User Accounts. Table 2.1 briefly describes the configurable options in the User Accounts option in Control Panel.

TABLE 2.1 Configurable user-account options in Control Panel

Option	Explanation
Change Your Password	Allows you to change a user's password.
Change Your Account Name	Allows you to rename the account.
Change Your Account Type	Allows you to change your account type between the standard user and administrator account type.
Manage Another Account	Allows you to configure other accounts on the Windows 10 machine.
Change User Account Control Settings	Allows you to set the level of notification displayed through pop-up messages when changes are made to your computer. These notifications can prevent potentially hazardous programs from being loaded onto the operating system.
Manage Your Credentials	Allows you to set up credentials so you can easily connect to websites that require usernames and passwords or computers that require certificates.
Manage Your File Encryption Certificates	Allows you to manage your file-encryption certificates.
Configure Advanced User Profile Properties	Takes you directly to the User's Profile dialog box in Control Panel ➤ System ➤ Advanced ➤ System Settings.
Change My Environment Variables	Allows you to access the Environment Variables dialog box directly.

Creating New Users

To create users on a Windows 10 computer, you must be logged on as a user with permission to create a new user, which means your account must be a member of the Administrators group.

When you create a new user, there are many options that you have to configure. Table 2.2 describes all the options available in the New User dialog box. (You access this dialog box through the MMC, which is detailed in Exercise 2.3 later in this chapter.)

TABLE 2.2   User account options available in the New User dialog box

Option	Description
User Name	Defines the username for the new account. Choose a name that is consistent with your naming convention (e.g., WPanek). This is the only required field. Usernames are not case sensitive.
Full Name	Allows you to provide more-detailed name information. This typically consists of the user's first and last names (e.g., Will Panek). By default, this field contains the same name as the User Name field.
Description	Typically used to specify a title and/or location (e.g., Sales-Nashville) for the account, but it can be used to provide any additional information about the user.
Password	Assigns the initial password for the user. For security purposes, avoid using readily available information about the user. Passwords are case sensitive.
Confirm Password	Confirms that you typed the password the same way two times to verify that you entered the password correctly.
User Must Change Password At Next Logon	If enabled, forces the user to change the password the first time they log on. This is done to increase security. By default, this option is selected.
User Cannot Change Password	If enabled, prevents a user from changing their password. This is useful for accounts such as Guest and accounts that are shared by more than one user. By default, this option is not selected.
Password Never Expires	If enabled, specifies that the password will never expire, even if a password policy has been specified. For example, you might enable this option if this is a service account and you do not want the administrative overhead of managing password changes. By default, this option is not selected.
Account Is Disabled	If enabled, specifies that this account cannot be used for logon purposes. For example, you might select this option for template accounts or if an account is not currently being used. It helps keep inactive accounts from posing security threats. By default, this option is not selected.

In the following sections, you will learn about username rules and conventions and security identifiers.

Username Rules and Conventions

The only real requirement for creating a new user is that you provide a valid username. To be valid, the name must follow the Windows 10 rules for usernames. However, it's also a good idea to have your own rules for usernames, which form your naming convention.

The following are the Windows 10 rules for usernames:

- A username must be from 1 to 20 characters.

- The username must be unique among all the other user and group names stored on the computer.

- The username cannot contain any of the following characters:

  / \ [ ] : ; | = , + ? < > " @

- A username cannot consist exclusively of periods or spaces.

Keeping the Windows 10 rules in mind, you should choose a naming convention (a consistent naming format) for your company. For example, your naming convention might be to use the last name and first initial, so for a user named William Panek, the username would be WillP or WilliamP. Another naming convention might use the first initial and last name, for the username WPanek. This is the naming convention followed by many midsize and larger organizations. You could base usernames on the naming convention your company has defined for email names so that the logon name and the name in the email address match.

You should also provide a mechanism that will accommodate duplicate names. For example, if you have a user named Jane Smith and a user named John Smith, you might use a middle initial for usernames, such as JDSmith and JRSmith. It is also a good practice to come up with a naming convention for groups, printers, and computers.

 Real World Scenario

Naming-Convention Considerations

As an IT manager, I don't recommend using first name, first initial of last name (WilliamP) as a naming convention. In a midsize-to-large company, there is the possibility of having two WilliamPs, but the odds that you will have two WPaneks are rare.

If you choose to use the first name, first initial of last name option, it can be a lot of work to go back and change this format later if the company grows. Choose a naming convention that can grow with the company.

When creating users, it's important to make sure your usernames and passwords are as strong as possible. The reason you want strong security is because when a user logs into a system, the user's credentials are placed into the computer's Local Security Authority Subsystem Service (LSASS) process memory. This is done so that the credentials can be used by the account during a session connection.

Credentials will also get stored on the Windows 10 authoritative databases, such as the SAM database and in the database that is used by Active Directory Domain Services (AD DS). Therefore, it's important to make your usernames and passwords strong so that hackers have the hardest time to hack into a system and steal these cached credentials.

Now let's take a look at how user accounts get security ID numbers associated with them and how those numbers affect your accounts.

Security Identifiers

When you create a new user account, a *security identifier (SID)* is automatically created for the user account. The username is a property of the SID. For example, a user SID might look like this:

```
S-1-5-21-823518204-746137067-120266-629-500
```

It's apparent that using SIDs for user identification would make administration a nightmare. Fortunately, for your administrative tasks, you see and use the username instead of the SID.

SIDs have several advantages. Because Windows 10 uses the SID as the user object, you can easily rename a user while retaining all the user's properties. All security settings get associated with the SID, not the user account. Every time you create a new user, a unique SID gets associated. This ensures that if you delete and re-create a user account with the same username, the new user account will not have any of the properties of the old account because it is based on a new, unique SID. Even if the username is the same as a previously deleted account, the system still sees the account as a new user.

Because every user account gets a unique SID number, it is a good practice to disable rather than delete accounts for users who leave the company or have an extended absence. If you ever need to access the disabled account again, you have the ability to do so.

Secure Channel

Another part of authentication and encrypted communications between a client and a server is a mechanism called *Secure Channel*. Secure Channel, also known as Schannel, is a set of security protocols that help offer secure encrypted communications and authentication between a client and a server.

Schannel is a security package that uses the following four protocols on the Windows platforms:

- Transport Layer Security (TLS 1.1)
- Transport Layer Security (TLS 1.2)
- Secure Sockets Layer (SSL 3.0)
- Secure Sockets Layer (SSL 2.0)

To create a Schannel connection, the clients and servers are both required to obtain Schannel credentials and create a security session. Once the client and server connection is obtained, the security credentials become available. If a connection is lost for any reason, the client and server can automatically renegotiate the connection and finish all communications.

Creating a New Local User Account

Complete Exercise 2.3 to create a new local user account. Before you complete the following steps, make sure you are logged on as a user with permissions to create new user accounts and have already added the Local Users and Groups Snap-in to the MMC (Exercise 2.1). I created bogus usernames; you can change these to whatever names you want to use, but I refer to the ones I created in other exercises.

EXERCISE 2.3

Creating New Users via the MMC

1. Open the Local Users and Groups MMC Desktop shortcut that you created in Exercise 2.1, and expand the Local Users and Groups Snap-in. If a dialog box appears, click Yes.

2. Highlight the Users folder and select Action ➢ New User. The New User dialog box appears, as shown in Figure 2.5.

FIGURE 2.5   New User dialog box

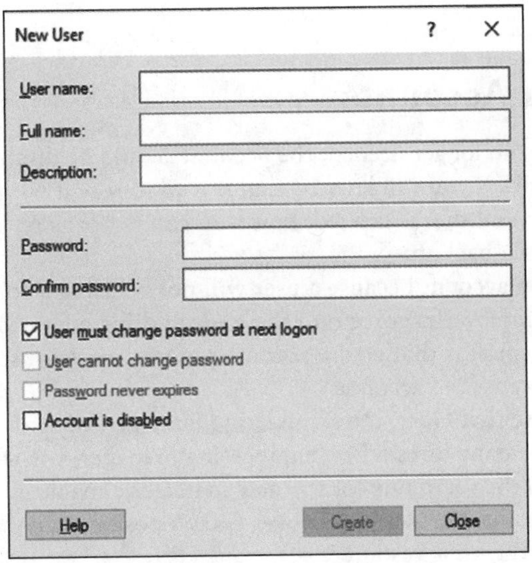

3. In the User Name text box, type **APanek**.

4. In the Full Name text box, type **Alexandria Panek**.

5. In the Description text box, type **Operations Manager**.

6. Leave the Password and Confirm Password text boxes empty. Make sure you uncheck the User Must Change Password At Next Logon option, and accept the defaults for the remaining check boxes. Click the Create button to add the user.

7. Use the New User dialog box to create four more users, filling out the fields as follows:

> User Name: **PPanek**; Full Name: **Paige Panek**
>
> User Name: **GWashington**; Full Name: **George Washington**
>
> User Name: **JAdams**; Full Name: **John Adams**
>
> User Name: **ALincoln**; Full Name: **Abe Lincoln**

8. After you've finished creating all of the users, click the Close button to exit the New User dialog box.

You can also create users through the command-line utility NET USER. For more information about this command, type **NET USER /?** at the command prompt.

Disabling User Accounts

When a user account is no longer needed, the account should be disabled or deleted. After you've disabled an account, you can later re-enable it to restore it with all of its associated user properties. An account that is deleted, however, can never be recovered unless you complete a restore from a backup.

You might disable an account because a user will not be using it for a period of time, perhaps because that employee is going on vacation or taking a leave of absence. Another reason to disable an account is that you're planning to put another user in that same function and would like to reuse the account.

For example, suppose that Gary, the engineering manager, quits. If you disable his account, when your company hires a new engineering manager, you can simply rename Gary's user account (to the username for the new manager), enable it, and reset the password. This ensures that the user who takes over Gary's position will have all the same user properties and own all the same resources.

Disabling accounts also provides a security mechanism for special situations. For example, if your company is laying off a group of people, as a security measure you could disable their accounts at the same time the layoff notices are given out. This prevents those users from inflicting any damage to the company's files after they receive their layoff notice. (Note, however, that this won't affect users who are already logged in.)

In Exercise 2.4, you will disable a user account. Before you complete this exercise, you should have created new users in Exercise 2.3.

EXERCISE 2.4

Disabling User Accounts

1. Open the Local Users and Groups MMC Desktop shortcut that you created in Exercise 2.1 and expand the Local Users and Groups Snap-in.

2. Open the Users folder (C:\Users). Double-click user PPanek to open her Properties dialog box.

3. In the General tab, check the Account Is Disabled box. Click OK.

4. Close the Local Users and Groups MMC.

5. Log off and attempt to log on as PPanek. This should fail because the account is now disabled.

6. Log back on using your user account.

You can also access a user's properties by highlighting the user, right-clicking, and selecting Properties.

When a user has left the company for a long period of time and you know you no longer need the user account, you can delete it. Let's take a look at how to delete user accounts.

Deleting User Accounts

As noted in the preceding section, you should disable a user account if you are not sure whether the account will ever be needed again. But if the account has been disabled and you know that the user account will never need to be accessed again, you should delete the account.

To delete a user, open the Local Users and Groups utility, highlight the user account you wish to delete, click Action to bring up the menu shown in Figure 2.6, and then select Delete. You can also delete an account by clicking the account and pressing the Delete key on the keyboard.

FIGURE 2.6   Deleting a user account

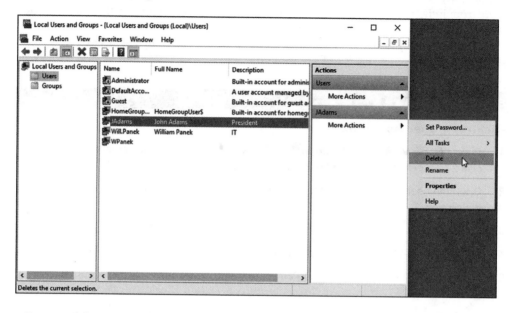

Because deleting an account is a permanent action, you will see the dialog box shown in Figure 2.7, asking you to confirm that you really wish to delete the account. After you click the Yes button here, you will not be able to re-create or re-access the account (unless you restore your local user accounts database from a backup).

FIGURE 2.7   Confirming account deletion

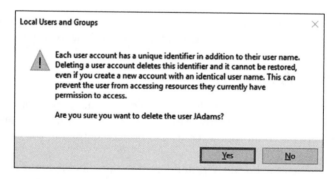

Complete Exercise 2.5 to delete a user account. These steps assume you have completed Exercises 2.2, 2.3, and 2.4.

EXERCISE 2.5

Deleting a User Account

1. Open the Local Users and Groups MMC Desktop shortcut and expand the Local Users and Groups Snap-in.

2. Expand the Users folder and single-click user JAdams to select his user account.

3. Select Action ➤ Delete. The dialog box for confirming user deletion appears.

4. Click the Yes button to confirm that you wish to delete this user.

5. Close the Local Users and Groups MMC.

Now that you have disabled and deleted accounts, let's take a look at how to rename a user's account.

Renaming User Accounts

Once an account has been created, you can rename it at any time. Renaming a user account allows the account to retain all the associated user properties such as group memberships and assigned permissions even though the username is being changed.

You might want to rename a user account because the user's name has changed (for example, the user gets married) or because the name was spelled incorrectly. Also, as explained in the section "Disabling User Accounts," you can rename an existing user's account for a new user, such as someone hired to take an ex-employee's position, when you want the new user to have the same properties.

Complete Exercise 2.6 to rename a user account. These steps assume you have completed Exercises 2.2 through 2.5.

EXERCISE 2.6

Renaming a User Account

1. Open the Local Users and Groups MMC Desktop shortcut and expand the Local Users and Groups Snap-in.

2. Open the Users folder and highlight user ALincoln.

3. Select Action ➤ Rename.

4. Type the username **RReagan** and press Enter. Notice that the Full Name field retains the original Full Name property of Abe Lincoln in the Local Users and Groups utility.

5. Double-click RReagan to open the properties and change the user's full name to Ronald Reagan.

6. Click the User Must Change Password At Next Logon check box.

7. Click OK.

8. Close the Local Users and Groups MMC.

Renaming a user does not change any hard-coded names, such as the name of the user's home folder. If you want to change these names as well, you need to modify them manually—for example, through Windows Explorer. (Note that there is a small possibility that you'll have to change the Registry to point to the new name.)

Another very common task that we must deal with is changing the user's password. Let's take a look at how to do that.

Changing a User's Password

What should you do if a user forgets their password and can't log on? As the administrator, you can change the user's password, which they can then use.

It is very important as IT managers and IT administrators that we teach our users proper security measures that go along with password protection. As you have all probably seen before, the users who tape their password to their monitors or under the keyboards are not following correct security precautions. It's our job as IT professionals to teach our users proper security, and it always amazes me when I do consulting how many IT departments don't teach their users properly.

Complete Exercise 2.7 to change a user's password. This exercise assumes you have completed Exercises 2.2 onward.

EXERCISE 2.7

Changing a User's Password

1. Open the Local Users and Groups MMC Desktop shortcut and expand the Local Users and Groups Snap-in.

2. Open the Users folder and highlight user APanek.

3. Select Action ➢ Set Password. The Set Password dialog box appears.

4. A warning appears, indicating the risks involved in changing the password. Select Proceed.

5. Type the new password and then confirm the password. Click OK.

6. Close the Local Users and Groups MMC.

Using Windows Hello, Pictures, and Biometrics

Now that we have looked at how to set up and manage local and domain accounts, let's look at how you can use other options to help you log into your system or network.

Those of us who have been certified for a long time are quite familiar with using a Microsoft account to log into the Microsoft websites. Now we can use this same account to log into our computer and networks.

Windows Hello is a Microsoft account that you can use to authenticate to a domain, to a cloud-based domain, or to a computer. To do this, you need to link your Microsoft account to your Windows 10 system.

Linking your Windows 10 system is an easy two-step verification process with Windows Hello enrollment. When you set up Windows Hello on the device, you can set up the system to use Windows Hello or a PIN.

Windows Hello allows you to sign in to your Windows 10 devices with just a look or a touch. Windows Hello can be set up so that you can use biometrics, face recognition, or even an iris scan. To configure Windows Hello options, click the Start menu and choose Settings. Once you're in the settings, choose Accounts.

You also have the ability to set up Windows Hello to use a personal identification number (PIN). This is a secure number that you input instead of a username and password. You may be thinking to yourself that a PIN doesn't seem as secure as a username and password, but actually that is not true.

PINs can be very complex and include special characters and letters, both uppercase and lowercase. So that means that you can have a PIN of 1234 or a PIN of 1234Wi!!Panek1001. Also, PINs are tied directly to a machine and not to an account, so when you set up a PIN, it's good for that machine only. Because of this, PINs are actually better than a password that can be used anywhere on the network. If someone steals your password, they can access your account from anywhere. This is not the case with a PIN, because anyone trying to use it would also need access to your machine.

Windows 10 also gives you the ability to set up your logon for use with a picture. When you decide to use a picture for authentication, you first choose your picture and then you add three gestures onto the picture. You can draw straight lines, circles, squares, or anything you want. Then when you log on to the system, you just re-create the gestures on the picture and the system logs you in.

Using Device Guard

So far we have been discussing how to secure your computer or network based on username, passwords, biometrics, and Windows Hello, but there are other ways to help lock your Windows 10 systems down. One of those ways is Device Guard.

Device Guard is an enterprise set of hardware and software security features that when used together can lock a system down so that only trusted applications can run on the operating system. Administrators have the ability to define policies, and it is these policies that help Windows 10 lock down applications that do not adhere to the policies that your organization has defined.

If an administrator has created a policy and an application does not meet the criteria of the defined policies, the application will not run. This is very useful when it comes to unauthorized people trying to access your network. Even if a hacker gets into the Windows 10 operating system and takes control of the kernel, because of the policies that you have created, it is almost impossible that any unauthorized software will be able to run.

As long as you are using Windows 10 Enterprise or Education, Device Guard can be used with virtualization-based security policies. This is possible because Device Guard works in conjunction with the Hyper-V hypervisor. Because of this, Device Guard can help protect applications and operating systems that run within the Hyper-V application.

The advantage to Device Guard is that it works on two levels, the kernel mode code integrity (KMCI) and user mode code integrity (UMCI). Because Device Guard works at both levels, it helps protect against hardware and software based threats.

Understanding Device Guard Protection

In Table 2.3, I will show you some of the different features available that can help protect against multiple types of threats.

TABLE 2.3   Device Guard features

Security Threat	Device Guard Feature
Boot attacks	To help protect against attacks at system startup, Device Guard includes a feature called Universal Extensible Firmware Interface (UEFI) Secure Boot. This feature protects the system from hacks during the boot process and also from malicious firmware installations. Because of the Device Guard security features, the UEFI is locked down (Boot order, Boot entries, Secure Boot, Virtualization extensions, IOMMU, Microsoft UEFI CA) and changes can't be made to compromise the system.
Control of kernel	To help protect against kernel invasions, Device Guard uses virtualization-based security (VBS). VBS helps guard the Hyper-V hypervisor, which in turn protects the kernel and the operating system. After an administrator enables VBS, VBS tightens the default kernel-mode code integrity policy (which help protect system files or bad drivers from being deployed) or the configurable code integrity policy.
Direct Memory Access (DMA) based attacks	With this policy, virtualization-based security (VBS) uses input/output memory management units (IOMMUs) to evaluate memory usage. This policy helps determine if the memory access is accepted or denied.
New malware	This policy helps protect against kernel invasions by protecting against code integrity policies. Administrators have the ability to control a white list of software that is allowed to run. This way, if a hacker tries to run a malicious piece of code that has not been white-listed, it will not run.
Unassigned code	When hackers build malicious code, the one advantage we have in IT is that the code is not signed by an authorized vendor. Because of this, Administrators can set up code integrity policies with catalog files. This policy will immediately help protect against many known and unknown threats. The one drawback to this policy is that many organizations use unsigned line-of-business (LOB) applications.

Managing Device Guard

There are many different ways that an administrator can configure Device Guard. Let's take a look at some of the different options available for managing and configuring Device Guard.

Group Policy

One of the ways that you can configure Device Guard is through the use of a Group Policy Object. You can configure the GPOs using the Windows Server 2019/2016 Group Policy Management console or directly through a local GPO within Windows 10.

GPOs provide a template that allows an administrator to manage and configure the hardware-based security features in Device Guard that you would like to enable and deploy. You can manage Device Guard settings and your other network settings within the same GPO.

Microsoft System Center Configuration Manager

Administrators also have the ability to use System Center Configuration Manager to easily deploy and manage catalog files, code integrity policies, and hardware-based security features.

Windows PowerShell

You can use Windows PowerShell to create and service code integrity policies. The following Table 2.4 shows Windows PowerShell commands for managing Device Guard.

TABLE 2.4   Device Guard PowerShell commands

PowerShell Command	Description
Add-SignerRule	Allows an administrator to create a signer rule and add that rule to a policy.
ConvertFrom-CIPolicy	This command allows an administrator to convert an XML file into binary format. These files contain code integrity policies.
Get-CIPolicy	Allows an administrator to view the rules in a code integrity policy.
Get-CIPolicyIdInfo	Allows an administrator to view code Integrity policy information.
Get-SystemDriver	Administrators can view the drivers on a system.
Merge-CIPolicy	This command allows an administrator to merge the rules of several code Integrity policy files.
New-CIPolicy	Allows an administrator to create a Code Integrity policy as an XML file.

TABLE 2.4   Device Guard PowerShell commands *(continued)*

PowerShell Command	Description
New-CIPolicyRule	Administrators can create code Integrity policy rules for drivers.
Set-CIPolicyIdInfo	This command allows an administrator to modify the name and ID of a code Integrity policy.
Set-CIPolicyVersion	This command allows an administrator to modify the version number of a policy.
Set-HVCIOptions	Administrators can change hypervisor code integrity options for a specific policy.
Set-RuleOption	This command allows an administrator to modify the rule options in a code Integrity policy.

Understanding Credential Guard

Another new security feature introduced with Windows 10 Enterprise and Windows Server 2016 is Credential Guard. Credential Guard relies on Hyper-V based security measure to help operating systems run only software with the appropriate security privileges. Credential Guard helps stop unauthorized access to credentials thus stopping many types of security threats.

When a user sends a username and password to a domain controller, after the domain controller authenticates the user and the Windows 10 system, a domain token (sometimes referred to as a Kerberos ticket) is issued to the user. Credential Guard helps protect against attacks that specifically target this authentication process.

Credential Guard Protection

One of the advantages of Credential Guard is that hardware can be secured. Credential Guard can help secure your hardware by using virtualization-based security and a feature called secure boot. By securing the Windows 10 hardware, you can also secure the Windows 10 operating system.

One of the nicest advantages of using Credential Guard is that it's easy to manage and deploy. Credential Guard can be configured by using a Group Policy Object, from a Windows 10 command prompt, or by using Windows PowerShell. But before we look at managing Credential Guard, let's take a look at each security measure.

Virtualization-Based Security

One of the greatest advantages of virtualization is that each guest operating system runs independently of every other guest operating system. So basically that means that each operating system works as if it's on its own physical piece of hardware. Credential Guard uses a security feature that works along the same way. The Windows services that manage domain authentication credentials are separated into their own special environment that is separated from the Windows 10 operating system.

It is because of this separation that you get added protection for your Windows environment. Virtualization-based security protects against credential theft attack techniques that are used in most credential attacks. Many types of attacks that run in the Windows operating system run using administrative privileges. Because Virtualization-based security separates authentication credentials into their own special environment, it protects system credentials from being extracted by the hackers or malware programs that are running on the operating system.

Secure Boot

Secure boot is another way that Windows 10 can help protect your hardware because secure boot verifies that only manufacturer-trusted firmware gets used by the system. This can protect your system from hackers and hacks that attack the system's firmware. But, as with any good thing, there could also be issues. Secure boot may possibly cause issues with things like hardware (high-end graphics cards) or operating systems such as Linux or previous version of Windows.

So one thing that you may need to know is actually how to disable secure boot in the event that is does conflict with some hardware. There are normally two ways that you can disable secure boot, through the BIOS or through the Windows 10 bootup process. If you need to disable secure boot, you would complete the following steps:

1. Open the PC BIOS menu or from the Windows 10 operating system and hold the Shift key while selecting Restart. Then choose Troubleshoot ➤ Advanced Options: UEFI Firmware Settings.

2. Under the Secure Boot setting (normally under the Security tab or Boot tab) and set it to Disabled.

3. Save the changes and reboot the system.

To re-enable secure boot, you would do the same procedure except you would choose Enable under the Secure Boot option.

Configuring Device Health Attestation

In today's Bring Your Own Device (BYOD) world, many companies allow users to bring their own personal devices into the workplace. The issue with this is that you have no idea what security measures they have on their machines. Something new with Windows 10 is the ability to check the health of your computers and make sure they meet certain system requirements. This is where Device Health Attestation comes into play.

As an administrator, you can use the Configuration Manager console in Device Health Attestation to view the status of Windows 10 machines on your network and make sure that they meet the minimum requirements that your organization sets.

Administrators can now view the computer systems that are on-site or even managed through the cloud using Microsoft Intune. Administrators have the ability to determine whether reporting is done through the on-site infrastructure or through the cloud. The advantage of being able to work with both cloud-based and internal computers is that if your company doesn't have a current Internet access, you can still use the Device Health Attestation utility.

Device Health Attestation allows an administrator to verify that client systems have TPM enabled and have proper BIOS configurations and that boot security measures are enabled.

Device Health Attestation Requirements

If you want to use Device Health Attestation on your network or in the cloud, your systems must meet some minimum requirements:

- Windows 10
- Windows Server 2016 with Device Health Attestation enabled
- TPM 2 enabled
- Internet communication needs to be established between your Configuration Manager client agent and has.spserv.microsoft.com (port 443) Health Attestation service

> System Center Configuration Manager (SCCM) is a Microsoft Server application that can be an add-on infrastructure for Windows 10 and Configuring Device Health Attestation. For more information on System Center, please check out Microsoft's website at:
>
> https://docs.microsoft.com/en-us/sccm/core/servers/manage/
> health-attestation

After you have met the minimum requirements for your systems, then you have to configure your systems to run Device Health Attestation.

1. In the Configuration Manager console, choose Administration ➤ Overview ➤ Client Settings. Choose the Computer Agent tab.

2. In the Default Settings dialog box, choose Computer Agent and then scroll down to Enable Communication With Health Attestation Service and choose Yes. Click OK.

You may also need to enable on-premises the Health Attestation service.

1. In the Configuration Manager console, navigate to Administration ➤ Overview ➤ Client Settings. You will then need to set Use On-Premises Healthy Attestation Service to Yes.

2. Specify the On-Premise Health Attestation Service URL and then click OK.

Managing User Properties

For more control over user accounts, you can configure user properties. Through the user's Properties dialog box, you can change the original password options, add the user to existing groups, and specify user profile information.

To open a user's Properties dialog box, access the Local Users and Groups utility, open the Users folder, and double-click the user account. The user's Properties dialog box has tabs for the three main categories of properties: General, Member Of, and Profile.

The General tab contains the information you supplied when you set up the new user account, including the full name and a description, the password options you selected, and whether the account is disabled. If you want to modify any of these properties after you've created the user, simply open the user's Properties dialog box and make the changes on the General tab (Figure 2.8).

FIGURE 2.8   General tab of the user's Properties dialog box

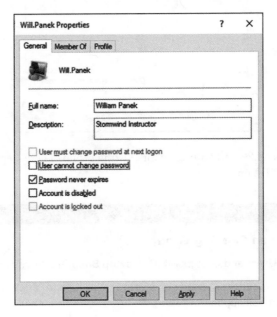

You can use the Member Of tab to manage the user's membership in groups, and the Profile tab lets you set properties to customize the user's environment. The following sections discuss the Member Of and Profile tabs in detail.

Managing User Group Membership

The Member Of tab of the user's Properties dialog box displays all the groups that the user belongs to, as shown in Figure 2.9. From this tab, you can add the user to an existing group or remove the user from a group. To add a user to a group, click the Add button and select the group that the user should belong to. If you want to remove the user from a group, highlight the group and click the Remove button.

FIGURE 2.9   The Member Of tab of the user's Properties dialog box

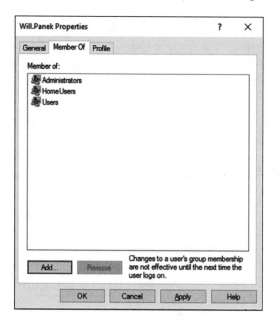

Complete Exercise 2.8 to add a user to an existing group. These steps assume you have completed Exercises 2.2 onward.

EXERCISE 2.8

Adding a User to an Existing Group

1. Open the Local Users and Groups MMC Desktop Snap-in that you created previously.

2. Open the Users (C:\Users) folder and double-click user APanek. The APanek Properties dialog box appears.

3. Select the Member Of tab and click the Add button. The Select Groups dialog box appears.

4. Under Enter The Object Names To Select, type **Backup Operators**, and click the Check Names button. After the name is confirmed, click OK.

5. Click OK to close the APanek Properties dialog box.

Now let's take a look at the Profile tab and what options can be configured within that tab.

Setting Up User Profiles, Logon Scripts, and Home Folders

The Profile tab of the user's Properties dialog box, shown in Figure 2.10, allows you to customize the user's environment. Here, you can specify the following items for the user:

- User profile path
- Logon script
- Home folder

FIGURE 2.10   The Profile tab of the user's Properties dialog box

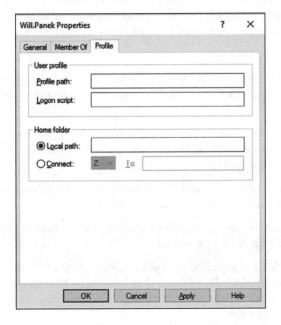

The following sections describe how these properties work and when you might want to use them.

Setting a User's Profile Path

User profiles contain information about the Windows 10 environment for a specific user. For example, profile settings include the Desktop arrangement, program groups, and screen colors that users see when they log on.

Each time you log on to a Windows 10 computer, the system checks to see if you have a local user profile in the Users folder, which was created on the boot partition when you installed Windows 10. The first time users log on, they receive a default user profile. A folder that matches the user's logon name is created for the user in the Users folder. The user profile folder that is created holds a file called NTUSER.DAT as well as subfolders that contain directory links to the user's Desktop items (as shown previously in Figure 2.10).

In Exercise 2.9, you'll create two new users and set up local user profiles.

EXERCISE 2.9

Setting Up User Profiles

1. Using the Local Users and Groups utility, create two new users: WPanek and CPanek. Deselect the User Must Change Password At Next Logon option for each user.

2. Right-click on the Start button and choose File Explorer. Click This PC and then double-click Local Disk (C:). Finally, double-click the Users folder. Notice that the Users folder does not contain user profile folders for the new users.

3. Log off and log on as WPanek.

4. Right-click an open area on the Desktop and select Personalize. In the Personalization dialog box, select a picture under Choose Your Picture, and then close the Settings app.

5. Right-click an open area on the Desktop and select New ≻ Shortcut. In the Create Shortcut dialog box, type **CALC** to open the Calculator program. Accept CALC as the name for the shortcut and click Finish.

6. Log off as WPanek and log on as CPanek. Notice that user PPanek sees the Desktop configuration stored in the default user profile.

7. Log off as CPanek and log on as WPanek. Notice that WPanek sees the Desktop configuration you set up in steps 4, and 5.

8. Log off as WPanek and log on as your user account. Right-click the Start button and choose File Explorer. Click This PC and then double-click Local Disk (C:). Finally, double-click the Users folder. Notice that this folder now contains user profile folders for WPanek and CPanek.

The drawback of local user profiles is that they are available only on the computer where they were created. For example, suppose all of your Windows 10 computers are a part of a domain and you use only local user profiles. User Rick logs on at Computer A and creates a customized user profile. When he logs on to Computer B for the first time, he will receive the default user profile rather than the customized user profile he created on Computer A. To enable users to access their user profile from any computer they log on to, you need to use roaming profiles; however, these require the use of a network server because they can't be stored on a local Windows 10 computer.

In the next sections, you will learn about how roaming profiles and mandatory profiles can be used. To have a roaming profile or a mandatory profile, your computer must be a part of a network with server access.

Using Roaming Profiles

A *roaming profile* is stored on a network server and allows a user to access their user profile regardless of the client computer to which they're logged on. Roaming profiles provide a consistent desktop for users who move around, no matter which computer they access. Even if the server that stores the roaming profile is unavailable, the user can still log on using a local profile.

If you are using roaming profiles, the contents of the user's systemdrive:\Users\ UserName folder will be copied to the local computer each time the roaming profile is accessed. If you have stored large files in any subfolders of your user profile folder, you may notice a significant delay when accessing your profile remotely as opposed to locally. If this problem occurs, you can reduce the amount of time the roaming profile takes to load by moving the subfolder to another location, such as the user's home directory, or you can use Group Policy Objects within Active Directory to specify that specific folders should be excluded when the roaming profile is loaded.

Using Mandatory Profiles

C:\Users\username ~~folder~~\ ntuser.man
↑
file

A *mandatory profile* is a profile that can't be modified by the user. Only members of the Administrators group can manage mandatory profiles. You can create mandatory profiles for a single user or a group of users. You might consider creating mandatory profiles for users who should maintain consistent Desktops.

For example, suppose you have a group of 20 salespeople who know enough about system configuration to make changes but not enough to fix any problems they create. For ease of support, you could use mandatory profiles. This way, all of the salespeople will always have the same profile, which they will not be able to change.

The mandatory profile is stored in a file named NTUSER.MAN. To create a mandatory profile, you just change the user's profile extension from .dat to .man and the profile will become mandatory. A user with a mandatory profile can set desktop preferences while logged on, but those settings will not be saved when the user logs off.

There are two folders where the profiles are stored. They are *Username* and *Username* .v2 (*Username* will be replaced with the user's name). The difference is that if you are using Windows XP, the profile gets placed in the *Username* folder. If the users are using Windows Vista, Windows 7 / 8 / 8.1, Windows 10, or Windows Server, the user profile gets placed in the *Username*.v# folder. The # will depend on the version of Windows that is getting used. For example, Windows 7 was v2. Table 2.5 was taken directly from Microsoft's website (at the time this book was written) and it shows what version number goes with each Microsoft operating system version.

To see current version numbers, please check out Microsoft's website at:

https://docs.microsoft.com/en-us/windows/client-management/
mandatory-user-profile

TABLE 2.5   User profile version numbers

Operating System	Profile Version Number
Windows Vista, Windows 7, and Windows Server 2008 / 2008 R2	<username>.V2
Windows 8 and Windows Server 2012	<username>.V2 (before the software update and registry key are applied). <username>.V3 (after the software update and registry key are applied)
Windows 8.1 and Windows Server 2012 R2	<username>.V2 (before the software update and registry key are applied). <username>.V4 (after the software update and registry key are applied)
Windows 10 versions 1507 to 1511	<username>.V5
Windows 10, versions 1607, 1703, 1709, 1803, and 1809 and Windows Server 2016	<username>.V6

You can use only roaming profiles as mandatory profiles. Mandatory profiles do not work for local user profiles.

Now let's look at a second type of mandatory profile called super-mandatory profile.

Using Super-Mandatory Profiles   C:\Users\username.man\ntuser.man

A *super-mandatory profile* is a mandatory user profile with an additional layer of security. With mandatory profiles, a temporary profile is created if the mandatory profile is not available when a user logs on. However, when super-mandatory profiles are configured, temporary profiles are not created if the mandatory profile is not available over the network, and the user is unable to log on to the computer.

The process for creating super-mandatory profiles is similar to that for creating mandatory profiles, except that instead of renaming the user folder *Username*.v2 as you would for a mandatory profile, you name the folder *Username*.man. User profiles become *super-mandatory* when the folder name of the profile path ends in .man, as in, for example, \\server\share\APanek.man\. Only system administrators can make changes to mandatory user profiles.

 Real World Scenario

Copying User Profiles

Within your company, you have a user, Paige, who logs in with two different user accounts. One account is a regular user account, and the other is an administrator account used for administration tasks only.

When Paige established all her Desktop preferences and installed the computer's applications, they were installed with the administrator account. Now, when she logs in with the regular user account, she can't access the Desktop and profile settings that were created for her as an administrative user.

To solve this problem, you can copy a local user profile from one user to another (for example, from Paige's administrative account to her regular user account) by choosing Start ➢ Windows System ➢ Control Panel ➢ System ➢ Advanced System Settings ➢ User Profiles Settings. When you copy a user profile, the following items are copied: favorites, cookies, documents, Start Menu items, and other unique user Registry settings.

Using Logon Scripts

Another configurable element within the Profile tab of the user's properties is logon scripts—files that run every time a user logs on to the network. They are usually batch files, but they can be any type of executable file. Logon scripts are either created by the admin or just grabbed off the Internet. Creating these scripts is beyond the scope of this book.

You might use logon scripts to set up drive mappings or to run a specific executable file each time a user logs on to the computer. For example, you could run an inventory-management file that collects information about the computer's configuration and sends that data to a central management database. Logon scripts are also useful for compatibility with non–Windows 10 operating systems for users who want to log on but still maintain consistent settings with their native operating system.

To run a logon script for a user, enter the script name in the Logon Script text box in the Profile tab of the user's Properties dialog box.

Setting Up Home Folders

Users usually store their personal files and information in a private folder called a home folder. In the Profile tab of the user's Properties dialog box, you can specify the location of a home folder as a local folder or a network folder. The main reason you give your users a home folder on the server is because the servers are usually the only machines that get backed up. Most companies do not back up individual users' machines. If your users place all their important documents in the home folder location on the network, those documents will get backed up as part of the nightly backup.

To specify a local folder, choose the Local Path option and type the path in the text box next to that option. To specify a network path for a folder, choose the Connect option and specify a network path using a Universal Naming Convention (UNC) path. A UNC consists of the computer name and the share that has been created on the computer. When you are connecting to a UNC name, the network folder you are connecting to should already be created and shared. For example, if you wanted to connect to a folder called \Users\Will on a server called SALES, you'd choose the Connect option, select a drive letter that would be mapped to the home directory, and then type **\\SALES\Users\Will** in the To box.

If the home folder you are specifying does not exist, Windows 10 will attempt to create the folder for you. You can also use the variable %username% in place of a specific user's name. The %username% will automatically change to the name of the user you are currently working on.

Be careful when you're specifying your home folder. If you make a mistake when typing in the path for the directory, Windows will create a bogus-named folder for you.

Complete Exercise 2.10 to assign a home folder to a user. These steps assume you have completed Exercises 2.2 onward.

EXERCISE 2.10

Assigning Home Folders

1. Open the Local Users and Groups MMC Desktop shortcut and expand the Local Users and Groups Snap-in.

2. Open the Users folder and double-click user GWashington. The GWashington Properties dialog box appears.

3. Select the Profile tab and click the Local Path radio button to select it.

4. Specify the home folder path by typing **C:\HomeFolders\GWashington** in the text box for the Local Path option. Then click OK.

5. Use Windows Explorer to verify that this folder was created.

6. Close the Local Users and Groups MMC.

⊕ **Real World Scenario**

Using Home Folders to Keep Files Backed Up

As an administrator for a large network, one of my primary responsibilities is to make sure all data is backed up daily. This has become difficult because daily backup of each user's local hard drive is impractical. You can also have problems with employees deleting important corporate information as they are leaving the company.

After examining the contents of a typical user's local drive, you will realize that most of the local disk space is taken by the operating system and the user's stored applications. This information does not change and does not need to be backed up. What you are primarily concerned with is backing up the user's data.

To more effectively manage this data and accommodate the necessary backup, you should create home folders for each user and store them on a network share. This allows the data to be backed up daily, to be readily accessible should a local computer fail, and to be easily retrieved if the user leaves the company.

Here are the steps to create a home folder that resides on the network:

1. Decide which server will store the users' home folders.

2. Create a directory structure that will store the home folders efficiently (for example, C:\HOME).

3. Create a single share to the user's home folder. (You can do this by right-clicking the home folder and choosing Properties.)

4. Use NTFS and share permissions to ensure that only the specified user has permissions to their home folder.

5. Specify the location of the home folder through the Profile tab of the user's Properties dialog box.

Troubleshooting User Account Authentication

When a user attempts to log on through Windows 10 and is unable to be authenticated, you will need to track down the reason for the problem.

If a local user is having trouble logging on, the problem may be with the username, the password, or the user account itself. The following are some common causes of local logon errors.

Because many of these same issues happen when logging on to a domain from a Windows 10 machine, these approaches can be used for both local logons and domain logons.

Incorrect Username   You can verify that the username is correct by checking the Local Users and Groups utility. Verify that the name was spelled correctly.

Incorrect Password   Remember that passwords are case sensitive. Is the Caps Lock key on? If you see any messages relating to an expired password or locked-out account, the reason for the problem is obvious. If necessary, you can assign a new password through the Local Users and Groups utility.

Prohibitive User Rights   Does the user have permission to log on locally at the computer? By default, the Log On Locally user right is granted to the Users group, so all users can log on to Windows 10 computers.

However, if this user right was modified, you will see an error message stating that the local policy of this computer does not allow interactive logon. The terms *interactive logon* and *local logon* are synonymous and mean that the user is logging on at the computer where the user account is stored on the computer's local database.

A Disabled or Deleted Account   You can verify whether an account has been disabled by checking the account properties through the Local Users and Groups utility. If the account is no longer in the database, then it has most likely been deleted.

A Domain Account Logon at the Local Computer   If a computer is a part of a domain, the logon dialog box has options for logging on to the domain or to the local computer. Make sure the user has chosen the correct option.

Managing and Creating Groups

Groups are an important part of network management. Many administrators are able to accomplish the majority of their management tasks through the use of groups; they rarely assign permissions to individual users.

Windows 10 includes built-in local groups (such as Administrators and Backup Operators) that already have all the permissions needed to accomplish specific tasks. Windows 10 also uses built-in special groups in which users are placed automatically when they meet certain criteria.

You can create and manage local groups (but not special groups) through the Local Users and Groups utility. With this utility, you can add groups, change group membership, rename groups, and delete groups.

One misconception about groups is that they have to work with Group Policy Objects (GPOs). This is not correct. Group Policy Objects are sets of rules that allow you to set computer-configuration and user-configuration options that apply to users or computers. Group Policies, on the other hand, are typically used with Active Directory and are applied as Group Policy Objects.

Using Built-In Groups

On a Windows 10 computer, built-in local groups have already been created and assigned all necessary permissions to accomplish basic tasks. In addition, there are built-in special groups that the Windows 10 system handles automatically. These groups are described in the following sections.

Built-In Local Groups

A local group is a group that is stored on the local computer's accounts database. You can add users to these groups and can manage the groups directly on a Windows 10 computer. By default, some the following local groups are created on Windows 10 computers:

- Administrators
- Backup Operators
- Cryptographic Operators
- Distributed COM Users
- Event Log Readers
- Guests
- IIS_IUSRS
- Network Configuration Operators
- Performance Log Users
- Performance Monitor Users
- Power Users
- Remote Desktop Users
- Replicator
- Users

I will briefly describe each group, its default permissions, and the users assigned to the group by default.

If possible, you should add users to the built-in local groups rather than creating new groups from scratch. This simplifies administration because the built-in groups already have the appropriate permissions. All you need to do is add the users you want to be members of the group.

Administrators The Administrators group has full permissions and privileges. Its members can grant themselves any permissions they do not have by default to manage all the objects on the computer. (Objects include the filesystem, printers, and account management.) By default, the Administrator account, which is disabled by default, and the Initial User account are members of the Administrators local group.

> Assign users to the Administrators group with caution since they will have full permissions to manage the computer.

Members of the Administrators group can perform the following tasks:

- Install the operating system.
- Install and configure hardware device drivers.
- Install system services.
- Install service packs, hotfixes, and Windows updates.
- Upgrade the operating system.
- Repair the operating system.
- Install applications that modify the Windows system files.
- Configure password policies.
- Configure audit policies.
- Manage security logs.
- Create administrative shares.
- Create administrative accounts.
- Modify groups and accounts that have been created by other users.
- Remotely access the Registry.
- Stop or start any service.
- Configure services.
- Increase and manage disk quotas.
- Increase and manage execution priorities.
- Remotely shut down the system.
- Assign and manage user rights.
- Re-enable locked-out and disabled accounts.
- Manage disk properties, including formatting hard drives.
- Modify systemwide environment variables.
- Access any data on the computer.
- Back up and restore all data.

Backup Operators Members of the Backup Operators group have permissions to back up and restore the filesystem, even if the filesystem is NTFS and they have not been assigned permissions to access the filesystem. However, the members of Backup Operators can access the filesystem only through the Backup utility. To access the filesystem directly, Backup Operators must have explicit permissions assigned. There are no default members of the Backup Operators local group.

Cryptographic Operators   The Cryptographic Operators group has access to perform cryptographic operations on the computer. There are no default members of the Cryptographic Operators local group.

Distributed COM Users   The Distributed COM Users group has the ability to launch and run Distributed COM objects on the computer. There are no default members of the Distributed COM Users local group.

Event Log Readers   The Event Log Readers group has access to read the event log on the local computer. There are no default members of the Event Log Readers local group.

Guests   The Guests group has limited access to the computer. This group is provided so that you can allow people who are not regular users to access specific network resources. As a general rule, most administrators do not allow Guest access because it poses a potential security risk. By default, the Guest user account is a member of the Guests local group.

IIS_IUSRS   The IIS_IUSRS group is used by Internet Information Services (IIS). The NT AUTHORITY\IUSR user account (premade for IIS) is a member of the IIS_IUSRS group by default.

Network Configuration Operators   Members of the Network Configuration Operators group have some administrative rights to manage the computer's network configuration, for example, editing the computer's TCP/IP settings.

Performance Log Users   The Performance Log Users group has the ability to access and schedule logging of performance counters and can create and manage trace counters on the computer. There are no default members of this group.

Performance Monitor Users   The Performance Monitor Users group has the ability to access and view performance counter information on the computer. Users who are members of this group can access performance counters both locally and remotely. There are no default members of this group.

Power Users   The Power Users group is included in Windows 10 for backward compatibility to ensure that computers upgraded from Windows XP function as before with regard to folders that allow access to members of the group. Otherwise, the Power Users group has limited administrative rights. There are no default members of this group.

Remote Desktop Users   The Remote Desktop Users group allows members of the group to log on remotely for the purpose of using the Remote Desktop service. There are no default members of this group.

Replicator   The Replicator group is intended to support directory replication, which is a feature used by domain servers. Only domain users who will start the replication service should be assigned to this group. The Replicator local group has no default members.

Users   The Users group is intended for end users who should have very limited system access. If you have installed a fresh copy of Windows 10, the default settings for the Users group prohibit its members from compromising the operating system or program files. By default, all users who have been created on the computer, except Guest, are members of the Users local group.

Special Groups

Special groups are premade groups that can be used by the system or by administrators. Membership in special groups is automatic if certain criteria are met. You cannot manage special groups through the Local Users and Groups utility, but an administrator can add special groups to resources. The following text describes the special groups that are built into Windows 10.

Anonymous Logon   This group includes users who access the computer through anonymous logons. When users gain access through special accounts created for anonymous access to Windows 10 services, they become members of the Anonymous Logon group.

Authenticated Users   This group includes users who access the Windows 10 operating system through a valid username and password. Users who can log on belong to the Authenticated Users group.

Batch   This group includes users who log on as a user account that is used only to run a batch job.

Creator Owner   This is the account that created or took ownership of an object. This is typically a user account. Each object (files, folders, printers, and print jobs) has an owner. Members of the Creator Owner group have special permissions to resources. For example, if you are a regular user who has submitted 12 print jobs to a printer, you can manipulate your print jobs as Creator Owner, but you can't manage any print jobs submitted by other users.

Dialup   This group includes users who log on to the network from a dial-up connection.

Everyone   This group includes anyone who could possibly access the computer—all users who have been defined on the computer (including Guest), plus (if your computer is a part of a domain) all users within the domain. If the domain has trust relationships with other domains, all users in the trusted domains are part of the Everyone group as well. The exception to automatic group membership with the Everyone group is that members of the Anonymous Logon group are not included as a part of the Everyone group.

Interactive   This group includes all users who use the computer's resources locally.

Network   This group includes users who access the computer's resources over a network connection.

Service   This group includes users who log on as a user account that is used only to run a service. You can configure the use of user accounts for logon through the Services program.

System   There are times when the Windows 10 operating system will access functions within the system. When the operating system accesses these functions, it does it as a system user. When the system accesses specific functions as a user, that process becomes a member of the System group.

Terminal Server User   This group includes users who log on through Terminal Services.

Creating Groups

To create a group, you must be logged on as a member of the Administrators group. The Administrators group has full permissions to manage users and groups.

Keep your naming conventions in mind when assigning names to groups, just as you do when choosing usernames. Consider the following guidelines:

- The group name should be descriptive; for example, Accounting Data Users.

- The group name must be unique to the computer and different from all other group names and usernames that exist on that computer.

- Group names can be up to 256 characters. It is best to use alphanumeric characters for ease of administration. The backslash (\) character is not allowed.

Creating groups is similar to creating users, and it is a fairly easy process. After you've added the Local Users and Groups MMC or used Local Users and Groups through the Computer Management utility, expand it to see the Users and Groups folders. Right-click the Groups folder and select New Group from the context menu. This brings up the New Group dialog box, shown in Figure 2.11.

FIGURE 2.11   The New Group dialog box

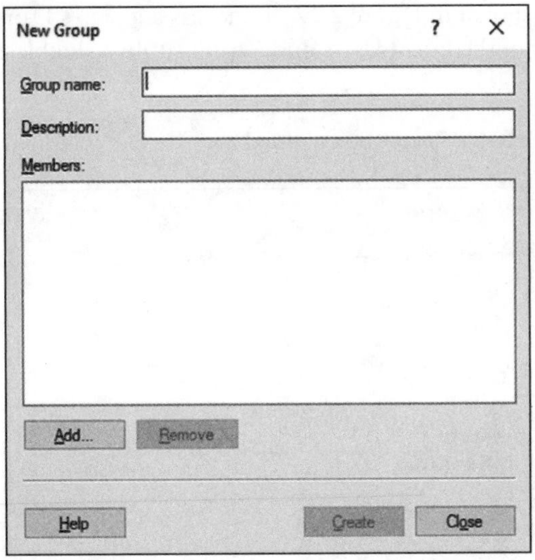

The only required entry in the New Group dialog box is the group name. If appropriate, you can enter a description for the group, and you can add (or remove) group members. When you're ready to create the new group, click the Create button.

Complete Exercise 2.11 to create two new local groups. (Creating domain groups is beyond the scope of this book.)

EXERCISE 2.11

Creating Local Groups

1. Open the Admin Console MMC Desktop shortcut you created and expand the Local Users and Groups Snap-in.

2. Right-click the Groups folder and select New Group.

3. In the New Group dialog box, type **Data Users** in the Group Name text box. Click the Create button.

4. Repeat step 3, but type **Application Users** in the Group Name text box.

After the groups are created, you will have to manage the groups and their membership. In the next section, we will look at managing groups.

Managing Group Membership

After you've created a group, you can add members to it. As mentioned earlier, you can put the same user in multiple groups. You can easily add and remove users through a group's Properties dialog box, shown in Figure 2.12. To access a group's Properties dialog box from the Groups folder in the Local Users and Groups utility, double-click the name of the group you want to manage.

FIGURE 2.12   IT Group's Properties dialog box

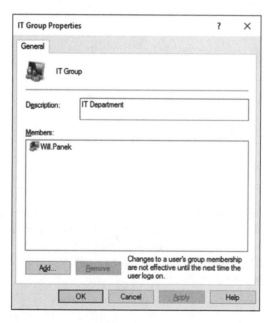

From the group's Properties dialog box, you can change the group's description and add or remove group members. When you click the Add button to add members, the Select Users dialog box appears (Figure 2.13).

FIGURE 2.13 The Select Users dialog box

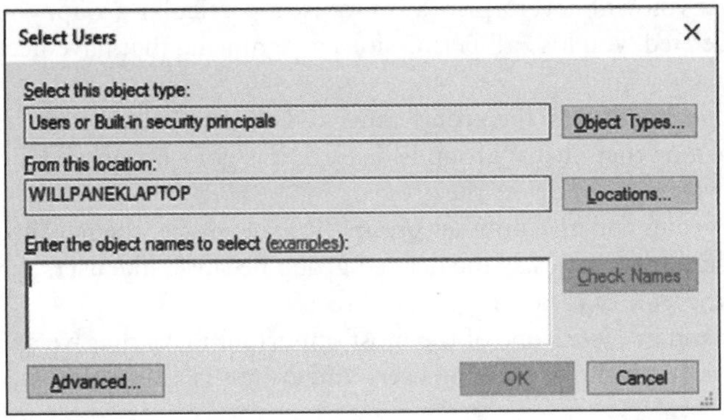

In the Select Users dialog box, you enter the object names of the users you want to add. You can use the Check Names button to validate the users against the database. Select the user accounts you wish to add and click Add. Click the OK button to add the selected users to the group.

To remove a member from the group, select the member in the Members list of the Properties dialog box and click the Remove button.

In Exercise 2.12, you'll create new user accounts and then add these users to one of the groups you created in the previous exercises.

EXERCISE 2.12

Adding Accounts to Groups

1. Open the Local Users and Groups MMC shortcut you created and expand the Local Users and Groups Snap-in.

2. Create two new users: JDoe and DDoe. Deselect the User Must Change Password At Next Logon option for each user.

3. Expand the Groups folder.

4. Double-click the Data Users group.

5. In the Data Users Properties dialog box, click the Add button.

6. In the Select Users dialog box, type the username **JDoe**; then click OK.

7. Click Add and type the username **DDoe**; then click OK.

8. In the Data Users Properties dialog box, you will see that the users have both been added to the group. Click OK to close the group's Properties dialog box.

There may come a point when a specific group is no longer needed. In the next section, we will look at how to delete a group from the Local Users and Groups utility.

Deleting Groups

If you are sure that you will never again want to use a particular group, you can delete it. Once a group is deleted, you lose all permissions assignments that have been specified for the group.

To delete a group, right-click the group name and choose Delete from the context menu. You will see a warning that once a group is deleted, it is gone for good. Click the Yes button if you're sure you want to delete the group.

If you delete a group and give another group the same name, the new group won't be created with the same properties as the deleted group because, like users, groups get unique SIDs assigned at the time of creation.

Creating users and groups is one of the most important tasks that we as IT members can do. On a Windows 10 machine, creating users and groups is an easy and straightforward process.

Now that you understand how to create users and groups, you need to know how to manage Windows 10 security using GPOs and LGPOs. We'll look at that next.

Managing Security Using GPOs and LGPOs

Windows 10 offers a wide variety of security options. If the Windows 10 computer is a part of a domain, then you can apply security through a Group Policy Object using the Group Policy Management Console. If the Windows 10 computer is not a part of a domain, then you use Local Group Policy Objects to manage local security.

Additionally, you can use policies to help manage user accounts. Account policies control the logon environment for the computer, such as password and logon restrictions. Local policies specify what users can do once they log on and include auditing, user rights, and security options. You can also manage critical security features through the Windows Security Center.

Understanding the GPO and LGPO Basics

The tools you use to manage Windows 10 computer security configurations depend on whether the Windows 10 computer is a part of a Windows Server domain environment.

If the Windows 10 client is not a part of a domain, then you apply security settings through *Local Group Policy Objects (LGPOs)*. LGPOs are sets of security configuration settings that are applied to users and computers. LGPOs are created and stored locally on the Windows 10 computer.

If your Windows 10 computer is a part of a domain, which uses the services of Active Directory, then you typically manage and configure security through *Group Policy Objects (GPOs)*. Active Directory is the database that contains all your domain user and group accounts along with all other domain objects.

Group Policy Objects are policies that can be applied to either users or computers in the domain. The Group Policy Management Console (GPMC) is a Microsoft Management Console (MMC) Snap-in that is used to configure and manage GPOs for users and computers via Active Directory. You can access the LGPO console by typing **gpedit.msc** in the Windows 10 Search box.

Windows 10 computers that are part of a domain still have LGPOs, and you can use LGPOs in conjunction with the Active Directory group policies (GPOs).

 Usage of Group Policy Objects for domains is covered in greater detail in my book *MCSA Windows Server 2016 Complete Study Guide: Exam 70-740, Exam 70-741, Exam 70-742 and Composite Upgrade Exam 70-743 2nd Edition* (Wiley, 2018).

The settings you can apply through the Group Policy utility within Active Directory are more comprehensive than the settings you can apply through LGPOs. Table 2.6 lists some of the options that can be set for GPOs within Active Directory and which of those options can be applied through LGPOs.

TABLE 2.6   Group Policy and LGPO setting options

Group Policy Setting	Available for LGPO?
Software installation	No
Remote Installation Services	Yes
Scripts	Yes
Printers	Yes
Security settings	Yes
Policy-based QOS	Yes
Administrative templates	Yes
Folder redirection	No
Internet Explorer configuration	Yes
Windows Update settings	Yes

Now that we have looked at LGPOs, let's look at some of the tools available for creating and managing them.

Using the Group Policy Result Tool

When a user logs on to a computer or domain, a resulting set of policies to be applied is generated based on the LGPOs, site GPOs, domain GPOs, and OU GPOs. The overlapping nature of group policies can make it difficult to determine what group policies will actually be applied to a computer or user.

To help determine what policies will actually be applied, Windows 10 includes the Group Policy Result Tool, also known as the *Resultant Set of Policy (RSoP)*. You can access this tool through the GPResult command-line utility. The gpresult command displays the set of policies that were enforced on the computer and the specified user during the logon process.

The gpresult command will display the RSoP for the computer and user who is currently logged in. Several switches that can be used with the gpresult command are listed in Table 2.7.

TABLE 2.7   gpresult switches

Switch	Explanation
/F	Forces gpresult to override the filename specified in the /X or /H command
/H	Saves the report in an HTML format
/P	Specifies the password for a given user context
/R	Displays RSoP summary data
/S	Specifies the remote system to connect to
/U	Specifies the user context under which the command should be executed
/V	Specifies that verbose information should be displayed
/X	Saves the report in XML format
/Z	Specifies that the super-verbose information should be displayed
/?	Shows all the gpresult command switches
/scope	Specifies whether the user or the computer settings need to be displayed
/User	Specifies the username for which the RSoP data is to be displayed

In the next section, we will look at how to create and apply Local Group Policy Objects to the Windows 10 machine.

Managing and Applying LGPOs

Policies that have been linked through Active Directory will, by default, take precedence over any established local group policies. Local group policies are typically applied to computers that are not part of a network or are in a network that does not have a domain controller and thus does not use Active Directory.

Pre-Vista versions of Windows contained only one Local Group Policy Object that applied to all of the computer's users unless NTFS permissions were applied to the LGPO. However, Windows 10 and Windows Vista changed that with the addition of *Multiple Local Group Policy Objects (MLGPOs)*. MLGPOs are applied in the following hierarchical order:

1. Local Computer Policy
2. Administrators and Non-Administrators Local Group Policy
3. User-Specific Group Policy

The Local Computer Policy is the only LGPO that includes computer and user settings; the other LGPOs contain only user settings. Settings applied here will apply to all users of the computer.

The Administrators LGPO is applied to users who are members of the built-in local Administrators group. As you might guess, the Non-Administrators LGPO is applied to users who are not members of the local Administrators group. Because each user of a computer can be classified as an administrator or a non-administrator, either one policy or the other will apply.

User-Specific LGPOs are also included with Windows 10. These LGPOs make it possible for specific policy settings to apply to a single user.

As with Active Directory GPOs, any GPO settings applied lower in the hierarchy will override GPO settings applied higher in the hierarchy by default. For example, any User-Specific GPO settings will override any conflicting Administrator/Non-Administrator GPO settings or Local Computer Policy settings. And, of course, any AD GPO settings will still override any conflicting LGPO settings.

Domain administrators can disable LGPOs on Windows 10 computers by enabling the Turn Off Local Group Policy Objects Processing Domain GPO setting under `Computer Configuration\Administrative Templates\ System\Group Policy`.

You apply an LGPO to a Windows 10 computer through the Group Policy Object Editor Snap-in within the MMC. Figure 2.14 shows the Local Computer Policy for a Windows 10 computer.

FIGURE 2.14   Local Computer Policy

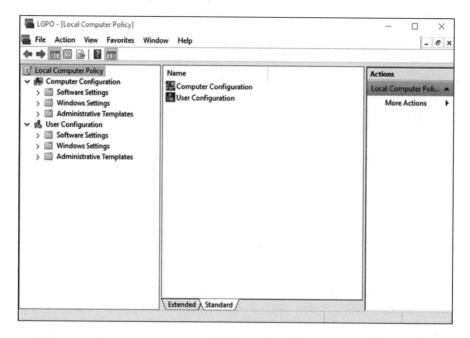

Complete Exercise 2.13 to add the Local Computer Policy Snap-in to the MMC.

EXERCISE 2.13

Adding the Local Computer Policy Snap-In

1. Open the Local Users and Groups MMC shortcut by typing **MMC** in the Search Programs And Files box.

2. A User Account Control dialog box appears. Click Yes.

3. Select File ➢ Add/Remove Snap-in.

4. Highlight the Group Policy Object Editor Snap-in and click the Add button.

5. The Group Policy Object specifies Local Computer by default. Click the Finish button.

6. In the Add Or Remove Snap-Ins dialog box, click OK.

7. In the left pane, right-click the Local Computer Policy and choose New Windows From Here.

8. Choose File ➢ Save As and name the console **LGPO**. Make sure you save it to the Desktop. Click Save.

9. Close the Local Users and Groups MMC.

Now we will look at how to open an LGPO for a specific user account on a Windows 10 machine. Complete Exercise 2.14 to access the Administrators, Non-Administrators, and User-Specific LGPOs.

EXERCISE 2.14

Accessing an LGPO

1. Open the Local Users and Groups MMC shortcut by typing **MMC** in the Windows 10 Search box.

2. Select File ➤ Add/Remove Snap-in.

3. Highlight the Group Policy Object Editor Snap-in and click the Add button.

4. Click Browse so that you can browse for a different GPO.

5. Click the Users tab.

6. Select the user you want to access and click OK.

7. In the Select Group Policy Object dialog box, click Finish.

8. In the Add Or Remove Snap-Ins dialog box, click OK. You may close the console when you have finished looking at the LGPO settings for the user you chose.

 Notice that the Administrators, Non-Administrators, and User-Specific LGPOs contain only User Configuration settings, not Computer Configuration settings.

Now let's take a look at the different security settings that can be configured in the LGPO.

Configuring Local Security Policies

Through the use of the Local Computer Policy, you can set a wide range of security options under `Computer Configuration\Windows Settings\Security Settings`.

This portion of the Local Computer Policy is also known as the Local Security Policy. The following list describes in detail how to apply security settings through LGPOs. The main areas of security configuration of the LGPO are as follows:

Account Policies Account policies are used to configure password and account lockout features. Some of these settings include password history, maximum password age, minimum password age, minimum password length, password complexity, account lockout duration, account lockout threshold, and whether to reset the account lockout counter afterward.

Local Policies   Local policies are used to configure auditing, user rights, and security options.

Windows Firewall with Advanced Security   Windows Firewall with Advanced Security provides network security for Windows computers. Through this LGPO, you can set domain, private, and public profiles. You can also set this LGPO to authenticate communications between computers and inbound/outbound rules.

Network List Manager Policies   This section allows you to set the network name, icon, and location group policies. Administrators can set Unidentified Networks, Identifying Networks, and All Networks.

Public Key Policies   Use the Public Key Policies settings to specify how to manage certificates and certificate life cycles.

Software Restriction Policies   The settings under Software Restriction Policies allow you to identify malicious software and control that software's ability to run on the Windows 10 machine. These policies allow an administrator to protect the Microsoft Windows 10 operating system against security threats such as viruses and Trojan horse programs.

Application Control Policies   This section allows you to set up AppLocker. You can use AppLocker to configure a Denied list and an Accepted list for applications. Applications that are configured on the Denied list will not run on the system, and applications on the Accepted list will operate properly.

IP Security Policies on Local Computer   This section allows you to configure the IPsec policies. IPsec is a way to secure data packets at the IP level of the message.

Advanced Audit Policy Configuration   Advanced Audit Policy Configuration settings can be used to provide detailed control over audit policies. This section also allows you to configure auditing to help show administrators either successful or unsuccessful attacks on their network.

You can also access the Local Security Policy by running secpol.msc or by opening Control Panel and selecting Administrative Tools ≻ Local Security Policy.

Now that you have seen all the options in the security section of the LGPO, let's take a look at account policies and local policies in more detail.

Using Account Policies

Account policies are used to specify the user account properties that relate to the logon process. They allow you to configure computer security settings for passwords and account-lockout specifications.

If security is not an issue—perhaps because you are using your Windows 10 computer at home—then you don't need to bother with account policies. If, on the other hand, security is important—for example, because your computer provides access to payroll information—then you should set very restrictive account policies.

Account policies at the LGPO level apply only to local user accounts, not domain accounts. To ensure that user account security is configured for domain user accounts, you need to configure these policies at the domain GPO level.

To access the `Account Policies` folder from the MMC, follow this path: Local Computer Policy ➤ Computer Configuration ➤ Windows Settings ➤ Security Settings ➤ Account Policies. In the following sections, you will learn about the password policies and account-lockout policies that define how security is applied to account policies.

Setting Password Policies

Password policies ensure that security requirements are enforced on the computer. It is important to understand that password policies are set on a per-computer basis; they cannot be configured for specific users. Figure 2.15 shows the password policies, which are described in Table 2.8.

FIGURE 2.15   The password policies

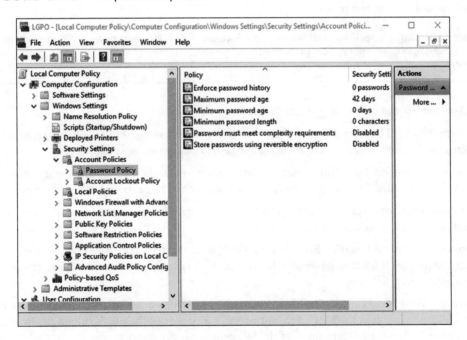

TABLE 2.8   Password policy options

Policy	Description	Default	Minimum	Maximum
Enforce Password History	Keeps track of user's password history	Remember 0 passwords	Same as default	Remember 24 passwords
Maximum Password Age	Determines maximum number of days user can keep valid password	Keep password for 42 days	Keep password for 1 day	Keep password for up to 999 days
Minimum Password Age	Specifies how long password must be kept before it can be changed	0 days (Password can be changed immediately.)	Same as default	998 days
Minimum Password Length	Specifies minimum number of characters password must contain	0 characters (No password required.)	Same as default	14 characters
Password Must Meet Complexity Requirements	Requires that passwords meet minimum levels of complexity	Disabled	No minimum	No maximum
Store Passwords Using Reversible Encryption	Specifies higher level of encryption for stored user passwords	Disabled	No minimum	No maximum

You can use the password policies in Table 2.8 as follows:

Enforce Password History   Prevents users from repeatedly using the same passwords. Users must create a new password when their password expires or is changed.

Maximum Password Age   Forces users to change their passwords after the maximum password age is exceeded. Setting this value to 0 will specify that the password will never expire.

Minimum Password Age   Prevents users from changing their passwords several times in rapid succession in order to defeat the purpose of the Enforce Password History policy.

Minimum Password Length   Ensures that a user creates a password and specifies the length requirement for that password. If this option isn't set, users are not required to create a password at all.

Password Must Meet Complexity Requirements   Passwords must be six characters or longer and cannot contain the user's account name or any part of the user's full name. In addition, passwords must contain three of the following four character types:

- English uppercase characters (A through Z)
- English lowercase characters (a through z)

- Decimal digits (0 through 9)
- Symbols (such as !, @, #, $, and %)

Store Passwords Using Reversible Encryption   Provides a higher level of security for user passwords. This is required for Challenge Handshake Authentication Protocol (CHAP) authentication through remote access or Network Policy Server and for Digest Authentication with Internet Information Services (IIS).

Complete Exercise 2.15 to configure password policies for your computer. These steps assume that you have added the Local Computer Policy Snap-in to the MMC in Exercise 2.1.

EXERCISE 2.15

Configuring Password Policy

1. Open the LGPO MMC shortcut that you created earlier.

2. Expand the Local Computer Policy Snap-in.

3. Expand the folders as follows: Computer Configuration ➤ Windows Settings ➤ Security Settings ➤ Account Policies ➤ Password Policy.

4. Open the Enforce Password History policy. On the Local Security Setting tab, specify that five passwords will be remembered. Click OK.

5. Open the Maximum Password Age policy. On the Local Security Setting tab, specify that the password expires in 60 days. Click OK.

Let's now look at how to set and manage the policies in the Account Lockout Policies section.

Setting Account-Lockout Policies

The account-lockout policies specify how many invalid logon attempts should be tolerated. You configure the account-lockout policies so that after x number of unsuccessful logon attempts within y number of minutes, the account will be locked for a specified amount of time or until the administrator unlocks it.

Account-lockout policies are similar to a bank's arrangements for ATM access-code security. You have a certain number of chances to enter the correct PIN. That way, anyone who steals your card can't just keep guessing your access code until they get it right. Typically, after three unsuccessful attempts, the ATM takes the card. Then you need to request a new card from the bank. Figure 2.16 shows the account-lockout policies, which are described in Table 2.9.

FIGURE 2.16   Account-lockout policies

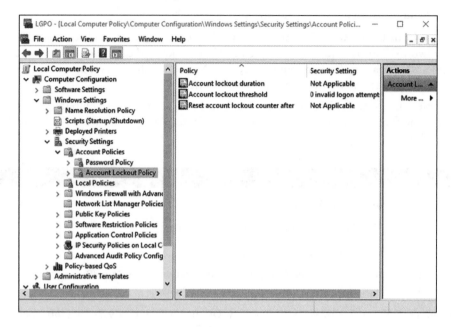

TABLE 2.9   Account-lockout policy options

Policy	Description	Default	Minimum	Maximum
Account Lockout Duration	Specifies how long account will remain locked if the account lockout threshold is reached	Disabled (If Account Lockout Threshold is enabled, 30 minutes)	Same as default	99,999 minutes
Account Lockout Threshold	Specifies number of invalid attempts allowed before account is locked out	0 (Disabled; account will not be locked out.)	Same as default	999 attempts
Reset Account Lockout Counter After.	Specifies how long counter will remember unsuccessful logon attempts	Disabled (If Account Lockout Threshold is enabled, 30 minutes)	Same as default; if enabled, must be equal to or less than the Account Lockout Duration value	99,999 minutes

The Account Lockout Duration and Reset Account Lockout Counter After policies will be disabled until a value is specified for the Account Lockout Threshold policy. After the Account Lockout Threshold policy is set, the Account Lockout Duration and Reset Account Lockout Counter After policies will be set to 30 minutes. If you set Account Lockout Duration to 0, the account will remain locked out until an administrator unlocks it.

  The Reset Account Lockout Counter After value must be equal to or less than the Account Lockout Duration value.

Complete Exercise 2.16 to configure account-lockout policies and test their effects.

EXERCISE 2.16

Configuring Account-Lockout Policies

1. Open the LGPO MMC shortcut.

2. Expand the Local Computer Policy Snap-in.

3. Expand the folders as follows: Computer Configuration ➤ Windows Settings ➤ Security Settings ➤ Account Policies ➤ Password Policy.

4. Open the Account Lockout Threshold policy. On the Local Security Setting tab, specify that the account will lock after three invalid logon attempts. Click OK.

5. Accept the suggested value changes for the Account Lockout Duration and Reset Account Lockout Counter After policies by clicking OK.

6. Open the Account Lockout Duration policy. On the Local Security Setting tab, specify that the account will remain locked for 5 minutes. Click OK.

7. Accept the suggested value changes for the Reset Account Lockout Counter After policy by clicking OK.

8. Log off your Administrator account. Try to log on as one of the accounts that have been created on this Windows 10 machine and enter an incorrect password four times.

9. After you see the error message stating that the referenced account has been locked out, log on as an administrator.

10. To unlock the account, open the Local Users and Groups Snap-in in the MMC, expand the Users folder, and double-click the user.

11. On the General tab of the user's Properties dialog box, click to remove the check mark from the Account Is Locked Out check box. Then click OK.

Using Local Policies

As you learned in the preceding section, account policies are used to control logon procedures. When you want to control what a user can do after logging on, you use local policies. With local policies, you can implement auditing, specify user rights, and set security options.

To use local policies, first add the Local Computer Policy Snap-in to the MMC. Then, from the MMC, follow this path to access the Local Policies folders: Local Computer Policy ➤ Computer Configuration ➤ Windows Settings ➤ Security Settings ➤ Local Policies. Figure 2.17 shows the three Local Policies folders: Audit Policy, User Rights Assignment, and Security Options. We will look at Audit Policy and User Rights Assignment in the following sections.

FIGURE 2.17   Accessing the Local Policies folders

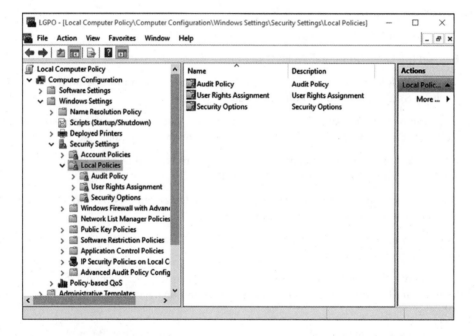

Setting Audit Policies

Audit policies can be implemented to track the success or failure of specified user actions. You audit events that pertain to user management through the audit policies. By tracking certain events, you can create a history of specific tasks, such as user creation and successful or unsuccessful logon attempts. You can also identify security violations that arise when users attempt to access system management tasks for which they do not have permission.

Real World Scenario

Auditing Failed Attempts

As an IT manager, you have to make sure that you monitor failed attempts to access resources. A failed attempt to access a resource usually means that someone tried to access the resource and was denied because of insufficient privileges.

Users who try to go to areas for which they do not have permission usually fall into two categories: hackers and people who are just curious to see what they can get away with. Both are very dangerous.

If a user is trying to access an area in which they do not belong, make sure to warn the user. This is very common on a network and needs to be nipped in the bud.

When you define an audit policy, you can choose to audit success or failure of specific events. The success of an event means that the task was successfully accomplished. The failure of an event means that the task was not successfully accomplished.

By default, auditing is not enabled, and it must be manually configured. Once auditing has been configured, you can see the results of the audit in the security log using the Event Viewer utility.

Only members of the Administrators group can view the security log in Event Viewer.

Figure 2.18 shows the audit policies, which are described in Table 2.10.

FIGURE 2.18 Audit policies

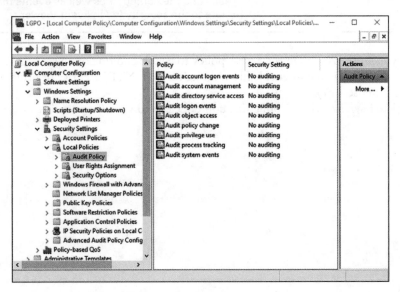

TABLE 2.10   Audit-policy options

Policy	Description
Audit Account Logon Events	Tracks when a user logs on or logs off either their local machine or the domain (if domain auditing is enabled).
Audit Account Management	Tracks user and group account creation, deletion, and management actions, such as password changes.
Audit Directory Service Access	Tracks directory service accesses.
Audit Logon Events	Audits events related to logon, such as running a logon script, accessing a roaming profile, and accessing a server.
Audit Object Access	Enables auditing of access to files, folders, and printers.
Audit Policy Change	Tracks any changes to the audit policies, trust policies, or user rights assignment policies.
Audit Privilege Use	Tracks users exercising a user right.
Audit Process Tracking	Tracks events such as activating a program, accessing an object, and exiting a process.
Audit System Events	Tracks system events such as shutting down or restarting the computer as well as events that relate to the security log in Event Viewer.

After you set the Audit Object Access policy to enable auditing of object access in the object's properties, you must enable file auditing through NTFS security or print auditing through printer security.

Complete Exercise 2.17 to configure audit policies and view their results.

EXERCISE 2.17

Configuring Audit Policies

1. Open the LGPO MMC shortcut.

2. Expand the Local Computer Policy Snap-in.

3. Expand the folders as follows: Computer Configuration ➢ Windows Settings ➢ Security Settings ➢ Local Policies ➢ Audit Policy.

4. Open the Audit Account Logon Events policy. Check the Success and Failure boxes. Click OK.

5. Open the Audit Account Management policy. Check the Success and Failure boxes. Click OK.

6. Log off of your Administrator account. Attempt to log back on to your Administrator account using an incorrect password. The logon should fail (because the password is incorrect).

7. Log on as an administrator.

8. Select Start, right-click Computer, and choose Manage to open Event Viewer.

9. From Event Viewer, open the security log by selecting Windows Logs ➢ Security. You should see the audited events listed with a Task Category of Credential Validation.

Assigning User Rights

The user-rights policies determine what rights a user or group has on the computer. User rights, also called privileges, apply to the system. They are not the same as permissions, which apply to a specific object. An example of a user right is Back Up Files And Directories. This right allows a user to back up files and folders even if the user does not have permissions that have been defined through NTFS filesystem permissions. The other user rights are similar because they deal with system access as opposed to resource access.

Figure 2.19 shows the first several user-rights policies; all of the policies are described in Table 2.11.

FIGURE 2.19   User-rights policies

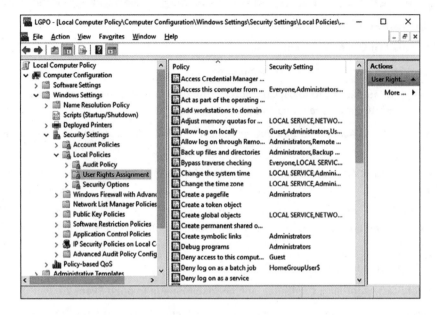

TABLE 2.11   User Rights Assignment policy options

Right	Description
Access Credential Manager As A Trusted Caller	Used to back up and restore Credential Manager.
Access This Computer From The Network	Allows a user to access the computer from the network.
Act As Part Of The Operating System	Allows low-level authentication services to authenticate as any user.
Add Workstations To Domain	Allows a user to create a computer account on the domain.
Adjust Memory Quotas For A Process	Allows you to configure how much memory can be used by a specific process.
Allow Log On Locally	Allows a user to log on at the physical computer.
Allow Log On Through Remote Desktop Services	Gives a user permission to log on through Remote Desktop Services.

Right	Description
Back Up Files And Directories	Allows a user to back up all files and directories regardless of how the file and directory permissions have been set.
Bypass Traverse Checking	Allows a user to pass through and traverse the directory structure, even if that user does not have permissions to list the contents of the directory.
Change The System Time	Allows a user to change the internal time and date on the computer.
Change The Time Zone	Allows a user to change the time zone.
Create A Pagefile	Allows a user to create or change the size of a page file.
Create A Token Object	Allows a process to create a token if the process uses an internal API to create the token.
Create Global Objects	Allows a user to create global objects when connected using Terminal Server.
Create Permanent Shared Objects	Allows a process to create directory objects through Object Manager.
Create Symbolic Links	Allows a user to create a symbolic link.
Debug Programs	Allows a user to attach a debugging program to any process.
Deny Access To This Computer From The Network	Allows you to deny specific users or groups access to this computer from the network. Overrides the Access This Computer From The Network policy for accounts present in both policies.
Deny Log On As A Batch Job	Allows you to prevent specific users or groups from logging on as a batch file. Overrides the Log On As A Batch Job policy for accounts present in both policies.
Deny Log On As A Service	Allows you to prevent specific users or groups from logging on as a service. Overrides the Log On As A Service policy for accounts present in both policies.
Deny Log On Locally	Allows you to deny specific users or groups access to the computer locally. Overrides the Log On Locally policy for accounts present in both policies.

TABLE 2.11 User Rights Assignment policy options *(continued)*

Right	Description
Deny Log On Through Terminal Services	Specifies that a user is not able to log on through Terminal Services.
Enable Computer And User Accounts To Be Trusted For Delegation	Allows a user or group to set the Trusted For Delegation setting for a user or computer object. A user or computer that is trusted for delegation can access resources on another computer using delegated credentials of a client.
Force Shutdown From A Remote System	Allows the system to be shut down by a user at a remote location on the network.
Generate Security Audits	Allows a user, group, or process to make entries in the security log.
Impersonate A Client After Authentication	Enables programs running on behalf of a user to impersonate a client.
Increase A Process Working Set	The working set of a process is the current set of pages in the virtual address space of the process that resides in physical memory. This setting allows you to increase the size of the process working set.
Increase Scheduling Priority	Specifies that a process can increase or decrease the priority that is assigned to another process.
Load And Unload Device Drivers	Allows a user to dynamically unload and load device drivers. This right does not apply to Plug and Play drivers.
Lock Pages In Memory	Allows an account to create a process that runs only in physical RAM, preventing it from being paged.
Log On As A Batch Job	Allows a process to log on to the system and run a file that contains one or more operating system commands.
Log On As A Service	Allows a service to log on in order to run.

Right	Description
Manage Auditing And Security Log	Allows a user to enable object access auditing for files and other Active Directory objects. This right does not allow a user to enable general object access auditing in the Local Security Policy.
Modify An Object Label	Allows a user to change the integrity level of files, folders, or other objects.
Modify Firmware Environment Variables	Allows a user to install or upgrade Windows. It also allows a user or process to modify the firmware environment variables stored in NVRAM of non-x86-based computers. This right does *not* affect the modification of system environment variables or user environment variables.
Perform Volume Maintenance Tasks	Allows a user to perform volume maintenance tasks such as defragmentation and error checking.
Profile Single Process	Allows a user to monitor nonsystem processes through performance-monitoring tools.
Profile System Performance	Allows a user to monitor system processes through performance-monitoring tools.
Remove Computer From Docking Station	Allows a user to undock a laptop through the Windows 10 user interface.
Replace A Process Level Token	Allows a process, such as Task Scheduler, to call an API to start another service.
Restore Files And Directories	Allows a user to restore files and directories regardless of file and directory permissions.
Shut Down The System	Allows a user to shut down the Windows 10 computer locally.
Synchronize Directory Service Data	Allows a user to synchronize Active Directory data.
Take Ownership Of Files Or Other Objects	Allows a user to take ownership of system objects, such as files, folders, printers, and processes.

In Exercise 2.18, you'll apply a user-rights policy.

EXERCISE 2.18

Applying a User-Rights Policy

1.   Open the LGPO MMC shortcut.

2.   Expand the Local Computer Policy Snap-in.

3.   Expand the folders as follows: Computer Configuration ➢ Windows Settings ➢ Security Settings ➢ Local Policies ➢ User Rights Assignment.

4.   Open the Log On As A Service user right.

5.   Click the Add User Or Group button. The Select Users Or Groups dialog box appears.

6.   Click the Advanced button, and then select Find Now.

7.   Select a user. Click OK.

8.   Click OK in the Select Users Or Groups dialog box.

9.   In the Log On As A Service Properties dialog box, click OK.

Configuring User Account Control

Most administrators have had to wrestle with the balance between security and enabling applications to run correctly. In the past, some applications simply would not run correctly under Windows unless the user running the application was a local administrator.

Unfortunately, granting local administrator permissions to a user also allows the user to install software and hardware, change configuration settings, modify local user accounts, and delete critical files. Even more troubling is the fact that malware that infects a computer while an administrator is logged in is able to perform administrative functions.

The problem is that many applications require that users have permissions to write to protected folders and to the Registry. Windows 10's solution is *User Account Control (UAC)*. When any standard user tries to run an application that requires an administrator access token, the UAC requires that the user provide valid administrator credentials.

Privilege Elevation

UAC protects computers by requiring privilege elevation for all users, even users who are members of the local Administrators group. As you have no doubt seen by now, UAC will prompt you for permission when performing a task that requires privilege elevation. This prevents malware from silently launching processes without your knowledge.

Privilege elevation is required for any feature that contains the security shield. For example, the small shield shown on the Change Date And Time button in the Date And Time dialog box indicates an action that requires privilege elevation.

Now let's take a look at how to elevate privileges for users and executables.

Elevated Privileges for Users

By default, local administrators are logged on as standard users. When administrators attempt to perform a task that requires privilege escalation, they are prompted for confirmation by default. This can require administrators to authenticate when performing a task that requires privilege escalation by changing the User Account Control: Behavior Of The Elevation Prompt For Administrators In Admin Approval Mode policy setting to Prompt For Credentials. On the other hand, if you don't want UAC to prompt administrators for confirmation when elevating privileges, you can change the policy setting to Elevate Without Prompting.

Non-administrator accounts are called standard users. When standard users attempt to perform a task that requires privilege elevation, they are prompted for a password of a user account that has administrative privileges. You cannot configure UAC to automatically allow standard users to perform administrative tasks, nor can you configure UAC to prompt a standard user for confirmation before performing administrative tasks. The UAC does this automatically. If you do not want standard users to be prompted at all for credentials when attempting to perform administrative tasks, you change the User Account Control: Behavior Of The Elevation Prompt For Standard Users policy setting to Automatically Deny Elevation Requests.

The built-in Administrator account, though disabled by default, is not affected by UAC. UAC will not prompt the built-in Administrator account for elevation of privileges. Thus, it is important to use a normal user account whenever possible and use the built-in Administrator account only when absolutely necessary.

With the Default UAC setting enabled, a user's desktop will be dimmed when they are notified of a change to the computer. The administrator or user must either approve or deny the request in the UAC dialog box before the user can do anything else on that computer. This is known as the *secure desktop*. You have the ability to turn off the secure desktop by modifying either the Local Security Policy or the Registry.

Complete Exercise 2.19 to see how UAC affects administrator and non-administrator accounts differently.

EXERCISE 2.19

Seeing How UAC Affects Accounts

1. Log on to Windows 10 as a non-administrator account.

2. Click Start ➢ Windows System ➢ Control Panel ➢ Large Icons View ➢ Windows Firewall.

3. Click the Turn Windows Firewall On Or Off link on the left side. The UAC box should prompt you for permission to continue. Click Yes. You should be denied access to the Windows Firewall Settings dialog box.

4. In the Users and Groups MMC, enable the Administrator account and also reset the Administrator's password.

5. Log off and log on as the Administrator account.

6. Click Start ➤ Windows System ➤ Control Panel ➤ *Large Icons View* ➤ Windows Firewall.

   Click the Turn Windows Firewall On Or Off link.

   You should automatically be taken to the Windows Firewall screen. Close the Windows Firewall screen.

Let's now take a look at elevating privileges for executable applications.

Elevated Privileges for Executables

You can also enable an executable file to run with elevated privileges. To do so, you can right-click a shortcut or executable and select Run As Administrator. The elevation applies to this session only.

But what if you need to configure an application to always run with elevated privileges for a user? To do so, log in as an administrator, right-click a shortcut or executable, and select Properties. On the Compatibility tab, check the Run This Program As An Administrator check box. If the Run This Program As An Administrator check box is unavailable, the program is blocked from permanently running as an administrator because the program doesn't need administrative privileges or you are not logged on as an administrator.

Registry and File Virtualization

Many applications that are installed on a Windows 10 machine need to have access to the Registry. By default, Windows 10 protects the Registry from non-administrator accounts, but a feature called Registry and File Virtualization enables non-administrator users to run applications that previously required administrative privileges to run correctly. As discussed earlier, some applications write to the Registry and to protected folders, such as C:\Windows and C:\Program Files. For non-administrator users, Windows 10 redirects any attempts to write to protected locations to a per-user location. By doing so, Windows 10 enables users to use the application successfully while it protects critical areas of the system.

Understanding Smart Cards

Another way to help secure Windows 10 is by using smart cards. *Smart cards* are plastic cards (the size of a credit card) that can be used in combination with other methods of authentication. This process of using a smart card along with another authentication method is called two-factor authentication or *multi-factor authentication.* Authentication is the process of using user credentials to log on to either the local Windows 10 machine or the domain.

Multi-factor authentication support allows you to increase the security of many critical functions of your company, including client authentication, interactive logon, and document signing.

Multi-factor authentication (using smart cards) is now easier than ever to use and deploy because of the new features included with all versions of Windows 10.

Enhanced Support for Smart Card–Related Plug and Play and the Personal Identity Verification (PIV) Standard   This allows users of Windows 10 to use smart cards from vendors who publish their drivers through Windows Update, allowing Windows 10 to use the smart card without special middleware. These drivers are downloaded in the same way as drivers for other Windows devices. When a smart card that is PIV-compliant is placed into a smart card reader, Windows 10 will try to download a current driver from Windows Update. If a driver is not available, the PIV-compliant minidriver that is included with Windows 10 is used for the smart card.

Encrypting Drives with BitLocker   If your users are using Windows 10 Enterprise or Professional, the users can choose to encrypt their removable media by turning on BitLocker and then choosing the smart-card option to unlock the drive. Windows will then retrieve the correct minidriver for the smart card and allow the operation to complete.

Smart-Card Domain Logon   When using Windows 10, the correct minidriver for a smart card is automatically retrieved. This allows a new smart card to authenticate with the domain controller without requiring the user to install or configure additional middleware.

Document and Email Signing   Windows 10 users can use smart cards to sign an email or document. XML Paper Specification (XPS) documents can also be signed without additional software.

Use with Line-of-Business Applications   Using Windows 10 smart cards allows applications that use Cryptography Next Generation (CNG) or CryptoAPI to retrieve the correct minidriver at runtime. This eliminates the need for middleware.

When you decide to use multi-factor authentication, you are deciding to use a process that will require certificate authorities (CAs). CAs are servers that are running the certificate services on them. When you move forward with the decision to use smart cards, you will then need to install and configure CAs to make all of the components work together.

CAs are built on Windows Server operating systems, and if your Windows 10 users are having issues logging into the Windows 10 operating systems using smart cards, then you must check the server CAs to make sure that they are configured and running properly.

 Certificate servers are covered in greater detail in *MCSA Windows Server 2016 Complete Study Guide: Exam 70-740, Exam 70-741, Exam 70-742 and Composite Upgrade Exam 70-743 2nd Edition* by William Panek (Wiley, 2018).

There are two types of smart cards: physical and virtual. Physical smart cards are cards that look like ATM cards. Most of them have either a magnetic strip or chip built into the physical card. To use a physical smart card, you need a smart card reader. This is a device that either connects to a computer or is built into a computer and you place the physical smart card into the reader. You then enter a PIN into the system and the machine is unlocked or logged into the network.

There is a downside to using physical smart cards, which is that they can get lost or misplaced. When I implemented a smart card system into a previous company, we ended up replacing one-fourth of all cards in the first month due to loss or damage.

This is where virtual smart cards can be an advantage. Virtual smart cards use a cryptographic key technology that is stored on the actual Windows 10 computer, as long as that computer has a Trusted Platform Module (TPM) installed on the motherboard.

Virtual smart cards offer the security benefits of two-factor authentication without the price of physical cards and readers. This is possible because of the TPM technology. TPM devices allow us to use cryptographic capabilities, the same as physical smart cards do, but without the cards. Virtual smart cards give us the same benefits as physical cards, including non-exportability, anti-hammering, and isolated cryptography.

Non-Exportability   TPM technology is built to be tamperproof. When a system uses TPM encryption, the TPM encryption is specific to the machine that installed it. Because of this, you can't take a virtual smart card from one system and use it on another.

Anti-Hammering (Lockout)   Smart cards use PINs to unlock the system. If a PIN is entered incorrectly, the TPM uses an Anti-hammering technology that locks the system from further attempts for a specific amount of time.

Isolated Cryptography   TPMs are the only mechanism on a Windows 10 system that loads a copy of the private keys. These keys are not loaded into the system's memory, and because only TPM has the keys, the keys stay isolated and inaccessible to anything or anyone.

Virtual smart cards function the same way as physical smart cards that are continuously inserted into a system. The machine gets the same benefits and results. To set up virtual smart cards, you need to build a certificate authority (CA) server in your organization, and all of your Windows clients need to be Windows 8 or higher.

After the CA is built, you then need to build a certificate template for the virtual smart cards to use. Then, to create the TPM virtual smart card for a Windows 10 system, open a command prompt with administrative credentials on a Windows 10 domain computer and type in the following command:

```
tpmvscmgr.exe create /name tpmvsc /pin default /adminkey random /generate
```

After you run this command, you will create a virtual smart card with the name tpmvsc. The system will then prompt you for a PIN. You will need to enter and confirm a PIN of at least eight characters. After a few seconds, the process will complete. The TPM application (tpmvscmgr.exe) will then provide you with the device instance ID for the virtual smart card. You may want to store this ID in case you will need it to manage or remove the virtual smart card later.

Finally, you will need to enroll the certificate into the CA by requesting a new certificate and then choosing the TPM Virtual Smart Card Logon check box. When you are prompted for a device, select the Microsoft virtual smart card that you created earlier.

Configuring Remote Management

End-user support is a major concern and a time-consuming endeavor for most IT departments. Anything you can do to provide a more efficient solution to user issues is a major benefit. Basic telephone or chat support works in many cases, but what if you could see what the end user sees or even interface with their machine? By using Remote Assistance and Remote Desktop, you can.

Remote Assistance in Windows provides many enhancements over previous versions, including improvements in security, performance, and usability. Windows 10 goes even further by adding a technology integrated with Remote Assistance called Easy Connect. This makes it even easier for novice users to request help from expert users. Group Policy support has been increased. There is command-line functionality (meaning you can add scripting), bandwidth optimization, logging, and even more.

Remote Desktop is a tool that allows you to take control of a remote computer's keyboard, video, and mouse. This tool does not require someone collaborating with you on the remote computer. Remote Desktop is used to access remote machines' applications and troubleshoot issues as well as meet end-user needs where you want complete control of the remote machine. Let's start the discussion with Remote Assistance.

In the following sections, we will also look at how to use virtual private networks (VPNs). We will look at how to configure VPNs and the protocols that work with VPNs.

Remote Assistance

Remote Assistance provides a method for inviting help by instant message, email, or a file. To use Remote Assistance, the computer requesting help and the computer providing help must have Remote Assistance capabilities and the feature enabled, and both computers must have network connectivity (they have to be able to talk to each other).

Remote Assistance is designed to have an expert user (the assistor) provide assistance to a novice user (assistee). When assisting a novice user, the expert can use text-based chat built into Remote Assistance. The expert can also take control of a novice user's desktop (with permission, of course). Here are two common examples of when you would use Remote Assistance:

- Diagnosing problems that are difficult to explain or reproduce. Remote Assistance can allow an expert to remotely view the computer, and the novice user can show the expert an error or problem.

- Guiding a novice user to perform a complex set of actions. The expert can also take control of the computer and complete the tasks if necessary.

Easy Connect

Easy Connect is a technology integrated with Remote Assistance and it's a method for getting remote assistance that is integrated with Windows 10. Easy Connect uses Peer Name Resolution Protocol (PNRP) to set up direct peer-to-peer transfer using a central machine on the Internet to establish the connection. PNRP uses IPv6 and Teredo tunneling to register a machine as globally unique. You're not using IPv6? You are with PNRP; Windows 10 (as well as Windows 7 / 8 / 8.1 and Windows Server) has IPv6 turned on natively as well as the currently used standard of IPv4. We'll discuss IPv6 in more detail in a later chapter, but to give you an idea, you can see the structure of the PNRP Teredo IPv6 packet in Figure 2.20.

FIGURE 2.20   Teredo and IPv6 PNRP structure

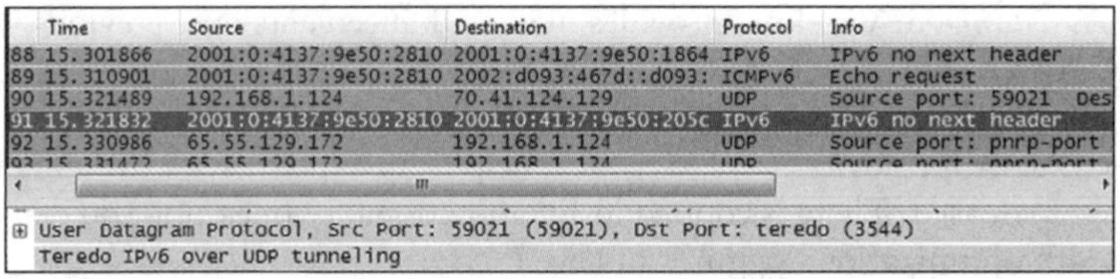

To establish a Remote Assistance session with a user, the novice should open the Windows Remote Assistance screen by typing **msra** in the integrated search box next to the Start Menu.

Remote Assistance can also be incorporated in Group Policy in an enterprise environment by having the expert user configured as a Helper for users in the enterprise (by domain or OU). Once configured as a Helper, the expert can initiate a Remote Assistance session by issuing the command msra /offerra. This will bring up the Who Do You Want To Help Remote Assistance screen.

The expert can also include the novice user's IP address or computer name as an option to the offerRA switch to initiate the Remote Assistance session in one stop (e.g., msra /offerra *ipaddress* | *computername*).

There are several msra.exe switches available to further control the establishment of the Remote Assistance session for both the novice and the expert user. Table 2.12 highlights many of the switches.

TABLE 2.12   MSRA command-line switches

Switch	OS Availability	Functionality
/?	Vista and above	Displays the help options.
/novice	Vista and above	Starts Remote Assistance at the Invite screen.

Switch	OS Availability	Functionality
/expert	Vista and above	Starts Remote Assistance at the Help Someone screen.
/offerRA *ip* | *computer*	Vista and above	Starts Remote Assistance at the Expert Initiated screen or with the options, by automatically initiating with the novice user (used with Group Policy configured in an enterprise environment).
/email *password*	Vista and above	Creates an email invitation to be sent to an expert user to request assistance using the novice's default email program; a random password will be generated and needs to be conveyed to the expert, or alternatively a password can be specified with the password option and conveyed to the expert.
/saveasfile *path password*	Vista and above	Creates a file invitation to be given to an expert user to request assistance; a random password will be generated, or optionally a password can be specified with the *password* option and conveyed to the expert.
/openfile *path*	Vista and above	Used to open the invitation file sent to the expert; can be local or on a shared network drive; the expert will enter the password given to the user when the session was initiated.
/geteasyhelp	Windows 7 and above	Starts a novice user's Remote Assistance session using Easy Connect; presents the novice with the password to convey to the expert user.
/offereasyhelp	Windows 7 and above	Starts an expert user's Remote Assistance session using Easy Connect; presents the expert user with the screen to enter the password from the novice user.
/getcontacthelp *address*	Windows 7 and above	Reestablishes a Remote Assistance session from a novice user's machine to the address from the previous session. The address is in the RAContactHistory .xml file as a 20-byte hexadecimal string with a .RAContact extension.
/offercontacthelp *address*	Windows 7 and above	Reestablishes a Remote Assistance session from an expert user's machine to the address from the previous session. The address is in the RAContactHistory .xml file as a 20-byte hexadecimal string with a .RAContact extension.

Whichever way the novice or the expert launches the feature, the Windows Remote Assistance screen will become available (see Figure 2.21). To start using Easy Connect, the novice user will select Invite Someone You Trust To Help You.

FIGURE 2.21   Remote Assistance initial screen

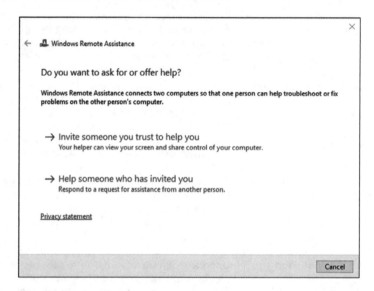

One nice feature of Easy Connect is that if the novice user has established an Easy Connect session previously with an expert user, the screen after selecting Use Easy Connect will offer the novice the ability to connect to the same expert. The novice user can also choose to invite someone new and/or delete the old contact. The expert user will have the same option after choosing Use Easy Connect from the machine used for a previous Easy Connect session.

After the Use Easy Connect option is selected, Windows 10 will verify network connectivity briefly. This is the point at which the PNRP actions take place and the novice user's information is added to a cloud on the Internet. The cloud is the group of machines holding little pieces of information—the identifiers of users needing connectivity, set up in a peer-to-peer sharing environment. PNRP uses this distributed infrastructure for its peer-to-peer name resolution. The novice user's contact information is entered into the PNRP cloud, and an associated password is created and displayed to the novice user.

The novice user will now relay the password to the expert by text message, telephone, or any convenient conversation method. The novice will simply have to wait for the expert to initiate their part. The novice user will still have to accept the connection once the expert starts the remote assistance session.

The expert user needs to start a Remote Assistance session the same way the novice did in Figure 2.21, but the expert will choose Help Someone Who Has Invited You from the Windows Remote Assistance screen.

The expert user will be presented with a dialog box to Use an invitation file and then after you choose the file, you will be prompted to enter the password (Figure 2.22) to connect to the Remote Assistance session.

FIGURE 2.22   Remote Assistance screen

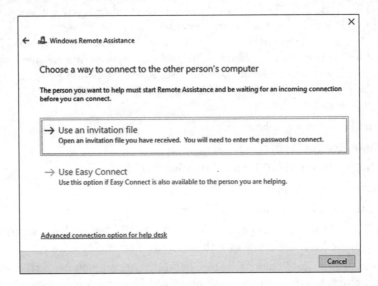

After a few moments of querying the PNRP cloud and finding the connection information that provides the path back to the novice user, Remote Assistance presents the novice user with a confirmation box verifying that the user wants to allow help from the expert.

The novice user will then have a control bar on their screen indicating that the Remote Assistance session is active. From this control bar, the novice can initiate a chat session with the expert and modify some general session settings (bandwidth, logging, contact information exchange, and sharing control).

The expert user will be shown the novice user's Desktop within a separate Remote Assistance window. The expert user will also have some general configuration-setting capabilities as well as an option to request control of the novice user's desktop. The novice user will, of course, be allowed to accept or reject the expert's request.

The expert and novice user can now have an interactive session in which the necessary assistance can be provided. This method of help really takes out the "can you tell me what you see on your screen" issues between two users. The Easy Connect feature takes one more problem out of the equation, getting a novice user to send an invitation to another user. The one caveat here is that both users must be using Windows 10 for Easy Connect to be an option.

Now what if the user is not available to send you the invitation? You can still connect to a user's computer using Remote Desktop, which I will discuss in the next section.

Remote Desktop

Remote Desktop is a tool in Windows 10 that allows you to take control of a remote computer's keyboard, video, and mouse. This tool does not require someone to be available to collaborate with you on the remote computer. While the remote computer is being accessed, locally it remains locked and any actions that are performed remotely will not be visible to the monitor that is attached to the remote computer.

Windows 10 Remote Desktop is, again, an enhanced version of the remote desktop functionality that has been with us for many of the previous versions of Windows, both client and server operating systems. Remote Desktop uses Remote Desktop Protocol (RDP) to provide the data between a host and a client machine. Windows 10 Remote Desktop features are as follows:

- RDP Core Performance Enhancements

- True Multi-Monitor Support

- Direct 2D and Direct 3D 10.1 Application Support

- Bi-directional Audio Support

- Multimedia and Media Foundation Support

- Remote FX has a few end-user enhancements for RDP. These enhancements allow for an enhanced desktop environment within your corporate network.

There are many uses for Remote Desktop, but the most common use is that of the administrator attempting to perform a task on an end user's machine (or on a server).

Another use is the end user connecting to a machine from their home or on the road. If you have noticed the enhancements of Remote Desktop (which are enhancements to RDP), you can see that one of the main goals of enhancing Remote Desktop is to make the user experience as comfortable and seamless as possible.

 Real World Scenario

Using Remote Desktop Functionality

I have mentioned many times using Remote Desktop for troubleshooting client computers. As an administrator, I like to just take control of an end-user machine and fix it. Although this can be done in Remote Assistance, the end user is required to allow us to have access and then can watch what we do. In Remote Desktop, we just take control and close the interactive session at the remote machine (yes, the remote end user can block us or take over the session, but not if they want their problem solved).

But there are other uses as well. We provide servers with resources to our clients, and that server may need to be changed or updated on a regular basis (sometimes a couple of changes in a day). Remote Desktop allows us to maintain our servers from wherever we are without impacting the clients or other administrators.

Remote Desktop Connection Options

When connecting to a Remote Desktop host machine, several options are available to enhance the client user session. The options allow configuration for general settings, display options, local resource access, programs to be executed on startup, the user experience, and advanced options for security and Remote Desktop gateway access. The options become available by clicking the Options button in the lower-left area of the initial Remote Desktop Connection screen. Figure 2.23 shows the options window displayed.

FIGURE 2.23   Remote Desktop options

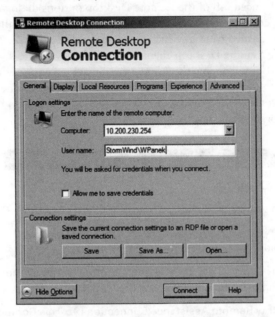

From the General tab, you can select the target remote computer and username. You can save the user credentials from this tab as well. You can save the connection settings to a file or open an existing RDP file from the General tab.

From the Display tab you can choose the size of the display screen. This is also where you select the option to use multiple monitors. The color depth (color quality) is also selected in the Display tab. The option to display the connection bar when using full-screen display is available here as well.

From the Local Resources tab, you can configure remote audio settings, keyboard settings, and local device and resource access.

The Programs tab for Remote Desktop options allows the selection of a program to run at connection startup. The program name and path are specified, as is a startup folder if necessary.

The end-user experience is important to the overall success of using Remote Desktop in the user environment. Remote Desktop can be used to provide a user with the ability to connect to their machine and "remote in." The most seamless environment from the user to the remote location is desirable, but that will be dependent on the bandwidth available. The more bandwidth, the more high-end features can be made available to the end user.

This is also nice for the administrator who is working on an end-user machine. The Experience tab allows the configuration of the end-user experience.

Controlling the behavior of the Remote Desktop connection with regard to security is configured on the Advanced tab of the Remote Desktop options dialog box. The Advanced tab also supports the configuration of a Remote Desktop gateway to allow Remote Desktop connections to be established from any Internet location through SSL. The user must still be authorized and the Remote Desktop client must still be available.

In Exercise 2.20, you will enable the Windows 10 machine to allow Remote Desktop connections. It is up to the company to decide whether all user machines are to be configured this way when you install Windows 10 or whether you should do this only when it becomes necessary for a given computer.

EXERCISE 2.20

Enabling Remote Desktop

1. Open the System tool by right clicking Start ➢ Windows System ➢ Control Panel ➢ System.

2. In the left-hand side, click the Remote Settings link.

3. In the Remote Desktop section, click the radio button that allows connections from computers running any version of Remote Desktop (Less Secure).

4. Make sure the Allow Remote Assistance Connections To This Computer check box is checked.

5. Click OK.

6. Close the System Properties screen.

Enabling PowerShell Remoting

PowerShell is one way to remotely configure and maintain Windows 10. This is becoming more and more popular as newer versions of Windows get released. You need to make sure that your Windows systems (including Windows 10) can accept remote PowerShell commands. If this feature is not already enabled on your system, you can enable this feature by running the `Enable-PSRemoting` cmdlet. To enable remote PowerShell commands, you must be an administrator when running the `Enable-PSRemoting` cmdlet. After PowerShell is enabled, you can then enter a PowerShell session on the Windows 10 system by using the `New-PSSession`. To exit the PowerShell session when completed, you can run the `Exit-PSSession` cmdlet.

Many PowerShell commands do not require an active PowerShell session when running commands remotely (as long as remote commands are enabled). If you are running a PowerShell command that has the computer name in the command, you can specify the Windows 10 machine in the command. For example, the following PowerShell command shows the computer name (our Windows 10 systems are named Computer01 and Computer02).

```
Restart-Computer -ComputerName "Computer01", "Computer02", "localhost"
```

So now that you can connect and run commands on a remote Windows 10 system, you can also run scripts on Windows 10. After you write a PowerShell script (file that ends in .ps1) for Windows 10, you can then run that command remotely by using the `Invoke-Command` cmdlet. The following example is running a PowerShell script on a Windows 10 machine named Computer01.

```
Invoke-Command -ComputerName Computer01 -FilePath c:\Scripts\DataCollect.ps1
```

PowerShell Remoting

If you would like to see additional commands and information about PowerShell remote connections, visit Microsoft's website:

https://docs.microsoft.com/en-us/powershell/scripting/learn/remoting/running-remote-commands?view=powershell-6

Configuring a VPN Connection

A virtual private network is a way to establish a connection between a client machine (VPN client) and server machine (VPN server). A VPN gives you the ability to connect (called *tunneling*) to a server through the use of the Internet or a dial-up connection (hopefully not dial-up), typically with the intention of accessing resources that are available on the network where the VPN server is connected. The VPN server acts as a bridge for the external user connecting from the Internet or other external connections points to the internal network. In a nutshell, a VPN allows you to connect to a private network from a public network.

VPN connections can be secured using various protocols. The following list shows you some of the tunneling protocols that can be used when connecting a Windows 10 machine to a remote server:

Internet Key Exchange Version 2 (IKEv2) Windows 10 can connect to a Windows Server VPN using the *Internet Key Exchange version 2 (IKEv2)* VPN tunneling protocol. The IKEv2 VPN protocol is the newest VPN protocol out of all of the following protocols and can be used with Windows Server 2012 and above. The main advantage of using the IKEv2 VPN protocol is that it allows for the interruptions of the network connection. IKEv2 will then automatically restore the VPN connection after the network connection is restored. This feature is referred to as VPN Reconnect and it is automatically built into the IKEv2 protocol.

Secure Socket Tunneling Protocol *Secure Socket Tunneling Protocol (SSTP)* was released with Windows Server 2008 and is one of the tunneling protocols available with a Windows Server 2008 / 2008 R2 server and Windows 7 machines and later. SSTP works by allowing encapsulated Point-to-Point Protocol (PPP) packets to be transmitted over an HTTPS connection. Because of this, firewalls or Network Address Translation (NAT) devices allow SSTP VPN connections to be more easily established. SSTP is the best choice for securing a VPN connection.

Point-to-Point Tunneling Protocol *Point-to-Point Tunneling Protocol (PPTP)* is one of the predecessors to SSTP, and it also allows point-to-point packets to have encryption for secure connections. PPTP uses TCP/IP for the encryption. PPTP encapsulates PPP frames in IP and uses the TCP for the management side of PPTP.

Layer 2 Tunneling Protocol *Layer 2 Tunneling Protocol (L2TP)* is a tunneling protocol that has no encryption included in the protocol. L2TP uses the IP Security protocol (IPSec) to make L2TP secure. L2TP with IPSec is a much more secure tunneling option than PPTP.

To set up an outbound client VPN connection in Windows 10, you use the Network and Sharing Center. In Exercise 2.21, you will set up a new VPN connection.

EXERCISE 2.21

Setting Up a VPN Connection

1. Start the Network and Sharing Center by right clicking Start ➤ Windows System ➤ Control Panel ➤ Network And Sharing Center.

2. Choose the Set Up A New Connection Or Network link.

3. Choose Connect To A Workplace. Click Next.

4. Choose the Use My Internet Connection (VPN) option.

5. The Connect To A Workplace screen appears. You need to type in the TCP/IP address of a VPN Server and name this VPN connection. In this window, you also have the

ability to use a smart card, to allow other people to use this connection, and to set up the VPN but not connect at this time (the option I chose). After you type in a TCP/IP address and name the VPN connection, click Next.

6. The next screen asks you for your logon credentials. Type in your username, password, and domain name. Click Create.

   Now that the connection is created, I'll show you the steps needed to use it.

7. In the lower-right corner, click on your network connection.

8. A box appears showing your connections. To connect to the VPN connection, choose the corresponding link.

9. When the Connect dialog box appears, make sure your username, password, and domain name are present and click the Connect button.

10. After the connection is established, close it and close the Network and Sharing Center.

Transparent Caching

Windows 10 has a feature called *transparent caching* to help reduce the time needed for retrieving shared files and folders. Transparent caching reduces the time required to access files for the second and subsequent times across a slow network.

In previous versions of Windows, to access a file across a slower network, client computers had to retrieve the file from the server computer. But now with Windows 10 transparent caching, computers can cache these remote files, thus reducing the number of times a computer might retrieve the same data.

When a user opens a file for the first time, Windows 10 accesses the file from the server and then stores the file in the cache of the local disk. From that point on, the user reads the same cached file instead of reading it from the server computer.

To make sure the file is accurate; the Windows 10 client always contacts the server to ensure the cached copy is up-to-date. The file would not be accessible if the server is unavailable. Transparent caching is not enabled by default on fast networks. Transparent caching can be enabled through the use of a group policy.

Broadband Tethering

One nice advantage to Windows 10 and mobility is Broadband Tethering. Let's all pretend that we are at a large Microsoft conference and only one of us in our group can get onto the Internet. Windows 10 Broadband Tethering allows at least 10 devices to connect to your Internet connection and use your Internet for their access. As long as their devices have Broadband enabled capabilities, they will be able to connect to your system and use the Internet.

When you set up the Broadband Tethering, you can set up a connection name and password for all of the other users in your group to connect to your system.

All you need to do is go to your Windows 10 mobile device (in Figure 2.24), I'm using a Windows 10 Surface Pro, and you just need to open your internet connection by sharing the connection.

FIGURE 2.24   Manage Wi-Fi Settings

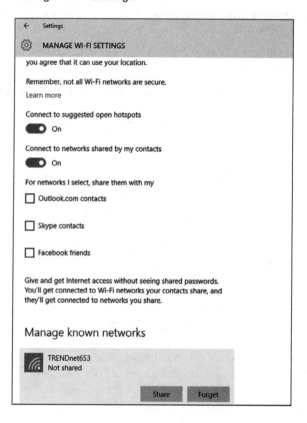

As you can see in Figure 2.25, once you open the connection up, you need to set up a password (at least 8 characters) and then you can share that password with the other members of your group who you want to allow your Internet to be shared with.

FIGURE 2.25   Manage Wi-Fi Settings Password

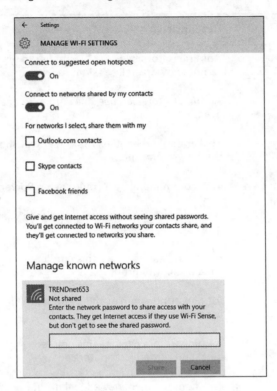

Using PowerShell

PowerShell commands are becoming more important when managing and maintaining Windows devices. Table 2.13 shows some of the common PowerShell commands for user management and remote access.

TABLE 2.13   Common PowerShell commands for Windows 10

Command	Description
Add-LocalGroupMember	This command adds members to a local group.
Disable-LocalUser	Administrators can use this cmdlet to disable a local user account.

TABLE 2.13   Common PowerShell commands for Windows 10 *(continued)*

Command	Description
Disconnect-PSSession	Administrators can use this cmdlet to disconnect from a remote PowerShell session.
Enable-LocalUser	Administrators can use this cmdlet to enable a local user account.
Enable-PSRemoting	This command enables remote PowerShell commands on a Windows computer.
Exit-PSSession	This command allows you to exit a PowerShell session.
Get-LocalGroup	Administrators can use this cmdlet to view a local security group.
Get-LocalGroupMember	Administrators can use this cmdlet to view the members of a local security group.
Get-LocalUser	Administrators can use this cmdlet to view a local user account.
Invoke-Command	Administrators can use this cmdlet to run commands on local and remote computers.
New-LocalGroup	This command creates a local group.
New-LocalUser	This command creates a local user account.
New-PSSession	This command allows you to start a PowerShell session.
New-PSSessionConfigurationFile	Administrators can use this cmdlet to create a file that defines a session's configuration.
Remove-LocalGroup	This command deletes a local group.
Remove-LocalUser	This command deletes a local user account.
Rename-LocalGroup	Administrators can use this cmdlet to rename a local group.
Rename-LocalUser	Administrators can use this cmdlet to rename a local user account.
Set-LocalUser	This command allows an administrator to modify a local user account.

Summary

In this chapter, you learned how to create and manage user and group accounts. We looked at the different tools that can be used to create users in Windows 10.

We also looked at Windows 10 security. We reviewed the difference between LGPOs, which are applied at the local computer level, and GPOs, which are applied through a Windows domain, and how they are applied.

We looked at account policies, which control the logon process. The two types of account policies are password and account lockout policies. We also looked at local policies, which control what a user can do at the computer. The three types of local policies are audit, user rights, and security options policies.

Finally we looked at how administrators can do remote administration and many of the different utilities that we can use to make sure that our hardware and boot up process is secure.

Exam Essentials

Be able to create and manage user accounts.   When creating user accounts, be aware of the requirements for doing so. Understand User Account Control. Know how to rename and delete user accounts. Be able to manage all user properties.

Know how to configure and manage local user authentication.   Understand the options that can be configured to manage local user authentication and when these options would be used to create a more secure environment. Be able to specify where local user authentication options are configured.

Know how to manage local groups.   Understand the local groups that are created on Windows 10 computers by default, and be familiar with the rights each group has. Know how to create and manage new groups.

Know how to set local group policies.   Understand the purpose of account policies and local policies. Know the purpose and implementation of account policies for managing password policies and account lockout policies. Understand the purpose and implementation of local policies and how they can be applied to users and groups for audit policies, user rights assignments, and security options.

Understand User Account Control.   Understand the purpose and features of User Account Control. Be familiar with Registry and file virtualization. Understand privilege escalation. Know the basics of the new UAC Group Policy settings.

Video Resources

There are videos available for the following exercises:

    2.1
    2.3
    2.4

You can access the videos at http://www.wiley.com/go/sybextestprep.

Review Questions

1. You are the network administrator for a Fortune 500 company. The Accounting department has recently purchased a custom application for running financial models. To run properly, the application requires that you make some changes to the computer policy. You decide to deploy the changes through a Local Group Policy setting. You suspect that the policy is not being applied properly because of a conflict somewhere with another Local Group Policy setting. What command should you run to see a list of how the group policies have been applied to the computer and the user?

   A. gpresult

   B. gporesult

   C. gpaudit

   D. gpinfo

2. You have a Windows 10 computer that is located in an unsecured area. You want to track usage of the computer by recording user logon and logoff events. To do this, which of the following auditing policies must be enabled?

   A. Audit Account Logon Events

   B. Audit Account Management

   C. Audit Process Tracking

   D. Audit System Events

3. You are the administrator for a printing company. After you configure the Password Must Meet Complexity Requirements policy, several users have problems when changing their passwords. Which of the following passwords meet the minimum complexity requirements? (Choose all that apply.)

   A. aBc-1

   B. Abcde!

   C. 1247445Np

   D. !@#$%^&*(-[]

4. You are the administrator for StormWind Studios. You want to configure some Local Group Policy Objects (LGPOs) on your Windows 10 machines. Which of the following is not configurable through a LGPO on Windows 10?

   A. Administrative templates

   B. Folder redirection

   C. Internet Explorer settings

   D. Windows Update settings

5. You are the administrator of a large company. You believe that your network's security has been compromised. You do not want hackers to be able to repeatedly attempt user logon with different passwords. What Local Security Policy box should you define?

    A. Password Policy

    B. Audit Policy

    C. Security Options

    D. Account Lockout Policy

6. You have recently hired Will as an assistant for network administration. You have not decided how much responsibility you want Will to have. In the meantime, you want Will to be able to restore files on Windows 10 computers in your network, but you do not want Will to be able to run the backups. What is the minimum assignment that will allow Will to complete this task?

    A. Add Will to the Administrators group.

    B. Grant Will the Read right to the root of each volume he will back up.

    C. Add Will to the Backup Operators group.

    D. Grant Will the user right Restore Files and Directories.

7. You are the network administrator of a medium-size company. Your company requires a fair degree of security, and you have been tasked with defining and implementing a security policy. You have configured password policies so that users must change their passwords every 30 days. Which password policy would you implement if you want to prevent users from reusing passwords they have used recently?

    A. Passwords Must Be Advanced

    B. Enforce Password History

    C. Passwords Must Be Unique

    D. Passwords Must Meet Complexity Requirements

8. Your network's security has been breached. You are trying to redefine security so that a user cannot repeatedly attempt user logon with different passwords. To accomplish this, which of the following items in the Local Security Policy box should you define?

    A. Password Policy

    B. Account Lockout Policy

    C. Audit Policy

    D. Security Options

9. You have been asked to create a new local user on Windows 10 by using Windows Power-Shell. Which of the following PowerShell commands allow you to create a new local user on Windows 10?

    A. Add-LocalUser

    B. New-WindowsUser

    C. New-LocalUser

    D. Add-WindowsUser

10. You are setting up a machine for a home user who does not know much about computers. You do not want to make the user a local administrator, but you do want to give this user the right to change Windows Updates manually. How can you configure this?

    A. Modify the LGPO for Windows Update to allow the user to make changes manually.

    B. Explain to the user how to log on as the Administrator account.

    C. Set Windows Update modifications to anyone.

    D. This can't be done. Only administrators can change Windows Update.

Chapter

3

Managing Data

MICROSOFT EXAM OBJECTIVES COVERED IN THIS CHAPTER:

✓ **Configure data access and protection.**

  - Configure NTFS permissions; configure shared permissions

One of the most fundamental tasks in network management is setting up users' rights and permissions. This is by far one of the most important tasks that we as IT members face every day. Too much access and your users can cause issues. Not enough access and your users can't do their job.

One way to help make sure your users don't have more permissions or security than they need is to use groups. Groups are used to ease network administration by grouping users together who have similar permission requirements. Groups are an important part of network management.

When setting up network data, one of the most important topics that you need to understand are how NTFS and Shared resources work together and how to secure the network hardware. So that's where this chapter comes into play.

In this chapter I will also talk about users accessing resources on a network. If you think about it, that's one of the main reasons we set up networks, to share resources. If we didn't have resources that users needed access to, why even bother setting up a network? So I will talk about sharing resources and assigning permissions to those shares.

You will then learn about NTFS security and share permissions and how they work independently and together. Finally, I will introduce you to some of the Windows 10 security options, including BitLocker. So let's start exploring ways to make your data more secure.

Managing File and Folder Security

Setting up proper file and folder security is one of the most important tasks that an IT professional can perform. If permissions and security are not properly configured, users will be able to access resources that they shouldn't. File and folder security defines what access a user has to local resources. You can limit access by applying security for files and folders. You should know what NTFS security permissions are and how they are applied.

A powerful feature of networking is the ability to allow network access to local folders. In Windows 10, it is very easy to share folders. You can also apply security to shared folders in a manner that is similar to applying NTFS permissions. Once you share a folder, users with appropriate access rights can access the folders through a variety of methods.

When a user is created on a local Windows 10 system or if the user is created on an Active Directory domain, the user gets a Security Identification (SID) number. It is important to remember that when you assign rights to a user, those rights and permissions get associated to the user's SID number and not the username. It's because of this that we can rename user accounts without any issues.

Before diving into the security nitty-gritty, you need to know about the folder options. So let's start with that discussion.

Folder Options

The Windows 10 Folder Options dialog box allows you to configure many properties associated with files and folders, such as what you see when you access folders and how Windows searches through files and folders. To open the Folder Options dialog box, right click Start ➤ File Explorer and then select View and then Options. You can also access Folder Options by choosing Start ➤ Windows System ➤ Control Panel ➤ Large Icons View ➤ File Explorer Options. The Folder Options dialog box has three tabs: General, View, and Search. The options on each of these tabs are described in the following sections.

Folder General Options

The General tab, shown in Figure 3.1, includes the following options:

- Whether folders are opened all in the same window when a user is browsing folders or each folder is opened in a separate window

- Whether a user opens items with a single mouse click or a double-click

- Whether to have the navigation pane show all folders and automatically expand to the current folder

FIGURE 3.1   The General tab of the Folder Options dialog box

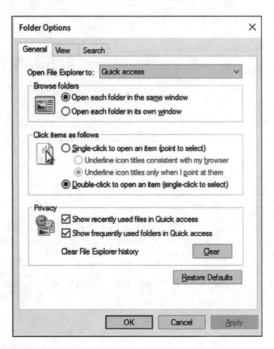

Folder View Options

The View tab of the Folder Options dialog box, shown in Figure 3.2, is used to configure what users see when they open files and folders. For example, you can change the default setting so that hidden files and folders are displayed. Table 3.1 describes the View tab options.

FIGURE 3.2   The View tab of the Folder Options dialog box

TABLE 3.1   Folder view options

Option	Description	Default
Always Show Icons, Never Thumbnails	Shows icons for files instead of thumbnail previews.	Not selected
Always Show Menus	Shows the File, Edit, View, Tools, and Help menus when you're browsing for files.	Not selected
Display File Icon On Thumbnails	Displays the file icon on thumbnails.	Selected

Option	Description	Default
Display File Size Information In Folder Tips	Specifies whether the file size is automatically displayed when you hover your mouse over a folder.	Selected
Display The Full Path In The Title Bar	Specifies whether the title bar shows an abbreviated path of your location. Selecting this option displays the full path as opposed to showing an abbreviated path.	Not selected
Hidden Files And Folders	Specifies whether files and folders with the Hidden attribute are listed. Choosing Show Hidden Files, Folders, Or Drives displays these items.	Don't Show Hidden Files, Folders, Or Drives
Hide Empty Drives	Prevents drives that are empty from being displayed.	Selected
Hide Extensions For Known File Types	By default, filename extensions, which identify known file types (such as .doc for Word files and .xls for Excel files) are not shown. Disabling this option displays all filename extensions.	Selected
Hide Folder Merge Conflicts	When this box is checked, If you move a folder from one directory to another and that folder already exists, folders will be merged without any warning.	Selected
Hide Protected Operating System Files (Recommended)	By default, operating system files are not shown, which protects operating system files from being modified or deleted by a user. Deselecting this option displays the operating system files.	Selected
Launch Folder Windows In A Separate Process	By default, when you open a folder, it shares memory with the previous folders that were opened. Selecting this option opens folders in separate parts of memory, which increases the stability of Windows 10 but can slightly decrease the performance of the computer.	Not selected

TABLE 3.1 Folder view options *(continued)*

Option	Description	Default
Show Drive Letters	Specifies whether drive letters are shown in the folder. When disabled, only the name of the disk or device will be shown.	Selected
Show Encrypted Or Compressed NTFS Files In Color	Displays encrypted or compressed files in an alternate color when they are displayed in a folder window.	Selected
Show Pop-up Description For Folder And Desktop Items	Displays whether a pop-up tooltip is displayed when you hover your mouse over files and folders.	Selected
Show Preview Handlers In Preview Pane	Shows the contents of files in the pre-view pane.	Selected
Use Check Boxes To Select Items	Adds a check box next to each file and folder so that one or more of them may be selected. Actions can then be performed on selected items.	Not selected
Use Sharing Wizard (Recommended)	Allows you to share a folder using a simplified sharing method.	Selected
When Typing Into List View	Selects whether text is automatically typed into the search box or whether the typed item is selected in the view.	Select The Typed Item In The View

Search Options

The Search tab of the Folder Options dialog box, shown in Figure 3.3, is used to configure how Windows 10 searches for files. You can choose for Windows 10 to search by filename only, by filenames and contents, or by a combination of the two, depending on whether indexing is enabled. You can also select from the following options:

- Include subfolders
- Find partial matches
- Use natural language searches
- Don't use the index when searching in file folders for system files
- Include system directories in non-indexed locations
- Include compressed files in non-indexed locations

FIGURE 3.3   The Search tab of the Folder Options dialog box

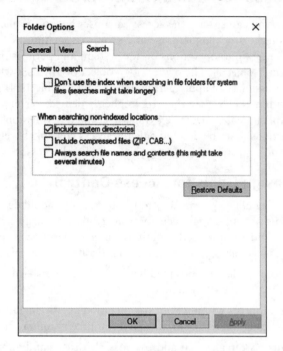

To search for files and folders, click Start ➤ Search and type your query in the search box.

Understanding Dynamic Access Control

One of the advantages of Windows Server and Windows 10 is the ability to apply data governance to your file server. This will help control who has access to information and auditing. We get these advantages through the use of Dynamic Access Control (DAC). Dynamic Access Control allows you to identify data by using data classifications (both automatic and manual) and then control access to these files based on these classifications.

DAC also gives administrators the ability to control file access by using a central access policy. This central access policy will also allow an administrator to set up audit access to files for reporting and forensic investigation.

DAC can be configured to automatically encrypt Microsoft Office documents with Active Directory Rights Management Service (AD RMS) based upon these classifications. For example, you can set up encryption for any documents that contain financial information.

DAC gives an administrator the flexibility to configure file access and auditing to domain based file servers. To do this, DAC uses the claims of the user for controlling access to the resource.

Administrators have the ability to give users access to files and folders based on Active Directory attributes. For example; a user named Dana is given access to the file server share because in the user's Active Directory (department attribute) properties, the value contains the value Sales.

Securing Access to Files and Folders

On NTFS partitions, you can specify the access each user has to specific folders or files on the partition based on the user's logon name and group associations. Access control consists of rights (which pertain to operations on the system) and permissions (which pertain to operations on specific objects). The owner of an object or any user who has the necessary rights to modify permissions can apply permissions to NTFS objects. If permissions are not explicitly granted within NTFS, then they are implicitly denied. Permissions can also be explicitly denied; explicit denials override explicitly granted permissions.

The following sections describe design goals for access control as well as how to apply NTFS permissions and some techniques for optimizing local access.

Considering Design Goals for Access Control

Before you start applying NTFS permissions to resources, you should develop design goals for access control as a part of your overall security strategy. Basic security strategy suggests that you provide each user and group with the minimum level of permissions needed for job functionality. The following list includes some of the considerations when planning access control:

- Defining the resources that are included within your network—in this case, the files and folders residing on the filesystem

- Defining which resources will put your organization at risk, including defining the resources and defining the risk of damage if a resource is compromised

- Developing security strategies that address possible threats and minimize security risks

- Defining groups that security can be applied to based on users within the group membership who have common access requirements, and applying permissions to groups as opposed to users

- Applying additional security settings through Group Policy if your Windows 10 clients are part of an Active Directory network

- Using additional security features, such as Encrypted File System (EFS), to provide additional levels of security or file auditing to track access to critical files and folders

After you have decided what your design goals are, you can start applying your NTFS permissions.

Applying NTFS Permissions

NTFS permissions control access to NTFS files and folders. Ultimately, the person who owns an object has complete control over the object. The owner or administrator can configure access by allowing or denying NTFS permissions to users and groups.

Normally, NTFS permissions are cumulative, based on group memberships. The user gets the highest level of security from all the different groups they belong to. However, if the user had been denied access through user or group membership, those deny permissions override the allowed permissions. Windows 10 offers seven levels of NTFS permissions, plus special permissions:

Full Control   This permission allows the following rights:

- Traverse folders and execute files (programs) in the folders. The ability to traverse folders allows you to access files and folders in lower subdirectories, even if you do not have permissions to access specific portions of the directory path.
- List the contents of a folder and read the data in a folder's files.
- See a folder's or file's attributes.
- Change a folder's or file's attributes.
- Create new files and write data to the files.
- Create new folders and append data to the files.
- Delete subfolders and files.
- Delete files.
- Compress files.
- Change permissions for files and folders.
- Take ownership of files and folders.

If you select the Full Control permission, all permissions will be checked by default and can't be unchecked.

Any user with Full Control access can manage the security of a folder. However, to access folders, a user must have physical access to the computer as well as a valid logon name and password. By default, regular users can't access folders over the network unless the folders have been shared.

Modify   This permission allows the following rights:

- Traverse folders and execute files in the folders.
- List the contents of a folder and read the data in a folder's files.
- See a file's or folder's attributes.
- Change a file's or folder's attributes.
- Create new files and write data to the files.
- Create new folders and append data to the files.
- Delete files.

If you select the Modify permission, the Read & Execute, List Folder Contents, Read, and Write permissions will be checked by default and can't be unchecked.

Read & Execute   This permission allows the following rights:

- Traverse folders and execute files in the folders.
- List the contents of a folder and read the data in a folder's files.
- See a file's or folder's attributes.

If you select the Read & Execute permission, the List Folder Contents and Read permissions will be checked by default and can't be unchecked.

List Folder Contents   This permission allows the following rights:

- Traverse folders.
- List the contents of a folder.
- See a file's or folder's attributes.

Read   This permission allows the following rights:

- List the contents of a folder and read the data in a folder's files.
- See a file's or folder's attributes.
- View ownership.

Write   This permission allows the following rights:

- Overwrite a file.
- View file ownership and permissions.
- Change a file's or folder's attributes.
- Create new files and write data to the files.
- Create new folders and append data to the files.

Special Permissions   This allows you to configure any permission beyond the normal per-missions, such as auditing, and to take ownership. To apply NTFS permissions, right-click the file or folder to which you want to control access, select Properties from the context menu, and then select the Security tab. The Security tab lists the users and groups who have been assigned permissions to the file or folder. When you click a user or group in the top half of the dialog box, you see the permissions that have been allowed or denied for that user or group in the bottom half (see Figure 3.4).

FIGURE 3.4   The object's Security tab

Exercise 3.1 walks you through assigning NTFS permissions.

EXERCISE 3.1

Managing NTFS Permissions

1. Right-click the file or folder to which you want to control access, select Properties from the context menu, and click the Security tab.

2. Click the Edit button to modify permissions.

3. Click the Add button to open the Select Users Or Groups dialog box. You can select users from the computer's local database or from the domain you are in (or trusted domains) by typing in the user or group name in the Enter The Object Names To Select portion of the dialog box and clicking OK.

    Through the Advanced button of the Security tab, you can configure more granular NTFS permissions, such as Traverse Folder and Read Attributes permissions.

4. You return to the Security tab of the folder Properties dialog box. Highlight a user or group in the top list box, and in the Permissions list, specify the NTFS permissions to be allowed or denied. When you have finished, click OK. To remove the NTFS permissions for a user, computer, or group, highlight that entity in the Security tab and click the Remove button. Be careful when you remove NTFS permissions. You won't be asked to confirm their removal as you are when deleting most other types of items in Windows 10.

Controlling Permission Inheritance

Normally, the directory structure is organized in a hierarchical manner. This means you are likely to have subfolders in the folders to which you apply permissions. In Windows 10, by default, the parent folder's permissions are applied to any files or subfolders in that folder as well as any subsequently created objects. These are called inherited permissions.

You can specify how permissions are inherited by subfolders and files by clicking the Advanced button on the Security tab of a folder's Properties dialog box. This calls up the Permissions tab of the Advanced Security Settings dialog box. To edit these options, click the Disable Inheritance button. You can edit the following options:

- Convert Inherited Permissions Into Explicit Permissions On This Object
- Remove All Inherited Permissions From This Object

If an Allow or a Deny item in the Permissions list on the Security tab has a shaded check mark, this indicates that the permission was inherited from an upper-level folder. If a check mark is not shaded, it means the permission was applied at the selected folder. This is known as an explicitly assigned permission. Knowing which permissions are inherited and which are explicitly assigned is useful when you need to troubleshoot permissions.

Understanding Ownership and Security Descriptors

When an object is initially created on an NTFS partition, an associated security descriptor is created. A security descriptor contains the following information:

- The user or group who owns the object
- The users and groups who are allowed or denied access to the object
- The users and groups whose access to the object will be audited

After an object is created, the owner of the object has full permissions to change the information in the security descriptor, even for members of the Administrators group. You can view the owner of an object from the Security tab of the specified folder's Properties dialog box by clicking the Advanced button.

Although the owner of an object can set the permissions of an object so that the administrator can't access the object, the administrator or any member of the Administrators group can take ownership of an object and thus manage the object's permissions. When you take ownership of an object, you can specify whether you want to replace the owner on subdirectories and subobjects of the object. If you would like to see who owns a directory from the command prompt, type **dir /q**.

Determining and Viewing Effective Permissions for NTFS

To determine a user's effective permissions (the aggregate permissions the user has to a file or folder), add all of the permissions that have been allowed through the user's assignments based on that user's username and group associations. After you determine what the user is allowed, you subtract any permissions that have been denied the user through the username or group associations.

As an example, suppose that user Marilyn is a member of both the Accounting and Execs groups. The following assignments have been made to the Accounting group permissions:

Permission	Allow	Deny
Full Control		
Modify	X	
Read & Execute	X	
List Folder Contents		
Read		
Write		

The following assignments have been made to the Execs group permissions:

Permission	Allow	Deny
Full Control		
Modify		
Read & Execute		
List Folder Contents		
Read	X	
Write		

To determine Marilyn's effective rights, you combine the permissions that have been assigned. The result is that Marilyn's effective rights are Modify, Read & Execute, and Read, so she effectively has Modify (the highest right).

As another example, suppose that user Dan is a member of both the Sales and Temps groups. The following assignments have been made to the Sales group permissions:

Permission	Allow	Deny
Full Control		
Modify	X	
Read & Execute	X	
List Folder Contents	X	
Read	X	
Write	X	

The following assignments have been made to the Temps group permissions:

Permission	Allow	Deny
Full Control		
Modify		X
Read & Execute		
List Folder Contents		
Read		
Write		X

To determine Dan's effective rights, you start by seeing what Dan has been allowed: Modify, Read & Execute, List Folder Contents, Read, and Write permissions. You then remove anything that he is denied: Modify and Write permissions. In this case, Dan's effective rights are Read & Execute, List Folder Contents, and Read.

If permissions have been applied at the user and group levels and inheritance is involved, it can sometimes be confusing to determine what the effective permissions are. To help identify which effective permissions will actually be applied, you can view them from the Effective Access tab of Advanced Security Settings, or you can use the icacls command-line utility.

To see what the effective permissions are for a user or group, you click the Select button and then type in the user or group name. Then click OK. If a box is checked and not shaded, then explicit permissions have been applied at that level. If the box is shaded, then the permissions to that object were inherited.

The icacls command-line utility can also be used to display or modify user access permissions. The options associated with the icacls command are as follows:

- /grant grants permissions.

- /remove revokes permissions.

- /deny denies permissions.

- /setintegritylevel sets an integrity level of Low, Medium, or High.

One issue that IT people run into is what happens to the security when you move or copy a file or folder. Let's take a look at NTFS permissions when they are moved or copied.

Determining NTFS Permissions for Copied or Moved Files

When you copy or move NTFS files, the permissions that have been set for those files might change. The following are guidelines to predict what will happen:

- If you move a file from one folder to another folder on the same volume, the file will retain the original NTFS permissions.

- If you move a file from one folder to another folder between different NTFS volumes, the file is treated as a copy and will have the same permissions as the destination folder.

- If you copy a file from one folder to another folder on the same volume or on a different volume, the file will have the same permissions as the destination folder.

- If you copy or move a file or folder to a FAT partition, it will not retain any NTFS permissions.

Managing Network Access

In every network, there are resources to which the users need to gain access. As IT professionals, we share these resources so that our users can do their jobs.

Sharing is the process of allowing network users access to a resource located on a computer. A network share provides a single location to manage shared data used by many users. Sharing also allows an administrator to install an application once, as opposed to installing it locally at each computer, and to manage the application from a single location.

The following sections describe how to create and manage shared folders and configure share permissions.

Creating and Managing Shared Folders

You can share a folder in two ways. To use the Sharing Wizard, right-click a folder and select Share. If the Sharing Wizard feature is enabled, you will see the File Sharing screen, where you can add local users. Alternatively, you can access the wizard by right-clicking a folder and then selecting Properties ➢ Sharing tab ➢ Share button.

However, you cannot use the Sharing Wizard to share resources with domain users. To share a folder with domain users, right-click the folder and select Properties and then select the Sharing tab, shown in Figure 3.5.

FIGURE 3.5   The Sharing tab of a folder's Properties dialog box

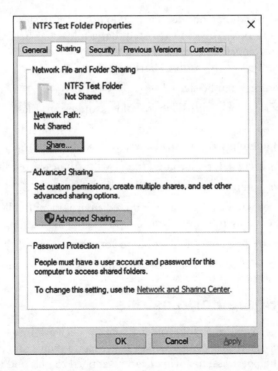

The Share button will take you to the Sharing Wizard. To configure Advanced Sharing, click the Advanced Sharing button, which will open up the Advanced Sharing dialog box.

When you share a folder, you can configure the options listed in Table 3.2.

TABLE 3.2   Shared folder options

Option	Description
Share This Folder	Makes the folder available through local access and network access.
Share Name	A descriptive name by which users will access the folder.
Comments	Additional descriptive information about the share (optional).
Limit The Number Of Simultaneous Users To	The maximum number of connections to the share at any one time (No more than 20 users can simultaneously access a share on a Windows 10 computer.)
Permissions	How users will access the folder over the network.
Caching	How folders are cached when the folder is offline.

If you share a folder and then decide that you do not want to share it, just deselect the Share This Folder check box. You can easily tell that a folder has been shared by the group icon located at the bottom left of the folder icon.

Keep in mind the following regarding sharing:

- Only folders, not files, can be shared.

- Share permissions can be applied only to folders and not to files.

- If a folder is shared over the network and a user is accessing it locally, then share permissions will not apply to the local user; only NTFS permissions will apply.

- If a shared folder is copied, the original folder will still be shared but not the copy.

- If a shared folder is moved, the folder will no longer be shared.

- If the shared folder will be accessed by a mixed environment of clients, including some that do not support long filenames, you should use the 8.3 naming format for files.

- Folders can be shared through the Net Share command-line utility.

Now let's take a look at configuring share permissions for your users.

Configuring Share Permissions

You can control users' access to shared folders from the network by assigning share permissions. Share permissions are less complex than NTFS permissions and can be applied only to folders (unlike NTFS permissions, which can be applied to files and folders).

To assign share permissions, click the Permissions button in the Advanced Sharing dialog box. This brings up the Share Permissions dialog box, shown in Figure 3.6.

FIGURE 3.6 The Share Permissions dialog box

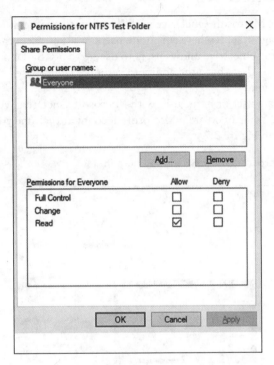

You can assign three types of share permissions:

Full Control   Allows full access to the shared folder.

Change   Allows users to change data within a file or to delete files.

Read   Allows a user to view and execute files in the shared folder. Read is the default permission on shared folders for the Everyone group.

Shared folders do not use the same concept of inheritance as NTFS folders. If you share a folder, there is no way to block access to lower-level resources through share permissions. One thing that is the same between shared and NTFS is that all shared permission are additive if you belong to multiple groups. This means that you add up all the permissions of the groups and get the highest permission.

When applying conflicting share and NTFS permissions, the most restrictive permissions win. Remember that share and NTFS permissions are both applied only when a user is accessing a shared resource over a network. Only NTFS permissions apply to a user accessing a resource locally. So, for example, if a user's NTFS security setting on a resource is Read and the share permission on the same resource is Full Control, the user would have only Read permission when they connect to the shared resource. The most restrictive set of permissions wins.

Configuring OneDrive

Windows 10 includes Microsoft OneDrive with the operating system. Microsoft OneDrive is a cloud-based storage system where corporate users or home users can store their data in the cloud. Microsoft OneDrive allows users to use up to 5 GB of cloud storage for free without a subscription. Users have the ability to get more cloud-based storage by purchasing a higher subscription.

To setup a corporate user or home user with Microsoft OneDrive, you must first have a Microsoft account. You can create a Microsoft account at the time you are accessing OneDrive, as shown in Figure 3.7.

FIGURE 3.7 Microsoft OneDrive Sign-in screen

Once you have a Microsoft account, you then sign into the Microsoft OneDrive system where you can begin uploading data. Figure 3.8 shows Microsoft OneDrive from the Internet browser. Using the Internet browser, you can control the files that are located in the cloud.

FIGURE 3.8   Microsoft OneDrive

In Exercise 3.2, I will show you how to sign into your Microsoft OneDrive application.

EXERCISE 3.2

Logging into OneDrive

1.   Click on the Start button and click the OneDrive tile as shown in Figure 3.9.

FIGURE 3.9   OneDrive tile

EXERCISE 3.2 *(continued)*

2. A dialog box will prompt you for your email address, where you will enter your email address for your Microsoft Account. If Microsoft does not recognize the email address associated with a Microsoft Account, you can click Sign Up for a New Account.

3. If a Microsoft Account is associated with your email, the next screen will prompt you for your Microsoft Account and Password as shown in Figure 3.10.

FIGURE 3.10   OneDrive Login

4. The next screen will allow you to Start using OneDrive (shown in Figure 3.11).

FIGURE 3.11   Start Using OneDrive

At this point you can start using OneDrive to create and upload files to the OneDrive cloud. You can modify OneDrive settings by clicking the icon for OneDrive (cloud) in the Notification Tray, selecting the three dots (More), and then Settings in the context menu that appears. You can choose which folders are synchronized to OneDrive by clicking the Choose Folders button on the Account tab. You can then choose which folders to synchronize, as shown in Figure 3.12.

FIGURE 3.12   Changing the OneDrive Settings

Inside the settings, you have the ability to change how much bandwidth will be used to sync with the cloud, which accounts will be associated to this OneDrive, and many other settings. The OneDrive cloud-based storage is a good way to back up some documents for protection of data loss.

Understanding Hardware Security

One issue that IT members have to face is the protection of not only our data but the hardware that the data resides on. You may remember a case a few years back when an individual stole some hard drives from a VA office. Well let's take a look at a security measure that will help you protect your data drives from physically being taken.

We must make sure that if anyone steals hardware from our corporation or from our server rooms that the data that they are stealing is secured and can't be used. This is where BitLocker can help.

Using BitLocker Drive Encryption

To prevent individuals from stealing your computer and viewing personal and sensitive data found on your hard disk, some editions of Windows come with a new feature called *BitLocker Drive Encryption*. BitLocker encrypts the entire system drive. New files added to this drive are encrypted automatically, and files moved from this drive to another drive or computers are decrypted automatically.

Only Windows 7 Enterprise and Ultimate, Windows 8 Pro and Enterprise, Windows 10 Pro and Enterprise, and Windows Server 2008 and above include BitLocker Drive Encryption, and only the operating system drive (usually C:) or internal hard drives can be encrypted with BitLocker. Files on other types of drives must be encrypted using BitLocker To Go. BitLocker To Go allows you to put BitLocker on removable media such as external hard disks or USB drives.

BitLocker uses a Trusted Platform Module (TPM) version 1.2 or higher to store the security key. A TPM is a chip that is found in newer computers. If you do not have a computer with a TPM, you can store the key on a removable USB drive. If you don't have a system with TPM, you will need to turn off the TPM setting in local computer settings as shown in Figure 3.13. The USB drive will be required each time you start the computer so that the system drive can be decrypted.

FIGURE 3.13   Changing the TPM settings

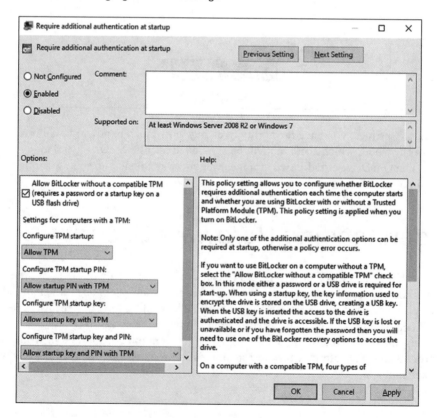

If the TPM discovers a potential security risk, such as a disk error or changes made to BIOS, hardware, system files, or startup components, the system drive will not be unlocked until you enter the 48-digit BitLocker recovery password or use a USB drive with a recovery key as a recovery agent.

BitLocker must be set up either within the Local Group Policy editor or through the BitLocker icon in Control Panel.

BitLocker Recovery Password

The BitLocker recovery password is very important. Do not lose it or you may not be able to unlock the drive. Even if you do not have a TPM, be sure to keep your recovery password in case your USB drive becomes lost or corrupted.

BitLocker requires that you have a hard disk with at least two partitions, both formatted with NTFS. One partition will be the system partition that will be encrypted. The other partition will be the active partition that is used to start the computer. This partition will remain unencrypted.

Features of BitLocker

As with any version of Windows, Microsoft continues to improve on technologies for Windows Server and Windows 10. The following sections cover some of the features of BitLocker.

BitLocker Provisioning

In previous versions of BitLocker (Windows 7) the BitLocker provisioning (system and data volumes) was completed during the post-installation of the BitLocker utility. The BitLocker provisioning was done either through the command-line interface (CLI) or Control Panel. In the Windows 8, Windows 10, and Windows Server (2012 and above) version of BitLocker, an administrator can choose to provision BitLocker before the operating system is even installed.

Administrators have the ability to enable BitLocker, prior to the operating system deployment, from the Windows Preinstallation Environment (WinPE). BitLocker is applied to the formatted volume and encrypts the volume prior to running the Windows setup process.

If an administrator wants to check the status of BitLocker on a particular volume, the administrator can view the status of the drive in either the BitLocker Control Panel applet or Windows Explorer.

Used Disk Space Only Encryption

Windows 10 BitLocker has a requirement that all data and free space on the drive has to be encrypted. Because of this, the encryption process can take a very long time on larger volumes. In Windows 10 BitLocker, administrators have the ability to encrypt either the entire volume or just the space being used. When you choose to encrypt the Used Disk Space Only option, only the section of the drive that has data will be encrypted. Because of this, encryption is completed much faster.

Standard User PIN and Password Change

One issue that BitLocker has had is that you need to be an administrator to configure BitLocker on operating system drives. This can be an issue in a large organization due to the fact deploying the Trusted Platform Module (TPM) + PIN to a large number of computers can be very challenging.

Even with the new operating system changes, administrative privileges are still needed to configure BitLocker, but now your users have the ability to change the BitLocker PIN for the operating system or change the password on the data volumes.

When a user gets to choose their own PIN and password, they normally choose something that has meaning and something easy for them to remember. That is a good thing and a bad thing. It's good because when your users choose their own PIN and password, normally they don't need to write it down—they just know it. It's bad because if anyone knows the user well, they can have an easier time figuring out the person's PIN and password. Even when you allow your users to choose their own PIN and password, make sure you set a GPO to require password complexity.

Network Unlock

One of the new features of BitLocker is called Network Unlock. *Network Unlock* allows administrators to easily manage desktop and servers that are configured to use BitLocker. Network Unlock allows an administrator to configure BitLocker to unlock automatically an encrypted hard drive during a system reboot when that hard drive is connected to their trusted corporate environment. For this to function properly on a machine, there has to be a DHCP driver implementation in the system's firmware.

If your operating system volume is also protected by the TPM + PIN protection, the administrator has to be sure to enter the PIN at the time of the reboot. This protection can actually make using Network Unlock more difficult to use, but they can be used in combination.

Support for Encrypted Hard Drives for Windows

One of the new advantages of using BitLocker is *Full Volume Encryption (FVE)*. BitLocker provides built-in encryption for Windows data files and Windows operating system files. The advantage of this type of encryption is that encrypted hard drives that use *Full Disk Encryption (FDE)* get each block of the physical disk space encrypted. Because each physical block gets encrypted, it offers much better encryption. The only downside to this is because each physical block is encrypted, it adds some degradation to the hard drive speed. So, as an administrator, you have to decide if you want better speeds or better security on your hard disk.

Windows 7 vs. Windows 10

The real question is what's the difference between Windows 7 versus Windows 10. Table 3.3 shows you many of the common features and how they worked then and now.

TABLE 3.3   BitLocker then and now

Feature	Windows 7	Windows 10
Reset the BitLocker PIN or password	The user's privileges must be set to an administrator if you want to reset the BitLocker PIN on an operating system drive and the password on a fixed or removable data drive.	Standard users now have the ability to reset the BitLocker PIN and password on operating system drives, fixed data drives, and removable data drives.
Disk encryption	When BitLocker is enabled, the entire disk is encrypted.	When BitLocker is enabled, users have the ability to choose whether to encrypt the entire disk or only the used space on the disk.
Hardware Encrypted Drive support	Not supported.	If the Windows logo hard drive comes pre-encrypted from the manufacturer, BitLocker is supported.
Unlocking using a network-based key to provide dual-factor authentication	Not available.	If a computer is rebooted on a trusted corporate wired network, key protector then allows a key to unlock and skip the PIN entry.
Linking a BitLocker key protector to an Active Directory account	Not available.	BitLocker allows a user, group, or computer account in Active Directory to be tied to a key protector. This key protector allows a protected data volumes to be unlocked.

In Exercise 3.3, you will enable BitLocker on the Windows 10 system.

EXERCISE 3.3

Using BitLocker in Windows 10

1. Open Control Panel by typing **Control Panel** in the Windows 10 Search box.

2. Change the View By: Category option to Large Icons by using the pull-down.

3. Choose the BitLocker Drive Encryption icon as shown in Figure 3.14.

FIGURE 3.14   Choosing the BitLocker icon

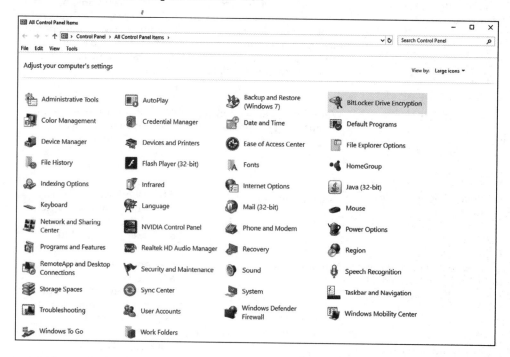

4. Click on the link that says "Turn on BitLocker."

5. At the Choose How To Unlock The Drive screen, click the Enter A Password link.

6. Enter a password and reenter the password and click the Next button.

7. At the How Do You Want To Save The Recovery Key screen, pick one of the options, and after you configure the option, click Next.

8. At the Choose How Much You Want To Encrypt screen, choose to encrypt used disk space or the entire drive. I am choosing the entire drive.

9. At the Are You Ready To Encrypt The Drive screen, click Continue.

10. The drive will be encrypted. You can unencrypt the drive at any time by choosing Unencrypt Drive from the BitLocker icon in Control Panel.

Using the BitLocker Administration and Monitoring Utility

Microsoft BitLocker Administration and Monitoring (MBAM) will allow the IT department to use enterprise-based utilities for managing and maintaining BitLocker and BitLocker To Go. As mentioned earlier, one of the hardest components of BitLocker is managing and maintaining BitLocker deployment and key recovery. This is where MBAM comes in to play.

MBAM helps IT departments simplify BitLocker deployment and key recovery while also providing centralized compliance monitoring and reporting. MBAM also helps minimize the money related to provisioning and supporting encrypted BitLocker drives.

As explained, BitLocker helps protect against the theft of hardware, and MBAM helps an IT department administer BitLocker in an easy-to-use administrative Microsoft Management Console (MMC) interface.

Overview of MBAM

Microsoft has created MBAM 2.5 to help administrators handle and administer BitLocker and BitLocker To Go. MBAM offers many of the following features:

- Allows IT administrators to automatically set up client computers to use encrypted volumes across the entire enterprise.

- Allows corporate security personnel to rapidly determine if the corporate compliances have been met and it also allows them to check the state of individual computers throughout the network.

- IT members can use Microsoft System Center Configuration Manager to have a centralized reporting and hardware management utility that works with MBAM.

- Helps IT departments to rapidly assist end users with BitLocker PIN and recovery key requests.

- Allows corporate users to recover their own encrypted devices by using the MBAM Self-Service Portal.

- Give corporations piece of mind that their users can work anywhere in the world with the knowledge that corporate data is being protected.

MBAM is a downloadable Microsoft utility, but your network must meet certain requirements (MBAM requires the Microsoft Desktop Optimization Pack (MDOP)). Many of these requirements require server installations and are beyond the scope of this book. To learn more about MBAM, go to Microsoft's website to see all of the requirements:

```
https://docs.microsoft.com/en-us/
microsoft-desktop-optimization-pack/mbam-v25/
```

Understanding Smart Cards

Another way to help secure Windows 10 is by using smart cards. *Smart cards* are plastic cards (the size of a credit card) that can be used in combination with other methods of authentication. This process of using a smart card along with another authentication method is called two-factor authentication or *multi-factor authentication*. Authentication is the process of using user credentials to log on to either the local Windows 10 machine or the domain.

Smart card support allows you to increase the security of many critical functions of your company, including client authentication, interactive logon, and document signing.

Smart cards are now easier than ever to use and deploy because of the new features included with all versions of Windows 10.

Enhanced Support for Smart Card–Related Plug and Play and the Personal Identity Verification (PIV) Standard   This allows users of Windows 10 to use smart cards from vendors who publish their drivers through Windows Update, allowing Windows 10 to use the smart card without special middleware. These drivers are downloaded in the same way as drivers for other Windows devices. When a smart card that is PIV-compliant is placed into a smart-card reader, Windows 10 will try to download a current driver from Windows Update. If a driver is not available, the PIV-compliant minidriver that is included with Windows 10 is used for the smart card.

Encrypting Drives with BitLocker   If your users are using Windows 10 Enterprise or Professional, the users can choose to encrypt their removable media by turning on BitLocker and then choosing the smart-card option to unlock the drive. Windows will then retrieve the correct minidriver for the smart card and allow the operation to complete.

Smart-Card Domain Logon   When using Windows 10, the correct minidriver for a smart card is automatically retrieved. This allows a new smart card to authenticate with the domain controller without requiring the user to install or configure additional middleware.

Document and Email Signing   Windows 10 users can use smart cards to sign an email or document. XML Paper Specification (XPS) documents can also be signed without additional software.

Use with Line-of-Business Applications   Using Windows 10 smart cards allows applications that use Cryptography Next Generation (CNG) or CryptoAPI to retrieve the correct minidriver at runtime. This eliminates the need for middleware.

Summary

In this chapter, we started looking at how to set up and configure folders on Windows 10 and Windows Server systems. You learned about sharing those folders and how to grant access to those folders by using NTFS and Shared Permissions.

The chapter also covered Dynamic Access Control (DAC) and how Dynamic Access Control allows an administrator to identify data by using data classifications and then controlling access to these files based on these classifications.

DAC also gives administrators the ability to control file access by using a central access policy. This central access policy will also allow an administrator to set up audit access to files for reporting and forensic investigation.

You also learned about BitLocker and BitLocker To Go, including Data Recovery Agent and Microsoft BitLocker Administration and Monitoring (MBAM). The chapter ended with a discussion of two-factor authentication using Smart Cards.

Exam Essentials

Understand Folder Options.   Understand the purpose and features of using folders and files. Properly configuring folders and folder access is one of the most important tasks that we do on a daily basis.

Understand NTFS and Share permissions.   Be able to configure security permissions and know the difference between NTFS and Share permissions.

Know how to use BitLocker Drive Encryption.   Understand the purpose and requirements of BitLocker Drive Encryption. Know which editions of Windows 10 (Enterprise, Education, and Professional) include BitLocker.

Know Microsoft BitLocker Administration and Monitoring (MBAM).   Understand the purpose and requirements of MBAM. MBAM allows an IT department to manage all of your BitLocker settings through the use of one application.

Understand smart cards.   You need to understand smart cards and two-factor authentication. The reason it is called two-factor authentication is because you need the smart cards and the pin number (two factors).

Video Resources

There are videos available for the following exercises:

3.1

You can access the videos at http://www.wiley.com/go/sybextestprep.

Review Questions

1. You are the IT manager for your company. You have been asked to give the Sales group the rights to read and change documents in the StormWind Documents folder. The following table shows the current permissions on the Stormwind Documents shared folder:

Group/User	NTFS	Shared
Sales	Read	Read
Marketing	Modify	Change

   What do you need to do to give the Sales group the rights to do their job? (Choose all that apply.)

   A.   Give Sales Change to shared permissions.

   B.   Give Sales Modify to NTFS security.

   C.   Give Marketing Change to shared permissions.

   D.   Give Sales Full Control to NTFS security.

2. You are the network administrator for a large organization. You have a Windows 10 machine that needs to prevent data from being accessed if the hard drive is stolen. How do you accomplish this task?

   A.   Within the System icon in Control Panel, set the BitLocker Drive Encryption.

   B.   Within the Hardware icon in Control Panel, set the BitLocker Drive Encryption.

   C.   Within the Device Manager icon in Control Panel, set the BitLocker Drive Encryption.

   D.   Within a Local Group Policy, set the BitLocker Drive Encryption.

3. In which editions of Windows 10 can you enable BitLocker? (Choose all that apply).

   A.   Windows 10 Education Edition

   B.   Windows 10 Basic Edition

   C.   Windows 10 Professional Edition

   D.   Windows 10 Enterprise Edition

4. You have a network folder that resides on an NTFS partition on a Windows 10 computer. NTFS permissions and share permissions have been applied. Which of the following statements best describes how share permissions and NTFS permissions work together if they have been applied to the same folder?

   A.   The NTFS permissions will always take precedence.

   B.   The share permissions will always take precedence.

   C.   The system will look at the cumulative share permissions and the cumulative NTFS permissions. Whichever set is less restrictive will be applied.

   D.   The system will look at the cumulative share permissions and the cumulative NTFS permissions. Whichever set is more restrictive will be applied.

5. You are the network administrator for a medium-sized company. Rick was the head of HR and recently resigned. John has been hired to replace Rick and has been given Rick's laptop. You want John to have access to all of the resources to which Rick had access. What is the easiest way to manage the transition?

A. Rename Rick's account to John.

B. Copy Rick's account and call the copied account John.

C. Go into the Registry and do a search and replace to replace all of Rick's entries with John's name.

D. Take ownership of all of Rick's resources and assign John Full Control to the resources.

6. Jeff, the IT manager for Stormwind, has been asked to give Tom the rights to read and change documents in the Stormwind Documents folder. The following table shows the current permissions on the shared folder:

Group/User	NTFS	Shared
Sales	Read	Change
Marketing	Modify	Change
R&D	Deny	Full Control
Finance	Read	Read
Tom	Read	Change

Tom is a member of the Sales and Finance groups. When Tom accesses the Stormwind Documents folder, he can read all the files, but the system won't let him change or delete files. What do you need to do to give Tom the minimum amount of rights to do his job?

A. Give Sales Full Control to shared permissions.

B. Give Tom Full Control to NTFS security.

C. Give Finance Change to shared permissions.

D. Give Finance Modify to NTFS security.

E. Give Tom Modify to NTFS security.

7. You are the IT manager for your company. You have been asked to give the Admin group the rights to read, change, and assign permissions to documents in the Stormwind Documents folder. The following table shows the current permissions on the Stormwind Documents shared folder:

Group/User	NTFS	Shared
Sales	Read	Change
Marketing	Modify	Change
R&D	Deny	Full Control
Finance	Read	Read
Admin	Change	Change

What do you need to do to give the Admin group the rights to do their job? (Choose all that apply.)

A. Give Sales Full Control to shared permissions.

B. Give Full Control to NTFS security.

C. Give Admin Full Control to shared permissions.

D. Give Finance Modify to NTFS security.

E. Give Admin Full Control to NTFS security.

8. Vincent is an instructor for Stormwind and he is talking to Paige, the company IT Manager. Vince asks Paige to implement some type of two-factor authentication. What can Paige install to complete this request?

A. Passwords and Usernames

B. Retina Scanners

C. Fingerprint scanners

D. Smartcards

9. You are using Windows 10 and you have created a file called "my text," and it was created in Notepad and has a `.txt` extension type. You need to change the extension type from `.txt` to `.vbx`. What setting do you need to change on the folder so that you can see the extension types?

A. Uncheck Hide Extensions For Known File Types.

B. Check Unhide Extensions For Files.

C. Check Show Extensions For Files.

D. Uncheck Hide All File Types.

10. The owner of your company has come to you and stated that they want all of the hardware on all systems to use BitLocker and BitLocker To Go. What utility should you install to help manage and maintain BitLocker and BitLocker To Go?

A. MAAM

B. MBAM

C. MNBM

D. MABM

Chapter

4

Managing the Windows 10 Environment

MICROSOFT EXAM OBJECTIVES COVERED IN THIS CHAPTER:

✓ **Perform post-installation configuration**

  ▪ Configure Edge and Internet Explorer; configure mobility settings; configure sign-in options; customize the Windows desktop.

Now that Windows 10 is installed, it's time to start setting up some of the configuration options that we have. In this chapter, we will look at performing post-installation tasks like setting up and configuring the Start Menu, Device Manager, and Cortana.

Another tool that we use in IT to configure the Windows 10 operating systems is Control Panel. Control Panel is one of the most important configuration tools for Windows 10. It includes many icons that can help you optimize, maintain, and personalize the operating system. One of the most important icons in Control Panel is the System icon. The System icon not only has operating-system information, but it also allows you to configure devices, remote settings, and system protection.

All of the same configuration settings that you can set in Control Panel can also be set in the Settings section of Windows 10. Microsoft has been slowly moving away from Control Panel and more to using the Setting section of Windows 10. You can still use Control Panel in Windows 10 while also getting used to the newer Setting section.

Next, we will talk about laptop users. If you use Windows 10 on a laptop computer, it is important to properly configure your power and mobility options. Configuring these options on a laptop will allow you to get the most out of your laptop and Windows 10. There are many different mobility options that you can choose from to help customize the laptop to each individual user.

We will also examine how services operate and how to configure your services to start manually or automatically. We will examine how to configure services in the event of a service error.

Managing Windows

Once the operating system is installed, the next thing we need to do in IT is manage the operating system. If Windows 10 is not properly configured, it may cause your IT department issues for a long time.

When you are the IT administrator for a company, you need to make sure that the Windows client systems are configured properly and, in most cases, the same.

There are many ways to do this, from individually configuring the Windows 10 systems to using Group Policy Objects (GPOs). Most companies are going to set Windows 10 configurations through the use of Windows Server and GPOs, but you still need to understand each component and what it does so you can configure the proper settings.

The following sections describe many of the configuration options for customizing Windows 10 for each user's needs. We will start with configuring the Windows 10 Desktop environment.

Manipulating the Desktop Environment

The Windows 10 Desktop is the interface that appears when a user logs into the operating system. The Desktop includes the wallpaper, Start Menu, tiles, and icons (see Figure 4.1).

FIGURE 4.1   The default Windows 10 Desktop

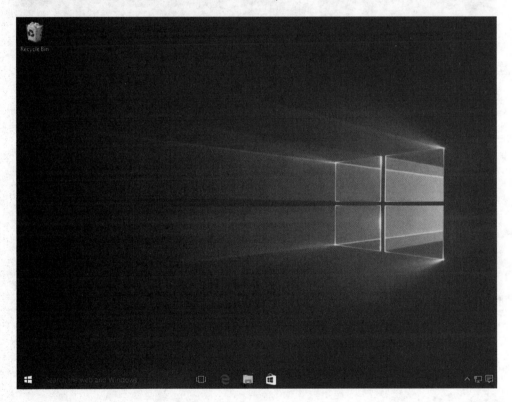

The Windows 10 Start Menu, located at the bottom left of the Desktop by default, includes the default All Apps section shown in Figure 4.2.

FIGURE 4.2 The All Apps section

The Windows 10 default Desktop appears after a user has logged onto a Windows 10 computer for the first time. When you install a new instance of Windows 10, you will notice that the Desktop is clean except for the Recycle Bin. You may also have a message on the Desktop that states that the Windows 10 system has not been activated (as shown in Figure 4.3).

FIGURE 4.3   The desktop with activation notice

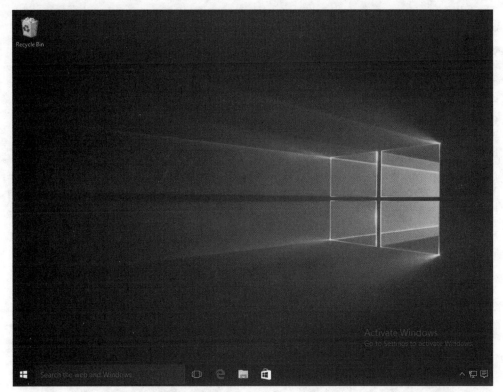

Users can then configure their Desktop to suit their personal preferences and to work more efficiently. The following list describes some of the common default options that appear on the Start Menu, in the Most Used section, Control Panel, and All Apps section. This list includes some of the more commonly used applications and shortcuts; it's not a complete list of every application available to you.

 Depending on which version of Windows 10 you are using, these options may vary a bit. Also, many options are unavailable for configuration until you activate Windows 10.

Windows 10 Applications

The following are some of the applications for Windows 10. These are not all of the applications installed by default on Windows 10 but just a few to get you started.

Calculator   This shortcut starts the Calculator program. The Calculator works like any other store-bought calculator, and it can even be changed from a Standard calculator to a Scientific, Programmer, Converter, Volume, Length, Weight & Mass, or Temperature calculator.

Cortana   With this application, you can speak or type into the Windows 10 system and your personal assistant, Cortana, will try to find answers to any queries that you may have.

Maps   This app allows you to see the current location and area of the Windows 10 system. You can use Maps to search for locations and services (food, gas, directions, etc.), as shown in Figure 4.4.

FIGURE 4.4   Maps

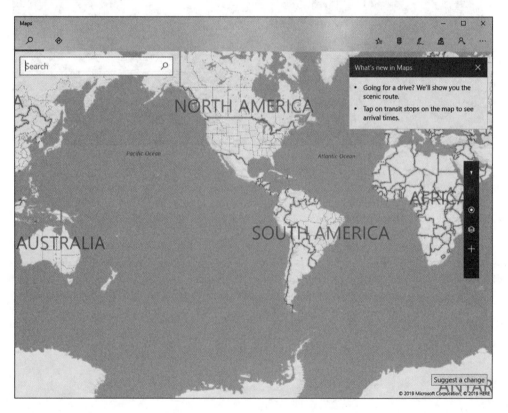

Microsoft Edge   This shortcut starts the built-in web browser. When used with an Internet connection, Microsoft Edge provides an interface for accessing the Internet or a local intranet.

OneDrive   This application allows you to connect with the Microsoft OneDrive cloud-based utility. You can use this application to share documents between the Windows 10 system and the OneDrive cloud-based subscription.

People   This application allows you to look up and work with your contacts. It enables you to use social media to connect to people and contacts.

Tips   The Tips app (see Figure 4.5) in Windows 10 allows a user to see Windows 10 tips and tricks that help any user get the most out of Windows 10. Every tip has a button in it that allows you to try the tip out with a single click.

FIGURE 4.5   Tips

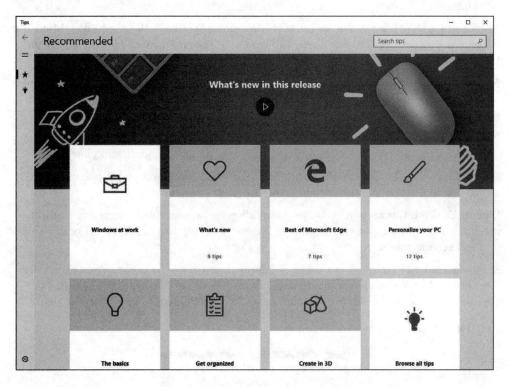

Windows Update   This shortcut allows you to receive updates and security patches for the Windows 10 operating system. You can receive updates from either Microsoft's web server or a Windows Server Update Services (WSUS) machine.

XPS Viewer   This application allows you to view Microsoft XML Paper Specification (.xps) files. The XPS viewer also allows you to print these files. Depending on your version release, the XPS viewer may be installed by default. New versions of Windows 10 have stopped installing the XPS viewer by default and you may need to install it manually if you need the application. If you need to install the application, you can do so by opening Settings ➢ Apps ➢ Apps & Features ➢ Manage Optional Features ➢ Add A Feature ➢ XPS Viewer.

Windows 10 Accessories

Windows Accessories are some basic tools that are included with Windows 10 to help you do tasks from surfing the Net to playing DVDs.

Internet Explorer   This shortcut starts the built-in web browser. When used with an Internet connection, Internet Explorer provides an interface for accessing the Internet or a local intranet.

Microsoft Edge   There is another Internet browser on Windows 10 called Edge. Microsoft Edge gives you new ways to find pages and read and write on the web plus get help from Cortana when you need it.

Microsoft Store   This application allows you to download and purchase applications from the Microsoft Store. The Microsoft Store has thousands of business and personal applications that you can use on Windows 10.

Notepad   This application allows you to create text files. This is a great way to store notes on the Windows 10 system without using a full word processing application like Word.

Paint   This shortcut starts the Paint program. The Paint program is an application that allows you to change or manipulate graphics files.

Remote Desktop Connection   This program allows a user to connect remotely to another machine. To connect to another computer, Remote Desktop Connection must be enabled on the receiving computer.

Snipping Tool   This tool allows a user to capture an item on the Desktop (see Figure 4.6). The user clicks the Snipping Tool and drags the cursor around an area that will then be captured. The captured area can then be drawn on, highlighted, or saved as a file.

FIGURE 4.6   Snipping Tool

Sticky Notes   This application places a sticky note on the Desktop, as shown in Figure 4.7. You can then type a message or reminder into the sticky note. It will remain on the Desktop until you delete it.

FIGURE 4.7 Sticky Notes application

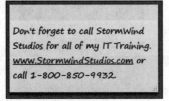

Don't forget to call StormWind Studios for all of my IT Training. www.StormWindStudios.com or call 1-800-850-9932.

Settings This application opens the Settings window. Inside the Settings window, you can configure options in the following areas: System, Devices, Network & Internet, Personalization, Accounts, Time & Language, Ease Of Access, Privacy, and Update & Security (see Figure 4.8).

FIGURE 4.8 Settings window

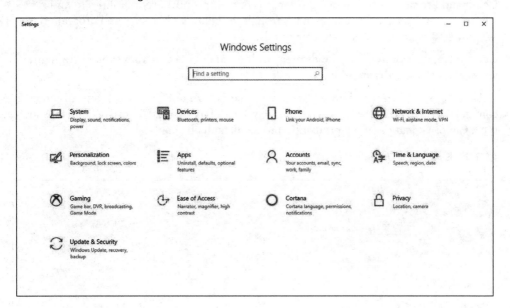

Windows Fax And Scan This application allows you to create and manage scans and faxes. Windows Fax And Scan allows users to send or receive faxes from their workstation.

Windows Media Player With this application, you can play all your media files, including videos, music, pictures, and recorded TV.

Windows Ease Of Access Tools

These tools are installed on a Windows 10 system to help individuals who have difficulty seeing the screen. The Ease Of Access tools can be accessed via Start ➤ All Apps ➤ Ease Of Access and include a magnifier, narrator, onscreen keyboard, and Windows Speech Recognition, as shown in Figure 4.9.

FIGURE 4.9 Ease Of Access tools

Windows System Utilities

These utilities are the ones that help most IT administrators manage and control Windows systems. These are the tools that help us start, manage, and control the Windows 10 systems and applications.

Command Prompt The command prompt is one of the most useful utilities to an IT administrator. You can run commands through the command prompt and program the Windows 10 system using system commands.

Control Panel Control Panel holds many utilities and tools that allow you to configure your computer. It is discussed in greater detail later in this chapter.

Default Apps When you choose Default Apps (as shown in Figure 4.10), four different configuration items can be accessed: Choose your Default Apps, Choose default apps by file type, Choose default apps by protocols, and Set defaults by app.

FIGURE 4.10 Default Apps

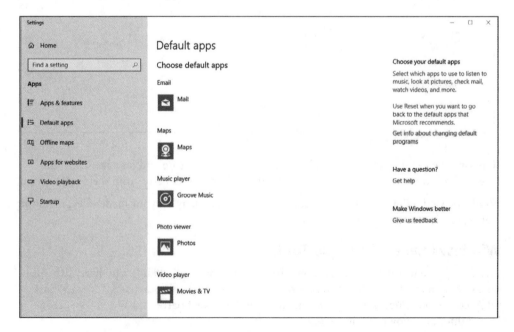

Devices   This shortcut opens the Devices section, where you can add or configure any of your hardware devices.

File Explorer   By default, this application shows all of the folders and files that are on the Windows 10 system. You can use this application to look at all of the files located on the Windows 10 system.

Run   You can either put in commands or run applications from the Run dialog box.

Task Manager   This is one of the few applications that I used as an IT director on a daily basis. The Task Manager allows you to see what applications are running on the Windows systems (including servers). The Task Manager also allows you to stop applications from running on a system. This utility will be explained in greater detail throughout this book.

This PC   This shortcut allows you to centrally manage your computer's files, hard drives, and devices with removable storage. It also allows you to manage system tasks and to view details about your computer.

Windows User's Tools

The Windows User's tools are the utilities we use to store and access user's data and documents. These are the applications and folders that we use to keep user data.

Desktop   This folder shows all of the applications that are located on the desktop.

Documents   By default, this folder stores the documents that are created. Each user has a unique Documents folder, so even if a computer is shared, each user will have his or her own personal folder.

Downloads   This folder allows you to store all of the applications and files that you download. By storing downloaded applications and files in this folder, you can always use these files to reinstall applications or files when needed. In many instances, when you download files from the Internet, they are placed into this folder by default. Some downloads allow you to choose a file location, but many downloads are placed in the Downloads folder automatically.

Pictures   This application shows any pictures that are in the user's Pictures folder.

Music   This shortcut will show any music that is in the Music folder.

Videos   This shortcut shows you all of the videos that are stored on this Windows 10 system.

Shut Down Or Restart   This button is used to shut down or restart the computer. There is an arrow next to the button that you can use to restart the machine or shut down the system.

The Desktop also includes the Recycle Bin. The Recycle Bin is a special folder that holds the files and folders that have been deleted, assuming that your hard drive has enough free space to hold the deleted files. You can restore or permanently delete a file from the Recycle Bin by opening the Recycle Bin and right-clicking that file.

When configuring the Desktop, you have the ability to decide between configuring a background of your choice as your Desktop backdrop or you can choose one of the built-in

Desktop themes. Desktop themes are a preset package containing graphical appearance details used to customize the look and feel of an operating system.

Backgrounds are just the graphics that you decide to set as your wallpaper. To switch between different themes, right-click an area of open space on the Desktop and select Personalize. In the Theme Settings dialog box, you can select the theme you want to use. You can additionally configure the Desktop by customizing the Taskbar and Start Menu, adding shortcuts, and setting display properties.

Configuring Personalization

To configure the Windows Desktop and how it looks, right-click the Desktop and select Personalize. When you choose to personalize the Desktop, you have five different settings that you can configure (as shown in Figure 4.11).

FIGURE 4.11   Personalization screen

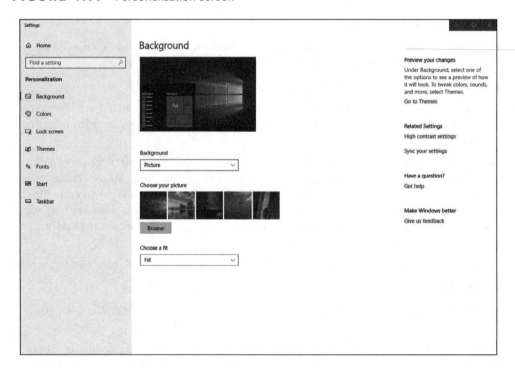

Background

This lets you pick your Desktop background, which uses a picture or an HTML document as wallpaper. Setting up a desktop background can be as easy as picking a solid color and placing a picture of your favorite sports team or pet on top of it.

Windows 10 comes with some pictures already in the system, but you can basically turn any picture into your background Desktop picture. As you can see in Figure 4.11, you can click the Browse button and choose the pictures that you want in your background.

Colors

This allows you to fine-tune the color and style of your windows background and accent. Windows 10 gives you the ability to automatically pick an accent color for your background, as shown in Figure 4.12.

FIGURE 4.12   Colors screen

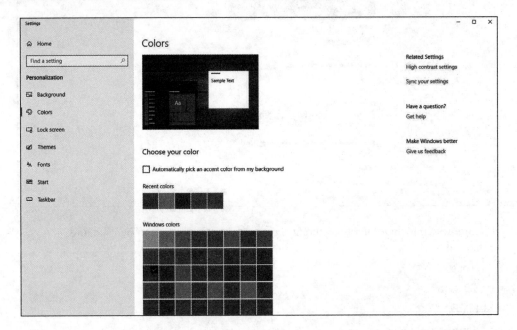

Windows 10 users also have the ability to automatically choose their own background colors. You can show colors on the Start screen, Taskbar, and Action Center. You can also make the Start screen, Taskbar, and Action Center transparent.

Lock Screen

This lets you select a screensaver that will start after the system has been idle for a specified amount of time. You can also specify a password that must be used to access the system after it has been idle. When the idle time has been reached and the screensaver is activated, the computer can also be set so that the Windows 10 system is locked (shown in Figure 4.13) and the password (or other authentication method) of the user who is currently logged on must be entered to unlock the computer again.

FIGURE 4.13 Lock screen options

Windows 10 includes many different screensaver options that can be used and configured:

- None
- 3D Text
- Blank
- Bubbles
- Mystify
- Photos
- Ribbons

Personalization Themes

This screen allows you to set the different themes that you can have for your Desktop. Themes allow you to change the color pattern for the Desktop and all applications in one setting. The Themes screen (shown in Figure 4.14) also allows you to change the advanced sound settings, Desktop icon settings, and mouse pointer settings.

FIGURE 4.14   Themes screen

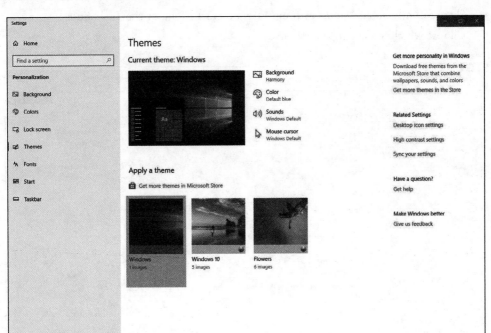

Advanced Sound Settings   This lets you choose the sounds that will be played based on the action taken. Each action can have its own sound. The Sound options also allow you to set up the external or internal speakers and microphones that you want to use. You can also calibrate different pieces of hardware.

Desktop Icon Settings   This allows you to customize the Desktop icons. You also have the ability to change shortcut icons. Some of the icons that you can add to the Desktop are the Computer icon, User's Files icon, Network icon, Recycle Bin icon, and Control Panel icon. You also have the ability to change icons at the screen.

Mouse Cursor Settings   This allows you to customize the appearance of the mouse pointers. It allows you to go from the traditional pointer to a Help Select, Busy, and Precision Select, to just name a few. You can also change the Button options, Pointer options, Wheel options, and Hardware options.

Personalization Start Screen

The Start section allows you to configure what you are going to see on your Start Menu and which folders appear on the Start Menu. As you can see in Figure 4.15, you have the ability to set the following settings;

- Show most used apps.
- Show recently added apps.

- Use Start full screen.
- Show recently opened items in Jump Lists on Start Menu or the Taskbar.
- Choose which folders appear on Start.

FIGURE 4.15   Start options

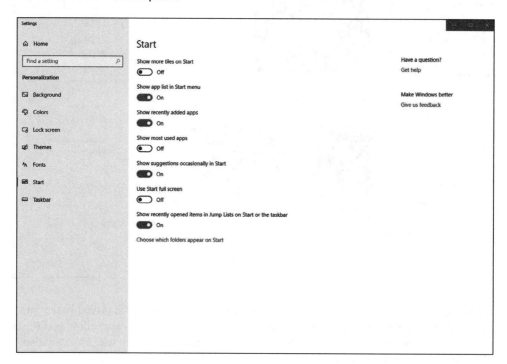

Now that we have looked at how to configure the Windows 10 Desktop, let's go ahead and practice doing just that. Exercise 4.1 will walk you through the process of configuring your theme and choosing additional options.

EXERCISE 4.1

Configuring Windows 10 Desktop Options

1. Right-click an open area of the Desktop and choose Personalize.

2. On the Background screen, either choose a new picture or use the pull-down under Background and choose Solid Color or Slideshow.

3. After you have set your new Desktop, go to the Lock Screen page.

4. Scroll down and choose the link Screen Saver Settings.

5. Under the Screen Saver pull-down, choose 3D Text.

6. Click the Settings button. Make sure the radio button is set for Custom Text and put in the text you would like to see. Go ahead and change the font or size or rotation speed. Once that's completed, click the OK button. At the Screen Saver Settings screen, change the Wait Time value to 15 minutes and then click the OK button.

7. Click the Themes screen. Click the Theme Settings link and choose a new theme that you like. You can also keep the current theme if you like that one. Hit the upper-right X to close the window once you're finished.

8. Click the Start screen. Make any changes that you want for your Start Menu. Once you are finished, close the Personalization window.

 Real World Scenario

Configuring Personal Preferences

One thing that I noticed as an IT manager is that the most common configuration change made by users is to configure their Desktop. This lets them use the computer more efficiently and often makes them more comfortable with the computer.

To help users work more efficiently with their computers, it's good to determine which applications or files are frequently and commonly used and verify that shortcuts or Start Menu items are added for those elements. You can also remove shortcuts or Start Menu items for elements that are seldom used or not used at all, helping to make the work area less cluttered and confusing.

Less-experienced users will feel more comfortable with their computer if they have a Desktop that has been personalized to their preferences. This might include their choice of a Desktop theme and screensaver.

Windows 10 includes several utilities for managing various aspects of the operating system configuration. In the following sections, you will learn how to configure your operating system using Control Panel and the Registry Editor.

We will start with Control Panel and the different utilities included within it.

Using Control Panel

Control Panel is a set of GUI utilities that allow you to configure Registry settings without the need to use a Registry Editor. The Registry is a database used by the operating system to store configuration information.

You can configure the system by using the Registry Editor REGEDIT or REGEDT32. Windows 10 actually only uses the REGEDIT command. If you type REGEDT32, it just opens the REGEDIT command utility.

If you don't want to open the Registry directly but you still want to do some Registry changes, you can just use Control Panel. So let's take a closer look at the utilities that are available through Control Panel. I have set Control Panel to Large Icons view, but you can set it to Small Icons view if you prefer (see Figure 4.16).

FIGURE 4.16   Control Panel

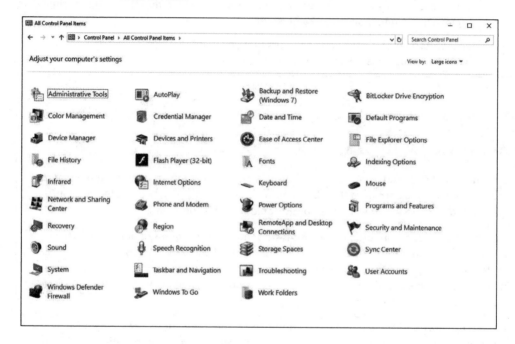

 If you keep the Control Panel view set to Category, you will not be able to follow along and see all the different items I am going to cover. The Category view has all of these settings, but they are in different sections. I feel it's easier to understand each item using the Large Icons view.

Administrative Tools   This icon has multiple administrative tools that can help you configure and monitor the Windows 10 operating system. The following tools are included:

- Component Services
- Computer Management
- Defragment and Optimize Drives
- Disk Cleanup
- Event Viewer
- iSCSI Initiator
- Local Security Policy
- ODBC Data Sources (32-bit)
- ODBC Data Sources (64-bit)
- Performance Monitor
- Print Management
- Recovery Drive
- Resource Monitor
- Services
- System Configuration
- System Information
- Task Scheduler
- Windows Firewall with Advanced Security
- Windows Memory Diagnostics

AutoPlay This icon lets you configure media disks and will autoplay when inserted into the media player (see Figure 4.17). Each media type has different configuration settings, but the basic choices are as follows:

- Use AutoPlay for All Media And Devices
- Removable Drive
- Camera Storage
- DVDs
- Blue-Ray Discs
- CDs
- Software
- Devices

FIGURE 4.17 AutoPlay options

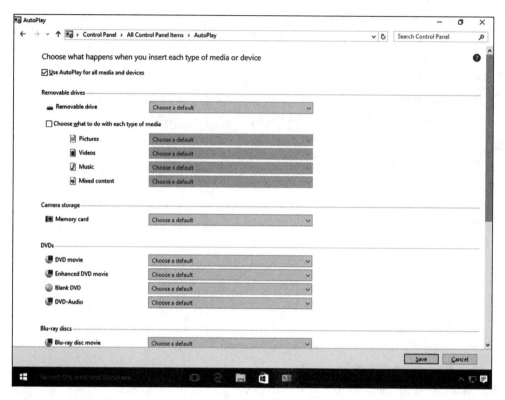

Backup And Restore (Windows 7) The Backup And Restore icon allows you to configure your backup media. Users can make copies of all important data on their machine to avoid losing it in the event of a hardware failure or disaster. Backups will be discussed in greater detail in Chapter 7, "Configuring Recovery."

BitLocker Drive Encryption BitLocker Drive Encryption helps prevent unauthorized users from accessing files stored on hard drives by encrypting the drive in its entirety. The user is able to use the computer as they normally would, but unauthorized users cannot read or use any of their files if the hard drive is stolen from the original machine.

Color Management The Color Management icon allows you to configure some of the video adapter's settings. You can configure the Windows color system defaults, the ICC Rendering Intent to WCS Gamut Mapping settings, and the display calibration. You can also change the system defaults to indicate how these items should be handled.

Credential Manager Users can use the Credential Manager to store credentials such as usernames and passwords. These usernames and passwords get stored in vaults so that you can easily log onto computers or websites.

There are two sections in the Credential Manager: Web Credentials and Windows Credentials. You can add credentials by clicking the link next to each of the two credential sections.

Date And Time   The Date And Time icon allows you to configure your local date and time for the Windows 10 machine. You also have the ability to synchronize your clock with the Internet, as shown in Figure 4.18. Be aware that if your computer is a member of a domain, you will not see this screen and will not be able to synchronize your time with an Internet time server.

FIGURE 4.18   Time synchronization

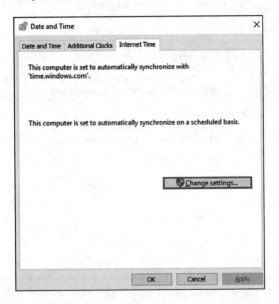

Default Programs   The Default Programs icon allows you to choose the programs that Windows will use by default. For example, you can set Internet Explorer to be the default web browser.

Device Manager   The Device Manager icon allows you to configure the different devices on your Windows 10 machine. You can configure such devices as disk drives, display adapters, DVD/CD-ROM drives, monitors, and network adapters.

Devices And Printers   The Devices And Printers icon lets you add or configure the devices on your machine and your printers. This is where you add the printers that you have on your network.

Ease Of Access Center   The Ease Of Access Center icon allows you to set up your accessibility options. These are settings that you can set for people with vision issues. The Ease of Access center allows you to configure voice narration (a computer voice tells you what you're mousing over) and an onscreen keyboard or start the magnifier (allows you to see everything magnified).

File Explorer Options   The Folder Options icon allows you to configure how you view folders on the Windows 10 machine by default. You have the ability to set up how you browse and navigate folders, which files and folders you can view (see Figure 4.19), and how folders are searched.

FIGURE 4.19 File Explorer Options window

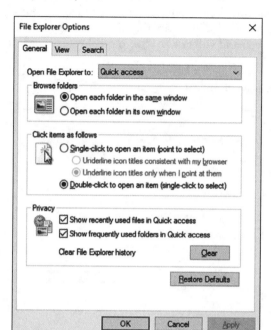

File History   File History allows users to save copies of their files so that you can get them back in the event of a file being lost or damaged. You have the ability to restore personal files, select drives, exclude folders, and even set advanced settings on the File History settings.

Flash Player (32-bit)   The Flash Player application allows you to set up how your Flash Player is going to operate and which applications the Flash Player will be associated with.

Fonts   This icon displays a screen where you can install, preview, delete, show, hide, and configure the fonts that the applications on your Windows 10 operating system can use. It enables you to get fonts online, adjust cleartext, find a character, and change font size.

Indexing Options   Windows uses indexing to perform very fast searches of common files on your computer. The Indexing Options feature gives you the ability to configure which files and applications get indexed.

Infrared   If a support device allows Infrared transfers, Infrared allows you to send and receive files and images to your Windows 10 computer. Many digital cameras today allow you to use Infrared to transfer images to your Windows 10 computer.

Internet Options   The Internet Options icon allows you to configure how the Internet will operate (see Figure 4.20). From this icon you can configure your home page, browsing history, tabs, security, privacy, content, connections, and programs.

FIGURE 4.20   Internet Properties dialog box

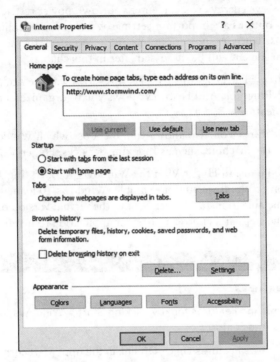

Keyboard   The Keyboard properties allow you to configure how the keyboard will react when used. You can set the character repeat speed (how fast the keyboard will repeat what you are typing) and the cursor speed. You can also use these properties to configure the keyboard drivers.

Mouse   Mouse properties give you the ability to configure how the mouse will operate. You can configure the buttons, click speed, ClickLock, pointer type, pointer options, center wheel, and hardware properties.

Mail   You may or may not have this Mail application in Control Panel. If you have a mail client, such as Outlook, then the Mail application icon will be in Control Panel. If you don't have a mail client, then this icon will be missing from Control Panel.

When you configure the Mail properties, you set up your client-side mail settings. In the Mail properties, you can set up different user profiles (mailboxes) and the local mail servers or Internet mail servers to which they connect.

Network And Sharing Center   The Network And Sharing Center properties configure your Windows 10 machine to connect to a local network or the Internet. You can configure TCP/IP, set up a new network, connect to a network, choose a homegroup, and configure the network adapter.

Phone And Modem   The Phone And Modem properties are used to set up local dialing properties and modem options. You can set up your dialing location, modem properties, and telephony providers.

Power Options   Power options allow a user to maximize their Windows 10 machine's performance and/or conserve energy. You can enter your own power restrictions to customize your machine. Power options are important settings when you are dealing with laptops. Since many laptops use batteries, power options allow you to get the most time from their batteries. Power management will be discussed later in this chapter.

Programs And Features   The Programs And Features icon was the Add/Remove Programs icon in Windows XP. Programs And Features allows you to organize, uninstall, change, or repair programs and features.

The Programs And Features icon also allows you to choose which Windows 10 features you want installed on the machine, such as Indexing Services, Hyper-V, and so on.

In Exercise 4.2, you'll install Hyper-V on the Windows 10 operating system. If you are using a virtual version of Windows 10 (for example, Windows 10 loaded onto a Hyper-V server), you will not be able to install Hyper-V onto the virtual version of Windows 10. But you can still follow the steps and choose a different application to install.

Installing New Features

1. Open the Programs And Features tool by clicking Start ➤ Windows System ➤ Control Panel ➤ Programs And Features.

2. Click the Turn Windows Features On Or Off link in the upper-left corner. Scroll down the features list and check the Hyper-V check box (shown in Figure 4.21).

FIGURE 4.21   Hyper-V check box

3. Click OK.

Recovery   The Recovery icon allows a user or administrator to recover the Windows 10 system to a previously captured restore point. System Restore is one of the first recovery options that should be considered when your Windows 10 system is experiencing problems.

Region   The Region tool allows you to configure your local regional settings as well as configure date and time formats.

RemoteApp And Desktop Connections   RemoteApp And Desktop Connections allows you to access programs and desktops on your network. To connect to these resources (remote applications and desktops), you must have the proper permission.

With RemoteApp And Desktop Connections, you can connect to either a remote computer or a virtual computer. To create a new connection, use the Set Up A New Connection Wizard included with the RemoteApp And Desktop Connections menu option.

Security And Maintenance   The Security And Maintenance utility has two configurable sections: Security and Maintenance. The Security section allows you to configure three different options:

- Spyware and unwanted software protection allows you to update Windows Defender.
- Virus protection allows you to install and configure virus protection.
- Windows Update allows you to update Windows 10.

The Maintenance section allows you to set up a Windows 10 Maintenance schedule.

Sound   The Sound icon allows you to configure your machine's audio. You can configure output (speakers and audio drivers) and your input devices (microphones).

Speech Recognition   The Speech Recognition icon allows you to configure your speech properties. Speech Recognition allows you to speak into the computer and have that speech be displayed on the system. Many programs, including Microsoft Office, can display the words onscreen as you speak them into the system. You can complete the following actions via the Speech Recognition icon:

- Start Speech Recognition.
- Set up a microphone.
- Take speech tutorials.
- Train your computer to better understand you.
- Open the Speech Reference Card, which allows you to view and print a list of common commands.

Storage Spaces   Storage Spaces in Windows 10 is another way to give your Windows 10 users data redundancy. Windows 10 administrators have the ability to group hard drives together into a storage pools. Windows 10 users can then use these storage pool capacities to turn the pools into individual Storage Spaces. You can configure your Storage Pools in this application.

Sync Center   The Sync Center allows you to configure synchronization between the Windows 10 machine and a network server. The Sync Center also allows you to see when synchronization occurred, if the synchronization was successful, and if there were any errors.

System   The System icon is one of the most important icons in Control Panel. The System icon allows you to view which operating system your machine is using, view installed system resources (processor, RAM), change the computer name/domain/workgroup, and activate Windows 10. From the System icon, you can also configure the following settings:

- Device Manager
- Remote Settings
- System Protection
- Advanced System Settings

Taskbar And Navigation   The Taskbar And Navigation icon allows you to configure how the Taskbar, Start Menu, and toolbars will operate.

Troubleshooting   The Troubleshooting icon in Control Panel allows you to troubleshoot common Windows 10 problems within the following categories:

- Programs
- Hardware And Sound
- Network And Internet
- System And Security

User Accounts   The User Accounts icon allows you to create and modify local user accounts. With the User Account icon, you can perform the following tasks:

- Change user passwords.
- Remove passwords.
- Change the account picture.
- Change the account name.
- Change the account type.
- Manage user accounts.
- Change user-account control settings.

Windows Defender Firewall   Windows Defender Firewall helps prevent unauthorized users or hackers from accessing your Windows 10 machine from the Internet or the local network.

Windows To Go   Windows To Go gives an administrator or user the ability to provision Windows 10 onto an external USB drive. You can then use the USB drive (known as a Windows To Go workspace) to load a complete and managed Windows 10 system image into a managed or unmanaged Windows 10 host computer to boot and run the Windows 10 operating system.

Work Folders   Work Folders allows a user to make data files available on all of the devices that they use. You can access that data even when the devices are offline.

Using the Microsoft Management Console

One really cool advantage of using Windows is the ability to create your own windows. All of the command windows that we have talked about run through the Microsoft

Management Console (MMC). Knowing this, you can create your own MMC windows. So let's take a look at creating a window with Disk Administrator and Services in the same console window. To do this, you would just complete the following steps:

1. Type **MMC** in Cortana and hit Enter.
2. Click Yes at the UAC dialog box.
3. In the MMC console, click File and then Add/Remove Snap-in.
4. Click Disk Management and click the Add button. Make sure This Computer is chosen and click Finish.
5. Scroll down and choose Services and click the Add button. Choose Local Computer and click Finished.
6. Click the OK button.
7. Click File Save As and choose Desktop in the left pane. Name your console "Test" and click Save.
8. The new console should be on your Desktop. Now when you want to open either the Disk Administrator or Services console, just open Test. Close the MMC.

Using the System Icon

The System icon (shown in Figure 4.22) in Control Panel is the gateway to a very useful set of utilities and tasks that can enable you to specify remote settings, device settings, system protection, and the computer name, among other things.

FIGURE 4.22   The System page

Let's look at the different utilities and tasks that can be configured in the System page:

Windows Edition   The Windows Edition section shows you which edition of Windows the machine currently has installed. The Windows Edition section also shows whether service packs are installed.

System   The System section shows the following information about the system hardware:

- Processor
- Installed memory (RAM)
- System type
- Pen and touch-screen availability

Computer Name, Domain, And Workgroup Settings   In the Computer Name, Domain, And Workgroup Settings section, you can change the name of the computer system and also change the workgroup or domain. Windows 10 works well with Windows Server domains and Azure AD domains.

Windows Activation   The Windows Activation section allows you to activate your Windows 10 operating system and change your product key before activating.

If you look to the left side of the System windows, you will see that there are four additional links: Device Manager, Remote Settings, System Protection, and Advanced System Settings. Let's take a look at some of these settings.

Device Manager   The Device Manager icon allows you to configure the different devices on your Windows 10 machine. You can configure such devices as disk drives, display adapters, DVD/CD-ROM drives, monitors, and network adapters.

Remote Settings   In the Remote section, you can set the Remote Assistance and Remote Desktop settings for the Windows 10 system. Windows Remote Assistance allows an administrator to connect to a machine and control the mouse and keyboard while the user is logged on with the administrator. This option can be enabled or disabled.

System Protection   The System Protection section is for configuring restore points and recoverability for the Windows 10 operating system. You can also manage disk space and all of your restore points from the System Protection section.

Advanced System Settings   The Advanced System Settings section allows you to set up such items as visual effects, processor scheduling, memory usage, virtual memory, desktop settings, system startup, and recoverability.

There are three main sections within the Advanced System Settings section:

Performance   The Performance section allows you to configure the visual effects, the virtual memory, processor scheduling, and Data Execution Prevention for the Windows 10 operating system.

The virtual memory is a section of the hard drive that is used by the system and RAM. Think of RAM as a pitcher of water. As the water fills up the pitcher, the pitcher becomes full. Once it's full, more water would cause it to overflow. The virtual memory is the overflow for RAM. When RAM fills up, the oldest data in RAM gets put into the virtual memory. This way, the system does not need to look at an entire hard drive for that data. It finds it in the virtual memory.

The Data Execution Prevention section (found under the Settings button) helps protect against damage from viruses and other security threats.

User Profiles   The User Profiles section allows you to copy, delete, or move a user's Desktop profile to another location or user account.

Startup And Recovery   The Startup And Recovery section allows you to configure which operating system will be booted by default (important for dual-booting machines) and what should happen when the system gets a startup error.

Let's now look at how to configure some of the options using the System icon. Complete Exercise 4.3 to change the computer name.

EXERCISE 4.3

Changing the Computer Name

1. Open the System tool by Clicking Start ➤ Windows System ➤ Control Panel ➤ System.

2. Under the Computer Name, Domain, And Workgroup Settings section, click the Change Settings link.

3. Click the Change button in the To Rename This Computer section.

4. In the Computer Name field, rename your computer. Click OK.

5. A dialog box asking you to reboot the machine will appear. Click the OK button.

6. Click the Close button, and then click the Restart Now button.

Now that you have renamed the computer, let's look at how to configure performance options. Complete Exercise 4.4 to manipulate your system's virtual memory.

EXERCISE 4.4

Changing the System's Virtual Memory

1. Open the System tool by clicking Start ➤ Windows System ➤ Control Panel ➤ System.

2. In the left side, click the Advanced System Settings link.

3. Under the Performance section, click the Settings button.

4. When the Performance option screen appears, click the Advanced tab.

5. In the Virtual Memory section, click the Change button.

EXERCISE 4.4 *(continued)*

6. Uncheck the Automatically Manage Paging File Size For All Drives check box.

7. Click the Custom Size radio button.

8. Set the Minimum and Maximum settings to two times the size of your RAM. For example, if your RAM is 4,096 MB, set it to 8,192 MB.

9. Click the Set button.

10. Click OK. Then click OK again at the Performance Options screen.

11. Close the System Properties screen.

Microsoft Windows 10 handles the virtual memory requirements by default, but I recommend increasing the virtual memory on your machine if hard drive space is available. I use the rule of thumb of one and a half to two times the size of RAM.

We have now talked about the Control Panel and the System icon, but we have not yet talked about the new Windows 10 Settings shortcut app. So in the next section, we are going to look at the Settings window.

Understanding the Settings Window

As stated earlier in the book, Microsoft took the best of both Windows 7 and Windows 8 and created Windows 10. When you click the Start Menu, you will see an option called Settings (see Figure 4.23).

FIGURE 4.23 The Settings option

The Settings screen is a new way to configure different parts of the Windows 10 system. When you click the Settings option from the Start Menu, you will see the Settings screen appear, as shown in Figure 4.24.

FIGURE 4.24   The Settings screen

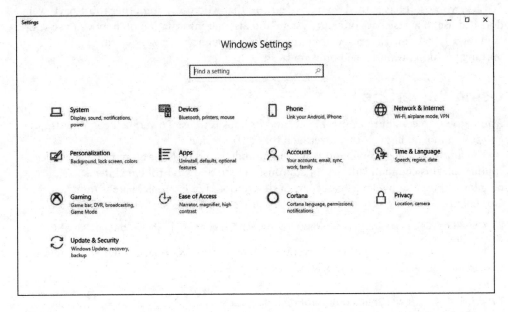

As you can see from Figure 4.24, the Settings window has multiple sections of Windows 10 that you can configure. The following areas are settings that can be configured using the Settings screen:

- System
- Devices
- Phone
- Network & Internet
- Personalization
- Apps
- Accounts
- Time & Language
- Gaming
- Ease Of Access
- Cortana
- Privacy
- Updates & Security

Most of these sections have already been covered previously in this chapter, and many of the other sections (such as Accounts) will be covered in other chapters of the book. I just wanted to make sure you understand that it's another way to configure many of the same options that we have already looked at.

The one area that I would recommend that you look at right away is the choice for Privacy. Microsoft has turned on many features that Microsoft and other third-party vendors can use to access data on your system and also get information on how you use your Windows 10 system. Take a few minutes to look through the Privacy section and make sure nothing you don't want turned on is on by default.

Using PowerShell

Another way to configure Control Panel and its apps is to use PowerShell commands. So let's take a look at how to use PowerShell for configuration.

The first PowerShell command you need to understand is the `Get-ControlPanelItem` command. This command allows an administrator to find Control Panel items on a local computer by name, category, or description. For example, here is the `Get-ControlPanelItem` command you would use to configure the Windows Firewall:

```
PS C:\> Get-ControlPanelItem –Name "Windows Firewall" | Show-ControlPanelItem
```

Table 4.1 includes some of the PowerShell configuration commands that you would use to help manage and configure the Windows 10 system.

TABLE 4.1 PowerShell configuration commands

Command	Description
Clear-EventLog	Allows an administrator to delete all entries from the event logs on a local or remote computer
Debug-Process	Debugs processes running on a local computer
Get-ComputerInfo	Returns the computer's system information
Get-EventLog	Finds an event in a specific event log
Get-Service	Finds a service on a Windows 10 system
Get-TimeZone	Gets the systems time zone
New-EventLog	Creates a new event log
New-Service	Allows an administrator to create a new service
Remove-EventLog	Deletes an event log
Rename-Computer	Allows an administrator to rename a computer
Restart-Computer	Reboots your system

Command	Description
Restart-Service	Restarts a service
Resume-Service	Resumes a service
Set-TimeZone	Sets the system's time zone
Start-Process	Starts a process
Start-Service	Starts a service
Stop-Computer	Shuts down a system
Stop-Service	Stops a service
Test-Connection	Sends a ping to test NIC adapter settings
Write-EventLog	Writes an event to an event log

Now that we have looked at how to do configurations for Windows 10, let's go ahead and take a look at how Windows 10 mobility works.

Configuring Mobility Options

So far in this chapter, you have learned about all of the different icons in Control Panel. Now we need to dive into a few of them in greater detail. The ones that we are going to discuss all have to deal with Windows 10 mobility.

Windows 10 is designed to be mobile and it has many features that revolve around that. The mobility issues that are covered in the following sections are how to configure offline file policies and sync options using the Sync Center, power policies, and Windows to Go.

Configuring Offline Files and Synchronization

One of the advantages of Windows 10 is how the operating system works and synchronizes with other systems and data.

The term *synchronization* could mean different things to different people. We could be talking about synchronization of offline files and data, or we can be talking about synchronization between two systems like a Windows 10 system and cloud-based Azure or OneNote.

In this section, we will talk about both. We will address synchronization between offline and online files, and we will discuss synchronization between Windows 10 and cloud-based services.

Offline Files allows network files to be available to clients even when a network connection to the server is unavailable or slow. When a user is accessing a server that is unavailable or when the network connection is slower than a configurable threshold, files are then retrieved from the Offline Files folders.

The Offline Files feature is enabled by default on the following client computer operating systems: Windows 10 Professional, Windows 10 Enterprise, and Windows Education. This feature is turned off by default on Windows Server operating systems.

Because in many organizations Windows 10 will be loaded onto a laptop computer, offline file access can be an important part of how Windows clients stay current even while off the network.

When you decide to turn synchronization on, Windows will automatically keep track of your synchronization choices for you on all of your Windows 10 devices (as long as you are logged on to all of the Windows devices using the same account or have set up synchronization with the other accounts and your Microsoft account).

Users have the ability to choose what items that they want to synchronize. For example, users can synchronize passwords, web browser settings, File Explorer settings, and even notifications.

To truly have synchronization work the way that Microsoft has intended, you need to link all of your devices together using your Microsoft account or have your other accounts linked to your Microsoft account. This includes having your school or work accounts all tied into one Microsoft account.

As an IT director for many years, I feel a bit uneasy about this idea. I truly believe that linking your personal accounts together to synchronize all of your personal data is a good way to go, but for obvious security reasons, I don't agree with corporate users linking into their personal accounts.

So how do we go about synchronizing everything in Windows 10 easily? The best method is to use the Sync Center in Control Panel (just click Start ➤ Windows System ➤ Control Panel ➤ Sync Center).

The Sync Center is built into Windows 10, and it's a one-stop shop for all of your synchronization needs, including working with offline files (see Figure 4.25).

FIGURE 4.25   The Sync Center

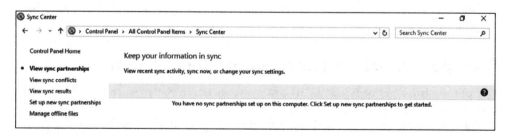

As you can see in Figure 4.25, you can set up synchronization between other devices and partnerships. The figure shows you can also manage offline files. To manage offline files, you have to enable that on the Windows 10 system (done through Sync Center) and then also configure offline folder access with the Windows servers that you have at your company.

When you click the Manage Offline Files link and enable offline folder access, you then have three tabs that can help you set up offline folder access properly:

Disk Usage   The Disk Usage tab will show you how much disk space is currently being reserved on the Windows 10 system for keeping offline files. You can change the amount of space that is set for the Windows 10 system by clicking the Change Limits button.

Encryption   To make sure the offline files are encrypted while on the system, click the Encryption button. The files will get encrypted based on your user's Security Identifier (SID) number. When you log into the Windows 10 account using the account with the matching SID number, the files will become automatically decrypted when they are opened. If someone with a different user ID (SID) number tries to access these files, they will be denied access.

Network   The Network tab allows you to set a time interval (such as 5 minutes), and when that interval is hit, the Windows 10 system will automatically check the network connection to make sure that the connection is not on a slow connection. For example, when you are at home and you don't have direct access to your network, the Windows system will automatically revert to using the offline files due to the connection being slow or not available.

Configuring Power Policies

Earlier in the chapter, we started talking about the Windows 10 Power options. Power options allow a user or administrator to maximize their Windows 10 machine's performance and/or conserve energy.

As an administrator or user, you have the ability to enter your own power restrictions to customize your machine. Power options are important settings when you are dealing with laptops. Since many laptops use batteries, power options allow you to get the most time from their batteries.

Now here is the kicker! Depending on what type of system you are on, you will see different power plan options. For example, Figure 4.26 shows the power plan options for a desktop system. You can tell that the only real options you have is what happens when you choose when to turn off the display or change your power consumption options.

FIGURE 4.26   Desktop power plan options

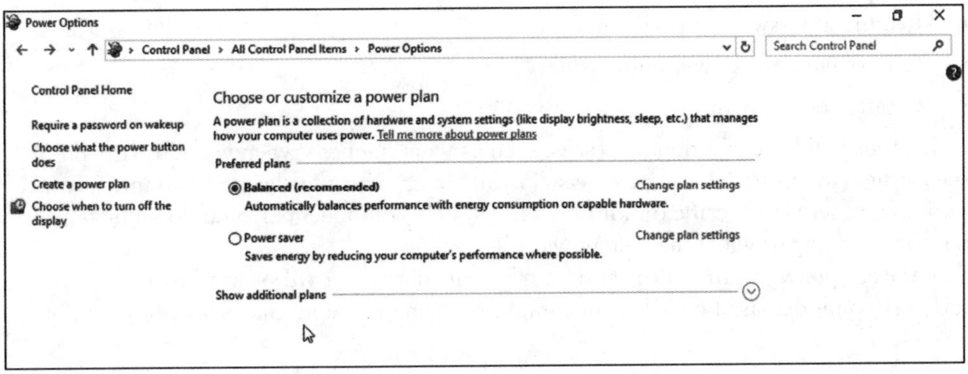

However, if you look at Figure 4.27, you can see that you have additional options based on whether your laptop or tablet is plugged in. You will not have those options on a desktop, because most desktops can't work when unplugged (unless you have a magical desktop).

FIGURE 4.27   Laptop power plan options

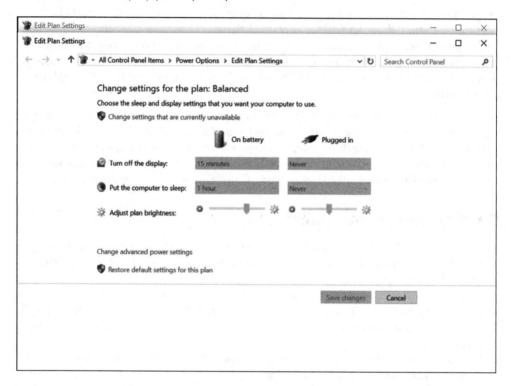

So setting up your power options really depends on what type of machine or tablet you're using. But some of the settings are the same no matter which one you use. The following are just some of the options that are the same no matter what type of Windows 10 system you're on:

- Require a password on wakeup.
- Choose what the power button does.
- Create a power plan.

Laptops will have additional choices, such as what happens when you close the lid of the laptop. No matter what type of system you are on, you can choose to go into advanced options and set very specific options on what system components would do while the system was running or while the system was idle.

For example, you can tell the system when the network card or hard drive can go into a sleep mode based on idle time (amount of time while no one is working on the system). So if you want to configure each individual component and how it should work while active or idle, you can go into the advanced options and configure each component separately.

Managing Power States

In Windows 10, the Advanced Configuration Power Interface (ACPI) specifies different levels of power states:

- Fully active PC
- Sleep
- Hibernation
- Complete shutdown of PC

The Sleep power option allows your computer to use very little power (while you're away from the computer) but it also allows your computer to start up faster and you will be instantly back to the spot where you left off. Users won't have to be concerned that they will lose their work because of their battery draining while they are away from the computer. Sleep allows Windows to automatically save all of your work and turn off the computer if the battery gets too low. Using the sleep option is good for when you're going to be away from your computer for just a short amount of time.

Hibernation mode falls short of a complete shutdown of the computer and it may not be available on all Windows 10 computers (depending on if you are working on a laptop or desktop). With hibernation, the computer saves your desktop state as well as any open files to the hard drive. To use the computer again, you need to press the power button. The computer should start more quickly than from a complete shutdown because it does not have to go through the complete startup process. You will have to again log onto the computer. Similar to when the computer is put into sleep mode, all the documents that were open when the computer went into hibernation are still available. With hibernation, you can easily resume work where you left off. You can configure your computer to hibernate through Power Options or by choosing Start and then clicking the arrow and selecting Hibernate from the drop-down menu. This option will appear only if hibernation has been enabled through Power Options.

As stated earlier, the hibernation mode may not be available on your Windows 10 laptop machine by default. You must make sure your firmware can support hibernation before attempting to enable it. Now let's take a look at the different types of power options that you can configure.

Managing Power Options

You configure power options through the Power Options Properties dialog box. To access this dialog box, click Start ➤ Windows System ➤ Control Panel ➤ Power Options. The Power Options dialog box provides the ability to manage power plans and to control power options, such as when the display is turned off, when the computer sleeps, and what the power button does.

Configuring Power Plans

Windows 10 includes three configurable power plans: Balanced, Power Saver, and High Performance. Power plans control the trade-off between quick access to an existing computer session and energy savings. In Windows 10, each power plan contains default options that can be customized to meet the needs of various scenarios.

The Balanced power plan, as its name suggests, provides a balance between power savings and performance. By default, this plan is configured to turn off the display after 20 minutes and to put the computer to sleep after 1 hour of idle time. You can modify these times as needed. Other power options that you can modify include Wireless Adapter settings and Multimedia settings. Wireless adapters can be configured for maximum power savings or maximum performance. By default, the Balanced power plan configures wireless adapters for maximum performance. Additionally, you can configure the Multimedia settings so that the computer will not be put into sleep mode when sharing media. For example, if the computer is acting as a Media Center device, then you can configure the computer to remain on by setting the Prevent Idling To Sleep option so that other computers can connect to it and stream media from it even when the computer is not being used for other purposes.

The Power Saver power plan is optimized for power savings. By default, the display is configured to be turned off after 20 minutes of inactivity, and the computer will be put into sleep mode after 1 hour of inactivity. Additionally, this power plan configures hard disks to be turned off after 20 minutes of inactivity.

The High Performance power plan is configured to provide the maximum performance for portable computers. By default, the computer will never enter sleep mode, but the display will be turned off after 20 minutes. When this setting is configured, by default the Multimedia settings are configured with the new Allow The Computer To Enter Away Mode option. Away mode configures the computer to look like it's off to users but remain accessible for media sharing. For example, the computer can record television shows when in Away mode. You can modify the existing power plans to suit your needs by clicking Change Plan Settings, or you can use the preconfigured power plans listed in Table 4.2.

TABLE 4.2   Windows 10 power plans

Power Plan	Turn Off Display	Put Computer to Sleep	Turn Hard Disks Off
Balanced	After 20 minutes	1 hour	
Power Saver	After 20 minutes	1 hour	After 20 minutes
High Performance	After 20 minutes	Never	

In Exercise 4.5, I will show you how to configure a power plan for your computer.

EXERCISE 4.5

Configuring a Power Plan

1. Click Start ➤ Windows System ➤ Control Panel ➤ Power Options.

2. Select a power plan to modify from the Preferred Plans list, and click Change Plan Settings.

3. Configure the power-plan options for your computer based on your personal preferences. Click Change Advanced Power Settings to modify the advanced power settings. When all changes have been made, click Save Changes.

4. Close Control Panel.

Other desktop options you can use are the power button and switching users. Let's take a look at these features.

Configuring the Power Button

Unless you decide to run your computer 24 hours a day, you will eventually want to shut it down. By default, the Start Menu has a power button. When you click this button, your machine will power off. But the power button does not have to be set to the Shut Down option. You can configure this button to Switch User, Logoff, Lock, Restart, or Shut Down.

You may have a machine that is shared by multiple users, and it may be better for you to have the Switch User button instead of the Shut Down button on the Start menu. Configuring the Switch User option would make it easier on your users.

In Exercise 4.6, you will configure the power button to use the Hibernate mode.

EXERCISE 4.6

Configuring the Power Button for Hibernate Mode

1. Click Start ➤ Windows System ➤ Control Panel ➤ Power Options.

2. On the left side, click Choose What The Power Button Does.

3. From the Power Button Settings drop-down menu, choose Hibernate.

4. Click OK.

5. Click the power button and see if the system goes into the Hibernate mode. Once the system is brought out of the Hibernate mode, redo this exercise and choose Shut Down in step 3 to return the system to normal (if it was set to turn off).

After you decide how the power button is going to be used, you may want to configure some of the advanced power options. In the next section, we will look at the different power options.

Configuring Advanced Power Settings

Each power plan contains advanced settings that can be configured, such as when the hard disks will be turned off and whether a password is required on wakeup. To configure these advanced settings, Click Start ➤ Windows System ➤ Control Panel ➤ Power Options and select the power plan to use. Then click Change Advanced Power Settings to open the Advanced Settings tab of the Power Options dialog box and modify the settings as desired (or restore the plan defaults).

For example, one option that you might want to change if you are using a mobile computer is the Power Buttons And Lid option, which configures what happens when you press the power button or close the lid of the mobile computer. When either of these actions occurs, the computer can be configured to do nothing, shut down, go into sleep mode, or go into hibernation mode.

Configuring Hibernation

Although sleep is the preferred power-saving mode in Windows 10, hibernation is still available for use. Hibernation for a computer means that anything stored in memory is written to your hard disk. This ensures that when your computer is shut down, you do not lose any of the information that is stored in memory. When you take your computer out of hibernation, it returns to its previous state by loading the hibernation reserved area of hard disk back into memory. To configure your computer to hibernate, complete the same steps as you did previously in Exercise 4.6.

Command-Line Configuration

Microsoft gives you the ability to configure and manage your power settings through the use of the command line. The Powercfg.exe tool allows you to control power settings and configure computers to default to hibernate or standby mode. The Powercfg.exe tool is installed with Windows 10 by default. Powercfg.exe has a few switches that provide you with better functionality. Table 4.3 describes some of these switches.

TABLE 4.3   Powercfg.exe switches

Switch	Description
-change	Changes a setting in the current power scheme.
-changename	Changes the name of a power scheme. Also gives you the ability to change the description.
-delete	Deletes the power scheme of the GUID specified.
-deletesetting	Deletes a power setting.

Switch	Description
-energy	Looks for common energy-efficiency and battery-life issues and displays these issues in an HTML format. This switch is used to identify problems with the power scheme.
-list	Shows all the power schemes in the current user's environment.
-query	Shows the content of a power scheme.
-qh	Displays the content (including hidden content) of the power scheme.
-waketimers	Enumerates the wake timers. If this is enabled, when the wake timer expires, the system will wake from hibernation or sleep state.

For a complete list of `Powercfg.exe` switches, visit the Microsoft website here:

https://docs.microsoft.com/en-us/windows-hardware/design/device-experiences/powercfg-command-line-options

There is a useful tool when you're using a laptop on battery power that allows you to see how much time you have left until the battery dies. Let's take a look at the battery meter.

Managing Power Consumption Using the Battery Meter

Windows 10 includes a battery meter that you can use to monitor the battery-power consumption on your mobile computer (laptop or tablet). The battery meter also provides notification as to what power plan is being used.

The battery meter appears in the notification area of the Windows Taskbar and indicates the status of the battery, including the percentage of battery charge. As the battery charge gets lower, the battery meter provides a visual indication of the amount of charge left. For example, when the battery charge reaches the low-battery level, a red circle with a white *X* is displayed.

The battery meter also provides a quick method for changing the power plan in use on the computer. By clicking the battery-meter icon, you can select among the preferred power plans available with Windows 10.

Configuring Windows To Go

As stated earlier, Windows To Go gives an administrator or user the ability to provision Windows 10 onto an external USB drive. You can then use the USB drive (known as a Windows To Go workspace) to load a complete and managed Windows 10 system image into a managed or unmanaged Windows 10 host computer to boot and run the Windows 10 operating system.

Many of us carry a USB drive with us or maybe even on your key ring. Well, think about having a copy of Windows 10 with you wherever and whenever you want to use it. So what are the requirements to set up a Windows To Go drive? Well, you need a USB drive certified for Windows To Go use and an image of Windows 10 Enterprise. If you try to load a USB that isn't certified, you will receive the error, as shown in Figure 4.28.

FIGURE 4.28   USB non-compatible error

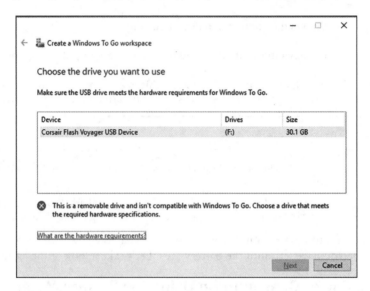

At the time that this book was written, the following list of USB drives are certified for Windows To Go:

- IronKey Workspace W700
- IronKey Workspace W500
- IronKey Workspace W300
- Kingston DataTraveler Workspace for Windows To Go
- Spyrus Portable Workplace
- Spyrus Secure Portable Workplace
- Spyrus Worksafe
- Super Talent Express RC4 for Windows To Go
- Super Talent Express RC8 for Windows To Go
- Western Digital My Passport Enterprise

To stay current with all of the available USB drives compatible with Windows 10 Windows To Go, please visit Microsoft's website at:

https://docs.microsoft.com/en-us/windows/deployment/planning/windows-to-go-overview

The information in Table 4.4 was taken directly from the Microsoft website regarding what is needed on the host's computer to be able to accept Windows To Go.

TABLE 4.4   Windows To Go Host requirements

Item	Requirement
Boot Process	Capable of USB boot
Firmware	USB boot enabled (PCs certified for use with Windows 7 or later can be configured to boot directly from USB; check with the hardware manufacturer if you are unsure of the ability of your PC to boot from USB.)
Processor architecture	Must support the image on the Windows To Go drive
External USB Hubs	Not supported; connect the Windows To Go drive directly to the host machine.
Processor	1 GHz or faster
RAM	2 GB or greater
Graphics	DirectX 9 graphics device with WDDM 1.2 or greater driver
USB port	USB 2.0 port or greater

To configure a Windows To Go USB drive, you need to complete the following steps:

1. Place a copy of a Windows 10 Enterprise image (.iso file) on the host computer you will use for image storage.

2. Open your Downloads folder on the host computer where you placed the .iso image, right-click the Windows image .iso file, and select Mount. The .iso file will then appear as a disk drive on the host computer.

3. Click Start ➤ Windows System ➤ Control Panel.

4. In Control Panel, select Windows To Go.

5. Insert a compatible USB drive into a USB port on the host computer.

6. On the Choose The Drive You Want To Use page, all attached USB drives appear. Choose the compatible USB drive you want to use, and then click Next.

7. The mounted .iso file should now appear on the Choose A Windows 10 Image page. If for some reason you don't see the .iso file, select Add Search Location to choose the mounted .iso file. Select the file, and then click Next.

8. On the Set A BitLocker Password (Optional) page, select the Use BitLocker With My Windows To Go Workspace check box to protect the drive with BitLocker Drive Encryption.

9. Enter a BitLocker password, confirm it, and then click Next.

10. On the Ready To Create Your Windows To Go Workspace page, select Create to create the Windows To Go workspace.

11. Choose a boot (startup) option, and then select Yes to modify the Windows Boot Manager configuration to boot automatically from your Windows To Go workspace when the drive is connected to this host computer.

12. When provisioning is complete, select Save And Restart to restart the host computer.

Managing Windows 10 Services

A *service* is a program, routine, or process that performs a specific function within the Windows 10 operating system. You can manage services through the Services window, which can be accessed in a variety of ways. If you go through the Computer Management utility, you can just click Start ➤ Windows System ➤ Computer Management ➤ Services And Applications. You can also go through Administrative Tools in Control Panel.

The Services window lists the name of each service, a short description, the status, the startup type, and the logon account that is used to start it. To configure the properties of a service, double-click it to open its Properties dialog box, shown in Figure 4.29. This dialog box contains four tabs of options for services: General, Log On, Recovery, and Dependencies.

FIGURE 4.29   The Properties dialog box for a service

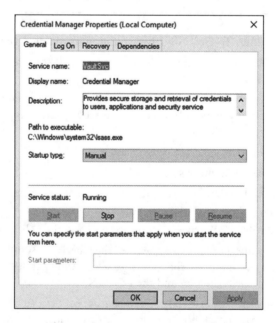

General   This tab allows you to view and configure the following options:

- The service display name
- The display name
- A description of the service
- The path to the service executable
- The startup type, which can be automatic, manual, or disabled
- The current service status
- Start parameters that can be applied when the service is started

In addition, the buttons across the lower part of the dialog box allow you to change the service state to start, stop, and pause, and if paused, you can also resume the service.

Log On   The Log On tab allows you to configure the logon account that will be used to start the service. Choose the local system account or specify another logon account.

Recovery   The Recovery tab allows you to designate what action will be taken if the service fails to load. For the first, second, and subsequent failures, you can select a discrete action from the following list:

- Take No Action
- Restart The Service
- Run A Program
- Restart The Computer

If you choose Run A Program, specify it along with any command-line parameters. If you choose Restart The Computer, you can configure a message that will be sent to users who are connected to the computer before it is restarted. You can also specify how long until a machine is restarted if an error occurs.

Dependencies   The Dependencies tab lists any services that must be running in order for the specified service to start. If a service fails to start, you can use this information to examine the dependencies and then make sure each one is running. In the bottom panel, you can verify whether any other services depend on this service before you decide to stop it.

In Exercise 4.7, you will complete the steps needed to configure services in the Windows 10 operating system.

EXERCISE 4.7

Configuring Services

1. Start Computer Management by Clicking Start ➤ Windows System ➤ Computer Management ➤ Services And Applications.

2. Click the Services link.

3. Scroll down the list and double-click Remote Desktop Configuration.

4. Under Startup Type, choose Automatic.

5. Under the Logon tab, click the This Account radio button.

6. Click the Browse button and choose the local administrator account. Click OK.

7. In the Password boxes, type and verify the administrator password.

8. In the Recovery tab, make sure the following settings are configured:

> Action: Response
>
> First Failure: Restart The Service
>
> Second Failure: Restart The Service
>
> Subsequent Failures: Take No Action
>
> Reset Fail Count After: 1 Day
>
> Restart Service After: 10 Minutes

9. Click the OK button.

10. Close the Computer Management MMC.

Using services is just another troubleshooting and configuring tool that is part of your arsenal of troubleshooting techniques. Just remember that when your services are working properly, your Windows 10 operating system will be working properly.

Configuring Internet Browsers

Windows 10 comes with two ways to browse the Internet; Edge and IE11. Windows Internet Explorer 11, or IE11, is the latest web browser developed and released by Microsoft Corporation in the popular Internet Explorer series. IE11 is available for Windows 10 and Windows Server 2012 R2 versions and above.

With the explosion of Internet use—even for the inexperienced end user browsing the Internet for personal reasons as well as for those who use it for work-related tasks—enhancing the user interface (UI) while providing better levels of security (which include privacy) has been the focus in the development of both Edge and IE11.

Both browsers are loaded with user features to provide end users with a better and simpler way to get the information they desire from their browsing experience.

The features added to Edge and IE11 are designed to give end users an easy way to browse the Internet for the information they're looking for while providing a secure environment for networks by recognizing potentially bad sites (those attempting to sneak viruses or Trojan horses into the network), phishing sites (those that attempt to steal private information about the user), or invasive sites that users may go to either on purpose or inadvertently.

When comparing the two browsers, Edge and IE11, Edge has taken browsing a step further with the implementation of Cortana. Cortana can assist you while working with Edge.

Cortana

One of the configuration options that I see asked about on the Internet all the time is how to turn off Cortana. Before we turn it off, though, let's talk about what Cortana can do for you.

Cortana is a powerful search and help utility. If you system has a microphone, you can ask Cortana questions and Cortana will help find an answer. If you don't have a microphone, you can type in your questions and Cortana will try to help find an answer.

To configure Cortana, click you mouse in the Cortana box. This will open Cortana. Once Cortana is open, click on the little settings wheel to configure Cortana (see Figure 4.30).

FIGURE 4.30   Cortana Settings

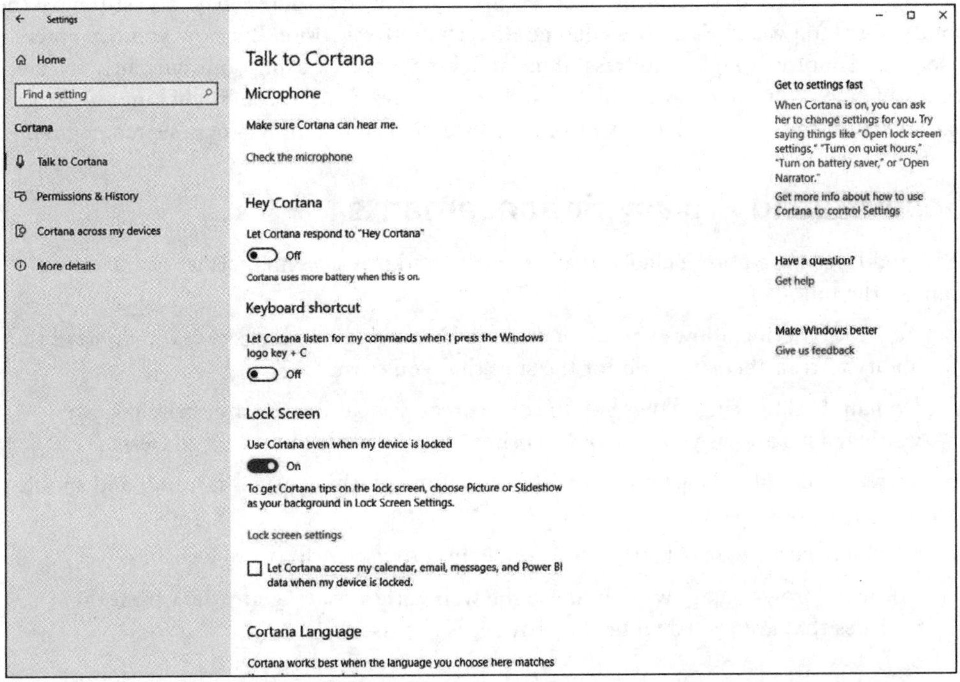

These settings allow you to configure Cortana or even turn off Cortana. If you decide to leave Cortana active, you can clear your search history from the Cortana settings and you can also have Cortana search the local system for an answer or search the web. After you set the configuration options that you want, close the Cortana settings box.

Browser Controls

When you open either Edge or IE11, one of the first things that will catch your attention is the simplified design. The most common controls, like tools and favorite buttons, are just a click away. You also have the ability to customize how the browser will look and which tools that you can use with the browser.

Pinning Sites to the Taskbar

Pinning sites to your Taskbar allows you to access websites by clicking the pinned site at the bottom of the Taskbar. Pinning a site is a very easy process. Just drag the tab of the website to the Taskbar. An icon for the website will stay pinned until you remove it. When you click the pinned icon, the website will open within the Internet browser.

Searchable Address Bar

You have the ability to search the Internet directly from the Address bar. You still have the ability to enter a website's address and go directly to the website. But now you can enter a search term or incomplete address, thus launching a search using your currently selected search engine. You can choose which search engine you want to use by clicking the Address bar and choosing the search engine from the listed icons or adding a new search engine.

Security and Privacy Enhancements

IE11 and Edge have both included many security and privacy enhancements, including some of the following:

- ActiveX Filtering allows you to block ActiveX controls for any sites. You do have the ability to turn them back on for the sites that you trust.

- Domain highlighting allows you to see the real web address of a website you are visiting. This allows you to avoid websites that use misleading web addresses.

- SmartScreen Filter helps protect you from online phishing attacks, fraud, and spoofed or malicious websites.

- 128-bit Secure Sockets Layer (SSL) connection to use with secure websites.

- InPrivate Browsing allows you to use the web without saving any data from the websites that are visited while the browser is in this mode.

Using the Browser's Compatibility View

Windows Internet Explorer 11 and Edge are the new releases of Microsoft's web browsers, and some websites may not be updated to use the new features or display their content correctly. Problems may exist displaying misaligned images or text. When you use

Compatibility View, the browsers will display a web page the way it would have been displayed in previous versions, which should correct any display issues. To display a page in Compatibility View, click the Compatibility View option in the tools (shown in Figure 4.31).

FIGURE 4.31 Compatibility View Settings

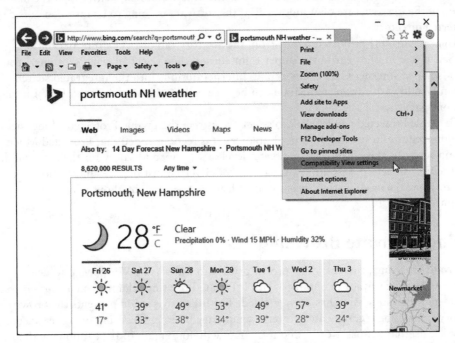

Once you have chosen Compatibility View for a website, you will not need to make the choice again. The browsers will display the site in Compatibility View the next time you browse to it. If the website gets updated in the future or you decide you would prefer to see it in the native standard mode, you can simply click the Compatibility View button again to return to the standard view. The Compatibility View option can also be selected from the Tools menu's Compatibility View menu option.

There is also a Compatibility View Settings option you can use to manage the sites currently set to be viewed in Compatibility View mode by adding or deleting sites by name. Many companies have extensive websites, and it may take time to update them to features. The Compatibility View Settings page has the default setting for all intranet sites to be displayed in Compatibility View. You also have to the choice to display all websites in Compatibility View.

Using Protected Mode for IE11

Protected Mode is a feature of Windows 10 for Windows Internet Explorer 11 that forces IE to run in a protected, isolated memory space, preventing malicious code from directly writing data outside the `Temporary Internet Files` folder unless the program trying to write the information is specifically granted access by the user. Protected Mode is enabled by default and displayed in the lower-right section of Windows Internet Explorer 11.

You can install software through IE11, but you will need to explicitly allow the modification of the file structure of Windows 10 if the software is going to be installed outside the protected directory.

You can turn off Protected Mode from the Security tab of IE11's Internet options (via the Settings icon, the gear in the upper right corner, then select Internet Options). You can also open Internet Options by typing **Internet options** into the integrated search box in Windows 10. Protected Mode can be accessed on the Security tab of the Internet Options page.

To toggle Protected Mode, click to select or deselect the Enable Protected Mode check box (this requires restarting Internet Explorer). It is recommended that Protected Mode remain active because it provides a greater level of security and safety for the user and does not prohibit an action (installing a program from IE11); it just requires interaction from the user to allow the modification, prompting at least a little thought about what's happening within Windows 10.

Using InPrivate Browsing

InPrivate Browsing provides some level of privacy to users using Windows Internet Explorer 11. The privacy maintained with InPrivate Browsing relates to a current browser where an InPrivate session has been enabled. The InPrivate session prevents the browsing history from being recorded and prevents temporary Internet files from being retained. Cookies, usernames, passwords, and form data will not remain in IE11 following the closing of the InPrivate session, nor will there be any footprints or data pertaining to the InPrivate Browsing session.

InPrivate Browsing keeps information from being saved to the local machine while the session is active, but don't get lulled into a false sense of security; malware, phishing, and other methods that send data out of the local machine are still valid and can provide personal information to a cybercriminal. In addition, employees visiting forbidden sites from work, for instance, could still be detected via forensics.

InPrivate Browsing is a good method of protecting user data if you are not surfing from your own machine or are surfing from a public location (always a bad place to leave personal information). InPrivate Browsing can also be used if you don't want anyone to be able to see data from your Internet browsing session.

There are several ways to launch an IE11 InPrivate Browsing session. One way is to open a new tab and select the Open An InPrivate Browsing Window option from the Browse With InPrivate section. This will open a new tab, and the tab will be an InPrivate session. You can also choose to open Windows Internet Explorer 11 and start an InPrivate session directly by choosing the Safety menu and selecting the InPrivate Browsing menu choice. Alternatively, you can open a new IE11 browser and press Ctrl+Shift+P.

Configuring Windows Internet Explorer 11 Options

In addition to security and usability options that you can configure in IE11, you can configure other options for managing the browser. Many of the configurations we have discussed in this chapter (i.e., the Safety or Tools menu options) and have used to quickly change individual parameters are also available for modification within the Internet Options tabbed dialog box. The general parameters, security parameters, privacy configurations, content controls, connection settings, program options, and advanced settings available within Internet Options are discussed in the following sections.

General Parameters

You can open the Internet Properties tabbed dialog box by selecting the Tools menu and choosing the Internet Properties menu item or simply typing **Internet options** into the integrated search box of Windows 10. The General tab (Figure 4.32) allows you to change the default home page that appears when Windows Internet Explorer 11 is launched. An interesting feature here is that you can have more than one default home page. When you enter more than one page in the Home Page text box, each time IE11 is launched, all pages will open in their own tab.

FIGURE 4.32   General tab of IE11's Internet Properties

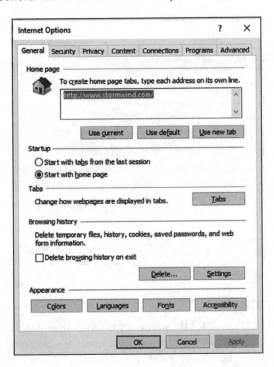

The General tab also allows you to control your Browsing History, Search, Tabs, and Appearance (including accessibility options) settings for the IE11 interface.

Security Parameters

The Security tab of IE11's (Figure 4.33) Internet Properties dialog box not only gives you access to control Protected Mode as discussed earlier in this section, it also gives you the ability to set security settings on the specific zones you may browse to as understood by Windows Internet Explorer 11. The zones are Internet, Local Intranet, Trusted Sites, and Restricted Sites. You can set the behavior of IE11 individually for each zone and even individual sites within each zone. For example, if you add a website to the Local Intranet settings, you will not be asked to authenticate your credentials when connecting to the website.

FIGURE 4.33   Security tab of IE11's Internet Properties

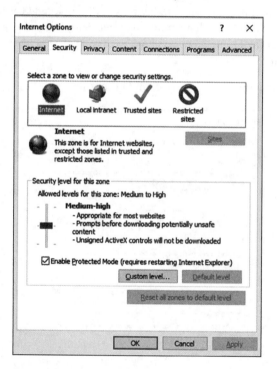

Privacy Configurations

The Privacy tab of IE11's (Figure 4.34) Internet Properties allows the management of privacy settings for the Internet zone; this is the cookie management for specific sites. You can also control the settings for the pop-up blocker and your InPrivate Filtering and InPrivate Browsing here.

FIGURE 4.34   Privacy tab of IE11's Internet Properties

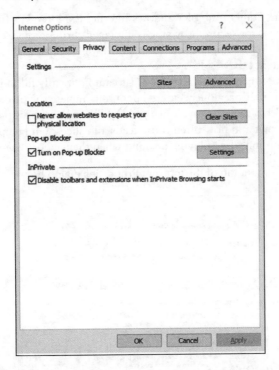

The pop-up blocker allows you to prevent unwanted Internet pop-ups from appearing while you are online. We have all been on websites where pop-up windows start appearing. With the IE11 pop-up blocker, you can prevent this from happening. To access the Pop-up Blocker settings, you will need to open Internet Explorer and choose Settings. In the Settings section, scroll down and choose View Advanced Settings. You will see an option to block pop-ups. Make sure that option is turned on. You can also configure pop-ups by using Control Panel and choosing Internet Options and then the Privacy tab.

To block cookies from any websites that do not have a compact privacy policy, you should set the privacy setting to High. The High setting prevents IE11 from saving cookies for websites that do not contain a compact privacy policy and cookies that have the potential of saving information that can be used to contact you without your explicit consent. Compact policies are used to indicate the privacy practices of a web service that uses cookies.

If you want to block any website from accessing cookies stored on the local computer, you should set the privacy setting to Block All Cookies. The Block All Cookies setting prevents cookies from being saved on the computer and prevents any existing cookies from being read by websites.

Content Control

Figure 4.35 shows the Content tab of Windows Internet Explorer 11's Internet Properties. Certificate management for secure browsing is managed through the Content tab. You have the ability to manage AutoComplete functionality as well as RSS feeds and Web Slice data from within the Content tab.

The AutoComplete functionality allows IE11 to automatically fill in fields as you complete forms in IE11. It uses previously entered data to complete the fields on the form.

The Feeds And Web Slices section allows you to fill in what subscription feeds you belong to on the Internet and how often those feeds and slices will be updated along with other configuration options (i.e., playing a sound when the feed or slice is updated).

FIGURE 4.35 Content tab of the Internet Properties dialog box

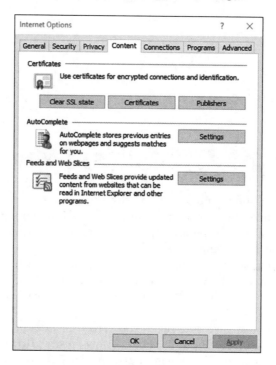

Connection Settings

The Connections tab of Windows Internet Explorer 11's Internet Properties dialog box allows you to manage the way IE11 gains access to the network. You can initiate the Connect to The Internet Wizard from this tab as well as set up a virtual private network (VPN). If you are using dial-up networking, this connection is also configured from the Connections tab. Local area network (LAN) general settings, which includes specifying a proxy server if you need to use one (this is typical across many corporate sites, to provide a better level of anonymity for Internet surfing), are configured here as well.

Program Options

The Programs tab of the IE11 Internet Properties dialog box allows you to establish a default web browser. You can manage add-ons specific to IE11 in the Programs tab as well. Additionally, you can set up an application to allow for HTML editing and set up default programs to be used for Internet services such as email.

Advanced Options

The Advanced tab allows you to configure accessibility settings, browsing settings, international browsing settings, encoding settings, multimedia parameters, printing parameters, and general security settings. You can control whether links are underlined, whether pictures should be displayed, which versions of the secure communication protocols or SSL are used, background colors, and many other parameters.

In addition to being able to change the advanced settings, you have the option to restore advanced settings to their original configurations or to even reset Internet Explorer settings, which resets all IE11 settings (not just the advanced settings) to the default configuration.

Summary

Besides actually installing Windows 10, configuring the operating system properly is one of the most important tasks that an IT team can perform.

Configuring the Desktop environment allows an administrator to configure an environment that is comfortable for the end user, which in turn makes the user more productive.

Understanding the Start Menu and Control Panel icons allows you to configure and operate the Windows 10 applications more efficiently. Knowing how to configure the System icon properly in Control Panel allows you to fine-tune the Windows 10 operating system and get the best performance possible out of it.

In addition to using Control Panel to configure the Windows 10 operating system, you can edit the Registry directly using the REGEDIT or REGEDT32 utility. In Windows 10, REGEDT32 just opens REGEDIT.

Another important consideration when configuring Windows 10 is how the operating system will function when installed on a laptop or tablet (Windows Mobility). By configuring the mobility options on a laptop, you can allow that laptop to connect to their data in multiple ways.

We also looked at services that run on Windows 10 and how to configure and troubleshoot them when they don't run properly.

Exam Essentials

Be able to configure Desktop settings.   Understand how to customize and configure the Windows 10 Desktop settings. This includes setting a Desktop and also setting up Desktop personalization. It is also important to know how to configure the Taskbar and Start Menu.

Be able to support mobile computers through power-management features.   Understand the new power features that are available in Windows 10 and be able to configure a laptop computer to use them.

Understand remote connections.   Know how to configure and connect to machines through remote connections. You can use Remote Assistance, Remote Desktop, and a VPN.

Know how to configure services.   Understand how to stop, start, monitor, pause, and configure services on the Windows 10 operating system. Know how to configure the different properties available through services.

Video Resources

There are videos available for the following exercises:

    4.1

    4.3

You can access the videos at http://www.wiley.com/go/sybextestprep.

Review Questions

1. You are the Network Administrator for StormWind Studios. You need to remove an old Registry key from a Windows 10 machine. Which of the following options could you use to remove the old Registry key?

   A. REGEDIT

   B. RGEDIT

   C. RGEDIT32

   D. REGEDITOR

2. You have a user, Rob, who uses a laptop computer running Windows 10. You have configured the laptop to enter sleep mode after 30 minutes of inactivity. What will occur when the computer enters sleep mode?

   A. The data will be saved to the hard disk, and the computer will shut down.

   B. The data will be erased from RAM, and the computer will shut down.

   C. The monitor will be turned off, but the hard disks will remain active.

   D. The data will be saved to memory, and the computer will be put into a power-saving state.

3. You want to speed up the resume time on your computer after it is put into hibernation mode. You have installed a hybrid hard disk drive into your Windows 10 computer. Which technology should you use to accomplish your goal?

   A. ReadyDrive

   B. ReadyBoost

   C. Superfetch

   D. SuperDrive

4. A new employee named Crystal has been supplied with a Windows 10 laptop computer. You have configured Crystal's computer with the Power Saver power plan, and you used the default options. Which of the following will occur after 20 minutes of inactivity on Crystal's computer?

   A. The display will be turned off, but the hard disk will remain active.

   B. The hard disk will be turned off, but the display will remain active.

   C. Both the hard disk and the display will be turned off.

   D. No components will be turned off.

5. You are the network administrator for a medium-size company. You support all user Desktop issues. Gary is using the default Windows 10 Desktop on his laptop computer. Gary wants to change his Desktop settings. Which of the following options should Gary use to configure the Desktop in Windows 10?

    A. Right-click an empty space on the Desktop and choose Personalize from the context menu.

    B. Select Control Panel ➢ System.

    C. Right-click My Computer and choose Manage from the context menu.

    D. Right-click My Computer and choose Properties from the context menu.

6. You work on the help desk for a large company. One of your users calls you and reports that they just accidentally deleted their `C:\Documents\Timesheet.xls` file. What is the easiest way to recover this file?

    A. In Folder Options, click the Show Deleted Files option.

    B. In Folder Options, click the Undo Deleted Files option.

    C. Click the Recycle Bin icon on the Desktop and restore the deleted file.

    D. Restore the file from your most recent tape backup.

7. You are the system administrator for your company. You are configuring the services on a Windows 10 computer. You want to ensure that if a service fails to load, it will attempt to restart. Which tab of the service's Properties dialog box should you use?

    A. General

    B. Log On

    C. Recovery

    D. Dependencies

8. The system administrator of your network wants to edit the Registry, including setting security on the Registry keys. What primary utilities that support full editing of the Windows 10 Registry should the system administrator use? (Choose all that apply.)

    A. REGEDIT

    B. REDIT

    C. REGEDT32

    D. REGEDITOR

9. Kayla is dissatisfied with the configuration of her keyboard and mouse. She wants to reset the keyboard speed and the mouse pointer rate. Which utility should she use to configure the keyboard and mouse properties?

    A. Control Panel

    B. Computer Management

    C. Microsoft Management Console

    D. Registry Editor

10. Denise is using a laptop computer that uses ACPI. She wants to see what percentage of the battery power is still available. She also wants to know if hibernation has been configured. Which of the following utilities should she use?

   A. Device Manager

   B. Computer Manager

   C. Battery meter

   D. MMC

Configuring Security and Devices

MICROSOFT EXAM OBJECTIVES COVERED IN THIS CHAPTER:

✓ **Manage Windows security**

- Configure user account control (UAC); configure Windows Defender Firewall; implement encryption.

When configuring Windows 10, we need to look at how the filesystems are configured and some of the security settings you can choose with your different options. Depending on how the filesystem is configured depends on how we can set up security for data and devices.

Then we need to take a look at how hardware is set up and configured. Getting hardware up and running in today's operating systems is not usually a problem. With Plug and Play technology, the initial installation and configuration will typically go smoothly. However, the software controlling the hardware (drivers) will usually need to be updated over time and may need to be rolled back in case of an issue in a new package.

There will also be times when the drivers need to be installed manually for legacy hardware. You may also need to verify the hardware configuration and make adjustments. The utility provided to perform these functions is Device Manager.

Device Manager displays all installed hardware. It also keeps information on storage, both removable and fixed, and communication devices like network interface cards and wireless and Bluetooth devices.

What you won't see for hardware in Device Manager are printers, unless of course they're USB. In that case, you will see the USB port and thus the printer will be identified, but you won't be able to configure the printer from Device Manager. You will use the Devices And Printers applet for configuring and troubleshooting printers in Control Panel or use Printers & Scanners in the Settings ➤ Devices section.

User Account Control

User Account Control (UAC) falls under the objective of Windows Security but UAC was covered in Chapter 2, "Configuring Users." Since UAC was covered in Chapter 2, it will not be covered in this chapter. It's listed in the exam objectives at the beginning of this chapter because it was the exam objective header.

Understanding Filesystems

A partition is a logical division of hard-drive space. Each partition you create under Windows 10 must have a filesystem associated with it. Partitions allow a single physical hard drive to be represented in the operating system as multiple drive letters and to be used as if there were multiple hard drives installed in the machine.

When selecting a filesystem, you can select FAT32 or NTFS. You typically select a filesystem based on the features you want to use and whether you will need to access the filesystem using other operating systems. If you have a FAT32 partition and want to update it to NTFS, you can use the Convert utility. The features of each filesystem and the procedure for converting filesystems are covered in the following sections.

Filesystem Selection

Your filesystem is used to track the storage of files on your hard drive in a way that is easily understood by end users while still allowing the operating system the ability to retrieve the files as requested. One of the fundamental choices associated with file management is the choice of your filesystem's configuration. It is recommended that you use the NTFS filesystem with Windows 10 because doing so will allow you to take advantage of features such as local security, file compression, and file encryption. You should choose the FAT32 filesystem only if you want to dual-boot your computer with a version of Windows that does not support NTFS because FAT32 is backward compatible with other operating systems.

Table 5.1 summarizes the capabilities of each filesystem, and they are described in more detail in the following sections. These volume size numbers were the values at the time this book was written. Make sure you continue to check with Microsoft to see if the volume sizes have increased since this book's publication.

TABLE 5.1   Filesystem capabilities

Feature	Fat32	NTFS
Supporting operating systems	All Windows operating systems above Windows 95	Windows NT, Windows 2000, Windows XP, Windows Server 2003, Windows Vista, Windows 7, Windows 8, Windows 10, Windows Server 2008/2008 R2, Windows Server 2012/2012 R2, and Windows Server 2016/2019
Long filename support	Yes	Yes
Efficient use of disk space	Yes	Yes
Compression support	No	Yes
Encryption support	No (Before Windows 10) Yes (if formatted using Windows 10)	Yes

TABLE 5.1   Filesystem capabilities *(continued)*

Feature	Fat32	NTFS
Support for local security	No	Yes
Support for network security	Yes	Yes
Maximum volume size	32 GB	16 TB with 4 KB clusters or 256 TB with 64 KB clusters

Windows 10 also supports Compact Disk Filesystem (CDFS). However, CDFS cannot be managed. It is used only to mount and read CDs. Let's start looking at the supported disk filesystems.

FAT32

FAT32 is an updated version of File Allocation Table (FAT). The FAT32 version was first shipped with Windows 95 OSR2 (Operating System Release 2) and can be used by every Windows operating system since.

One of the main advantages of FAT32 is its support for smaller cluster sizes, which results in more efficient space allocation than was possible with FAT16. Files stored on a FAT32 partition can use 20 to 30 percent less disk space than files stored on a FAT16 partition. FAT32 supports drive sizes from 512 MB up to 2 TB, although if you create and format a FAT32 partition through Windows 10, the FAT32 partition can only be up to 32 GB. Because of the smaller cluster sizes, FAT32 can also load programs up to 50 percent faster than FAT16 partitions can.

The main disadvantages of FAT32 compared to NTFS are that it does not provide as much support for larger hard drives and it does not provide very robust security options. It also doesn't offer native support for disk compression. Now that you understand FAT32, let's take a look at NTFS.

NTFS

NTFS, which was first used with the NT operating system, offers the highest level of service and features for Windows 10 computers. NTFS partitions can be up to 16 TB with 4 KB clusters or 256 TB with 64 KB clusters.

NTFS offers comprehensive folder-level and file-level security. This allows you to set an additional level of security for users who access the files and folders locally or through the network. For example, two users who share the same Windows 10 computer can be assigned different NTFS permissions so that one user has access to a folder but the other user is denied access to that folder. This is not possible on a FAT32 filesystem.

NTFS also offers disk-management features—such as compression and encryption capabilities—and data-recovery features. NTFS includes some of the following features:

1. When files are read or written to a disk, they can be automatically encrypted and decrypted.

2. Reparse points are used with mount points to redirect data as it is written or read from a folder to another volume or physical disk.

3. There is support for sparse files, which are used by programs that create large files but allocate disk space only as needed.

4. Remote storage allows you to extend your disk space by making removable media (for example, external tapes) more accessible.

5. It gives you the ability to resize volumes and partitions.

6. You use recovery logging on NTFS metadata, which is used for data recovery when a power failure or system problem occurs.

Now that you have seen the differences between FAT32 and NTFS, let's discuss how to convert a FAT32 drive to an NTFS drive.

Filesystem Conversion

In Windows 10, you can convert FAT32 partitions to NTFS. Filesystem conversion is the process of converting one filesystem to another without the loss of data. If you format a drive, as opposed to converting it, all the data on that drive will be lost.

To convert a partition, you use the Convert command-line utility. The syntax for the Convert command is as follows:

```
Convert [drive:]/fs:ntfs
```

For example, if you wanted to convert your D: drive to NTFS, you would type the following from a command prompt:

```
Convert D:/fs:ntfs
```

When the conversion process begins, it will attempt to lock the partition. If the partition cannot be locked—perhaps because it contains the Windows 10 operating system files or the system's page file—the conversion will not take place until the computer is restarted.

Using the Convert Command

You can use the /v switch with the Convert command. This switch specifies that you want to use verbose mode, and all messages will be displayed during the conversion process. You can also use the /NoSecurity switch, which specifies that all converted files and folders will have no security applied by default, so they can be accessed by anyone.

Configuring NTFS

As mentioned earlier, NTFS has many advantages over FAT32. The main advantages are NTFS Security, compression, encryption (EFS), and quotas. Let's take a look at some of these advantages in greater detail.

NTFS Security   One of the biggest advantages of NTFS is security. NTFS Security is one of the most important aspects of an IT administrator's job. An advantage of NTFS Security is that the security can be placed on individual files and folders. It does not matter whether you are local to the share (in front of the machine where the data is stored) or remote to the share (coming across the network to access the data); the security is always in place with NTFS. The default security permission is Users = Read on new folders or shares. Configuring NTFS security and managing how it works with Shared Permissions are covered in Chapter 3, "Managing Data."

Compression   *Compression* helps compact files or folders to allow for more efficient use of hard drive space. For example, a file that usually takes up 20 MB of space might use only 13 MB after compression. To enable compression, just open the Advanced Attributes dialog box for a folder and check the Compress Contents To Save Disk Space box.

Encryption   *Encrypting Filesystem (EFS)* allows a user or administrator to secure files or folders by using encryption. Encryption employs the user's security identifier (SID) number to secure the file or folder. To implement encryption, open the Advanced Attributes dialog box for a folder, and check the Encrypt Contents To Secure Data box.

If files are encrypted using EFS and an administrator has to unencrypt the files, there are two ways to do this. First, you can log in using the user's account (the account that encrypted the files) and unencrypt the files. Second, you can become a recovery agent and manually unencrypt the files. When configuring encryption in the command line or PowerShell utilities, administrators can use the Cipher command to manage and maintain encryption.

FAT32 Encryption

Until Windows 10 and Windows Server, FAT32 did not support encryption. With the release of Windows 10 and Windows Server 2016, if you format FAT32 using one of these operating systems, encryption is now available.

Quotas   Disk *quotas* give administrators the ability to limit how much storage space a user can have on a hard drive. You have a few options available to you when you set up disk quotas. You can set up disk quotas based on volume or on users.

Setting Quotas by Volume   One way to set up disk quotas is by setting the quota by volume, on a per-volume basis. This means that if you have a hard drive with C:, D:, and E: volumes, you would have to set up three individual quotas (one for each volume). This is your umbrella. This is where you set up an entire disk quota based on the volume for all users.

Setting Quotas by User   You have the ability to set up quotas on volumes by user. Here is where you would individually let users have independent quotas that exceed your umbrella quota.

Specifying Quota Entries   You use quota entries to configure the volume and user quotas. You do this on the Quotas tab of the volume's Properties dialog box.

Creating Quota Templates   Quota templates are predefined ways to set up quotas. Templates allow you to set up disk quotas without needing to create a disk quota from scratch. One advantage of using a template is that when you want to set up disk quotas on multiple volumes (C:, D:, and E:) on the same hard drive, you do not need to re-create the quota on each volume.

Configuring Hardware

Configuring hardware properly is one of the most important tasks when setting up Windows 10. Windows 10 has included some tools to help users and administrators configure their hardware properly.

In Windows 10, there is built-in functionality called Devices (under Settings). Devices offers an enhanced graphic output, giving better details about and functionality to installed devices such as cameras.

Hardware today follows the Plug and Play standard, so most of the time simply connecting hardware will allow Devices to automatically configure it. Devices that are not Plug and Play compatible can be installed manually from Devices as well.

Understanding Devices

Throughout the evolution of technologies and PCs, one of the greatest features is how we can use such a wide array of devices on PCs. Device Manager has allowed us to see all the hardware connected and make configuration changes, but utilizing the features of the devices themselves has been left up to programs outside the Windows interface. Windows 10 includes a specification for hardware vendors (knowing that most hardware comes with software for the user to interface with), allowing them to provide user access within Windows Settings ➢ Devices. Windows 10 Printers & Scanners (Figure 5.1) is the interface for displaying and accessing supported printers and scanners.

FIGURE 5.1   Printers & Scanners

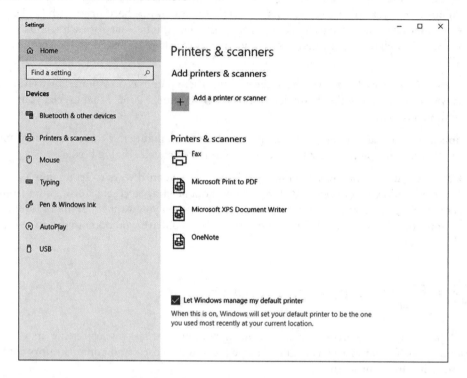

Take, for example, a digital camera. Generally, when you connect a camera to a PC, the PC recognizes the device (this immediate recognition is called Plug and Play) and typically displays the camera as a mass storage device. Users wanting advanced features like downloading and editing the photos must use another program. When you plug in a device that is supported by Devices technology, on the other hand, Devices displays a single window that gives you easy access to common device tasks, such as, in the case of a camera, importing pictures, launching the vendor-supplied editing programs, and simply browsing pictures, all from one interface.

With Windows 10, you'll be able to access all of your connected and wireless devices from the single Devices screen under Settings, and some devices will be displayed in the Windows 10 enhanced Taskbar. From here, you can work with your devices, browse files they might contain, and manage device settings.

Wireless and Bluetooth devices are also supported by Devices, making management of these resources much easier for the end user. As portable devices are disconnected and reconnected, the Devices screen will update in real time. Exercise 5.1 will guide you through opening and viewing devices recognized on your Windows 10 machine.

EXERCISE 5.1

Opening Devices

1. Click Start ➤ Settings ➤ Devices.

2. Look through the different Devices sections to see what is attached to your current PC.

Next, we'll take a look at using Device Manager to configure devices.

Using Device Manager

Device Manager is the component in Windows 10 you'll use to see which devices are connected to your machine. You can use Device Manager to ensure that all devices are working properly and to troubleshoot misbehaving devices. For each device installed, you can view specific properties down to the resources being used, such as the assigned I/O (input/output) port and IRQs (interrupt requests). Through Device Manager, you can take the following specific actions:

- View a list of all hardware installed on your computer.
- Determine which device driver is installed for each device.
- Manage and update device drivers.
- Install new devices.
- Disable, enable, and uninstall devices.
- Use driver rollback to return to a previous version of a driver.
- Troubleshoot device problems.

More importantly, you can see which devices Windows 10 has recognized. That is, if you install or connect a new piece of hardware and Windows 10 doesn't recognize it at all, it won't be seen in Device Manager. This would be an unusual occurrence given the sophistication of today's hardware vendors and the Plug and Play standards that are implemented. However, using Device Manager is an important tool in seeing just which devices are known to Windows 10. Keep in mind that we've been using Device Manager for many versions of Windows, so what I'm discussing is applicable to legacy versions as well. In Exercise 5.2, you will view devices using Device Manager.

EXERCISE 5.2

Viewing Devices Using Device Manager

1. Click Start ➤ Windows System ➤ Control Panel ➤ Device Manager.

2. Click the triangle next to Network Adapters (or double-click Network Adapters) to expand Network Adapters.

The steps in Exercise 5.2 show one way to launch Device Manager, through Control Panel. This is a valid method that shows you where the application resides, but administrators can launch Device Manager in other ways.

You may want to try the following method to open Device Manager: right-click Start and then choose Device Manager. I also sometimes type **Device Manager** (or just **device**) into the Windows integrated search box and press Enter. All of these are means to the same end.

As shown in Figure 5.2, Device Manager has a fairly simple opening screen, but it has a lot of functionality behind it. From the opening screen, you get a good first feeling for the hardware that's installed and recognized and for any major issues, such as a device that's recognized but has no drivers installed or is not working correctly. You'll see a warning symbol displayed over the misbehaving device. For example, suppose you have just installed a new network adapter but the device does not seem to be working. You can open Device Manager and open the Network Adapter option to start the troubleshooting process. Figure 5.2 shows just such a network adapter.

FIGURE 5.2   Device Manager screen

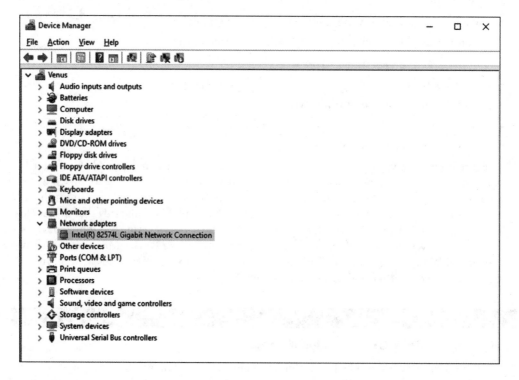

To continue troubleshooting the network adapter within Device Manager, you would right-click the misbehaving adapter and choose Properties to see its Properties dialog box (Figure 5.3). This is just a small part of the functionality within Device Manager.

FIGURE 5.3   Device Manager network adapter properties

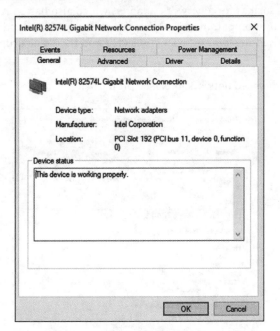

There are many reasons to view the devices installed and configured on a machine. One reason is to verify the type and status of hardware. For example, if someone in your organization has given you documentation for a specific user machine that includes the machine's hardware specifications and you are concerned that the stated network adapter for the machine may not be the one actually installed, you can use Device Manager on the machine in question to see the network adapters Windows 10 recognizes in the machine.

Device Properties Available within Device Manager

Once you have opened Device Manager and have access to the installed devices on your machine, you can view their Properties dialog boxes. From there, you can view and change configuration parameters if necessary. You will find that the tabs available in the Properties dialog boxes will vary from device to device because the parameters that are available will vary with different hardware. Most devices will have at a minimum a General tab, a Driver tab, and a Details tab.

The Properties dialog box for most devices will include more specific tabs for the hardware configuration, such as for a network adapter, which also has an Advanced tab for more specific configuration parameters. Figure 5.4 shows a network adapter's Advanced tab selected with Adaptive Inter-Frame Spacing selected and the Value drop-down box active to show possible choices.

FIGURE 5.4   Advanced network interface properties

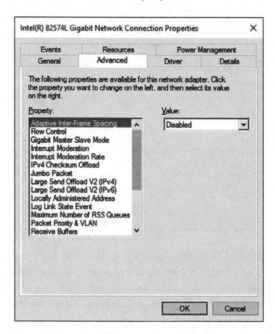

If you need to change the hardware configuration properties, Device Manager is the best way to access the parameters. Exercise 5.3 will show you how to view configurable properties for a network adapter through the Advanced tab.

EXERCISE 5.3

Configuring Network Adapter Advanced Properties

1. Choose Start ➢ Windows System ➢ Control Panel ➢ Device Manager.

2. Click the triangle next to Network Adapters (or double-click Network Adapters) to expand it.

3. Right-click your network adapter and select Properties.

4. Choose the Advanced tab.

5. Select various properties and view the parameters.

In addition to setting up devices, you will need to install and configure device drivers, which I will cover in the next section.

Installing and Updating Device Drivers

Device drivers are the controlling code actually interfacing the hardware components with the operating system. The commands are specific to each piece of hardware, and there may be different commands, memory locations, or actions even within the same type of hardware. A network interface card (NIC) from one vendor may actually have a different set of instructions than a NIC from a different manufacturer.

An operating system or software works best when it can issue a standard command and have the same functionality across the hardware regardless of vendor. This is where *drivers* come in; the driver takes a standard instruction from the operating system and interprets and then issues the command to the hardware to perform the desired function.

Drivers need to be updated. For example, a command set for a driver may perform a function incorrectly. This can produce errors and would need to be fixed. The hardware vendor will typically update the driver to fix the problem. Oftentimes, new or improved functionality may be necessary, so the hardware vendor would need to change the driver code to add functionality or provide better performance, in turn leading to an update.

There are different ways to download and install drivers. Microsoft drivers can be downloaded using the Windows Update utility. Drivers from different manufacturers can normally be downloaded from the manufacturer's website. Just access their website, search the product, and download the latest drivers. Then you can install those drivers using the Device Manager.

 Real World Scenario

Driver Code Causing an Arbitrary Nonreproducible Error

While working on a consulting job for a company where I was installing a new program and hardware to provide bar code scanning, I was plagued by the bar code readers connected to PCs randomly failing.

The bar code readers seemed to install correctly, and they showed as functioning properly within Device Manager. However, periodically the hardware readers would fail to input data into the application I was using. I could reboot the affected machine and the bar code reader would work fine again (for a while). It's easy to blame the operating system because the reboot seemed to fix the problem, but the operating system wasn't to blame.

After several days of troubleshooting and working with the manufacturer, it was determined that the driver interfacing the operating system with the hardware was not releasing memory resources correctly, causing the driver to fail. We received an updated driver and applied the update to the machines and the problem was resolved. Be careful not to blame the operating system prematurely, and be sure to investigate other areas for possible problems.

Typical first-time installation of drivers today happens automatically with the Plug and Play specification. After the hardware is installed, Windows 10 will recognize it and launch the driver installation program. Let's take, for example, the connection of a digital camera to the USB port of your computer.

Windows 10 will recognize that a device has been plugged in and will gather the information about the USB device. Windows 10 will then install the best driver it knows about (and if it doesn't know about the device, it will ask you how to proceed). Figure 5.5 shows the message indicating that the operating system found a driver and is installing it automatically.

FIGURE 5.5   Automatic driver installation

The installation completes and the device is now available in Device Manager. If you need to review the driver details for your newly installed device, the network adapter in this case, you can right-click the device in Device Manager and choose Properties. Figure 5.6 shows the right-click menu (also known as the context menu); note that the top choice in this menu is a quick launch to update the driver software.

FIGURE 5.6 Right-click menu for a device in Device Manager

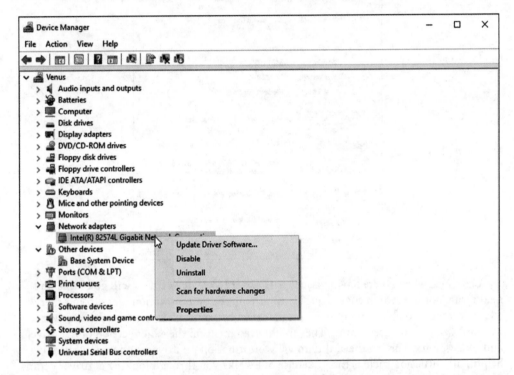

You may want to verify general information about the driver, like the provider or version. You can see that information in the Driver tab of the Properties dialog box. You can also choose to view the driver details, which are the supporting files and associated paths. Figure 5.7 shows the Properties dialog box of the network adapter that shows the Driver Details button on the Driver tab of the Properties dialog box for the network adapter.

FIGURE 5.7   Driver details within Device Manager

Sometimes when you're having issues with a hardware device, you will go online and read forums or use search engine queries to attempt to find resolution ideas from other administrators. Someone might mention that they had a problem with a specific driver for the hardware you're researching. They might even mention the exact version of the driver and suggest a fix. Having the ability to view information on drivers and update them is helpful in a situation such as this. Exercise 5.4 walks you through looking at driver details.

EXERCISE 5.4

Viewing Driver Details

1. Click Start ➢ Windows System ➢ Control Panel ➢ Device Manager (or type **device manager** in the integrated search window).

2. Click the triangle next to the category in which you want to view driver details to expand the item list; you can also double-click the category name. For example, double-click the Network Adapters category to see the network connection to the machine.

3. Choose the Driver tab.

4. View the driver version.

5. Click the Driver Details button to see the files associated with the hardware.

Another task may be to update the drivers. In Exercise 5.5 we will look at updating a driver.

EXERCISE 5.5

Updating a Driver

1. Click Start ➢ Windows System ➢ Control Panel ➢ Device Manager (or type **device manager** in the integrated search window).

2. Click the triangle next to category for which you want to update the driver to expand the item list; you can also double-click the category name.

3. Right-click the hardware item and select Properties.

4. Choose the Driver tab.

5. Click the Update Driver button; a window launches asking how you want to search for the driver.

6. Choose Search Automatically For Updated Driver Software to have Windows 10 search for you, or choose Browse My Computer For Driver Software if you have the new drivers already.

7. Windows 10 searches for and updates the drivers or reports back that you have the most current version.

Not only will you often need to update drivers because of a failure or hardware issue, but you will at times install new drivers for new or updated functionality. There will also be times when a hardware driver gets updated and the update breaks a piece of functioning hardware or doesn't solve a problem. In these cases, you will want to go back to the previous version, or "roll back" the driver. In Exercise 5.6, you will learn how to do a driver rollback.

EXERCISE 5.6

Rolling Back a Driver

1. Click Start ➢ Windows System ➢ Control Panel ➢ Device Manager (or type **device manager** in the integrated search window).

2. Click the triangle next to the category for which you want to roll back the driver to expand the item list; you can also double-click the category name.

3. Right-click the hardware item and select Properties.

4. Choose the Driver tab.

5. Click the Roll Back Driver button. Note that if the Roll Back Driver button is grayed out, there isn't a previous version of the driver available.

6. The previous driver will be installed and the hardware will return to its previous state of functionality.

The Driver tab for a piece of installed hardware in Device Manager also provides functionality for disabling and uninstalling a driver. Why would you want to disable a driver? There are several possibilities, but troubleshooting is one of the most common reasons.

Disabling the driver effectively disables the hardware; it will no longer function in the system. Uninstalling the device driver has a similar effect, but if the hardware is still installed, you can uninstall the driver and perform a scan to ensure that the hardware is still recognized and force a reinstallation.

I have often disabled a device from Device Manager to eliminate one part of an issue I am having with a system. If I'm confident that the problem is with the hardware, I will uninstall the driver and let the operating system reinstall it as part of the troubleshooting procedure. This works much of the time and is a good place to start. In Exercise 5.7, you will disable and enable a device driver.

EXERCISE 5.7

Disabling and Enabling a Device in Device Manager

1.   Click Start ➤ Windows System ➤ Control Panel ➤ Device Manager (or type **device manager** in the integrated search window).

2.   Click the triangle next to the appropriate category to expand the item list; you can also double-click the category name.

3.   Right-click the hardware item and select Properties. Note that you can select Disable directly from the context menu if desired.

4.   Choose the Driver tab.

5.   Click the Disable button. (This is a toggle button; it will be labeled Disable if the device is enabled and Enable if the device is disabled.)

6.   The device driver and hence the device will be disabled and will no longer function. There will be a down arrow on the item in Device Manager, and the General tab will show that the device is disabled. Close the Properties dialog box for that device.

7.   Right-click the hardware item and select Properties.

8.   Choose the Driver tab.

9.   Click the Enable button. (Remember that this is a toggle button.)

10. The device driver will become enabled and the hardware will work as designed (barring any other issues).

11. Close Device Manager.

It may be beneficial at times to uninstall and reinstall a device driver. Many times when you do that, the default configuration parameters will be reset to their original specifications.

Any changes you have made will need to be reconfigured, but if the device driver worked previously and has stopped for some unknown reason (if you knew the reason, you'd simply fix it), uninstalling and reinstalling is worth a try. You may also consider using a different device driver than Windows 10 is set up to use via Plug and Play. Note that uninstalling a device driver does not delete the driver files from the machine; uninstalling the device driver removes the operating system configuration for the hardware.

You may want or need to find the driver files and delete them manually in some cases. Remember, you can find the files (and thus the filenames) from Driver Details within the Driver's tab of the Properties dialog box of the hardware within Device Manager.

If you have determined that the device driver for your misbehaving hardware is potentially causing the problem you are having, you can choose to uninstall and reinstall (automatically) the drivers. In Exercise 5.8, you will uninstall and then reinstall a device driver.

EXERCISE 5.8

Uninstalling and Reinstalling a Device Driver

1. Click Start ➤ Windows System ➤ Control Panel ➤ Device Manager (or type **device manager** in the integrated search window).

2. Click the triangle next to the category for the device you want to uninstall to expand the item list; you can also double-click the category name.

3. Right-click the hardware item and select Properties. Note that you can select Uninstall directly from the context menu.

4. Choose the Driver tab.

5. Click the Uninstall button.

6. Click OK in the Confirm Device Uninstall dialog box. A progress box appears as the device driver is uninstalled. Once the driver is uninstalled, Device Manager will no longer show the device.

7. From Device Manager, choose the Action menu item and select Scan For Hardware Changes; alternatively, you can right-click the machine name in Device Manager and select Scan For Hardware Changes from the context menu.

8. Windows 10 will initiate the process of discovering the Plug and Play device and will reinstall the device driver configuration into the operating system. The hardware will be available again within Device Manager.

A lot of hardware manufacturers would like you to install the driver files and some software for their device before the operating system has a chance to discover it. This is often so that the software program controlling some of the hardware functionality will be installed first so its configuration file can accurately reference the installed drivers, or it can also be to add the driver files to the driver configuration directories of the operating system before the operating system discovers the device.

The process of adding the drivers is usually done by inserting and running a setup program from a provided CD or DVD. I will say the hardware vendors know what's best. As an admin, it's sometimes hard not to just install the hardware and go from there, but following the vendor's recommendations will most often produce a better result.

 Real World Scenario

Follow the Hardware Vendor's Recommendation

Like many other admins, I sometimes think I know the right way to proceed in installing a piece of hardware. Seriously, how hard can it be? I once installed a new wireless USB adapter into a machine I was using by just plugging it in despite the great big red sticker that said, "Run the setup on the CD FIRST!"

Sure enough, Windows found the adapter and proceeded to install the drivers. The hardware showed up in Device Manager but would not work. Now, being the good troubleshooter I am, I decided to run the Setup program on the CD. It turns out the driver files on the CD were a different version (actually older) than the installed files and Windows would not replace the installed drivers.

Even after I manually uninstalled them? Yes. I had to go back and find five different files in numerous locations and delete each one. Finding the files to delete was not a simple operation; a lot of online research went into solving this problem, and several hours of my time were wasted.

Simply following the hardware-vendor instructions would have been much easier. I did the same installation on another machine following the vendor recommendations and everything worked perfectly. But then again, that's how we all learn these valuable lessons in life.

There are also situations we run into requiring a manual installation of hardware. There may be multiple reasons, including installation of legacy hardware, situations when drivers are not supplied in the operating system distribution files, or when drivers that may perform different functions from the default drivers are available. You can perform manual installations from Device Manager through the Add Hardware Wizard.

In the manual installation process, you can have Windows 10 go out to the Internet to find a current driver, or you can specify a location of your choosing locally. From Device Manager, you launch the Add Hardware Wizard (Figure 5.8) by choosing Add Legacy Hardware from either the Action menu or the context menu of the machine.

FIGURE 5.8 Add Hardware Wizard initial window

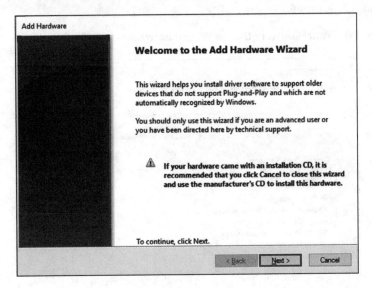

The next step is to tell Windows 10 where to look for the driver. This is the next page of the Add Hardware Wizard, as Figure 5.9 shows.

FIGURE 5.9 Driver file location choices

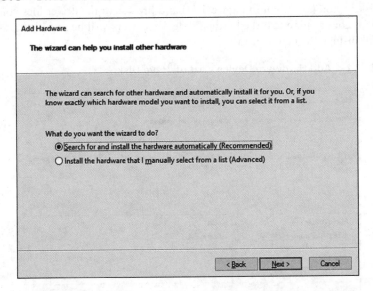

To choose a piece of hardware from a list of supplied drivers or, more important, to choose a specific path, select the option Install The Hardware That I Manually Select From A List (Advanced) and choose Next. This allows you to select a device type or choose Show

All Devices (Figure 5.10); selecting Show All Devices and clicking Next will give you the ability to choose a location.

FIGURE 5.10   Add Hardware Device Wizard hardware-selection window

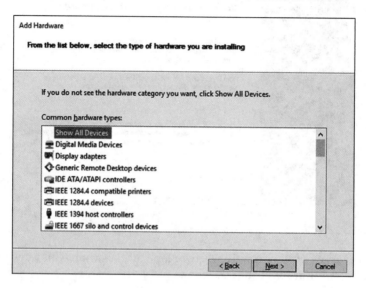

If you have a disk or have the appropriate drivers stored in an accessible location, click the Have Disk button (as shown in Figure 5.11) and browse to the driver files you need to install. If all goes as planned, the hardware device drivers will be installed and Device Manager will display the newly installed hardware.

FIGURE 5.11   Add Hardware Device Wizard, Have Disk

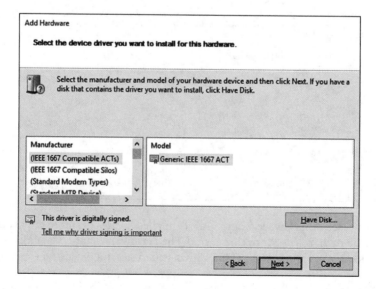

Driver Signing

In this world of hackers and viruses, one issue that needs to be addressed is the possibility that drivers that are downloaded come from an unrepeatable source and have viruses or worms contained within the files. To help combat this problem, drivers that are created from reputable companies (like Dell or HP Compaq) assign a digital file certificate to the driver to show its validity.

One way to ensure that all the drivers on your machine are verified is to run Sigverif.exe from the Search Programs And Files box on the Start menu. Exercise 5.9 walks you through the steps of verifying the drivers on your machine.

EXERCISE 5.9

Verifying Signed Drivers

1. Run the Sigverif.exe program by typing **Sigverif.exe** in the Search The Web And Windows box, and then pressing Enter.

2. The File Signature Verification box appears. Click Start.

3. You will notice that the system scan begins. When the system has finished verifying the drivers, a message will appear stating that your files were all scanned. Click OK.

4. If there are any programs with unsigned drivers, they will be displayed at this time. Click Close to close the dialog box and then click Close to close the Sigverif.exe program.

Knowing how to properly install and configure drivers is an important part of an IT professional's job. Another task that we must perform is managing input/output devices.

Managing I/O Devices

The devices you use to get information into and out of your Windows 10 machine are your I/O (input/output) devices. I/O devices include removable storage, keyboard, mouse, scanner, and printer. Your devices may be connected to your computer by standard cabling or by USB, or they may use a wireless technology such as IrDA (infrared) or RF (radio frequency).

Configuring Removable Storage Devices

Removable storage devices have been part of our computing world since the beginning. CDs, DVDs, and floppy disks are examples of removable storage. Today, we're using other types of removable storage as well, including flash-based electronics like USB sticks, memory cards, USB or FireWire external hard drives, cameras, phones, and so on. Windows 10 installs drivers for these devices (or media) dynamically as the devices are connected.

We'll be concentrating in this section on dynamically connected devices utilizing the USB/FireWire connectivity and memory cards. These devices present challenges to the administrative team, because end users utilizing the technology may not follow guidelines for protecting their data from loss or for keeping it secure.

Windows 10 includes improvements to the Safely Remove Hardware (eject) menu. For example, it's now possible to eject just one memory card (from a single hub) and keep the ports available for future use. Removable media are now listed under their label through Devices and Printers in Fig. 5.12 rather than just their drive letter as they were in previous versions of Windows. This is also part of the Devices functionality of Windows 10; hardware vendors can include configuration information about portable devices and give users more resources from one location.

FIGURE 5.12   Devices And Printers with USB stick installed

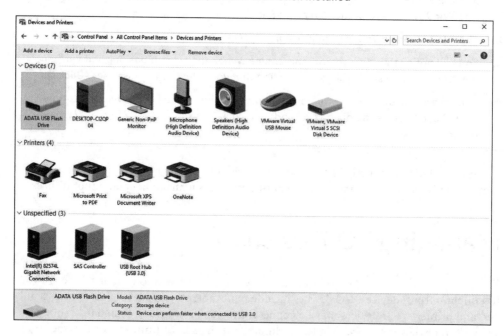

There are considerations in terms of data access performance with the portable devices as well. To make data access and saves faster, it's possible to have the operating system cache the data and write it to the portable device later when there's free processor time. However, this allows the possibility of a user removing the portable device before the write is actually made, which would result in a loss of data.

Windows 10 defaults to writing the data immediately, minimizing the chance of data loss at the cost of performance. The configuration for optimizing the portable device for quick removal or better performance is found in the Policies tab of the Properties dialog box for the hardware device in Device Manager.

In Exercise 5.10, we will walk through the steps to configure input/output devices through the use of Device Manager.

EXERCISE 5.10

Configuring an Input/Output Device

1. Click Start ➤ Windows System ➤ Control Panel ➤ Device Manager (under Printers & Scanners) or type **device manager** into the integrated search window of Windows 10.

2. Click the triangle next to Disk Drives (or double-click Disk Drives) to expand the item.

3. Right-click on one of the storage device items and select Properties.

4. Choose the Policies tab (see Figure 5.13).

FIGURE 5.13 Policies tab

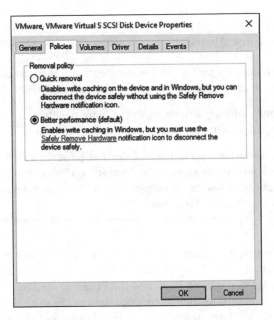

5. Select the Better Performance radio button and then click OK.

In Exercise 5.10, you changed the storage device to a write cache policy for better performance; this means writes to the portable device may be saved and written at a later time when the processor has clock cycles available. To ensure no loss of data, it is fairly important to properly eject the device through Windows 10 before physically removing it.

Choosing the icon in the Taskbar to eject the device initiates a stop for the hardware, forcing any cached writes in memory to be written to the device.

The device will close, meaning the writes have been made, and you will be presented with a window saying it's safe to remove the hardware.

Another important piece of hardware that needs to be configured is the printer. In the next section, we will discuss managing printers.

Managing Printers

Printers have been an issue for IT teams around the world and will continue to be as far as I can tell. Every new update/release/version of an operating system has new software intelligence to make the installation and maintenance easier, but printer technology continues to grow and hardware vendors continue to make changes.

The driver base for all the different printers out there is huge, and even for the same printer there are numerous variations. Printers themselves have lots of options that can be made available, and this all has to be controlled by the operating system, through the drivers.

The Printer vs. the Print Device

I have referred in the preceding portion of this chapter to printers and devices; I have been talking about the physical piece of hardware and its functions.

In the IT world, we need to distinguish between the functionality of the hardware and of the software (both the driver software and the controlling software).

To this end, a lot of us know the physical device that has paper in it as the print device, not "the printer." The printer is the software application on the local machine controlling the print device. The printer driver is the software shim between the operating system and the locally installed software (the printer).

You will find in most organizations that there is not a print device attached to every computer. They are usually shared among users. This is cost effective on many levels, but it tends to cause issues. Most of us, end users and the IT team, need to print something once in a while, and so we send our documents or web pages to the print device to be printed.

The print device may be connected to someone's machine and shared for others to use, or it may be a stand-alone device. You may have a server on your network that has one or more print devices attached, and everyone sends their documents to a central location. Each user machine will have a printer installed and the appropriate drivers to allow Windows 10 to send the document to the print device through the printer with the appropriate instructions.

Of course, the print device can't physically print a document at the speed at which the printer can send the data to it. This is where a software component called the spool (spooler, print spool, and so on) comes in. There need to be software components that can buffer the print job until the print device can complete it. In fact, there may be more than one user sending documents to be printed to the same print device at the same time, and the spool handles this as well.

What, No Spool?

I was working on a networking problem for a local veterinary clinic. The employees were complaining about issues they were having with their PCs being extremely slow sometimes but faster other times, and they were sure the network hardware was the cause. We discussed things that had changed recently—they had upgraded a piece of their software package to allow more functionality, which included having a couple of centralized printers for the docs and techs to use. It seemed as though every time someone printed, the network bogged down to the point of uselessness.

Casual discussions ensued. The network bog-down affected only the machine (or machines) actively sending a print job. Looking into the problem a little further showed that the vendor installation defaulted to printing directly to the print device, with no spooling. Each machine had to wait for the print job to complete before releasing any local resources (yes, that's right, not even background printing), and the other machines on the network ended up waiting as well. Allowing the machines to spool their print jobs solved the problem of slow networking (clearly not a networking issue in the end).

Installing Printers

Installing printers to a machine is done in two distinct ways: one where the print device is physically connected to the machine and one where it is not (it's connected over the network). There have to be software drivers in either case, and they can be on a CD/DVD, on a network share, downloaded on the Internet from the vendor, or even in the Windows distribution files. Printers in Windows 10 will be located in the Printers & Scanners window (under Settings ➤ Devices) and will allow the device configuration to accommodate a full range of functionality from this one location.

To add a printer to a machine locally, you will usually run the Setup program on the CD/DVD (following the manufacturer's instructions). The manufacturer's Setup program in a wizard format will ask the appropriate questions. You can set up the printer through Windows 10 as well as by using the Add Printer functionality of Printers & Scanners. To add a printer using the Windows 10 functionality, click Settings ➤ Devices ➤ Printers & Scanners ➤ Add A Printer Or Scanner, as shown in Figure 5.14. When USB printers are plugged in, they will be automatically detected and their drivers will be installed (or at least looked for automatically).

FIGURE 5.14   Adding a printer from Printers & Scanners

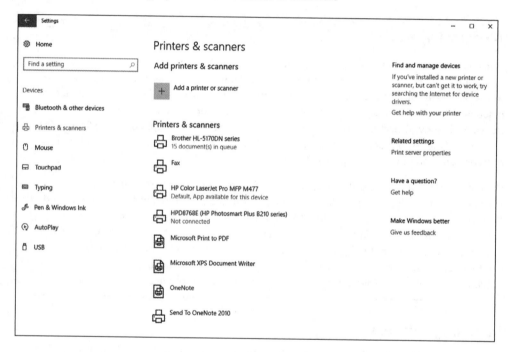

Choosing the Add A Printer Or Scanner menu item launches the Add Wizard and you will notice that Windows 10 will automatically try to find the printer. If the printer that you want to install is not in the list, you can choose The Printer That I Want Isn't Listed. If the printer wasn't listed, then the next screen (shown in Figure 5.15) allows you to make the choice of installing the printer by the printer name, TCP/IP address, or Bluetooth discovery or by adding a local printer or network printer.

FIGURE 5.15   Add Printer Wizard local or remote choice

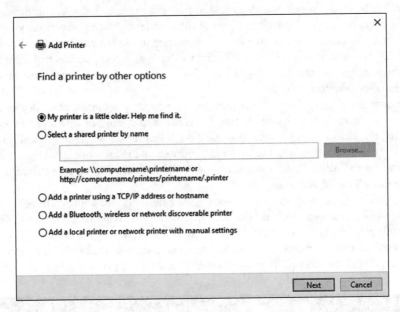

From the opening screen you can follow the steps in Exercise 5.11 to install the printer for a physically connected print device to a machine. We're going on the premise that the Setup program on the CD/DVD (if one existed) was not run and we're installing the printer from the wizard associated with Windows.

EXERCISE 5.11

Installing a Printer

1. Click Settings ➤ Devices ➤ Printers & Scanners.

2. Choose Add A Printer Or Scanner.

3. Select the option The Printer I Want Isn't Listed.

4. Choose the option "Add a local printer or network printer with manual settings" and click Next.

5. Use the option LPT1: (printer port) and click Next.

6. Under Manufacture, choose Generic and then choose Generic / Text Only. Click Next.

7. For the printer name, leave the default Generic / Text. Click Next.

8. On the Printer Sharing screen, choose Do Not Share This Printer and click Next.

9. Make sure the check box Set As Default Printer is unchecked and click the Finish button.

Do not remove the printer you just installed in this exercise 5.11.

Once you have completed the Add Printer Wizard to install your printer, you can open the Printers & Scanners window and see it. Using the context menu, you will have access to the Properties dialog box as well as some of the standard printing functions you've had in Windows in the past. As hardware vendors continue to implement functionality for Windows 10, you will have access to a full array of software components from the Printers & Scanners window, at least for the vendors who are going to participate in the Devices specifications for Windows 10.

What about installing a printer on a machine that needs to access a print device connected to another machine or on the network? In order to configure a printer to connect to a remote print device, you must launch the Add A Printer Or Scanner Wizard and go through the process of installing the printer, but point to a shared or stand-alone network printer by using the Add A Bluetooth, Wireless, Or Network Discoverable Printer option or by putting in its TCP/IP address.

Knowing that not all machines on any company's network are going to have print devices physically attached, there is functionality to allow sharing of networked devices and to install printers (software) on client machines. In Exercise 5.12, we will look at how to connect to a network printer. To complete this exercise, you need to have a network printer that you can connect to. If you do not have a network printer, skip this exercise.

EXERCISE 5.12

Installing a Shared Network Print Device

1. Click Settings ➤ Devices ➤ Printers & Scanners.

2. Choose Add A Printer Or Scanner.

3. Select the option The Printer I Want Isn't Listed.

4. Choose the option Add A Bluetooth, Wireless, Or Network Discoverable Printer and click Next.

5. The Add Printer Wizard will search the local network for print devices that are available.

6. Select the networked print device from the Select A Printer section. If the device is not listed, you can choose The Printer That I Want Is Not Listed and enter the parameters for the networked print device.

7. The print device will be detected, the driver will be discovered and installed, and you will be able to use the printer. It will be available at this time in Printers & Scanners.

Configuring Printers

Once the printer is installed for either a print device physically connected to the local machine or a network-connected print device, you can view the configuration parameters of the printer and modify them if necessary from the Properties dialog box. Access the property pages from either Control Panel ➤ Devices And Printers (Figure 5.16) or Settings ➤ Devices ➤ Printers And Scanners. Right-click the printer and select Properties for the hardware properties or Printer Properties for the software components.

FIGURE 5.16 Printer context menu from Devices And Printers

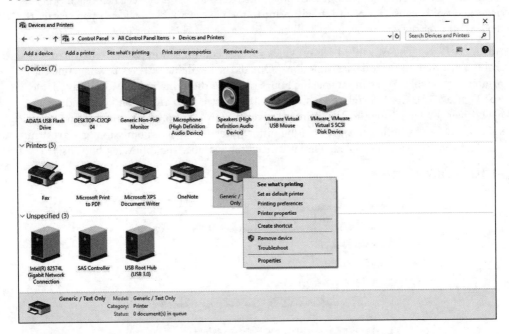

The Properties dialog boxes for printers follow a standard that Microsoft has in place, but the content is really up to the manufacturer. Some vendors will supply more information than others. Most printers will provide a basic set of pages (tabs):

General Tab The printer name, location, and comment are displayed here. The model is typically shown as well as the features of the specific print device and available paper. The printer preferences page is available by clicking the Preferences button, and you can print a test page by clicking the Print Test Page button.

Sharing Tab The Sharing tab allows you to share a printer if it wasn't shared during its installation or to stop sharing it if it was previously shared. You can also add drivers for other flavors of operating systems so the locally installed and shared printer can supply drivers for other machines attempting to connect and use it.

Ports Tab Available ports and print devices connected to them can be viewed on the Ports tab. You can add a port, delete a port, and configure ports from the tab as well. Normally, operating systems just talk to the print device, but some print devices need to communicate with the operating system. This is known as bidirectional support (sending codes back from the print device to the printer for control).

Printer pooling is also available here. Printer pooling gives the IT staff the ability to config-ure multiple print devices (using identical drivers) to appear as one printer to connected users. The print jobs will be printed on one of the devices in the pool (first available print device prints the job). If a print device fails, the others will keep working, making life bet-ter for the users (always a goal). It is important to keep all print devices near each other in a printing pool because the print job will print to the next available device. If you scatter the devices all over the company, users will have to search for their print jobs.

Advanced Tab   The Advanced tab provides various configuration parameters to con-trol the printer and print device functions. One of the available settings is what time the printer is available. You can set specific hours or allow the printer to always be available (see Figure 5.17). Configuring the installed print driver is also an option, as is adding a new driver (by launching the Add Printer Driver Wizard). Spool options include whether to spool or not and whether to start printing immediately upon job submission or start print-ing after the last page is spooled. The Advanced tab includes the following buttons:

FIGURE 5.17   The Advanced tab

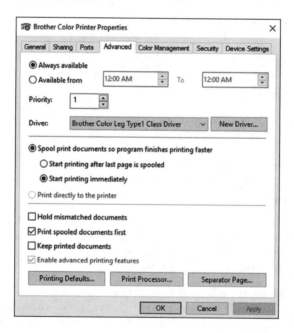

Printing Defaults Button   Launches the printer properties for the vendor as they apply to the documents.

Print Processor Button   Let's you choose whether to use the vendor-supplied print processor or the built-in Windows print processor. You can also choose the default data type to be sent to the print device.

Separator Page Button   Allows a specific page to be inserted between print jobs, making the separation of different documents easier.

Color Management Tab   If the print device has the capabilities of printing in color, there will be a color management tab. This tab gives you the ability to adjust the color management settings.

Security Tab   Group or user access permissions are controlled in the Security tab. Advanced permissions can be controlled here as well.

Device Settings Tab   Device settings–specific parameters for each print device are set up on the Device Settings tab (Figure 5.18). Items like Form To Tray Assignment, Font Substitution, and other installable options for the print device are configurable here.

FIGURE 5.18   The Device Settings tab

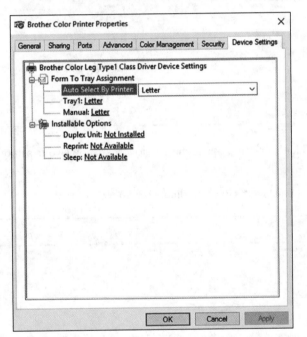

Managing Documents

Once the configuration is complete and the printer and print device are working in harmony, life is good. You can see the status of the document currently being printed as well as documents waiting to be printed. This is what we call the queue. The queue used to be viewed by choosing the queue option in the context menu for the printer. Windows 10 calls it See What's Printing (Figure 5.19).

FIGURE 5.19   See What's Printing

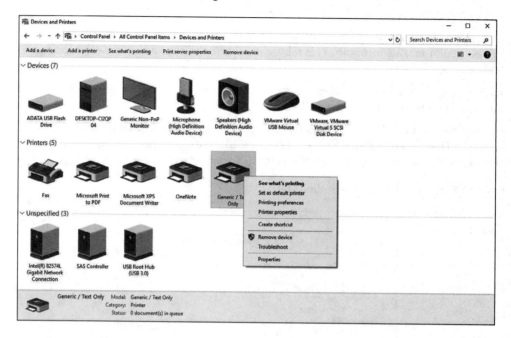

Selecting See What's Printing opens the window that shows your printer's document/job control (Figure 5.20).

FIGURE 5.20   See What's Printing display window

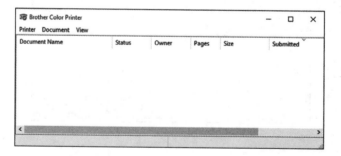

The Devices section allows you to select the context window from Printers & Scanners. To get a graphical view of Devices, double-click the printer in Printers & Scanners to get a consolidated view and the popular (as decided by the vendor) menu choices. Figure 5.21 shows a printer and its options as seen when you double-click it in Printers & Scanners.

FIGURE 5.21   Printer window from Printers & Scanners

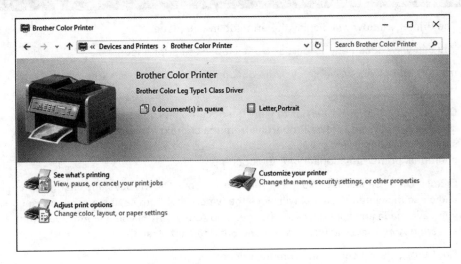

In Exercises 5.11 and 5.12, you installed printers for both a locally connected and a network-connected printer. In Exercise 5.13, let's take a look at sending a print job to the locally connected printer that you set up in Exercise 5.11 and view the document properties.

EXERCISE 5.13

Managing Documents in the Local Queue

1. Click Settings ➤ Devices ➤ Printers & Scanners.

2. Click on the Generic printer that you installed during Exercise 5.11.

3. You will see three option buttons appear, Open Queue, Manage, and Remove Device. Click the Open Queue button.

4. Choose Printer ➤ Pause Printing from the menu.

5. View the status bar of the printer to verify that the printer is paused; there will also be a check mark next to Pause Printing in the menu.

   Now let's send a test document to the paused locally connected printer:

1. From the Printer window, select Printer ➤ Properties.

2. On the General tab of the Properties window, click the Print Test Page button.

3. An information box will appear stating that a test page has been sent to the printer; click the Close button.

4. Click the OK button in the printer Properties window.

5.   The Printer window will display the print job in the queue.

     You can view document properties from a job in the print queue:

1.   In the Printer window, single-click the document you want to view (the print job you want to view).

2.   Choose Document ➢ Properties to view the document properties; you can also right-click the print job and select Properties from the context menu. The General tab will show you the document properties; the other tabs are vendor supplied to control additional printer functionality for the document.

3.   Choose OK or Cancel to close the Properties window. OK will save any changes made and close the window; Cancel will close the window without saving any changes. If you have made any configuration changes, the Apply button will become available; selecting Apply saves any changes made but does not close the window.

     Now, let's delete a document from the queue:

1.   In the Printer windows, single-click the job you want to cancel (the document you want to delete).

2.   Choose the menu choice Document ➢ Cancel to delete the document. You can also right-click the document and select Cancel to delete the print job. Either method will prompt a confirmation message box asking Are You Sure You Want To Cancel The Document? Choose Yes.

3.   The document will no longer be in the queue in the Printer window.

4.   Choose Printer ➢ Close to close the Printer window.

Deleting Printers

There may also be times you will want to delete a printer, either one that's locally connected or a network printer, from your Windows 10 machine. This may be due to a replacement of an older print device or may be necessary when moving a user to a new print device. The removal will be performed from the Printers & Scanners window. Removing a printer will remove the software configuration but not necessarily the driver files from the local machine. In Exercise 5.14, we will remove a printer.

Removing a Printer from Printers & Scanners

1.   Click Settings ➢ Devices ➢ Printers & Scanners.

2.   Click on the Generic printer that you installed during Exercise 5.11.

3. You will see three option buttons appear, Open Queue, Manage, and Remove Device. Click the Remove Device button.

4. A dialog box will appear asking if you are sure you want to remove this device. Click Yes.

5. The printer will be removed.

Print Management Tool

The Print Management MMC Snap-in is available in the `Administrative Tools` folder on computers running Windows 7/8/8.1/10, Windows Server 2008 and above. Administrators can use the Print Management tools to install, manage, import/export print server settings, and view all of the printers and print servers throughout your company.

Administrators can use Print Management to install printers and to monitor print queues remotely. Print Management allows administrators to use filters to find printers that are in an error condition and to also receive email notifications or run scripts when a printer or print server needs attention. Depending on your printer, Print Management can also show administrators if a printer is low on ink or paper.

Print Management allows print administrators to have a single application where they can monitor and manage their printers. For example, Print Management allows an administrator to export print server information to a file and then take that file to another Windows system and import those print server settings into a new machine. This process is referred to as Print Server Migration.

Administrators can also use Print Management tools along with Group Policies. Group Policies are rules and policies that an administrator can set on a server and those policies will be deployed to your users and computers automatically through the network.

Print Management also gives administrators the ability to automatically search for and install network printers on their local network. Besides the Print Management MMC, there is a command-line utility that administrators can use, called `Printbrm.exe`, to manage their printers and print servers. When using the `Printbrm.exe` command, you must be in a command prompt with administrative privileges.

Print Management allows a printer administrator to complete some of the following tasks:

- Update and manage printer drivers.
- Control printer driver installation.
- Create new printer filters.
- View extended features of the printers.
- Pause or resume printing.
- Cancel all print jobs.
- List or remove printers from Active Directory.
- Delete printers.
- Import and export printer settings.

In Exercise 5.15, we will use the Print Migration Tools to export our print server settings to a file. You can then take that file and import the settings into another print server. This is a way to export printers from one server and load them onto another.

EXERCISE 5.15

Using the Print Migration Tools

1. In the Windows 10 search box, type **Print Management**. Click the Print Management tool that appears.

2. When the Print Management tool appears, right-click on Print Management and choose Migrate Printers (as shown in Figure 5.22).

FIGURE 5.22   Migrate Printers option

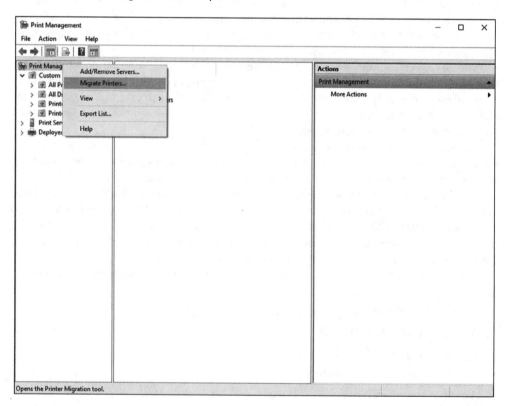

3. At the Getting Started With Print Migration screen, choose to export printer queues and print drivers to a file. Click Next.

4. Choose your print server and click Next.

5. A screen will appear showing you which objects will be exported. Click Next.

6. Type in a file name and location or click Browse to choose the file name and location. Click Next once completed.

7. The settings will be exported. Once the export is complete, click the Finish button as shown in Figure 5.23.

FIGURE 5.23   Export Complete screen

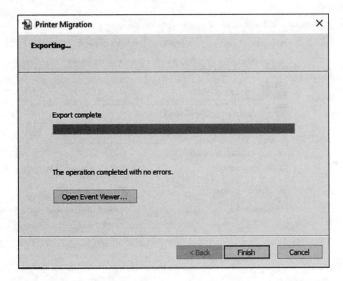

Now that the print server settings have been exported to a file, an administrator can take that file to another machine and import those setting using the Print Migration tools. This is an easy way for administrators to move print servers without manually rebuilding the print server settings.

Configuring Windows Defender Firewall

Windows Defender Firewall, which is included with Windows 10, helps prevent unauthorized users or malicious software from accessing your computer. Windows Defender Firewall does not allow unsolicited traffic, which is traffic that was not sent in response to a request, to pass through the firewall.

Understanding the Windows Defender Firewall Basics

You configure Windows Defender Firewall by clicking Start ➤ Windows System ➤ Control Panel ➤ Large Icons View ➤ Windows Firewall. You can then decide what firewall options you want to set (as seen in Figure 5.24) like Changing Firewall notifications, turning the Windows Defender Firewall on or off, Restoring defaults, setting advanced settings, and Troubleshooting.

FIGURE 5.24   Windows Firewall settings dialog box

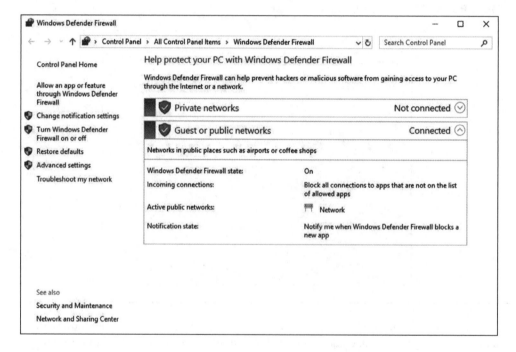

The Windows Firewall settings dialog box allows you to turn Windows Firewall on or off for both private and public networks. The On setting will block incoming sources and the Turn off Windows Firewall setting will allow incoming sources to connect.

There is also a check box for Block All Incoming Connections. This feature allows you to connect to networks that are not secure. When Block All Incoming Connections is enabled, all incoming connections (even ones allowed in the allowed apps list) will be blocked by Windows Firewall.

Windows Defender Firewall with Advanced Security

You can configure more-advanced settings by configuring Windows Firewall with Advanced Security (WFAS) via the Start ➤ Windows System ➤ Control Panel ➤ Large Icons

View ➤ Windows Defender Firewall ➤ Advanced Settings link. The Windows Defender Firewall With Advanced Security dialog box appears, as shown in Figure 5.25.

FIGURE 5.25   Windows Defender Firewall With Advanced Security

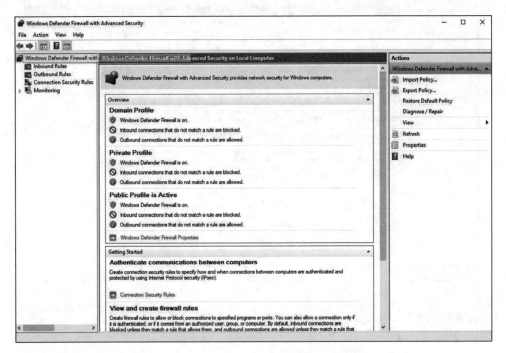

The scope pane to the left shows that you can set up specific inbound and outbound rules, connection security rules, and monitoring rules. The central area shows an overview of the firewall's status when no rule is selected in the left pane. When a rule is selected, the central area shows the rule's settings. The right pane shows the same actions as the Action menu on the top. These are just shortcuts to the different actions that can be performed in Windows Firewall. Let's take a more detailed look at some of the elements in Windows Firewall.

Inbound and Outbound Rules

Inbound and outbound rules consist of many preconfigured rules that can be enabled or disabled. Obviously, inbound rules (see Figure 5.26) monitor inbound traffic, and outbound rules monitor outbound traffic. By default, many are disabled. Double-clicking a rule will bring up its Properties dialog box (Figure 5.27).

FIGURE 5.26 Inbound rules

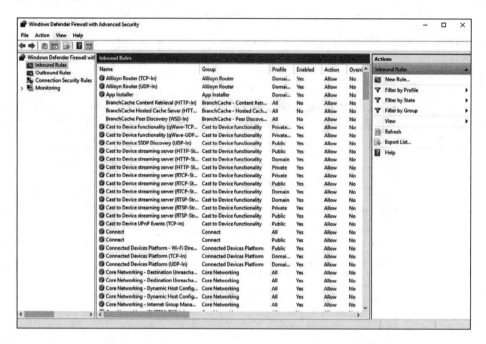

FIGURE 5.27 An inbound rule's Properties dialog box

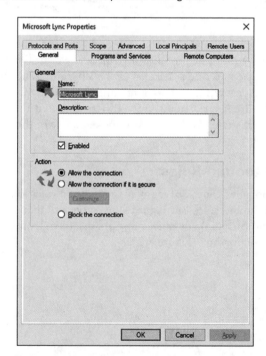

You can filter the rules to make them easier to view. Filtering can be based on the profile the rule affects, on whether the rule is enabled or disabled, or on the rule group. You can filter a rule by clicking which filter type you want to use in the right pane or by clicking the Action menu on the top of the screen.

If you can't find a rule that is appropriate for your needs, you can create a new rule by right-clicking Inbound Rules or Outbound Rules in the scope pane and then selecting New Rule. The New Inbound (or Outbound) Rule Wizard will launch, and you will be asked whether you want to create a rule based on a particular program, protocol or port, predefined category, or custom settings.

As you are setting up the firewall rules, you have the ability to configure authenticated exceptions. No matter how well your system security is set up, there are almost always times when computers on your network can't use IPsec. This is when you set up authenticated exceptions. Now it's important to understand that when you set up these authenticated exceptions, you are reducing the security of the network because it allows computers to send unprotected IPsec network traffic. So make sure the computers that are added to the authenticated exceptions list are managed and trusted computers only.

Complete Exercise 5.16 to create a new inbound rule that will allow only encrypted TCP traffic.

EXERCISE 5.16

Creating a New Inbound Rule

1. Click Start ➤ Windows System ➤ Control Panel ➤ Large Icons View ➤ Windows Defender Firewall.

2. Click Advanced Settings on the left side.

3. Right-click Inbound Rules and select New Rule.

4. Choose a rule type. For this exercise, choose Custom so you can see all the options available to you. Then click Next.

5. At the Program screen, choose All Programs. Then click Next.

6. Choose the protocol type as well as the local and remote port numbers that are affected by this rule. For this exercise, choose TCP, and ensure that All Ports is selected for both Local Port and Remote Port. Click Next to continue.

7. At the Scope screen, choose Any IP Address for both local and remote. Then click Next.

8. At the Action screen, choose Allow The Connection Only If It Is Secure. Click Next.

9. At the Users screen, you can experiment with these options if you want by entering users to both sections. Once you click on one of the check boxes, the Add and Remove buttons become available. Click Next to continue.

10. At the Computers screen, you can choose what computers you will authorize or allow through this rule (exceptions). Again, you can experiment with these options if you want. Click Next to continue.

11. At the Profiles screen, choose which profiles will be affected by this rule. Select one or more profiles and click Next.

12. Give your profile a name and description, and then click Finish. Your custom rule will appear in the list of inbound rules, and the rule will be enabled.

13. Double-click your newly created rule. Notice that you can change the options that you previously configured.

14. Delete the rule by right-clicking it and choosing Delete. A dialog box will appear asking you if you are sure. Click Yes.

15. Close the Windows Firewall.

Connection Security Rules

Connection security rules are used to configure how and when authentication occurs. These rules do not specifically allow connections; that's the job of inbound and outbound rules. You can configure the following connection security rules:

- Isolation: To restrict a connection based on authentication criteria
- Authentication Exemption: To specify computers that are exempt from authentication requirements
- Server-to-Server: To authenticate connections between computers
- Tunnel: To authenticate connections between gateway computers
- Custom

Monitoring

The Monitoring section shows detailed information about the firewall configurations for the Domain Profile, Private Profile, and Public Profile settings. These network location profiles determine what settings are enforced for private networks, public networks, and networks connected to a domain.

 Real World Scenario

Use More Than Just Windows Defender Firewall

When doing consulting, it always makes me laugh when I see small to midsize companies using Microsoft Windows Defender Firewall and no other protection. Microsoft Windows Defender Firewall should be your *last* line of defense. You need to make sure that you have good hardware firewalls that separate your network from the world.

Also watch Windows Defender Firewall when it comes to printing. I have run into many situations where a printer that needs to communicate with the operating system has issues when Windows Defender Firewall is enabled. If this happens, make sure that the printer is allowed in the Allowed Programs section.

Summary

There are two different ways that you can format your hard disk in a Windows 10 operating system: FAT32 and NTFS. NTFS has many advantages over FAT32, including security, encryption (before Windows 10 and Server 2016), disk quotas, and compression, just to name a few.

Devices and hardware are two very important components that must be properly configured in Windows 10 to guarantee the best possible machine performance. Using Device Manager and Devices (under Settings) is an effective way to help manage these devices and drivers.

Another important task that we have to configure is setting up our print devices. The print devices are the physical machines that spit the print jobs out. The printer is the drivers that allow the print device to communicate with Windows 10.

Finally, we also discussed using Windows Firewall with Advanced Security. Windows Firewall helps prevent unauthorized users from connecting to the Windows 10 operating system. Windows Firewall is an extra line of defense, but it should not replace a perimeter firewall for your network.

Exam Essentials

Understand the different file format options.   There are two ways to format a hard disk in Windows 10: FAT32 and NTFS. Understand that NTFS offers many benefits over FAT32, including security, compression, and disk quotas.

Know how to verify whether drivers are signed.   Microsoft includes with Windows 10 a utility called Sigverif.exe for users to verify whether their drivers are digitally signed on their machines. Sigverif.exe will scan your machine and verify that all drivers are properly signed. If they are not signed, Sigverif.exe will show you which drivers are not signed.

Know how to configure devices and drivers.   Understand how to configure devices and drivers in Device Manager. Know how to roll back drivers and how to update drivers when newer versions are released. Know how to use Devices (under Settings) and how to add devices in Device Manager.

Know how to configure printers and print devices.   Understand how to configure printers and print devices in Printers & Scanners. Know how to connect to a print device and how to manage the jobs that are sent to the printer.

Know how to configure Windows Firewall.   Know how to set up and maintain Windows Firewall with Advanced Security. Know that you can set up inbound and outbound rules by using Windows Firewall. Know how to allow or deny applications by using Windows Firewall.

Video Resources

There are videos available for the following exercises:

5.7

5.12

You can access the videos at `http://www.wiley.com/go/sybextestprep`.

Review Questions

1. You are the network administrator for your organization. You have been asked by the owner of the company to verify that all drivers installed on the Windows 10 machines are signed drivers. How do you accomplish this task?

   A. Run `Verify.exe` at the command prompt.

   B. Run a scan in Device Manager.

   C. Run `Sigverif.exe` at the command prompt.

   D. Run `Drivers.exe` at the command prompt.

2. You are the network administrator for your organization. You have a Windows 10 Enterprise system called PS1 that is configured with multiple shared print queues. You need to migrate the print queues to a new machine called PS2. How do you do that?

   A. Use the Migrate Printers utility in the Print Management tool.

   B. Use the Migrate Printers utility in the Control Panel.

   C. Use the Migrate Printers utility in the Printers & Scanners utility.

   D. Use the Export Printers tool in the Print Management tool.

3. Your computer uses a SCSI adapter that supports a SCSI drive, which contains your Windows 10 system and boot partitions. After updating the SCSI driver, you restart your computer, but Windows 10 will load but with errors. You need to get this computer up and running as quickly as possible. Which of the following strategies should you try first to correct your problem?

   A. Restore your computer's configuration with your last backup.

   B. Boot your computer with the System Image reload.

   C. Boot your computer and do a driver rollback.

   D. Boot your computer to the Recovery Console and manually copy the old driver back to the computer.

4. You are about to install a new driver for your CD-ROM drive, but you are not 100 percent sure that you are using the correct driver. Which of the following options will allow you to *most easily* return your computer to the previous state if the new driver is not correct?

   A. Safe Mode

   B. Roll Back Driver

   C. System Restore utility

   D. Startup Repair tool

5. You are the network administrator for your organization. Your organization has been using Windows 10 Enterprise. You need to run the Print Management tools from the command prompt. What command do you run?

   A. `Printmgmt.exe`

   B. `PrintMig.exe`

    C. Prtmgmt.exe

    D. Printbrm.exe

6. You are using Windows 10 Professional and you have a hardware component that is no longer needed. You do not want to delete the drivers but you do not want them active. What can you do to the drivers?

    A. Remove the drivers using Device Manager.

    B. Disable the drivers using Device Manager.

    C. Upgrade the drivers using Device Manager.

    D. Roll back the drivers using Device Manager.

7. You are the network administrator for a small organization. Your organization has implemented Windows 10 on all client machines. You want to implement another line of security on the Windows 10 machine so unauthorized users can't access the machines. What can you implement on the Windows 10 machines?

    A. Windows Data Protection

    B. Windows Encryption Protection

    C. Windows Defender Firewall

    D. Windows Secure Data Protocol

8. You are the network administrator for a large organization. One of your users calls you and states that they think they are having issues with their network card. What tool can you use to see if the hardware is working properly?

    A. Device Hardware

    B. Manage Hardware

    C. Device Manager

    D. Device Configuration

9. You are the network administrator for a large organization. You have a Windows 10 machine that is working fine, but you downloaded and installed a newer version of the network adapter driver. After you load the driver, the network device stops working properly. Which tool should you use to help you fix the problem?

    A. Driver rollback

    B. Driver Repair utility

    C. Reverse Driver application

    D. Windows 10 Driver Compatibility tool

10. You are using Windows 10 and you want to update your video drivers. How do you accomplish this?

    A. Install new drivers using Driver Manager.

    B. Upgrade the drivers using Device Manager.

    C. Upgrade the drivers using Driver Manager.

    D. Install new drivers using Device Manager.

Chapter

6

Configuring Network Connectivity

MICROSOFT EXAM OBJECTIVES COVERED IN THIS CHAPTER:

✓ **Configure networking**

- Configure client IP settings; configure mobile networking; configure VPN client; troubleshoot networking; configure Wi-Fi profiles.

When it comes to Windows 10, I think it's important to understand how to set up a network. In most IT departments, you install applications through the network. Also, when your users authenticate, they normally authenticate onto a network.

For most of us, our Windows 10 devices will be configured on some type of a network. It doesn't matter if it's a home network or a corporate network, Windows 10 will normally belong to some type of network.

Because of this, it is very important to know how to properly configure and design a Windows network. In this chapter, we discuss Active Directory and how to configure Windows 10 to work within the Windows Server domain environment.

So let's begin this chapter with the basics and what networking is all about.

Understanding the Basics

Microsoft uses three networking models: domain-based networks, workgroup networks, and HomeGroup networks. HomeGroup networks and workgroup networks are basically the same type of network, called peer-to-peer. The difference between a workgroup and HomeGroup network is just how you set up the network.

The way you design your network is going to determine how you set up the rest of the computers and servers on that network. The choice you make here will be determined by many factors, including the number of users on your network and the amount of money you can spend.

Peer-to-Peer Networks

When setting up a Microsoft Windows *peer-to-peer network* (also referred to as a *workgroup*), it is important to understand that all computers on the network are equal. All of the peer-to-peer computers, also referred to as *nodes*, simultaneously act as both clients and servers.

Peer-to-peer networks are typically any combination of Microsoft Windows XP, Windows Vista, Windows 7, Windows 8 / 8.1, and Windows 10 machines connected by a centralized device such as a router, switch, or hub (see Figure 6.1).

FIGURE 6.1   Peer-to-peer model

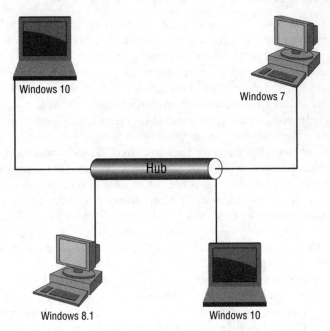

One of the biggest debates among IT professionals is when to use a peer-to-peer net-work. These types of networks have their place in the networking world. Most home net-works use this type of configuration—where all of the computers are connected by a small Internet router. It's often the same for companies. You would use this network configura-tion in a small environment with 10 users or fewer. This enables small organizations to still share resources without needing expensive equipment, server software, or an internal IT department.

But there is a downside to peer-to-peer networks; the biggest issues are manageability and security. Many new IT people like working on a small peer-to-peer network because of its size, but no matter what, a network with 10 users and 10 computers can be very dif-ficult to manage, and security is extremely difficult to set up. Because there is no server to centralize user accounts on a peer-to-peer network, each Microsoft Windows 7, Windows 8/8.1, and Windows 10 computer must have a user account and password. So if you have 10 users and 10 computers and all 10 users must be able to access all 10 computers, you end up creating 100 accounts: 10 accounts on each machine times 10 machines.

Another disadvantage of peer-to-peer networks is backups. Most IT departments do not back up individual user machines, and because there is no centralized server for data stor-age when using a peer-to-peer network, data recoverability can be an issue.

Now that you have seen the advantages and disadvantages of a peer-to-peer network, let's discuss the advantages and disadvantages of a domain-based network.

On-site Active Directory Networks

A *domain-based* network uses Microsoft's *Active Directory*, which is a single distributed database that contains all the objects in your network. A domain is a logical grouping of objects into a distributed database. Some of these objects are user accounts, group accounts, and published objects (folders and printers).

The first of many advantages to Active Directory is centralized management. As just stated, the Active Directory database contains all the network information within a single, distributed data repository. Because these network objects are all located in the same database, an administrator can easily manage the domain from one location.

Another major advantage to using Active Directory is domain security. An administrator has the advantage of creating a unique username and password for each user within the domain. These usernames and passwords can be used to access all resources that an individual has the proper rights to access. An administrator can determine, based on job function or position, which files or folders on the network a user should be granted access to and assign access to the user's single account. In our earlier peer-to-peer example, you needed to create 100 user accounts. With a domain, you would need to create only the 10 accounts, one per person.

An Active Directory structure is made up of one or more domains. As explained, a *domain* is a logical grouping of objects within your organization. For example, if we had the WillPanek.com domain, all users in that domain should be members of the WillPanek.com organization. The objects that are contained within a domain do not need to be in the same physical location. Domains can span the entire globe even though they are part of the same organization.

One of the advantages to using domains is the ability to have a *child domain*, which is a subdomain of another domain. You can build child domains based on physical locations, departments, and so forth. Figure 6.2 shows the hierarchy structure of WillPanek.com with its child domains (based on geographic location).

 Microsoft Active Directory domains are represented as triangles. It is important to remember that when taking any Microsoft exam.

Child domains give you greater scalability. Active Directory has the ability to store millions of objects within a single domain, but child domains give an administrator the flexibility to design a structure that meets an organization's needs. For example, you may have a site located in a different state. Creating a child domain for that office allows that office to be an independent domain, and thus they can have their own security and domain settings. One or more domains that follow the same contiguous namespace are called a tree. For example, if my domain name is WillPanek.com and the child domains are NH.WillPanek.com, Arizona.WillPanek.com, and Florida.WillPanek.com, this would be a tree. All of these domains follow the WillPanek.com namespace.

FIGURE 6.2   Domain structure

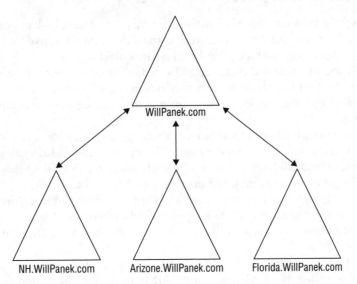

When you set up child domains, the parent and child domains automatically establish a trust relationship. *Trusts* allow users to be granted access to resources in a domain even when their accounts reside in a different domain. To make administration of trust relationships easier, Microsoft has made transitive two-way trusts the default relationship between domains within a forest. A forest is all the trees that are part of your Active Directory structure, and they share a schema and global catalog. This means that by default, all domains within the same forest automatically trust one another. As shown in Figure 6.2, WillPanek.com automatically trusts NH.WillPanek.com, Arizona.WillPanek.com, and Florida.WillPanek.com. This means that all of the child domains implicitly trust one another.

The last Active Directory advantage that we will discuss is an extensible schema. The Active Directory schema contains all the objects and attributes of the database. For example, when you create a new user by using the Active Directory Users and Computers Snap-in, the system asks you to fill in the user's first name, last name, username, password, and so forth. These fields are the attributes of the user object, and the way that the system knows to prompt for these fields is that the user object has these specific attributes assigned to it within the Active Directory schema. An administrator has the ability to change or expand these fields based on organizational needs.

The major disadvantage to an Active Directory model is cost. When setting up an Active Directory domain, an organization needs a machine that's powerful enough to handle the Windows Server operating system. Also, most companies that decide to use a domain-based organization will require the IT personnel to manage and maintain the network infrastructure.

Cloud-Based Azure Active Directory

Now that you have been introduced to Active Directory, let's take a look at how you can have Microsoft manage your Active Directory with its cloud-based Active Directory called *Azure*. Azure is Microsoft's subscription-based Active Directory service.

If you are a small to midsized company and you don't want to worry about employing a full-time multi-person IT department, then this may be a great option for you. This allows Microsoft to deal with the worries of managing and maintaining a server room and all of the hardware.

All your company would need to do is hire or train someone who would add and maintain the actual Azure Active Directory accounts. This person could also work as the help desk or support individual. Now you have Microsoft worrying about the hardware and your IT people can focus on helping and maintaining users and accounts.

So how does Azure Active Directory compare when it comes to adding Windows 10 to the domain? It really doesn't matter. As long as you have Internet access to the cloud-based system, your Windows 10 accounts will work the same way as if the Active Directory was on premise.

Windows 10 includes a new feature for configuring and deploying corporation-owned Windows devices called Azure AD Join. Azure AD Join registers the Windows 10 devices in the Azure Active Directory, which then allows them to be accessible and managed by your organization.

The one nice advantage is that with Azure Active Directory, Windows 10 devices authenticate directly to Azure AD without the need of an on-site domain controller. But, if you want, you can still have a domain controller on-site that works with the cloud-based Azure Active Directory.

When you are adding Windows 10 to Azure Active Directory, end users or domain admins can join their Windows 10 device (computer, tablet, or phone) to Azure AD during the out-of-box experience (OOBE). Because of this, organizations can assign devices to their users with no IT interaction or staging time.

Because of the Azure AD Join built into Windows 10, during the OOBE, the IT department would just add the device to the Azure Active Directory network.

Now that you understand the difference between a workgroup and a domain, let's go ahead and make sure that you understand some of the other networking terms that you will need to know.

Other Microsoft Networking Terms and Roles

Now that you have seen the different Microsoft networking models, let's talk about some of the server terminology that is used in the remainder of this chapter. You may be familiar with some of these terms, but it's always good to get a refresher.

Server   A *server* is a machine that users connect to so they can access resources located on that machine. These resources can be files, printers, applications, and so forth. Usually, the type of server is dependent on the resource that the user needs. For example, a print server is a server that controls printers. A file server contains files. Application servers can run applications for the users. Sometimes you will hear a server referred to by the specific application that it may be running. For example, someone may say, "That's our SQL server" or "We have an Exchange server."

Domain Controller   This is a server that contains a replica of the Active Directory database. As mentioned earlier in this chapter, Active Directory is the database that contains all the security objects in your network along with any resources that you publish to Active Directory. A *domain controller* is a server that contains this database. All domain controllers are equal in a Windows Server network, and each can read from and write to the directory database unless it's a Read Only Domain Controller (RODC). Some domain controllers may contain extra roles, but they are all part of the same Active Directory network.

Member Server   A *member server* is a server that is a member of a domain-based network but does not contain a copy of Active Directory. For example, it is recommended by Microsoft that a Microsoft Exchange server be loaded on a member server instead of a domain controller. Both domain controllers and member servers can act as file, print, or application servers. Your choice of server type depends on whether you need that server to have a replica of Active Directory.

Network Discovery   *Network Discovery* is a setting that determines whether your Windows 10 system can locate other computers and devices on the network and if other computers on the network can see your computer. To enable or disable Network Discovery, you need to complete the following steps:

1. Click the Start button ➤ Windows System ➤ Control Panel.
2. Choose Network and Sharing Center, then Change Advanced Sharing Settings.
3. Click Turn On/Turn Off Network Discovery, and then click the Save Changes button.

Stand-Alone Server   A *stand-alone server* is not a member of a domain. Many organizations may use this type of server for virtualization. For example, say you load Windows Server with Hyper-V (Microsoft's virtualization server) on a stand-alone server. You can then create virtual machines that act as domain controllers to run the network.

Client Machine   A *client machine* is a computer that normally is used by a company's end users. The most common operating systems for a client machine are Windows XP, Windows Vista, Windows 7, Windows 8/ 8.1, and Windows 10.

DNS Server   A *Domain Name Service (DNS)* server has the DNS service running on it. DNS is a name-resolution service that resolves a hostname to a TCP/IP address (called forward lookup). DNS also has the ability to resolve a TCP/IP address to a name (called reverse lookup). When you install an operating system onto a computer, you assign that computer a hostname. The problem is that computers talk to each other by using TCP/IP addresses, such as, for example, 192.168.1.100. It would be very difficult for most users to remember all the different TCP/IP addresses on a network. So normally you connect to a machine by using its hostname. DNS does the conversion of hostname to TCP/IP address for you.

The easiest way to understand how this works is to think of your phone number. If someone wants to call you but doesn't have your telephone number, they can call Information. They give Information your name, and they get your phone number. This is basically how a network works as well. DNS is Information on your network. You give DNS a hostname, and it returns a network telephone number (TCP/IP address). DNS is a requirement if you want to install Active Directory. You can install DNS before or during the Active Directory installation, but DNS is required for an Active Directory installation to occur. DNS can help resolve either IPv4 or IPv6 TCP/IP addresses, both of which are explained later in this chapter, in the section "Understanding TCP/IP."

The reason that DNS can resolve both IPv4 and IPv6 is because of the Link Local Multicast Name Resolution, or LLMNR, protocol, which is based on DNS packet formats that allow both IPv4 and IPv6 hosts to perform name resolution for hosts on the same local network.

DHCP Server   *A Dynamic Host Configuration Protocol (DHCP)* server runs the DHCP service, which assigns TCP/IP information to your computers dynamically. Every computer needs three settings to operate properly (with the Internet and an intranet): a TCP/IP address, a subnet mask, and a default gateway (router address). Your computers can get this minimum information two ways: manually, where someone manually types in the TCP/IP information on the machine, or dynamically, where the DHCP service automatically assigns the machine an address. DHCP can assign more than just these three settings. DHCP can assign any TCP/IP configuration information, including the address of a DNS server, WINS server, time servers, and so forth.

Continuing with our scenario from the DNS server description, DHCP would be the phone company. DHCP is the component that assigns the telephone number (TCP/IP number).

If you are using DHCP and your Windows 10 machine receives a 169.254.*x*.*x* TCP/IPv4 address, your client is not able to connect to the DHCP server. Windows 10 machines will automatically assign themselves a 169.254.*x*.*x* TCP/IPv4 number when DHCP is unavailable. This is called Automatic Private IP Addressing (APIPA). DHCP can issue both IPv4 or IPv6 TCP/IP addresses.

Global Catalog   The *Global Catalog* is a database of all Active Directory objects in a forest with only a subset of the object attributes. Think of the Global Catalog as an index. If you needed to look something up in this Windows 10 book, you would go to the index and find what page you need to turn to. You would not just randomly look through the book for the information. This is the same purpose the Global Catalog serves in your Active Directory forest. When you need to find a resource in the domain (user, published printer, and so forth), you can search the Global Catalog to find its location.

Domain controllers need to use a Global Catalog to help with user authentication. Global Catalogs are a requirement on an Active Directory domain. All domain controllers can be

Global Catalogs, but this is not always a good practice. Your network should have at least two Global Catalogs for redundancy, but too many can cause too much Global Catalog replication traffic unless you have a single-domain model.

Port Numbers   Port numbers are used by applications and services so that they can communicate with a network or a computer system. Think of port numbers as doorways that are used for the application or service. So for example, if a user wants to connect to the Internet, they use port number 80.

Configuring NIC Devices

Before you can connect a Windows 10 machine to the domain, you must set up the *network interface card (NIC)*—a hardware component used to connect computers or other devices to the network to allow the machines to communicate with each other. NICs are responsible for providing the physical connection that recognizes the physical address of the device where they are installed.

 The Open Systems Interconnection (OSI) model defines the encapsulation technique that builds the basic data structure for data transport across an internetwork. The OSI model provides interoperability among hardware vendors, network protocols, and applications. The physical address is the OSI model Layer 2 address or, for Ethernet technologies, the MAC (Media Access Control) address. This is not an IP address, which is the OSI Layer 3, or Network layer, also generically defined as the logical address.

We generically call the interface between our network devices and the software components of the machines *network adapters* (also referred to as a NICs). Most commonly, you see network adapters installed on computers, but you also see network adapters installed in network printers and specialized devices such as intrusion detection systems (IDSs) and firewalls. Network adapters do not need to be separate cards; they can be built in, as in the case of most PCs today or other network-ready devices, such as network cameras and network media players. These adapters (and all other hardware devices) need a driver to communicate with the Windows 10 operating system.

Before you physically install a network adapter, it's important to read the vendor's instructions that come with the hardware. Most network adapters you get today should be self-configuring, using Plug and Play capabilities. After you install a network adapter that supports Plug and Play, it should work following the installation procedure (which should be automated if the vendor says it is). You might have to restart, but our operating systems are getting much better with this, and you might just get lucky and be ready to use the device immediately.

If you happen to have a network adapter that is not Plug and Play, the operating system should detect the new piece of hardware and start a wizard that leads you through the process of loading the adapter's driver and setting initial configuration parameters. You can see your network connection and manage the network connection properties through the Network and Sharing Center.

Configuring a Network Adapter

After you have installed the network adapter, you configure it through its Properties dialog box. You can get to the network adapter properties pages via the Network and Sharing Center (detailed in the section "Configuring Wireless Network Settings" later in this chapter), through Computer Management, or through Device Manager.

To use the Device Manager applet for the network adapter configuration, right-click Start and choose Device Manager. This launches the Device Manager MMC (Microsoft Management Console), shown in Figure 6.3.

FIGURE 6.3   Device Manager MMC

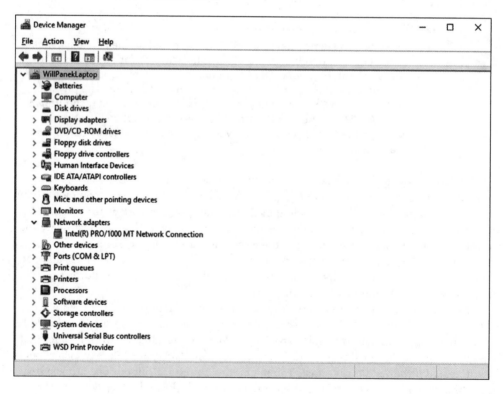

Figure 6.3 shows the Network Adapters device category expanded, and the adapter is installed in the machine. Accessing the network adapter properties allows us to view and change configuration parameters of the adapter. You do this by right-clicking the adapter in Device Manager and selecting Properties from the context menu. Each tab is detailed in the following list.

General Tab   The General tab of the Network Adapter's Properties dialog box (Figure 6.4) shows the name of the adapter, the device type, the manufacturer, and the location. The Device Status box reports whether the device is working properly. If not, the Device Status box gives you an error code and a brief description of what Windows 10 identifies as the issue. You can perform an Internet search for the error code(s) if the text is not sufficient.

FIGURE 6.4   General tab of the Network Adapter's Properties page

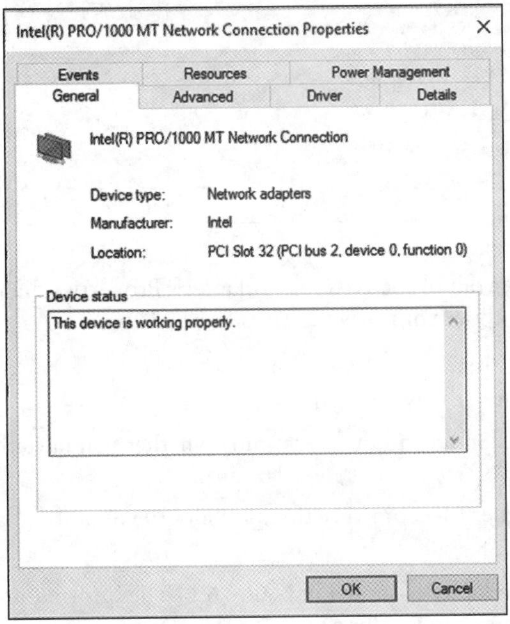

Advanced Tab   The contents of the Advanced tab of a Network Adapter's Properties dialog box vary depending on the network adapter and driver that you are using. Figure 6.5 shows an example of the Advanced tab for my Fast Ethernet adapter. To configure options in this dialog box, choose the property you want to modify in the Property list box and specify the desired value for the property in the Value box on the right.

FIGURE 6.5   Advanced tab of the Network Adapter's Properties page

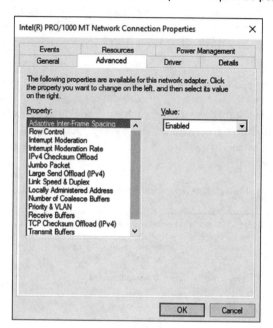

Driver Tab   The Driver tab of the Network Adapter's Properties dialog box provides the following information about your driver:

- The driver provider

- The date the driver was released

- The driver version (useful in determining whether you have the latest driver installed)

- The digital signer (the company that provides the digital signature for driver signing)

The Driver tab for my adapter is shown in Figure 6.6. The information here varies from driver to driver and even from vendor to vendor. The Driver Details button on the Driver tab brings up the Driver File Details dialog box that provides the following details about the driver:

- The location of the driver file (useful for troubleshooting)

- The original provider of the driver

- The file version (useful for troubleshooting)

- Copyright information about the driver

- The digital signer for the driver

The Update Driver button starts a wizard to step you through upgrading the driver for an existing device. The Roll Back Driver button allows you to roll back to the previously installed driver if you update your network driver and encounter problems. In Figure 6.6, the Roll Back Driver button is grayed out (not available) because I have not updated the driver or a previous driver is not available. The Disable button is used to disable the device. After you disable the device, the Disable button changes into an Enable button, which you can use to enable the device. The Uninstall button removes the driver from your computer's configuration. You would uninstall the driver if you were going to remove the device from your system or if you want to completely remove the driver configuration from your system so you can reinstall it from scratch either automatically or manually.

FIGURE 6.6 Driver tab of the Network Adapter's Properties page

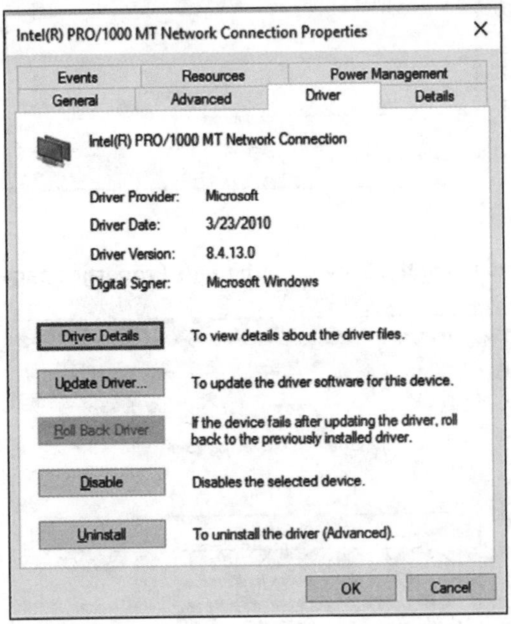

Details Tab   The Details tab of the network adapter's Properties dialog box lists the resource settings for your network adapter. Information found on the Details tab varies by hardware device. I have included the Details tab information from my adapter in Figure 6.7, with the Property drop-down list box set to Device description.

Events Tab   The Events tab (Figure 6.8) of the network adapter's Properties dialog box shows you some of the device events that have happened to this piece of hardware. There is also a View All Events button that opens the Event Viewer MMC, which shows you all events for this device. This is a good way to look to see if there have been any events or issues (like errors or warnings) for the device.

FIGURE 6.7   Details tab of the Network Adapter's Properties page

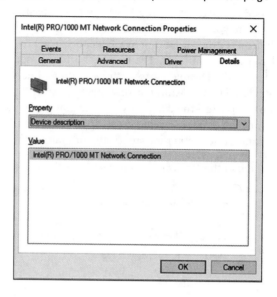

FIGURE 6.8   Events tab of the Network Adapter's Properties page

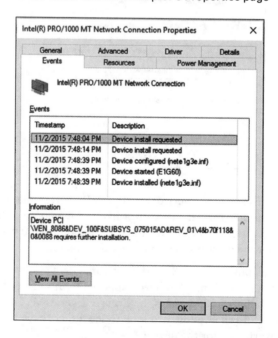

Resources Tab   The Resources tab of the Network Adapter's Properties dialog box
(Figure 6.9) lists the resource settings for your network adapter. Resources include interrupt request (IRQ), memory, and input/output (I/O) resources. This information can be

important for troubleshooting if other devices are trying to use the same resource settings. This is not normally the case because Windows 10 and the Plug and Play specification should set up nonconflicting parameters. If there are issues, the Conflicting Device List box at the bottom of the Resources tab will show the conflicts.

FIGURE 6.9   Resources tab of the Network Adapter's Properties page

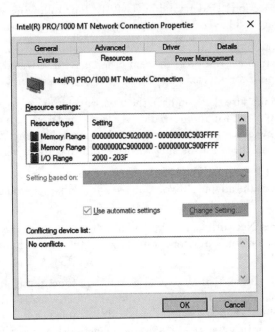

Power Management Tab   The Power Management tab (Figure 6.10) of the network adapter's Properties dialog box allows you to set up how this device can save power on the system. For example, you can allow the system to turn off this device and also allow this device to wake the system from sleep mode.

FIGURE 6.10   Power Management tab of the Network Adapter's Properties page

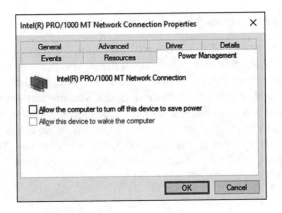

Troubleshooting a Network Adapter

When installing the NIC, you may encounter some problems or errors. Let's take a look at some NIC troubleshooting.

If your network adapter is not working, the problem might be with the hardware, the driver software, or the network protocols. I discuss the Layer 3 (Network layer) issues later in this chapter in the section "Understanding TCP/IP." The following are some common Layer 1 (Physical layer) and Layer 2 (Data Link layer) causes for network adapter problems:

Network Adapter Not on the HCL If the device is not on the Hardware Compatibility List (HCL), use your Internet resources to see if others have discovered a solution, or contact the hardware vendor for advice.

Outdated Driver Make sure that you have the most current driver for your adapter. You can have Windows 10 check for an updated driver from the Driver tab of the Properties page for the adapter by clicking the Update Driver button and having Windows search for a better driver, or you can check for the latest driver on the hardware vendor's website.

Network Adapter Not Recognized by Windows 10 Check Device Manager to see whether Windows 10 recognizes the adapter. If you don't see your adapter, you can try to manually install it.

Improperly Configured Network Card Verify that the settings for the network card are correct for the parameters known within your network and for the hardware device the machine is connected to.

Cabling Problem Make sure that all network cables are functioning and are the correct type. This includes making sure that the connector is properly seated, the cable is straight or crossed (depending on where it's plugged in), and the cable is not broken. This is usually done by looking at the little green light (LGL) on the network adapter card. This does not guarantee a good connection even if the LGLs are illuminated. A single conductor failure in a cable can still have a link light on, but data is not passing.

Bad Network Connection Device Verify that all network connectivity hardware is properly working. For example, on a Fast Ethernet network, make sure the switch and port being used are functioning properly.

Configuring Wireless NIC Devices

Wireless technology has matured to the point of becoming cost effective and secure. The use of wireless network adapters is increasingly popular, scaling well out of the home and into the workplace. Windows 10 supports wireless auto-configuration, which makes wireless network connections easy to use. Windows 10 will automatically discover the wireless networks available and connect your machine to the preferred wireless network.

One of the advantages to setting up Windows 10 and wireless connections is that once you have connected to a wireless access point (WAP), your Windows 10 will remember that and reconnect you to that preferred wireless network when your Windows 10 system is in range.

Configuring Wireless Network Settings

If you have a wireless network adapter compatible with Windows 10, it will be automatically recognized by the operating system. This can be a built-in adapter such as those most modern laptops come with, a wireless card you install in the machine, or even a wireless USB adapter. After it is installed, it is shown in Device Manager as well as in the Network and Sharing Center within the View Your Active Networks section.

We used Device Manager in the previous section for the network adapter configuration, so let's use the Network and Sharing Center for the wireless network configuration. Figure 6.11 shows the Network and Sharing Center with one active network, the wireless network connection called Trend.

FIGURE 6.11   Network and Sharing Center

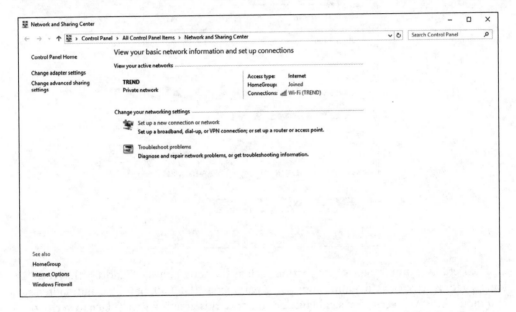

You can perform any of the following steps to access the Network and Sharing Center:

- Type **Network and Sharing Center** in the integrated search box of Windows 10.

- Click Start ➢ Windows System ➢ Control Panel ➢ Network And Internet ➢ Network And Sharing Center (if Control Panel view is Category).

- Click Start ➢ Windows System ➢ Control Panel ➢ Network And Sharing Center (if Control Panel view is Large Icons or Small Icons).

- Right-click the network icon in the lower-right Taskbar and choose Open Network And Sharing Center.

- Click Start ➢ Settings ➢ Network And Internet and then choose either the Wi-Fi or Ethernet Connection link.

Viewing the Wireless Network Connection Status

From the Network and Sharing Center, you have easy access to the Wireless Network Connection Status window, which gives you an initial look at the status by providing the Layer 3 connectivity status (IPv4 and IPv6), media state, service set identifier (SSID) being used, how long the connection has been active (Duration), the negotiated speed of the connection, and the signal quality, as shown in Figure 6.12.

FIGURE 6.12 Wireless Network Connection Status window

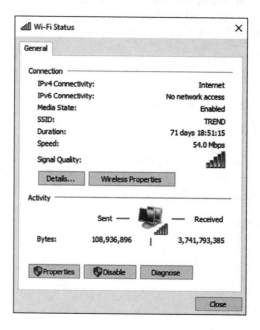

The Details button provides information such as the actual physical address (Layer 2), logical address (Layer 3), dynamic addressing parameters (DHCP), name-resolution items, and more. After you verify Physical layer parameters, this area is a great place to verify or troubleshoot logical (driver/software) issues.

Viewing Wireless Network Connection Details

If you have a wireless adapter in your machine, perform Exercise 6.1 to view the network connection details for your wireless network connection.

EXERCISE 6.1

Viewing the Network Connection Details

1. Click Start ➢ Windows System ➢ Control Panel ➢ Network And Internet ➢ Network And Sharing Center (if Control Panel view is Category).

2. Select the Wireless Network Connection menu item from the View Your Active Networks section.

3. Click the Details button.

4. Review the network connection details for this connection.

The Wireless Network Connection Status window has an Activity section showing real-time traffic (in bytes) being sent from and received by the wireless network. From the Wireless Network Connection Status window, you also have access to the Wireless Network Connection Properties, which includes access to the wireless adapter configuration pages.

You access the properties page by clicking the Properties button in the Activity section (refer back to Figure 6.12). The Wi-Fi Properties page has a Networking tab (see Figure 6.13) that shows which network adapter is being used for this connection (which you can change if you have more than one available).

FIGURE 6.13   Wi-Fi Properties window's Networking tab

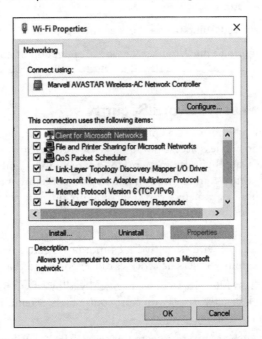

The section that begins with "This connection uses the following items" displays the various clients, services, and protocols that are currently available for this connection.

You can install or uninstall network clients, network services, and network protocols by clicking the appropriate button. You can also view the client, service, or protocol properties if they are available by first highlighting the item from the list and then clicking the

Properties button for the selected item. If the Properties button is gray, a properties page is not available for the item. From the Wireless Network Connection Properties window, you even have access to the network adapter's hardware configuration property pages. These are the same pages you have access to from Device Manager.

Perform Exercise 6.2 to access the network adapter properties from the Wireless Network Connection Properties page.

EXERCISE 6.2

Viewing Wireless Network Connection Properties

1. Click Start ➤ Windows System ➤ Control Panel ➤ Network And Internet ➤ Network And Sharing Center (if Control Panel view is Category).

2. Select the Wireless Network Connection menu item in the View Your Active Networks section.

3. Click the Properties button in the Activity section.

4. Click the Configure button.

5. View the various tabs regarding the network adapter properties.

6. Choose Cancel to return to the Wireless Network Connection Status window.

Configuring Wireless Network Security

Wireless network security is a very large piece of setting up our wireless networks. The focal point for this is the wireless access point or wireless router to which we connect. Whether you are using a small wireless network or a large wireless infrastructure, you should have a plan for secure communication and should configure wireless network security. There are several basic parameters you can configure on your network access devices to increase the security of a wireless network:

▪ Disable broadcast of the SSID, which is the name of the wireless network. When SSID broadcast is disabled, the wireless network cannot be detected automatically until you manually configure your wireless network card to connect to that SSID.

▪ Create a MAC address filter list so only specifically allowed wireless devices can connect to the wireless network, or you can require users attempting to connect to supply connection credentials.

▪ Enable encryption such as Wi-Fi Protected Access (WPA) or WPA2.

Real World Scenario

Wireless Connection Infrastructure or Ad Hoc?

You might not always be connecting to an access point or router; these connections are considered infrastructure mode connections. An infrastructure mode connection is similar to a wired connection of a PC to an outlet. Instead, you might connect in an ad hoc fashion, which could be a computer-to-computer connection to share information with other wireless network devices without another wireless device acting as an intermediary.

Ad hoc connections exist in a wired environment as well, when we connect two PCs' NICs together by using an Ethernet crossover cable. Securing data transfer in an ad hoc wireless setup is just as important as it is in infrastructure mode because the data is still traversing between devices using radio frequency (RF) and network sniffers today running the wireless adapter promiscuously (in monitor mode) have no problem viewing the data stream. If the data stream is not encrypted, sniffers will have access to it.

For large implementations, there are several vendors supplying wireless access points under the control of a wireless director, which consists of software-based controllers that are responsible for allowing access points on the network, providing user access control, and enforcing encryption policies. For smaller implementations, this control functionality is done manually as the wireless routers or access points are set up.

The security policies put in place are configured on the wireless access device and the wireless client. Windows 10 client components must be set up to match the security settings of the wireless network access devices. During the setup of most wireless access devices provided by the hardware vendor, the administrator will configure the security parameters. Configuring can be done during the setup process and/or through a web browser that can access the wireless access device configuration pages.

Most of our current devices have a built-in web server to allow the HTTP connection from a web browser. Windows 10 also has the ability to configure the wireless access device if the hardware vendor makes it available. If there is no specific component written, you can launch the web browser–based configuration from a convenient location—the Network and Sharing Center.

Whether you have Windows 10 configure the wireless network connection or you perform the setup through the manufacturer's process, you still need to configure your Windows 10 client access.

If you have performed the simplest configuration and there are no security parameters configured (bad idea, by the way), Windows 10 will connect automatically with a quick window showing the wireless network it's connecting to and providing access without much user intervention. Even canceling the screens will produce a successful (nonsecure) connection. This simple configuration process makes connecting a home or small network easy and straightforward for nontechnical users. However, this is not a good solution.

If you have configured wireless network security (a good idea!), then you need to configure the Windows 10 client with the correct settings. Once again, the configuration screens are available from the convenient location known as the Network and Sharing Center.

In Exercise 6.3, you will access the Windows 10 client wireless network properties.

EXERCISE 6.3

Accessing the Windows 10 Wireless Properties

1. Click Start ≻ Windows System ≻ Control Panel ≻ Network And Internet ≻ Network And Sharing Center (if Control Panel view is Category).

2. Choose the Wireless Network Connection item within the View Your Active Networks section of the Network and Sharing Center.

3. Click the Wireless Properties button (shown in Figure 6.14) within the Connection area of the Wi-Fi Status window.

4. The Wireless Network Properties tabbed dialog box opens, displaying the current setup for the wireless network. Click Finish to close the window.

FIGURE 6.14   Wireless Properties button

From the Wireless Network Properties tabbed dialog box, you have the ability to set or change the Windows 10 client configuration. The first tab of the dialog box is the Connection tab (Figure 6.15), which displays the following information.

FIGURE 6.15   Wireless Network Properties dialog box's Connection tab

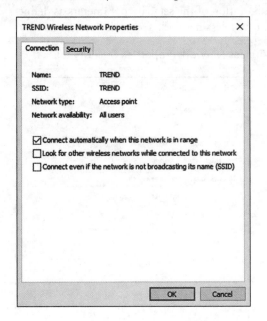

Name   The name assigned to the wireless network.

SSID   The SSID of the wireless connection. This defines a friendly name for the wireless network. This is normally an ASCII string and is usually broadcast by default, allowing a machine or users to select a wireless network with which to connect. Some wireless access devices will allow more than one SSID to be available (broadcast) at the same time, creating more than one wireless network within the same device.

Network Type   Displays the mode the wireless network is operating in. If the wireless network is in infrastructure mode, this parameter will be Access Point. If the wireless network is ad hoc, this will display Computer-To-Computer.

Network Availability   Displays to whom the wireless network is available—All Users or Me Only, for example.

Connect Automatically When This Network Is In Range   This option, when selected, allows automatic connection for this wireless network. Deselecting (clearing the check mark) requires the user to choose this wireless network for connection.

Look For Other Wireless Networks While Connected To This Network   Windows 10 will attempt to look for other wireless network connections even though you are connected to a network at the time. This allows a user to see if there is a better network connection available even after you have connected to your wireless access point.

Connect Even If The Network Is Not Broadcasting Its Name (SSID)   If the wireless network you are attempting to connect to is not broadcasting its SSID, you must select this option to allow Windows 10 to automatically connect.

The second tab on the Wireless Network Properties dialog box is Security (Figure 6.16), which allows the configuration of the security parameters as defined in your security policy and configured on your wireless network access devices.

FIGURE 6.16   Wireless Network Properties Security tab

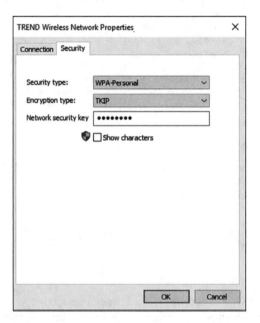

Figure 6.16 shows the Security tab's Security Type drop-down box with the WPA-Personal security choice selected and Encryption Type with TKIP (Temporal Key Integrity Protocol) selected. You can also see the network security key as hidden text because the Show Characters check box is unchecked.

Configuring Wi-Fi Direct

Think about being able to connect to devices without the use of a WAP. What if we could connect devices directly to each other through the high-speed wireless adapters in those devices? That is exactly what Wi-Fi Direct enables us to do.

Wi-Fi Direct is a technology that allows us to directly access other devices without requiring a separate Wi-Fi access point. Windows 10 uses near-field communication (better known as NFC) technology to allow the Windows 10 system to locate other NFC Wi-Fi enabled devices so that they can be paired together.

When devices are trying to pair together, the Near Field Proximity (NFP) receives pairing information from the device that is trying to connect. NFP then passes the pairing information to Windows 10. Windows 10 Wi-Fi Direct will then automatically follow the Wi-Fi Alliance Out-Of-Box pairing procedures for the connection.

If the pairing process connects, Windows will prompt the user for permission for the connection. If permission is given, Windows 10 will then attempt to finalize the connection. From that point on, there is no other user interaction needed.

Windows 10 gives you the ability to set whether you want to pair with other devices or not. Figure 6.17 shows the Windows 10 Privacy settings and how Windows 10 will sync with other devices.

FIGURE 6.17   Sync with devices

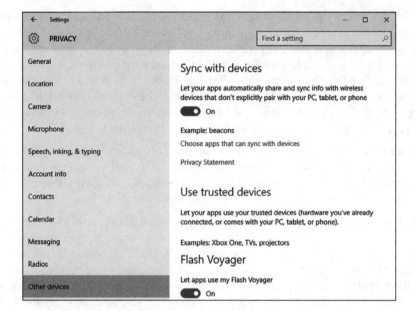

As you can see in Figure 6.17, you also have the ability to choose which applications can sync with devices. This gives an administrator or user better flexibility on whether to allow all applications to connect to all devices or only specific applications to connect.

Troubleshooting Wireless Connectivity

There are a few common issues with wireless networking you can look at if you're having problems connecting to your wireless network. Following are a few problems and solutions:

Ensure that your wireless network card is enabled.   Here's one I see regularly: Many newer laptops and tablets have either a switch or a hot-key setting that enables and disables the wireless device. Often, a laptop switch will somehow be turned off, or a user will somehow press the key sequence to shut off the PC's wireless radio. The Physical layer is always a good place to start looking.

Ensure that your wireless card and the access devices are compatible.   Cards that are compatible with the 802.11b standard can connect to only 802.11b or 802.11b/g access devices configured to accept b. Cards using 802.11a can connect to only 802.11a or 802.11a/b/g access devices configured to accept a. An 802.11n card needs to connect to an 802.11n access device for efficiency, although most will auto-negotiate to the best specification available. The specification you're using on the card has to be available and turned on in the wireless access device.

Ensure that the access point signal is available.   I find radio frequency (RF) to be a funny thing. You can't see it, and you assume that it is everywhere. Not a good assumption. The output power of the signal might be fine, but the RF power is absorbed or attenuated as it goes through walls, insulation, or water. You need to make sure there is nothing that might be causing interference of the wireless signal.

Ensure that the security parameters are configured alike.   The SSID, encryption type, encryption algorithm, and passphrase/security key have to be set the same on both the wireless access device and the wireless client. Here's another one I see quite often: In the desire to make the initial setup and the secure setup easier for end users, some hardware vendors have a nice little button that allows the network access device to negotiate a secure set of parameters with the client. In one instance, after the wireless network had been working correctly for a while, a failure showed the parameters to be incompatible, thanks in large part to someone pressing the easy button just before the failure.

Ensure automatic connections if the SSID is not being broadcast.   If you are having trouble connecting to a network that does not broadcast its SSID, select the Connect Even If The Network Is Not Broadcasting check box in the Wireless Network Properties dialog box. I have solved several wireless network connection issues with this fix.

Consider how a wireless router interfaces with hard-wired devices.   Many times when I go into a small or midsized network, I find that the company (or home user) is connected to a multifunction type of device. The wireless routers that are often deployed are really quite technologically sophisticated. They have switch ports for connecting hard-wired devices on the private network as well as an Internet port to connect to the outside world. The wireless portion of the device is like another switch port on the private side, allowing the wireless devices to interact with the hard-wired devices.

When I troubleshoot and eliminate issues, I start with the hard-wired devices and see whether they can communicate to each other and the outside (the other side of your wireless router). Try to communicate between the hard-wired and wireless as well, to eliminate the router components. It's also not the best idea to use the wireless network to configure the wireless devices. Configuring through the wireless interface will ultimately cause you to lose connectivity in the middle of a configuration and may force you to connect with the cable, often leaving the access point unusable until you complete the task you started wirelessly.

Understanding TCP/IP

Another item that we need to configure before we can connect a Windows 10 machine to the domain is the protocol that will allow the Windows 10 machine to communicate with other machines. *Transmission Control Protocol/Internet Protocol (TCP/IP)* is the most commonly used network protocol. It is actually a suite of protocols that have evolved into the industry standard for network, internetwork, and Internet connectivity.

As I explained earlier in this chapter, when I teach my Microsoft Windows classes (both server and client classes), I like to use the following example for TCP/IP. Don't think of TCP/IP as IP addresses, think of them as telephone numbers. That's right, think of them as telephone numbers. When you need to contact a server or a website, you call its telephone number (TCP/IP).

Just like telephone numbers, you may need to call Information to get someone's telephone number. Well, we have a form of information on our networks also. We call it Domain Name Service (DNS) servers. That's all DNS does. Its turns a name into a telephone number (name resolution). So when you type in www.willpanek.com, DNS turns willpanek.com into a TCP/IP number so that you can make your call to my website.

Now, just as with telephone numbers, there must be some device that acts like the telephone company that issues us our telephone numbers. Well there is, and it's called a Dynamic Host Configuration Protocol (DHCP) server. DHCP gives your users a telephone (TCP/IP) number.

If you think of TCP/IP numbers as telephone numbers, I think it makes it much easier for anyone to understand why we use them and how they work.

 The main protocols providing basic TCP/IP services include Internet Protocol (IP), Transmission Control Protocol (TCP), User Datagram Protocol (UDP), Address Resolution Protocol (ARP), Internet Control Message Protocol (ICMP), and Internet Group Management Protocol (IGMP).

Benefits and Features of TCP/IP

TCP/IP as a protocol suite was accepted as an industry standard in the 1980s and continues to be the primary internetworking protocol today. For a default installation of Windows 10, IPv4 and IPv6 are both installed by default. TCP/IP has the following benefits:

- TCP/IP is the most common protocol and is supported by almost all network operating systems. It is the required protocol for Internet access.

- TCP/IP is dependable and scalable for use in small and large networks.

- Support is provided for connectivity across interconnected networks, independent of the operating systems being used at the upper end of the OSI model or the physical components at the lower end of the OSI model.

- TCP/IP provides standard routing services for moving packets over interconnected network segments. Dividing networks into multiple subnetworks (or subnets) optimizes network traffic and facilitates network management.

- TCP/IP is designed to provide data reliability by providing a connection at the Transport layer and verifying that each data segment is received and passed to the application requiring the data by retransmitting lost information.

- TCP/IP allows for the classification of data in regard to its importance with Quality of Service. This allows important time-sensitive streams of data, such as Voice over IP, to get preferential treatment.

- TCP/IP is designed to be fault tolerant. It is able to dynamically reroute packets if network links become unavailable, assuming alternate paths exist.

- Applications can provide services such as Dynamic Host Configuration Protocol (DHCP) for TCP/IP configuration and Domain Name Service (DNS) for hostname-to-IP-address resolution.

- Windows 10 continues to support Automatic Private IP Addressing (APIPA) used by small, local-connection-only networks without a DHCP server to allow Windows 10 to automatically assign an IP address to itself.

- Support for NetBIOS over TCP/IP (NetBT) is included in Windows 10. NetBIOS is a software specification used for identifying computer resources by name as opposed to IP address. We still use TCP/IP as the network protocol, so we map the NetBIOS name to an IP address.

- The inclusion of Alternate IP Configuration allows users to have a static and a DHCP-assigned IP address mapped to a single network adapter. This feature supports mobile users who roam between different network segments.

- IPv6 incorporates a much larger address space compared to IPv4 and, more important, incorporates many of the additional features of TCP/IP into a standardized protocol. This is important because a vendor that claims to support TCP/IP only has to support the 1980s version and may not support additional features such as Internet Protocol Security (IPSec). IPv6 as a standard includes these features, allowing a more robust network protocol.

Several of the features of TCP/IP included with Windows 10 are as follows:

- Allows a common structure for network communications across a wide variety of hardware and operating systems and a lot of applications that are specifically written to configure and control it.

- TCP/IP connectivity tools allowing access to a variety of hosts across a TCP/IP network. TCP/IP tools in Windows 10 include clients for HTTP, FTP, TFTP, Telnet, Finger, and so forth. Server components for the tools are available to install as well.

- Inclusion of a Simple Network Management Protocol (SNMP) agent that can be used to monitor performance and resource use of a TCP/IP host, server, or network hardware devices.

- TCP/IP management and diagnostic tools for maintenance and diagnostic support. TCP/IP management and diagnostic commands include `ipconfig`, `arp`, `ping`, `nbtstat`, `netsh`, `route`, `nslookup`, `tracert`, and `pathping`.

- Support for TCP/IP network printing, enabling you to print to networked print devices.

- Logical and physical multihoming, enabling multiple IP addresses on a single computer for single or multiple network adapters. Multiple network adapters installed on a single computer are normally associated with routing for internetwork connectivity.

- Support for internal IP routing, which enables a Windows 10 computer to route packets among multiple network adapters installed in one machine.

- Support for virtual private networks, which enable you to transmit data securely across a public network via encapsulated and encrypted packets.

Basics of IP Addressing and Configuration

Before you can configure TCP/IP, you should have a basic understanding of TCP/IP configuration and addressing. Let's review TCP/IP addressing. To configure a TCP/IP client, you must specify an IP address, subnet mask, and default gateway (if you're going to communicate outside your local network). Depending on your network, you might want to configure a DNS server and a domain name.

You can see the Windows 10 IPv4 Properties window in Figure 6.18. I have included it here because I am going to discuss the different configuration items in the following sections. Although normally set up for automatic configuration, these parameters have been manually assigned in this figure for clarity.

FIGURE 6.18   Windows 10 TCP/IP version 4 properties

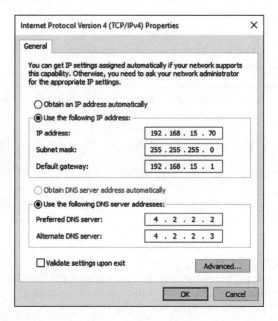

Understanding IPv4 Address Types

The IPv4 address scheme is one of two used by the Internet today, and TCP/IP is the only network protocol used by the Internet. There are three types of IPv4 addresses: broadcast, multicast, and unicast.

A *broadcast address* is read by all hosts that hear it (the broadcast will not go across a router, so only local devices hear the broadcast). The IPv4 broadcast address is 255.255.255.255; every single bit is a 1.

A *multicast address* is a special address that one or more devices will listen for by joining a multicast group. Only the local devices configured to listen for the address will respond and process the data in the multicast packet. A multicast address will have a value between 224 and 239 in the first octet (the leftmost number in the dotted decimal representation). A multicast example is 224.0.0.5.

A *unicast address* uniquely identifies a computer or device on the network. An IPv4 unicast address is a 32-bit address represented as dotted decimal (an example is 131.107.1.200). Each number in the dotted decimal notation is a decimal representation of 8 bits, and the value of each is between 0 and 255 (255 is the numerically largest value that 8 bits can represent). A portion of the IPv4 unicast address is used to identify the network the device is on (or the network of a destination device), and a portion is used to identify the individual host on the local network or the unique host on a remote network.

IPv4 Address Classes

There are three classes of unicast IP addresses defined. Depending on the class you use, different parts of the address show the default network portion of the address and the host address. Table 6.1 shows the three classes of network addresses and the number of networks and hosts available for each network class.

TABLE 6.1   IPv4 class assignments

Network Class	Address Range of First Octet	Number of Unique Networks Available	Number of Unique Hosts per Network
A	1–126	126	16,777,214
B	128–191	16,384	65,534
C	192–223	2,097,152	254

As you probably noticed, 127 is missing from the address ranges. 127.0.0.1 is the diagnostic loopback address, and because of that, no commercial TCP/IP range can start with 127.

The number of octets you can use for either the network ID or the host ID depends on which class you use for your network. For example, if I own a Class B address of 131.107.0.0, the first two octets (131.107) would be the network ID and the last two octets would be the host ID. Table 6.2 shows you the different classes and which octets are the network ID (represented by X) and which octets are the host ID (represented by Y). You are allowed to manipulate only the host IDs (Y) for your organization unless you are using a private IP address scheme.

TABLE 6.2   IPv4 network and host octets

Class	Example	Network ID	Host ID
A	17.1.10.10 (X.Y.Y.Y)	17 (X)	1.10.10 (Y.Y.Y)
B	131.107.14.240 (X.X.Y.Y)	131.107 (X.X)	14.240 (Y.Y)
C	192.168.1.10 (X.X.X.Y)	192.168.1 (X.X.X)	10 (Y)

IPv4 Subnet Mask

The *subnet mask* is used to specify which portion of the unicast IPv4 address defines the network value and which portion defines the unique host value. The subnet mask can be shown either as a dotted decimal, as with 255.255.255.0, or as a slash notation (called Classless Inter-Domain Routing, or CIDR), as in/24. The CIDR representation is the number of bits turned on in the subnet mask. For example, 255.255.224.0 is actually 11111111.11111111.11100000.00000000 (1s are on bits and 0s are off), which equals 19 bits turned on, or/19.

The standard for classful network addressing defines subnet masks for each class, as shown in Table 6.3.

TABLE 6.3   IPv4 default class subnet masks

Class	Default Mask	Slash Notation (CIDR)
A	255.0.0.0	/8
B	255.255.0.0	/16
C	255.255.255.0	/24

Another task of the subnet mask is to break down the ranges of your network. For example, 255.255.255.224 allows for six subnets. There should be six TCP/IP ranges that go with the six subnets. Table 6.4 shows the ranges for the different subnet masks.

TABLE 6.4   Subnet mask ranges

Subnet Mask Number	Ranges
255	1
254	2
252	4
248	8
240	16
224	32
192	64
128	128

What does this chart mean to you? Well, let's say that you have a subnet mask of 255.255.255.224. Because 224 allows for six subnets, the six ranges are in increments of 32. Table 6.5 shows a Class C subnet range for 224. Remember, in any range, you can't use the first number of the range (network ID) or the last number of any range (broadcast).

TABLE 6.5   Class C 224 subnet mask ranges

Subnets	Range	Usable
Range 1	0–31	1–30
Range 2	32–63	33–62
Range 3	64–95	65–94
Range 4	96–127	97–126
Range 5	128–159	129–158
Range 6	160–191	161–190
Range 7	192–223	193–222
Range 8	224-255	225-254

If this were a Class B subnet mask, the ranges would include a second octet that you would work with. Table 6.6 shows a Class B 224 subnet mask.

TABLE 6.6   Class B 224 subnet mask range

Subnets	Range	Usable
Range 1	0.0–31.255	0.1–31.254
Range 2	32.0–63.255	32.1–63.254
Range 3	64.0–95.255	64.1–95.254
Range 4	96.0–127.255	96.1–127.254
Range 5	128.0–159.255	128.1–159.254
Range 6	160.0–191.255	160.1–191.254
Range 7	192.0–223.255	192.1–223.254
Range 8	224.0-255.255	224.1-255.254

If this were a Class A subnet mask, the ranges would include three octets that you would work with. Table 6.7 shows a Class A 224 subnet mask.

TABLE 6.7   Class A 224 subnet mask range

Subnets	Range	Usable
Range 1	0.0.0–31.255.255	0.0.1-31.255.254
Range 2	32.0.0–63.255.255	32.0.1–63.255.254
Range 3	64.0.0–95.255.255	64.0.1–95.255.254
Range 4	96.0.0–127.255.255	96.0.1–127.255.254
Range 5	128.0.0–159.255.255	128.0.1–159.255.254
Range 6	160.0.0–191.255.255	160.0.1–191.255.254
Range 7	192.0.0–223.255.255	192.0.1–223.255.254

Using IPv6 Addresses

Through most of this discussion, we have been referencing TCP/IP as the network protocol. However, you should remember that it is really a suite of protocols running in Layer 3
and Layer 4 of the OSI model. Internet Protocol (IP) is the Layer 3 protocol responsible for
assigning devices globally unique addresses (that is, unique in a whole company for private
addresses and unique across the whole Internet for public addresses).

When the TCP/IP standard was adopted in the 1980s, it was unimaginable that we
would ever need more than 4 billion addresses that are possible with IPv4, but with the
dramatic growth of the use of computers in the home and workplace today, we do. In the
1990s, programmers realized that a new Layer 3 was going to be needed. This was not an
easy task, and integration into the existing infrastructure was going to take a long time.
An interim solution known as Network Address Translation (NAT) and Port Address
Translation (PAT) emerged. NAT/PAT allowed more than one device to use the same IP
address on a private network as long as there was one Internet address available. Cool
enough, but this is not the real solution. IPv6 is the solution to the IPv4 address depletion.

As time has progressed from the IPv4 standard acceptance in the 1980s, we have needed
new and better functionality. However, the way the standards process works around the
world is that you can add functionality, but it may or may not be supported in any vendor's
TCP/IPv4 network stack. What happened in IPv6 is that not only did the address space
increase in size, but the additional functionality that may or may not have been included
before has become part of the IPv6 standard.

For example, IPv4 is defined as having a variable-length header, which is cumbersome
because we need to read an additional piece of data to see how big the header is. Most of
the time, the header stays the same, so why not just fix its length and add an extension to
the header if we need to carry more information? IPv6 uses a fixed-length IP header with
the capability of carrying more information in an extension to the header, known as an
extension header.

Microsoft has been including IPv6 in its operating systems since NT 4.0; it just has not
been enabled by default. Windows 10 (as did Vista and Windows 7/8/8.1) natively supports
both IPv4 and IPv6. The main differences you will notice between IPv4 and IPv6 are the
format and size of the IP address. IPv6 addresses are 128 bits, typically written as eight
groups of four hexadecimal characters. IPv4 addresses, as you saw earlier, are 32 bits—
four decimal representations of eight bits. Each of the eight groups of characters in an
IPv6 address is separated by a colon; for example, 2001:4860:0000:0000:0012:10FF:
FECD:00EF.

Leading zeros can be omitted, so we can write our example address as 2001:4860:0:0:
12:10FF:FECD:EF. Additionally, a double colon can be used to compress a set of consecu-
tive zeros, so we could write our example address as 2001:4860::12:10FF:FECD:EF. The
IPv6 address is 128 bits; when you see a double colon, it's a variable that says to fill enough
zeros within the colons to make the address 128 bits. You can have only one set of double
colons; two variables in one address won't work.

Will IPv6 take over the global address space soon? Even with IPv4's lack of address
space, we are going to continue to use it for many years. The integration of IPv6 into the

infrastructure is going to happen as a joint venture with IPv4 and IPv6 running at the same time in the devices and on some networks.

There are many mechanisms for enabling IPv6 communications over an IPv4 network, including the following:

- Dual Stack: A computer or device running both the IPv4 and IPv6 protocol stacks at the same time

- ISATAP: Intra-Site Automatic Tunnel Addressing Protocol

- 6to4: An encapsulation technique for putting IPv6 addresses inside IPv4 addresses

- Teredo Tunneling: Another encapsulation technique for putting IPv6 traffic inside an IPv4 packet

Some IPv6-to-IPv4 dynamic translation techniques require that a computer's IPv4 address be used as the last 32 bits of the IPv6 address. When these translation techniques are used, it is common to write the last 32 bits as you would typically write an IPv4 address, such as 2001:4850::F8:192.168.122.26.

There are two ways to receive a TCP/IP address (for either IPv4 or IPv6): You can manually assign a TCP/IP address to the Windows 10 machine, or the Windows 10 machine can use DHCP.

There are several elements of the IPv4 protocol that could use some enhancements. Other elements have been added to IPv4 as extras to provide more functionality. IPv6 is designed to incorporate these enhancement/changes directly into the protocol specification.

The new concepts and new implementation of old concepts in IPv6 include the following:

- Larger address space (128-bit vs. 32-bit).

- Auto-configuration of Internet-accessible addresses with or without DHCP (without DHCP it's called stateless auto-configuration).

- More efficient IP header (fewer fields and no checksum).

- Fixed-length IP header (IPv4 header is variable length) with extension headers beyond the standard fixed length to provide enhancements.

- Built-in IP mobility and security (although available in IPv4, the IPv6 implementation is much better implementation).

- Built-in transition schemes to allow integration of the IPv4 and IPv6 spaces.

- ARP broadcast messages are replaced with a multicast request.

128-bit Address Space   The new 128-bit address space will provide unique addresses for the foreseeable future. I would like to say we will never use up all the addresses, but history may prove me wrong. The number of unique addresses in the IPv6 space is 2^{128}, or 3.4×10^{38} addresses. How big is that number? Enough for toasters and refrigerators (and maybe even cars) to all have their own addresses? Why yes, I believe it is.

For a point of reference, the nearest black hole to Earth is 1,600 light years away. If you were to stack 4 mm BB pellets from here to the nearest black hole and back, you would need 7.6×10^{21} BBs. This means you could uniquely address each BB from Earth to the black hole and back and still have quite a few addresses left over.

Or how about this: The IPv6 address space is big enough to provide well over 1 million addresses per square inch of the surface area of the earth (oceans included). No more running out of addresses for the Internet!

Stateful vs. Stateless Auto-Configuration   Auto-configuration is another added/improved feature of IPv6. When you are choosing to use DHCP in IPv6, you can choose to set your systems up for Stateful or Stateless configuration. Stateful is what we currently do today with IPv4. Stateful means that DHCP is going to give our IPv6 clients all of their TCP/IP data (IP address, default gateway, and all DHCP options).

What if a Windows 10 client could ask the network itself what network it's on and, based on that information, create its own IP address and determine the default gateway. Well, that is what Stateless configuration does. Stateless configuration means that the client's address is based on the router's advertisement messages. What this means is that the client creates their own IP address and default gateway based on the router's advertisement message and the machine's MAC address. They can still get all of the other DHCP options, but they will not get an IP address and default gateway from DHCP.

Improved IPv6 Header   The IPv6 header is more efficient than the IPv4 header because it is fixed length (with extensions possible) and has only a few fields. The IPv6 header consists of a total of 40 bytes, which is broken down as follows: 32 bytes for source and destination IPv6 addresses and 8 bytes for the version field, traffic class field, flow label field, payload length field, next header field, and hop limit field.

We don't waste time with a checksum validation anymore, and we don't have to include the length of the IP header since it's fixed in IPv6; the IP header is variable length in IPv4, so the length must be included as a field.

IPv6 Mobility   IPv6 is only a replacement of the OSI Layer 3 component, and we are going to continue to use the TCP (and UDP) components as they currently exist; however, a TCP issue is addressed by IPv6. TCP is connection oriented, meaning we establish an end-to-end communication path with sequencing and acknowledgments before we ever send any data, and then we have to acknowledge all pieces of data sent. This is done through a combination of an IP address, port number, and port type (socket).

If the source IP address changes, the TCP connection may be disrupted. But then, how often does this happen? More and more often, because more people are walking around with a wireless laptop or a wireless Voice over IP (VoIP) telephone. IPv6 mobility adds the capability by establishing a TCP connection with a home address, and when changing networks, it continues to communicate with the original endpoint from a care-of address as it changes LANs, which sends all traffic back through the home address. The handing off of network addresses does not disrupt the TCP connection state (the original TCP port number and address stay intact).

Improved Security   IPv6 has security built in. Internet Protocol security (IPSec) is a component we use today to authenticate and encrypt secure tunnels from a source to a destination. This can be from the client to the server or between gateways. IPv4 lets us do this by enhancing IP header functionality (basically adding a second IP header while encrypting everything behind it). In IPv6, we add this as standard functionality by using extension headers. Extension headers are inserted into the packet only if they are needed. Each header has a "next header" field, which identifies the next piece of information. The extension headers currently identified for IPv6 are Hop-By-Hop Options, Routing, Fragment, Destination Options, Authentication, and Encapsulating Security Payload. The Authentication header and Encapsulating Security Payload header are the IPSec-specific control headers.

IPv4-to-IPv6 Transmission   There are several mechanisms in place in IPv6 to make the IPv4 to IPv6 transition easy:

- A simple dual-stack implementation where both IPv4 and IPv6 are installed and used is certainly an option. In most situations (so far), this doesn't work so well because most of us aren't connected to an IPv6 network and our Internet connection is not IPv6 even if we're using IPv6 internally. So Microsoft includes other mechanisms that can be used in several different circumstances.

- *Intra-Site Automatic Tunnel Addressing Protocol (ISATAP)* is an automatic tunneling mechanism used to connect an IPv6 network to an IPv4 address space that does not use NAT. ISATAP treats the IPv4 space as one big logical link connection space.

- *6to4* is a mechanism used to transition to IPv4. This method, like ISATAP, treats the IPv4 address space as a Logical Link Layer with each IPv6 space in transition using a 6to4 router to create endpoints using the IPv4 space as a point-to-point connection (kind of like a WAN, eh?). 6to4 implementations still do not work well through a NAT, although a 6to4 implementation using an Application Layer Gateway (ALG) is certainly doable.

- *Teredo* is a mechanism that allows users behind a NAT to access the IPv6 space by tunneling IPv6 packets in UDP.

Pseduointerfaces are used in these mechanisms to create a usable interface for the operating system. Another interesting feature of IPv6 is that addresses are assigned to interfaces (or pseudointerfaces), not simply to the end node. Your Windows Server will have several unique IPv6 addresses assigned.

New Broadcast Methods   IPv6 has moved away from using broadcasting. The three types of packets used in IPv6 are unicast, multicast, and anycast. IPv6 clients then must use one of these types to get the MAC address of the next Ethernet hop (default gateway). IPv6 makes use of multicasting for this along with new functionality of neighbor discovery. Not only does ARP utilize new functionality, but ICMP (also a Layer 3 protocol) is redone and known as ICMP6. ICMP6 is used for messaging (packet too large, time exceeded, and so on) as it was in IPv4, but it also is used for the messaging of IPv6 mobility. ICMP6 echo request and ICMP6 echo reply are still used for **ping**.

Additionally, there are several concepts to consider in IPv6 addressing. The format of the address has changed since IPv4 and we must get used to seeing/using it. There are three types of addresses we will use as well as predefined values used within the address space. You need to get used to seeing these addresses and being able to identify their uses.

IPv6 Address Format

For the design of IPv4 addresses, remember that we present addresses as octets or the decimal (base 10) representation of 8 bits. Four octets add up to the 32 bits required. IPv6 expands the address space to 128 bits, and the representation is for the most part shown in *hexadecimal* (a notation used to represent 8 bits using the values 0–9 and A–F). The following is an example of a full IPv6 address: 2001:0DB8:0000:0000:1234:0000:A9FE:133E.

You can tell the implementation of DNS will make life a lot easier for even those of us who like to ping the address in lieu of the name. Fortunately, DNS already has the ability to handle IPv6 addresses with the use of an AAAA record. (*A* is short for *alias*.) An A record in IPv4's addressing space is 32 bits, so an AAAA record—4 *As*—is 128 bits. The Windows Server DNS server handles the AAAA and the reverse pointer (PTR) records for IPv6.

IPv6 Address Shortcuts

Here are some shortcuts you can use for writing an IPv6 address:

- :0: stands for:0000:
- You can leave out preceding 0s in any 16-bit word.

   For example, :DB8: and:0DB8: are equivalent.

- :: is a variable standing for enough zeros to round out the address to 128 bits.
- :: can be used only once in an address.

You can use these shortcuts to represent the example address 2001:0DB8:0000:0000:1234:0000:A9FE:133E as shown here:

- Compress :0000: into :0:

   2001:0DB8:0000:0000:1234:0:A9FE:133E

- Eliminate preceding zeros:

   2001:DB8:0000:0000:1234:0:A9FE:133E

- Use the special variable shortcut for multiple zeros:

   2001:DB8::1234:0:A9FE:133E

You can also use *prefix notation* or slash notation when discussing IPv6 networks. The network of the example address can be represented as 2001:DB8:0000:0000:0000:0000:0000:0000. This can also be expressed as 2001:DB8::/32. The /32 indicates 32 bits of network, and 2001:DB8: is 32 bits of network.

IPv6 Address Assignment

We can let Windows Server dynamically or automatically assign its IPv6 address, or we can still assign it manually. With dynamic/automatic assignment, the IPv6 address is assigned either by a DHCPv6 server or by the Windows Server machine itself. If no DHCPv6 server is configured, Windows Server can query the local LAN segment to find a router with a configured IPv6 interface. If so, the server will assign itself an address on the same IPv6 network as the router interface and set its default gateway to the router interface's IPv6 address.

To see your configured IP addresses (IPv4 and IPv6), you can still use the `ipconfig` command. I have configured a static IPv4 and IPv6 address on my server. The IPv6 address is the same as used in the previous example IPv6 address.

IPv6 Address Types

There are multiple types of addresses in IPv6.

> **NOTE** You will notice that there is an absence of the broadcast type that is included in IPv4. IPv6 does not use broadcasts; they're replaced with multicasts.

Anycast Addresses   Anycast addresses are not really new. The concept of anycast existed in IPv4 but was not widely used. An anycast address is an IPv6 address assigned to multiple devices (usually different devices). When an anycast packet is sent, it is delivered to one of the devices, usually the closest one.

Unicast Addresses   A unicast packet uniquely identifies an interface of an IPv6 device. The interface can be a virtual or *pseudointerface* or a real (physical) interface.

 Real World Scenario

Unicast vs. Anycast

Unicast and anycast addresses look the same and may be indistinguishable from each other; it only depends on how many devices have the same address. If only one device has a globally unique IPv6 address, it's a unicast address; if more than one device has the same address, it's an anycast address. Both unicast and anycast are considered one-to-one communication, although you could say anycast is one-to-"one of many."

There are several types of unicast addresses, as described here:

Global Unicast Address   As of this writing, the *global unicast address* space is defined as 2000:: /3. 2001::/32 are the IPv6 addresses being issued to business entities. I mentioned before that Microsoft has been allocated 2001:4898:: /32. You'll find most example addresses listed as 2001:DB8:: /32; this space has been reserved for documentation. A DHCPv6 server would be set up with scopes (ranges of addresses to be assigned) within this address space. There are some special addresses and address formats you will see in use as well. Do you remember the loopback address in IPv4—127.0.0.1? In IPv6, the loopback address is ::1 (or 0:0:0:0:0:0:0:0001). You may also see an address with dotted decimal used. A dual-stack Windows Server 2016 may also show you 2001:DB8::4:2:165.55.4.2. This address form is used in an integration/migration model of IPv6 (or if you just can't leave the dotted decimal era).

Link-Local Address   *Link-local addresses* are defined as FE80:: /10. If you look at the ipconfig command, you will see the link-local IPv6 address as FE80::a425:ab9d:7da4:ccba. The last 8 bytes (64 bits) are random to ensure a high probability of randomness for the link-local address.

The link-local address is to be used on a single link (network segment) and will never be routed.

There is another form of the link-local IPv6 address called the Extended User Interface 64-bit (EUI-64) format. This is derived by using the MAC address of the physical interface and inserting an FFFE between the third and fourth bytes of the MAC. Again, looking at ipconfig, the EUI-64 address would take the physical (MAC) address 00–03–FF–11–02–CD and make the link-local IPv6 address FE80::0203:FFFF:FE11:02CD. I've left the preceding zeros in the link-local IPv6 address to make it easier for you to pick out the MAC address with the FFFE inserted.

AnonymousAddress   Microsoft Server uses the random address by default instead of EUI-64. The random value is called the AnonymousAddress in Microsoft Server. It can be modified to allow the use of EUI-64.

Unique Local Address   The unique local address can be FC00 or FD00 and is used like the private address space of IPv4. Unique local addresses are described in RFC 4193. They are not expected to be routable on the global Internet. They are routable inside a more limited area, such as a site. They may also be routed between a limited set of sites.

Multicast Address   Multicast addresses are one-to-many communication packets. Multicast packets are identifiable by their first byte (most significant byte, leftmost byte, leftmost 2 nibbles, leftmost 8 bits, etc.). A multicast address is defined as FF00::/8.

In the second byte shown (the 00 of FF00), the second 0 is what's called the scope. Interface local is 01; link-local is 02. FF01:: is an interface local multicast.

There are several well-known (already defined) multicast addresses. For example, if you want to send a packet to all nodes in the local link scope, you send the packet to FF02::1 (also shown as FF02:0:0:0:0:0:0:1). The all-routers multicast address is FF02::2.

We also use multicasting to get the logical link layer address (MAC address) of a device we are trying to communicate with. Instead of using the ARP mechanism of IPv4, IPv6 uses the ICMPv6 neighbor solicitation (NS) and neighbor advertisement (NA) messages. The NS and NA ICMPv6 messages are all part of the new Neighbor Discovery Protocol (NDP). This new ICMPv6 functionality also includes router solicitation and router advertisements as well as redirect messages (similar to the IPv4 redirect functionality).

Table 6.8 outlines the IPv6 address space known prefixes and some well-known addresses.

TABLE 6.8   IPv6 address space known prefixes and addresses

Address Prefix	Scope of Use
2000:: /3	Global unicast space prefix
FE80:: /10	Local link address prefix
FC00:: /7	Unique local unicast prefix
FF00:: /8	Multicast prefix
2001:DB8:: /32	Global unicast prefix used for documentation
::1	Reserved local loopback address
2001:0000: /32	Teredo prefix
2002:: /16	6to4 prefix

IPv6 Integration/Migration

It's time to get into the mindset of integrating IPv6 into your existing infrastructure with the longer goal of migrating over to IPv6. This is not going to be an "OK, Friday the Internet is changing over" rollout. We are going to bring about the change as a controlled implementation. It could easily be three to five years before a solid migration occurs and probably longer. The migration is just below getting the world migrated to the metric system on the overall timeline. The process of integration/migration is made up of several mechanisms:

Dual Stack: Simply running both IPv4 and IPv6 on the same network, utilizing the IPv4 address space for devices only using IPv4 addresses and utilizing the IPv6 address space for devices using IPv6 addresses

Tunneling: Using an encapsulation scheme for transporting one address space inside another

Address Translation: Using a higher-level application to transparently change one address type (IPv4 or IPv6) to the other so end devices are unaware one address space is talking to another

IPv6 Dual Stack

The default implementation in Windows 10 is an enabled IPv6 configured along with IPv4; this is dual stack. The implementation can be dual IP Layer or dual TCP/IP stack. Windows 10 uses the dual IP Layer implementation. When an application queries a DNS server to resolve a hostname to an IP address, the DNS server may respond with an IPv4 address or an IPv6 address. If the DNS server responds with both, Windows 10 will prefer the IPv6 addresses. Windows 10 can use both IPv4 and IPv6 addresses as necessary for network communication. When looking at the output of the ipconfig command, you will see both address spaces displayed.

IPv6 Tunneling

Windows 10 includes several tunneling mechanisms for tunneling IPv6 through the IPv4 address space. They include the following:

ISATAP: Intra-Site Automatic Tunnel Addressing Protocol used for unicast IPv6 communication across an IPv4 infrastructure. ISATAP is enabled by default in Windows Server 2008 and above.

6to4: Used for unicast IPv6 communication across an IPv4 infrastructure.

Teredo: Used for unicast IPv6 communication with an IPv4 NAT implementation across an IPv4 infrastructure.

With multiple tunneling protocols available and enabled by default, you might ask what the difference is and why one is used over the others. They all allow us to tunnel IPv6 packets through the IPv4 address space (a really cool thing if you're trying to integrate/migrate).

ISATAP ISATAP is the automatic tunnel addressing protocol providing IPv6 addresses based on the IPv4 address of the end interface (node). The IPv6 address is automatically configured on the local device, and the dual-stack machine can use either its IPv4 or IPv6 address to communicate on the local network (within the local network infrastructure). ISATAP can use the neighbor discovery mechanism to determine the router ID and network prefix where the device is located, thus making intrasite communication possible even in a routed infrastructure.

The format of an ISATAP address is [64 bits of prefix] [32 bits indicating ISATAP] [32 bits IPv4 address].

The center 32 bits indicating ISATAP are actually 0000:5EFE (when using private IPv4 addresses). The ISATAP address of my Windows 10 machine using the link-local IPv6 address is FE80::5EFE. Each node participating in the ISATAP infrastructure must support ISATAP. If you're routing through an IPv4 cloud, a border router (a router transitioning from an IPv6 to IPv4 space) must support ISATAP. Windows 10 can be configured as a border router and will forward ISATAP packets. ISATAP is experimental and is defined in RFC 4214.

6to4 6to4 specifies a procedure for IPv6 networks to communicate with each other through an IPv4 space without having the IPv6 nodes having to know what's going on.

The IPv6 nodes do not need to be dual stacked to make this happen. The border router is the device responsible for knowing about the IPv6-to-IPv4 transition. The IPv6 packets are encapsulated at the border router and decapsulated at the other end or on the way back. There is an assigned prefix for the 6to4 implementation; 2002:: /16. 6to4 is defined in RFC 3056.

Teredo   Teredo (named after a genus of shipworm that drills holes in the wood of ships) is a protocol designed to allow IPv6 addresses to be available to hosts through one or more layers of NAT. Teredo uses a process of tunneling packets through the IPv4 space using UDP. The Teredo service encapsulates the IPv6 data within a UDP segment (packet) and uses an IPv4 address to get through the IPv4 cloud. Having a Layer 4 (Transport Layer) available to use as a translation functionality is what gives us the ability to be behind a NAT. Teredo provides host-to-host communication and dynamic addressing for IPv6 nodes (dual stack), allowing the nodes to have access to resources in an IPv6 network and the IPv6 devices to have access to the IPv6 devices that have connectivity only to the IPv4 space (just as home users who have an IPv6-enabled operating system connecting to IPv6 resources and their home ISP have only IPv4 capabilities). Teredo is defined in RFC 4380.

In Windows 10, an IPv4 Teredo server is identified and configured (using the netsh command interface). The Teredo server provides connectivity resources (address) to the Teredo client (the node that has access to the IPv4 Internet and needs access to an IPv6 network/ Internet). A Teredo relay is a component used by the IPv6 router to receive traffic destined for Teredo clients and forward the traffic appropriately. The defined prefix for Teredo addresses is 2001:: /32 (does it look better like this? – 2001:0000:: /32). Teredo does add overhead like all the implementations discussed. It is generally accepted that we should use the simplest model available. However, in the process of integration/migration for most of us behind a NAT, Teredo will be the process to choose.

From Windows 10, use the ipconfig /all command to view the default configurations including IPv4 and IPv6. You may notice a notation we didn't discuss: the percent sign at the end of the IPv6 address. The number after the percent sign is the virtual interface identifier used by Windows 10.

Information Commands Useful with IPv6

There are numerous commands you can use to view, verify, and configure the network parameters of Windows 10. You can use the netsh command set and the route command set as well as the standard ping and tracert functions.

Use the netsh command interface to examine and configure IPv6 functionality (as well as the provided dialog boxes if you like). The netsh command issued from the command interpreter changes into a network shell (netsh) where you can configure and view both IPv4 and IPv6 components.

Don't forget to use the ever-popular route print command to see the Windows 10 routing tables (IPv4 and IPv6). The other diagnostic commands are still available for IPv4 as well as IPv6. In previous versions of Microsoft operating systems, ping was the IPv4 command and ping6 was the IPv6 command.

This has changed for Windows 10; ping works for both IPv4 and IPv6 to test Layer 3 connectivity to remote devices. The command is now tracert for both IPv4 and IPv6 and will show you every Layer 3 (IP) hop from source to destination (assuming all the administrators from here to there want you to see the hops and are not blocking ICMP and also assuming there are not IP tunnels your packets are traversing; you won't see the router hops in the tunnel either).

Overall, the consortium of people making up development of the Internet and Internet protocols have tried to make all changes to communication infrastructures easy to implement (this is a daunting task with so many vendors and various infrastructures currently in place).

The goal is not to daze and confuse administrators; it's to provide the most flexibility with the greatest functionality. IPv6 is going to provide the needed Layer 3 (Network Layer, Global Addressing Layer, Logical Addressing Layer... call it what you like) functionality for the foreseeable future.

Configuring TCP/IP on Windows 10

Windows 10 can use either IPv4 or IPv6 to communicate with other machines on a network, but the Windows 10 machine must receive the TCP/IP address. There are two ways that a Windows 10 machine can get a TCP/IP address: statically or dynamically.

Assigning Static TCP/IP Numbers

As an administrator, it may be necessary to configure a Windows 10 machine manually (static configuration). To do so, you must know the following:

- Which TCP/IP address the machine will receive
- What the subnet mask is for the segment
- What the default gateway (router's TCP/IP address) is
- What the DNS server TCP/IP addresses are

Complete Exercise 6.4 to configure a Windows 10 machine to use a static TCP/IP address. This example uses TCP/IP addresses for a local network, but you can use your own TCP/IP addresses if you know what they should be.

EXERCISE 6.4

Configuring a Static TCP/IP Address

1. Click Start ➢ Windows System ➢ Control Panel ➢ Network And Internet ➢ Network And Sharing Center (if Control Panel view is Category).

2. In the Network And Sharing Center window, click the Ethernet item in the View Your Active Networks section.

3. Click the Properties button from the Activity section of the Local Area Connection Status box.

4. In the Ethernet Properties dialog box, click to highlight (do not deselect the check box) Internet Protocol Version 4 (TCP/IPv4) and click the Properties button. Manual configuration will work with both IPv4 and IPv6.

5. Under the General tab, click the Use The Following IP Address radio button. Type in the following (unless you want or know your own settings):

   IP Address: **192.168.1.50**

   Subnet Mask: **255.255.255.0**

   Default Gateway: **192.168.1.1**

6. Click the Use The Following DNS Server Addresses radio button and type **8.8.8.8** (unless you want to use your own settings) in the TCP/IP Address field.

7. Click OK.

Configuring a Windows 10 Machine to Use DHCP

Dynamic IP configuration assumes that you have a DHCP server on your network that is reachable by the DHCP clients. DHCP servers are configured to automatically provide DHCP clients with all their IP configuration information, including IP address, subnet mask, and DNS server.

For large networks, DHCP is the easiest and most reliable way of managing IP configurations. By default, a Windows 10 machine is configured as a DHCP client for dynamic IP configuration.

Complete Exercise 6.5 to configure a Windows 10 machine to use a dynamic IP configuration.

EXERCISE 6.5

Using DHCP

1. Click Start ➤ Windows System ➤ Control Panel ➤ Network And Internet ➤ Network And Sharing Center (if Control Panel view is Category).

2. In the Network And Sharing Center window, click the Ethernet item in the View Your Active Networks section.

3. Click the Properties button from the Activity section of the Local Area Connection Status box.

4. In the Ethernet Properties dialog box, click to select (do not deselect the check box) Internet Protocol Version 4 (TCP/IPv4) and click the Properties button. DHCP will work with both IPv4 and IPv6.

5. Choose the Obtain An IP Address Automatically radio button from the General tab of the Internet Protocol Version 4 (TCP/IPv4) Properties dialog box.

6. Choose the Obtain DNS Server Address Automatically radio button from the General tab of the Internet Protocol Version 4 (TCP/IPv4) Properties dialog box.

7. To use this configuration, click OK to accept the selection and close the dialog box. To exit without saving (if you had a valid static configuration), choose Cancel.

If you are using DHCP and you are not connecting to other machines properly, you can type ipconfig /all at a command prompt to see what your TCP/IP address is. If your TCP/IP address starts with 169.254.*x.x*, you are not connecting to the DHCP server. Instead, your Windows 10 machine is using APIPA.

Understanding APIPA

Automatic Private IP Addressing (APIPA) is used to automatically assign private IP addresses for home or small business networks that contain a single subnet, have no DHCP server, and are not using static IP addressing. If APIPA is being used, clients will be able to communicate only with other clients on the same subnet that are also using APIPA. The benefit of using APIPA in small networks is that it is less tedious and has less chance of configuration errors than statically assigning IP addresses and configuration.

APIPA is used with Windows 10 under the following conditions:

- When the client is configured as a DHCP client but no DHCP server is available to service the DHCP request

- When the client originally obtained a DHCP lease from a DHCP server but when the client tried to renew the DHCP lease, the DHCP server was unavailable and the lease period expired

APIPA uses a Class B network address space that has been reserved for its use. The address space is the 169.254.0.0 network, where the range of 169.254.0.1–169.254.255.254 is available for the host to assign to itself. APIPA uses the following process:

1. The Windows 10 client attempts to use a DHCP server for its configuration, but no DHCP servers respond.

2. The Windows 10 client selects a random address from the 169.254.0.1–169.254.255.254 range of addresses and will use a subnet mask of 255.255.0.0.

3. The client uses a duplicate address-detection method to verify that the address it selected is not already in use on the network.

4. If the address is already in use, the client repeats steps 1 and 2. If the address is not already in use, the client configures its network interface with the address it randomly selected. Given the number of the address the APIPA client can select from (65,534 addresses), the odds of selecting a duplicate are very slim.

5. The Windows 10 network client continues to search for a DHCP server every five minutes. If a DHCP server replies to the request, the APIPA configuration is dropped, and the client receives new IP configuration settings from the DHCP server.

You can determine whether your network interface has been configured using APIPA by looking at your IP address from the command prompt by using the ipconfig /all command.

Testing Your IP Configuration

After you have installed and configured the TCP/IP settings, you can test the IP configuration by using the ipconfig, ping, and nbtstat commands. These commands are also useful in troubleshooting IP configuration errors. You can also graphically view connection details through the Ethernet Status section of the Network and Sharing Center.

Using the *ipconfig* Command

The ipconfig command displays your IP configuration. Table 6.9 lists the command switches that you can use with the ipconfig command.

TABLE 6.9   ipconfig switches

Switch	Description
/?	Shows all of the help options for ipconfig
/all	Shows verbose information about your IP configuration, including your computer's physical address, the DNS server you are using, and whether you are using DHCP
/allcompartments	Shows IP information for all compartments
/release	Releases an IPv4 address that has been assigned through DHCP
/release6	Releases an IPv6 address that has been assigned through DHCP
/renew	Renews an IPv4 address through DHCP
/renew6	Renews an IPv6 address through DHCP
/flushdns	Purges the DNS resolver cache
/registerdns	Refreshes DHCP leases and re-registers DNS names
/displaydns	Displays the contents of the DNS resolver cache
/showclassid	Lists the DHCP class IDs allowed by the computer
/setclassID	Allows you to modify the DHCP class ID

Using Other TCP/IP Commands

You can use numerous commands to view, verify, and configure the network parameters of Windows 10. Specifically, you can use the netsh command set and the route command set as well as the standard ping and tracert functions.

Use the netsh command interface to examine and configure IPv6 functionality (as well as the provided dialog boxes if you want). The netsh command issued from the command interpreter changes into a network shell (netsh) where you can configure and view both

IPv4 and IPv6 components. Don't forget to use the ever-popular route print command to see the Windows 10 routing tables (IPv4 and IPv6). Ping works for both IPv4 and IPv6 to test Layer 3 connectivity to remote devices. As already mentioned, the command is tracert for both IPv4 and IPv6 and will show you every Layer 3 (IP) hop from source to destination (assuming all the administrators from here to there want you to see the hops and are not blocking ICMP and also assuming there are no IP tunnels your packets are traversing, or you won't see the router hops in the tunnel either).

TCP/IP Troubleshooting

If you are having trouble connecting to network resources, consider the following:

- If you can access resources on your local subnet but not on a remote subnet, check the default gateway settings on your computer. Pinging a remote host and receiving a Destination Unreachable message is also related to default gateway misconfiguration.

- If you can access some but not all resources on your local subnet or remote subnet, you should check your subnet mask settings, the wiring to those resources, or the devices between your computer and those resources.

- Use the ipconfig utility to ensure that you are not configured with an APIPA address. If you are, determine why you are not receiving IP settings from your DHCP server.

- If you can access a resource (for example, by pinging a computer) by IP address but not by name, check the DNS settings on your computer.

After we have TCP/IP set up on our Windows 10 machine, we can connect the Windows 10 machine to the network. In the next section, we will look at how to do that.

Configuring Windows 10 on a Network

In a corporate environment, the client machines (Windows 7/8/8.1, and Windows 10) will be connected to the domain environment either from the Windows 10 operating system domain or from Active Directory. Having the Windows 10 machine on the network offers many benefits to administration:

- You can deploy GPOs from one location instead of LGPOs on each machine.

- Users can store their data on a server. This way, the nightly backups capture user information. Most Windows 10 machines will *not* be backed up separately.

- You can manage users and groups from one central location (Active Directory) instead of on each Windows 10 machine.

- You can manage resource security on servers instead of on each Windows 10 machine.

Adding Windows 10 to the Domain

It does not matter which way you choose to connect the machine to the domain. I usually connect the Windows 10 machine through the Windows operating system. Many IT administrators add the Windows 10 system by using the Active Directory Users and Computers MMC, but either way does the same task.

Complete Exercise 6.6 to connect a Windows 10 machine to a Windows Server domain via the Windows 10 OS. To complete this exercise, you will need to have a Windows Server domain that the Window 10 machine can connect to.

EXERCISE 6.6

Connecting a Windows 10 Machine to the Domain

1. On the Windows 10 machine, click Start ➢ Windows System ➢ Control Panel, then choose System. If you choose System from right-clicking on the Start button, you will see different options. So open the System applet in Control Panel.

2. Change the View By to Large Icons and select System.

3. Under the Computer Name, Domain, And Workgroup section, click the Change Settings link.

4. Click the Change button next to the To Rename This Computer Or Change Its Domain Or Workgroup section.

5. In the Member Of section, click the Domain radio button (shown in Figure 6.19) and type in the name of your Windows Server 2016 domain.

FIGURE 6.19   Computer Name/Domain Changes screen

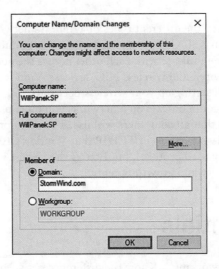

6. A Credentials box appears, asking for a username and password. Enter an account with administrative credentials to join the machine to the domain. Click OK.

7. A dialog box stating that you are part of the domain appears. Click OK and reboot the machine.

8. From the Windows 10 machine, log on to the domain with your username and password.

You also have the ability to create the computer account in the Active Directory Users and Computers MMC Snap-in. Complete Exercise 6.7 to add the Windows 10 machine to the domain from the Active Directory Snap-in. To complete this exercise, you will need a Windows Server domain that you can add the Windows 10 machine to.

EXERCISE 6.7

Adding Windows 10 to the Domain via Active Directory

1. From the Windows Server domain controller machine, click Start ➢ Administrative Tools ➢ Active Directory Users And Computers.

2. Expand the domain and right-click the Computers OU. Choose New ➢ Computer.

3. In the Computer Name field, type the name of the Windows 10 computer. Click OK.

4. Double-click the new Windows 10 computer in the right-hand window to open the properties.

5. Take a look at the different tabs, and then click the Cancel button.

Summary

In this chapter, we discussed the different types of Windows networks: domain based and peer-to-peer (workgroup) based. Computers need to use a communication device called a NIC device in order to communicate with each other across the network. You can set up Windows 10 to use both wired and wireless NIC devices. Windows 10 also has new features included to help with setting up your wireless networks.

To allow computers to communicate on a network, you must use a *protocol*—a set of communication standards that all computers will use. The main protocol that Windows 10 uses is TCP/IP. There are two versions of TCP/IP that Windows 10 can use, IPv4 and IPv6. IPv4 is the most commonly used protocol, but IPv6 is the newest version of TCP/IP and gives organizations flexibility and growth potential.

Exam Essentials

Understand Microsoft networking.   Know the difference between the Microsoft networks that you can set up. Know the difference between workgroups and domains. Know about working with Azure Active Directory vs. on-site Active Directory.

Understand how to configure network settings.   Know how to install and configure both wired and wireless networks. Understand how Windows 10 has built-in wireless network support. Know how to set up your preferred wireless network.

Understand IPv4 and IPv6.   Know and understand IPv4 and IPv6. Understand how to configure and maintain both IPv4 and IPv6 networks. Know how to subnet an IPv4 network. Understand that APIPA will automatically assign an IP address to a Windows 10 machine if DHCP is not available.

Video Resources

There are videos available for the following exercises:

    6.1

    6.2

    6.4

You can access the videos at http://www.wiley.com/go/sybextestprep.

Review Questions

1. You have two DHCP servers on your network. Your computer accidentally received the wrong IP and DNS server configuration from a DHCP server that was misconfigured. The DHCP server with the incorrect configuration has been disabled. What commands could you use to release and renew your computer's DHCP configuration? (Choose two.)

   A. `ipconfig /release`

   B. `ipconfig /registerdhcp`

   C. `ipconfig /renew`

   D. `ipconfig /flushdhcp`

2. You are the network administrator for your company. Your service provider has assigned you the network address 192.168.154.0. You have been granted the entire range to use. What class of address have you been assigned?

   A. Class A

   B. Class B

   C. Class C

   D. Class D

3. You are the network administrator for your company. After configuring a new computer and connecting it to the network, you discover that you cannot access any of the computers on the remote subnet by IP address. You can access some of the computers on the local subnet by IP address. What is the most likely problem?

   A. Incorrectly defined IP address

   B. Incorrectly defined subnet mask

   C. Incorrectly defined default gateway

   D. Incorrectly defined DNS server

4. A user cannot access a server in the domain. After troubleshooting, you determine that the user cannot access the server by name but can access the server by IP address. What is the most likely problem?

   A. Incorrectly defined IP address

   B. Incorrectly defined subnet mask

   C. Incorrectly defined DHCP server

   D. Incorrectly defined DNS server

5. You have a Windows 10 machine that needs to have a static TCP/IP address. You assign the IP address to the machine and you now want to register the computer with DNS. How can you do this from the Windows 10 machine?

   A. `ipconfig /renewdns`

   B. `ipconfig /flushdns`

   C. `ipconfig /dns`

   D. `ipconfig /registerdns`

6. You have been hired as a TCP/IP contractor for an organization who wants to redo their network. The company currently uses a 192.168.*x.x* class but they are projecting a hiring of over 500 new employees this year. They currently have 175 employees. They do not want to buy a new TCP/IP class. What can you do to help them? (Choose all that apply.)

   A. Change the network to 10.0.0.0/8.

   B. Change the network to 172.16.0.0/16.

   C. Change the network to 224.10.0.0/24.

   D. Change the network to 192.10.0.0/24.

7. You are hired by a small company to set up a network. The company sells pocket watches and they have only five employees. They can't afford a server and client access licenses. What type of network can you set up for them?

   A. Set up all Windows 10 clients on a workgroup.

   B. Create a HomeGroup.

   C. Set them up on Azure Active Directory.

   D. Load Windows Server onto a Windows 10 system.

8. Which of the following IP addresses are Class A addresses? (Choose all that apply.)

   A. 131.107.10.15

   B. 128.10.14.1

   C. 10.14.100.240

   D. 65.102.17.9

9. Which of the following IP addresses are Class B addresses? (Choose all that apply.)

   A. 131.107.10.150

   B. 189.10.14.1

   C. 10.14.100.240

   D. 198.102.17.9

10. You are the network administrator for a large organization with many laptop users who go on the road. Your organization would like to start moving away from users connecting in by VPN to get data. They have decided that they want to start moving the entire IT department to the cloud. What version of Active Directory can they start using?

    A. Azure Active Directory

    B. OneDrive

    C. Windows Server Active Directory

    D. DirectAccess

Chapter

7

Configuring Recovery

MICROSOFT EXAM OBJECTIVES COVERED IN THIS CHAPTER:

✓ **Configure system and data recovery**

- Perform file recovery (including OneDrive); recover Windows 10; troubleshoot startup/boot process.

✓ **Monitor and manage Windows**

- Configure and analyze event logs; manage performance; manage Windows 10 environment.

One of the tasks that administrators will need to do on a daily basis is fixing Windows 10 systems that are having issues.

There are many ways to determine what issues a Windows 10 system may be having, and there are many tools to help you solve the issues.

The best way to protect any Windows 10 system is to make sure the users' files are stored on a network server and backed up daily. But there may be times when you need to back up the Windows 10 system.

Windows 10 includes a full backup and restore application (Backup and Restore [Windows 7]) that allows a user or an administrator to maintain a backup copy of any of the Windows 10 component files and data files that are considered critical to the operation of your day-to-day business.

There may also be times when Windows 10 doesn't start properly and an administrator will need to identify and resolve the Windows error to get the system booting up properly again. There are many different utilities that allow you to troubleshoot and fix startup issues, including Safe Mode, Startup Repair tool, Backup and Restore Center, Driver Rollback, and doing a System Restore.

Finally, there will be times when an administrator needs to monitor the Windows 10 system. Sometimes, performance optimization can feel like a luxury, but it can be very important, especially if you can't get your Windows 10 system to run applications the way they are intended to run. The Windows 10 operating system has been specifically designed to keep your mission-critical applications and data accessible even in times of failures.

The most common cause of such problems is a hardware configuration issue. Poorly written device drivers and unsupported hardware can cause problems with system stability. Failed hardware components (such as system memory) may do so as well. Memory chips can be faulty, electrostatic discharge can ruin them, and other hardware issues can occur. No matter what, a problem with your memory chip spells disaster for your Windows 10 system.

Usually, third-party hardware vendors provide utility programs with their computers that can be used for performing hardware diagnostics on machines to help you find problems. These utilities are a good first step to resolving intermittent problems, but Windows 10 comes with many utilities that can help you diagnose and fix your issues.

In this chapter, I'll cover the tools and methods used for measuring performance and troubleshooting failures in Windows 10. Before you dive into the technical details, however, you should thoroughly understand what you're trying to accomplish and how you'll meet this goal.

One of the Microsoft objectives under Monitoring Windows is using Windows Defender. Windows Defender is not covered in this chapter because it was covered in detail in Chapter 5, "Configuring Security and Devices."

Understanding Recovery

One of the worst events you may experience is a computer that won't boot. An even worse experience is discovering that there is no recent backup for that computer. The first step in preparing for disaster recovery is to expect that a disaster will happen at some point and ensure that you take proactive measures to plan your recovery before the failure occurs. Here are some of the preparations you can take:

- Keep your computer up-to-date with Windows Update (covered in Chapter 1, "Windows 10 Installation").

- Perform regular system backups.

- Use current software to scan for malware (such as viruses, spyware, and adware), and make sure you have the most recent updates.

- Perform regular administrative functions, such as monitoring the logs in the Event Viewer utility.

No matter how many safeguards you enact, eventually you'll likely need to recover a system. Table 7.1 summarizes all of the Windows 10 utilities and options you can use to assist in performing system recovery. All these Windows 10 recovery techniques are covered in detail in this chapter.

TABLE 7.1   Windows 10 recovery techniques

Recovery Technique	When to Use
Event Viewer	If the Windows 10 operating system can be loaded through normal mode or Safe Mode, one of the first places to look for hints about the problem is Event Viewer. Event Viewer displays system, security, and application logs.
Safe Mode	This is generally your starting point for system recovery. Safe Mode loads the absolute minimum of services and drivers that are needed to boot Windows 10. If you can boot your computer to Safe Mode and you suspect that you have a system conflict, you can temporarily disable an application or processes, troubleshoot services, or uninstall software.
Startup Repair tool	If your computer will not boot to Safe Mode, you can use the Startup Repair tool to replace corrupted system files. This option will not help if you have hardware errors, however.
Backup and Restore	You should use this utility to safeguard your computer. If necessary, you can use the Backup and Restore (Windows 7) utility to restore personal files from backup media and to restore a complete image of your computer.

TABLE 7.1   Windows 10 recovery techniques *(continued)*

Recovery Technique	When to Use
Driver Rollback	If you install a driver that causes issues on your system, you can use the Driver Rollback utility to return the driver to its previous version. Use Device Manager to access the Driver Rollback utility. Right-click the hardware component and choose Properties. Then click the Driver tab, and the Roll Back Driver button (Driver Rollback) will be there.
System Restore	System Restore is used to create known checkpoints of your system's configuration. In the event that your system becomes misconfigured, you can restore the system configuration to an earlier version of the checkpoint.

Knowing the Startup/Boot Options

The Windows 10 advanced boot options can be used to troubleshoot errors that keep Windows 10 from successfully booting. Figure 7.1 shows the Advanced Boot Options screen. These advanced boot options are covered in the following sections.

FIGURE 7.1   Advanced Options screen

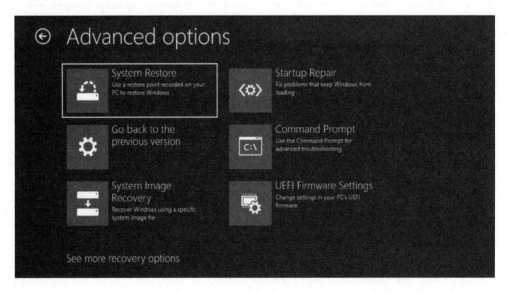

In Windows 7 and earlier versions, to access the advanced boot options, you used the F8 key during startup. Starting with Windows 8, Microsoft changed this. To access the Windows 10 advanced boot options, hold the Shift key down and choose the Restart option (from either the login screen or the Start Menu). This will bring up the Advanced Boot Options menu, which offers numerous options for booting Windows 10.

Starting in Safe Mode

When your computer will not start, one of the fundamental troubleshooting techniques is to simplify the configuration as much as possible. This is especially important when you do not know the cause of your problem and you have a complex configuration. After you have simplified the configuration, you can determine whether the problem is in the basic configuration or is a result of your complex configuration.

If the problem is in the basic configuration, you have a starting point for troubleshooting. If the problem is not in the basic configuration, you should proceed to restore each configuration option you removed, one at a time. This helps you to identify what is causing the error.

If Windows 10 will not load, you can attempt to load the operating system in *Safe Mode*. When you run Windows 10 in Safe Mode, you are simplifying your Windows configuration as much as possible. Safe Mode loads only the drivers needed to get the computer up and running.

The Windows Recovery Environment (WinRE) will automatically boot after two failed attempts to boot the operating system. You can then perform a Safe Mode boot from the advanced boot options.

The drivers that are loaded with Safe Mode include basic ones for the mouse, monitor, keyboard, hard drive, standard video driver, and default system services.

Safe Mode is considered a diagnostic mode, so you do not have access to all of the features and devices in Windows 10 that you have access to when you boot normally, including networking capabilities.

Windows 10 offers a few startup settings when you're trying to repair your Windows 10 system. Figure 7.2 shows the settings that are offered when you boot into Startup Settings.

When the Startup Settings screen appears, you then have the ability to choose to enter a Safe Mode (three versions). Once a computer is booted into Safe Mode, you will see the text *Safe Mode* in the four corners of your Desktop, as shown in Figure 7.3.

FIGURE 7.2 Startup Settings screen

FIGURE 7.3 A computer running in Safe Mode

If you boot to Safe Mode, check all of your computer's hardware and software settings in Device Manager and try to determine why Windows 10 will not boot properly. After you take steps to fix the problem, try to boot to Windows 10 as you normally would.

In Exercise 7.1, you will boot your computer to Safe Mode.

EXERCISE 7.1

Booting Your Computer to Safe Mode

1. Turn on the Windows 10 system.

2. After boot up, press and hold the Shift key and select Reboot from the Start Menu.

3. At the Choose An Option screen, choose the Troubleshoot option shown in Figure 7.4.

FIGURE 7.4 Windows Recovery Environment

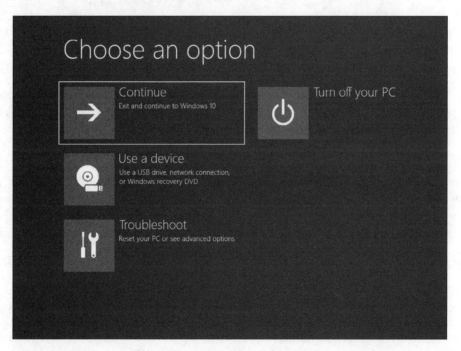

4. At the Troubleshoot screen, choose Advanced Options (shown in Figure 7.5).

FIGURE 7.5   Troubleshoot screen

5.   At the Advanced Options screen, choose See More Recovery Options, then choose Startup Settings.

6.   At the Startup Settings screen, click the Restart button. The system will reboot into the Startup Settings screen.

7.   At the Startup Settings screen, choose 5) Enable Safe Mode With Networking.

8.   When Windows 10 starts, log in.

Don't restart your computer yet; you will do this as a part of the next exercise.

Enabling Boot Logging

Boot logging creates a log file that tracks the loading of drivers and services. When you choose the Enable Boot Logging option from the Advanced Boot Options menu, Windows 10 loads normally, not in Safe Mode. This allows you to log all of the processes that take place during a normal boot sequence.

This log file can be used to troubleshoot the boot process. When logging is enabled, the log file is written to \WINDOWS\Ntbtlog.txt. A sample of the Ntbtlog.txt file is shown in Figure 7.6.

FIGURE 7.6 A Windows 10 boot log file

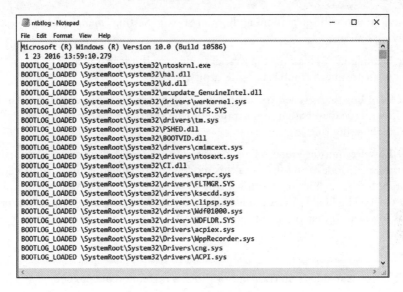

In Exercise 7.2, you will examine the boot log file that was created by default during Exercise 7.1.

EXERCISE 7.2

Using Boot Logging

1. Click File Explorer (the folder icon on the Taskbar) and browse to C:\WINDOWS\Ntbtlog.txt. Double-click this file.

2. Examine the contents of your boot log file.

3. Shut down your computer and restart it without using Advanced Boot Options.

The boot log file is cumulative. Each time you boot to Safe Mode, you are writing to this file. This enables you to make changes, reboot, and see whether you have fixed any problems. If you want to start from scratch, you should manually delete this file and reboot to an Advanced Boot Options menu selection that supports logging (Enable Boot Logging).

Using Other Startup Setting Options

In this section, you will learn about additional Startup Settings menu modes. These include the following options:

1) Enable Debugging   This runs the Kernel Debugger, if it is installed. The Kernel Debugger is an advanced troubleshooting utility.

2) Enable Boot Logging   When you enable boot logging, a file is created called Ntbtlog.txt. This file lists all the drivers that are installed during startup and that might be useful for advanced troubleshooting.

3) Enable Low-Resolution Video   This loads a standard VGA driver without starting the computer in Safe Mode. You might use this mode if you changed your video driver, did not test it, and tried to boot to Windows 10 with a bad driver that would not allow you to access video. The Enable VGA mode bails you out by loading a default driver, providing access to video so that you can properly install (and test!) the correct driver for your computer.

Safe Mode starts Windows 10 at a resolution of 800×600.

4) Enable Safe Mode   As explained previously, entering into Safe Mode allows the system to boot up with only the minimum drivers needed to make the system operate.

5) Enable Safe Mode With Networking   This is the same as the Safe Mode option but adds networking features. You might use this mode if you need networking capabilities to download drivers or service packs from a network location.

6) Enable Safe Mode With Command Prompt   This starts the computer in Safe Mode, but after you log in to Windows 10, only a command prompt is displayed. This mode does not provide access to the desktop. Experienced troubleshooters use this mode.

7) Disable Driver Signature Enforcement   This allows drivers to be installed even if they do not contain valid signatures.

8) Disable Early Launch Anti-malware Protection   Windows 10 has a feature called Secure Boot. Secure Boot helps protect the Windows boot configuration and its components. Secure Boot also loads an Early Launch Anti-malware (ELAM) driver. Choosing this option disables the Early Launch Anti-malware driver.

9) Disable Automatic Restart After Failure   This prevents Windows from restarting when a critical error causes Windows to fail. This option should be used only when Windows fails every time you restart, preventing you from accessing the desktop or any configuration options.

10) Press Enter to Return to Your Operating System   This boots the Windows 10 system in the default manner. This option is on the Advanced Boot Options menu in case you accidentally hit F8 during the boot process but really wanted to boot Windows 10 normally.

11) Launch Recovery Environment   The Windows 10 Recovery Environment (WinRE) is used to repair common causes of bootable operating systems problems. By default, WinRE is preloaded into the Windows 10 for Desktop editions (Home, Pro, Enterprise, and Education).

Understanding System Restore

System restores are actually a two-part process to make work. First in the Windows 10 operating system, you create system restore points. These are snapshots of the Windows 10 system so in the event that you need to revert to one of these snapshots, you can.

So after you create some system restore points, the System Restore option in the Advanced Options allows you to revert your PC to an earlier point in time. Restore points are generated when an administrator or user installs a new application, driver, or Windows update or when you manually create a restore point.

When you restore to a previous point, the user's personal files won't be affected, but restores do remove applications, drivers, and updates installed after the restore point was made.

To enable System Protection (needed to create restore points), in Control Panel, choose the System icon. When the System Properties window appears, choose System Protection on the left side of the window. Click the Configure button (see Figure 7.7) to turn System Protection on.

FIGURE 7.7   Configure button for System Protection

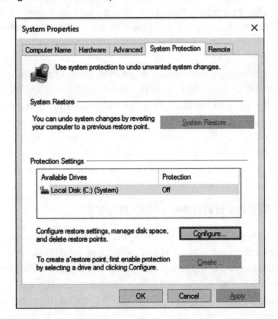

Once you have enabled System Protection in Control Panel, you then need to open the System Restore application. To do that, you follow these steps:

1. Click the Start button ➢ Windows System and then select Control Panel.

2. Choose Recovery in the Control Panel.

3. In the Recovery window, choose Configure System Restore (as shown in Figure 7.8).

FIGURE 7.8   Open System Restore

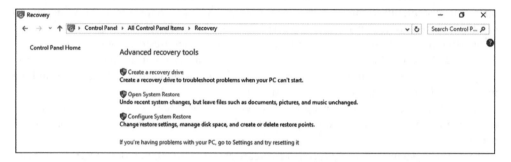

4. At the next screen, click the Create button. This will allow you to create a system restore point.

The steps to create restore points as well as restore and clean up old restore points will be explained in the section "Maintaining Windows 10 with Backup and Restore" later in this chapter.

Before you can use System Restore to fix a crashed computer, you need to create a recovery drive. Recovery drives allow you to create a backup drive in the event that a PC can't start. After the recovery drive is created, you can then use that drive to recover from a system crash.

To use the recovery drive to fix a crashed computer, boot the system into the Advanced Options and then choose System Restore. You will be asked for a username and then a password and the system will continue using one of the restore points that was selected.

Using the System Image Recovery

Another way to protect your Windows 10 computer system is to create and use system images. System images are exact copies of the Windows 10 drive. System images, by default, include the drives that are needed for Windows to function properly. System images include Windows and all of the system settings, programs, and files.

System images work well in the event of a major hard disk or computer crash. System images allow you to restore all of the contents of the crashed system and get the system back up and running. When you restore a crashed system from an image, the entire system is restored. It's a complete restore of the computer system. This means that you can't pick and choose what programs you want to install. It's an all-or-nothing restore.

This is the reason you should also make sure that you do regular backups. By making sure all of your backups are up-to-date and by making sure you have a system image, you are completely covered in the event of a major crash.

To create a system image, right-click the Start Menu and choose Control Panel. In the Control Panel, open File History. Once you're in the File History application, click the System Image Backup link in the lower-left corner (see Figure 7.9).

FIGURE 7.9   System Image Backup link

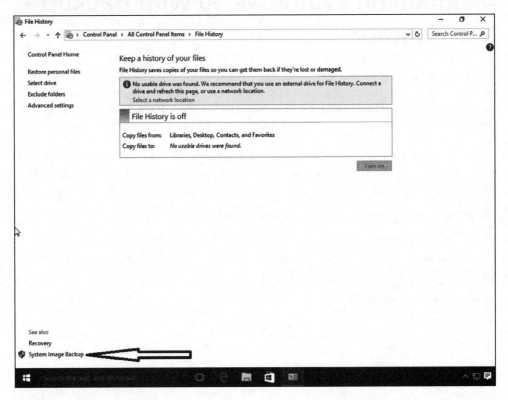

The steps to create a System Image Backup will be explained later in this chapter in the section "Maintaining Windows 10 with Backup and Restore."

Using the Startup Repair Tool

Another option that is available in the Advanced Options menu is the Startup Repair tool. If your Windows 10 computer will not boot because of missing or corrupted system files, you can use the *Startup Repair tool* to correct these problems. Startup Repair cannot repair hardware failures. Additionally, Startup Repair cannot recover personal files that have been corrupted, damaged by viruses, or deleted. To ensure that you can recover your personal files, you should use the Backup and Restore utility discussed in the next section.

If Startup Repair is unable to correct the problem, you might have to reinstall Windows 10, but this should be done as a last resort. This is one reason you should always back up your Windows 10 machine.

Maintaining Windows 10 with Backup and Restore

The Windows 10 *Backup and Restore utility* enables you to create and restore backups. Backups protect your data in the event of system failure by storing the data on another medium, such as a hard disk, CD, DVD, or network location. If your original data is lost because of corruption, deletion, or media failure, you can restore the data by using your backup.

Choose Start ➢ Windows System ➢ Control Panel, choose either the small or large icon view, and then click Backup And Restore (Windows 7). Backup and Restore is shown in Figure 7.10.

FIGURE 7.10   Windows 10 Backup and Restore

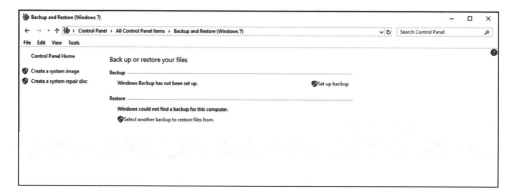

Creating a Backup

You can see in Figure 7.10 that no backups of this Windows 10 machine have been made. To set up a backup, choose the Set Up Backup link in the right side of the **Backup And Restore** window. Choosing Set Up Backup launches a wizard that takes you through the process of creating a backup. The Backup Wizard first asks you for a location to save your backup. This location can be a hard disk (removable or fixed), a CD, a DVD, or even a network location (if you have Windows 10 Premium or Ultimate).

Next, you are asked to either let Windows 10 choose the files and folders to back up or let you manually select the resources you want to back up. In your manual selection, you can choose just the data libraries of Windows 10 for you as a user or other users. You can also choose to create a backup of the Windows 10 system files. If you want to choose other files and folders, you have the option of selecting any resources individually on your hard disk(s).

The final page of the wizard enables you to view the items you have selected as well as set up a schedule for your backups to occur. If you're happy with the setup, click the Save Settings And Run Backup button. The backup commences, and you are able to restore the resources if necessary in the future. Figure 7.11 shows my Windows 10 machine right after I chose to save the settings and run a backup. You can see the backup in progress and the date and time of my last backup.

FIGURE 7.11 Windows 10 backup status

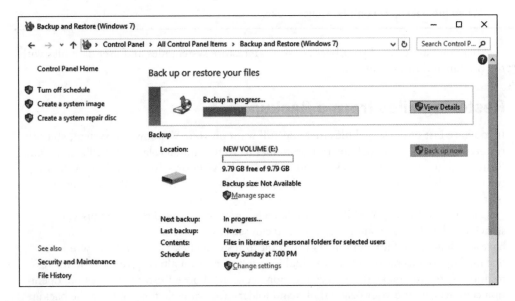

Windows 10 *cannot* back up encrypted files. To back up encrypted files, you need to manually copy all encrypted files to an external hard drive or decrypt the files before the backup.

In Exercise 7.3, you will make a backup of your files. This exercise assumes that you haven't yet configured an automatic backup.

EXERCISE 7.3

Backing Up Files

1. Click Start ➢ Windows System ➢ Control Panel ➢ Backup And Restore (Windows 7).

2. Click the Back Up Now button.

3. Select the location where you want to save your backup, and then click Next. In this example, I will use my D: drive.

4. The What Do You Want To Back Up? screen appears. Click the Let Me Choose radio button and then click Next.

5. Select the files that you would like to back up. Click Next.

6. At the Review Your Backup Settings screen, you can select how often you want a backup to be automatically performed. To start the backup, click the Save Settings And Run Backup button.

   Windows begins backing up files, and a progress indicator indicates how the backup is progressing.

7. When the backup is complete, click Close.

After you have created your backup, you can restore system files and user data files with the Backup and Restore utility.

Restoring Files from a Backup

If you have lost or destroyed files that you still want on your Windows 10 system, you can restore them from your backup. To restore files to your computer, launch the Backup and Restore program by typing **backup and restore** in the Windows 10 search box. Assuming the media where your backup was saved is available, you can click the Restore My Files button.

Clicking the Restore My Files button launches a restore wizard that prompts you to search for the files you want to restore. You can select multiple files and folders. When you have selected all the files and folders you want to restore, click Next, and you will have one final option: to restore to the original location or pick an alternative location for restoration. After you make the restore-location decision, choose Restore. The restore operation commences, and your original files and folders are available for you from the backup media.

You also have options in the Backup And Restore window to restore all users' files or to select another backup to restore files from. You would use this second option if you saved your backup to multiple locations and the last one (the one listed in the backup section) is not the set of backup files you want to use in your current session. Other than just restoring files and folders, you have the choice to use other advanced backup options.

In Exercise 7.4, you will restore some files. This exercise assumes that you created a backup in Exercise 7.3.

EXERCISE 7.4

Restoring Files

1. Click Start ➤ Windows System ➤ Control Panel ➤ Backup And Restore (Windows 7).

2. Click the Restore My Files button.

3. At the Restore Files screen, click the Browse For Folders button.

4. Click the Microsoft Windows Backup link in the left window. Then double-click the backup that you created in the previous exercise. Choose the folder that you want to restore (I chose the Program Files folder, but you need to choose a folder with enough free space) and click Add. Click Next to continue.

5. Select whether you want files saved in the original location or a different location. To begin the restore, click Restore.

6. When the restore is complete, click Finish.

Recovering Files from OneDrive

As explained in Chapter 3, "Managing Data" Microsoft has a subscription-based storage system called OneDrive. Microsoft's OneDrive is built into Windows 10 by default. OneDrive is a cloud-based storage subscription service so home users can store their documents and then access those documents from anywhere in the world (provided that you have Internet access).

OneDrive was designed for the average home user who is looking to store data in a safe, secure, cloud-based environment. OneDrive, when first released, was also a consideration for corporate environments, but with the release of Windows Azure, OneDrive is really intended for the home user or corporate user who wants to store some of their own personal documents in the cloud. Corporations would be more inclined to use Microsoft Azure with all of its corporate benefits.

Exercise 7.5 will show you how to set up a OneDrive account for your user account. To do this, you must have a Microsoft account. You get 5 GB for free from Microsoft on the OneDrive cloud-based storage.

If you did Exercise 3.2 in Chapter 3, "Managing Data," please skip the following exercise.

EXERCISE 7.5

Configuring OneDrive

1. Open OneDrive.

2. Log into OneDrive using your Microsoft account.

3. You will get a screen that shows where your files will be located on your system. Click the Next button.

4. At the Sync Files screen, choose what folders you want to sync with Microsoft and then click Next.

   A screen will appear telling you that your OneDrive is set up and ready to go.

5. Click the Open My OneDrive Folder button to open your folders and Microsoft OneDrive.

6. Close OneDrive.

Now that the OneDrive subscription has been set up, you can recover files and folders by clicking Windows Explorer and then choosing OneDrive from the left side. You can recover any of the files and folders that were stored on OneDrive.

Using the Wbadmin Command Utility

Administrators have the ability to configure and manage backups and restores through the command prompt using a utility called Wbadmin. The Wbadmin.exe command replaces the Ntbackup.exe command that was released with previous versions of Windows. Wbadmin allows you to back up and restore your operating system, volumes, files, folders, and applications all from a command prompt.

You must be a member of the Administrators group to configure a regularly scheduled backup. To perform any other tasks using Wbadmin, you must be a member of either the Backup Operators group or the Administrators group, or you must have been delegated the appropriate permissions.

To run the Wbadmin.exe command, you must start it from an elevated command prompt. To do this, click Start, right-click the command prompt, and then click Run As Administrator.

Table 7.2 shows the Windows 10 Wbadmin command switches and their descriptions.

TABLE 7.2   Wbadmin switches

Command	Description
Wbadmin Start Backup	Runs a one-time backup
Wbadmin Stop job	Stops the currently running backup or recovery job
Wbadmin get versions	Shows the details of a backup
Wbadmin get items	Lists items contained in a backup
Wbadmin get status	Shows the status of the currently running operation

Using Advanced Backup Options

In the main Backup And Restore window, you have options in the left pane to turn off the schedule, create a system image, and create a system repair disk.

Choosing the Turn Off Schedule option lets you take your backup out of the current backup scheduling as seen in Task Scheduler. Creating a system image lets you back up critical operating system files for restoration later if your operating system becomes corrupt. Creating a system repair disc allows you to create a bootable disc with which you will have a limited set of repair utilities and the ability to restore your backup files if necessary.

Creating a System Image

A *system image* enables you to take a snapshot of the entire hard disk and capture that image to a specific location so you can restore that image at a later date.

To create a system image of your entire computer, select the Create A System Image link on the left side of the Backup and Restore utility. When creating a system image, you can save that image to a hard disk, a DVD, or a network location.

In Exercise 7.6, you will create a system image and save it to a local hard disk.

EXERCISE 7.6

Creating a System Image

1. Click Start ➢ Windows System ➢ Control Panel ➢ Backup And Restore (Windows 7).

2. Click the Create A System Image link on the left side.

3. Choose the location where you want to save the image. I am choosing the local D: drive. Click Next.

4. At the Confirm screen, click Start Backup.

5. A dialog box may appear, asking whether you want to create a system repair disc. Click the No button. If you want to create a system repair disc, you will need a DVD burner and a DVD.

6. When the image is complete, click the Close button.

After you create a system image, you may need to restore it. Let's take a look at the steps needed to complete a restore.

Restoring an Image

When you need to restore an image, you will use the System Image Recovery tool. To restore an image using this tool, you must perform the following steps:

1. Boot your computer by using the Windows 10 media, or use the recovery partition instructions provided by your computer manufacturer.

2. When the Install Windows dialog box appears, select the language, the time and currency format, and the keyboard or input method. Click Next to continue.

3. The Install Now button appears in the center of the screen. Click Repair Your Computer in the lower-left corner.

4. This opens the Windows Recovery Environment (WinRE), where you will choose the Troubleshoot option, then choose Advanced Options.

5. The Advanced Options dialog box appears. You can choose one of the following options:

    -   System Restore
    -   Startup Repair
    -   Uninstall Updates
    -   Command Prompt
    -   System Image Recovery
    -   UEFI Firmware Settings (if applicable)

    Choose System Image Recovery to continue.

6. Select the user account that has administrative privileges and then enter the password for that user account.

7. The Re-image Your Computer wizard will appear and the Use The Latest Available System Image (Recommended) option will be selected by default. If the image is okay, you can click Next to continue.

8. If you want to select a different image, you can choose Select A System Image, then click Next and follow the prompts to select the location of the image and the image you want to restore.

9. You will then be presented with a dialog box where you can select additional restore options, such as installing drivers, and formatting and repartitioning disks as well as choosing if the system will automatically install updates and reboot. Click Next.

10. You will be asked to review your selections. Click Finish to continue.

11. You will be warned one final time that all the data on the drive is to be replaced; you can then choose Yes to continue.

 If you were not provided with the Windows 10 media when you purchased your computer, the computer manufacturer might have placed the files on a recovery partition. Check with the manufacturer for more information.

Using System Protection

System Protection is a feature of Windows 10 that creates a backup and saves the configuration information of your computer's system files and settings on a regular basis. System Protection saves multiple previous versions of saved configurations rather than just overwriting them. This makes it possible to return to multiple configurations in your Windows 10 history, known as *restore points*. These restore points are created before most significant events, such as installing a new driver. Restore points are also created automatically every seven days. System Protection is turned on by default in Windows 10 for any drive formatted with NTFS.

You manage System Protection and the restore points from the System Protection tab of the System Properties dialog box. You can also access this tab directly by typing **restore point** into the Windows 10 search box or by clicking the Recovery icon in Control Panel.

Clicking the System Restore button launches the System Restore Wizard, which walks you through the process of returning Windows 10 to a previous point in time.

Also within the System Protection tab of the System Properties dialog box is the Protection Settings section, where you can configure any of your available drives. Select the drive for which you would like to modify the configuration and click the Configure button. The System Protection configuration dialog box for the drive appears.

The System Protection dialog box allows you to enable or disable system protection for the drive. When you enable protection, you can opt for previous versions of files or previous versions of files and system settings. You also have the ability to set the maximum disk space that your restore points will use for storage. Another function of the System Protection dialog box for the selected disk is to delete all restore points (including system settings and previous versions of files) by clicking the Delete button.

One tool included with restore points is shadow copies. Shadow copies are copies of files and folders that Windows automatically saves as part of a restore point. Normally, restore points are made only once a day if you have enabled System Protection. If System Protection is enabled, Windows will then automatically create shadow copies of files that have been modified since the last restore point was made.

One advantage of using restore points and shadow copies is the ability to restore files and folders using the Previous Versions tab. When you click any folder and choose Properties, the last tab on the right is Previous Versions. You can easily restore any folder by choosing one of these previous versions.

Creating Restore Points

Restore points contain Registry and system information as it was at a certain point in time. These restore points are created at the following times:

- Weekly
  - Before installing applications or drivers
  - Before significant system events
  - Before System Restore is used to restore files (so you can undo the changes if necessary)
  - Manually upon request

In Exercise 7.7, you will manually create a restore point.

EXERCISE 7.7

Creating a Restore Point

1. Click Start ➤ Windows System ➤ Control Panel ➤ System ➤ System Protection.

2. Click the Create button on the bottom of the screen.

3. At the System Protection dialog box, enter a description for the restore point. Click Create.

4. A dialog box states that the restore point was created. Click Close.

Restoring Restore Points

You can restore previously created restore points with System Restore. The restore operation will restore system files and settings but will not affect your personal files.

WARNING   System Restore will also remove any programs that have been installed since the restore point was created.

In Exercise 7.8, you will revert your system configuration to a previously captured restore point.

EXERCISE 7.8

Restoring a Restore Point

1. Click Start ➤ Windows System ➤Control Panel ➤ System ➤ System Protection.

2. Click the System Restore button. Click Next at the Restore System Files And Settings screen to continue.

3. Choose the restore point created in the previous exercise and click Next to continue.

4. Review your restore point selection, and click Finish to continue.

5. Click Yes to confirm that you want System Restore to continue.

6. System Restore will restore your system and reboot your computer to apply the changes. You should see a message stating that System Restore has restored your computer. Click OK to close the dialog box.

Cleaning Up Old Restore Points

One problem with creating multiple restore points is that they start to take up a large amount of your hard disk. You will need to clean up old restore points from time to time, and you can accomplish this task by using the Disk Cleanup utility.

The Disk Cleanup utility removes temporary files, empties the Recycle Bin, and removes a variety of system files and other items that you no longer need. When using the Disk Cleanup utility, you can also click the More Options tab and choose Programs And Features and System Restore And Shadow Copies to clean them up as well.

> The More Options tab is available when you choose to clean up files from all users on the computer.

To use the Disk Cleanup utility, click Start ➤ Windows System ➤ Control Panel ➤ Administrative Tools ➤ Disk Cleanup.

Using the Recycle Bin

Now we are going to talk about an icon that we have seen on our desktop for many years called the Recycle Bin. The Recycle Bin is a temporary storage container that holds deleted files. The advantage of having a temporary storage container is that you can restore or recycle the files to their original location. So basically, it allows you to undelete a deleted file.

When a file or folder is deleted on a computer, it isn't actually deleted. When files or folders get deleted, they get placed into the Recycle Bin. This works well because if you change your mind or realize that you actually need the file or folder, you can undelete it and it gets restored. The Recycle Bin allows you to perform a refresh or recycle of files that were deleted but shouldn't have been.

The Recycle Bin allows you to restore files or folders multiple ways. You can right-click the item and choose Restore or you can use the Manage tab (as shown in Figure 7.12).

FIGURE 7.12   Manage tab in Recycle Bin

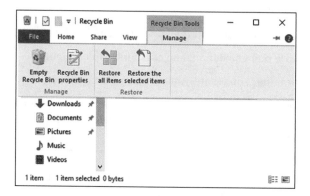

In Exercise 7.9, you will create a document and then delete the document. Then you will use the Recycle Bin to restore the document to its original location.

EXERCISE 7.9

Using the Recycle Bin

1.   On the Windows 10 desktop, right-click and choose New Text Document.

2.   Create a new test document called **Test.txt**.

3.   After the document is created, right-click the document and choose Delete.

4.   Double-click to open the Recycle Bin.

5.   You can either right-click the Test.txt document and choose Restore or click the document, and then on the Manage tab, choose Restore The Selected Item.

6.   Close the Recycle Bin, and the document should be back on the desktop.

Monitoring Windows

Because performance monitoring and optimization are vital functions in network environments of any size, Windows 10 includes several monitoring and performance tools.

Introducing Performance Monitor

The first and most useful tool is the Windows 10 *Performance Monitor*, which was designed to allow users and system administrators to monitor performance statistics for various operating system parameters. Specifically, you can collect, store, and analyze information about CPU, memory, disk, and network resources using this tool, and these are only a handful of the things you can monitor. By collecting and analyzing performance values, system administrators can identify many potential problems.

You can use the Performance Monitor in the following ways:

Performance Monitor ActiveX Control   The Windows 10 Performance Monitor is an ActiveX control that you can place within other applications. Examples of applications that can host the Performance Monitor control include web browsers and client programs such as Microsoft Word and Microsoft Excel. This functionality can make it easy for application developers and system administrators to incorporate the Performance Monitor into their own tools and applications.

Performance Monitor MMC   For more common performance monitoring functions, you'll want to use the built-in Microsoft Management Console (MMC) version of the Performance Monitor.

Data Collector Sets   Windows 10 Performance Monitor includes the Data Collector Set. This tool works with performance logs, telling Performance Monitor where the logs are stored and when the log needs to run. The Data Collector Sets also define the credentials used to run the set.

To access the Performance Monitor MMC, you open Administrative Tools and then choose Performance Monitor. This launches the Performance MMC and loads and initializes Performance Monitor with a handful of default counters.

You can choose from many different methods of monitoring performance when you are using Performance Monitor. A couple of examples are listed here:

- You can look at a snapshot of current activity for a few of the most important counters. This allows you to find areas of potential bottlenecks and monitor the load on your servers at a certain point in time.

- You can save information to a log file for historical reporting and later analysis. This type of information is useful, for example, if you want to compare the load on your servers from three months ago to the current load.

You'll get to take a closer look at this method and many others as you examine Performance Monitor in more detail.

In the following sections, you'll learn about the basics of working with the Windows 10 Performance Monitor and other performance tools. Then you'll apply these tools and techniques when you monitor the performance of your network.

Your Performance Monitor grows as your system grows, and whenever you add services to Windows 10, you also add to what you can monitor. You should make sure that, as you install services, you take a look at what it is you can monitor.

Deciding What to Monitor

The first step in monitoring performance is to decide *what* you want to monitor. In Windows 10, the operating system and related services include hundreds of performance statistics that you can track easily. For example, you may want to monitor the processor. This is just one of many items that can be monitored. All performance statistics fall into three main categories that you can choose to measure:

Performance Objects   A *performance object* within Performance Monitor is a collection of various performance statistics that you can monitor. Performance objects are based on various areas of system resources. For example, there are performance objects for the processor and memory as well as for specific services.

Counters   *Counters* are the actual parameters measured by Performance Monitor. They are specific items that are grouped within performance objects. For example, within the Processor performance object, there is a counter for % Processor Time. This counter displays one type of detailed information about the Processor performance object (specifically, the amount of total CPU time all of the processes on the system are using). Another set of counters you can use will allow you to monitor print servers.

Instances   Some counters will have *instances*. An instance further identifies which performance parameter the counter is measuring. A simple example is a server with two CPUs. If you decide you want to monitor processor usage (using the Processor performance object)—specifically, utilization (the % Total Utilization counter)—you must still specify *which* CPU(s) you want to measure. In this example, you would have the choice of monitoring either of the two CPUs or a total value for both (using the Total instance).

To specify which performance objects, counters, and instances you want to monitor, you add them to Performance Monitor using the Add Counters dialog box. Figure 7.13 shows the various options that are available when you add new counters to monitor using Performance Monitor.

The items that you will be able to monitor will be based on your hardware and software configuration. For example, if you have not installed and configured Hyper-V, the options available within the Hyper-V Server performance object will not be available. Or, if you have multiple network adapters or CPUs on the Windows 10 system, you will have the option of viewing each instance separately or as part of the total value.

FIGURE 7.13   Adding a new Performance Monitor counter

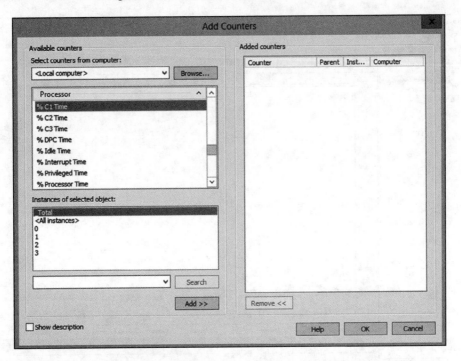

Viewing Performance Information

The Windows 10 Performance Monitor was designed to show information in a clear and easy-to-understand format. Performance objects, counters, and instances may be displayed in each of three views. This flexibility allows system administrators to quickly and easily define the information they want to see once and then choose how it will be displayed based on specific needs. Most likely, you will use only one view, but it's helpful to know what other views are available depending on what it is you are trying to assess.

You can use the following main views to review statistics and information on performance:

Graph View   The *Graph view* is the default display that is presented when you first access the Windows 10 Performance Monitor. The chart displays values using the vertical axis and time using the horizontal axis. This view is useful if you want to display values over a period of time or see the changes in these values over that time period. Each point that is plotted on the graph is based on an average value calculated during the sample interval for the measurement being made. For example, you may notice overall CPU utilization starting at a low value at the beginning of the chart and then becoming much higher during later measurements. This indicates that the server has become busier (specifically, with CPU-intensive processes). Figure 7.14 provides an example of the Graph view.

FIGURE 7.14 Viewing information in Performance Monitor Graph view

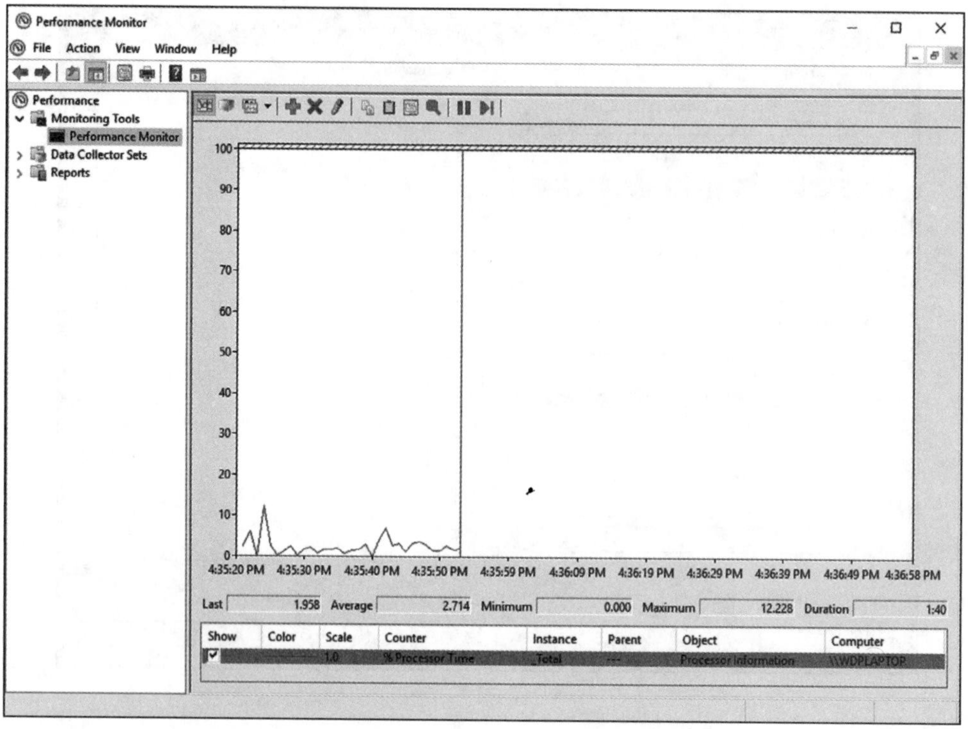

Histogram View The *Histogram view* shows performance statistics and information using a set of relative bar charts. This view is useful if you want to see a snapshot of the latest value for a given counter. For example, if you were interested in viewing a snapshot of current system performance statistics during each refresh interval, the length of each of the bars in the display would give you a visual representation of each value. It would also allow you to compare measurements visually relative to each other. You can set the histogram to display an average measurement as well as minimum and maximum thresholds. Figure 7.15 shows a typical Histogram view.

Report View Like the Histogram view, the *Report view* shows performance statistics based on the latest measurement. You can see an average measurement as well as minimum and maximum thresholds. This view is most useful for determining exact values because it provides information in numeric terms, whereas the Chart and Histogram views provide information graphically. Figure 7.16 provides an example of the type of information you'll see in the Report view.

FIGURE 7.15   Viewing information in Performance Monitor Histogram view

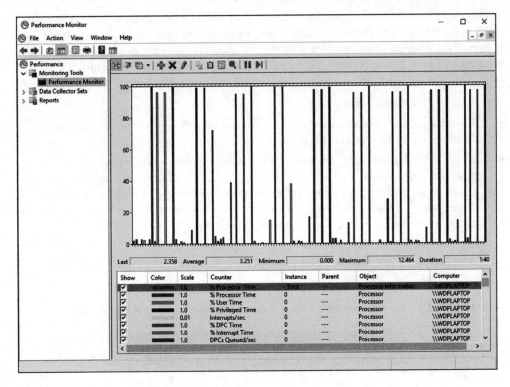

FIGURE 7.16   Viewing information in Performance Monitor Report view

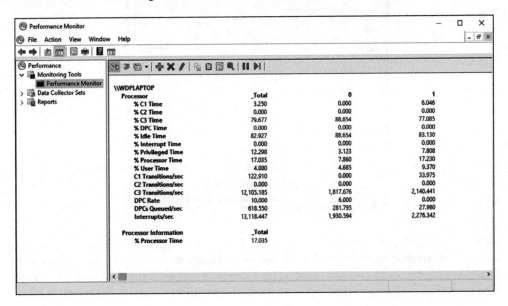

Managing Performance Monitor Properties

You can specify additional settings for viewing performance information within the properties of Performance Monitor. You can access these options by clicking the Properties button in the Taskbar or by right-clicking the Performance Monitor display and selecting Properties. You can change these additional settings by using the following tabs:

General Tab   On the General tab (shown in Figure 7.17), you can specify several options that relate to Performance Monitor views:

- You can enable or disable legends (which display information about the various counters), the value bar, and the toolbar.

- For the Report and Histogram views, you can choose which type of information is displayed. The options are Default, Current, Minimum, Maximum, and Average. What you see with each of these options depends on the type of data being collected. These options are not available for the Graph view because the Graph view displays an average value over a period of time (the sample interval).

- You can also choose the graph elements. By default, the display will be set to update every second. If you want to update less often, you should increase the number of seconds between updates.

FIGURE 7.17   General tab of the Performance Monitor Properties dialog box

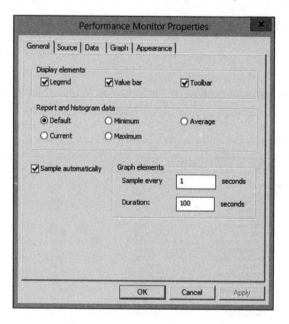

Source Tab   On the Source tab (shown in Figure 7.18), you can specify the source for the performance information you want to view. Options include current activity (the default setting) or data from a log file. If you choose to analyze information from a log file, you can also specify the time range for which you want to view statistics. I'll cover these selections in the next section.

FIGURE 7.18   Source tab of the Performance Monitor Properties dialog box

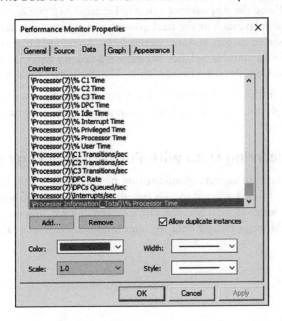

Data Tab   The Data tab (shown in Figure 7.19) lists the counters that have been added to the Performance Monitor display. These counters apply to the Chart, Histogram, and Report views. Using this interface, you can also add or remove any of the counters and change the properties, such as the width, style, and color of the line and the scale used for display.

FIGURE 7.19   The Data tab of the Performance Monitor Properties dialog box

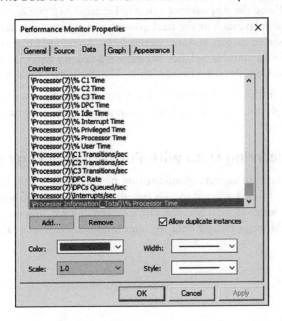

Graph Tab   On the Graph tab (shown in Figure 7.20), you can specify certain options that will allow you to customize the display of Performance Monitor views. First, you can specify what type of view you want to see (Line, Histogram, or Report). Then you can add a title for the graph, specify a label for the vertical axis, choose to display grids, and specify the vertical scale range.

FIGURE 7.20   The Graph tab of the Performance Monitor Properties dialog box

Appearance Tab   Using the Appearance tab (see Figure 7.21), you can specify the colors for the areas of the display, such as the background and foreground. You can also specify the fonts that are used to display counter values in Performance Monitor views. You can change settings to find a suitable balance between readability and the amount of information shown on one screen. Finally, you can set up the properties for a border.

Now that you have an idea of the types of information Performance Monitor tracks and how this data is displayed, we'll take a look at another feature—saving and analyzing performance data.

Saving and Analyzing Data with Performance Logs and Alerts

One of the most important aspects of monitoring performance is that it should be done over a given period of time (referred to as a *baseline*). So far, I have shown you how you can use Performance Monitor to view statistics in real time. I have, however, also alluded to using Performance Monitor to save data for later analysis. Now let's take a look at how you can do this.

FIGURE 7.21 The Appearance tab of the Performance Monitor Properties dialog box

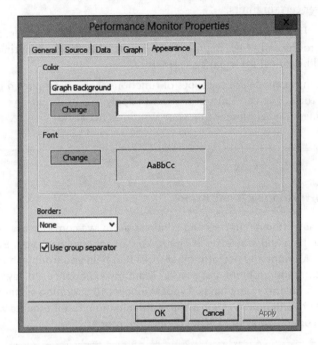

When viewing information in Performance Monitor, you have two main options with respect to the data on display:

View Current Activity When you first open the Performance icon from the Administrative Tools folder, the default option is to view data obtained from current system information. This method of viewing measures and displays various real-time statistics on the system's performance.

View Log File Data This option allows you to view information that was previously saved to a log file. Although the performance objects, counters, and instances may appear to be the same as those viewed using the View Current Activity option, the information itself was actually captured at a previous point in time and stored into a log file.

Log files for the View Log File Data option are created in the Performance Logs And Alerts section of the Windows 10 Performance tool.

Three items allow you to customize how the data is collected in the log files:

Counter Logs *Counter logs* record performance statistics based on the various performance objects, counters, and instances available in Performance Monitor. The values are updated based on a time interval setting and are saved to a file for later analysis.

Circular Logging In *circular logging*, the data that is stored within a file is overwritten as new data is entered into the log. This is a useful method of logging if you want to record information only for a certain time frame (for example, the past four hours). Circular logging also conserves disk space by ensuring that the performance log file will not continue to grow over certain limits.

Linear Logging   In *linear logging*, data is never deleted from the log files, and new information is added to the end of the log file. The result is a log file that continually grows. The benefit is that all historical information is retained.

Now that you have an idea of the types of functions that are supported by the Windows 10 Performance tools, you can learn how you can apply this information to the task at hand—monitoring and troubleshooting your Windows network.

 Real World Scenario

Real-World Performance Monitoring

In our daily jobs as system engineers and administrators, we come across systems that are in need of our help and may even ask for it. You, of course, check your Event Viewer and Performance Monitor and perform other tasks that help you troubleshoot. But what is really the most common problem that occurs? From my experience, I'd say that you suffer performance problems many times if your Windows 10 operating system is installed on a subpar system. Either the system's hardware minimum requirements weren't addressed or the operating system is not configured properly.

Using Other Performance-Monitoring Tools

Performance Monitor allows you to monitor different parameters of the Windows 10 operating system and associated services and applications. However, you can also use three other tools to monitor performance in Windows 10. They are Reliability Monitor, Task Manager, and Event Viewer. All three of these tools are useful for monitoring different areas of overall system performance and for examining details related to specific system events. In the following sections, you'll take a quick look at these tools and how you can best use them.

Reliability Monitor

Windows 10 Reliability Monitor is part of the Windows Reliability and Performance Monitor Snap-in for Microsoft Management Console (MMC). The easiest way to access the Reliability Monitor is to type **perfmon /rel** in the Start Search box and press Enter.

The Reliability Monitor provides a system stability overview and allows an administrator to get details about events that may be impacting the Windows 10 reliability. Reliability Monitor calculates a stability index based on a certain period of time and it then shows that stability index in the System Stability Chart.

The Reliability Monitor shows information, all on their own separate lines, about application failures, Windows failures, miscellaneous failures, warnings, and information.

The Reliability Monitor shows an administrator a period of time on the Windows 10 system and the administrator can click on any of the events during that specific period of time and see what Information, Warnings, or Errors that may have happened during that time period.

Administrators can then use the information gathered by the Reliability Monitor to help diagnose the issues that the Windows 10 system may be having.

Task Manager

Performance Monitor is designed to allow you to keep track of specific aspects of system performance over time. But what do you do if you want to get a quick snapshot of what the local system is doing? Creating a System Monitor chart, adding counters, and choosing a view is overkill. Fortunately, the Windows 10 Task Manager has been designed to provide a quick overview of important system performance statistics without requiring any configuration. Better yet, it's always readily available.

You can easily access Task Manager in several ways:

- Right-click the Windows Taskbar, and then click Task Manager.

- Press Ctrl+Alt+Del, and then select Task Manager.

- Press Ctrl+Shift+Esc.

- Type **Taskman** in the Windows Search box.

Each of these methods allows you to access a snapshot of the current system performance quickly.

Once you access Task Manager, you will see the following seven tabs:

 These tabs can be different on Windows client machines. For example, Windows 10 Home can vary from Windows 10 Enterprise.

Processes Tab   The Processes tab shows you all the processes that are currently running on the local computer. By default, you'll be able to view how much CPU time and memory a particular process is using. By clicking any of the columns, you can quickly sort by the data values in that particular column. This is useful, for example, if you want to find out which processes are using the most memory on your server.

By accessing the performance objects in the View menu, you can add columns to the Processes tab. Figure 7.22 shows a list of the current processes running on a Windows 10 computer.

FIGURE 7.22 Viewing process statistics and information using Task Manager

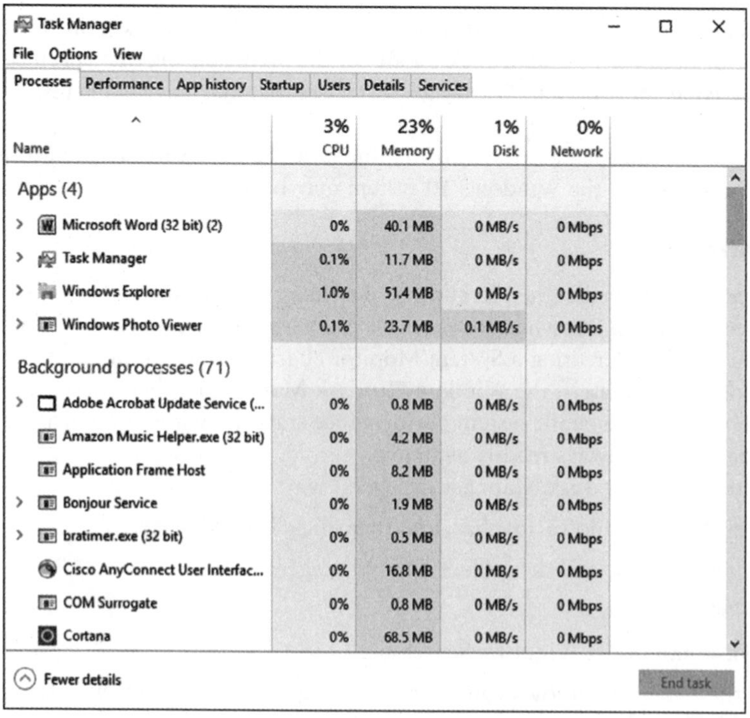

Performance Tab   One of the problems with using Performance Monitor to get a quick snapshot of system performance is that you have to add counters to a chart. Most system administrators are too busy to take the time to do this when all they need is basic CPU and memory information. That's where the Performance tab of Task Manager comes in. Using the Performance tab, you can view details about how memory is allocated on the computer and how much of the CPU is utilized (see Figure 7.23).

App History   This tab shows you all of the recent applications that have been running on the Windows 10 system. Users have the ability to Delete Usage History from this tab.

Startup   The Startup tab shows an administrator or user which applications get started when the machine first starts up. Some applications require that services start at system startup for the applications to run properly.

Users Tab   The Users tab (see Figure 7.24) lists the currently active user accounts. This is particularly helpful if you want to see who is online and quickly log off or disconnect users.

FIGURE 7.23   Viewing CPU and memory performance information using Task Manager

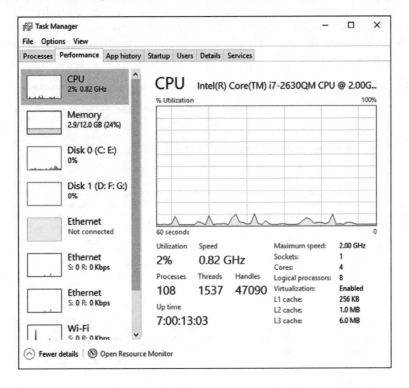

FIGURE 7.24   Viewing user information using Task Manager

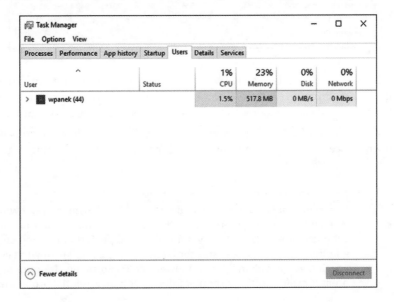

Details Tab   The Details tab (see Figure 7.25) shows you what applications are currently running on the system. From this location, you can stop an application from running by right-clicking the application and choosing Stop. You also have the ability to set your affinity level here. By setting the affinity, you can choose which applications will use which processors on your system.

FIGURE 7.25   Viewing currently running applications using Task Manager

Name	PID	Status	User name	CPU	Memory (p...	Description
Amazon Music Help...	5720	Running	wpanek	00	4,256 K	Amazon Music Help...
AppleMobileDeviceS...	2860	Running	SYSTEM	00	2,144 K	MobileDeviceService
ApplicationFrameHo...	1328	Running	wpanek	00	8,376 K	Application Frame ...
armsvc.exe	2396	Running	SYSTEM	00	860 K	Adobe Acrobat Upd...
audiodg.exe	1496	Running	LOCAL SE...	00	4,884 K	Windows Audio Dev...
bratimer.exe	2356	Running	SYSTEM	00	544 K	bratimer.exe
conhost.exe	12740	Running	SYSTEM	00	948 K	Console Window H...
csrss.exe	616	Running	SYSTEM	00	1,132 K	Client Server Runtim...
csrss.exe	6180	Running	SYSTEM	00	892 K	Client Server Runtim...
dasHost.exe	1360	Running	LOCAL SE...	00	9,020 K	Device Association F...
dkab1err.exe	11296	Running	wpanek	00	1,552 K	Printer Alert Utility
dkabcoms.exe	2376	Running	SYSTEM	00	59,436 K	Printer Communicat...
dllhost.exe	1468	Running	wpanek	00	800 K	COM Surrogate
dllhost.exe	14112	Running	wpanek	00	24,524 K	COM Surrogate
dwm.exe	6472	Running	DWM-2	01	25,960 K	Desktop Window M...
explorer.exe	10000	Running	wpanek	01	52,812 K	Windows Explorer
FAHWindow.exe	8864	Running	wpanek	01	1,840 K	File Association Hel...
Fitbit Connect.exe	12592	Running	wpanek	00	4,140 K	Fitbit Connect Deskt...
FitbitConnectService...	2936	Running	NETWORK...	00	10,508 K	Fitbit Connect Servi...
FLxHClm.exe	4972	Running	wpanek	00	1,200 K	Fresco Logic
FspUip.exe	13416	Running	wpanek	00	3,608 K	Finger Sensing Pad -...
GfExperienceService....	2424	Running	SYSTEM	00	2,724 K	NVIDIA GeForce Exp...
HPCustPartic.exe	6532	Running	wpanek	00	2,320 K	HP Customer Partici...

Services Tab   The Services tab (see Figure 7.26) shows you what services are currently running on the system. From this location, you can stop a service from running by right-clicking the service and choosing Stop. The Open Services link launches the Services MMC.

As you can see, Task Manager is useful for providing important information about the system quickly. Once you get used to using Task Manager, you won't be able to get by without it!

Make sure that you use Task Manager and familiarize yourself with all that it can do; you can end processes that have become intermittent, kill applications that may hang the system, view NIC performance, and so on. In addition, you can access this tool quickly to get an idea of what could be causing you problems. Event Viewer and Performance Monitor are both great tools for getting granular information on potential problems.

FIGURE 7.26   Viewing services information using Task Manager

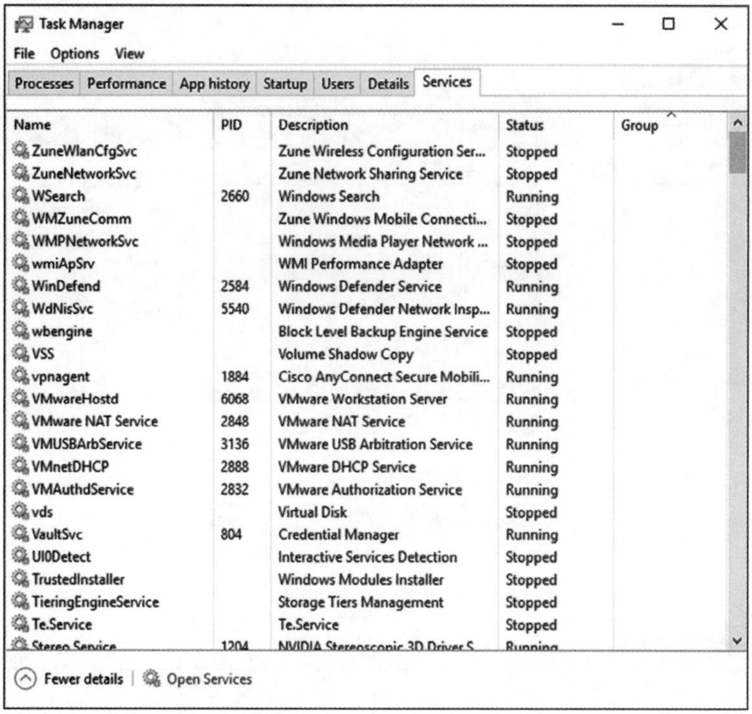

Event Viewer

Event Viewer is also useful for monitoring network information. Specifically, you can use the logs to view any information, warnings, or alerts related to the proper functioning of the network (see Figure 7.27). You can access Event Viewer by selecting Windows Administrative Tools ➤ Event Viewer or by right-clicking the Start button and choosing Event Viewer. Clicking any of the items in the left pane displays the various events that have been logged for each item.

Each event that is preceded by a blue "i" icon designates that these events are informational and do not indicate problems with the network. Rather, they record benign events such as Microsoft Office startup or a service starting.

Problematic or potentially problematic events are indicated by a yellow warning icon or a red error icon (see Figure 7.28). Warnings usually indicate a problem that wouldn't prevent a service from running but might cause undesired effects with the service in question.

FIGURE 7.27 Event Viewer

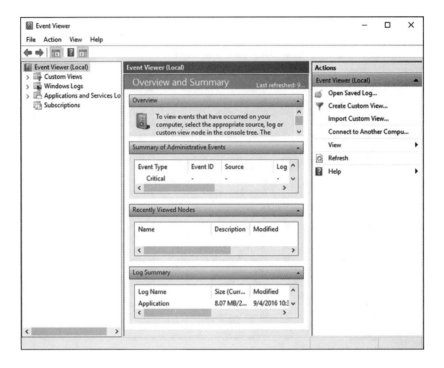

FIGURE 7.28 Information, errors, and warnings in Event Viewer

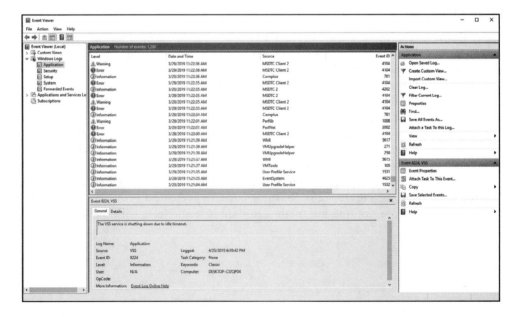

Error events almost always indicate a failed service, application, or function. For instance, if the dynamic registration of a DNS client fails, Event Viewer will generate an error. As you can see, errors are more severe than warnings because, in the case of DNS, the DNS client cannot participate in DNS at all because of the error.

Double-clicking any event opens its Event Properties dialog box, as shown in Figure 7.29, which displays a detailed description of the event.

FIGURE 7.29 An Event Properties dialog box

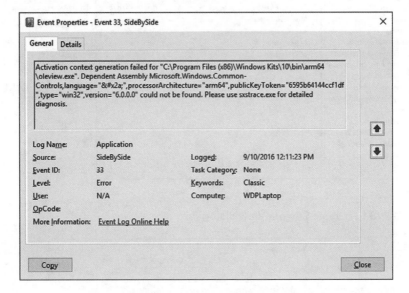

Event Viewer can display thousands of different events, so it would be impossible to list them all here. The important points of which you should be aware are the following:

- Information events are always benign.

- Warnings indicate noncritical problems.

- Errors indicate showstopping events.

Let's discuss some of the logs and the ways that you can view data:

Applications and Services The *applications and services logs* are part of Event Viewer where applications (for example, Hardware events) and services log their events. Internet Explorer events would be logged in this part of Event Viewer. An important log in this section is the Key Management Service log (see Figure 7.30). This is where all of your Key Management Service events get stored.

Custom Views *Custom views* allow you to filter events (see Figure 7.31) to create your own customized look. You can filter events by event level (critical, error, warning, and so on), by logs, and by source. You also have the ability to view events occurring within a specific time frame. This allows you to look only at the events that are important to you.

FIGURE 7.30 The applications and services logs

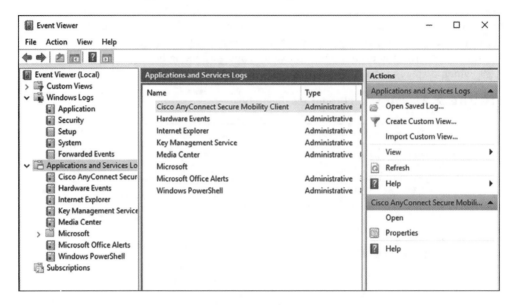

FIGURE 7.31 Create Custom View dialog box

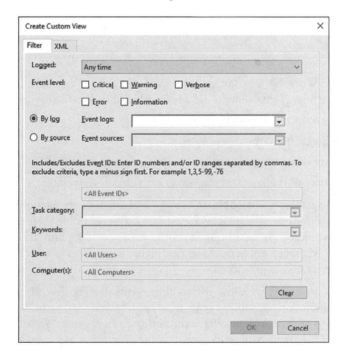

Subscriptions   *Subscriptions* allow a user to receive alerts about events that you predefine. In the Subscription Properties dialog box (see Figure 7.32), you can define what type of events you want notifications about and the notification method. The Subscriptions section is an advanced alerting service to help you watch for events.

FIGURE 7.32   Subscription Properties dialog box

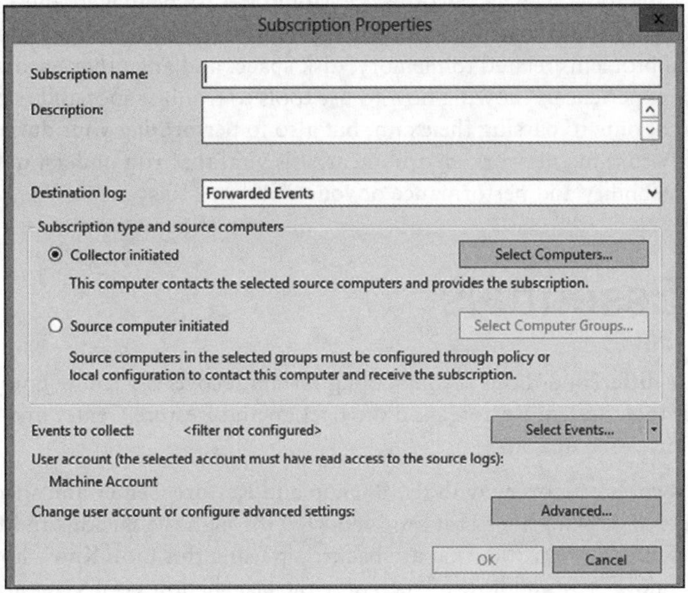

Summary

In this chapter, you looked at the different ways to recover and protect your Windows 10 machine from hardware and software issues. We discussed using the Advanced Boot Options such as Safe Mode and VGA Mode.

Another important item that needs to be completed on a Windows 10 machine is Backup and Restore (Windows 7). Backing up a Windows 10 machine protects data in the event of a hardware or software failure.

We also discussed how to back up a complete copy of Windows 10 by using images. An image allows you to copy the entire Windows 10 machine and then reimage the machine in the event of a major failure. Another way to protect data is by the use of shadow copies. Shadow copies, which are a part of System Protection, allow you to keep previous versions of data and revert to a previous version in the event of a problem.

The chapter also covered monitoring the Windows 10 system. Monitoring performance on Windows 10 is imperative to rooting out any issues that may affect your network. If your systems are not running at their best, your end users may experience issues such as latency, or worse, you may experience corruption in your network data. Either way, it's important to know how to monitor the performance of your systems.

We also examined how to use the various performance-related tools that are included with Windows 10. Tools such as Performance Monitor, Task Manager, and Event Viewer can help you diagnose and troubleshoot system performance issues. These tools will help you find typical problems related to memory, disk space, and any other hardware-related issues you may experience. Knowing how to use tools to troubleshoot and test your systems is imperative, not only to passing the exam, but also to performing your duties at work. To have a smoothly running network environment, it is vital that you understand the issues related to the reliability and performance of your Windows 10 systems.

Exam Essentials

Understand the different options for managing system recovery.   Know how to use the Startup Repair tool, System Restore, and the Backup and Restore Center and when it is appropriate to use each option.

Be able to perform file recovery with the Backup and Restore Center and shadow copies.   Understand the options that are supported through the Backup and Restore (Windows 7) Center and the files that are backed up using this tool. Know how to manually create a shadow copy and how to keep only the last shadow copy version.

Know how to troubleshoot using Advanced Boot Options.   Be able to list the options that can be accessed through Advanced Boot Options, and know when it is appropriate to use each option. Know the difference between Safe Mode and Enable Low-Resolution Video.

Know the importance of common performance counters.   Several important performance-related counters deal with general system performance. Know the importance of monitoring memory, print server, CPU, and network usage on a busy server.

Understand the role of other troubleshooting tools.   Windows Task Manager and Event Viewer can both be used to diagnose and troubleshoot configuration- and performance-related issues.

Understand how to troubleshoot common sources of server reliability problems.
Windows 10 has been designed to be a stable, robust, and reliable operating system. Should you experience intermittent failures, you should know how to troubleshoot device drivers and buggy system-level software.

Video Resources

There are no videos for this chapter.

Review Questions

1. You need to stop an application from running in Task Manager. Which tab would you use to stop an application from running?

   A. Performance

   B. Users

   C. Options

   D. Details

2. You have a computer that runs Windows 10. You upgrade the network adapter driver on the computer. After the upgrade, you can no longer access network resources. You open Device Manager and see a warning symbol next to the network adapter. You need to restore access to network resources. What should you do?

   A. Roll back the network adapter driver.

   B. Assign a static IP address to the network adapter.

   C. Disable the network adapter and scan for hardware changes.

   D. Uninstall the network adapter and scan for hardware changes.

3. You need to back up the existing data on a computer before you install a new application. You also need to ensure that you are able to recover individual user files that are replaced or deleted during the installation. What should you do?

   A. Create a system restore point.

   B. Perform an Automated System Recovery (ASR) backup and restore.

   C. In the Backup And Restore Center window, click the Back Up Now button.

   D. In the Backup And Restore Center window, click the Back Up Computer button.

4. Your data-recovery strategy must meet the following requirements:

   - Back up all data files and folders in C:\Data.

   - Restore individual files and folders in C:\Data.

   - Ensure that data is backed up to and restored from external media.

   What should you do?

   A. Use the Previous Versions tab to restore the files and folders.

   B. Use the System Restore feature to perform backup and restore operations.

   C. Use the NTBackup utility to back up and restore individual files and folders.

   D. Use the Backup and Restore Center to back up and restore files.

5. You need to ensure that you can recover system configuration and data if your computer hard disk fails. What should you do?

   A. Create a system restore point.

   B. Create a backup of all file categories.

   C. Create a Backup and Restore image.

   D. Perform an Automated System Recovery (ASR) backup.

6. You have a computer that runs Windows 10. Your computer has two volumes, C: and D:. Both volumes are formatted by using the NTFS filesystem. You need to disable previous versions on the D: volume. What should you do?

   A. From System Properties, modify the System Protection settings.

   B. From the properties of the D: volume, modify the Quota settings.

   C. From the properties of the D: volume, modify the Sharing settings.

   D. From the Disk Management Snap-in, convert the hard disk drive that contains the D: volume to Dynamic.

7. You have a computer that runs Windows 10. You configure a backup job to back up all files and folders on an external NTFS filesystem hard disk drive. The backup job fails to back up all files that have the encryption attribute set. You need to back up all encrypted files. The backed-up files must remain encrypted. What should you do?

   A. Manually copy the encrypted files to the external hard disk drive.

   B. Schedule a backup job to occur when you are not logged on to the computer.

   C. Enable Volume Shadow Copy on the external drive and schedule a backup job.

   D. Add the certificate of the local administrator account to the list of users who can transparently access the files, and schedule a backup job.

8. You have a computer that runs Windows 10. You use Windows Backup and Restore to create a backup image. You need to perform a complete restore of the computer. What are two possible ways to begin the restore? (Each correct answer presents a complete solution. Choose two.)

   A. Open the Windows Backup and Restore Center and click Advanced Restore.

   B. Open the Windows Backup and Restore Center and click Restore Computer.

   C. Start your computer. From the Advanced Boot Options menu, select Repair Your Computer.

   D. Start the computer by using the Windows 10 installation media. Select Repair Your Computer.

9. You are the network administrator for your organization. You are asked by a junior administrator when he should create restore points. Which of the following are times when restore points should be created? (Choose all that apply.)

   A. Every day

   B. Before installing applications or drivers

   C. Before significant system events

   D. Before System Restore is used to restore files (so you can undo the changes if necessary)

10. You install Windows 10 on a new computer. You update the video card driver and restart the computer. When you start the computer, the screen flickers and then goes blank. You restart the computer and receive the same result. You need to configure the video card driver. What should you do first?

    A. Restart the computer in Safe Mode.

    B. Restart the computer in Debugging Mode.

    C. Restart the computer in low-resolution video mode.

    D. Insert the Windows 10 installation media into the computer, restart, and use System Recovery to perform a startup repair.

Exam MD-101

Chapter 8

Installing and Updating Windows 10

MICROSOFT EXAM OBJECTIVES COVERED IN THIS CHAPTER:

✓ **Plan and implement Windows 10 by using dynamic deployment**

- Evaluate and select an appropriate deployment options; pilot deployment; manage and troubleshoot provisioning packages.

✓ **Plan and implement Windows 10 by using Windows Autopilot**

- Evaluate and select an appropriate deployment options; pilot deployment; create, validate, and assign deployment profile; extract device HW information to CSV file; import device HW information to cloud service; troubleshoot deployment.

✓ **Upgrade devices to Windows 10**

- Identify upgrade and downgrade paths; manage in-place upgrades; configure a Windows analytics environment; perform Upgrade Readiness assessment; migrate user profiles.

✓ **Manage updates**

- Configure Windows 10 delivery optimization; configure Windows Update for Business; deploy Windows updates; implement feature updates; monitor Windows 10 updates.

This book is for exam MD-101, and this is the second of two Windows 10 exams (MD-100 and MD-101) for the Microsoft 365 Certified: Modern Desktop Administrator Associate. If you are using both of the Sybex books for the Microsoft 365 Certified: Modern Desktop Administrator Associate, you will notice that some of the topics in Chapter 1 are the same in both books. The reason for this is that no matter what test you take, installing Windows 10 is the same. Where the two books start to differ is with automated installations. Many of these automated installations will require an Azure subscription along with Intune.

But as with the start of any journey, we must take our first steps. The first steps for this exam is with learning about the Windows 10 installation process. It is important that you understand the different versions of Windows 10 and which one is right for you and your organization.

Understanding the Basics

Microsoft Windows 10 is the latest version of Microsoft's client operating system software and according to Microsoft, it's the last. Microsoft has announced that Windows 10 will be the last client operating system and they will just continue to do edition updates. Windows 10 combines the best of Windows 7 and Windows 8 and it also makes it much easier to work within the cloud.

Microsoft has released many different editions of the Windows 10 operating system. The following list is just a few of the more popular editions:

- Windows 10 Home
- Windows 10 Pro
- Windows 10 Pro for Workstation
- Windows 10 Enterprise
- Windows 10 Enterprise E3
- Windows 10 Enterprise E5
- Windows 10 Education

Microsoft also offers some of these operating systems as slimmed down versions called "Windows 10 IoT Core." This edition is one of the above Windows 10 versions that don't require a monitor or system. For example, suppose you are building a toy robot and you want to load Windows 10 into his core computer. You can use the IoT versions to run the robot's functionality.

Windows 10 has been improved in many of the weak areas that plagued Windows 8. Windows 10 has a much faster boot time and shutdown compared to Windows 8. It also brings back the Start button that we are all so familiar with from previous editions.

The Windows 10 operating system functions are also faster than their previous counterparts. The processes for opening, moving, extracting, compressing, and installing files and folders are more efficient than they were in previous versions of Microsoft's client operating systems.

Let's take a look at some of the features of each Windows 10 edition (this is just an overview of some of the benefits to using Windows 10). Table 8.1 and Table 8.2 show each edition and what some of the features are for those editions.

 The information in Table 8.1 and Table 8.2 was taken directly from Microsoft's website and documentation.

TABLE 8.1 Windows 10 Security and Protection

Description	Home	Pro	Pro for Workstation	E3	E5
Integrity enforcement of operating system boot up process	■	■	■	■	■
Integrity enforcement of sensitive operating system components	■	■	■	■	■
Advanced vulnerability and zero-day exploit mitigations	■	■	■	■	■
Reputation based network protection for Microsoft Edge, Internet Explorer, and Chrome	■	■	■	■	■
Host based firewall	■	■	■	■	■
Ransomware mitigations	■	■	■	■	■
Pre-execution emulation executables and scripts	■	■	■	■	■
Runtime behavior monitoring	■	■	■	■	■
In memory anomaly and behavior monitoring	■	■	■	■	■

TABLE 8.1 Windows 10 Security and Protection *(continued)*

Description	Home	Pro	Pro for Workstation	E3	E5
Machine learning and AI based protection from viruses and malware threats	▪	▪	▪	▪	▪
Cloud protection for fastest responses to new/unknown web-based threats	▪	▪	▪	▪	▪
Protection from fileless based attacks	▪	▪	▪	▪	▪
Industry standards based multifactor authentication	▪	▪	▪	▪	▪
Support for biometrics (Facial and Fingerprints)	▪	▪	▪	▪	▪
Support for Microsoft Authenticator	▪	▪	▪	▪	▪
Support for Microsoft compatible security devices	▪	▪	▪	▪	▪
Automatic encryption on capable devices	▪	▪	▪	▪	▪
Advanced encryption configuration options		▪	▪	▪	▪
Removable storage protection		▪	▪	▪	▪
Supports for Active Directory and Azure Active Directory		▪	▪	▪	▪
Hardware based isolation for Microsoft Edge		▪	▪	▪	▪
Application control powered by the Intelligent Security Graph		▪	▪	▪	▪
Device Control (e.g.: USB)		▪	▪	▪	▪
Personal and business data separation		▪	▪	▪	▪
Application access control		▪	▪	▪	▪

Description	Home	Pro	Pro for Workstation	E3	E5
Copy and paste protection		▪	▪	▪	▪
Removable storage protection		▪	▪	▪	▪
Integration with Microsoft Information Protection		▪	▪	▪	▪
Network protection for web-based threats				▪	▪
Enterprise management of hardware-based isolation for Microsoft Edge				▪	▪
Hardware isolation of single sign-in tokens				▪	▪
Direct Access & Always On VPN device Tunnel				▪	▪
Centralized configuration mgmt, analytics, reporting, and security operations					▪
Centralized management, analytics, reporting, and operations					▪
Customizable network protection for web-based threats					▪
Host intrusion prevention rules					▪
Device-based conditional access					▪
Tamper protection of operating system					▪
Advanced monitoring, analytics, and reporting for attack surface					▪
Advanced machine learning and AI based protection for apex level viruses and malware threats					▪
Advanced cloud protection that includes deep inspection and detonation					▪

TABLE 8.1 Windows 10 Security and Protection *(continued)*

Description	Home	Pro	Pro for Workstation	E3	E5
Emergency outbreak protection from the Intelligent Security Graph					▪
ISO 27001 compliance					▪
Geolocation and sovereignty of sample data					▪
Sample data retention policy					▪
Monitoring, analytics- and reporting for Next Generation Protection capabilities					▪

TABLE 8.2 Windows 10 Updates

Description	Home	Pro	Pro for Workstation	E3	E5
In-place upgrades	▪	▪	▪	▪	▪
Express updates	▪	▪	▪	▪	▪
Delivery optimization	▪	▪	▪	▪	▪
Windows Analytics Upgrade Readiness		▪	▪	▪	▪
Windows Analytics Update Compliance		▪	▪	▪	▪
Windows Update for Business		▪	▪	▪	▪
Windows Analytics Device Health				▪	▪
30 months of support for September targeted releases				▪	▪
Windows 10 LTSC Access				▪	▪

Windows 10 Features

Now that you have seen which editions contain which features, let's take a look at some of the Windows 10 features in greater detail. This section describes only a few of these features, but all features will be explained throughout this book.

Cortana Integration   Windows 10 comes with Cortana integration. Cortana is your very own personal assistant. You can type in or ask Cortana a question and Cortana will seek out the best possible answer based on your question.

Secure Boot   Windows 10 provides the ability for securely booting the operating system. Secure boot validates all drivers and operating system components before they are loaded against the signature database. If you are going to implement the Secure Boot feature of Windows 10, then make sure the system firmware is set up as Unified Extensible Firmware Interface (UEFI) and not BIOS. You also need to make sure the disks are converted from Master Boot Record (MBR) disks to a GUID Partition Table (GPT) disk.

Virtual Smart Cards   Windows 10 has started offering a new way to do two-factor authentication with virtual smart cards. Virtual smart cards help an IT department that doesn't want to invest in extra hardware and smart cards. Virtual smart cards use Trusted Platform Module (TPM) devices that allow for the same capabilities as physical smart cards with the physical hardware.

Miracast   Windows 10 allows you to project your Windows 10 laptop or mobile device to a projector or television. Miracast allows you to connect to an external device through the use of your mobile wireless display (WiDi) adapter.

Hyper-V   Windows 10 (except Home version) comes with Hyper-V built into the operating system. Hyper-V is Microsoft's version of a Virtual Server.

Enterprise Data Protection   Windows 10 Enterprise Data Protection (EDP) helps protect corporate data in a world that is increasingly becoming a Bring Your Own Device (BYOD) environment. Since many organizations are allowing employees to connect their own devices to their network, the possibility of corporate data being compromised because of noncorporate programs running on these personnel devices is increasing. For example, many third-party apps may put corporate data at risk by accidentally disclosing corporate information through the application.

Enterprise Data Protection helps protect information by separating corporate applications and corporate data from being disclosed by personal devices and personal applications.

Device Guard   Because employees can use multiple types of Windows 10 devices (Surface Pros, Windows Phones, and Windows 10 computer systems), Device Guard is a feature that helps guarantee that only trusted applications will run on any of these devices.

Device Guard uses both hardware and software security features to lock down a device so it can run only trusted and approved applications. This also helps protect against hackers running malicious software on these devices.

Microsoft Passport / Windows Hello   Microsoft has introduced two security features for Windows 10 called Windows Hello and Microsoft Passport. Windows Hello is a biometrics system integrated into Windows 10 and it is a piece of the user's authentication experience. Microsoft Passport allows users to use a two-factor authentication system that combines a PIN or biometrics with an encrypted key from a user's device to provide two-factor authentication.

Start Menu   Windows 10 has brought back the Start Menu that users are familiar with. The Windows 10 Start Menu combines the best of both Windows 7 and Windows 8. So the Start Menu gives you a menu that we were familiar with in Windows 7 as well as the Live Tiles that users liked in Windows 8.

Microsoft Edge and Internet Explorer 11   Windows 10 has introduced a new way to surf the Internet with Microsoft Edge. But Windows 10 also still comes with Internet Explorer 11 in the event that you need to run ActiveX controls or run backward-compatible web services or sites.

Microsoft Edge allows users to start using many new Microsoft features, including Web Note (allows you to annotate, highlight, and call things out directly on web pages), Reading View (allows you to print and save as a PDF for easy reading), and Cortana (personal assistant).

Domain Join and Group Policy   Depending on the version of Windows 10 that you are using, administrators have the ability to join Windows 10 clients to either a corporate version of Active Directory or a cloud-based version of Azure Active Directory.

Microsoft Store for Business   Microsoft Store has included many applications that allow users to get better functionality and productivity out of their Windows 10 devices. One advantage for corporations is that they can create their own applications and load them into the Microsoft Store for users to download (called *sideloading*).

Mobile Device Management   Mobile Device Management (MDM) allows administrators to set up Windows 10 policies that can integrate many corporate scenarios, including the ability to control users' access to the Windows Store and the ability to use the corporate VPN. MDM also allows administrators to manage multiple users who have accounts set up on Microsoft Azure Active Directory (Azure AD). Windows 10 MDM support is based on the Open Mobile Alliance (OMA) Device Management (DM) protocol 1.2.1 specification.

Understanding the Windows 10 Architecture

Windows 10 has limited the number of files that load at system startup to help with the core performance of the operating system. Microsoft has also removed many of the fluff items that Windows Vista used, allowing for better performance.

Microsoft offers both a 32-bit version and a 64-bit version of Windows 10. The terms *32-bit* and *64-bit* refer to the CPU, or processor. The number represents how the data is processed. It is processed either as 2^{32} or 2^{64}. The larger the number, the larger the amount of data that can be processed at any one time.

To get an idea of how 32-bit and 64-bit processors operate, think of a large highway with 32 lanes. Vehicles can travel on those 32 lanes only, so when traffic gets backed up, the result is delays. Now think of how many more vehicles can travel on a 64-lane highway. The problem here is that a 32-lane highway can't handle the number of vehicles a 64-lane highway can. You need to have the infrastructure to allow for that volume of vehicles. The same is true for computers. Your computer has to be configured to allow you to run a 64-bit processor.

So what does all of this mean to the common user or administrator? It's all about random access memory, or RAM. A 32-bit operating system can handle up to 4 GB of RAM, and a 64-bit processor can handle up to 16 exabytes (EB) of RAM. None of this is new. Although 64-bit processors are just starting to get accepted with Windows systems, other operating systems, such as Apple, have been using 64-bit processors for many years.

When you're installing or upgrading Windows 10, the version of Windows 10 must match the CPU version. For example, if your system is a 32-bit system, you must use a 32-bit OS. If your system is a 64-bit system, you can install either the 32-bit or 64-bit version of Windows 10.

Computer processors are typically rated by speed. The speed of the processor, or central processing unit (CPU), is rated by the number of clock cycles that can be performed in 1 second. This measurement is typically expressed in gigahertz (GHz). One GHz is one billion cycles per second. Keep in mind that processor architecture must also be taken into account when considering processor speed. A processor with a more efficient pipeline will be faster than a processor with a less-efficient pipeline at the same CPU speed.

Preparing to Install Windows 10

Installing Windows 10 can be relatively simple because of the installation wizard. The installation wizard will walk you through the entire installation of the operating system.

The most difficult part of installing Windows 10 is preparing and planning for the installation. One thing I often say to IT pros is, "An hour of planning will save you days of work." Planning a Windows 10 rollout is one of the hardest and most important tasks that you will perform when installing Windows 10.

There are many decisions that should be made before you install Windows 10. The first decision is which edition of Windows 10 you want to install. As mentioned previously, Microsoft has six different editions of the Windows 10 operating system. This allows an administrator to custom-fit a user's hardware and job function to the appropriate version of Windows 10. Many times, Microsoft releases multiple editions of the operating system contained within the same Windows 10 media disk. You can choose to unlock the one you want based on the product key you have. Let's take a closer look at the different versions of Windows 10.

> In this book, I will not talk much about Windows 10 Education. Windows 10 Education is the counterpart to Windows 10 Enterprise, but it is a volume-licensed version of Windows 10 that is specifically priced for educational institutions. Educational institutions receive the same Enterprise functionality, but they pay much less than a corporation.

Windows 10 Pro

Windows 10 Pro is designed for small-business owners. Microsoft designed Windows 10 Pro for users to get more done and safeguard their data. Pro offers the following features:

- Broad application and device compatibility with unlimited concurrent applications.
- A safe, reliable, and supported operating system.
- Microsoft Passport/Windows Hello.
- Domain Join.
- Improved Taskbar and Jump Lists.
- Enterprise Mode Internet Explorer (EMIE).
- Advanced networking support (ad hoc wireless networks and Internet connection sharing).
- View Available Networks (VAN). Windows 10 by default has the ability, when you use a wireless network adapter, to choose the wireless network that you want to connect to by using the wireless network adapter properties.
- Mobility Center.
- Action Center, which makes it easier to resolve many IT issues yourself.
- Easy networking and sharing across all your PCs and devices.
- Group Policy Management.
- Windows Update and Windows Update for Business.
- Multitouch.
- Improved handwriting recognition.
- Domain Join, which enables simple and secure server networking.
- BitLocker, which protects data on removable devices.
- Device Encryption.
- Encrypting File System, which protects data.

- Client Hyper-V.
- Location Aware Printing, which helps find the right printer when moving between the office and home.
- Start Menu that includes Live Tiles.

Windows 10 Enterprise

Windows 10 Enterprise is the version designed for midsize and large organizations. This operating system has the most features and security options of all Windows 10 versions. Here are some of the features:

- Broad application and device compatibility with unlimited concurrent applications.
- A safe, reliable, and supported operating system.
- Microsoft Passport/Windows Hello.
- Enterprise Mode Internet Explorer (EMIE).
- Group Policy Management.
- Windows Update and Windows Update for Business.
- Advanced networking support (ad hoc wireless networks and Internet connection sharing).
- View Available Networks (VAN). Windows 10 by default has the ability, when you use a wireless network adapter, to choose the wireless network that you want to connect to by using the wireless network adapter properties.
- Mobility Center.
- Easy networking and sharing across all your PCs and devices.
- Multitouch.
- Start Menu that includes Live Tiles.
- Improved handwriting recognition.
- Domain Join, which enables simple and secure server networking.
- Device Encryption.
- Encrypting File System, which protects data.
- Location Aware Printing, which helps find the right printer when you are moving between the office and home.
- Client Hyper-V.
- Credential Guard.
- Device Guard.
- BitLocker, which protects data on removable devices.
- DirectAccess, which links users to corporate resources from the road without a virtual private network (VPN).

- BranchCache, which makes it faster to open files and web pages from a branch office.

- AppLocker, which restricts unauthorized software and also enables greater security hardware requirements

Windows 10 Enterprise E3 and E5

Microsoft has released a new cloud-based way to deploy Windows 10 Enterprise with the introduction of Windows 10 Enterprise E3 and E5. Windows 10 Enterprise E3 and E5 are subscription-based versions of Windows 10 for organizations that like to work with Microsoft Office 365.

When Microsoft released Windows 10 version 1703, it included a Windows 10 Enterprise E3 and E5 benefit for Microsoft customers with either Enterprise Agreements (EA) or Microsoft Products & Services Agreements (MPSA).

One of the advantages of using the subscription-based service for Windows 10 E3 and E5 is that the Windows 10 license can be purchased per user or per device. If the licenses are per user, the users can then choose to download the corporate version of Windows 10 E3 or E5 onto either their work systems or personal systems (depending on corporate policies).

As you saw in Table 8.1 and Table 8.2, by purchasing the Windows 10 E3 and E5 subscriptions, you get many additional features, including enterprise-level security and control. Some of the E3 and E5 components are available if you would like to purchase them separately.

New Install or Upgrade?

Once you've determined that your hardware meets the minimum requirements, you need to decide whether you want to do an upgrade or a clean install. An upgrade allows you to retain your existing operating system's applications, settings, and files.

The bad news is that if you are moving from Windows Vista, Windows XP, or earlier versions of Windows to Windows 10, you must perform a clean install. You can perform an upgrade to Windows 10 if the following conditions are true:

- You are running Windows 7 or Windows 8.

- You want to keep your existing applications and preferences.

- You want to preserve any local users and groups you've created.

You must perform a clean install of Windows 10 if any of the following conditions are true:

- There is no operating system currently installed.

- You have an operating system installed that does not support an in-place upgrade to Windows 10 (such as DOS, Windows 9x, Windows NT, Windows Me, Windows 2000 Pro, Windows Vista, or Windows XP).

- You want to start from scratch, without keeping any existing preferences.

- You want to be able to dual-boot between Windows 10 and your previous operating system.

Table 8.3 shows each operating system that can be upgraded and the edition of Windows 10 to which it should be upgraded.

TABLE 8.3 Windows 7 and Windows 8 upgrade options

From Current Edition	Windows 10 Edition
Windows 7 Pro	Windows 10 Pro
Windows 7 Ultimate	Windows 10 Pro
Windows 7 Enterprise	Windows 10 Enterprise
Windows 8.1 Home	Windows 10 Home
Windows 8.1 Pro	Windows 10 Pro
Windows 8.1 Enterprise	Windows 10 Enterprise
Windows 8.1 Pro for Students	Windows 10 Pro

Upgrade Considerations

Almost all Windows 7 and Windows 8 applications should run with the Windows 10 operating system. However, possible exceptions to this statement include the following:

- Applications that use file-system filters, such as antivirus software, may not be compatible.
- Custom power-management tools may not be supported.

Before upgrading to Windows 10, be sure to stop any antivirus scanners, network services, or other client software. These software packages may see the Windows 10 install as a virus and cause installation issues.

If you are performing an upgrade installation to the same partition as an existing version of Windows, the contents of the existing Users (or Documents and Settings), Program Files, and Windows directories will be placed in a directory named Windows.old, and the old operating system will no longer be available.

Another issue that you may need to look at is the user's profile. Depending if your company uses roaming profiles, these profiles will be stored on a local server. Starting with Windows 7, Microsoft started using roaming profile version numbers to identify what operating system is using what profile. The following list shows some of the different operating systems and what roaming profile version numbers go with the operating system:

- Windows XP and Windows Server 2003 \\<servername>\<fileshare>\<username>
- Windows Vista and Windows Server 2008 \\<servername>\<fileshare>\<username>.V2

- Windows 7 and Windows Server 2008 R2 \\<servername>\<fileshare>\<username>.V2
- Windows 8 and Windows Server 2012 (after updates) \\<servername>\<fileshare>\ <username>.V3
- Windows 8.1 and Windows Server 2012 R2 (after updates) \\<servername>\<fileshare> \<username>.V4
- Windows 10 (before version 1607) \\<servername>\<fileshare>\<username>.V5
- Windows 10 (after version 1607) \\<servername>\<fileshare>\<username>.V6

Hardware Compatibility Issues

You need to ensure that you have Windows 10 device drivers for your hardware. If you have a video driver without a Windows 10–compatible driver, the Windows 10 upgrade will install the Standard VGA driver, which will display the video with an 800×600 resolution. Once you get the Windows 10 driver for your video, you can install it and adjust video properties accordingly.

Application Compatibility Issues

Not all applications that were written for earlier versions of Windows will work with Windows 10. After the upgrade, if you have application problems, you can address the problems in any of the following ways:

- If the application is compatible with Windows 10, reinstall the application after the upgrade is complete.
- If the application uses dynamic-link libraries (DLLs) and there are migration DLLs for the application, apply the migration DLLs.
- Use the Microsoft Application Compatibility Toolkit (ACT) to determine the compatibility of your current applications with Windows 10. ACT will determine which applications are installed, identify any applications that may be affected by Windows updates, and identify any potential compatibility problems with User Account Control and Internet Explorer. Reports can be exported for detailed analysis.
- If applications were written for earlier versions of Windows but are incompatible with Windows 10, use the Windows 10 Program Compatibility Wizard. From the Control Panel, click the Programs icon, and then click the Run Programs From Previous Versions link to start the Program Compatibility Wizard. If the application is not compatible with Windows 10, upgrade your application to a Windows 10–compliant version.

An Upgrade Checklist

Once you have made the decision to upgrade, you should develop a plan of attack. The following upgrade checklist (valid for upgrading from Windows 7 or Windows 8/8.1) will help you plan and implement a successful upgrade strategy:

- Verify that your computer meets the minimum hardware requirements for Windows 10.
- Make sure you have the Windows 10 drivers for the hardware. You can verify this with the hardware manufacturer.

- To audit the current configuration and status of your computer, run the Get Windows 10 App tool from the Microsoft website, which also includes documentation on using the utility. It will generate a report of any known hardware or software compatibility issues based on your configuration. You should resolve any reported issues before you upgrade to Windows 10.

- Make sure your BIOS is current. Windows 10 requires that your computer has the most current BIOS. If it does not, it may not be able to use advanced power-management features or device-configuration features. In addition, your computer may cease to function during or after the upgrade. Use caution when performing BIOS updates because installing the incorrect BIOS can cause your computer to fail to boot.

- If you are going to implement the Secure Boot feature of Windows 10, then make sure the system firmware is set up as Unified Extensible Firmware Interface (UEFI) and not BIOS. You also need to make sure the disks are converted from Master Boot Record (MBR) disks to a GUID Partition Table (GPT) disk.

- Take an inventory of your current configuration. This inventory should include documentation of your current network configuration, the applications that are installed, the hardware items and their configuration, the services that are running, and any profile and policy settings.

- Back up your data and configuration files. Before you make any major changes to your computer's configuration, you should back up your data and configuration files and then verify that you can successfully restore your backup. Chances are, if you have a valid backup, you won't have any problems. Likewise, if you don't have a valid backup, you will likely have problems.

- Delete any unnecessary files or applications, and clean up any program groups or program items you don't use. Theoretically, you want to delete all the junk on your computer before you upgrade. Think of this as the spring-cleaning step.

- Verify that there are no existing problems with your hard drive prior to the upgrade. Perform a disk scan, a current virus scan, and defragmentation. These too are spring-cleaning chores. This step just prepares your hard drive for the upgrade.

- Perform the upgrade. In this step, you upgrade from the Windows 7 or Windows 8/8.1 operating system to Windows 10.

- Verify your configuration. After Windows 10 has been installed, use the inventory to compare and test each element that was inventoried prior to the upgrade to verify that the upgrade was successful.

Handling an Upgrade Failure

Before you upgrade, you should have a contingency plan in place. Your plan should assume the worst-case scenario. For example, what happens if you upgrade and the computer doesn't work anymore? It is possible that, after checking your upgrade list and verifying that everything should work, your attempt at the actual upgrade may not work. If this happens, you may want to return your computer to the original, working configuration.

Indeed, I have made these plans, created my backups (two, just in case), verified them, and then had a failed upgrade anyway—only to discover that I had no clue where to find the original operating system CD. A day later, with the missing CD located, I was able to get up and running again. My problem was an older BIOS, and the manufacturer of my computer did not have an updated BIOS.

Disk Partitioning

Disk partitioning is the act of taking the physical hard drive and creating logical partitions. A logical drive is how space is allocated to the drive's primary and logical partitions. For example, if you have a 500 GB hard drive, you might partition it into three logical drives:

- C: drive, which might be 200 GB
- D: drive, which might be 150 GB
- E: drive, which might be 150 GB

The following list details some of the major considerations for disk partitioning:

Partition Size   One important consideration in your disk-partitioning scheme is determining the partition size. You need to consider the amount of space taken up by your operating system, the applications that will be installed, and the amount of stored data. It is also important to consider the amount of space required in the future.

Microsoft recommends that you allocate at least 16 GB of disk space for Windows 10. This allows room for the operating system files and for future growth in terms of upgrades and installation files that are placed with the operating system files.

The System and Boot Partitions   When you install Windows 10, files will be stored in two locations: the system partition and the boot partition. The system partition and the boot partition can be the same partition.

The system partition contains the files needed to boot the Windows 10 operating system. The system partition can be set as either a Master Boot Record (MBR) disk or a GUID Partition Table (GPT) disk. It is often the first physical hard drive in the computer and normally contains the necessary files to boot the computer. The files stored on the system partition do not take any significant disk space. The active partition is the system partition that is used to start your computer. The C: drive is usually the active partition.

The boot partition contains the Windows 10 operating system files. By default, the Windows operating system files are located in a folder named Windows.

Disk Partition Configuration Utilities   If you are partitioning your disk prior to installation, you can use several utilities, such as the DiskPart utility, or a third-party utility, such as Paragon Partition Magic. You can also configure the disks during the installation of the Windows 10 operating system.

You might want to create only the first partition where Windows 10 will be installed. You can then use the Disk Management utility in Windows 10 to create any other partitions you need.

Language and Locale

Language and locale settings determine the language the computer will use. Windows 10 supports many languages for the operating system interface and utilities.

Locale settings are for configuring the format for items such as numbers, currencies, times, and dates. For example, English for the United States specifies a short date as mm/dd/yyyy (month/day/year), while English for South Africa specifies a short date as yyyy/mm/dd (year/month/day).

It is very important to only choose the locales that this machine will need to use. The reason for this is that for every locale you choose, your system will get updates for all chosen locales that you set up.

Installing Windows 10

The first step to installing Windows 10 is to know what type of media you need to install the Windows 10 operating system. Windows 10 gives you multiple ways to do an install.

You can install Windows 10 either from the bootable DVD or through a network installation using files that have been copied to a network share point or USB device. You can also install Windows 10 by using a virtual hard drive (vhd). You can also launch the setup.exe file from within the Windows 10 operating system to upgrade your operating system.

To start the installation, you simply restart your computer and boot to the DVD. The installation process will begin automatically. You will walk through the steps of performing a clean install of Windows 10 from the DVD in Exercise 8.1.

If you are installing Windows 10 from the network, you need a distribution server and a computer with a network connection. A distribution server is a server that has the Windows 10 distribution files copied to a shared folder. The following steps are used to install Windows 10 over the network:

1. Boot the target computer.

2. Attach to the distribution server and access the share that has the files copied to it.

3. Launch setup.exe.

4. Complete the Windows 10 installation using either the clean install method or the upgrade method. These methods are discussed in detail in the following sections.

Performing a Clean Install of Windows 10

On any installation of Windows 10, there are three stages.

Collecting Information   During the collection phase of the installation, Windows 10 gathers the information necessary to complete the installation. This is where Windows 10 gathers your local time, location, keyboard, license agreement, installation type, and installation disk partition information.

Installing Windows   This section of the installation is where your Windows 10 files are copied to the hard disk and the installation is completed. This phase takes the longest because the files are installed.

Setting Up Windows   In this phase, you set up a username, computer name, and password; enter the product key; configure the security settings; and review the date and time. Once this is finished, your installation will be complete.

As explained earlier, you can run the installation from the optical media, from a USB, or over a network. The only difference in the installation procedure is your starting point: from your optical drive or USB or a network share. The steps in Exercise 8.1 and Exercise 8.2 assume you are using the Windows 10 DVD to install Windows 10.

When you boot to the Windows 10 installation media, the Setup program will automatically start the Windows 10 installation. In Exercise 8.1, you will perform a clean install of Windows 10. This exercise assumes that you have access to Windows 10 Enterprise; other editions may vary slightly. You can also download an evaluation version of Windows 10 from the Microsoft website.

Also, I may list steps that you may not see or I may not list steps that you see—this is because my version of Windows may be different. For example, I am installing an MSDN Windows 10 Enterprise edition. At this time, I am not required to enter a license number during install. A normal version bought from a vendor may ask for the license during the actual install.

I am loading Windows 10 Enterprise into a Hyper-V virtual machine. Again, this may make your installation a little different than the steps listed in Exercise 8.1. Plus, depending on your version and license model, not all screens may appear.

EXERCISE 8.1

Performing a Clean Install of Windows 10

1.   Insert the Windows 10 DVD or .iso image in the machine or virtual machine with no operating system and start the computer.

2.   If you are directed to "Hit any key" to start the DVD, press Enter.

3.   The first screen will ask you to enter your language, time and currency format, and keyboard or input method (see Figure 8.1). After filling in these fields, click Next.

FIGURE 8.1   Windows Setup screen

4.   On the next screen, click the Install Now button (see Figure 8.2).

FIGURE 8.2   Windows install screen

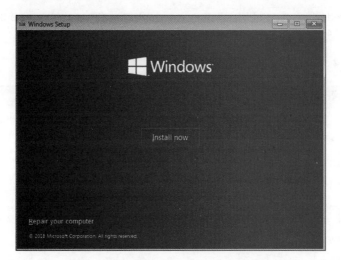

5.   Depending on your installation media, the next screen will ask you which version of Windows 10 you want to install. I am choosing Windows 10 Enterprise (see Figure 8.3).

FIGURE 8.3 Windows version screen

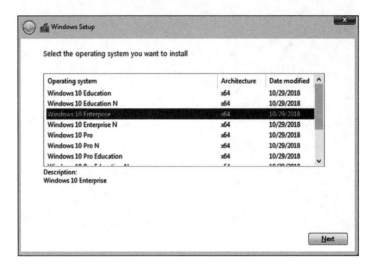

6. A message appears to tell you that the setup is starting. The licensing screen will be first. Read the license agreement and then check the I Accept The License Terms check box. Click Next.

7. When asked which type of installation you want, click Custom (Advanced) as shown in Figure 8.4.

FIGURE 8.4 Type of install screen

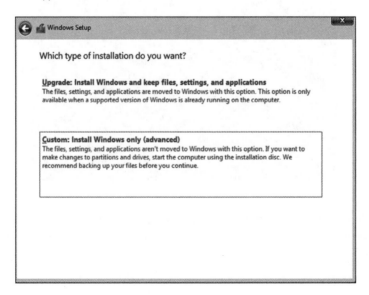

8. The next screen asks you to identify the disk to which you would like to install Windows 10. Choose an unformatted free space or a partition (partition will be erased) with at least 32 GB available. You can also click the Drive Options (Advanced) link to create and format your own partition as shown in Figure 8.5. Click the New link and click Apply to create the new partition for Windows 10. A message will appear stating that Windows 10 will set some partitions for system files. Just click the OK button. After you choose your partition, click Next.

FIGURE 8.5   Windows disk setup screen

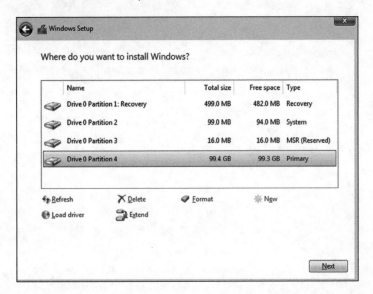

9. When your partition is set, the installation will start (as shown in Figure 8.6). You will see the progress of the installation during the entire process. When the installation is complete, the machine will reboot.

FIGURE 8.6   Windows installation status screen

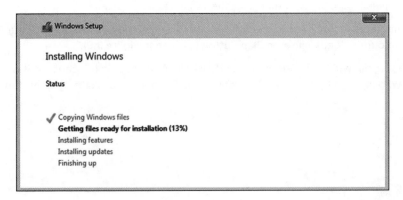

10. After the restart, a screen appears that asks you to choose your region. Select your region (see Figure 8.7), and then click the Next button.

FIGURE 8.7 Choose your region screen

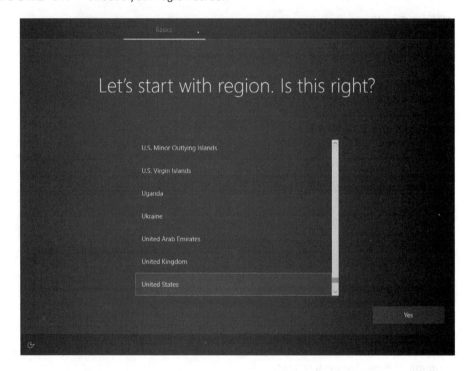

11. The next screen will ask you about your keyboard layout. Choose your keyboard layout (see Figure 8.8) and then click the Yes button.

12. The next screen will ask you if you have a second keyboard. If you do, click the Add Layout button. If not, click the Skip button (as seen in Figure 8.9).

13. At the sign in with Microsoft screen, choose the Domain Join Instead link. It will ask you who is going to use this PC. Enter your username and click the Next button.

FIGURE 8.8 Choosing your keyboard layout

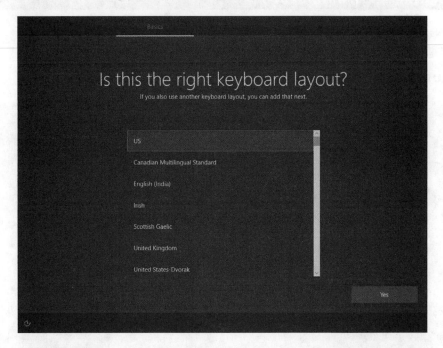

FIGURE 8.9 Adding a second keyboard

14. Next it's going to ask you to enter a super memorable password (as shown in Figure 8.10). Type in your password and click the Next button.

FIGURE 8.10   Windows 10 screen

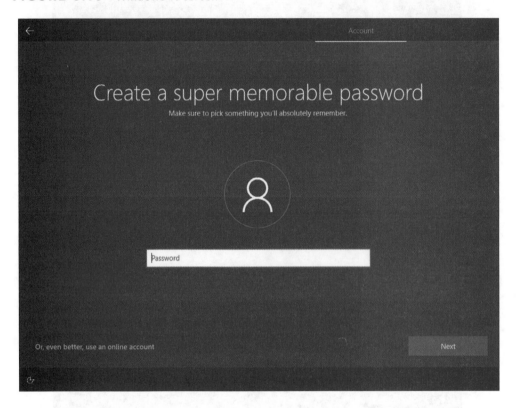

15. You will be asked to reenter your password. Enter your password again and click the Next button.

16. Depending on your version, you may be asked to create three security questions. If your edition asks this, put in your security questions and click the Next button for each security question. After the third question, click the Next button to move on.

17. The next screen will ask if you want to make Cortana your personal assistant. You can choose either Accept or Decline. I am going to choose Decline.

18. The next screen will ask if you want Microsoft to save your activity history. If you accept this, you will send Microsoft information about all activities that you are doing. This allows you to continue to finish these activities from any other device. Since this is a corporate machine, I will choose not to send Microsoft my activity history by choosing the No button (see Figure 8.11).

FIGURE 8.11   Windows activity screen

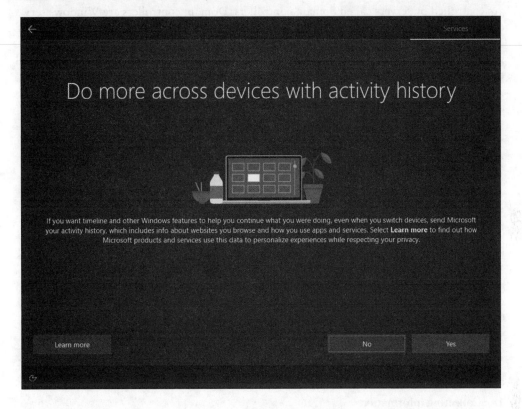

19. The next screen will be the privacy settings screen. Enable or disable any of the privacy settings that you want disabled (all will be enabled by default). Once you're complete, click the Accept button.

20. A different screen will appear letting you know that the system is being set up. This may take a few minutes. Be sure not to turn off the machine during this process. Once this is all completed, the system may ask you to log in. Put in your password and click the right arrow next to the password box. Your installation is now complete.

Before we talk about the Windows 10 upgrade procedure, I want to quickly explain something that you saw during the Windows 10 install. In step 13, I had you choose "Domain Join Instead" instead of using a Microsoft account. We will explore both of the choices in greater detail, but I wanted to quickly explain why we chose one over the other.

Microsoft offers two main networks: workgroup-based or domain-based. *Workgroups* (also referred to also as peer-to-peer networks) is when you just connect your computers together directly to each other. A perfect example for most of us is what you do in your home network. Most home users connect their machines together without the use of a main server.

Corporations normally do things a bit differently than that. *Domains* are networks that are controlled by servers called domain controllers. Domain controllers are Windows servers that have a copy of a database called Active Directory (AD). Recently Microsoft took domain-based networks a step further by allowing companies to set up a cloud-based version of an Active Directory domain (Azure AD). This means that companies no longer need to maintain and manage their own domain controllers.

Most companies that decide to start moving to an Azure based network will also have an onsite domain. This is a hybrid network that includes both on-site and cloud-based networks. This book will focus heavily on that type of hybrid set up.

Performing an Upgrade to Windows 10

This section describes how to perform an upgrade to Windows 10 from Windows 8.1. Similar to a clean install, you can run the installation from the installation DVD, from a USB drive, or over a network. The only difference in the installation procedure is your starting point: from your optical or USB drive or from a network share. For the steps in this section, it is assumed that you are using the Windows 10 DVD to install the Windows 10 operating system.

Upgrading a Windows 7 or Windows 8/8.1 system to Windows 10 will save you a lot of time and trouble. Because we are upgrading the system, all of the user's data and applications will remain installed and most likely still work the exact same way. Sometimes when we upgrade a system, we run into problems with applications. But many times that is caused by a driver or a needed software update that will most likely solve the issue.

The three main steps in the Windows 10 upgrade process are very similar to the ones for a clean install. The three steps of upgrading to Windows 10 are as follows:

1. Collecting information

2. Installing Windows

3. Setting up Windows

In Exercise 8.2, you will go through the process of installing Windows 10 by upgrading Windows 8.1. I have a Windows 8.1 Enterprise system that I will update to Windows 10 Enterprise.

EXERCISE 8.2

Upgrading Windows 8.1 to Windows 10

1. Insert the Windows 10 DVD. (We are upgrading Windows 8.1 Enterprise to Windows 10 Enterprise.)

2. If Autorun does not start, navigate to the DVD drive and click setup.exe. Once the setup starts (via either setup.exe or Autorun), click Run Setup.exe as shown in Figure 8.12.

FIGURE 8.12   DVD setup screen

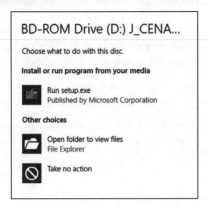

3. If a pop-up box appears for User Account Control, click the Yes button (see Figure 8.13).

FIGURE 8.13   User Account Control screen

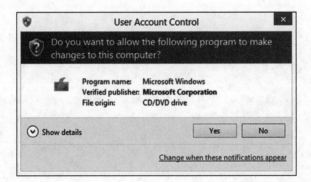

You should then see a message appear stating that Windows is preparing the system, as shown in Figure 8.14.

FIGURE 8.14   Preparing screen

4. You may be prompted to Get Important Updates. You can choose to either download the updates or not do them at this time. Make a choice and click the Next button. (During my installation, I decided to download the updates.)

5. The Microsoft Windows 10 license terms appear. Read the terms and then click Accept. (The installation will not allow you to continue until you click Accept.)

6. At the Ready To Install screen (shown in Figure 8.15), you can change what files and/ or apps you want to keep by clicking the Change What To Keep link. Once you're ready, click the Install button.

FIGURE 8.15 Ready To Install screen

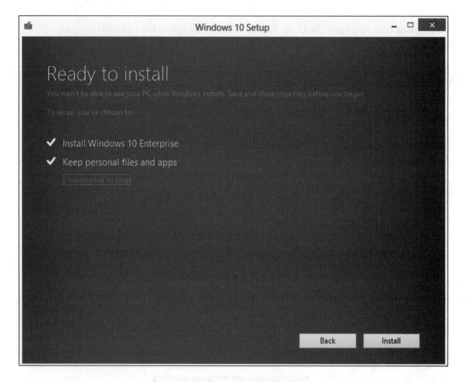

7. Windows 10 will begin to install (as shown in Figure 8.16). Your computer may restart multiple times. This is normal. As the upgrade status screen states, "Sit back and relax."

8. After the upgrade has completed, a welcome screen will be displayed, similar to the one shown in Figure 8.17. Click Next.

FIGURE 8.16   Installing status screen

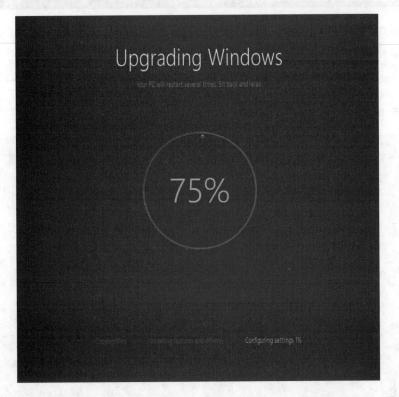

FIGURE 8.17   Welcome screen

9. At the Get Going Fast screen, click the Use Express Settings button.

10. At the New Apps screen, just click Next.

And that's it—Windows 10 is installed (see Figure 8.18). Congrats.

FIGURE 8.18 Windows 10 screen

Now that we have installed the Windows 10 operating system, let's take a look at how to change your system's locales. Earlier I explained that the locale settings help you with the system's language format, settings, and region specific details.

In Exercise 8.3, I will show you how to change your current locale. This helps when you take your Windows 10 laptop, tablet, or phone to another part of the world.

EXERCISE 8.3

Configuring Locales

1. Click the Start button and choose Settings.

2. Once in the Settings screen, choose Time And Language.

3. This should place you on the Date & Time screen. Make sure your time zone is set correctly. If it's not, pull down the time zone options and choose your time zone.

4. Scroll down and make sure the date and time formats are set the way you want. If they are not, click the Change Date And Time Formats link. Change the formats to the way you want them set.

5. Click the Region And Language link on the left-hand side.

6. Make sure the country or region is set properly. If you want to add a second language to this Windows 10 system, click the Add A Language link. Choose the language you want.

7. Once completed, close the Settings screen.

Troubleshooting Installation Problems

The Windows 10 installation process is designed to be as simple as possible. The chances for installation errors are greatly minimized through the use of wizards and the step-by-step process. However, it is possible that errors will occur.

Identifying Common Installation Problems

As most of you are aware, installations sometimes do get errors. You might encounter some of the following installation errors:

Media Errors   Media errors are caused by defective or damaged DVDs. To check the disc, put it into another computer and see if you can read it. Also check your disc for scratches or dirt—it may just need to be cleaned.

Insufficient Disk Space   Windows 10 needs at least 16 GB for the 32-bit OS and 20 GB for the 64-bit OS to execute properly. If the Setup program cannot verify that this space exists, the program will not let you continue.

Not Enough Memory   Make sure your computer has the minimum amount of memory required by Windows 10 (1 GB for 32-bit or 2 GB for 64-bit). Having insufficient memory may cause the installation to fail or blue-screen errors to occur after installation.

Not Enough Processing Power   Make sure your computer has the minimum processing power required by Windows 10 (1 GHz or faster processor or system-on-a-chip (SoC)). Having insufficient processing power may cause the installation to fail or blue-screen errors to occur after installation.

Hardware That Is Not on the HCL   If your hardware is not listed on the Hardware Compatibility List, Windows 10 may not recognize the hardware or the device may not work properly.

Hardware with No Driver Support   Windows 10 will not recognize hardware without driver support.

Hardware That Is Not Configured Properly   If your hardware is Plug and Play (PnP) compatible, Windows 10 should configure it automatically. If your hardware is not Plug and Play compatible, you will need to manually configure the hardware per the manufacturer's instructions.

Incorrect Product Key   Without a valid product key, the installation will not go past the Product Key screen. Make sure you have not typed in an incorrect key (check your Windows 10 installation folder or your computer case for this key).

Incorrect CPU Version   When installing or upgrading Windows10, the version of Windows 10 that is installed must match the CPU version. For example, if your system is a 32-bit system, you must use a 32-bit version of Windows 10. If your system is a 64-bit system, you can install either the 32-bit or 64-bit version of Windows 10.

Failure to Access TCP/IP Network Resources   If you install Windows 10 with typical settings, the computer is configured as a DHCP client. If there is no DHCP server to provide IP configuration information, the client will still generate an autoconfigured IP address but be unable to access network resources through TCP/IP if the other network clients are using DHCP addresses.

Installing Nonsupported Hard Drives   If your computer is using a hard disk that does not have a driver included on the Windows 10 media, you will receive an error message stating that the hard drive cannot be found. You should verify that the hard drive is properly connected and functional. You will need to obtain a disk driver for Windows 10 from the manufacturer and then specify the driver location by selecting the Load Driver option during partition selection.

Troubleshooting with Installation Log Files

When you install Windows 10, the Setup program creates several log files. You can view these logs to check for any problems during the installation process. Two log files are particularly useful for troubleshooting:

- The action log includes all of the actions that were performed during the setup process and a description of each action. These actions are listed in chronological order. The action log is stored as \Windows\panther\setupact.log.

- The error log includes any errors that occurred during the installation. For each error, there is a description and an indication of the severity of the error. This error log is stored as \Windows\panther\setuperr.log.

In Exercise 8.4, you will view the Windows 10 Setup logs to determine whether there were any problems with your Windows 10 installation.

EXERCISE 8.4

Troubleshooting Failed Installations with Setup Logs

1. Select Start ➤ This PC.

2. Double-click Local Disk (C:).

3. Double-click Windows.

4. Double-click Panther.

5. In the Windows folder, double-click the Setupact.log file to view your action log in Notepad. When you are finished viewing this file, close Notepad.

6. Double-click the Setuperr.log file to view your error file in Notepad. If no errors occurred during installation, this file will be empty. When you are finished viewing this file, close Notepad.

7. Close the directory window.

Supporting Multiple-Boot Options

You may want to install Windows 10 but still be able to run other operating systems. *Dual-booting* or multibooting allows your computer to boot multiple operating systems. Your computer will be automatically configured for dual-booting if there was a dual-boot–supported operating system on your computer prior to the Windows 10 installation, you didn't upgrade from that operating system, and you installed Windows 10 into a different partition.

One reason for dual-booting is to test various systems. If you have a limited number of computers in your test lab and you want to be able to test multiple configurations, you should dual-boot. For example, you might configure one computer to dual-boot with Windows 7, Windows 8/8.1, and Windows 10.

Here are some keys to successful dual-boot configurations:

- Make sure you have plenty of disk space.

- Windows 10 must be installed on a separate partition in order to dual-boot with other operating systems.

- Install older operating systems before installing newer operating systems. If you want to support dual-booting with Windows 7 and Windows 10, Windows 7 must be installed first. If you install Windows 10 first, you cannot install Windows 7 without ruining your Windows 10 configuration.

- Do not install Windows 10 on a compressed volume unless the volume was compressed using NTFS compression.

Once you have installed each operating system, you can choose the operating system that you will boot to during the boot process. You will see a boot-selection screen that asks you to choose which operating system you want to boot.

The Boot Configuration Data (BCD) store contains boot information parameters that were previously found in boot.ini in older versions of Windows. To edit the boot options in the BCD store, use the bcdedit utility, which can be launched only from a command prompt. To open a command prompt window, you can do the following:

1. Launch \Windows\system32\cmd.exe.

2. Open the Run command by pressing the [Windows] key + R and then entering **cmd**.

3. Type **cmd.exe** in the Search Programs And Files box and press Enter.

Once the command-prompt window is open, type **bcdedit** to launch the bcdedit utility. You can also type **bcdedit/?** to see all the different bcdedit commands. A few bcdedit commands may be needed when dual-booting a machine. Table 8.4 shows some of the bcdedit commands that may be needed when dual-booting.

TABLE 8.4   Bcdedit commands for dual-booting

Command	Explanation
/createstore	Creates a new empty boot configuration data store
/default	Allows you to specify which operating system will start when the time-out expires
/deletevalue	Allows you to delete a specified element from a boot entry
/displayorder	Shows the display order that the boot manager uses when showing the display order to the user
/export	Allows you to export the contents of the system store into a file
/import	Restores the system store by using the data file previously generated by using the /export option
/set	Allows you to set an entry option value
/store	Specifies the store to be used
/timeout	Specifies the amount of time used before the system boots into the default operating system

Using Windows Activation

Windows Activation is Microsoft's way of reducing software piracy. Unless you have a corporate license for Windows 10, you will need to perform post installation activation. This can be done online or through a telephone call. Windows 10 will attempt automatic activation three days after you log on to it for the first time. There is a grace period when you will be able to use the operating system without activation. After the grace period expires, a permanent watermark is displayed. Until the activation key is entered certain personalization settings are not configurable until Windows 10 is activated. When the grace period runs out, Windows will automatically lock you out of the system.

To access the Windows Activation screen, click the Start button and choose settings (the spoke icon). Scroll down to Update And Security and click on that link. On the left side, you will see a link for Activation. When you click on Activation, you will see the Activation screen (shown in Figure 8.19). Scroll down to the Activate Windows Now section. You may need to click the Change Product Key button and put in the license number that came with your Windows 10 copy. Once Windows 10 is activated, it will show that you are activated.

FIGURE 8.19   The Windows Activation Wizard screen

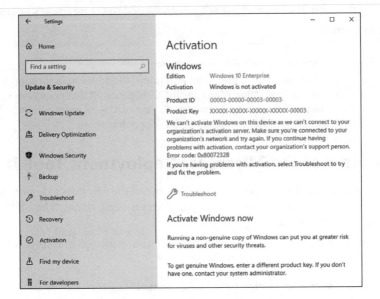

Understanding Automated Deployment Options

If you need to install Windows 10 on multiple computers, you could manually install the operating system on each computer. However, automating the deployment process will make your job easier, more efficient, and more cost effective if you have a large number of client computers on which to install Windows 10.

Windows 10 comes with several utilities that can be used for deploying and automating the Windows 10 installation. With access to multiple utilities with different functionality, administrators have increased flexibility in determining how to best deploy Windows 10 within a large corporate environment.

The following sections contain overviews of the automated deployment options, which will help you choose which solution is best for your requirements and environment. Each utility will then be covered in more detail throughout this chapter. The options for automated deployment of Windows 10 are as follows:

- Microsoft Deployment Toolkit (MDT)

- Unattended installation, or unattended setup, which uses `Setup.exe`

- Windows Automated Installation Kit (Windows AIK)
- Windows Assessment and Deployment Kit for Windows 10
- Windows Deployment Service (WDS), which requires Windows Server for deployment
- System Preparation Tool (Sysprep.exe), which is used to create images or clones
- Windows Autopilot

> Another option that you have to deploy Windows 10 is through System Center Configuration Manager (SCCM). Since SCCM is its own application, it is beyond the scope of this book. You can learn more about SCCM on the Microsoft website at http://www.microsoft.com.

An Overview of the Microsoft Deployment Toolkit

Microsoft released a deployment assistance toolset called the *Microsoft Deployment Toolkit (MDT)*. It is used to automate desktop and server deployment. The MDT provides an administrator with the following benefits:

- Administrative tools that allow for the deployment of desktops and servers through the use of a common console (see Figure 8.20)

FIGURE 8.20   Microsoft Deployment Toolkit console

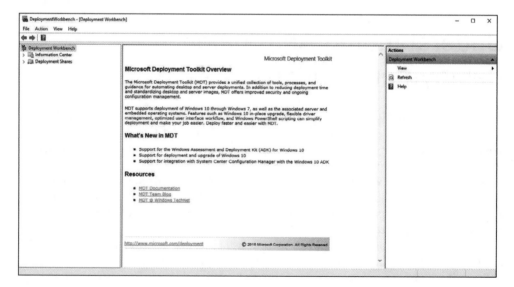

- Quicker deployments and the capabilities of having standardized desktop and server images and security
- Zero-touch deployments of Windows 10, Windows Server, and Windows 7/ 8/8.1

To install the MDT package onto your computer (regardless of the operating system being deployed), you must first meet the minimum requirements of MDT. These components need to be installed only on the computer where MDT is being installed:

- Windows 10, Windows 7, Windows 8, Windows 8.1, or Windows Server.
- The Windows Assessment and Deployment Kit (ADK) for Windows 10 is required for all deployment scenarios.
- System Center 2012 R2 Configuration Manager Service Pack 1 with the Windows ADK for Windows 10 is required for zero-touch installation (ZTI) and user-driven installation (UDI) scenarios.
- If you are using ZTI and/or UDI, you are allowed to add the MDT SQL database to any version of System Center Configuration Manager with SQL Technology; if you are using LTI, you must use a separately licensed SQL Server product to host your MDT SQL database.

You can install MDT without installing Windows (ADK) first, but you will not be able to use the package fully until Windows (ADK) is installed.

In Exercise 8.5, you will download and install MDT. You can install MDT on the Windows 10 operating system machine that you installed earlier in this chapter. If you decide to install the MDT onto a server or production machine, I recommend that you perform a full backup before completing Exercise 8.5. Installing MDT will replace any previous version of MDT that the machine may currently be using.

EXERCISE 8.5

Downloading and Installing MDT

1. Download the MDT Update 1 utility from Microsoft's website (https://www.microsoft.com/en-us/download/details.aspx?id=54259).

2. Click the Download button.

3. You get a screen with the message "Choose the download you want." Choose the x64 or x86 version. Click Next.

4. A message box may appear asking if you want to run or save the MDT. I clicked the down arrow next to Save and saved the files into the downloads directory.

5. Double-click MicrosoftDeploymentToolkit_xxx.exe to start the installation.

6. At the Welcome screen, click Next as shown in Figure 8.21.

FIGURE 8.21   Microsoft Deployment Toolkit setup screen

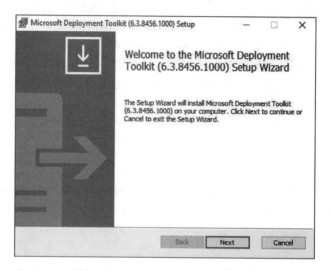

7. At the License screen, click the I Accept The Terms In The License Agreement radio button and click Next.

8. At the Custom Setup screen, click the down arrow next to Microsoft Deployment Toolkit and choose Entire Feature Will Be Installed On Local Hard Drive. Click Next as shown in Figure 8.22.

FIGURE 8.22   Microsoft Deployment Toolkit Custom Setup screen

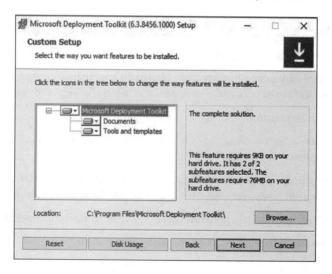

9. At the Customer Experience Improvement Program screen, choose if you want to participate or not and click Next.

10. At the Ready To Install screen, click the Install button.

11. If a User Account Control dialog box appears, click the Yes button.

12. When the installation completes, click the Finish button.

Now that you have installed MDT, you are going to configure the package. In Exercise 8.6, you will configure MDT and set up a distribution share and database. I am creating the MDT on a Windows Server so that we can distribute Windows 10. Make sure the Windows Assessment and Deployment Kit (ADK) for Windows 10 is installed because it is required for all deployment scenarios.

EXERCISE 8.6

Configuring MDT

1. Create a shared folder on your network called Distribution, and give the Everyone group full control to the folder for this exercise.

2. Open the MDT workbench by choosing Start ➤ then the down arrow ➤ Microsoft Development Toolkit ➤ Deployment Workbench.

3. If the User Account Control box appears, click Yes.

4. In the left-hand pane, click Deployment Shares, and then right-click the deployment shares and choose New Deployment Share.

5. The New Deployment Share Wizard begins (as shown in Figure 8.23). At the first screen, you will choose the directory where the deployments will be stored. Click the Browse button and choose the Distribution share that you created in step 1. Then click Next.

6. At the Share Name screen, accept the default, Distribution. Click Next.

7. At the Descriptive Name screen, accept the default description name (as shown in Figure 8.24) and click Next.

FIGURE 8.23 New Deployment Share Wizard screen

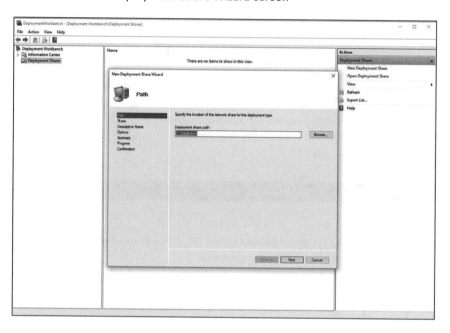

FIGURE 8.24 Descriptive Name screen

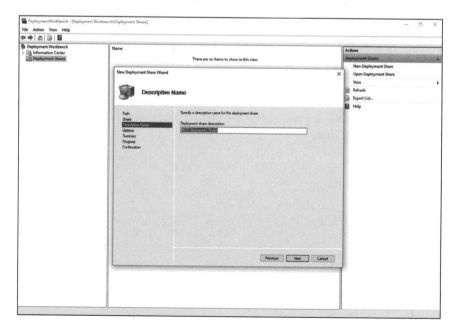

8. At the Options screen, make sure all check boxes are checked as shown in Figure 8.25.

FIGURE 8.25   Options screen

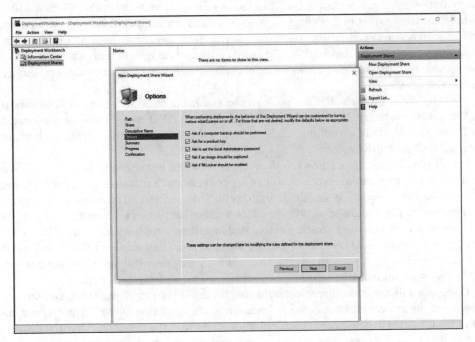

9. At the Summary screen, look over the options and choose the Next button.

10. The Installation will progress screen will show you how the installation is performing. Once it's finished, click the Finish button.

11. The new deployment share is set up and ready to start deploying. Now an operating system needs to be set up in the MDT for deployment.

12. Close the MDT workbench.

Now that you have seen how to install the MDT utility, let's take a look at some other ways to automatically install Windows 10.

An Overview of Unattended Installation

Unattended installation is a practical method of automating deployments when you have a large number of clients to install and the computers require different hardware and software configurations. Unattended installations allow you to create customized installations that are specific to your environment. Custom installations can support custom hardware and software installations.

Unattended installations utilize an answer file called autounattend.xml to provide configuration information during the installation process. Think about the Windows 10 installation from earlier in this chapter. You are asked for your locale, type of installation, and so on. The answer file allows these questions to be answered without user interaction. In addition to providing standard Windows 10 configuration information, the answer file can provide installation instructions for applications, additional language support, service packs, and device drivers.

With an unattended installation, you can use a distribution share to install Windows 10 on the target computers. You can also use a Windows 10 DVD with an answer file located on the root of the DVD, on a floppy disk, or on a universal flash device (UFD), such as an external USB flash drive.

Unattended installations allow you to create customized installations that are specific to your environment. Custom installations can support custom hardware and software installations. Since the answer file for Windows 10 is in XML format, all custom configuration information can be contained within the autounattend.xml file. This is different from past versions of Windows, where creating automated installation routines for custom installations required multiple files to be used. In addition to providing standard Windows 10 configuration information, you can use the answer file to provide installation instructions for applications, additional language support, service packs, and device drivers.

If you use a distribution share, it should contain the Windows 10 operating system image and the answer file to respond to installation configuration queries. The target computer must be able to connect to the distribution share over the network. After the distribution share and target computers are connected, you can initiate the installation process. Figure 8.26 illustrates the unattended installation process.

FIGURE 8.26   Unattended installation with distribution share and a target computer

Distribution Share   Target

Stores: Requires:
Windows 10 Image File   Network Connection
Answer File (Unattend.xml)

Advantages of Unattended Installation

In a midsize or large organization, it just makes sense to use automated setups. As stated earlier, it is nearly impossible to install Windows 10 one at a time on hundreds of machines.

But there are many advantages to using unattended installations as a method for automating Windows 10:

- Unattended installation saves time and money because users do not have to interactively respond to each installation query.

- It can be configured to provide automated query response while still selectively allowing users to provide specified input during installations.

- It can be used to install clean copies of Windows 10 or upgrade an existing operating system (providing it is on the list of permitted operating systems) to Windows 10.

- It can be expanded to include installation instructions for applications, additional language support, service packs, and device drivers.

- The physical media for Windows 10 does not need to be distributed to all computers on which it will be installed.

Disadvantages of Unattended Installation

As stated earlier, a manual installation is not practical for mass installations. But one of the biggest disadvantages to performing an unattended installation is that an administrator does not physically walk through the installation of Windows 10. A client operating system is one of the most important items that you will install onto a machine. As an IT manager and consultant, I have always felt better physically installing a client operating system. This way, if there are any glitches, I can see and deal with them immediately. If something happens during an unattended install, you may never know it, but the end user may experience small issues throughout the lifetime of the machine.

Two other disadvantages of using unattended installations as a method for automating Windows 10 installations are listed here:

- They require more initial setup than a standard installation of Windows 10.

- Someone must have access to each client computer and must initiate the unattended installation process on the client side.

An Overview of Windows Deployment Services

Windows Deployment Services (WDS) is a suite of components that allows you to remotely install Windows 10 on client computers.

A WDS server installs Windows 10 on the client computers, as illustrated in Figure 8.27. The WDS server must be configured with the Preboot Execution Environment (PXE) boot files, the images to be deployed to the client computers, and the answer file. WDS client computers must be PXE-capable. PXE is a technology that is used to boot to the network when no operating system or network configuration has been installed and configured on a client computer.

FIGURE 8.27 Windows Deployment Services (WDS) uses a WDS server and WDS clients.

WDS Server

WDS Client

Stores:
PXE Boot Files and Boot Images
Windows 10 Boot Images
Answer File(s)

Requires:
PXE-Compatible Boot

The WDS clients access the network with the help of a Dynamic Host Configuration Protocol (DHCP) server. This allows the WDS client to remotely install the operating system from the WDS server. The network environment must be configured with a DHCP server, a Domain Name System (DNS) server, NTFS volumes, and Active Directory to connect to the WDS server. No other client software is required to connect to the WDS server. Remote installation is a good choice for automatic deployment when you need to deploy to large numbers of computers and the client computers are PXE-compliant.

Advantages of WDS

The advantages of using WDS as a method for automating Windows 10 installations are as follows:

- Allows an IT department to remotely install Windows operating systems through the network. This advantage helps reduce the difficulty and IT man power cost compared to a manual installation.

- Allows an IT department to deploy multiple images for mixed environments including Windows 7, Windows 8/8.1, Windows 10, and Windows Server.

- Allows IT departments to use Windows setups including Windows Preinstallation Environment (Windows PE), .wim files, and image-based setups.

- WDS can use multicasting to allow for the transmitting and image data to communicate with each other.

- An IT department can create reference images using the Image Capture Wizard, which is an alternative to the ImageX tool.

- Allows an IT Administrator to install a driver package to the server and configure the drivers to be deployed to client computers at the same time the image is installed.

- Allows IT departments to standardize Windows 10 installations throughout a group or organization.

- The physical media for Windows 10 does not need to be distributed to all computers that will be installed.

- End-user installation deployment can be controlled through the Group Policy utility. For example, you can configure what choices a user can access or are automatically specified through the end-user Setup Wizard.

Disadvantages of WDS

The disadvantages of using WDS as a method for automating Windows 10 installations include the following:

- WDS can be used only if your network is running Windows Server 2008 and above with Active Directory installed.
- The clients that use WDS must be PXE-capable.

You can configure WDS on a Windows Server computer by using the Windows Deployment Services Configuration Wizard or by using the WDSUTIL command-line utility. Table 8.5 describes the WDSUTIL command-line options.

TABLE 8.5   WDSUTIL command-line options

WDSUTIL Option	Description
/initialize-server	Initializes the configuration of the WDS server
/uninitialized-server	Undoes any changes made during the initialization of the WDS server
/add	Adds images and devices to the WDS server
/convert-ripimage	Converts Remote Installation Preparation (RIPrep) images to WIM images
/remove	Removes images from the server
/set	Sets information in images, image groups, WDS servers, and WDS devices
/get	Gets information from images, image groups, WDS servers, and WDS devices
/new	Creates new capture images or discover images
/copy-image	Copies images from the image store
/export-image	Exports to WIM files images contained within the image store
/start	Starts WDS services
/stop	Stops WDS services
/disable	Disables WDS services
/enable	Enables WDS services

TABLE 8.5   WDSUTIL command-line options *(continued)*

WDSUTIL Option	Description
/approve-autoadddevices	Approves Auto-Add devices
/reject-autoadddevices	Rejects Auto-Add devices
/delete-autoadddevices	Deletes records from the Auto-Add database
/update	Uses a known-good resource to update a server resource

An Overview of the System Preparation Tool and Disk Imaging

The *System Preparation Tool*, or *Sysprep* (Sysprep.exe), is used to prepare a computer for disk imaging, and the disk image can then be captured using DISM (an imaging-management tool included with Windows 10) or third-party imaging software. Sysprep is a free utility that comes on all Windows operating systems. By default, the Sysprep utility can be found on Windows Server and Windows 10 operating systems in the \Windows\system32\sysprep directory.

Disk imaging is the process of taking a checkpoint of a computer and then using that checkpoint to create new computers, thus allowing for automated deployments. The reference, or source, computer has Windows 10 installed and is configured with the settings and applications that should be installed on the target computers. The image (checkpoints) is then created and can be transferred to other computers, thus installing the operating system, settings, and applications that were defined on the reference computer.

Using Imaging Software

Using the System Preparation Tool and disk imaging is a good choice (and the one most commonly used in the real world) for automatic deployment when you have a large number of computers with similar configuration requirements or machines that need to be rebuilt frequently.

For example, StormWind Studios, an online computer education company, reinstalls the same software every few weeks for new classes. Imaging is a fast and easy way to simplify the deployment process.

Most organizations use images to create new machines quickly and easily, but they also use them to reimage end users' machines that crash.

In most companies, end users will have space on a server (home folders) to allow them to store data. IT departments give our end users space on the server because this way we need to back up only the servers at night and not the end users' machines. If your end users place all of their important documents on the server, that information gets backed up.

Now, if we are also using images in our company and an end user's machine crashes, we just reload the image and they are back up and running in minutes. Since their documents are being saved on the server, they do not lose any of their information.

Many organizations use third-party imaging software (such as Ghost) instead of using Sysprep.exe and Image Capture Wizard. This is another good way of imaging your Windows 10 machines. Just make sure your third-party software supports the Windows 10 operating system.

To perform an unattended installation, the System Preparation Tool prepares the reference computer by stripping away any computer-specific data, such as the security identifier (SID), which is used to uniquely identify each computer on the network, any event logs, and any other unique system information. The System Preparation Tool also detects any Plug and Play devices that are installed and can adjust dynamically for any computers that have different hardware installed.

When the client computer starts an installation using a disk image, you can customize what is displayed on the Windows Welcome screen and the options that are displayed through the setup process. You can also fully automate when and how the Windows Welcome screen is displayed during the installation process by using the /oobe option with the System Preparation Tool and an answer file named oobe.xml.

Sysprep is a utility that is good only for setting up a new machine. You do not use Sysprep to image a computer for upgrading a current machine. There are a few switches that you can use in conjunction with Sysprep to configure the Sysprep utility for your specific needs. Table 8.6 shows you the important Sysprep switches and what they will do for you when used.

TABLE 8.6 Sysprep switches

Switch	Explanation
/pnp	Forces a mini-setup wizard to start at reboot so that all Plug and Play devices can be recognized.
/generalize	This allows Sysprep to remove all system-specific data from the Sysprep image. If you're running the GUI version of Sysprep, this is a check-box option.
/oobe	Initiates the Windows Welcome screen at the next reboot.

TABLE 8.6   Sysprep switches *(continued)*

Switch	Explanation
/audit	Initiates Sysprep in audit mode.
/nosidgen	Sysprep does not generate a new SID on the computer restart. Forces a mini-setup on restart.
/reboot	Stops and restarts the computer system.
/quiet	Runs without any confirmation dialog messages being displayed.
/mini	Tells Sysprep to run the mini-setup on the next reboot.

 Real World Scenario

The SID Problem with Deployment Software

For many years, when you had to create many machines that each had a Microsoft operating system on it, you would have to use files to help deploy the multiple systems.

Then, multiple third-party companies came out with software that allowed you to take a picture of the Microsoft operating system, and you could deploy that picture to other machines. One advantage of this is that all the software that is installed on the system could also be part of that picture. This was a great way to copy all the software on a machine over to another machine.

There was one major problem for years—*security identifier (SID)* numbers. All computers get assigned a unique SID that represents them on a domain network. The problem for a long time was that when you copied a machine to another machine, the SID number was also copied.

Microsoft released Sysprep many years ago, and that helped solve this problem. Sysprep would allow you to remove the SID number so that a third-party software package could move the image to another machine without issues. Many third-party image software products now also remove the SID numbers, but Sysprep was one of the first utilities to help solve this problem.

When you decide to use Sysprep to set up your images, there are a few rules that you must follow for Sysprep to work properly:

- You can use images to restart the Windows activation clock. The Windows activation clock starts to decrease as soon as Windows starts for the first time. You can restart the Windows activation clock only three times using Sysprep.

- The computer on which you're running Sysprep has to be a member of a workgroup. The machine can't be part of a domain. If the computer is a member of the domain, when you run Sysprep, the computer will automatically be removed from the domain.

- When installing the image, the system will prompt you for a product key. During the install you can use an answer file, which in turn will have all the information needed for the install, and you will not be prompted for any information.

- A third-party utility or Image Capture Wizard is required to deploy the image that is created from Sysprep.

- If you are using Sysprep to capture an NTFS partition, any files or folders that are encrypted will become corrupt and unreadable.

One advantage to Sysprep and Windows 10 is that you can use Sysprep to prepare a new machine for duplication. You can use Sysprep to image a Windows 10 machine. The following steps are necessary to image a new machine:

1. Install the Windows 10 operating system.

2. Install all components on the OS.

3. Run sysprep /generalize to get the Windows 10 system ready to be imaged.

When you image a computer using the Windows Sysprep utility, a Windows image (.wim) file is created. Most third-party imaging software products can work with the Windows image file.

Advantages of the System Preparation Tool

The following are advantages of using the System Preparation Tool as a method for automating Windows 10 installations:

- For large numbers of computers with similar hardware, it greatly reduces deployment time by copying the operating system, applications, and desktop settings from a reference computer to an image, which can then be deployed to multiple computers.

- Using disk imaging facilitates the standardization of desktops, administrative policies, and restrictions throughout an organization.

- Reference images can be copied across a network connection or through DVDs that are physically distributed to client computers.

Disadvantages of the System Preparation Tool

There are some disadvantages of using the System Preparation Tool as a method for automating Windows 10 installations:

- Image Capture Wizard, third-party imaging software, or hardware disk-duplication devices must be used for an image-based setup.

- The version of the System Preparation Tool that shipped with Windows 10 must be used. An older version of Sysprep cannot be used on a Windows 10 image.

- The System Preparation Tool will not detect any hardware that is not Plug and Play compliant.

Overview of the Windows Assessment and Deployment Kit

Another way to install Windows 10 is to use the *Windows Assessment and Deployment Kit (ADK)*. The Windows (ADK) is a set of utilities and documentation that allows an administrator to configure and deploy Windows operating systems. An administrator can use the Windows (ADK) to access the following utilities:

- Windows Configuration Designer

- Windows Assessment Toolkit

- Windows Performance Toolkit

The Windows (ADK) can be installed and configured on the following operating systems:

- Windows 10

- Windows 7 with SP1

- Windows 8/8.1

- Windows Server 2019

- Windows Server 2016

- Windows Server 2012 R2

- Windows Server 2012

- Windows Server 2008

- Windows Server 2008 R2

The Windows (ADK) is a good solution for organizations that need to customize the Windows deployment environments. The Windows (ADK) allows an administrator to have the flexibility needed for mass deployments of Windows operating systems. Since every organization's needs are different, the Windows (ADK) allows you to use all or just some of the deployment tools available. It allows you to manage deployments by using some additional tools.

Windows Configuration Designer The tools included with this part of the Windows (ADK) will allow an administrator to easily create a provisioning package.

Windows Assessment Toolkit When new Windows operating systems are installed, applications that ran on the previous version of Windows may not work properly. The Windows Assessment Toolkit allows an administrator to help solve these issues before they occur.

Windows Performance Toolkit The Windows Performance Toolkit is a utility that will locate computers on a network and then perform a thorough inventory of them. This inventory can then be used to determine which machines can have Windows 10 installed.

Summary of Windows 10 Deployment Options

Table 8.7 summarizes the installation tools and files that are used with unattended and automated installations of Windows 10. Table 8.7 shows the associated installation method and a description of each tool.

TABLE 8.7 Summary of Windows 10 unattended deployment utilities

Tool or File	Automated Installation Option	Description
setup.exe	Unattended installation	Program used to initiate the installation process
autounattend.xml	Unattended installation	Answer file used to customize installation queries
Windows System Image Manager	Unattended installation	Program used to create answer files to be used for unattended installations
DISM.exe	DISM	Command-line utility that works in conjunction with Sysprep to create and manage Windows 10 image files for deployment
sysprep.exe	Sysprep	System Preparation Tool, which prepares a source reference computer that will be used in conjunction with a distribution share or with disk duplication through Image Capture Wizard, third-party software, or hardware disk-duplication devices

The Windows 10 installation utilities and resources relating to automated deployment are found in a variety of locations. Table 8.8 provides a quick reference for each utility or resource and its location.

TABLE 8.8 Location of Windows 10 deployment utilities and resources

Utility	Location
DISM.exe	Included with Windows 10; installed to %WINDIR%\system32\DISM
sysprep.exe	Included with Windows 10; installed to %WINDIR%\system32\sysprep
Windows System Image Manager	Installed with the Windows ADK; installed to C:\Program Files (x86)\Windows Kits\10\Assessment and Deployment Kit\ Deployment Tools\WSIM\ImgMgr.exe

Deploying Unattended Installations

You can deploy Windows 10 installations or upgrades through a Windows 10 distribution DVD or through a distribution server that contains Windows 10 images and associated files, such as autounattend.xml for unattended installations. Using a DVD can be advantageous if the computer on which you want to install Windows 10 is not connected to the network or is connected via a low-bandwidth network. It is also typically faster to install a Windows 10 image from DVD than to use a network connection.

Unattended installations rely on options configured in an answer file that is deployed with the Windows 10 image. Answer files are XML files that contain the settings that are typically supplied by the installer during attended installations of Windows 10. Answer files can also contain instructions for how programs and applications should be run.

The Windows Setup program is run to install or upgrade to Windows 10 from computers that are running compatible versions of Windows. In fact, Windows Setup is the basis for the other types of installation procedures I'll be discussing in this chapter, including unattended installations, WDS, and image-based installations.

The Windows Setup program (setup.exe) replaces winnt32.exe and winnt.exe, which are the setup programs used in versions of Windows prior to Windows Vista. Although it's a graphical tool, Windows Setup can be run from the command line. For example, you can use the following command to initiate an unattended installation of Windows 10:

```
setup.exe /unattend:answerfile
```

The Windows Setup program has several command-line options that can be applied. Table 8.9 describes the setup.exe command-line options.

TABLE 8.9   Setup.exe command-line options and descriptions

Setup.exe Option	Description
/1394debug: *channel* [baudrate:*baudrate*]	Enables kernel debugging over a FireWire (IEEE 1394) port for troubleshooting purposes. The [baudrate] optional parameter specifies the baud rate for data transfer during the debugging process.
/debug:port [*baudrate:baudrate*]	Enables kernel debugging over the specified port for troubleshooting purposes. The [baudrate] optional parameter specifies the baud rate for data transfer during the debugging process.
/DynamicUpdate {enable | disable}	Used to prevent a dynamic update from running during the installation process.

Setup.exe Option	Description
/emsport:{com1|com2| usebiossettings|off} [/emsbaudrate:*baudrate*]	Configures EMS to be enabled or disabled. The [baudrate] optional parameter specifies the baud rate for data transfer during the debugging process.
/m:*folder_name*	Used with Setup to specify that replacement files should be copied from the specified location. If the files are not present, Setup will use the default location.
/noreboot	Normally, when the down-level phase of Setup.exe is complete, the computer restarts. This option specifies that the computer should not restart so that you can execute another command prior to the restart.
/tempdrive:*drive letter*	Specifies the location that will be used to store the temporary files for Windows 10 and the installation partition for Windows 10.
/unattend:[*answerfile*]	Specifies that you will be using an unattended installation for Windows 10. The answerfile variable points to the custom answer file you will use for installation.

Using the System Preparation Tool to Prepare an Installation for Imaging

You can use disk images to install Windows 10 on computers that have similar hardware configurations. Also, if a computer is having technical difficulties, you can use a disk image to quickly restore it to a baseline configuration.

To create a disk image, you install Windows 10 on the source computer with the configuration that you want to copy and use the System Preparation Tool to prepare the installation for imaging. The source computer's configuration should also include any applications that should be installed on target computers.

Once you have prepared the installation for imaging, you can use imaging software such as Image Capture Wizard to create an image of the installation.

The System Preparation Tool (Sysprep.exe) is included with Windows 10, in the %WINDIR%\system32\sysprep directory. When you run this utility on the source computer, it strips out information that is unique for each computer, such as the SID. Table 8.10 defines the command options that you can use to customize the sysprep.exe operation.

TABLE 8.10 System Preparation Tool command-line options

Switch	Description
/audit	Configures the computer to restart into audit mode, which allows you to add drivers and applications to Windows or test the installation prior to deployment
/generalize	Removes any unique system information from the image, including the SID and log information
/oobe	Specifies that the Windows Welcome screen should be displayed when the computer reboots
/quiet	Runs the installation with no user interaction
/quit	Specifies that the System Preparation Tool should quit after the specified operations have been completed
/reboot	Restarts the target computer after the System Preparation Tool completes
/shutdown	Specifies that the computer should shut down after the specified operations have been completed
/unattend	Indicates the name and location of the answer file to use

In the following sections, you will learn how to create a disk image and how to copy and install from it.

Preparing a Windows 10 Installation

To run the System Preparation Tool and prepare an installation for imaging, take the following steps:

1. Install Windows 10 on a source computer. The computer should have a similar hardware configuration to that of the destination computer(s). The source computer should not be a member of a domain.

2. Log on to the source computer as Administrator and, if desired, install and configure any applications, files (such as newer versions of Plug and Play drivers), or custom settings (for example, a custom desktop) that will be applied to the target computer(s).

3. Verify that your image meets the specified configuration criteria and that all applications are properly installed and working.

4. Select Start ➤ This PC, and navigate to C:\%WINDIR%\System32\sysprep. Double-click the Sysprep application icon.

5. The Windows System Preparation Tool dialog box appears. Select the appropriate options for your configuration.

6. If configured to do so, Windows 10 will shut down after Sysprep is run. The next time it is rebooted, the setup process will begin as if the PC is brand new.

7. You will now be able to use imaging software to create an image of the computer to deploy to other computers.

In Exercise 8.7, you will use the System Preparation Tool to prepare the computer for disk imaging. The Sysprep utility must be run on a machine with a clean version of Windows 10. If you upgraded a Windows 7/8/8.1 machine to Windows 10, you will not be able to run the Sysprep utility.

EXERCISE 8.7

Prepare a System for Imaging by Using the System Preparation Tool

1. Log on to the source computer as Administrator and, if desired, install and configure any applications that should also be installed on the target computer.

2. Select Start ➤ This PC, and navigate to C:\%WINDIR%\System32\sysprep. Double-click the Sysprep application icon.

3. In the System Preparation Tool dialog box, select Enter System Out-Of-Box Experience (OOBE) in the system cleanup action.

4. Depending on the shutdown options you selected, the System Preparation Tool will quit, the computer will shut down, or the computer will be rebooted into setup mode, where you will need to configure the setup options. Choose the Reboot option. Click OK.

5. After the computer has been shut down, the administrator will need to image the machine. Administrators can use an image capturing software to capture the image.

Using the Deployment Image Servicing and Management Tool

Deployment Image Servicing and Management (DISM.exe) is a command-line utility that allows you to manipulate a Windows image. DISM also allows you to prepare a Windows PE image. DISM replaces multiple programs that were included with Windows 7/8/8.1. These programs include Package Manager (Pkgmgr.exe), PEimg, and Intlcfg. These tools have been consolidated into one tool (DISM.exe), and new functionality has been added to improve the experience for offline servicing.

When DISM was first released, it was primarily used for servicing and managing Windows images. But now DISM has become even more powerful, including capturing images and deploying images.

DISM provides additional functionality when used with Windows 10 and Windows Server. You can use DISM to do the following:

- Capture Windows images
- Copy and move Windows images
- Install Windows images
- Add, remove, and enumerate packages
- Add, remove, and enumerate drivers
- Enable or disable Windows features
- Apply changes to an Unattend.xml answer file
- Configure international settings
- Upgrade a Windows image to a different edition
- Prepare a Windows PE 3.0 image
- Works with all platforms (32-bit, 64-bit, and Itanium)
- Allows for the use of Package Manager scripts

Table 8.11 shows the different commands that can be used with DISM.exe.

TABLE 8.11 DISM.exe command-line commands

Command	Description
/Add-Driver	Adds third-party driver packages to an offline Windows image.
/Get-CurrentEdition	Displays the edition of the specified image.
/Get-Drivers	Displays basic information about driver packages in the online or offline image. By default, only third-party drivers will be listed.
/Get-DriverInfo	Displays detailed information about a specific driver package.
/Get-Help /?	Displays information about the option and the arguments.
/Get-TargetEditions	Displays a list of Windows editions that an image can be changed to.
/Remove-Driver	Removes third-party drivers from an offline image.
/Set-ProductKey:<productKey>	Can only be used to enter the product key for the current edition in an offline Windows image.
/Online /Enable-Feature /All /FeatureName:Microsoft-Hyper-V	This command allows you to install Hyper-V into a Windows image while it's an actual image.

Using Windows System Image Manager to Create Answer Files

Answer files are automated installation scripts used to answer the questions that appear during a normal Windows 10 installation. You can use answer files with Windows 10 unattended installations, disk image installations, or WDS installations. Setting up answer files allows you to easily deploy Windows 10 to computers that may not be configured in the same manner, with little or no user intervention. Because answer files are associated with image files, you can validate the settings within an answer file against the image file.

You can create answer files by using the Windows System Image Manager (Windows SIM) utility. There are several advantages to using Windows SIM to create answer files:

- You can easily create and edit answer files through a graphical interface, which reduces syntax errors.

- It simplifies the addition of user-specific or computer-specific configuration information.

- You can validate existing answer files against newly created images.

- You can include additional application and device drivers in the answer file.

In the following section, you will learn about options that can be configured through Windows SIM, how to create answer files with Windows SIM, how to format an answer file, and how to manually edit answer files.

Configuring Components through Windows System Image Manager

You can use Windows SIM to configure a wide variety of installation options. The following list defines which components can be configured through Windows SIM and gives a short description of each component:

auditSystem   Adds additional device drivers, specifies firewall settings, and applies a name to the system when the image is booted into audit mode. Audit mode is initiated by using the sysprep/audit command.

auditUser   Executes RunSynchronous or RunAsynchronous commands when the image is booted into audit mode. Audit mode is initiated by using the sysprep/audit command.

generalize   Removes system-specific information from an image so that the image can be used as a reference image. The settings specified in the generalize component will be applied only if the sysprep/generalize command is used.

offlineServicing   Specifies the language packs and packages to apply to an image prior to the image being extracted to the hard disk.

oobeSystem   Specifies the settings to apply to the computer the first time the computer is booted into the Windows Welcome screen, which is also known as the Out-Of-Box

Experience (OOBE). To boot to the Welcome screen, the sysprep/oobe command should be used.

specialize   Configures the specific settings for the target computer, such as network settings and domain information. This configuration pass is used in conjunction with the generalize configuration pass.

Windows PE   Sets the Windows PE specific configuration settings as well as several Windows Setup settings, such as partitioning and formatting the hard disk, selecting an image, and applying a product key.

Deploying with Windows Autopilot

So far, we have talked about automating the deployment of Windows 10 on-site. Now it's time to look at how to deploy Windows 10 machines from the cloud. Microsoft has introduced a new way to deploy Windows 10 by using Intune and Windows Autopilot.

Windows Autopilot is a group of multiple technologies that allow an administrator to set up and configure brand-new devices directly from the manufacturer. These devices can go directly into the production environment and when the user logs into Intune, the device will get automatically configured for your environment.

Administrators can also use Windows Autopilot to reconfigure, recover, and repurpose devices that are already in your corporate environment. This allows administrators to quickly and easily repurpose machines so that they can be assigned to different users. Since Windows Autopilot is a benefit with using Microsoft Intune, your IT department does not need to set up an onsite infrastructure to support this service. This helps reduce the cost of building machines for your IT department.

So, what does this actually mean to your IT department? Let's take a look at just a couple scenarios where Windows Autopilot can help your IT department quickly set up or repurpose Windows 10 devices.

When you purchase Windows 10 machines from different vendors, currently you need to make sure that you have custom images for each vendor. The reason for this is that each vendor puts in its own hardware and that hardware needs custom drivers to work properly. With Windows Autopilot, you can have the vendor send the machines directly to your remote users or IT department for immediate deployment.

When the user logs into Windows Azure with their email address and password, Windows Autopilot will automatically apply settings, policies, and applications and, if need be, even change the version of Windows 10 (for example, from Windows 10 Pro to Windows 10 Enterprise) on the machine. The machine will automatically be ready for use in your corporate environment without any need for the IT department to manually make any changes to the new machine.

Another scenario of using Windows Autopilot is when you need to repurpose machines within your organization. Currently, when many of us get a new machine for a user, we need to load an image onto that machine and set it up for that specific user. After the machine is given to the user, we normally take their machine, reimage it, and pass it on to someone with an older machine. This can result in a large chain of repurposed machines.

With Windows Autopilot, when a user gets a machine from another user, once they log into their Azure account, the machine can reload a clean operating system with all of the policies and applications that they need to do their job. The IT department doesn't need to reimage machines before they are redeployed.

After the IT department deploys or repurposes the Windows 10 machines, those machines can then be managed by using Microsoft Intune, System Center Configuration Manager, Windows Update for Business, and other compatible tools. Windows Autopilot allows your organization to complete the following tasks:

- Join Windows 10 devices automatically to Azure Active Directory (Azure AD) or to your on-site Active Directory (via Hybrid Azure AD Join).

- Automatically enroll your Windows 10 devices into MDM services, such as Microsoft Intune (this requires an Azure AD Premium subscription).

- Restrict the creation of the Administrator account.

- Build and automatically assign Windows 10 devices to configuration groups based on the Windows 10 device profile.

- Customizable OOBE content that is specific to your organization.

Windows Autopilot Requirements

So now that you understand the benefits of using Windows Autopilot, let's take a look at what's required so that you can use Windows Autopilot in your organization.

First off, and most importantly, Windows Autopilot depends on the version and specific capabilities of Windows 10. Secondly, you will need to have an Azure subscription set up with Azure Active Directory. Finally, you will need to add the Mobile Device Management (MDM) services along with Intune to your Azure subscription so that you can set up and manage Windows Autopilot.

Hardware Requirements

If an administrator wants to deploy a new machine directly from a vendor using Windows Autopilot, a unique hardware ID for the device needs to be captured and uploaded. This step can be done directly by the hardware vendor, but if an administrator needs to get this information manually, they can do this through a data gathering process that collects the device data. For this to be done, the version of Windows 10 must be version 1703 or later.

The hardware ID (commonly called a hardware hash) contains data details about the Windows 10 device. This data includes the manufacturer information (including the model), the device's serial number, the hard drive's serial number, and many other factors that are used to uniquely identify the device.

To manually gather this information, an administrator can use Microsoft System Center Configuration Manager (version 1802 or higher). System Center Configuration Manager automatically collects the hardware hashes for existing Windows 10 systems as long as the Windows 10 systems are using Windows 10 version 1703 and higher. After all of the hash information is collected, the data can be exported from System Center Configuration Manager into a CSV file.

Once you have met the hardware requirements, we need to look at the software requirements of Windows 10.

Software Requirements

So as stated above, one of the main requirements for Windows Autopilot is Windows 10. Windows 10 must meet the following minimum requirements:

- Windows 10 version 1703 (Semi-Annual Channel) or higher.
- Windows 10 must be one of the following editions in order to use Windows Autopilot:
  - Windows 10 Pro
  - Windows 10 Pro Education
  - Windows 10 Pro for Workstations
  - Windows 10 Enterprise
  - Windows 10 Education
  - Windows 10 Enterprise 2019 LTSC

Besides meeting the minimum software requirements, your organization must also meet minimum networking requirements

Networking Requirements

Windows Autopilot depends on multiple Microsoft cloud–based subscriptions. These include an Azure subscription setup with Azure Active Directory. Your organization is going to have to also subscribe to MDM services along with using Microsoft Intune.

After your organization sets up the Microsoft cloud–based subscriptions, you will need to ensure that the proper access to these services have been configured. Now this access may change based on how your Azure subscription is set up. For example, if you are using a hybrid setup (where you have an onsite network and an Azure network working together), you need to make sure that your firewall and DNS settings are set up properly. If you are using just an Azure network, then you need to make sure that access to the Azure network is set up properly.

Since Windows Autopilot requires access to Internet-based services, you need to ensure that the following settings are set up as a minimum:

- Administrators must properly configure DNS name resolution for their Internet DNS names.
- Firewalls must allow all hosts to have access to port 80 (HTTP), 443 (HTTPS), and 123 (UDP/NTP).
- If your organization requires that users authenticate before gaining Internet access, white-list access may be needed so your users can access the required services.

After you have met the required software and hardware configuration, the next step is to set up Windows Autopilot profiles.

Windows Autopilot Profiles

Windows Autopilot profiles allow an administrator to choose how the Windows 10 system will be set up and configured on Azure AD and Intune. This allows your organization to set up different options depending on the requirements needed for configuring the Windows 10 devices. The following Windows Autopilot profiles are available:

Skip Cortana, OneDrive and OEM Registration Setup Pages   Any device that registers with Windows Autopilot will automatically skip the Cortana, OneDrive, and OEM registration setup pages during the out-of-box experience (OOBE) process.

Automatically Set Up for Work or School   Any device that registers with Windows Autopilot will automatically be configured as a work or school device. Because of this, these questions will not be asked during the OOBE process.

Sign In Experience with Company Branding   Instead of presenting your user with a generic Azure Active Directory sign-in page, any device that registers with Windows Autopilot will automatically be presented with a customized sign-in page. This page can be configured with the organization's name, logon, and additional help text, as configured in Azure Active Directory.

Skip Privacy Settings   Any device that registers with Windows Autopilot will not be asked about privacy settings during the Windows 10 OOBE process. This setting is used if the organization is going to configure these privacy settings using Intune.

Disable Local Admin Account Creation on the Device   Organizations can decide whether the user who is registering with Windows Autopilot will have the ability to have administrator access once the process is finished.

Skip End User License Agreement   If your organization is using Windows 10 version 1709 or later, organizations can allow users to skip the End User License Agreement (EULA) page during the OOBE process. When an organization chooses this profile setting, the organization accepts the EULA terms on their user's behalf.

Disable Windows Consumer Features   If your organization is using Windows 10 version 1803 or later, organizations have the ability to disable certain Windows features. For example, the Windows 10 device would not automatically install any additional Microsoft Store apps once the user first signs into the Windows 10 device.

If you decide that you want to use PowerShell when configuring Windows Autopilot, after the software and hardware requirements are met, you can use the `Install-Module WindowsAutopilotIntune` cmdlet to configure Windows Autopilot.

Understanding Windows Updates

One task that is very important to any IT department is keeping the Windows operating systems up-to-date. This can happen in many different ways, depending on your infrastructure setup. If you are using an onsite network only, your users can update their own machines or you can set up a server to help you out.

Windows Update is a utility that can connect to the Microsoft update website, connect to your Azure network, or connect to a local onsite update server called a Windows Server Update Services (WSUS) server. Windows Update is used to ensure that the Windows 10 operating system (along with other Microsoft products) has the most up-to-date versions of Microsoft operating system files or software.

Some of the common update categories associated with Windows Update are as follows:

- Security updates

- Critical updates

- Service packs

- Drivers

- Product/Software updates

- Windows Store

To truly understand updates, you need to understand how the update process works with Microsoft. Microsoft normally releases updates to their products on the second Tuesday of the month (this is why we use the term Patch Tuesdays). But before that update gets released to the public, it has already been tested at Microsoft.

It all starts with the Windows engineering team adding new features and functionality to Windows using product cycles. These product cycles are comprised from three phases; development, testing, and release.

After the new Windows 10 features or functionality are developed, Microsoft employees test these updates out themselves on their own Windows 10 machines. This is referred to as "selfhost testing."

After the updates get tested at Microsoft, they then get released to the public. With Windows 10, Microsoft has introduced new ways to service updates. Microsoft's new servicing options are referred to as Semi-Annual Channel, Long-Term Servicing Branch (LTSB), and Windows Insider. Table 8.12 (taken directly from Microsoft's website) shows the different servicing options and the benefits of those options.

TABLE 8.12   Servicing options

From this channel	To this channel	You need to
Windows Insider Program	Semi-Annual Channel (Targeted)	Wait for the final Semi-Annual Channel release.
	Semi-Annual Channel	Not directly possible, because Windows Insider Program devices are automatically upgraded to the Semi-Annual Channel (Targeted) release at the end of the development cycle.
	Long-Term Servicing Channel	Not directly possible (requires wipe-and-load).
Semi-Annual Channel (Targeted)	Insider	Use the Settings app to enroll the device in the Windows Insider Program.
	Semi-Annual Channel	Select the **Defer upgrade** setting, or move the PC to a target group or flight that will not receive the next upgrade until it is business ready. Note that this change will not have any immediate impact; it only prevents the installation of the next Semi-Annual Channel release.
	Long-Term Servicing Channel	Not directly possible (requires wipe-and-load).
Semi-Annual Channel	Insider	Use the Settings app to enroll the device in the Windows Insider Program.
	Semi-Annual Channel (Targeted)	Disable the **Defer upgrade** setting, or move the device to a target group or flight that will receive the latest Current Semi-Annual Channel release.
	Long-Term Servicing Channel	Not directly possible (requires wipe-and-load).

TABLE 8.12 Servicing options *(continued)*

From this channel	To this channel	You need to
Long-Term Servicing Channel	Insider	Use media to upgrade to the latest Windows Insider Program build.
	Semi-Annual Channel (Targeted)	Use media to upgrade. Note that the Semi-Annual Channel build must be a later build.
	Semi-Annual Channel	Use media to upgrade. Note that the Semi-Annual Channel build must be a later build.

Windows Update Process

There are multiple ways a user can receive updates. The user can get updates directly from Microsoft. This is done by the user using the Updates section of Windows settings. This is how most of us get our updates at home. But this is a process that doesn't work well in a business environment. The reason for this is that if you have hundreds of users, they are all connecting directly with Microsoft and receiving the same updates. This can take up a lot of Internet bandwidth and the IT department has very little control over what updates get installed.

When it comes to company-based updates, there are better options. Administrators can set up either Group Policy Objects (GPOs) or Azure MDM solutions (such as Microsoft Intune) to configure the Windows Update for Business settings that control how and when Windows 10 devices are updated and which updates get accepted by the IT department. Windows Update for Business updates are updates that you receive from your Microsoft cloud-based services (MDM and Intune).

Administrators can also set up a Microsoft Windows Server Update Service (WSUS) server. WSUS runs on a Windows server, and that server goes out to the Microsoft website and downloads the updates for your Windows clients. This allows client machines to receive their updates from a server that is controlled by the IT department.

 WSUS is discussed in detail in *MCSA Windows Server 2016 Complete Study Guide: Exam 70-740, Exam 70-741, Exam 70-742, and Exam 70-743, 2nd Edition*, by William Panek (Wiley, 2018).

Using Windows Update for Business

Windows Update for Business allows an IT administrator to keep their organization's Windows 10 devices up-to-date with the latest Microsoft security defenses and Windows features by using Microsoft Azure. Windows Update for Business allows your Windows 10 systems to connect to Microsoft's Windows Update service.

Administrators have the ability to configure Windows Update for Business by using Group Policies or MDM solutions to configure the Windows Update for Business settings. These settings will control how and when Windows 10 devices are updated.

So, what does this mean for your organization? Administrators have total control over how updates are delivered and which updates will be delivered. Administrators can do this best by doing reliability and performance testing on a small group of systems (including just a single system for testing) before allowing updates to roll out to all of the computers in their organization. By testing updates, administrators can determine which updates will work best for their company.

Windows Update for Business Update Types

Windows Update for Business allows an organization to choose which updates an organization wants delivered to their Windows 10 systems. Administrators can do this by setting up management policies to help choose which updates they want delivered to their users. The following are different types of updates that Administrators can deploy to their Windows 10 devices:

Feature Updates   These updates were previously referred to as upgrades. Feature Updates not only contain security updates and revisions, but they also include major feature additions and changes. Feature Updates are released semi-annually in the spring and in the fall.

Quality Updates   Quality Updates are normally operating system updates that are usually released the second Tuesday of each month. Sometimes these updates, depending on their importance, can actually be released at any time. Quality Updates include security updates, critical updates, and driver updates.

Windows Update for Business also deploys non-Windows operating system updates (for example, Visual Studio) as part of the Quality Updates deployment.

Driver Updates   Driver Updates are updates for third-party devices that apply to your Windows 10 systems. For example, you may be using a printer that Microsoft Windows 10 has a driver for; these drivers get updated as part of the Driver Updates process. Administrators have the ability to enable or disable Driver Updates by using Windows Update for Business policies.

Microsoft Product Updates   Microsoft Product Updates are updates for Microsoft application or software products like Office. Administrators have the ability to enable or disable Microsoft Product Updates by using Windows Update for Business policies.

Deferring Updates

Windows Update for Business allows administrators to defer updates from being installed for a specific period of time. Administrators can defer the installation of both Feature Updates and Quality Updates for a specific period of time, but that specific period of time starts as soon as those updates are first made available through the Windows Update service.

Administrators can use this time to test and validate the updates before they are pushed to all of your Windows 10 devices. The way deferrals work is by allowing administrators to specify the amount of time after an update is released before it is offered to your Windows 10 devices.

For example, if an administrator decides to defer Feature Updates for 365 days, the Windows 10 devices will not install any Feature Update before the 365 days expire. Administrators can defer Feature Updates by using the *Select when Preview Builds and Feature Updates are Received* policy.

Table 8.13 shows you the different updates that can be deferred and the maximum time that they can be deferred for.

TABLE 8.13 Maximum Update Deferral

Update	Maximum Deferral
Feature Updates	365 days
Quality Updates	30 days
Non-deferrable	None

Pausing an Update

Administrators also have the ability to pause an update if they discover an issue while they are deploying Feature Updates or Quality Updates. Administrators can choose to pause the update for up to 35 days. This helps prevent other Windows 10 devices from experiencing the same issues.

If the administrator pauses the installation of a Feature Update, then Quality Updates are still deployed and vice versa. When an administrator sets a pause time period for an update, the pause time is calculated from the start date that the administrator sets.

To pause a Feature Update, the administrator uses the *Select when Preview Builds and Feature Updates are Received* policy. To pause a Quality Update, the administrator uses the *Select when Quality Updates are Received* policy.

Selecting Branch Readiness Level for Feature Updates

Windows Update for Business allows administrators to choose which channel of Feature Updates they want to receive. Currently Microsoft offers branch readiness level options to organizations for pre-release and released updates. The following options are included:

- Windows Insider Program for Business prerelease updates. These updates include Windows Insider Fast, Windows Insider Slow, and Windows Insider Release Preview.

- Semi-Annual Channel for released updates

Prior to version 1903 of Windows 10, there are only two channels for released updates: Semi-Annual Channel and Semi-Annual Channel (Targeted). Versions of Windows 10 released after version 1903 get a single release channel: Semi-Annual Channel.

Administrators have the ability to configure the branch readiness level by configuring the *Select when Preview Builds and Feature Updates are Received* policy. But if an administrator wants to manage pre-release builds, they need to enable preview builds by configuring the *Manage preview Builds* policy.

Monitoring Windows Updates

Administrators have the ability to monitor which Windows 10 computers are receiving their updates by using the Update Compliance utility. The Update Compliance utility lets administrators see a complete view of Windows 10 operating system updates Administrators can view which operating systems are meeting compliances, how the update deployments are progressing, and any errors that may have occurred on the Windows 10 devices.

The Update Compliance utility uses multiple factors to show you a complete view of the update process. These factors include diagnostic data from the installation progress, Windows Update configuration settings, and additional data (for example, Windows Defender Antivirus diagnostic data). This service is included free with your Azure subscription and there is no need to set up any additional infrastructure requirements.

Update Compliance Prerequisites

To use the Update Compliance utility, your organization must meet some prerequisites:

- Only Windows 10 Professional, Education, and Enterprise editions can be used with the Update Compliance utility. Update Compliance only gathers data for the standard desktop Windows 10 version. The Update Compliance utility is not currently compatible with other operating systems like Windows Server, Surface Hub, or IoT.

- Windows 10 devices must be on the Semi-Annual Channel and the Long-Term Servicing Channel. The Update Compliance utility will show administrators Windows Insider Preview devices. But currently Windows Insider Preview devices will not have any detailed deployment information.

- The Update Compliance utility requires at minimum the Basic level of diagnostic data and a Commercial ID to be enabled on the Windows 10 device.

- Administrators must opt in to the Windows Analytics to see device names for versions of Windows 10 version 1803 or higher.

- If administrators want to use the Windows Defender Status, Windows 10 devices must be E3 licensed and have Cloud Protection enabled. E5-licensed devices should use Windows Defender ATP instead.

- Administrators must add the Update Compliance utility to their Azure subscription. To do this, the administrator must log in to the Azure portal and select + Create A Resource. At the search for window, type **Update Compliance**. At the bottom of the screen, select the Create button to add the Update Compliance utility to your Azure subscription.

Summary

This chapter started with a discussion of the features included with Windows 10. We also took a look at installing Windows 10. Installation is an easy process, but you must first make sure the machine is compatible with the Windows 10 operating system.

There are two main ways to install Windows 10: upgrade or clean install. You can upgrade a Windows 7 or Windows 8/8.1 machine to Windows 10.

I discussed automated installation of Windows 10. Installing Windows 10 through an automated process is an effective way to install the Windows 10 operating system on multiple computers.

There are several methods for automated installation: unattended installations, Windows Deployment Services (WDS), Windows Assessment and Deployment Kit (ADK), third-party applications, unattended installations, and using the System Preparation Tool along with Image Capture Wizard.

Windows Deployment Services (WDS) is a suite of components that allows you to remotely install Windows 10 on client computers.

The Windows (ADK) is a set of utilities and documentation that allows an administrator to configure and deploy Windows operating systems.

You can use unattended answer files to automatically respond to the queries that are generated during the normal installation process.

You can also prepare an installation for imaging by using the System Preparation Tool (sysprep.exe) and creating a disk image by using the Image Capture Wizard utility or a third-party utility.

Microsoft Deployment Toolkit (MDT) is a way of automating desktop and server deployment. With the MDT, an administrator can deploy desktops and servers through the use of a common console, which allows for quicker deployments, having standardized desktop and server images and security and zero-touch deployments of Windows 10, Windows 8, Windows 7, and Windows Server.

I also talked about installing Windows 10 devices using Intune and Windows Autopilot. I explained how Windows Autopilot is used and configured and the requirements needed to use Windows Autopilot. I also explained the different profiles that you can use with Windows Autopilot.

After the Windows 10 installation is complete, you'll want to make sure all updates and service packs are installed. You can use Windows Update to complete that task on-site. I finally explained how to setup and configure cloud-based updates by using Windows Update for Business. I talked about how you can use The Update Compliance utility to get reporting data on how updates are being delivered to your Windows 10 devices.

Exam Essentials

Understand the Windows 10 hardware requirements.   The minimum hardware requirements to run Windows 10 properly are 1 gigahertz (GHz) or faster processor or SoC, 1 gigabyte (GB) for 32-bit or 2 GB for 64-bit of RAM, 16 GB for 32-bit OS or 20 GB for

64-bit OS of hard drive space, DirectX 9 or later with WDDM 1.0 video driver, and a DVD-R/W drive or compatible network interface card.

Understand how to complete a clean install. If your machine meets the minimum hardware requirements, you can install Windows 10. There are a few different ways to install Windows 10 onto a computer. You can use the installation disk or USB, install it over a network, or install it from an image.

Understand how to complete an upgrade. You can't upgrade a Windows Vista machine to Windows 10. To complete an upgrade on a Windows 7 or Windows 8/8.1 machine, insert the Windows 10 DVD into the Windows machine or connect to the Windows 10 files over the network and complete an upgrade on the computer.

You can't upgrade a Windows XP machine directly to Windows 10. If the machine is running Windows XP, you have to use a migration tool to migrate all the user data from Windows XP to a Windows 10 machine.

Know the difference between the various unattended installation methods. Understand the various options available for unattended installations of Windows 10 and when it is appropriate to use each installation method.

Understand the features and uses of WDS. Know when it is appropriate to use WDS to manage unattended installations. Be able to list the requirements for setting up WDS servers and WDS clients. Be able to complete an unattended installation using WDS.

Be able to use disk images for unattended installations. Know how to perform unattended installations of Windows 10 using the System Preparation Tool and disk images.

Understand the Microsoft Deployment Toolkit (MDT). Know that the MDT is a way of automating desktop and server deployment. Understand that the MDT allows an administrator to deploy desktops and servers through the use of a common console.

Be able to use Windows Autopilot. Windows Autopilot is a group of multiple technologies that allow an administrator to set up and configure brand-new devices, repurpose current machines, and even recover corporate machines.

Understand how to receive updates. You need to understand how to set up and receive Microsoft updates for Windows 10, Microsoft products, and the Windows Store. Make sure you know the different settings for configuring advanced update options.

Understand Windows Update for Business. You need to understand how to set up and receive Microsoft updates for Windows 10 using Windows Update for Business in Azure. Make sure you know the different settings for configuring Windows Update for Business options.

Review Questions

1. You are the network administrator for a large communications company. You have 25 computers that currently run Windows 7. These computers have the following configurations:

   ▪ A single MBR disk

   ▪ A disabled TPM chip

   ▪ Disabled hardware virtualization

   ▪ UEFI firmware running in BIOS mode

   ▪ Enabled Data Execution Prevention (DEP)

   You plan to upgrade the computers to Windows 10. You need to ensure that the computers can use Secure Boot. Which two actions should you perform? (Choose two).

   A. Convert the MBR disk to a GPT disk.

   B. Enable the TPM chip.

   C. Disable DEP.

   D. Enable hardware virtualization.

   E. Convert the firmware from BIOS to UEFI.

2. You are the network administrator for StormWind Studios. Your network contains an Active Directory domain. The domain contains 300 computers that run Windows 10.

   You have both an on-site Active Directory network and a Microsoft Azure Active Directory (Azure AD) with Microsoft Intune. You need to automatically register all the existing computers to the Azure AD network and also enroll all of the computers in Intune. What should you use?

   A. Use a DNS Autodiscover address record.

   B. Use a Windows Autopilot deployment profile.

   C. Use an Autodiscover service connection point (SCP).

   D. Set up a Group Policy Object (GPO).

3. You are the network administrator for a large company. You have 2 computers that run Windows 7. Computer 1 has a 32-bit CPU that runs Windows 7 Enterprise. Computer 2 has a 64-bit CPU that runs Windows 7 Enterprise. You plan to perform an in-place upgrade to the 64-bit version of Windows 10. Which computers can you upgrade to the 64-bit version of Windows 10?

   A. Computer1 only

   B. Computer2 only

   C. Computer1 and Computer2

   D. Neither

4. You are the network administrator for your organization. You have a reference computer that runs Windows 10. You need to create and deploy an image of the Windows 10 computer. You create an answer file named `answer.xml`. You have to make sure that the installation applies the answer file after you deploy the image. Which command should you run before you capture the image?

   A. `dism.exe /append answer.xml /check`

   B. `dism.exe /mount answer.xml /verify`

   C. `sysprep.exe /reboot /audit /unattend:answer.xml`

   D. `sysprep.exe /generalize /oobe /unattend:answer.xml`

5. You have a Windows 10 Windows Image (WIM) that is mounted. You need to view the list of third-party drivers installed on the WIM. What should you do?

   A. Run DISM and specify the `/get-drivers` parameter.

   B. Run `Driverquery.exe` and use the `/si` parameter.

   C. From Device Manager, view all hidden drivers.

   D. From Windows Explorer, open the `mount` folder.

6. You have computers that run Windows 10 Pro. The computers are joined to Microsoft Azure Active Directory (Azure AD) and enrolled in Microsoft Intune. You need to upgrade the computers to Windows 10 Enterprise. What should you configure in Intune?

   A. A device enrollment policy

   B. A device cleanup rule

   C. A device compliance policy

   D. A Windows Autopilot device profile

7. You are the network administrator for a large organization. You are in charge of developing a plan to install 200 Windows 10 computers in your company's data center. You decide to use WDS. You are using a Windows Server 2012 R2 domain and have verified that your network meets the requirements for using WDS. What command-line utility should you use to configure the WDS server?

   A. `dism`

   B. `wdsutil`

   C. `setup.exe`

   D. The WDS icon in Control Panel

8. Will is the network manager for a large company. He has been tasked with creating a deployment plan to automate installations for 100 computers that need to have Windows 10 installed. Will wants to use WDS for the installations. To fully automate the installations, he needs to create an answer file. Will does not want to create the answer files with a text editor. What other program can he use to create unattended answer files via a GUI interface?

   A. DISM

   B. Answer Manager

   C. Windows System Image Manager

   D. System Preparation Tool

9. You are using WDS to install 20 Windows 10 computers. When the clients attempt to use WDS, they are not able to complete the unattended installation. You suspect that the WDS server has not been configured to respond to client requests. Which one of the following utilities would you use to configure the WDS server to respond to client requests?

   A. Active Directory Users and Computers

   B. Active Directory Users and Groups

   C. WDS MMC snap-in

   D. WDSMAN

10. You want to install a group of 25 computers using disk images created in conjunction with the System Preparation Tool. Your plan is to create an image from a reference computer and then copy the image to all the machines. You do not want to create an SID on the destination computer when you use the image. Which sysprep.exe command-line option should you use to set this up?

    A. /specialize

    B. /generalize

    C. /oobe

    D. /quiet

Chapter

9

Managing Authentication

MICROSOFT EXAM OBJECTIVES COVERED IN THIS CHAPTER:

✓ **Manage device authentication**

- Manage authentication policies; manage sign-on options; perform Azure AD join.

✓ **Manage user profiles**

- Configure user profiles; configure Enterprise State Roaming in Azure AD; configure sync settings; implement Folder Redirection (including OneDrive).

Now that you understand how to create a Windows 10 device, it's time to work with Active Directory. There are different ways to set up Active Directory. Administrators can set up Active Directory on their local networks or in an Azure virtual machine. But you can also set up Active Directory within the Azure desktop.

For all of you administrators that currently work on an Active Directory network, Azure Active Directory is not really the Active Directory that we all know. It is a database that controls access, and yes, you can join computers to an Azure Active Directory network but that's almost where the similarities stop.

So I think the best way to talk about Active Directory in this chapter is to talk about what it does and how Azure Active Directory differs from that. Then I think the features and limitations of Azure Active Directory will be a lot clearer.

Active Directory vs. Azure Active Directory

One of the most confusing things that Microsoft can do at times is name a new feature or service similarly to a feature or service that already exists. This is what happened here with Active Directory and Azure Active Directory.

A perfect example of this is Universal Group Membership Caching (UGMC). UGMC has NOTHING to do with Universal Groups. Universal Groups are a type of group and UGMC helps a site, with no Global Catalog, with logins. But because they both have the words Universal Groups, people think that they are connected.

Azure Active Directory is not the Active Directory that most of us use on a daily basis. This might be overstating it a bit. Think of Azure Active Directory as Active Directory lite. So let's look at Active Directory and then look at Azure Active Directory so that you can see the differences between the two.

Understanding Active Directory

There are different ways that you can setup a network. If all of the machines can work both as clients and servers, this type of network is referred to as a Workgroup or Peer-to-Peer network. The downside of this type of network is that it is too small and that each computer has its own authentication database. This means that every user has to have an account on every computer. This can lead to all types of issues and it is also a very difficult network to manage.

This is where Active Directory comes in. Active Directory at its core is just a database. It's a single database that all of your users can belong to. This makes it much easier to manage a network and it also allows an administrator to have better control over the users and their permissions.

Active Directory is built on the database standard called Directory Services. Directory Services got its "claim to fame" with Novell. Novell used Directory Services to control access to their networks. When Microsoft decided to move their network over to Directory Services, they decided to name their version Active Directory.

Active Directory networks are grouped together in units known as Domains (as shown as triangles). A domain is a logical grouping of objects into a distributed database. Some of these objects are user accounts, group accounts, and published objects (folders and printers).

It is very important to understand that domains are a logical grouping of objects. Logical is the key word in this description. Domains are logical, not physical. For example, Microsoft.com is a worldwide entity. Not all of the domain users are located in Redmond, Washington. They are scattered all over the world.

Active Directory can be a local version by loading Active Directory onto an on-site server or setting up Active Directory in a virtual machine on Azure. But Active Directory is Active Directory no matter how you set it up. It's a database that you setup to help control access to your network. No matter if that network is on-site or in a VM in the cloud.

One of the advantages to using domains is the ability to have a *child domain*, which is a subdomain of another domain. You can build child domains based on physical locations, departments, and so forth.

Child domains give you greater scalability. Active Directory child domains give an administrator the flexibility to design a structure that meets an organization's needs. For example, you may have a site located in other states or countries. Creating a child domain for that office allows that office to be an independent domain, and thus they can have their own security and domain settings. One or more domains that follow the same contiguous namespace are called a tree. So if my domain name is Stormwind.com and the child domains are `NH.Stormwind.com`, `Arizona.Stormwind.com`, and `Florida.Stormwind.com`, this would be a tree. All domains here follow the `Stormwind.com` namespace.

Another Active Directory advantage is the ability to extend the Active Directory schema. The Active Directory schema contains all the objects and attributes of the database. For example, when you create a new user in Active Directory, the system asks you to fill in the user's first name, last name, username, password, and so forth. These fields are the attributes of the user object, and the way that the system knows to prompt for these fields is that the user object has these specific attributes assigned to it within the Active Directory schema. An administrator has the ability to change or expand these fields based on organizational needs.

Let's take a look at some of the advantages of Active Directory.

Active Directory Certificate Services   Active Directory Certificate Services (AD CS) provides a customizable set of services that allows you to issue and manage public key infrastructure (PKI) certificates. These certificates can be used in software security systems that employ public key technologies.

Active Directory Domain Services   Active Directory Domain Services (AD DS) includes new features that make deploying domain controllers simpler and lets you implement them faster. AD DS also makes the domain controllers more flexible, both to audit and to authorize access to files. Moreover, AD DS has been designed to make performing administrative tasks easier through consistent graphical and scripted management experiences.

Active Directory Rights Management Services   Active Directory Rights Management Services (AD RMS) provides management and development tools that let you work with industry security technologies, including encryption, certificates, and authentication. Using these technologies allows organizations to create reliable information protection solutions.

Kerberos Authentication   Windows Server uses the Kerberos authentication protocol and extensions for password-based and public-key authentication. The Kerberos client is installed as a security support provider (SSP), and it can be accessed through the Security Support Provider Interface (SSPI).

Kerberos Constrained Delegation   Kerberos constrained delegation (KCD) is an authentication protocol that administrators can setup for delegating client credentials for specific service accounts. For example, KCD may be a requirement for services in SharePoint 2019. If you are planning on using SharePoint 2019 Analysis Services and Power Pivot data, you will need to configure KCD. KCD allows a service account to impersonate another service account and this allows access to specific resources.

Managed Service Accounts   The *Managed Service Accounts* is a Windows Server account that is managed by Active Directory. Regular service accounts are accounts that are created to run specific services such as Exchange and SQL Server. Normally when an administrator creates a service account, it's up to that administrator to maintain the account (including changing the password). Managed Service Accounts are accounts that administrators create but the accounts are managed by Active Directory (including password changes). To create Managed Service Accounts, you must use the `New-ADServiceAccount` PowerShell command. You must use PowerShell in order to create a Managed Service Account.

Group Managed Service Accounts   The group Managed Service Account (gMSA) provides the same functionality within the domain as Managed Service Accounts, but gMSAs extend their functionality over multiple servers. These accounts are very useful when a service account needs to work with multiple servers as with a server farm (for Network Load Balancing).

There are times when the authentication process requires that all instances of a service use the same service account. This is where gMSAs are used. Once group Managed Service Accounts are used, Windows Server will automatically manage the password for the service account. The network administrator will no longer be responsible for managing the service account password.

Security Auditing   Security auditing gives an organization the ability to help maintain the security of an enterprise. By using security audits, you can verify authorized or unauthorized access to machines, resources, applications, and services. One of the best advantages of security audits is to verify regulatory compliance.

TLS/SSL (Schannel SSP)   Schannel is a security support provider (SSP) that uses the Secure Sockets Layer (SSL) and Transport Layer Security (TLS) Internet standard authentication protocols together. The Security Support Provider Interface (SSPI) is an API used by Windows systems to allow security-related functionality, including authentication.

Windows Deployment Services   Windows Deployment Services allows an administrator to install Windows operating systems remotely. Administrators can use Windows Deployment Services to set up new computers by using a network-based installation.

Now when it comes to setting up Active Directory on-site or on a virtual machine, that server becomes a Domain Controller. Microsoft only has three server types; Domain Controller, Member Server, or Stand Alone Server. So it's important that you understand how each server works. So let's take a look at servers and what types of Microsoft servers you can have.

Server   A *server* is a machine that users connect to so they can access resources located on that machine. These resources can be files, printers, applications, and so forth. Usually, the type of server is dependent on the resource that the user needs. For example, a print server is a server that controls printers. A file server contains files. Application servers can run applications for the users. Sometimes you will hear a server referred to by the specific application that it may be running. For example, someone may say, "That's our SQL server" or "We have an Exchange server."

Domain Controller   This is a server that contains a replica of the Active Directory database. As mentioned earlier in this chapter, Active Directory is the database that contains all the objects in your network. A *domain controller* is a server that contains this database. All domain controllers are equal in a Windows Server network and each can both read from and write to the directory database. Some domain controllers may contain extra roles, but they all have the same copy of Active Directory.

Member Server   A *member server* is a server that is a member of a domain-based network but does not contain a copy of Active Directory. For example, it is recommended by Microsoft that a Microsoft Exchange server be loaded on a member server instead of a domain controller. Both domain controllers and member servers can act as file, print, or application servers. Your choice of server type depends on whether you need that server to have a replica of Active Directory.

Stand-Alone Server   A *stand-alone server* is not a member of a domain. Many organizations may use this type of server for virtualization. For example, say you load Windows Server with Hyper-V (Microsoft's virtualization server) on a stand-alone server. You can then create virtual machines that act as domain controllers to run the network.

Another component of a Microsoft network is a Global Catalog. The *Global Catalog* is a database of all Active Directory objects in a forest with only a subset of the object attributes.

In other words, the Global Catalog is a partial representation of the Active Directory objects. Think of the Global Catalog as an index. If you needed to look something up in this Windows 10 book, you would go to the index and find what page you need to turn to. You would not just randomly look through the book for the information. This is the same purpose the Global Catalog serves in your Active Directory forest. When you need to find a resource in the forest (user, published printer, and so forth), you can search the Global Catalog to find its location.

Domain controllers need to use a Global Catalog to help with user authentication. Global Catalogs are a requirement on an Active Directory domain. All domain controllers can be Global Catalogs, but this is not always a good practice. Your network should have at least two Global Catalogs for redundancy, but too many can cause too much Global Catalog replication traffic unless you have a single-domain model.

Read-Only Domain Controllers

Windows Server supports another type of domain controller called the *read-only domain controller (RODC)*. This is a full copy of the Active Directory database without the ability to write to Active Directory. The RODC gives an organization the ability to install a domain controller in a location (on site or off site) where security is a concern.

RODCs need to get their Active Directory database from another domain controller. So if you have a network with no domain controllers set up yet for the domain, the RODC option will not be available (the option will be grayed out). Implementing an RODC is the same as adding another domain controller to a domain. The installation is exactly the same except that when you get to the screen to choose Domain Controller options, you check the box for RODC. Again, this is ONLY available if there are other domain controllers already in the domain.

Installing Active Directory On-Site or in Azure

Before you install Active Directory into your network, you must first make sure that your network and the server meet some minimum requirements. Table 9.1 will show you the requirements needed for Active Directory.

TABLE 9.1 Active Directory requirements

Requirement	Description
Adprep	When adding the first Windows Server domain controller to an existing Active Directory domain, Adprep commands run automatically as needed.
Credentials	When installing a new AD DS forest, the administrator must be set to local Administrator on the first server. To install an additional domain controller in an existing domain, you need to be a member of the Domain Admins group.
DNS	Domain Name System needs to be installed for Active Directory to function properly. You can install DNS during the Active Directory installation.

Requirement	Description
NTFS	The Windows Server drives that store the database, log files, and SYSVOL folder must be placed on a volume that is formatted with the NTFS file system.
RODCs	Read-only domain controllers can be installed as long as another domain controller (Windows Server 2008 or newer) already exists on the domain. Also, the forest functional level must be at least Windows Server 2003.
TCP/IP	You must configure the appropriate TCP/IP settings on your domain, and you must configure the DNS server addresses.

The Installation Process

Windows Server computers are configured as either member servers (if they are joined to a domain) or stand-alone servers (if they are part of a workgroup). The process of converting a server to a domain controller is known as *promotion*. Through the use of a simple and intuitive wizard in Server Manager, system administrators can quickly configure servers to be domain controllers after installation. Administrators also have the ability to promote domain controllers using Windows PowerShell.

The first step in installing Active Directory is promoting a Windows Server computer to a domain controller. The first domain controller in an environment serves as the starting point for the forest, trees, domains, and the operations master roles.

Exercise 9.1 shows the steps you need to follow to promote an existing Windows Server computer to a domain controller. To complete the steps in this exercise, you must have already installed and configured a Windows Server computer. I am using a Windows Server 2016 computer for this exercise. You also need a DNS server that supports SRV records. If you do not have a DNS server available, the Active Directory Installation Wizard automatically configures one for you. I would recommend that you do this lab on a test box. This lab is needed later so that I can show you how to connect your on-site setup with Azure.

EXERCISE 9.1

Setting Up an On-Site Domain Controller

1. Install the Active Directory Domain Services by clicking the Add Roles And Features link in Server Manager's Dashboard view.

2. At the Before You Begin screen, click Next.

3. The Select installation Type screen will be next. Make sure that the Role-Based radio button is selected and click Next.

4. At the Select Destination Server screen, choose the local machine. Click Next.

5. At the Select Server Roles screen, click the check box for Active Directory Domain Services.

6. After you check the Active Directory Domain Services box, a pop-up menu will appear asking you to install additional features. Click the Add Features button.

7. Click Next.

8. At the Select Features screen, accept the defaults and click Next.

9. Click Next at the information screen.

10. Click the Install button at the Confirmation Installation screen.

11. The Installation Progress screen will show you how the installation is progressing.

12. After the installation is complete, click the Close button.

13. On the left-side window, click the AD DS link.

14. Click the More link next to Configuration Required For Active Directory Domain Services.

15. Under the Post-Deployment Configuration section, click the Promote This Server To A Domain Controller link.

16. At this point, you will configure this domain controller. You are going to install a new domain controller in a new domain in a new forest. At the Deployment Configuration screen, choose the Add A New Forest radio button. You then need to add a root domain name. In this exercise, I will use StormWindAD.com (see Figure 9.1). Click Next.

FIGURE 9.1   New Forest screen

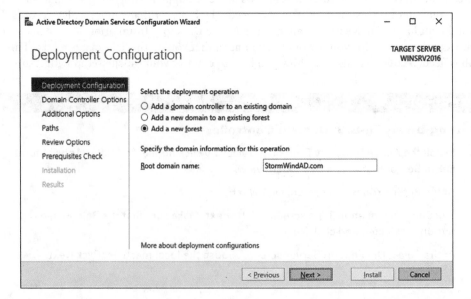

17. At the Domain Controller Options screen, set the following options (see Figure 9.2):

- Function levels: Windows Server 2016 (for both)

- Verify that the DNS and Global Catalog check boxes are checked. Notice that the RODC check box is grayed out. This is because RODCs need to get their Active Directory database from another domain controller. Since this is the first domain controller in the forest, RODCs are not possible. If you need an RODC, complete the previous steps on a member server in a domain where domain controllers already exist.

- Password: **P@ssw0rd**

Then click Next.

FIGURE 9.2   Domain Controller Options screen

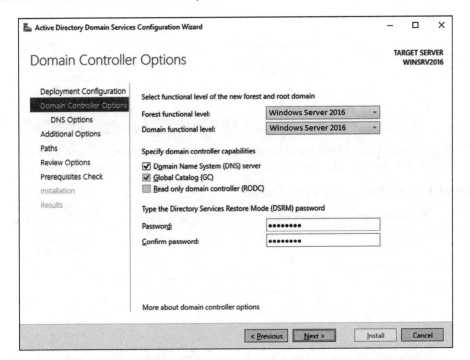

18. At the DNS screen, click Next.

19. At the Additional Options screen, accept the default NetBIOS domain name and click Next.

20. At the Paths screen, accept the default file locations and click Next.

21. At the Review Options screen (see Figure 9.3), verify your settings and click Next. At this screen, there is a View Script button. This button allows you to grab a PowerShell script based on the features you have just set up.

EXERCISE 9.1 *(continued)*

FIGURE 9.3 Review Options screen

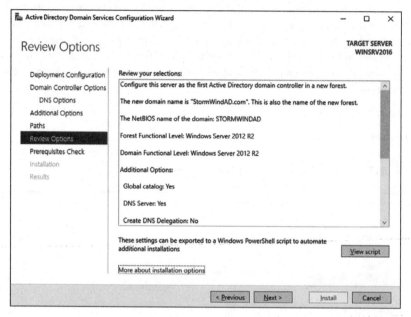

22. At the Prerequisites Check screen, click the Install button (as long as there are no errors). Warnings are OK just as long as there are no errors (see Figure 9.4).

FIGURE 9.4 Prerequisites Check screen

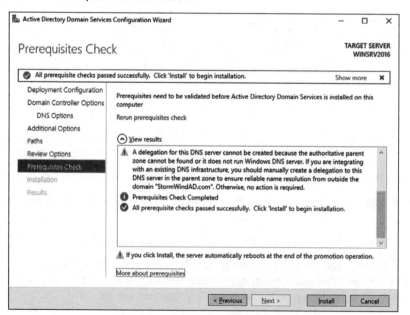

23. After the installation completes, the machine will automatically reboot. Log in as the administrator.

24. Close Server Manager.

25. Click the Start button on the keyboard and choose Administrative Tools.

26. You should see new MMC snap-ins for Active Directory.

27. Close the Administrative Tools window.

Using Active Directory Administrative Tools

After a server has been promoted to a domain controller, you will see that various tools are added to the Administrative Tools program group, including the following:

Active Directory Administrative Center   This is a *Microsoft Management Console (MMC)* snap-in that allows you to accomplish many Active Directory tasks from one central location. This MMC snap-in allows you to manage your directory services objects, including doing the following tasks:

- Reset user passwords
- Create or manage user accounts
- Create or manage groups
- Create or manage computer accounts
- Create or manage organizational units (OUs) and containers
- Connect to one or several domains or domain controllers in the same instance of Active Directory Administrative Center
- Filter Active Directory data

Active Directory Domains and Trusts   Use this tool to view and change information related to the various domains in an Active Directory environment. This MMC snap-in also allows you to set up shortcut trusts.

Active Directory Sites and Services   Use this tool to create and manage Active Directory sites and services to map to an organization's physical network infrastructure.

Active Directory Users and Computers   User and computer management is fundamental for an Active Directory environment. The Active Directory Users and Computers tool allows you to set machine- and user-specific settings across the domain. This tool is discussed throughout this book.

Active Directory Module for Windows PowerShell   *Windows PowerShell* is a command-line shell and scripting language. The Active Directory Module for Windows PowerShell is a group of cmdlets used to manage your Active Directory domains, Active Directory Lightweight Directory Services (AD LDS) configuration sets, and Active Directory Database Mounting Tool instances in a single, self-contained package. The Active

Directory Module for Windows PowerShell is a normal PowerShell window. The only difference is that the Active Directory PowerShell module is pre-loaded when you choose the Active Directory Module for Windows PowerShell.

A good way to make sure that Active Directory is accessible and functioning properly is to run the Active Directory Users and Computers tool. When you open the tool, you should see a configuration similar to that shown in Figure 9.5. Specifically, you should make sure the name of the domain you created appears in the list. You should also click the Domain Controllers folder and make sure that the name of your local server appears in the right pane. If your configuration passes these two checks, Active Directory is present and configured.

FIGURE 9.5   Viewing Active Directory information using the Active Directory Users and Computers tool

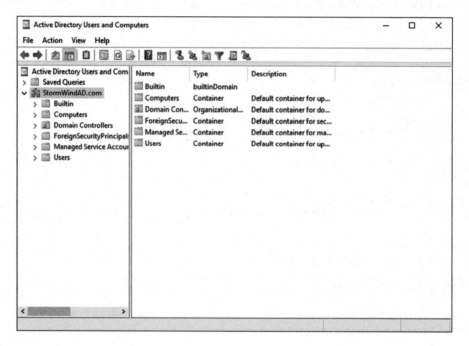

Understanding Azure Active Directory

So now that you understand how to install Active Directory on your on-site network, it's time to see how to configure your Azure Active Directory. One big misconception is that Azure Active Directory is set up and configured the same way that your on-site Active Directory is set up. The advantage of Azure Active Directory is that there is no installation. As soon as you set up your Azure subscription, Azure Active Directory is ready to go.

So before we begin setting up your Azure Active Directory, let's take a look at some of the features that Azure Active Directory delivers. The following features are just some of the features available in Azure AD managed domains.

Simple Deployment   Administrators can easily enable Azure AD Domain Services for their Azure AD directory. Managed domains include cloud-only user accounts and user accounts synchronized from an on-premises directory.

Domain-Join   Administrators have the ability to easily join computers to the Azure domain. Administrators can even combine the Azure domain with Windows 10 so that the clients can automatically join the domain with automated domain joining tools.

Setting Domain Names   Azure administrators have the ability to create custom domain names (for example, WillPanek.com) that are either verified or unverified with the Azure AD Domain Service wizards. Administrators can also create domain names using the Microsoft domain suffix of onmicrosoft.com. So if you want, you can create a domain of WillPanek.onmicrosoft.com. So as an administrator, you have a lot of flexibility when creating domain names for your organization.

AD Account Lockout Protection   Administrators can set up password protection with account lockout protection. If a user enters an improper password five times within two (2) minutes, the user account is locked out for 30 minutes. The nice advantage of this is that the user account will automatically unlock after the 30 minutes are up.

Group Policy Support   Azure administrators have the ability to create and use built-in GPOs for both the user and computer containers. This gives administrators the ability to enforce company compliances for security policies. Administrators can create custom GPOs that can be assigned to Organizational Units (OUs) and this in turn will help administrators manage and enforce company policies.

For example, you can set a GPO up so that your users will use Folder Redirection. Folder Redirection allows a user to place a file in one folder but it gets redirected to another (this includes OneDrive).

To use a Group Policy to redirect OneDrive, you need the OneDrive sync to be at least build 18.111.0603.0004 or later. You can see the OneDrive build number in the About tab of the OneDrive settings.

The Group Policy Object for "OneDrive Known Folder Move" won't work if an administrator has already set up a Windows Folder Redirection policy to redirect a user's Documents, Pictures, or Desktop folders to a storage location other than OneDrive. If this has been done, the administrator must first remove the Redirection Group Policy Object that has already been created. The redirection for OneDrive doesn't affect the Music and Videos folders. So, an administrator can keep them redirected with the Windows Group Policy object that is already created.

Azure AD Integration   One of the nice advantages of Azure is that administrators do not need to manage or configure Azure AD replication. Azure user accounts, group membership, or even user passwords are automatically replicated between Azure AD and Azure AD Domain Services. Azure AD tenant information is automatically replicated and synchronized to your onsite or Azure AD domains.

NTLM and Kerberos Authentication Support   Some applications, like Exchange, require Windows integrated authentication. Since Azure AD supports NTLM and Kerberos support, any service or application that needs to work with NTLM and Kerberos will work within the Azure AD domain.

LDAP Integration   Administrators have the ability to use any application, service, or LDAP security measure with Azure AD. LDAP is an industry standard and any LDAP-compatible application or feature can be integrated with your Azure AD network.

DNS Support   Administrators have the ability to set up, configure, and integrate DNS with their Azure network. DNS is a hostname resolution service and Azure allows administrators to easily configure DNS with many of the same DNS administration tools that they are currently familiar with.

Working with Organizational Units   Organizational Units (OUs) are Active Directory storage containers that administrators can use to manage users, computers, and groups accounts. One of the nice advantages of using OUs is the ability to set policies on each individual OU. So administrators have the ability to set different policies for different OUs and this gives an organization better control on how policies are administered.

High Availability   One of the most important requirements for any IT department is the ability to keep their network up and running. Some organizations require minimum downtime requirements. This means that your organization can only be down for a certain amount of time per year. Azure AD Domain Services offers an organization the ability to setup high availability for your Azure domains.

This feature guarantees higher service resiliency and uptime. With built-in health monitoring, Azure offers automatic failure recovery by spinning up a new instance to take over for any failed instances. This feature provides automatic and continued services for your organization's Azure network.

Management Tools Support   Administrators have the ability to use the same tools that they are familiar with for managing their current domains. The Active Directory Administrative Center and Active Directory PowerShell utilities can be used when managing their Azure AD domains.

Azure AD Questions and Answers

The following section is questions and answers about features and functionality of Azure Active Directory. The text was taken directly from Microsoft's website (https://docs .microsoft.com/en-us/azure/active-directory-domain-services/active-directory -ds-faqs). I recommend that you visit this page often for updates about features and Services.

Q. Can I create multiple managed domains for a single Azure AD directory?

Answer: No. You can only create a single managed domain serviced by Azure AD Domain Services for a single Azure AD directory.

Q. Can I enable Azure AD Domain Services in an Azure Resource Manager virtual network?

Answer: Yes. Azure AD Domain Services can be enabled in an Azure Resource Manager virtual network. Classic Azure virtual networks are no longer supported for creating new managed domains.

Q. Can I migrate my existing managed domain from a classic virtual network to a Resource Manager virtual network?

Answer: Not currently. Microsoft will deliver a mechanism to migrate your existing managed domain from a classic virtual network to a Resource Manager virtual network in the future.

Q. Can I enable Azure AD Domain Services in an Azure CSP (Cloud Solution Provider) subscription?

Answer: Yes. You can enable Azure AD Domain Services in Azure CSP subscriptions.

Q. Can I enable Azure AD Domain Services in a federated Azure AD directory? I do not synchronize password hashes to Azure AD. Can I enable Azure AD Domain Services for this directory?

Answer: No. Azure AD Domain Services needs access to the password hashes of user accounts, to authenticate users via NTLM or Kerberos. In a federated directory, password hashes are not stored in the Azure AD directory. Therefore, Azure AD Domain Services does not work with such Azure AD directories.

Q. Can I make Azure AD Domain Services available in multiple virtual networks within my subscription?

Answer: The service itself does not directly support this scenario. Your managed domain is available in only one virtual network at a time. However, you may configure connectivity between multiple virtual networks to expose Azure AD Domain Services to other virtual networks. See how you can connect virtual networks in Azure.

Q. Can I enable Azure AD Domain Services using PowerShell?

Answer: Yes. You can enable Azure AD Domain Services using PowerShell.

Q. Can I enable Azure AD Domain Services using a Resource Manager Template?

Answer: No, it is not currently possible to enable Azure AD Domain Services using a template. Instead use PowerShell to enable Azure AD Domain Services using PowerShell.

Q. Can I add domain controllers to an Azure AD Domain Services managed domain?

Answer: No. The domain provided by Azure AD Domain Services is a managed domain. You do not need to provision, configure, or otherwise manage domain controllers for this domain—these management activities are provided as a service by Microsoft. Therefore, you cannot add additional domain controllers (read-write or read-only) for the managed domain.

Q. Can guest users invited to my directory use Azure AD Domain Services?

Answer: No. Guest users invited to your Azure AD directory using the Azure AD B2B invite process are synchronized into your Azure AD Domain Services managed domain. However, passwords for these users are not stored in your Azure AD directory. Therefore, Azure AD Domain Services has no way to sync NTLM and Kerberos hashes for these users into your managed domain. As a result, such users cannot log in to the managed domain or join computers to the managed domain.

Q. Can I connect to the domain controller for my managed domain using Remote Desktop?

Answer: No. You do not have permissions to connect to domain controllers for the managed domain via Remote Desktop. Members of the AAD DC Administrators group can administer the managed domain using AD administration tools such as the Active Directory Administration Center (ADAC) or AD PowerShell. These tools are installed using the Remote Server Administration Tools feature on a Windows server joined to the managed domain.

Q. I've enabled Azure AD Domain Services. What user account do I use to domain-join machines to this domain?

Answer: Members of the administrative group AAD DC Administrators can domain-join machines. Additionally, members of this group are granted remote desktop access to machines that have been joined to the domain.

Q. Do I have domain administrator privileges for the managed domain provided by Azure AD Domain Services?

Answer: No. You are not granted administrative privileges on the managed domain. Both Domain Administrator and Enterprise Administrator privileges are not available for you to use within the domain. Members of the domain administrator or enterprise administrator groups in your on-premises Active Directory are also not granted domain/enterprise administrator privileges on the managed domain.

Q. Can I modify group memberships using LDAP or other AD administrative tools on managed domains?

Answer: No. Group memberships cannot be modified on domains serviced by Azure AD Domain Services. The same applies for user attributes. You may however change group memberships or user attributes either in Azure AD or on your on-premises domain. Such changes are automatically synchronized to Azure AD Domain Services.

Q. How long does it take for changes I make to my Azure AD directory to be visible in my managed domain?

Answer: Changes made in your Azure AD directory using either the Azure AD UI or PowerShell are synchronized to your managed domain. This synchronization process runs in the background. Once initial synchronization is complete, it typically takes about 20 minutes for changes made in Azure AD to be reflected in your managed domain.

Q. Can I extend the schema of the managed domain provided by Azure AD Domain Services?

Answer: No. The schema is administered by Microsoft for the managed domain. Schema extensions are not supported by Azure AD Domain Services.

Q. Can I modify or add DNS records in my managed domain?

Answer: Yes. Members of the AAD DC Administrators group are granted DNS Administrator privileges, to modify DNS records in the managed domain. They can use the DNS Manager console on a machine running Windows Server joined to the managed domain, to manage DNS. To use the DNS Manager console, install DNS Server Tools, which is part of the Remote Server Administration Tools optional feature on the server. More information on utilities for administering, monitoring and troubleshooting DNS is available on TechNet.

Q. What is the password lifetime policy on a managed domain?

Answer: The default password lifetime on an Azure AD Domain Services managed domain is 90 days. This password lifetime is not synchronized with the password lifetime configured in Azure AD. Therefore, you may have a situation where users' passwords expire in your managed domain, but are still valid in Azure AD. In such scenarios, users need to change their password in Azure AD and the new password will synchronize to your managed domain. Additionally, the password-does-not-expire and user-must-change-password-at-next-logon attributes for user accounts are not synchronized to your managed domain.

Q. Does Azure AD Domain Services provide AD account lockout protection?

Answer: Yes. Five invalid password attempts within 2 minutes on the managed domain cause a user account to be locked out for 30 minutes. After 30 minutes, the user account is automatically unlocked. Invalid password attempts on the managed domain do not lock out the user account in Azure AD. The user account is locked out only within your Azure AD Domain Services managed domain.

Q. Can I failover Azure AD Domain Services to another region for a DR event?

Answer: No. Azure AD Domain Services does not currently provide a geo-redundant deployment model. It is limited to a single virtual network in an Azure region. If you want to utilize multiple Azure regions, you need to run your Active Directory Domain Controllers on Azure IaaS VMs.

Q. Can I get Azure AD Domain Services as part of Enterprise Mobility Suite (EMS)? Do I need Azure AD Premium to use Azure AD Domain Services?

Answer: No. Azure AD Domain Services is a pay-as-you-go Azure service and is not part of EMS. Azure AD Domain Services can be used with all editions of Azure AD (Free, Basic, and, Premium). You are billed on an hourly basis, depending on usage.

Managing Azure AD

So now that we have looked at some of the features of Azure AD along with the common questions and answers about Azure AD, it's time to go through the Azure AD Dashboard. Figure 9.6 shows you the Azure AD Dashboard (you get to the Azure AD dashboard by clicking on Azure AD on the left side menu of the main dashboard). Let's take a look at some of the different options on the left side starting with Overview.

FIGURE 9.6 Viewing the Azure AD Dashboard

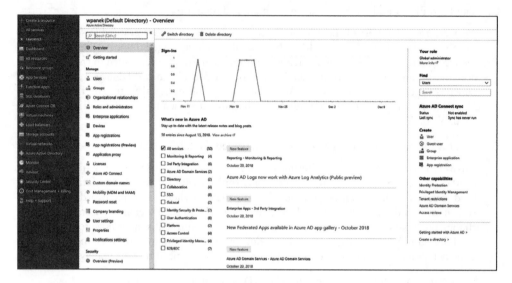

Overview

The Overview section of the Azure AD Dashboard is the figure you are looking at in Figure 9.6. The first thing you will notice in the center of the screen is the default Azure AD directory and the number of Sign-ins on Azure.

Below the Sign-ins section are all the different services that you have with Azure AD. You can click on the All services check box to see every service or you can click on an individual service and see the details of just those services on Azure AD.

On the right-hand side, you can see the role that your user is currently logged in as and you can also search for individual objects in the Find section.

Also, on the right-hand side you can add Users, Guest users, Groups, Enterprise applications, and App registrations. Below that you will see that you can access Other capabilities like Identity Protection, Privilege Identity Management, Tenant restrictions, Azure AD Domain Services, and Access reviews.

Below that section, you can view Getting started with Azure AD and you have the ability to Create a directory.

Getting Started

The Getting Started section (on the left side window under Overview) allows you to view videos and resources about how to accomplish tasks in Azure AD.

Users

The Users section (under Manage) on the left side allows you to view all of your current Azure AD user accounts (see Figure 9.7). Under the Users section, an administrator can also create New users, New guest users, Reset passwords, Delete users, Multi-Factor Authentication, Refresh your screen, or set up your columns.

FIGURE 9.7   Viewing User Section

Another task that can be created in the User's section is the ability to manipulate the user's settings. The User Settings link allows you to setup how the user can launch and view applications, how the user can register applications, and if the user can access the Azure AD administration portal. Administrators can also manage External user and access panel control from the settings section.

The User section also allows administrators to see how often the user is logging into Azure (this allows you to perform an access review) and administrators can also get audit information about the user account. Finally, in the User section, you can also troubleshoot user issues and also open a support ticket with Microsoft for additional help.

Groups

The Groups section allows an administrator to create and manage groups (see Figure 9.8). In the Groups section, you can create new groups, manage group settings for all groups, manage group membership, and delete groups. Administrators can also do auditing on groups along with troubleshooting group issues or opening a support ticket with Microsoft for additional help.

FIGURE 9.8 Viewing Group Section

Organizational Relationships

The Organizational Relationships section allows you to work with user accounts from other organizations. The Organizational relationship section also allows you to invite users who already own an Azure Active Directory account or a Microsoft Account. If they have one of these account types already setup, they can automatically sign in without any further configuration from an Administrator.

In the Settings section of Organizational relationships (see Figure 9.9), Administrators can setup what guest accounts can do regarding Azure. For example, an Administrator can decide if guest user access is limited or if users can invite other users to use your organization's Azure network. Finally, you can setup Collaboration restrictions (which domains you can invite users from) for your guest user accounts.

FIGURE 9.9 Viewing the Settings Section of Organizational Relationships

The Lifecycle Management section of Organizational relationships also allows an Administrator to setup Terms of use agreements while also allowing Administrators to have auditing of their guest users. Finally, Administrators can troubleshoot issues or opening a support ticket with Microsoft for additional help.

Roles and Administrators

The Roles and Administrators section allows you to see all of the available Azure AD roles and what each role does. In Table 9.2, I will show you the different roles that are available and what each role does in Azure AD.

Azure AD Roles

When you are in the Azure AD Roles and Administrators section, you can click on any of these roles to see who currently has this role in your organization.

TABLE 9.2   Azure Roles

Role	Description of Role Permission
Application administrator	This role allows you to create and manage all aspects of app registrations and enterprise apps.
Application developer	This role allows you to create application registrations independent of the "Users can register applications" setting.
Billing administrator	This role allows you to perform common billing related tasks like updating payment information.
Cloud application administrator	This role allows you to create and manage all aspects of app registrations and enterprise apps except App Proxy.
Cloud device administrator	This role allows you to have full access to manage devices in Azure AD.
Compliance administrator	This role allows you to read and manage compliance configuration and reports in Azure AD and Office 365.
Conditional Access administrator	This role allows you to manage conditional access capabilities.
Customer LockBox access approver	This role allows you to approve Microsoft support requests to access customer organizational data.
Desktop Analytics administrator	This role allows you to access and manage Desktop management tools and services.

TABLE 9.2 Azure Roles *(continued)*

Role	Description of Role Permission
Dynamics 365 administrator	This role allows you to manage all aspects of the Dynamics 365 product.
Exchange administrator	This role allows you to manage all aspects of the Exchange product.
Global administrator	This role allows you to manage all aspects of Azure AD and Microsoft services that use Azure AD identities.
Guest inviter	This role allows you to invite guest users independent of the "members can invite guests" setting.
Information Protection administrator	This role allows you to manage all aspects of the Azure Information Protection product.
Intune administrator	This role allows you to manage all aspects of the Intune product.
License administrator	This role allows you to have the ability to assign, remove, and update license assignments.
Message center reader	This role allows you to read messages and updates for their organization in Office 365 Message Center only.
Password administrator	This role allows you to reset passwords for non-administrators and Helpdesk Administrators.
Power BI administrator	This role allows you to manage all aspects of the Power BI product.
Privileged role administrator	This role allows you to manage role assignments in Azure AD and all aspects of Privileged Identity Management.
Reports reader	This role allows you to read sign-in and audit reports.
Security administrator	This role allows you to read security information and reports and manage configuration in Azure AD and Office 365.
Security reader	This role allows you to read security information and reports in Azure AD and Office 365.
Service administrator	This role allows you to read service health information and manage support tickets.
SharePoint administrator	This role allows you to manage all aspects of the SharePoint service.

Role	Description of Role Permission
Skype for Business administrator	This role allows you to manage all aspects of the Skype for Business product.
Teams Communications Administrator	This role allows you to manage calling and meetings features within the Microsoft Teams service.
Teams Communications Support Engineer	This role allows you to troubleshoot communications issues within Teams using advanced tools.
Teams Communications Support Specialist	This role allows you to troubleshoot communications issues within Teams using basic tools.
Teams Service Administrator	This role allows you to manage the Microsoft Teams service.
User administrator	This role allows you to manage all aspects of users and groups, including resetting passwords for limited admins.

Enterprise applications

The Enterprise applications section allows an Administrator to view, setup, and configure your organization's Enterprise applications (see Figure 9.10). Administrators can also setup an Application proxy within the Enterprise Applications section. An Application proxy allows an Administrator to provide single sign-on (SSO) and secure remote access for web applications hosted on your on-premise network.

FIGURE 9.10   Viewing the Enterprise Applications Section

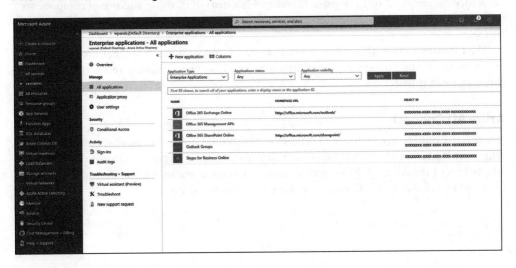

The Enterprise applications section also allows an Administrator to setup user settings for your Enterprise applications. These settings include users giving consent to applications accessing data on their company networks, users adding applications to their Access panel, and if users can only see Office 365 in the O365 portal.

The Enterprise applications section allows an Administrator to also setup Conditional access (setting up application policies), seeing who has logged into the applications, and auditing. Administrators can also troubleshoot application issues or opening a support ticket with Microsoft for additional help.

Application Menu Options

In the main Azure AD dashboard, there are three other menu options on the left hand side that have to do with Enterprise Applications. All three of these options (App registrations, App registrations (Preview), and Application Proxy) can be accessed in the Enterprise Applications section or directly using the Azure AD dashboard menu. Either link gets you to the same settings. Because of this, I will not add them below while explaining the Azure AD menu options.

Devices

The Devices section allows an Azure AD Administrator to setup which devices can access Azure AD. Administrators can also setup device settings and device roaming settings (Enterprise State Roaming). Finally, Administrators can do auditing and troubleshooting from the Device section.

Licenses

The Licenses section allows you to view purchased licensing for additional Azure AD components. If you purchase additional Azure AD components (for example: Azure Active Directory Premium P2 or Enterprise Mobility + Security E5), those additional components will show up in the Licenses section. You can also see if there are any licensing issues in this section.

The Licenses section also allows you to view additional components that are available and what those components do. Administrators can also view auditing and get troubleshooting from this section.

Azure AD Connect

Azure AD Connect (see Figure 9.11) allows an Administrator to integrate their Azure AD with your Windows Server AD or another directory on your network. One of the nice advantages of the Azure AD Connect section is that it allows an Administrator to download and install Azure AD Connect by using the Download link.

FIGURE 9.11   Viewing the Azure AD Connect Section

Azure AD Connect helps you integrate your on-premises Active Directory with Azure AD. This allows your users to be more productive by giving those users access to both cloud and on-premises resources by using a common user account for accessing both networks. By using Azure AD Connect, users and organizations can take advantage of the following features:

- Users can have a common hybrid identity that allows them to access on-site or cloud based services that use both Windows Server Active Directory and Azure Active Directory.

- Administrators have the ability to provide conditional access based on their device and user identity, network location, application resource, and multifactor authentication.

- Users can use this common identity in Azure AD, Office 365, Intune, SaaS apps, and third-party applications.

- Developers can create applications that use the common identity model thus integrating applications into on-site Active Directory or cloud based Azure applications.

To use Azure AD Connect, your on-site network must be using Windows Server 2008, Windows Server 2008 R2, Windows Server 2012, Windows Server 2012 R2, Windows Server 2016, and/or Windows Server 2019.

The Azure AD Connect section allows you to setup how your users will seamlessly pass through between both networks. Administrators can setup seamless connections by using a

Federation server (including Active Directory Federation Services (AD FS)), Seamless single sign-on, or Pass-through authentication.

Custom Domain Names

The Custom Domain Names section allows you to add and verify new domain names (see Figure 9.12). When you first build your Azure subscription, your new Azure AD tenant comes with an initial domain name (for example, willpanek.onmicrosoft.com).

FIGURE 9.12   Viewing the Custom Domain Names section

Administrators can't change or delete the initial domain name that is created, but they do have the ability to add their organization's domain names to the list of supported names. Adding custom domain names allows an administrator to create user names that are familiar to their users, such as wpanek@willpanek.com.

Mobility (MDM and MAM)

One feature that many organizations have started to implement is the ability for their employees to bring in their own devices to work (Bring Your Own Device, or BYOD). Because of this, Microsoft has tools like Mobile Device Management (MDM) and Mobile Application Management (MAM) to help IT administrators manage corporate data on personal devices.

Also, many organizations have started issuing devices like tablets to their employees, and many companies do not mind personal use of those devices. These are reasons Microsoft has implemented mobility tools into its Azure AD networks.

Windows 10 devices (either personal or corporate) have the ability to be connected to a corporate Azure AD network either by using the Windows 10 Settings app or through any of the Universal Windows Platform (UWP) apps.

Windows 10 Mobile Devices

When a user connects their personal device to a corporate network, the user should understand that corporate policies may affect their devices and settings.

Password Reset

The Password Reset section allows an administrator to determine if they want to enable self-service password reset (SSPR). If an organization decides to enable this feature, users will be able to reset their own passwords or unlock their accounts.

An administrator can allow all accounts to use SSPR (see Figure 9.13) or they can just choose certain groups that will have the ability to do SSPR.

FIGURE 9.13   Setting the self-service password reset

In the Password Reset section, administrators can also choose to use authentication methods. Authentication methods allow an organization to verify that the user is who they say they are. Methods for this include verification by mobile app notification, mobile app code, email, mobile phone, office phone, or security question. Administrators can choose between a single verification or multiple verifications.

Administrators can also require registrations when a user logs into Azure AD and can also set up password resets so that the user is notified if their password changes. Administrators can also choose to be notified when administrator passwords are reset.

Also, in the Password Reset section, admins can choose to enable a custom helpdesk link for users and finally you can configure password changes to be replicated back to an Active Directory network. Administrators can perform auditing and troubleshooting from the Password Reset section.

Company Branding

The Company Branding section allows an organization to set up custom text and graphics that your users will see when they sign in to Azure Active Directory.

Properties

The Properties section allows an Azure AD administrator to change the Default Directory properties. These settings include the Default Directory name, language, technical contact email, global privacy contact, privacy statement URL, and access management person for Azure.

Notifications Settings

The Notifications settings section (see Figure 9.14) allows an administrator to set up how often and what types of notifications they should receive. The Notifications settings section allows you to choose if you receive emails for Weekly status and educational content, service notifications, new features availability, and product research. Administrators also have the ability to set the Administrator email in the Notifications settings section.

FIGURE 9.14 Configuring the notifications settings

Security Overview (Preview)

The Overview (Preview) section (under the Security header on left side) allows an administrator to view an Overview of your security policies and security issues. Security is a big part of Azure AD because unlike an On-site network, the Azure AD network can be accessed from anywhere in the world. So making sure your Azure AD security is strong is a very important task for any Azure Administrator.

The Overview (Preview) allows an Administrator to view if there are any risky user accounts (deemed by Microsoft), configured user risk policies, new risky sign-ins, and sign-in risk remediation policies.

Identity Secure Score (Preview)

The Identity Secure Score section allows an Administrator to view their Azure AD Identity Secure Score. The Identity Secure Score is an indicator for how aligned Azure AD is with Microsoft's best practices recommendations for your organization's security setup.

The Identity Secure Score is an integer number between 1 and 248. The higher the number, the better your security settings align with Microsoft's recommendations. The score helps an organization objectively measure their identity security position, plan for identity security improvements, and review the successful implementation of your organization's improvements.

On this Identity Secure Score dashboard, an organization will be able to view your organization's score, comparison graph, trend graph, and a list of identity security best practices.

So the way this works is that Azure views your security configuration every 48 hours. Its then takes what it sees and compares your organization's settings against Microsoft's best practices. Based on that evaluation, your organization's security score is calculated. Based on that security score, an administrator can adjust their security settings and policies to make improvements.

Conditional Access

The Conditional Access section (see Figure 9.15) allows an Azure AD Administrator to set security policies. When it comes to Azure, one of the biggest concerns for organizations is cloud based security. Azure allows users to access their networks from anywhere in the world and from almost any device. Because of this, just securing resource access is not enough. This is where Conditional Access Policies come into play.

Conditional Access policies allow an organization to set how resources are accessed using access control decisions (who have access to resources) through Azure AD. Setting up Conditional Access policies allows an organization to have automated access control decisions based on the policies that your organization sets. Some of the situations that Conditional Access policies can help with are sign-in risk, network location risk, device management, and client applications.

FIGURE 9.15   Conditional Access Policies section

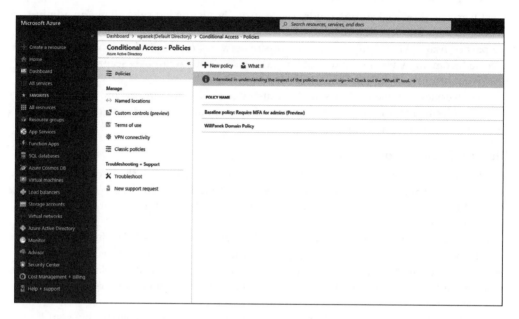

Configuring Objects

Now that we have looked at some of the different sections within Azure AD, let's look at how to create objects like users and groups.

User accounts allow employees to log into the Azure network. In Exercise 9.2, I will show you how to create a user account in Azure AD.

EXERCISE 9.2

Creating an Azure AD User Account

1. Log into the Azure portal at https://azure.microsoft.com.

2. Click on the Azure Active Directory link.

3. Under Manage, click the Users link.

4. Click the link +New User.

5. Type in the name of your user and a username. For this lab, I used George Washington as my user's name and GWashington@wpanek.onmicrosoft.com as the username (see Figure 9.16).

6. Click on Profile and put in the user's name and job information. Click the OK button when done filling in the profile information.

7. We are not going to add this user to a group yet. Make sure the Directory role is set to User.

FIGURE 9.16   New User information

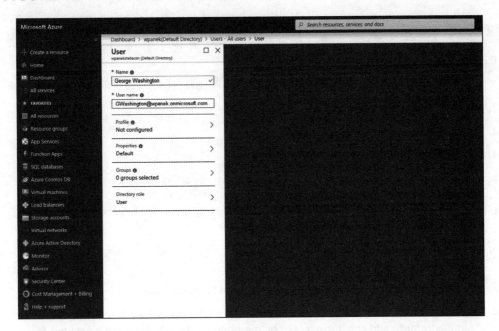

8. You can click on the Show Password box to see the temporary password assigned. Then click the Create button.

9. You should now see your user account (see Figure 9.17). If you would like to change any user information, double click on the user account and make changes. Be sure to save any changes that are made.

FIGURE 9.17   New User Created

In Exercise 9.3, I will show you how to create a group in Azure AD.

EXERCISE 9.3

Creating an Azure AD Group Account

1. Log into the Azure portal at https://azure.microsoft.com.

2. Click on the Azure Active Directory link.

3. Under Manage, click the Groups link.

4. Click on the link +New Group.

5. Under the Group Type pull down, choose Security. Security groups are the group type you use when you want the group to be assigned to resources. Office 365 groups allow users to collaborate with other users by giving them access to a shared mailbox, calendar, files, SharePoint site, and more.

6. In the Group Name box, type the name of your group. I used Marketing for my group name.

7. In the Group Description field, type a description for your group.

8. In the Membership Type pull down, choose Assigned. Assigned groups allow an administrator to add specific users to be members of the group and to have unique permissions. Dynamic user groups allow an administrator to use dynamic group rules to automatically add and remove members. Dynamic device groups allow an administrator to use dynamic group rules to automatically add and remove devices.

9. Click the Create button.

Self-Service Password Reset

As stated earlier, the Password Reset section allows an Administrator to determine if they want to enable Self-service password resets (SSPR). If an organization decides to enable this feature, users will be able to reset their own passwords or unlock their accounts.

An Administrator can allow all accounts to use the SSPR or they can just choose certain groups that will have the ability to do SSPR. To setup SSPR, the following Prerequisites must be met:

- An Azure AD tenant subscription with the minimum of at least one trial license enabled.

- Global Administrator account that can be used to enable SSPR.

- A non-administrator test account with a password that you know.

- A pilot group account to test with the non-administrator test account (the user account needs to be a member of this group).

In Exercise 9.4, I will show you how to setup the Self-Service Password Reset option in Azure Active Directory. To complete this exercise, you must have created a user and group in Exercise 3.2 and Exercise 3.3.

EXERCISE 9.4

Setting Up Self-Service Password Reset

1. From your existing Azure AD tenant, click the Azure Active Directory.

2. Select Password Reset.

3. From the Properties page, under the option Self Service Password Reset Enabled, choose the Selected option (see Figure 9.18).

FIGURE 9.18   Choosing the Selected option

4. From Select group, choose your pilot group.

5. Click Save.

6. From the Authentication methods page, make the following choices and then click Save:

> Number of methods required to reset: 1

> Methods available to users:

> Mobile phone

> Office phone

EXERCISE 9.4 *(continued)*

7. From the Registration page, make the following choices:

   Require users to register when they sign in: Yes

   Set the number of days before users are asked to

   reconfirm their authentication information: 365

In Exercise 9.5, I will show you how to test the Self-Service Password Reset option. For this exercise to be completed, you must have completed the previous exercise (Exercise 9.4). This test must be done with a normal user account. You can't run this test using an administrator account.

EXERCISE 9.5

Testing the Self-Service Password Reset

1. Open a new browser window in InPrivate or incognito mode, and browse to https://aka.ms/ssprsetup.

2. Sign in with a non-administrator test user, and register your authentication phone.

3. Once complete, click the button marked Looks Good and close the browser window.

4. Open a new browser window in InPrivate or incognito mode, and browse to https://aka.ms/sspr.

5. Enter your non-administrator test user's user ID, the characters from the CAPTCHA, and then click Next.

6. Follow the verification steps to reset your password.

Configuring Azure AD Identity Protection

One feature that can help any organization protect themselves is to add and configure Azure AD Identity Protection. Azure Active Directory Identity Protection is a feature of the Azure AD Premium P2 edition. Azure AD Identity Protection allows an organization to:

▪ Identify possible vulnerabilities that can affect your organization's identities

▪ Setup automated reactions to detected suspicious actions

▪ Identify suspicious events and take proper action to resolve those events

Azure AD Identity Protection allows an Azure Administrator to use the same type of protection that Microsoft uses to protect and secure users' identities.

One of the most common security breaches that hackers use to gain access to an organization is by stealing and using a current user's identity. In recent years, hackers have used more effective ways of stealing user data by using common attacks like phishing for data and hacking into third party organizations.

For an organization, detecting a compromised user account is no easy task. Azure AD helps an organization by using an adaptive learning algorithm and heuristics to determine irregularities and suspicious events. Once these events are recognized, Identity Protection produces a report and generates an alert that allows an Azure Administrator to view the issues and take appropriate actions to stop the attack.

There are advantages of using Identity Protection because Identity Protection is more than just a monitoring and reporting utility. Identity Protection allows an Azure Administrator to create policies that automatically detect and respond to events that meet a specific risk level. These policies can automatically stop the hack by blocking the user account and require that the user's password gets reset. During the password reset, multi-factor user authentication is then enforced.

To use Azure AD Identity Protection, an organization needs to add the service to their Azure subscription. In Exercise 9.6, I will show you how to add Azure AD Identity Protection.

EXERCISE 9.6

Adding Azure AD Identity Protection

1. Log into the Azure portal at `https://azure.microsoft.com`.

2. Click Marketplace.

3. Click Identity.

4. Click on Azure AD Identity Protection (see Figure 9.19).

FIGURE 9.19   Choosing Azure AD Identity Protection

5. When the Azure AD Identity Protection information page appears, click the Create button.

6. If a page appears showing that the Directory is Default Directory, you can choose a different directory you want this added to and then click Create. If the default directory is fine, don't click Create.

7. You should see a message (see Figure 9.20) that states that the Default Directory is protected. Click on that message to open the Azure AD Identity Protection dashboard. If this message does not appear, click the Create button and then click Azure Active Directory on left side. On the right side under Your Role, you should see a section called Other Capabilities. Click Identity Protection to see this message. This is also how you can access the Identity Protection dashboard later.

FIGURE 9.20   Clicking the message to open the Identity Protection Dashboard

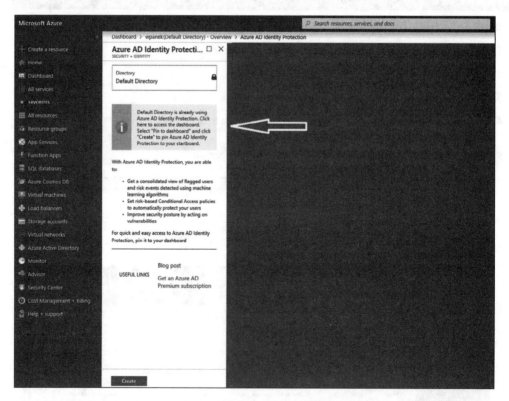

8. At this point, you should be seeing the Azure AD Identity Protection dashboard (as seen in Figure 9.21). Take a few minutes and look at the different sections within the

dashboard. Under the Investigation section, click on Users Flagged For Risk, Risk Events, and Vulnerabilities.

FIGURE 9.21   Identity Protection Dashboard

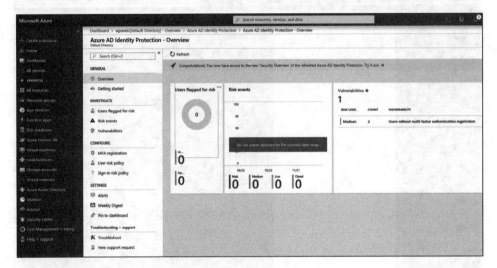

9. Under the Configure section, click User Risk Policy.

10. Under Users, make sure all users are selected.

11. Click Set Condition. Under User Risk, choose Select A Risk Level. Choose Medium And Above. Click the Select button. Choose the Done button.

12. Under Controls, select Choose Select a control. Under Select The Controls To Be Enforced, choose Allow Access and make sure the check box for Require Password Change is selected. Click the Select button.

13. Under Enforce Policy, choose On if you want to enforce this policy. If you do not want this policy to go live, do not choose On.

14. Click the Save button.

15. You can also set a sign-in risk policy by clicking on Sign-in Risk Policy. Under Users, choose All Users. Under Conditions, choose Medium And Above. Under Controls, Access, make sure you choose Allow Access and choose the Require Multi-factor Authentication check box. Choose either On or Off for Enforce Policy (choose Off if you just want to see how the policy is created) and then click the Save button.

16. Under Settings, click Alerts. Choose the level of risk you want to set. For this lab, I am choosing Medium. Click the link under Emails Are Sent To The Following Users and choose who the alerts should be sent to. Click the Add button and choose an email address. Then click the Done button (as seen in Figure 9.22). Click the Save button.

EXERCISE 9.6 *(continued)*

FIGURE 9.22   Setting an email for alerts

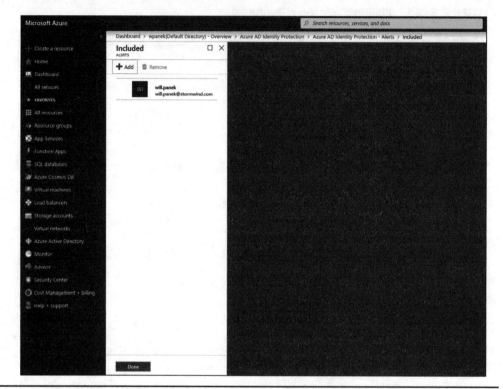

Managing Hybrid Networks

One nice feature of using both an on-site and Azure network is that Microsoft has many different tools to help you connect both networks. Connecting both networks is important so that users can seamlessly move between the two networks.

Microsoft's identity solutions extend your organization's on-site network with the Azure network features. These solutions create a common user identity for authentication and authorization to all resources. The advantage is that the users can access these resources no matter where they reside. This is what Microsoft refers to as *hybrid identity*.

To properly set up your hybrid identity, one of the following authentication methods can be used. Which one you decide to use is all depended on your environment scenario. The three available methods are:

- Password hash synchronization (PHS)

- Pass-through Authentication (PTA)

- Federation

So, what is the real advantage of setting up both networks using one of these methods? When you choose one of the authentication methods, you are providing your users with *Single Sign-On (SSO)* capabilities. Single sign-on allows your users to sign in once but have access to resources on both networks. This is what gives your users seamless access to all resources. So let's take a look at some of the available Identity solutions.

Password Hash Synchronization with Azure AD

One of the hybrid identity sign-in methods that you can use is called *Password hash synchronization*. Azure AD and your on-site Active Directory synchronize with each other by using a hash value. The hash value is created based on the user's password. This way the two systems can stay in sync with each other. Azure AD Connect is also required for this setup to function properly.

Password hash synchronization is a feature that is part of the Azure AD Connect sync and it allows you to log into Azure AD applications like O365. The advantage is that your users log into their account using their on-site username and password. This helps users because it reduces the number of username and passwords that they need to know.

Another advantage to your organization is that they can use password hash synchronization as a backup sign-on method if your organization decides to use Federation services with Active Directory Federation Services (AD FS). To setup password hash synchronization, your environment needs to implement the following:

- Azure AD Connect.
- Directory synchronization between your on-site Active Directory and your Azure AD instance.
- Have password hash synchronization enabled.

Azure Active Directory Pass-through Authentication

Another option for allowing your users to sign in to both on-site and cloud based applications using the same passwords is *Azure AD Pass-through Authentication*. Organizations can use Azure AD Pass-through Authentication instead of using Azure AD Password Hash Synchronization. The organizational benefits for using Azure AD Pass-through Authentication is the ability to enforce on-site Active Directory security and password policies.

Azure AD Pass-through Authentication utilizes an agent installed onto an on-premise server. This allows Azure Active Directory to validate the username and password directly on one of the on-premise Active Directory Domain Controllers.

This will help your organization with costs because your IT support desk will not be inundated by user's calls trying to remember their different passwords. This will help lower your IT department budget for total cost of ownership (TCO). Less calls to support means less support people needed. Some of the key benefits to using Azure AD Pass-through Authentication are as follows:

- Better User Experience
  - Users can use the same account password to sign into both your Azure AD and On-Site AD networks.

- Users don't need to talk to IT as often to reset passwords for multiple accounts.
- Azure AD allows your users to do their own password management using the Self-Service Password Management tools.

- Easy Deployment
  - There is no need to deploy a large infrastructure on-site. Azure AD network can handle most of your networking services.
  - Less budgeting needed for on-site IT departments. Since your Azure AD and your on-site AD can easily integrate with each other, there is no need for large IT departments on-site.

- Security
  - One nice advantage is that on-site passwords will never be stored in the Azure cloud.
  - Users' accounts are protected using Azure AD Conditional Access policies. These policies include Multi-Factor Authentication (MFA), filtering for brute force password attacks, and stopping legacy authentication.
  - The Azure agent will only allow outbound connections from within your network. The advantage of this means that you are not required to load an agent on your perimeter network.
  - With the use of certificate-based authentication, organizations get secure connections between the Azure agent and Azure AD.

- Highly Available
  - By installing additional Azure agents onto on-site servers, you can get high availability of Azure sign-in requests.

Federation with Azure AD

To understand what Federation can do for your organization, you must first understand Trusts. Federation, along with Active Directory Federation Services (AD FS), are just Trusts on steroids. Understanding what a Trust can do for your organization will help you understand why we use Federation services.

Understanding Trusts

Trust relationships make it easier to share security information and network resources between domains. As was already mentioned, standard transitive two-way trusts are automatically created between the domains in a tree and between each of the trees in a forest. Figure 9.23 shows an example of the default trust relationships in an Active Directory forest.

FIGURE 9.23   Default trusts in an Active Directory forest

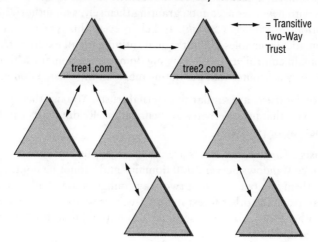

When configuring trusts, you need to consider two main characteristics:

Transitive Trusts   By default, Active Directory trusts are *transitive trusts*. The simplest way to understand transitive relationships is through this example: if Domain A trusts Domain B and Domain B trusts Domain C, then Domain A implicitly trusts Domain C. If you need to apply a tighter level of security, trusts can be configured as intransitive.

One-Way vs. Two-Way   Trusts can be configured as one-way or two-way relationships. The default operation is to create *two-way trusts* or *bidirectional trusts*. This makes it easier to manage trust relationships by reducing the trusts you must create. In some cases, however, you might decide against two-way trusts. In one-way relationships, the trusting domain allows resources to be shared with the trusted domain but not the other way around.

When domains are added together to form trees and forests, an automatic transitive two-way trust is created between them. Although the default trust relationships work well for most organizations, there are some reasons you might want to manage trusts manually:

- You may want to remove trusts between domains if you are absolutely sure you do not want resources to be shared between domains.

- Because of security concerns, you may need to keep resources isolated.

In addition to the default trust types, you can configure the following types of special trusts:

External Trusts   You use *external trusts* to provide access to resources on a Windows NT 4 domain or forest that cannot use a forest trust. Windows NT 4 domains cannot benefit from the other trust types that are used in Windows Server 2016. Thus, in some cases, external trusts could be your only option. External trusts are always nontransitive, but they can be established in a one-way or two-way configuration.

Default SID Filtering on External Trusts   When you set up an external trust, remember that it is possible for hackers to compromise a domain controller in a trusted domain. If this trust is compromised, a hacker can use the security identifier (SID) history attribute to associate SIDs with new user accounts, granting themselves unauthorized rights (this is called an *elevation-of-privileges attack*). To help prevent this type of attack, Windows Server 2016 automatically enables SID filter quarantining on all external trusts. SID filtering allows the domain controllers in the trusting domain (the domain with the resources) to remove all SID history attributes that are not members of the trusted domain.

Realm Trusts   *Realm trusts* are similar to external trusts. You use them to connect to a non-Windows domain that uses Kerberos authentication. Realm trusts can be transitive or nontransitive, one-way or two-way.

Cross-Forest Trusts   *Cross-forest trusts* are used to share resources between forests. They have been used since Windows Server 2000 domains and cannot be nontransitive, but you can establish them in a one-way or a two-way configuration. Authentication requests in either forest can reach the other forest in a two-way cross-forest trust. If you want one forest to trust another forest, you must set it (at a minimum) to at least the forest function level of Windows Server 2003.

Selective Authentication vs. Forest-wide Authentication   Forest-wide authentication on a forest trust means that users of the trusted forest can access all of the resources of the trusting forest. Selective authentication means that users cannot authenticate to a domain controller or resource server in the trusting forest unless they are explicitly allowed to do so.

Shortcut Trusts   In some cases, you may actually want to create direct trusts between two domains that implicitly trust each other. Such a trust is sometimes referred to as a *shortcut trust*, and it can improve the speed at which resources are accessed across many different domains. Let's say you have a forest, as shown in Figure 9.24.

FIGURE 9.24   Example of a forest

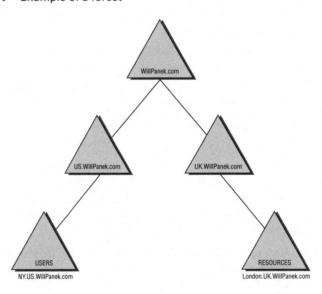

Users in the NY.us.WillPanek.com domain can access resources in the London.uk .WillPanek.com domain, but the users have to authenticate using the parent domains to gain access (NY.us.WillPanek.com to us.WillPanek.com to WillPanek.com to uk.WillPanek .com to finally reach London.uk.WillPanek.com). This process can be slow. An administrator can set up a one-way trust from London.uk.WillPanek.com (trusting domain) to NY.us.WillPanek.com (trusted domain) so that the users can access the resources directly.

> Perhaps the most important aspect to remember regarding trusts is that creating them only *allows* you to share resources between domains. The trust does not grant any permissions between domains by itself. Once a trust has been established, however, system administrators can easily assign the necessary permissions.

Understanding Federation

So now that you understand trusts, it's easier to understand Federation services because Federation is just a group of domains that have an established trust. These domains can be between sites or between separate organizations.

Remember, even though it's your company on Azure, Azure is owned by Microsoft. So you are technically setting up a trust between your company and Microsoft's network (onmicrosoft.com).

When setting up Federation, the trust level can be set to whatever the organization needs for their users. You do not need to just give open access to everyone. Also, Federation is just the mechanism to allow access across the trust. You still need to setup user's permissions to your resources.

When you setup authentication and authorization, using Federation, between your on-site network and Azure AD, all user authentications happen on-site. This allows an organization to have better levels of access control.

Federation services use claims that are passed to the application (resource) from the user domain after the user has initially authenticated. The username and password are never passed. Instead the application (resource) trusts the organization and this authenticates the user's claims.

Common Identity Scenarios

Table 9.3 was taken directly from Microsoft's website and it shows some of the common hybrid identity and access management scenarios along with Microsoft's recommendations as to which hybrid identity option would be suitable for each.

Understanding the Identity Table

In the following table, the three headers are abbreviated. Column 2, PHS and SSO, stands for Password hash synchronization with single sign-on. Column 3, PTA and SSO, stands for Pass-through authentication and single sign-on. Finally, Column 4 stands for Federated single sign-on using Active Directory Federation Services.

TABLE 9.3   Common Identity Scenarios and Recommendations

Scenario	PHS and SSO	PTA and SSO	AD FS
Sync new user, contact, and group accounts created in my on-premises Active Directory to the cloud automatically.	X	X	X
Set up my tenant for Office 365 hybrid scenarios.	X	X	X
Enable my users to sign in and access cloud services using their on-premises password.	X	X	X
Implement single sign-on using corporate credentials.	X	X	X
Ensure no password hashes are stored in the cloud.		X	X
Enable cloud multi-factor authentication solutions.		X	X
Enable on-premises multi-factor authentication solutions.			X
Support smartcard authentication for my users.			X
Display password expiry notifications in the Office portal and on the Windows 10 Desktop.			X

Azure AD Connect

Once you decide that you want your on-site network to be integrated with Azure AD, you need to install a component that allows both versions of Active Directory to work together. That component is called Azure AD Connect.

Azure AD Connect is a Microsoft utility that allows you to setup a hybrid design between Azure AD and your on-site AD. It provides some of the following features:

- Password hash synchronization
- Pass-through Authentication

- Federation integration
- Synchronization
- Health Monitoring

Azure AD Connect Health Monitoring

Azure AD Connect Health Monitoring is a way that an administrator can monitor their on-site identity infrastructure and maintain a constant connection to all of your Azure services.

To access the Azure AD Connect Health information, an administrator would need to connect to the Azure AD Connect Health portal. The portal can be used to view alerts, usage information, performance monitoring, and other key information. The Azure AD Connect Health portal gives you a one stop shop for all of your Azure AD Connect monitoring.

Installing Azure AD Connect

Before you can install Azure AD Connect, you need to make sure that your infrastructure and your Azure network have some prerequisites setup. The following is a list of requirements for installing Azure AD Connect:

- Azure AD
- On-site Active Directory
- Azure AD Connect server
- SQL Server database used by Azure AD Connect
- Azure AD Global Administrator account
- Enterprise Administrator account
- Connectivity between networks
- PowerShell and .Net Framework setup
- Enabled TLS 1.2 for Azure AD Connect

In Exercise 9.7, I will show you how to download and install Azure AD connect. To complete this exercise, you must have an on-site version of AD that can be connected to Azure.

EXERCISE 9.7

Installing Azure AD Connect

1. Log into the Azure portal at https://azure.microsoft.com.

2. Click on Azure Active Directory.

3. Click on Azure AD Connect.

4. Click the Download Azure AD Connect link.

EXERCISE 9.7 *(continued)*

5. Click on the Download button.

6. When the download box appears, choose to download the AzureADConnect.msi file to a network location. Once the download is complete, close the download box.

7. Log into the server (where you wish to install Azure AD Connect) as the local administrator.

8. Navigate to the AzureADConnect.msi file and double-click on the file to start the install.

9. On the Welcome screen, select the box to agree to the license terms and then click Continue.

10. On the Express Settings page, click Use Express Settings.

11. On the Connect To Azure AD page, enter the Azure Global administrator's username and password and then click Next.

12. The Connect To AD DS page will appear. Enter the username and password for an onsite enterprise admin and then click Next.

13. The Azure AD sign-in configuration page will appear. Review every domain marked Not Added and Not Verified. Make sure domains are verified in Azure AD. Once the domains are verified in Azure, click the Refresh symbol. If you need to verify your domains, go into Azure Active Directory, and then select Custom Domain Names. Enter the domain names for your onsite domain.

14. On the Ready to configure page, click Install.

15. When the installation completes, click Exit.

16. After the installation has completed, you will need to sign off and sign in again before you can use or set up any other services.

Azure VPN Gateway

As I have stated throughout this book, most (if not all) companies will have both an on-site network and an Azure network. Because of this, you will need to know how to connect both networks together. This is where you would use a Site-to-Site VPN (virtual private network) gateway connection.

Site-to-Site VPN gateway connections allow you to connect both networks together over a secure IPsec/IKE (Internet Key Exchange) VPN tunnel. To make this type of connection between networks, you need to have a VPN device located on-site. This VPN device will require a public IP address on the external side (the side facing the Internet) of the device.

To use a Site-to-Site VPN connection, you must meet the following requirements:

- Compatible VPN device with an administrator who can configure the device.

- An external public IP address for that VPN device.

- Knowledge of your on-site IP configuration and subnetting. None of your on-site IP subnets can overlap your Azure virtual network subnets.

Example Values for Site-to-Site VPN Connection

To help IT people better understand and configure Site-to-Site VPN connections, Microsoft released example values on their website. These example values can be used to setup a test environment or they can be used to help you better understand what values are needed to setup a Site-to-Site VPN connection.

Site-to-Site VPN Connection Examples

The following examples were taken directly from Microsoft's website, https://docs.microsoft.com/en-us/azure/vpn-gateway/vpn-gateway-howto-site-to-site-resource-manager-portal:

- VNet Name: TestVNet1

- Address Space: 10.1.0.0/16

- Subscription: The subscription you want to use

- Resource Group: TestRG1

- Location: East US

- Subnet: FrontEnd: 10.1.0.0/24, BackEnd: 10.1.1.0/24 (optional for this exercise)

- Gateway Subnet name: GatewaySubnet (this will auto-fill in the portal)

- Gateway Subnet address range: 10.1.255.0/27

- DNS Server: 8.8.8.8—Optional. The IP address of your DNS server.

- Virtual Network Gateway Name: VNet1GW

- Public IP: VNet1GWIP

- VPN Type: Route-based

- Connection Type: Site-to-site (IPsec)

- Gateway Type: VPN

- Local Network Gateway Name: Site1

- Connection Name: VNet1toSite1

- Shared Key: For this example, we use abc123. But you can use whatever is compatible with your VPN hardware. The important thing is that the values match on both sides of the connection.

Creating the VPN Gateway

Now that you have an understanding of why you would need a VPN gateway, let's look at what it takes to create a VPN gateway. Since every VPN device is different, I will show you how to create the actual Site-to-Site VPN connection in Exercise 9.8. You need to have someone create the connection on the VPN device.

EXERCISE 9.8

Creating the Site-to-Site VPN Connection

1. Log into the Azure portal at `https://azure.microsoft.com`.

2. On the left side of the portal page, click + Create A Resource and then type **Virtual Network Gateway** in the search box. In the Results section, click Virtual Network Gateway (as seen in Figure 9.25).

FIGURE 9.25 Choosing Virtual Network Gateway

3. On the Virtual Network Gateway page, click the Create button.

4. On the Create Virtual Network Gateway page, enter the values for your virtual network gateway settings.

   - **Name**: This is the name of your gateway object.

   - **Gateway Type**: Select VPN. VPN gateways use the VPN type.

   - **VPN Type**: Choose the VPN type that fits your configuration. Route-based VPNs are the most common type.

- **SKU**: Select your gateway SKU. This will depend on the VPN type you select.

- **Enable Active-Active Mode**: If you are creating an active-active gateway configuration, choose this check box. If you are not creating an active-active gateway configuration, leave this check box unselected.

- **Location**: Choose your appropriate geographical location.

- **Virtual Network**: Choose the virtual network you want for this gateway.

- **Gateway Subnet Address Range**: This setting will only be seen if you did not already create a gateway subnet for your virtual network. If you did create a valid gateway subnet, this setting will not appear.

- **Public IP Address**: This setting specifies the public IP address that gets associated to the VPN gateway. Make sure Create New is the selected radio button and type a name for your public IP address.

- Unless your configuration specifically requires BGP ASN, leave this configuration's check box unchecked. If BGP ASN is required, the default setting for ASN is 65515. You can change this if needed.

5. Click Create. The settings will be validated and you'll see the "Deploying Virtual network gateway" message on the dashboard. This can take up to 45 minutes. Refresh your portal page to see the current status.

Creating the Local Network Gateway

The next step that we must complete is creating the local network gateway. The local network gateway refers to your on-site network. What you need to do is give your on-site network a name that Azure can use to access that network.

After you name the on-site network on Azure, you then need to tell Azure what IP address that it needs to use to access the on-site VPN device. You also need to specify the IP address prefix (that is located on your on-site location) that will be used to route traffic through the VPN gateway and to the VPN device.

In Exercise 9.9, I will show you how to setup the local network gateway. To complete this exercise, you need to know the IP address information for your on-site test or live network.

EXERCISE 9.9

Creating the Local Network Gateway

1. Log into the Azure portal https://azure.microsoft.com.

2. On the left side of the portal page, click the + Create A Resource and then type **Local network gateway** in the search box. In the Results section, click Local network gateway (as seen in Figure 9.26).

FIGURE 9.26   Choosing a Local network gateway

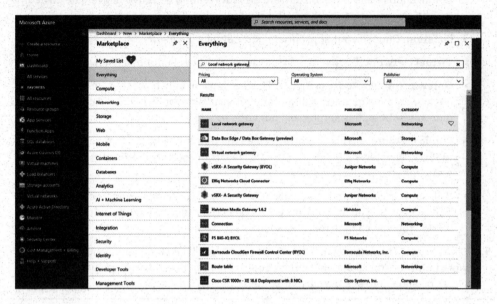

3.   On the Local network gateway page, click the Create button.

4.   On the Create Local Network Gateway page, enter the values for your local network gateway settings.

   ▪   **Name**: Specify the name of your local network gateway.

   ▪   **IP address**: This is the public IP address of the VPN device.

   ▪   **Address Space**: This is the IP address ranges for the local network.

   ▪   **Configure BGP settings**: Use this setting when configuring BGP. Otherwise, don't check this checkbox.

   ▪   **Subscription**: Verify your current Azure subscription is showing.

   ▪   **Resource Group**: You can create a new resource group or choose one that you have already created.

   ▪   **Location**: Choose your appropriate geographical location.

5.   Click the Create button.

Once you have finished creating the VPN connection, you will need to configure the company's VPN device. As stated above, Site-to-Site connections require a VPN device. Once the VPN device is configured properly, your Site-to-Site communications are completed.

Understanding ExpressRoute

ExpressRoute allows you to setup another way to connect your two networks. ExpressRoute allows you to connect your internal network to your external network using a private connection provided by your connection provider. Using ExpressRoute allows you to connect your internal network with any or all of the different Microsoft networks including Azure, Office 365, and Dynamics 365.

Since the connection is through your connection provider and not the internet, ExpressRoute is a much faster, more reliable, better security, and lower latencies connection over the Internet.

Implementing Active Directory Federation Services

Active Directory Federation Services (AD FS) demands a great deal of preparation and planning to ensure a successful implementation. The type of certificate authority used to sign the AD FS server's certificate must be planned. The SSL encryption level must be negotiated with the partnering organization. For instance, how much Active Directory information should be shared with the partnering organization? What should the DNS structure look like to support federation communications? You must explore all of these questions before implementing AD FS. In the following sections, I will discuss how to deploy AD FS and the configurations used to set up a federated partnership between your on-site network and Azure AD.

What Is a Claim?

A *claim* is an identifiable element (email address, username, password, and so on) that a trusted source asserts about an identity, such as, for example, the SID of a user or computer. An identity can contain more than one claim, and any combination of those claims can be used to authorize access to resources.

Windows Server extends the authorization identity beyond using the SID for identity and enables administrators to configure authorization based on claims published in Active Directory.

Today, the claims-based identity model brings us to cloud-based authentication. One analogy to the claim-based model is the old airport check-in procedure:

1. You first check in at the ticket counter.

2. You present a suitable form of ID (driver's license, passport, credit card, and so on). After verifying that your picture ID matches your face (authentication), the agent pulls up your flight information and verifies that you've paid for a ticket (authorization).

3. You receive a boarding pass (token). The boarding pass lets the gate agents know your name and frequent flyer number (authentication and personalization), your flight number and seating priority (authorization), and more. The boarding pass has bar-code information (certificate) with a boarding serial number proving that the boarding pass was issued by the airline and not a (self-signed) forgery.

Active Directory Federation Services is Microsoft's claims-based identity solution, providing browser-based clients (internal or external to your network) with transparent access to one or more protected Internet-facing applications.

When an application is hosted in a different network than the user accounts, users are occasionally prompted for secondary credentials when they attempt to access the application. These secondary credentials represent the identity of the users in the domain where the application is hosted. The web server hosting the application usually requires these credentials to make the most proper authorization decision.

AD FS makes secondary accounts and their credentials unnecessary by providing trust relationships that send a user's digital identity and access rights to trusted partners. In a federated environment, each organization continues to manage its own identities, but each organization can also securely send and accept identities from other organizations. This seamless process is referred to as *single sign-on (SSO)*.

Windows Server AD FS federation servers can extract Windows authorization claims from a user's authorization token that is created when the user authenticates to the AD FS federation server. AD FS inserts these claims into its claim pipeline for processing. You can configure Windows authorization claims to pass through the pipeline as is, or you can configure AD FS to transform Windows authorization claims into a different or well-known claim type.

Claims Provider

A *claims provider* is a federation server that processes trusted identity claims requests. A federation server processes requests to issue, manage, and validate security tokens. Security tokens consist of a collection of identity claims, such as a user's name or role or an anonymous identifier. A federation server can issue tokens in several formats. In addition, a federation server can protect the contents of security tokens in transmission with an X.509 certificate.

For example, when a StormWind user needs access to Fabrikam's web application, the StormWind user must request claims from the StormWind AD FS server claims provider. The claim is transformed into an encrypted security token, which is then sent to Fabrikam's AD FS server.

Relying Party

A *relying party* is a federation server that receives security tokens from a trusted federation partner claims provider. In turn, the relying party issues new security tokens that a local relying party application consumes. In the prior example, Fabrikam is the relying party that relies on the StormWind's claims provider to validate the user's claim. By using a relying-party federation server in conjunction with a claims provider, organizations can offer web single sign-on to users from partner organizations. In this scenario, each organization manages its own identity stores.

Endpoints

Endpoints provide access to the federation server functionality of AD FS, such as token issuance, information card issuance, and the publishing of federation metadata. Based on the type of endpoint, you can enable or disable the endpoint or control whether the endpoint is published to AD FS proxies.

Table 9.4 describes the property fields that distinguish the various built-in endpoints that AD FS exposes. The table includes the types of endpoints and their methods of client authentication. Table 9.5 describes the AD FS security modes.

TABLE 9.4   AD FS Endpoints

Name	Description
WS-Trust 1.3	An endpoint built on a standard Simple Object Access Protocol (SOAP)–based protocol for issuing security tokens.
WS-Trust 2005	An endpoint built on a prestandard, SOAP-based protocol for issuing security tokens.
WS-Federation Passive/SAML Web SSO	An endpoint published to support protocols that redirect web browser clients to issue security tokens.
Federation Metadata	A standard-formatted endpoint for exchanging metadata about a claims provider or a relying party.
SAML Artifact Resolution	An endpoint built on a subset of the Security Assertion Markup Language (SAML) version 2.0 protocol that describes how a relying party can access a token directly from a claims provider.
WS-Trust WSDL	An endpoint that publishes WS-Trust Web Services Definition Language (WSDL) containing the metadata that the federation service must be able to accept from other federation servers.
SAML Token (Asymmetric)	The client accepts a SAML token with an asymmetric key.

TABLE 9.5   AD FS Security Modes

Name	Description
Transport	The client credentials are included at the transport layer. Confidentiality is preserved at the transport layer (Secure Sockets Layer [SSL]).
Mixed	The client credentials are included in the header of a SOAP message. Confidentiality is preserved at the transport layer (SSL).
Message	The client credentials are included in the header of a SOAP message. Confidentiality is preserved by encryption inside the SOAP message.

Claim Descriptions

Claim descriptions are claim types based on an entity's or user's attribute like a user's email address, common name or UPN. AD FS publishes these claims types in the federation metadata and most common claim descriptions are pre-configured in the AD FS Management snap-in.

The claim descriptions are published to federation metadata which is stored in the AD FS configuration database. The claim descriptions include a claim type URI, name, publishing state, and description.

Claim Rules

Claim rules define how AD FS processes a claim. The most common rule is using a user's email address as a valid claim. The email address claim is validated through the partner's Active Directory email attribute for the user's account. If there is a match, the claim is accepted as valid.

Claim rules can quickly evolve into more complex rules with more attributes such as a user's employee ID or department. The key goal of claim rules is to process the claim in a manner that validates the user's claim and to assemble a user's profile information based on a sufficient number of attributes to place the user into a role or group.

The Attribute Store

Attribute stores are the repositories containing claim values. AD FS natively supports Active Directory by default as an attribute store. SQL Server, AD LDS, and custom attribute stores are also supported.

AD FS Role Services

The AD FS server role includes federation, proxy, and web agent services. These services enable the following:

- Web SSO
- Federated web-based resources

- Customizing the access experience
- Managing authorization to access applications

Based on your organization's requirements, you can deploy servers running any one of the following AD FS role services:

Active Directory Federation Service   Microsoft federation solution for accepting and issuing claims based token for users to experience a single sign-on to a partnered web application.

Federation Service Proxy   The Federation Service Proxy forwards user claims over the internet or DMZ using WS-Federation Passive Requestor Profile (WS-F PRP) protocols to the internal AD FS farm. Only the user credential data is forwarded to the Federation Service. All other datagram packets are dropped.

Claims-Aware Agent   The claims-aware agent resides on a web server with a claims-aware application to enable the Microsoft ASP.NET application to accept AD FS security token claims.

Windows Token-Based Agent   The Windows token-based agent resides on a web server with a Windows NT token-based application to translate an AD FS security token to an impersonation-level Windows NT token-based authentication.

AD FS in Windows Server 2016

The Active Directory Federation Services role in Windows Server 2016 introduced the following new features:

- HTTP.SYS
- Server Manager integration
- AD FS deployment cmdlets in the AD FS module for Windows PowerShell
- Interoperability with Windows authorization claims
- Web proxy service

HTTP.SYS

Prior AD FS versions relied on IIS components for the AD FS claim functions. Microsoft has improved the overall claims handling performance and SSO customization by building the AD FS 3.0 code on top of the standard kernel mode driver—HTTP.SYS. This approach also avoids the huge security "no-no" of hosting IIS on an AD FS server.

The classic netsh HTTP command can be entered to query and configure HTTP.SYS. The AD FS proxy server introduces interesting deployment nuisances and "gotchas" with HTTP.SYS, which I will discuss in the section "Web Proxy Service."

Improved Installation Experience

The installation experience for Active Directory Federation Services 3.0 was cumbersome, requiring multiple hotfixes as well as .NET Framework 3.5, Windows PowerShell, and the

Windows Identity Foundation SDK. Windows Server 2016's AD FS role includes all of the software you need to run AD FS for an improved installation experience.

Web Proxy Service

The kernel mode (HTTP.SYS) in Windows Server 2016 includes server name indication (SNI) support configuration. I strongly recommend verifying that your current load balancer/reverse proxy firmware supports SNI. This prerequisite is a sore spot for most AD FS 3.0 upgrade projects in the field. Therefore, it's worthwhile checking the following:

- Your preferred load balancer/device needs to support SNI.

- Clients and user agents need to support SNI and should not become locked out of authentication.

- All SSL termination endpoints vulnerable to the recent heartbleed bug (http://heartbleed.com) need to be patched, exposing OpenSSL libraries and certificates.

AD FS Dependency Changes in Windows Server 2016

Active Directory Federation Services was built on a claim-based identity framework called *Windows Identity Foundation (WIF)*. Prior to Windows Server 2016, WIF was distributed in a software development kit and the .NET runtime. WIF is currently integrated into version 4.5 of the .NET Framework, which ships with Windows Server 2016.

Windows Identity Foundation

WIF is a set of .NET Framework classes; it is a framework for implementing claims-based identity for applications. Any web application or web service that uses .NET Framework version 4.5 or newer can run WIF.

New Claims Model and Principal Object

Claims are at the core of .NET Framework 4.5. The base claim classes (Claim, ClaimsIdentity, ClaimsPrincipal, ClaimTypes, and ClaimValueTypes) all live directly in mscorlib. Interfaces are no longer necessary to plug claims in the .NET identity system. WindowsPrincipal, GenericPrincipal, and RolePrincipal now inherit from ClaimsPrincipal, WindowsIdentity, and GenericIdentity, and FormsIdentity now inherits from ClaimsIdentity. In short, every principal class will now serve claims. The integration classes and interfaces (WindowsClaimsIdentity, WindowsClaimsPrincipal, IClaimsPrincipal, and IClaimsIdentity) have thus been removed. The ClaimsIdentity object model also contains various improvements, which makes it easier to query the identity's claims collection.

   As you climb further up "Mount Federation," you will realize that not all vendor SAML flavors are compatible, and configuration challenges can bring even the most seasoned system integrators to their knees. SAML deserves an entire book, so to avoid this chapter reaching encyclopedia size, I will touch on just a few pointers.

AD FS negotiates SAML authentication in order of security strength from the weakest to the strongest, as shown in Table 9.6. The default mode, Kerberos, is considered the strongest method. The authentication precedence can be tuned by executing the PowerShell command `Set-AD FSProperties -AuthenticationContextOrder` to select an order to meet your organization's security requirements.

TABLE 9.6   SAML-supported authentication methods

Authentication Method	Authentication Context Class URI
Username/password	`urn:oasis:names:tc:SAML:3.0:ac:classes:Password`
Password-protected transport	`urn:oasis:names:tc:SAML:3.0:ac:classes:PasswordProtectedTransport`
Transport Layer Security (TLS) Client	`urn:oasis:names:tc:SAML:3.0:ac:classes:TLSClient`
X.509 certificate	`urn:oasis:names:tc:SAML:3.0:ac:classes:X509`
Integrated Windows authentication	`urn:federation:authentication:windows`
Kerberos	`urn:oasis:names:tc:SAML:3.0:classes:Kerberos`

Configuring a Web Application Proxy

One of the advantages of using the Remote Access role service in Windows Server is the Web Application Proxy. Normally, your users access applications on the Internet from your corporate network. The *Web Application Proxy* reverses this feature, and it allows your corporate users to access applications from any device outside the network.

Administrators can choose which applications to provide reverse proxy features, and this allows administrators the ability to give access selectively to corporate users for the application they want to set up for the Web Application Proxy service.

The Web Application Proxy feature allows applications running on servers inside the corporate network to be accessed by any device outside the corporate network. The process of allowing an application to be available to users outside of the corporate network is known as *publishing*.

Web Application Proxy works differently than a normal VPN solution because when an administrator publishes applications through Web Application Proxy, end users get access only to applications that the administrator published. Administrators have the ability to deploy the Web Application Proxy alongside a VPN as part of the Remote Access deployment for an organization.

Web Application Proxy can function as an AD FS proxy, and it also preauthenticates access to web applications using Active Directory Federation Services (AD FS).

Publishing Applications

One disadvantage to corporate networks is that the machines that access the network are normally devices issued by the organization. That's where Web Application Proxy publishing can help.

Web Application Proxy allows an administrator to publish an organization's applications, thus allowing corporate end users the ability to access the applications from their own devices. This is becoming a big trend in the computer industry called *Bring Your Own Device (BYOD).*

In today's technology world, users are buying and using many of their own devices, even for business work. Because of this, users are comfortable with their own devices. Web Application Proxy allows an organization to set up applications and enable their corporate users to use these applications with the devices the users already own, including computers, tablets, and smartphones.

The client side is easy to use as long as the end user has a standard browser or Office client. End users can also use apps from the Microsoft Windows Store that allow the client system to connect to the Web Application Proxy.

Configuring Pass-through Authentication

Now when setting up the Web Application Proxy (see Figure 9.27) so that your users can access applications, you must have some kind of security or everyone with a device would be able to access and use your applications.

FIGURE 9.27   Example of Web Application Proxy setup

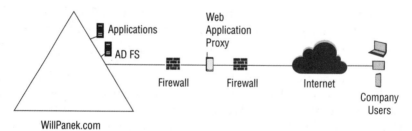

Because of this, Active Directory Federation Services (AD FS) should be deployed with a Web Application Proxy. AD FS gives you features such as single sign-on (SSO). Single sign-on allows you to log in one time with a set of credentials and use that set of credentials to access the applications over and over. To use a Web Application Proxy, you should set your firewall to allow for ports 443 and 49443.

When an administrator publishes an application using the Web Application Proxy, the method that users and devices use for authentication is known as preauthentication. The Web Application Proxy allows for two forms of preauthentication:

AD FS Preauthentication   AD FS preauthentication requires the user to authenticate directly with the AD FS server. After the AD FS authentication happens, the Web Application Proxy then redirects the user to the published web application. This guarantees that traffic to your published web applications is authenticated before a user can access it.

Pass-through Preauthentication   When using Pass-through Preauthentication, a user is not required to enter credentials before they are allowed to connect to published web applications.

Pass-through Authentication is truly a great benefit for your end users. Think of having a network where a user has to log in every time that user wants to access an application. The more times you make your end users log into an application, the more chances there are that the end user will encounter possible issues. Pass-through Authentication works in the following way:

1. The client enters a URL address on their device, and the client system attempts to access the published web application.
2. The Web Application Proxy sends the request to the web server.
3. If the backend server needs the user to authenticate, the end user needs to enter their credentials only once.
4. After the server authenticates the credentials, the client has access to the published web application.

To access applications easily that are published by the Web Application Proxy and use the AD FS preauthentication, end users need to use one of the following types of clients:

- Any HTTP client that supports redirection (web browsers). When Web Application Proxy receives an incoming message, the Web Application Proxy redirects the user to an authentication server and then back to the original web address authenticated.
- Rich clients that use HTTP basic.
- Clients that use MS-OFBA (Microsoft Office Forms Bases Authentication) protocol.
- Clients that use the Web Authentication Broker for authentication like Windows Store apps and RESTful applications.

Active Directory Federation Services Installation

I will now describe how to install and deploy Active Directory Federation Services roles on computers running Windows Server (see Exercise 9.10). I am using a Windows Server 2016 server for this exercise. You will learn about the following:

- Deploying AD FS role services using Windows PowerShell
- Supporting upgrade scenarios for AD FS

EXERCISE 9.10

Installing the AD FS Role on a Computer Using Server Manager

1. Start Server Manager.

2. Click Manage and click Add Roles And Features. Click Next.

3. The Add Roles And Features Wizard shows the Before You Begin screen. Click Next.

4. Click Role-Based Or Feature-Based Installation on the Select Installation Type screen. Click Next.

5. Click the server on which you want to install Active Directory Federation Services from the Server Pool list on the Select Destination Server screen. Click Next.

6. Select the Active Directory Federation Services check box on the Select Server Roles screen. Server Manager will prompt you to add other features associated with this role, such as management tools. Leave the default selections. Click Add Features to close the dialog.

7. Click Next on the Select Server Roles screen.

8. Click Next on the Select Features screen.

9. Server Manager shows the Active Directory Federation Services screen. This screen displays simple role introduction and important AD FS configuration information. Click Next.

10. From the Select Server Roles screen, select the check box next to the AD FS role services to install on the computer. Click Next.

11. Server Manager prompts you to add other features associated with this role, such as management tools. Leave the default selections. Click Add Features to close the dialog.

12. Read the Confirm Installation Selections screen. This screen provides a list of roles, role services, and features that the current installation prepares on the computer. Click Install to begin the installation.

Role Installation Using Windows PowerShell

To view the installation state of AD FS using Windows PowerShell, open an elevated Windows PowerShell console, type the following command, and press Enter:

```
Get-WindowsFeature "adfs*","*fed*"
```

Upgrading to Windows AD FS

Windows Server AD FS role supports upgrading version 3.0 of Active Directory Federation Services. You cannot upgrade versions of AD FS prior to version 3.0 using Windows Server.

Table 9.7 represents the support upgrade matrix for the AD FS role in Windows Server.

TABLE 9.7   Support upgrade matrix for the AD FS role in Windows Server

AD FS and Operating System Version	Windows Server 2016 / 2019 Upgrade Supported
AD FS 3.0 running on Windows Server 2008	Yes
AD FS 3.0 running on Windows Server 2008 R2	Yes
AD FS 3.0 Proxy running on Windows Server 2008	Yes
AD FS 3.0 Proxy running on Windows Server 2008 R2	Yes
AD FS 1.1 running on Windows Server 2008	No
AD FS 1.1 running on Windows Server 2008 R2	No
AD FS 1.1 Proxy running on Windows Server 2008	No
AD FS 1.1 Proxy running on Windows Server 2008 R2	No
AD FS 1.1 Web Agents on Windows Server 2008 or Windows Server 2008 R2	Yes

Configuring Active Directory Federation Services

Windows Server (should be Windows Server 2012 R2 or higher for full benefits) delineates role installation and role deployment. Role installations make staged role services and features available for deployment. Role deployment enables you to configure the role service, which enables the role service in your environment. AD FS in Windows Server uses the same deployment tools as AD FS 3.0. However, an entry point to start these tools is included in Server Manager. Server Manager indicates that one or more role services are eligible for deployment by showing an exclamation point inside a yellow triangle on the Action Flag notification.

AD FS Graphical Deployment

The AD FS Management snap-in link in Windows Server Manager is how you perform the initial configuration for the AD FS roles using the graphical interface. Administrators can also use PowerShell commands to install and configure AD FS.

Alternatively, you can start the AD FS management console using the AD FS Management tile on the Start screen. The Start screen tile points to the Microsoft .IdentityServer.msc file located in the C:\windows\adfs folder.

To configure AD FS, select Start ➤ Run and type FsConfigWizard.exe; alternatively, click the FsConfigWizard.exe file located in the C:\windows\adfs folder.

Exercise 9.11 uses the AD FS Federation Server Configuration Wizard. To complete this exercise, you'll need an active SSL certificate assigned to the server and a managed service account for the AD FS service.

EXERCISE 9.11

Configuring the AD FS Role on the Computer Using Server Manager

1. Select Create The First Federation Server In The Federation Server Farm.

2. Select the administrative account with permissions to configure the AD FS server and click Next.

3. Select the server certificate from the SSL certificate drop-down list.

4. Select the AD FS service name from the drop-down list.

5. Type **ADFS-Test** in the federation service's Display Name field and click Next.

6. Select Create A Database On This Server Using Windows Internal Database and click Next.

7. Click Next on the Review Options screen.

8. If the prerequisites check is successful, click Configure on the Prerequisite Check screen.

9. If the Result screen displays "This Server was successfully configured," you can click Close.

Deployment Using Windows PowerShell

Windows Server includes the Active Directory Federation Services module for Windows PowerShell when you install the AD FS role using Server Manager. The AD FS module for Windows PowerShell includes five new cmdlets to deploy the AD FS role:

- Add-AdfsProxy
- Add-AdfsFarmNode
- Export-AdfsDeploymentSQLScript
- Install-AdfsStand-alone
- Install-AdfsFarm

These AD FS cmdlets provide the same functionality as the command-line version of the AD FS Federation Server Configuration Wizard, fsconfig .exe. The AD FS role in Windows Server includes fsconfig.exe to remain compatible with previously authored deployment scripts. New deployments should take advantage of the deployment cmdlets included in the AD FS module for Windows PowerShell.

Add-AdfsProxy   Configures a server as a federation server proxy.

FederationServiceName   Specifies the name of the federation service for which a server proxies requests.

FederationServiceTrustCredentials   Specifies the credentials of the Active Directory identity that is authorized to register new federation server proxies. By default, this is the account under which the federation service runs or an account that is a member of the Administrators group on the federation server.

ForwardProxy   Specifies the DNS name and port of an HTTP proxy that this federation server proxy uses to obtain access to the federation service.

`Add-AdfsFarmNode`   Adds this computer to an existing federation server farm.

CertificateThumbprint   Specifies the value of the certificate thumbprint of the certificate that should be used in the SSL binding of the default website in IIS. This value should match the thumbprint of a valid certificate in the Local Computer certificate store.

OverwriteConfiguration   Must be used to remove an existing AD FS configuration database and overwrite it with a new database.

SQLConnectionString   Specifies the SQL Server database that will store the AD FS configuration settings. If not specified, AD FS uses Windows Internal Database to store configuration settings.

ServiceAccountCredential   Specifies the Active Directory account under which the AD FS service runs. All nodes in the farm must have the same service account.

PrimaryComputerName   Specifies the name of the primary federation server in the farm that this computer will join.

PrimaryComputerPort   Specifies the value of the HTTP port that this computer uses to connect with the primary computer in order to synchronize configuration settings. Specify a value for this parameter only if the HTTP port on the primary computer is not 80.

Active Directory Federation Services Certificates

There are three types of certificates used by an AD FS implementation:

- Service communications
- Token decrypting
- Token signing

The service communications certificate is required for communication with web clients over SSL and with Web Application Proxy services using Windows Communication Foundation (WCF) components. This certificate is specified at configuration time for AD FS.

The token decrypting certificate is required to decrypt claims and tokens received by the federation service. The public key for the decrypting certificate is usually shared with relying parties and others to encrypt the claims and tokens using the certificate.

The token signing certificate is required to sign all claims and tokens created by the server. You can have multiple token encrypting and signing certificates for an implementation, and new ones can be added within the AD FS management tool.

Relying-Party Trust

The federation service name originates from the SSL certificate used for AD FS. The SSL certificate can be template based and needs to be enrolled and used by IIS.

The next step in setting up AD FS is to configure a relying-party trust. A relying-party trust can be configured with a URL acquired from the relying party. The URL contains the federation metadata used to complete the federation trust configuration. The federation metadata may also be exported to a file that can then be imported into the relying-party trust. There is also a manual option for configuring a relying-party trust.

See Table 9.8 for the Federation Metadata fields.

TABLE 9.8   Federation Metadata Fields

Field	Description
Display Name	This is the friendly display name given to this relying party trust.
Profile	Select AD FS Profile for the standard Windows Server 2012 AD FS, or select AD FS 1.0 And 1.1 Profile for AD FS configurations that need to work with older versions of AD FS.
Certificate	This is the optional certificate file from the relying party for token encryption.
URL	This is the URL for the relying party. WS-Federation Passive Protocol URL or SAML 2.0 WebSSO protocols are supported.
Identifiers	This is the unique identifier used for this trust.
Authorization Rules	Selecting this permits all users to access the relying party or denies all users access to the relying party, depending on the needs of this trust.

Configuring Claims Provider and Transform Claims Rules

Claims provider trust rules are configured within the AD FS management console and are configured on a per-trust basis. Planning claims rules involves determining what claims are needed by the relying party to complete the authentication and authorization process and which users will need access to the relying-party trust. The relying party determines what claims need to be received and trusted from the claims provider.

Trust rules start with templates as the basis for the rule. There are different types of claims templates depending on the type of rule being used. The claims rule templates for transforms are described in Table 9.9.

TABLE 9.9   Transform claims rule templates

Template	Description
Send LDAP Attributes as Claims	Attributes found in an LDAP directory (such as Active Directory) can be used as part of the claim.
Send Group Membership as Claim	The group memberships of the logged-in user are sent as part of the claim.
Transform an Incoming Claim	This is used for configuring a rule to change an incoming claim. Changes include both the type and the value of an incoming claim.
Pass Through or Filter an Incoming Claim	This performs an action such as pass-through or filter on an incoming claim based on certain criteria, as defined in the rule.
Send Claims Using a Custom Rule	This creates a rule that's not covered by a predefined template, such as an LDAP attribute generated with a custom LDAP filter.

Defining Windows Authorization Claims in AD FS

Windows Server stores information that describes Windows authorization claims in the configuration partition of Active Directory. Windows refers to this information as *claim types*; however, Active Directory Federation Services typically refers to this information as claim descriptions. There are more than 40 new claim descriptions available in the AD FS Windows Server release.

The Active Directory Federation Services role included in Windows Server lets you configure AD FS to include Windows authorization claims in the AD FS claim pipeline. To simplify this configuration, you can create *claim descriptions* in AD FS. Claim types in Windows authorization claims are analogous to claim descriptions in AD FS. The Windows authorization claim ID maps to the AD FS claim description's claim identifier.

To simplify AD FS configuration using Windows authorization claims, create a claim description in AD FS for each Windows authorization claim you intend to deploy in AD FS.

Create Claim Pass-Through and Transformation Rules

You need to configure a claim rule with the Active Directory Claims Provider Trusts Wizard to insert Windows authorization claims into the AD FS claims pipeline.

Creating a claim description makes it easier to select the incoming claim type. Alternatively, you can type the claim type ID directly in the Incoming Claim Type list. A *pass-through claim rule* enables the Windows authorization claim to enter the AD FS claim pipeline. A pass-through claim leaves the claim type ID intact. Therefore, the pass-through claim ID begins with ad://ext, whereas most claim description URIs begin with http://. In addition, you can create a claim transformation claim rule on the Active Directory Claim Provider Trust Wizard to transform a Windows authorization claim into a well-known claim description.

Creating a claim provider trust claim rule enables the Windows authorization claim to enter the AD FS claim pipeline. However, this does not ensure that AD FS sends the Windows authorization claim. AD FS claim processing begins with the claim's provider. This allows the claim to enter the pipeline. Claim processing continues for the targeted relying party—first with the issuance authorization rules and then with the issuance transform rules.

You can configure Windows authorization claims in claims rules configured on a relying party. By default, a relying party does not have any issuance transform rules. Therefore, AD FS drops all claims in the pipeline destined for a relying party when the relying party does not have any rules that pass incoming claims. Additionally, issuance authorization rules determine whether a user can receive claims for a relying party and, therefore, access the relying party.

Choose the claim types from the list of inbound rules created in the Active Directory claims provider trust that you want to send to the designated relying party. Then create rules that continue to pass the selected claim types through the pipeline to the relying party. Alternatively, you can create a rule that passes all the inbound claims to the relying party.

> The AD FS role in Windows Server cannot provide claim information when the incoming authentication is not Kerberos. Clients must authenticate to AD FS using Kerberos authentication. If Windows authorization claims are not entering the AD FS claim pipeline, then make sure the client authenticates to AD FS using Kerberos and the correct service principal name is registered on the computer/service account.

Enabling AD FS to Use Compound Authentication for Device Claims: Compound Authentication

Windows Server enhances Kerberos authentication by introducing compound authentication. Compound authentication enables a Kerberos TGS request to include two identities: the identity of the user and the identity of the user's device. Windows accomplishes compound authentication by extending Kerberos Flexible Authentication Secure Tunneling (FAST) or Kerberos armoring.

During normal Kerberos authentication, the Kerberos client requesting authentication for a service sends the ticket-granting service (TGS) a request for that service. Using Kerberos armoring, the TGS exchange is armored using the user's ticket-granting ticket (TGT). Prior to sending the ticket-granting service reply (TGS-REP) to the client, the KDC checks the 0x00020000 bit in the value of the msDS-SupportedEncryptionTypes attribute of the security principal's object running the service. An enabled bit means that the service can accept compound authentication. The KDC sends the TGS-REP, which includes the service's ability to support compound authentication.

The Kerberos client receives the ticket-granting service TGS-REP that includes compound authentication information. The Kerberos client then sends another ticket-granting service request (TGS-REQ), with the difference being that this TGS-REQ is armored with the device's TGT rather than the user. This allows the KDC to retrieve authentication information about the principal and the device.

The Active Directory Federation Services role included in Windows Server automatically enables compound authentication when creating an AD FS web farm. During the creation of the first node in the farm, the AD FS configuration wizard enables the compound authentication bit on the msDS-SupportedEncryptionTypes attribute on the account that you designate to run the AD FS service. If you change the service account, then you must manually enable compound authentication by running the Set-ADUser -compoundIdentitySupported:$true Windows PowerShell cmdlet.

In Exercise 9.12, you will learn how to configure multi-factor authentication.

EXERCISE 9.12

Configuring Multi-factor Authentication

1. In the AD FS Management Console, traverse to Trust Relationships And Relying Party Trusts.

2. Select the relying party trust that represents your sample application (claimapp) and then either by using the Actions pane or by right-clicking this relying party trust, select Edit Claim Rules.

3. In the Edit Claim Rules For Claimapp window, select the Issuance Authorization Rules tab and click Add Rule.

4. In the Add Issuance Authorization Claim Rule Wizard, on the Select Rule Template screen, select Permit Or Deny Users Based On An Incoming Claim Rule Template and click Next.

5. On the Configure Rule screen, complete all of the following tasks and click Finish.

    a. Enter a name for the claim rule, for example **TestRule**.

    b. Select Group SID As Incoming Claim Type.

    c. Click Browse, type in **Finance** for the name of your AD test group, and resolve it for the Incoming Claim Value field.

    d. Select the Deny Access To Users With This Incoming Claim option.

    e. In the Edit Claim Rules For Claimapp window, make sure to delete the Permit Access To All Users rule that was created by default when you created this relying-party trust.

Verify Multifactor Access Control Mechanism

In this phase, you will verify the multi-factor access control policy that you set up in the previous phase. You can use the following procedure to verify that a test AD user can access your sample application because the test account belongs to the Finance group. Conversely, you will use the procedure to verify that AD users who do not belong to the Finance group cannot access the sample application.

1. On your client computer, open a browser window and navigate to your sample application. I am showing you an example of an application link below and what it should look like. But you must make sure that Webserv1 (in our example) is set up to successfully see a response: https://webserv1.contoso.com/claimapp. This action automatically redirects the request to the federation server, and you are prompted to sign in with a username and password.

2. Type in the credentials of a test AD account to be granted access to the application.

3. Type in the credentials of another test AD account that does not belong to the Finance group.

At this point, because of the access control policy that you set up in the previous steps, an access denied message is displayed for an AD account that does not belong to the Finance group. The default message text is "You are not authorized to access this site. Click here to sign out, and sign in again or contact your administrator for permissions." However, this text is fully customizable.

Using PowerShell Commands

In the following table (Table 9.10), I will show you some of the PowerShell commands available for Azure Active Directory. You must be using a newer version of PowerShell on your on-site servers or client machines. If you run into any issues trying to run these commands, please check out a newer version of Microsoft PowerShell on Microsoft's website.

TABLE 9.10 PowerShell commands for Azure Active Directory

Command	Description
Add-AzureADAdministrativeUnitMember	This command allows an Azure admin to add an administrative unit member.
Add-AzureADApplicationPolicy	Administrators can use this command to add an application policy.

Command	Description
`Add-AzureADScopedRoleMembership`	This command allows an Azure admin to add a scoped role membership to an administrative unit.
`Add-AzureADServicePrincipalPolicy`	Administrators can use this command to add a service principal policy.
`Get-AzureADAdministrativeUnit`	This command allows an Azure admin to view an administrative unit.
`Get-AzureADAdministrativeUnitMember`	Administrators can use this command to view a member of an administrative unit.
`Get-AzureADApplicationPolicy`	This command allows an Azure admin to view an application policy.
`Get-AzureADDirectorySetting`	Administrators can use this command to view a directory setting.
`Get-AzureADDirectorySettingTemplate`	This command allows an Azure admin to view a directory setting template.
`Get-AzureADObjectSetting`	Administrators can use this command to view an object setting.
`Get-AzureADPolicy`	This command allows an Azure admin to view a policy.
`Get-AzureADPolicyAppliedObject`	Administrators can use this command to view the objects to which a policy is applied.
`Get-AzureADScopedRoleMembership`	This command allows an Azure admin to view a scoped role membership from an administrative unit.
`Get-AzureADServicePrincipalPolicy`	Administrators can use this command to view the service principal policy.
`New-AzureADAdministrativeUnit`	This command allows an Azure admin to create an administrative unit.
`New-AzureADDirectorySetting`	Administrators can use this command to create a directory settings object.

TABLE 9.10 PowerShell commands for Azure Active Directory *(continued)*

Command	Description
New-AzureADObjectSetting	This command allows an Azure admin to create a settings object.
New-AzureADPolicy	Administrators can use this command to create a policy.
Remove-AzureADAdministrativeUnit	This command allows an Azure admin to remove an administrative unit.
Remove-AzureADAdministrativeUnitMember	Administrators can use this command to remove an administrative unit member.
Remove-AzureADDirectorySetting	This command allows an Azure admin to delete a directory setting in Azure Active Directory.
Remove-AzureADObjectSetting	Administrators can use this command to delete settings in Azure Active Directory.
Remove-AzureADPolicy	This command allows an Azure admin to delete a policy.
Remove-AzureADScopedRoleMembership	Administrators can use this command to remove a scoped role membership.
Set-AzureADDirectorySetting	Updates a directory setting in Azure Active Directory.
Set-AzureADObjectSetting	This command allows an Azure admin to update object settings.
Set-AzureADPolicy	Administrators can use this command to update a policy.
sGet-AzureADApplicationProxy ConnectorGroupMembers	Retrieve the members of an Application Proxy connector group

In Table 9.11, I will show you some of the PowerShell commands available for Azure and AD FS. You must be using a newer version of PowerShell on your on-site servers or client machines. If you run into any issues trying to run these commands, please check out a newer version of Microsoft PowerShell on Microsoft's website.

TABLE 9.11   PowerShell commands for Azure and AD FS

Command	Description
Add-AdfsAttributeStore	Administrators can use this command to add an attribute store to the Federation Service.
Add-AdfsCertificate	This command allows an administrator to add a new certificate to the AD FS server for signing, decrypting, or securing communications.
Add-AdfsClaimsProviderTrust	Administrators can use this command to add a new claims provider trust to the Federation Service.
Add-AdfsClient	This command allows an admin to register an OAuth 2.0 client with AD FS.
Add-AdfsFarmNode	Administrators can use this command to add a computer to an existing federation server farm.
Add-AdfsNativeClientApplication	This command allows an admin to add a native client application role to an application in AD FS.
Add-AdfsServerApplication	Administrators can use this command to add a server application role to an application in AD FS.
Disable-AdfsCertificateAuthority	This command allows an admin to disable a certificate authority.
Disable-AdfsLocalClaimsProviderTrust	This command allows an administrator to disable a local claims provider trust.
Disable-AdfsRelyingPartyTrust	Administrators can use this command to disable a relying party trust of the Federation Service.
Enable-AdfsApplicationGroup	This command allows an administrator to enable an application group in AD FS.
Enable-AdfsClaimsProviderTrust	Administrators can use this command to enable a claims provider trust in the Federation Service.

TABLE 9.11 PowerShell commands for Azure and AD FS *(continued)*

Command	Description
Enable-AdfsLocalClaimsProviderTrust	This command allows an administrator to enable a local claims provider trust.
Get-AdfsApplicationGroup	Administrators can use this command to view an application group.
Get-AdfsAttributeStore	This command allows an administrator to view the attribute stores of the Federation Service.
Get-AdfsAuthenticationProvider	Administrators can use this command to view a list of all authentication providers in AD FS.
Get-AdfsCertificate	This command allows an administrator to view the certificates from AD FS.
Get-AdfsCertificateAuthority	Administrators can use this command to view a certificate authority.
Get-AdfsClient	This command allows an administrator to view registration information for an OAuth 2.0 client.
Get-AdfsFarmInformation	Administrators can use this command to view AD FS behavior level and farm node information.
Initialize-ADDeviceRegistration	Admins can use this command to initialize the Device Registration Service configuration in the Active Directory forest.
New-AdfsApplicationGroup	This command creates a new application group.
New-AdfsClaimRuleSet	Administrators can use this command to create a set of claim rules.
New-AdfsOrganization	This command allows an administrator to create a new organization information object.
Register-AdfsAuthenticationProvider	Administrators can use this command to register an external authentication provider in AD FS.

Command	Description
Remove-AdfsApplicationGroup	This command allows an administrator to remove an application group.
Set-AdfsFarmInformation	This command allows an admin to remove a stale or offline farm node from the farm information table.
Set-AdfsProperties	Administrators can use this command to set the properties that control global behaviors in AD FS.
Set-AdfsServerApplication	This command allows an administrator to modify configuration settings for a server application role of an application in AD FS.
Set-AdfsWebConfig	Administrators can use this command to modify web customization configuration settings.

Summary

This chapter covered the basics of implementing an Active Directory within your organization. We looked at the different pieces of an Active Directory onsite (or Azure VM) setup.

We then examined the different components of Azure AD. I showed you all of the benefits and features of Azure AD in addition to the common questions and answers about Azure AD directly from Microsoft's website.

You were introduced to the Azure AD dashboard and many of its different sections. I showed you how to create an Azure AD users account and an Azure AD group. I then talked about the Azure AD Password Reset option and how to configure that feature.

This chapter also covered the benefits of using the Azure AD Identity Protection feature, and I showed you how to add that feature to your subscription. You learned how to configure Identity Protection and set up an email address so that you can receive alerts.

You saw how you can set up a hybrid network and the importance of setting up an on-site network along with your Azure AD network.

This chapter then covered the different authentication methods and what each method could do for you. I also explained Azure AD Connect and how it can link your onsite AD with Azure AD.

I explained the benefits of using Site-to-Site VPN gateway connections. I showed you the requirements and how to set up and configure the different components needed for Site-to-Site VPN gateway connections.

Finally, I explained Active Directory Federation Services, which provides Internet-based clients with a secure identity access solution that works on both Windows and non-Windows operating systems. You saw how to install and configure AD FS onto a Windows Server machine.

Exam Essentials

Know the prerequisites for promoting a server to a domain controller.   You should understand the tasks that you must complete before you attempt to upgrade a server to a domain controller. Also, you should have a good idea of the information you need in order to complete the domain controller promotion process.

Understand the steps of the Active Directory Installation Wizard.   When you run the Active Directory Installation Wizard, you'll be presented with many different choices. You should understand the effects of the various options provided in each step of the wizard.

Be familiar with the tools you will use to administer Active Directory.   Three main administrative tools are installed when you promote a Windows Server machine to a domain controller. Be sure that you know which tools to use for which types of tasks.

Understand the features of Azure AD.   Make sure you understand the features and benefits of using Azure AD. This is not only important for taking the Microsoft exams, but it is also important to determine if Azure AD is the correct choice for your organization.

Understand the Q&As of Azure AD.   This is very important for many reasons. First, and most obvious, for the Microsoft exam you need to understand what Azure AD can do and not do. Second, you need to make sure that Azure AD can handle all of the services your organization is trying to provide.

Know the Azure AD Dashboard.   You need to understand the Azure AD dashboard and where you set the different components for Azure AD. You also need to know how to access other dashboards (like the Azure AD Identity Protection dashboard) so that you can properly navigate Azure AD and its features.

Know how to set up and configure password resets.   You should understand what the process is for password resets and how to configure different authentication methods. Understand how to verify the users by using text messages or emails for verification.

Understand Azure AD Identity Protection.   Understand how to add Azure AD Identity Protection to your Azure subscription. Make sure you know how to configure the different policies and how to set alerts for an Azure administrator.

Know about hybrid networks.   It is important to understand why we use hybrid networks and the different authentication methods that can be used for setting up a hybrid network.

Understand Azure AD Connect.   Understand why we use Azure AD Connect. Azure AD Connect allows you to connect your onsite AD with Azure AD. This allows your user accounts and passwords to be replicated.

Know about Site-to-Site VPN Gateway Connections.   Know and understand what Site-to-Site VPN Gateways can do for your company. Site-to-Site VPN gateway connections allow you to connect both of your networks together over a secure IPsec/IKE VPN tunnel.

Understand Active Directory Federation Service.   Active Directory Federation Service gives users the ability to do a single sign-on and access applications on other networks without needing a secondary password. Organizations can set up trust relationships with other trusted organizations so that a user's digital identity and access rights can be accepted without a secondary password.

Know the Azure AD PowerShell commands.   Microsoft announced that all of their Microsoft exams would start asking questions about using PowerShell. This is going to be true for all chapters in this book, but make sure you understand the basic Azure AD PowerShell commands that can be used.

Review Questions

1. You are the system administrator of a large organization that has recently decided to add an Azure AD subscription. Your boss has asked you about Azure security and making sure that user logins are secure. What feature can you explain to your boss to ease their concerns?

   A. Azure AD User Security

   B. Azure AD Identity Protection

   C. Azure AD Security add-on

   D. Azure Identity Protection

2. You want to create a new Azure Active Directory policy for your users. What PowerShell command would you use to accomplish this task?

   A. New-AzurePolicy

   B. New-AzureActiveDirectoryPolicy

   C. Set-AzurePolicy

   D. New-AzureADPolicy

3. You want to look at an Azure Active Directory policy for your users. What PowerShell command would you use to accomplish this task?

   A. Get-AzureADPolicy

   B. Get-AzureADPolicy

   C. View-AzurePolicy

   D. View-AzureADPolicy

4. You are the administrator for a large organization that has subscribed to a new Azure AD subscription. You want your users to be able to reset passwords themselves. What Azure AD feature allows this to happen?

   A. User enabled password resets

   B. Azure password reset feature

   C. Self-service password reset

   D. Password reset service

5. You are the new Azure AD Global administrator for your organization. Your company wants to set up a way to integrate their on-site AD with Azure AD. What tool can you use to do this?

   A. Site-to-Site VPN Gateway Connectors.

   B. Azure AD Connect.

   C. Azure AD Replication.

   D. Active Directory Replicator.

6. You want to look at an Azure Active Directory application policy for your user's applications. What PowerShell command would you use to accomplish this task?

   A. `Add-AzureADPolicy`

   B. `Add-AzureADApplicationPolicy`

   C. `Create-AzurePolicy`

   D. `Install-AzureADPolicy`

7. You want to change an Azure Active Directory policy for your users. What PowerShell command would you use to accomplish this task?

   A. `New-AzureADPolicy`

   B. `Edit-AzureADPolicy`

   C. `New-AzurePolicy`

   D. `Set-AzureADPolicy`

8. You are the new Azure AD Global administrator for your organization. Your company has an Azure AD domain name of ContosoAzure.onmicrosoft.com. Your bosses want you to change the default domain name to Contoso.onmicrosoft.com. How can you change the initial domain name?

   A. Use the Custom Domain Names section of Azure AD and change the name.

   B. In Azure AD, go to default directories and change the domain name.

   C. Use PowerShell to change the default domain name.

   D. This can't be done.

9. You are the new Azure AD Global administrator for your organization. Your company has an Azure AD domain name of ContosoAzure.onmicrosoft.com. Your bosses want you to add a new domain name for Contoso.onmicrosoft.com. How can you add the new domain name to your existing domain?

   A. Use the Custom Domain Names section of Azure AD and change the name.

   B. In Azure AD, go to default directories and add the domain name.

   C. Use the Azure Administrative Center to add the new domain name.

   D. This can't be done.

10. You want to view your Azure AD directory settings for your Azure AD subscription. What PowerShell command would you use to accomplish this task?

    A. `View-AzureADDirectorySetting`

    B. `Get-AzureADDirectorySetting`

    C. `Add-AzureADDirectorySetting`

    D. `Set-AzureADDirectorySetting`

Chapter

10

Managing Devices

MICROSOFT EXAM OBJECTIVES COVERED IN THIS CHAPTER:

✓ **Implement conditional access and compliance policies for devices**

- Implement conditional access policies; manage conditional access policies; plan conditional access policies; implement device compliance policies; manage device compliance policies; plan device compliance policies

✓ **Configure device profiles**

- Implement device profiles; manage device profiles; plan device profiles.

✓ **Plan and implement co-management**

- Implement co-management precedence; migrate group policy to MDM policies; recommend a co-management strategy.

So now that you understand how to install Windows 10 and set up Active Directory, it's time to work with devices. In this chapter, I will show you how to set up and manage your Windows 10 devices both on site and using Intune and Azure AD.

When you install Windows 10, you designate the initial configuration for your disks. Through Windows 10's utilities and features, you can change that configuration and perform disk-management tasks.

For file-system configuration, it is recommended that you use NTFS, although you could also format the disk drive as FAT32. You can also convert a FAT32 partition to NTFS. This chapter covers the features of each file system and how to use the Convert utility to convert to NTFS.

Another factor in disk management is choosing the configuration for your physical drives. Windows 10 supports basic, dynamic, and GPT disks. Dynamic disks allow you to create simple volumes, spanned volumes, and striped volumes. If your system is configured as a Basic Disk, in order to utilize volumes, you must first convert the machine's basic disks to dynamic disks.

Once you decide how your disks should be configured, you implement the disk configurations through the Disk Management utility. This utility helps you view and manage your physical disks and volumes. In this chapter, you will learn how to manage multiple types of storage and how to convert from basic storage to dynamic storage.

Another item that needs to be discussed is Windows 10 configuration with Azure. One of the advantages to using Azure is the ability to connect to your Azure network using many different device styles (Microsoft, Apple, etc.). But that means that you have to set up Azure to accept these different device types.

Also, you have the ability to set up policies and rules for the devices that connect to your Azure network. This chapter is going to show you how to set up those policies.

Understanding File Systems

The Microsoft MD-101 exam primarily focuses on using Windows 10 with the cloud. But I am starting this chapter with basic Windows 10 configuration settings. The reason for this is twofold.

First, you will see test questions about Windows 10 and how a Windows 10 device is configured (nothing to do with the cloud). Second, and probably even more important, is that I not only want you to pass the exam but I want to make sure that you know how to do your day-to-day tasks at work. Part of this is properly setting up and configuring Windows 10 so that you can get it on the cloud. So let's take a look at setting up file systems.

A partition is a logical division of hard drive space. Each partition you create under Windows 10 must have a file system associated with it. Partitions allow a single physical hard drive to be represented in the operating system as multiple drive letters and to be used as if there were multiple hard drives installed in the machine.

When selecting a file system, you can select FAT32 or NTFS. You typically select a file system based on the features you want to use and whether you will need to access the file system using other operating systems. If you have a FAT32 partition and want to update it to NTFS, you can use the Convert utility. The features of each file system and the procedure for converting file systems are covered in the following sections.

File System Selection

Your file system is used to track the storage of files on your hard drive in a way that is easily understood by end users while still allowing the operating system the ability to retrieve the files as requested. One of the fundamental choices associated with file management is the choice of your file system's configuration. It is recommended that you use the NTFS file system with Windows 10 because doing so will allow you to take advantage of features such as local security, file compression, and file encryption. You should choose the FAT32 file system only if you want to dual-boot your computer with a version of Windows that does not support NTFS, since it is backward compatible with other operating systems.

Table 10.1 summarizes the capabilities of each file system, and they are described in more detail in the following sections. These volume size numbers are the current values at the time this book was written. Make sure you continue to check with Microsoft to see if the volume sizes have increased since this book's publication.

TABLE 10.1   File-system capabilities

Feature	FAT32	NTFS
Supporting operating systems	All Windows operating systems above Windows 95	Windows 7, 8, 10, Windows Server 2008 /2008 R2; Windows Server 2012/2012 R2, 2016, 2019 (Other previous versions of Windows supports NTFS but they are not mentioned since they are no longer supported.)
Long filename support	Yes	Yes
Efficient use of disk space	Yes	Yes

TABLE 10.1   File-system capabilities *(continued)*

Feature	FAT32	NTFS
Compression support	No	Yes
Encryption support	No before Windows 10 Yes after Windows 10	Yes
Support for local security	No	Yes
Support for network security	Yes	Yes
Maximum volume size	32 GB	16 TB with 4 KB clusters or 256 TB with 64 KB clusters

Windows 10 also supports Compact Disk File System (CDFS). However, CDFS cannot be managed. It is used only to mount and read CDs. Let's start looking at the supported disk file systems.

FAT32

FAT32 is an updated version of File Allocation Table (FAT). The FAT32 version was first shipped with Windows 95 OSR2 (Operating System Release 2) and can be used by every Windows operating system since.

One of the main advantages of FAT32 is its support for smaller cluster sizes, which results in more efficient space allocation than was possible with FAT16. Files stored on a FAT32 partition can use 20 to 30 percent less disk space than files stored on a FAT16 partition. FAT32 supports drive sizes from 512 MB up to 2 TB, although if you create and format a FAT32 partition through Windows 10, the FAT32 partition can only be up to 32 GB. Because of the smaller cluster sizes, FAT32 can also load programs up to 50 percent faster than FAT16 partitions can.

The main disadvantages of FAT32 compared to NTFS are that it does not provide as much support for larger hard drives and it does not provide very robust security options. It also doesn't offer native support for disk compression. Now that you understand FAT32, let's take a look at NTFS.

NTFS

NTFS, which was first used with the NT operating system, offers the highest level of service and features for Windows 10 computers. NTFS partitions can be up to 16 TB with 4 KB clusters or 256 TB with 64 KB clusters.

NTFS offers comprehensive folder-level and file-level security. This allows you to set an additional level of security for users who access the files and folders locally or through the network. For example, two users who share the same Windows 10 computer can be assigned different NTFS permissions so that one user has access to a folder but the other user is denied access to that folder. This is not possible on a FAT32 file system.

NTFS also offers disk-management features—such as compression and encryption capabilities—and data-recovery features.

You should also be aware that there are several different versions of NTFS. Every version of Windows 2000 uses NTFS 3.0. Windows 7/8/10, Windows Vista, Windows XP, Windows Server 2003, Windows Server 2008 / 2008 R2, and Windows Server 2012 / 2012 R2 use NTFS 3.1. NTFS versions 3.0 and 3.1 use similar disk formats, so Windows 2000 computers can access NTFS 3.1 volumes and Windows 10 computers can access NTFS 3.0 volumes. NTFS 3.1 includes the following features:

- When files are read or written to a disk, they can be automatically encrypted and decrypted.

- Reparse points are used with mount points to redirect data as it is written or read from a folder to another volume or physical disk.

- There is support for sparse files, which are used by programs that create large files but allocate disk space only as needed.

- Remote storage allows you to extend your disk space by making removable media (for example, external tapes) more accessible.

- You can use recovery logging on NTFS metadata, which is used for data recovery when a power failure or system problem occurs.

Now that you have seen the differences between FAT32 and NTFS, let's discuss how to convert a FAT32 drive to an NTFS drive.

File System Conversion

In Windows 10, you can convert FAT32 partitions to NTFS. File-system conversion is the process of converting one file system to another without the loss of data. If you format a drive, as opposed to converting it, all the data on that drive will be lost.

To convert a partition, you use the Convert command-line utility. The syntax for the Convert command is as follows:

```
Convert [drive:]/fs:ntfs
```

For example, if you wanted to convert your D: drive to NTFS, you would type the following from a command prompt:

```
Convert D:/fs:ntfs
```

When the conversion process begins, it will attempt to lock the partition. If the partition cannot be locked—perhaps because it contains the Windows 10 operating system files or the system's page file—the conversion will not take place until the computer is restarted.

In Exercise 10.1, you will convert your D: drive from FAT32 to NTFS. For this exercise, it is assumed that you have a D: drive that is formatted with the FAT32 file system. If you don't have a FAT32 drive, open Disk Management by right-clicking the Start button and choosing Disk Management. Click on your C: partition, right-click, and shrink the drive by only 5 to 10 GBs. Now create a simple volume and format it as FAT32 (follow the steps in Exercise 10.1 but choose FAT32).

Using the Convert Command

You can use the /v switch with the Convert command. This switch specifies that you want to use verbose mode, and all messages will be displayed during the conversion process. You can also use the /NoSecurity switch, which specifies that all converted files and folders will have no security applied by default so they can be accessed by anyone.

EXERCISE 10.1

Converting a FAT32 Partition to NTFS

1. Copy some folders to the D: drive.

2. Select Start, and then type **cmd** into the Search box to open a command prompt.

3. In the Command Prompt dialog box, type **Convert D:/fs:ntfs** and press Enter.

4. After the conversion process is complete, close the Command Prompt dialog box.

5. Verify that the folders you copied in step 1 still exist on the partition.

Stopping a Conversion

If you choose to convert a partition from FAT32 to NTFS and the conversion has not yet taken place because it is scheduled on next reboot, you can cancel the conversion by editing the registry with the REGEDIT or REGEDT32 command. The key that needs to be edited is

HKEY_LOCAL_MACHINE\System\CurrentControlSet\Control\SessionManager

The BootExecute value needs to be changed from autoconv\DosDevices\x:/FS:NTFS to autocheck autochk*.

Once you decide which file system you want to use, you need to decide what disk storage type you want to configure. Let's look at some of the disk storage options you have.

Be careful when converting your file system. Once you change a FAT32 file system to NTFS, you cannot change it back without formatting the disk and losing your data.

Configuring NTFS

As mentioned earlier, NTFS has many advantages over FAT32. The main advantages are NTFS Security, Compression, Encryption (EFS), and Quotas. Let's take a look at some of these advantages in greater detail.

NTFS Security   One of the biggest advantages of NTFS is security. NTFS Security (shown in Figure 10.1) is one of the most important aspects of an IT administrator's job. An advantage of NTFS security is that the security can be placed on individual files and folders. It does not matter whether you are local to the data (in front of the machine where the data is stored) or remote to the share (coming across the network to access the data); the security is always in place with NTFS. The default security permission is Users = Read on new folders or shares.

FIGURE 10.1   NTFS Security tab

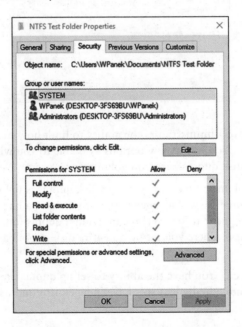

Compression   *Compression* helps compact files or folders to allow for more efficient use of hard drive space. For example, a file that usually takes up 20 MB of space might use only

13 MB after compression. To enable compression, just open the Advanced Attributes dialog box for a folder and check the Compress Contents To Save Disk Space box.

Encryption   *Encrypting File System (EFS)* allows a user or administrator to secure files or folders by using encryption. Encryption employs the user's security identification (SID) number to secure the file or folder. To implement encryption, open the Advanced Attributes dialog box for a folder and check the Encrypt Contents To Secure Data box (see Figure 10.2).

If files are encrypted using EFS and an administrator has to unencrypt the files, there are two ways to do this. First, you can log in using the user's account (the account that encrypted the files) and unencrypt the files. Second, you can become a recovery agent and manually unencrypt the files.

FIGURE 10.2   Setting up encryption on a folder

Quotas   Disk *quotas* give administrators the ability to limit how much storage space a user can have on a hard drive. You have a few options available to you when you set up disk quotas. You can set up disk quotas based on volume or on users.

>   **Setting Quotas by Volume**   One way to set up disk quotas is by setting the quota by volume, on a per-volume basis. This means that if you have a hard drive with C:, D:, and E: volumes, you would have to set up three individual quotas (one for each volume). This is your umbrella. This is where you set up an entire disk quota based on the volume for all users.

>   **Setting Quotas by User**   You have the ability to set up quotas on volumes by user. Here is where you would individually let users have independent quotas that exceed your umbrella quota.

>   **Specifying Quota Entries**   You use quota entries to configure the volume and user quotas. You do this on the Quotas tab of the volume's Properties dialog box. (See Exercise 10.2.)

Creating Quota Templates   Quota templates are predefined ways to set up quotas. Templates allow you to set up disk quotas without needing to create a disk quota from scratch. One advantage of using a template is that when you want to set up disk quotas on multiple volumes (C:, D:, and E:) on the same hard drive, you do not need to re-create the quota on each volume.

Exercise 10.2 will show you how to set up an umbrella quota for all users. This is the disk quota that all users will then follow for whichever drive you set this up on.

EXERCISE 10.2

Configuring Disk Quotas

1. Open Windows Explorer.

2. Right-click the local disk (C:), and choose Properties.

3. Click the Quotas tab.

4. Check the Enable Quota Management check box. Also check the Deny Disk Space To Users Exceeding Quota Limit box.

5. Click the Limit Disk Space To option, and enter **1000MB** in the box.

6. Enter **750MB** in the Set Warning Level To boxes.

7. Click the Apply button. If a warning box appears, click OK. This warning is just informing you that the disk may need to be rescanned for the quota.

8. Now that you have set up an umbrella quota to cover everyone, close the disk quota tool.

Configuring Disk Storage

Windows 10 supports three types of disk storage: basic, dynamic, and GUID Partition Table (GPT). Basic storage is backward compatible with other operating systems and can be configured to support up to four partitions. Dynamic storage is supported by Windows 2000, Windows XP, Windows Vista, Windows 7, Windows 8, Windows 10, and Windows Server 2003 (and above) and allows storage to be configured as volumes. GPT support begins with the Windows 2003 SP1 release and allows you to configure volume sizes larger than 2 TB and up to 128 primary partitions. The following sections describe the basic storage, dynamic storage, and GPT storage configurations.

Basic Storage

Basic storage consists of primary and extended partitions and logical drives that exist within the extended partition. The first partition that is created on a hard drive is called a primary partition and is usually represented as the C: drive. Primary partitions use all of the space that is allocated to the partition, and a single drive letter is used to represent the partition. Only a single extended partition is allowed on any basic disk. Each physical drive can have up to four partitions. You can set up four primary partitions, or you can have three primary partitions and one extended partition. With an extended partition, you can allocate the space however you like, and each suballocation of space (called a logical drive) is represented by a different drive letter. For example, a 500 MB extended partition could have a 250 MB D: partition and a 250 MB E: partition.

At the highest level of disk organization, you have a physical hard drive. You cannot use space on the physical drive until you have logically partitioned the physical drive.

One of the advantages of using multiple partitions on a single physical hard drive is that each partition can have a different file system. For example, the C: drive might be FAT32 and the D: drive might be NTFS. Multiple partitions also make it easier to manage security requirements.

Basic storage is the default, and this is the type that many users continue to use. But what if you want some additional functionality from your storage type? Let's look at some of the more advanced disk storage options.

Dynamic Storage

Dynamic storage is a Windows 10 feature that consists of a dynamic disk divided into dynamic volumes. Dynamic volumes cannot contain partitions or logical drives.

Dynamic storage supports three dynamic volume types: simple volumes, spanned volumes, and striped volumes. Dynamic storage also supports a Redundant Array of Independent Disks (RAID).

To set up dynamic storage, you convert or upgrade a basic disk to a dynamic disk. When converting a basic disk to dynamic, you do not lose any of your data. After the disk is converted, any partitions that existed on the basic disk are converted to dynamic simple volumes and you can then create any additional dynamic volumes required within the dynamic disk.

You create dynamic storage with the Windows 10 Disk Management utility, which is discussed in the section "Using the Disk Management Utility" later in this chapter. Let's take a closer look at the different types of dynamic volumes.

Simple Volumes

A *simple volume* contains space from a single dynamic drive. The space from the single drive can be contiguous or noncontiguous. Simple volumes are used when you have enough disk space on a single drive to hold your entire volume. Figure 10.3 illustrates two simple volumes on a physical disk.

FIGURE 10.3 Two simple volumes

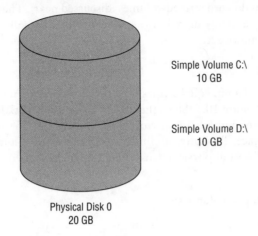

Simple Volume C:\
10 GB

Simple Volume D:\
10 GB

Physical Disk 0
20 GB

Spanned Volumes

A *spanned volume* consists of disk space on two or more dynamic drives; up to 32 dynamic drives can be used in a spanned volume configuration. Spanned volume sets are used to dynamically increase the size of a dynamic volume. When you create spanned volumes, the data is written sequentially, filling space on one physical drive before writing to space on the next physical drive in the spanned volume set. Typically, administrators use spanned volumes when they are running out of disk space on a volume and want to dynamically extend the volume with space from another hard drive.

You do not need to allocate the same amount of space to the volume set on each physical drive. This means you could combine 500 MB on one physical drive with two 750 MB volumes on other dynamic drives, as shown in Figure 10.4.

FIGURE 10.4 A spanned volume set

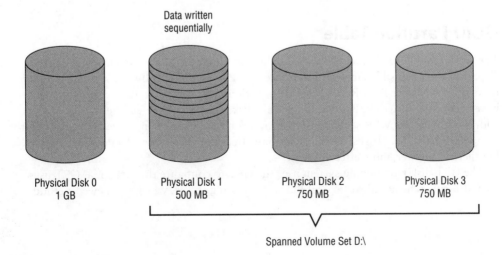

Data written
sequentially

Physical Disk 0
1 GB

Physical Disk 1
500 MB

Physical Disk 2
750 MB

Physical Disk 3
750 MB

Spanned Volume Set D:\

Because data is written sequentially, you do not see any performance enhancements with spanned volumes as you do with striped volumes (discussed next). The main disadvantage of spanned volumes is that if any drive in the spanned volume set fails, you lose access to all of the data in the spanned set.

Striped Volumes

A *striped volume* stores data in equal stripes between two or more (up to 32) dynamic drives, as illustrated in Figure 10.5. Since the data is written sequentially across the stripe, you can take advantage of multiple I/O performance and increase the speed at which data reads and writes take place. Typically, administrators use striped volumes when they want to combine the space of several physical drives into a single logical volume and increase disk performance.

FIGURE 10.5   A striped volume set

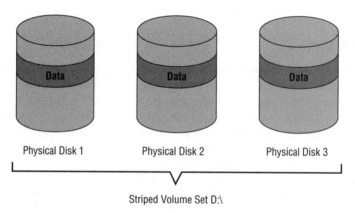

The main disadvantage of striped volumes is that if any drive in the striped volume set fails, you lose access to all of the data in the striped set.

GUID Partition Table

The *GUID Partition Table (GPT)* is available for Windows 10 and was first introduced as part of the Extensible Firmware Interface (EFI) initiative from Intel. Basic and dynamic disks use the Master Boot Record (MBR) partitioning scheme that all operating systems have been using for years. Basic and dynamic disks use Cylinder-Head-Sector (CHS) addressing with the MBR scheme. CHS allows computers to assign addresses to data on the computer's hard-disk drives. This has been an effective way to store data on a hard drive, but there is a newer, more effective way.

The GPT disk-partitioning system uses the GPT to configure the disk area. GPT uses an addressing scheme called Logical Block Addressing (LBA), which is a newer method of accessing hard-disk drives. LBA uses a unique sector number only instead of using the cylinder, head, and sector number. Another advantage is that the GPT header and partition table are written to both the front and the back ends of the disk, which provides for better redundancy.

The GPT disk-partitioning system gives you many benefits over using the MBR system:

- Allows a volume size larger than 2 TB
- Allows up to 128 primary partitions
- Used for both 32-bit and 64-bit Windows 10 editions
- Includes cyclic redundancy check (CRC) for greater reliability

However, there is one disadvantage to using the GPT drives. You can convert a GPT drive only if the disk is empty and unpartitioned. I will show you the steps to creating a GPT disk later in this chapter.

To convert any disk or format any volume or partition, you can use the Disk Management utility. I will show you how to manage your disks using the Disk Management utility in the section "Using the Disk Management Utility."

Cloud-Based Storage

One of the fastest growing parts of the IT world is cloud-based services. From cloud-based user storage to cloud-based corporate data storage, it seems like the cloud is all we hear about anymore.

Microsoft has cloud-based subscription services called Microsoft Azure and OneDrive.

Microsoft Azure

Microsoft Azure (https://azure.microsoft.com/en-us/) can be used by almost any operating system on the market (Windows, Linux, etc.), by most applications (Java, .Net, PHP, etc.), and by most device types (Windows, Android, and iOS).

Microsoft Azure is different than many other cloud-based systems because Microsoft Azure doesn't make you choose either your network or the cloud. Many cloud-based service providers want you to use their cloud to run all of your applications and/or storage from their location. Microsoft Azure allows you to extend your current network infrastructure into the cloud to take full advantage of both worlds.

This way you can still have a full IT server room with full-time IT employees but get the benefits of storing data both locally and also in a cloud environment which is then available from anywhere in the world.

One advantage to using Microsoft Azure is that you only pay for what you need. The more cloud-based storage you need, the more you pay for and the less you need means less money. Table 10.2 shows you the maximum amount of data that can be stored on Microsoft Azure.

TABLE 10.2 Microsoft Azure Data Size Availability

Operating System	Maximum Size of Data Source
Windows Server 2012 or above	54400 GB
Windows 8 or above	54400 GB
Windows Server 2008, Windows Server 2008 R2	1700 GB
Windows 7	1700 GB

If you decide that you want your company to use Microsoft Azure for some of its cloud-based storage or all of its cloud-based storage, please go to https://azure.microsoft.com/en-us/ to get the current subscription rates.

Microsoft OneDrive

Another Microsoft-based subscription is called OneDrive (used to be known as SkyDrive). Microsoft's OneDrive is built into Windows 10 by default (see Figure 10.6). OneDrive is a cloud-based storage subscription so home users can store their documents and then access those documents from anywhere in the world (provided that you have Internet access).

FIGURE 10.6 OneDrive Welcome Screen

OneDrive was designed for the average home user who is looking to store data in a safe, secure, cloud-based environment. OneDrive, when first released, was also a consideration for corporate environments, but with the release of Windows Azure, OneDrive is really intended for the home user or corporate user who wants to store some of their own personal documents in the cloud. Corporations would be more inclined to use Microsoft Azure and all of its corporate benefits.

If you or your company decides to purchase the Office 365 subscription, then OneDrive is included for cloud-based storage. If you didn't purchase Office 365, then you have to choose from one of the subscriptions shown in Table 10.3.

Please note that these are the current prices at the time this book was written and these prices may have changed. Be sure to check out Microsoft's OneDrive web page for current prices (https://onedrive.live.com/options/Upgrade).

TABLE 10.3 OneDrive Subscriptions

Amount of Storage	Subscription Monthly Fee
5 GB	Free
100 GB	$1.99
1000 GB	$6.99

Exercise 10.3 will show you how to set up a OneDrive account for your user account. To do this access, you must have a Microsoft account. You get 5 GB for free from Microsoft on the OneDrive cloud-based storage.

EXERCISE 10.3

Configuring OneDrive

1. Open OneDrive.

2. Log into OneDrive using your Microsoft Account as seen in Figure 10.7.

FIGURE 10.7 OneDrive sign-in screen

3. You will see a screen that will show you where your files will be located on your system, as seen in Figure 10.8. Click the Next button.

FIGURE 10.8 OneDrive File Location screen

4. At the Sync files screen, choose what folders that you want to sync with Microsoft and then click Next.

5. A screen will appear telling you that your OneDrive is set up and ready to go (see Figure 10.9).

FIGURE 10.9 OneDrive verification screen

6. Click the Open My OneDrive Folder button to open your folders and Microsoft's OneDrive.

7. Close OneDrive.

Using the Disk Management Utility

The Disk Management utility is a Microsoft Management Console (MMC) snap-in that gives administrators a graphical tool for managing disks and volumes within Windows 10. In the following sections, you will learn how to access the Disk Management utility and use it to perform basic tasks, including managing basic storage and dynamic storage. You will also learn about troubleshooting disks through disk status codes.

But before we dive into the Disk Management utility, let's explore the MMC. It is important to understand the MMC since Disk Management (like many other tools) is actually an MMC snap-in.

Using the Microsoft Management Console

The *Microsoft Management Console (MMC)* is the console framework for application management. The MMC provides a common environment for snap-ins. Snap-ins are administrative tools developed by Microsoft or third-party vendors. Some of the MMC snap-ins that you may use are Computer Management, Active Directory Users and Computers, Active Directory Sites and Services, Active Directory Domains and Trusts, and DNS Management. When you look at the administrative tools, you know that each one of these tools are running inside of an MMC (shown in Figure 10.10).

FIGURE 10.10   The Administrative Tools running in MMCs

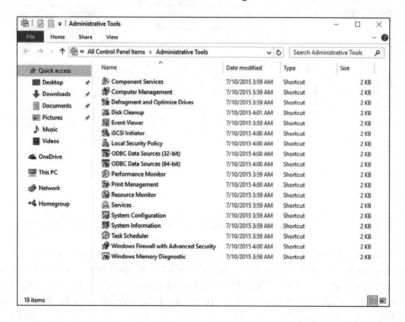

Knowing how to use and configure the MMC snap-ins will allow you to customize your work environment. For example, if you are in charge of Active Directory Users and

Computers and DNS, you can add both of these snap-ins into the same window. This would then allow you to open just one application to configure all your tasks. The MMC offers many other benefits:

- The MMC is highly customizable—you add only the snap-ins you need.

- Snap-ins use a standard, intuitive interface, so they are easier to use than previous versions of administrative utilities.

- You can save customized MMCs and share them with other administrators.

- You can configure permissions so that the MMC runs in authoring mode, which an administrator can manage, or in user mode, which limits what users can access.

- You can use most snap-ins for remote computer management.

As shown in Figure 10.11, by default, the MMC contains three panes: a console tree on the left, a details pane in the middle, and an optional Actions pane on the right. The console tree lists the hierarchical structure of all snap-ins that have been loaded into the console. The details pane contains a list of properties or other items that are part of the snap-in that is highlighted in the console tree. The Actions pane provides a list of actions that the user can access depending on the item selected in the details pane.

FIGURE 10.11   The MMC tree, details pane, and Actions pane

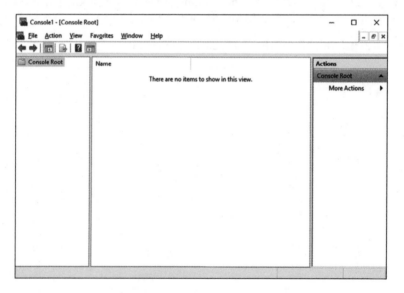

On a Windows 10 computer, to open the MMC, click the Start button and type **MMC** in the Search dialog box. When you first open the MMC, it contains only the Console Root folder, as shown in Figure 10.11. The MMC does not have any default administrative functionality. It is simply a framework used to organize administrative tools through the addition of snap-in utilities.

The first thing that you should decide when using the MMC is which of the different administrative mode types you will employ. You need to decide which mode type is best suited to use for your organization.

Configuring MMC Modes

You can configure the MMC to run in author mode for full access to the MMC functions or in one of three user modes, which have more limited access to the MMC functions. To set a console mode, while in the MMC editor, select File ➤ Options to open the Options dialog box. In this dialog box, you can select from the console modes listed in Table 10.4.

TABLE 10.4   MMC modes

Console Mode	Description
Author mode	Allows use of all the MMC functions.
User mode—full access	Gives users full access to window-management commands, but they cannot add or remove snap-ins or change console properties.
User mode—limited access, multiple window	Allows users to create new windows but not close any existing windows. Users can access only the areas of the console tree that were visible when the console was last saved.
User mode—limited access, single window	Allows users to access only the areas of the console tree that were visible when the console was last saved, and they cannot create new windows.

After you decide which administrative role you are going to run, it's time to start configuring your MMC snap-ins.

Adding Snap-Ins

The biggest advantage of using the MMC is to configure snap-ins the way your organization needs them. Adding snap-ins is a very simple and quick procedure. To add a snap-in to the MMC and save it, complete Exercise 10.4.

EXERCISE 10.4

Adding an MMC Snap-In

1. To start the MMC editor, click Start, type **MMC** into the search box, and press Enter.

2. From the main console window, select File ➤ Add/Remove Snap-In to open the Add Or Remove Snap-Ins dialog box.

3. Highlight the snap-in you want to add as seen in Figure 10.12, and click the Add button.

FIGURE 10.12 The MMC Add Or Remove Snap-ins screen

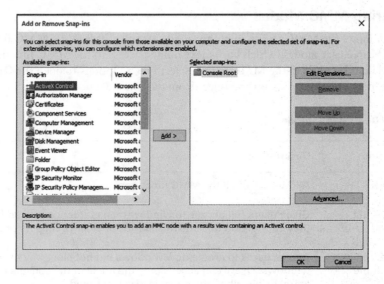

4. If prompted, specify whether the snap-in will be used to manage the local computer or a remote computer. After you choose the MMCs you want in your custom snap-in (shown in Figure 10.13), click the Finish button.

FIGURE 10.13 The MMC Console screen

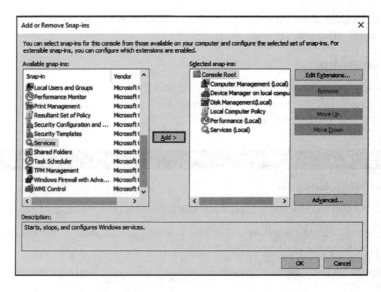

5. When you have finished adding snap-ins, click OK.

6. After you have added snap-ins to create a console, you can save it by selecting File ➤ Save As and entering a name for your console. Place the console on the Desktop as shown in Figure 10.14.

FIGURE 10.14   The MMC Console on the Desktop

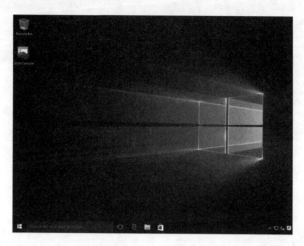

You can save the console to a variety of locations, including a program group or the Desktop. By default, custom consoles have a `.msc` filename extension.

Many applications that are MMC snap-ins, including Disk Management, are already configured for you under the Administrative Tools section of Windows 10. Next, let's look at the Disk Management utility.

Understanding the Disk Management Utility

The Disk Management utility, located under the Computer Management snap-in by default, is a one-stop shop for configuring your disk options.

First of all, to have full permissions to use the Disk Management utility, you must be logged on with local Administrative privileges. You can access the Disk Management utility a few different ways. You can right-click Computer from the Start menu and select Manage, and then in Computer Management, select Disk Management. You could also use Control Panel ➤ Administrative Tools ➤ Computer Management.

Once you have launched Computer Management, you must expand the storage section of the console in order to access the Disk Management toolset. The Disk Management utility's opening window, shown in Figure 10.15, displays the following information:

- The volumes that are recognized by the computer
- The type of disk, either basic or dynamic
- The type of file system used by each partition
- The status of the partition and whether the partition contains the system or boot partition
- The capacity (amount of space) allocated to the partition

- The amount of free space remaining on the partition
- The amount of overhead associated with the partition

FIGURE 10.15   The Disk Management window

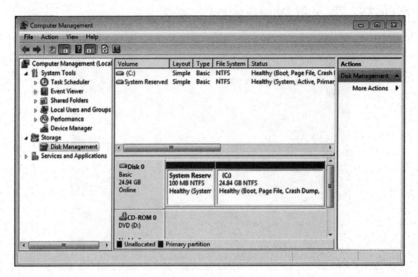

Windows 10 also includes a command-line utility called diskpart, which can be used as a command-line alternative to the Disk Management utility. You can view all of the options associated with the diskpart utility by typing **diskpart** (as seen in Figure 10.16) at a command prompt and then typing **?** at the diskpart prompt.

FIGURE 10.16   The diskpart window

The Disk Management utility allows you to configure and manage your disks. Let's take a look at some of the tasks that you can perform in disk administration.

Managing Administrative Hard-Disk Tasks

The Disk Management utility allows you to perform a variety of hard drive administrative tasks:

- View disk properties.
- View volume and local disk properties.
- Add a new disk.
- Create partitions and volumes.
- Upgrade a basic disk to a dynamic or GPT disk.
- Change a drive letter and path.
- Delete partitions and volumes.

These tasks are discussed in the sections that follow.

Viewing Disk Properties

To view the properties of a disk, right-click the disk number in the lower panel of the Disk Management main window and choose Properties from the context menu. This brings up the disk's Properties dialog box. Click the Volumes tab to see the volumes associated with the disk, as shown in Figure 10.17, which contains the following disk properties:

- The disk number
- The type of disk (basic, dynamic, CD-ROM, removable, DVD, or unknown)
- The status of the disk (online or offline)
- The partition style
- The capacity of the disk
- The amount of unallocated space on the disk
- The amount of space reserved on the disk
- The logical volumes that have been defined on the physical drive

If you click the General tab of a disk's Properties dialog box, the hardware device type, the hardware vendor that produced the drive, the physical location of the drive, and the device status are displayed.

FIGURE 10.17   The Volumes tab of a disk's Properties dialog box

Viewing Volume and Local Disk Properties

On a dynamic disk, you manage volume properties. On a basic disk, you manage partition properties. Volumes and partitions perform the same function, and the options discussed in the following sections apply to both. (The examples here are based on a dynamic disk using a simple volume. If you are using basic storage, you will view the partition properties rather than the volume properties.)

To see the properties of a volume, right-click the volume in the upper panel of the Disk Management main window and choose Properties. This brings up the volume's Properties dialog box. Volume properties are organized on seven tabs: General, Tools, Hardware, Sharing, Security, Previous Versions, and Quota. The Security tab and Quota tab appear only for NTFS volumes. All these tabs are covered in detail in the following items.

General   The information on the General tab of the volume's Properties dialog box, as shown in Figure 10.18, gives you a general idea of how the volume is configured. This dialog box shows the Label, Type, File system, Used and Free space, and Capacity of the volume. The label is shown in an editable text box, and you can change it if desired. The space allocated to the volume is shown in a graphical representation as well as in text form.

The label on a volume or local disk is for informational purposes only. For example, depending on its use, you might give a volume a label such as APPS or ACCTDB.

The Disk Cleanup button starts the Disk Cleanup utility, which you can use to delete unnecessary files, thereby freeing disk space.

FIGURE 10.18   General properties for a volume

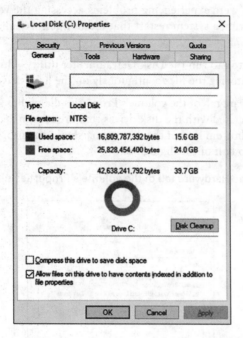

This tab also allows you to configure compression for the volume and to indicate whether the volume should be indexed.

Tools   The Tools tab of the volume's Properties dialog box, shown in Figure 10.19, provides access to two tools.

FIGURE 10.19   The Tools tab of the volume's Properties dialog box

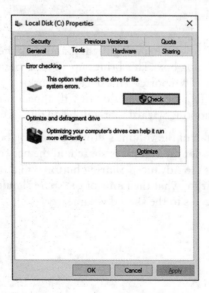

Click the Check button to run the Error-Checking utility to check the volume for errors. You may do this if you were experiencing problems accessing the volume or if the volume had been open during a system restart that did not go through a proper shutdown sequence.

Click the Optimize button to run the Disk Defragmenter utility. This utility defragments files on the volume by storing the files contiguously on the hard drive.

Hardware   The Hardware tab of the volume's Properties dialog box, shown in Figure 10.20, lists the hardware associated with the disk drives that are recognized by the Windows 10 operating system. The bottom half of the dialog box shows the properties of the device that is highlighted in the top half of the dialog box.

FIGURE 10.20   The Hardware tab of the volume's Properties dialog box

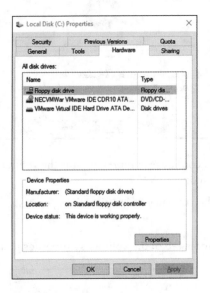

For more details about a hardware item, highlight it and click the Properties button in the lower-right corner of the dialog box. This brings up a Properties dialog box for the item. Your Device Status field should report, "This device is working properly." If that's not the case, you can click the Troubleshoot button (it will appear if the device is not working properly) to get a troubleshooting wizard that will help you discover the problem.

Sharing   On the Sharing tab of the volume's Properties dialog box, shown in Figure 10.21, you can specify whether or not the volume is shared on the network. Volumes are not shared by default. Clicking the Advanced Sharing button will allow you to specify whether the volume is shared and, if so, what the name of the share should be. You will also be able to specify who will have access to the shared volume.

FIGURE 10.21   The Sharing tab of the volume's Properties dialog box

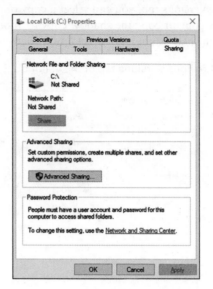

Security   The Security tab of the volume's Properties dialog box, shown in Figure 10.22, appears only for NTFS volumes. The Security tab is used to set the NTFS permissions for the volume.

FIGURE 10.22   The Security tab of the volume's Properties dialog box

Previous Versions   The Previous Versions tab displays shadow copies of the files that are created by System Restore, as shown in Figure 10.23. Shadow copies of files are backup

copies created by Windows in the background to allow you to restore the system to a previous state. On the Previous Versions tab, you can select a copy of the volume and either view the contents of the shadow copy or copy the shadow copy to another location. If System Restore is not enabled, then shadow copies of a volume will not be created.

FIGURE 10.23   The Previous Versions tab of the volume's Properties dialog box

Quota   Quotas give you the ability to limit the amount of hard-disk space that a user can have on a volume or partition (see Figure 10.24). By default, quotas are disabled. To enable quotas, check the Enable Quota Management check box. There are a few options that can be configured when enabling quotas.

FIGURE 10.24   The Quota tab of the volume's Properties dialog box

The Deny Disk Space To Users Exceeding Quota Limit check box is another option. When this box is enabled, any user who exceeds their quota limit will be denied disk storage. You can choose not to enable this option, which allows you to just monitor the quotas. You also have the ability to set the quota limit and warning size and to log all quota events as they happen.

Adding a New Disk

New hard disks can be added to a system to increase the amount of disk storage you have. This is a fairly common task that you will need to perform as your application programs and files grow larger.

How you add a disk depends on whether your computer supports hot swapping of drives. Hot swapping is the process of adding a new hard drive while the computer is turned on. Most desktop computers do not support this capability. Remember, your user account must be a member of the Administrators group to install a new drive. The following list specifies configuration options:

Computer Doesn't Support Hot Swapping   If your computer does not support hot swapping, you must shut down the computer before you add a new disk. Then add the drive according to the manufacturer's directions. When you've finished, restart the computer. You should find the new drive listed in the Disk Management utility.

Computer Supports Hot Swapping   If your computer does support hot swapping, you don't need to turn off your computer first. Just add the drive according to the manufacturer's directions. Then open the Disk Management utility and select Action ➤ Rescan Disks. You should find the new drive listed in the Disk Management utility.

Creating Partitions and Volumes   Once you add a new disk, the next step is to create a partition (on a basic disk) or a volume (on a dynamic disk). Partitions and volumes fill similar roles in the storage of data on disks, and the processes for creating them are the same.

Creating a Volume or a Partition

Creating a volume or partition is a fairly easy process. To create the new volume or partition, right-click the unformatted free space and start the wizard.

Exercise 10.5 walks you through the New Volume Wizard for creating a new volume.

EXERCISE 10.5

Creating a New Volume

1. In the Disk Management utility, right-click an area of free storage space and choose the type of volume to create. If only one drive is installed, you will be able to create only a simple volume. You can click New Simple Volume to create a new simple volume.

2. The Welcome To The New Simple Volume Wizard appears. Click the Next button to continue.

3. The Select Volume Size screen appears. Select the size of volume to create, and then click Next to continue.

EXERCISE 10.5 *(continued)*

4. You should see the Assign Drive Letter Or Path screen. You can specify a drive letter, mount the volume as an empty folder, or choose not to assign a drive letter or drive path. If you choose to mount the volume into an empty folder, you can have a virtually unlimited number of volumes, negating the drive-letter limitation. If you choose not to assign a drive letter or path, users will not be able to access the volume. Make your selections, and click Next to continue (shown in Figure 10.25).

FIGURE 10.25 Assign Drive Letter Or Path screen

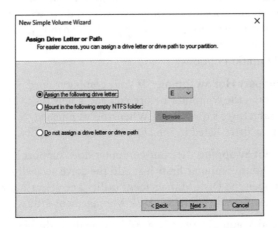

5. The Format Partition screen appears (see Figure 10.26). This screen allows you to choose whether you will format the volume. If you choose to format the volume, you can format it as FAT32 or NTFS. You can also select the allocation unit size, enter a volume label (for information only), specify whether or not you would like to perform a quick format, and choose whether or not to enable file and folder compression. After you've made your choices, click Next.

FIGURE 10.26 Format Partition screen

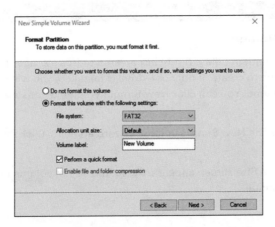

6. The Completing The New Volume Wizard screen appears. Verify your selections. If you need to change any of them, click the Back button to reach the appropriate screen. When everything is correctly set, click the Finish button.

Now that you know how to create a new volume or partition, let's see how to convert a basic disk to dynamic or GPT.

Upgrading a Basic Disk to a Dynamic or GPT Disk

When you perform a fresh installation of Windows 10, your drives are configured as basic disks. To take advantage of the features offered by Windows 10 dynamic or GPT disks, you must upgrade your basic disks to either of those disk configurations.

WARNING　Upgrading basic disks to dynamic disks is a one-way process as far as preserving data is concerned and is a potentially dangerous operation. Before you perform this upgrade (or make any major change to your drives or volumes), create a new backup of the drive or volume and verify that you can successfully restore the backup before proceeding with the change.

Any basic disk can be converted to a dynamic disk, but only a disk with all unformatted free space can be converted to a GPT disk. Exercise 10.6 walks you through converting an MBR based disk to a GPT disk.

EXERCISE 10.6

Converting a Basic Disk to a GPT Disk

1. If the disk that you want to convert has partitions or volumes defined, first delete the partition or volume.

2. Open the Disk Management utility by clicking the Start button, right-clicking Computers, and choosing Manage.

3. Click Disk Management in the lower-left section.

4. Right-click the disk and choose Convert To GPT Disk (shown in Figure 10.27).

EXERCISE 10.6 *(continued)*

FIGURE 10.27 Convert to GPT option

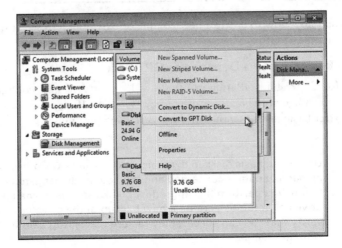

5. After the disk converts, you can right-click the disk and see that the Convert To MBR Disk option is now available.

There are a few other methods for converting an MBR based disk to a GPT disk. You can use the diskpart utility and type in the Convert GPT command. You can also create a GPT disk when you first install a new hard drive. After you install the new hard drive, during the initialization phase, you can choose GPT Disk.

Another type of conversion that you may need to perform is that from a basic disk to a dynamic disk. Complete Exercise 10.7 to convert a basic disk to a dynamic disk.

EXERCISE 10.7

Converting a Basic Disk to a Dynamic Disk

1. In the Disk Management utility, right-click the disk you want to convert and select the Convert To Dynamic Disk option.

2. In the Convert To Dynamic Disk dialog box, check the disk that you want to convert and click OK.

3. In the Disks To Convert dialog box, click the Convert button.

4. A confirmation dialog box warns you that you will no longer be able to boot previous versions of Windows from this disk. Click the Yes button to continue to convert the disk.

As you are configuring the volumes or partitions on the hard drive, other things that you may need to configure are the drive letters and paths.

Changing the Drive Letters and Paths

There may be times when you need to change drive letters and paths when you add new equipment. Let's suppose you have a hard drive with two partitions: drive C: assigned as your first partition and drive D: assigned as your second partition. Your DVD drive is assigned the drive letter E:. You add a new hard drive and partition it as a new volume. By default, the new partition is assigned as drive F:. If you want your logical drives to be listed before the DVD drive, you can use the Disk Management utility's Change Drive Letter And Paths option to reassign your drive letters.

When you need to reassign drive letters, right-click the volume for which you want to change the drive letter and choose Change Drive Letter And Paths. This brings up the dialog box shown in Figure 10.28. Click the Change button to access the Change Drive Letter Or Path dialog box. Use the drop-down list next to the Assign The Following Drive Letter option to select the drive letter you want to assign to the volume.

FIGURE 10.28   The dialog box for changing a drive letter or path

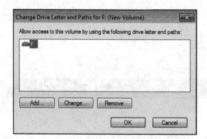

In Exercise 10.8, you will edit the drive letter of the partition you created.

EXERCISE 10.8

Editing a Drive Letter

1. Right-click Start ➤ Computer Management; then expand Storage ➤ Disk Management.

2. Right-click a drive that you have created and select Change Drive Letter And Paths.

3. In the Change Drive Letter And Paths dialog box, click the Change button.

4. In the Change Drive Letter Or Path dialog box, select a new drive letter and click OK.

5. In the dialog box that appears, click the Yes button to confirm that you want to change the drive letter.

Another activity that you may need to perform is deleting a partition or volume that you have created. The next section looks at these activities.

Deleting Partitions and Volumes

When configuring your hard disks, there may be a time that you want to reconfigure your drive by deleting the partitions or volumes on the hard drive. You may also want to delete a volume so that you can extend another volume. These are tasks that can be configured in Disk Management.

When deleting a volume or partition, you will see a warning that all the data on the partition or volume will be lost. You have to click Yes to confirm that you want to delete the volume or partition. This confirmation is important because once you delete a partition or volume, it's gone for good along with any data content that was contained within it.

 The system volume, the boot volume, or any volume that contains the active paging (swap) file can't be deleted through the Disk Management utility. If you are trying to remove these partitions because you want to delete Windows 10, you can use a third-party disk-management utility.

In Exercise 10.9, you will delete a partition that you have created. Make sure that if you delete a partition or volume, it is empty; otherwise, back up all the data that you would like to retain before the deletion.

EXERCISE 10.9

Deleting a Partition

1. In the Disk Management utility, right-click the volume or partition that you want to remove and choose Delete Volume.

2. A warning box appears, stating that once this volume is deleted, all data will be lost. Click Yes.

3. The volume will be removed and the area will be returned as unformatted free space.

You may be worried about your users removing devices from their Windows 10 machines. Microsoft has helped you in this situation. You can use removable-device policies to help restrict your users from removing their hardware. Removable-device policies can be created through the use of a Group Policy Object (GPO) on the server. GPOs are policies that are set on a computer or user and allow you to manipulate the Windows 10 environment.

Now that we have explored some of the basic administrative tasks of Disk Management, let's look at how to manage storage.

Managing Storage

The Disk Management utility offers support for managing storage. You can create, delete, and format partitions or volumes on your hard drives. You can also extend or shrink volumes on dynamic disks. Additionally, you can delete volume sets and striped sets.

Managing Dynamic Storage

As noted earlier in this chapter, a dynamic disk can contain simple, spanned, or striped volumes. Through the Disk Management utility, you can create volumes of each type. You can also create an extended volume, which is the process of adding disk space to a single simple volume. The following sections describe these disk-management tasks.

Creating Simple, Spanned, and Striped Volumes

As explained earlier, you use the New Volume Wizard to create a new volume. To start the New Volume Wizard, in the Disk Management utility right-click an area of free space where you want to create the volume. Then, you can choose the type of volume you want to create: simple, spanned, or striped.

When you choose to create a spanned volume, you are creating a new volume from scratch that includes space from two or more physical drives, up to a maximum of 32 drives.

When you choose to create a striped volume, you are creating a new volume that combines free space from 2 to 32 drives into a single logical partition. The free space on all drives must be equal in size in a striped volume. Data in the striped volume is written across all drives in 64 KB stripes. (Data in spanned and extended volumes is written sequentially.) Striped volumes offer you better performance and are normally used for temporary files or folders. The problem with a striped volume is if you lose one of the drives in the volume, the entire striped volume is lost.

Another option that you have with volumes is to extend the volumes to create a larger storage area. In the next section, we will look at that process.

Creating Extended Volumes

When you create an extended volume, you are taking a single, simple volume (maybe one that is almost out of disk space) and adding more disk space to it, using free space that exists on the same physical hard drive. When the volume is extended, it is seen as a single drive letter. To extend a volume, the simple volume must be formatted as NTFS. You cannot extend a system or boot partition.

An extended volume is created when you are using only one physical drive. A spanned volume is created when you are using two or more physical drives. Exercise 10.10 shows you how to create an extended volume.

EXERCISE 10.10

Creating an Extended Volume

1. In the Disk Management utility, right-click the volume you want to extend and choose Extend Volume.

2. The Extend Volume Wizard starts. Click Next.

3. The Select Disks screen appears (see Figure 10.29). You can specify the maximum size of the extended volume. The maximum size you can specify is determined by the amount of free space that exists in all of the dynamic drives on your computer. Click Next to continue.

FIGURE 10.29 The Select Disks screen

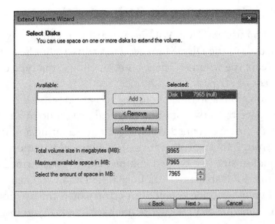

4. The Completing The Extend Volume Wizard screen appears. Click the Finish button. You will see the new volume.

Once a volume is extended, no portion of the volume can be deleted without losing data on the entire set. However, if there is unneeded space on a volume, you can shrink that volume without losing data by using the Shrink Volume option in Disk Management.

 Real World Scenario

You're Running Out of Disk Space

Crystal, a user on your network, is running out of disk space. The situation needs to be corrected so she can be brought back up and running as quickly as possible. Crystal has a 250 GB drive (C:) that runs a very large customer database. She needs additional space added to the C: drive so the database will recognize the data because it must be stored on a single drive letter. Crystal's computer has a single IDE drive with nothing attached to the second IDE channel.

You have two basic options for managing space in this circumstance. One is to upgrade the disk to a larger disk, but this will necessitate reinstalling the OS and the applications and restoring the user's data. The other choice is to add a temporary second drive and extend the volume. This will at least allow Crystal to be up and running—but it should not be considered a permanent solution. If you do choose to extend the volume and then either drive within the volume set fails, the user will lose access to both drives. When Crystal's workload allows time for maintenance, you can replace the volume set with a single drive.

One issue you may run into with hard drives is that they go bad from time to time. If you have ever heard a hard drive fail, you know the sound: it is a distinct clicking. Once you have experienced it, you will never forget it.

Windows 10 Devices in Azure

So now that we have looked at configuring the actual Windows 10 device, it's time to look at how we can use Azure to help set up and manage our Windows 10 devices.

The Devices section in Azure allows an Azure AD administrator to set up which devices can access Azure AD. Administrators can also configure device settings and device roaming settings (Enterprise State Roaming). Azure AD administrators can perform auditing and troubleshooting from the Devices section.

But to make sure that your users and devices can access Azure, you need to make sure that you purchase Azure licenses. The Licenses section in Azure AD allows you to view purchased licensing for additional Azure AD components. If you purchase additional Azure AD components (for example, Azure Active Directory Premium P2 or Enterprise Mobility + Security E5), those additional components will show up in this Licenses section. You can also see if there are any licensing issues in this section.

The Licenses section also allows you to view additional components that are available and what those components do. Azure AD administrators can also view auditing and get troubleshooting from this section.

So after you purchase your licenses and you are ready to go, you can then configure Azure AD with Compliance Policies. These policies allow you to setup and configure how Windows 10 devices will work within the Azure network.

Before we dive in to policies and profiles for your devices, let's take a look at Microsoft Intune. Intune will be discussed in detail in Chapter 11, "Planning and Managing Microsoft Intune," but I want to just explain a bit of what Intune can do for you. It's important to understand a little about Intune because even though these policies and profiles are added to devices and users, you create them in Intune.

Microsoft Intune is a device management system. Microsoft Intune allows administrators to manage mobile devices, mobile applications, and PC management capabilities all from the cloud.

Administrators using Intune can provide their users with access to corporate applications, data, and resources from almost anywhere and on almost any device while also keeping your corporate information secure.

Microsoft Intune also helps you save money because Intune allows you to license users instead of licensing devices. So, if you have a user that works from multiple devices (laptop, tablet, and Windows phone), you only pay once for the user license instead of multiple times for all of the user's devices.

Administrators can use Microsoft Intune to support and manage Windows 10. Administrators can use Intune on a Windows 10 device for the following:

- Enrollment
- Organization resource access
- Application management
- Policies
- Inventory
- Reporting
- Remote wipe

Microsoft Intune is an add-on to your Azure subscription, but if you want to deploy software using the cloud or set up rules for how your devices and users will function, Intune is a subscription that you should add to your cloud-based utilities. Let's now take a look at how you can set up policies and profiles for your devices and users.

Compliance Policies

One of the advantages to using Azure is the ability to protect the corporate data by ensuring that users and devices meet certain requirements. When using Intune, this is referred to as compliance policies. Compliance policies are rules and settings that your users and their devices must follow in order to connect and access Intune.

Compliance policies, along with Conditional Access, ensures that administrators can stop users and devices that don't follow the rules that your organization has determined as necessary for access. For example, the Intune administrator can require some of the following:

- Corporate users must enter a password on their mobile devices to access data.
- Ensures that the device hasn't been cracked, rooted, or jail broken. Administrators can ensure that devices are under a minimum threat level.
- Ensure that devices have a minimum operating system along with updates.

Azure Active Directory, along with Conditional Access, allows Intune to enforce the compliances that your organizations want to use. When devices enroll in Intune, the enrollment registration begins with Azure AD and the device information gets placed into

Azure AD. As part of this registration process is the device's compliance status. This device compliance status is then used by the policies in Conditional Access and based on that, corporate resources are either blocked or allowed.

One advantage that you get using compliance policies is that an administrator can assign the policy to either a user (using a user group) or a device (using a device group). If a policy is assigned to a user, all the user's devices are also checked for policy compliance.

Microsoft recommends that if you are using Windows 10 version 1803 or higher, the policy should be deployed to the device group if the user doesn't enroll the device. By using device groups, Azure administrators can use compliancy reporting to ensure that the devices meet complexity.

Conditional Access

The Conditional Access section (see Figure 10.30) allows an Azure AD administrator to set security policies. When it comes to Azure, one of the biggest concerns for organizations is cloud-based security. Azure allows users to access their networks from anywhere in the world and from almost any device. Because of this, just securing resource access is not enough. This is where Conditional Access Policies comes in to play.

FIGURE 10.30   Conditional Access Policies section

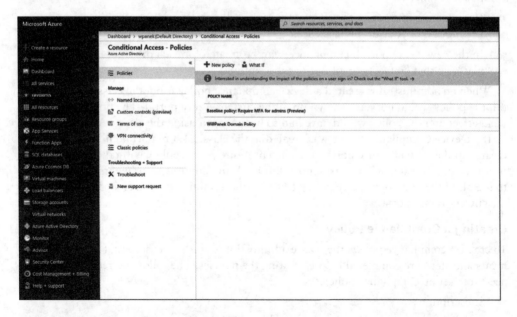

Conditional Access policies allow an organization to set how resources are accessed using access control decisions (who has access to resources) through Azure AD. Setting up Conditional Access policies allows an organization to have automated access control decisions based on the policies that your organization sets. Some of the situations that Conditional Access policies can help with are sign-in risk, network location risk, device management, and client applications.

With Conditional Access

If a device complies to the policy rules that you have configured, that device can get access to data, email, and other company resources. If the device does not meet the minimum policies that you have set up, then that device will not have access to any of the company's resources. This is how conditional access works when it is set up and enabled.

Without Conditional Access

If you decide that you do not want to use conditional access, you can still use compliance policies. If you decide to use compliance policies without conditional access, you can access reports showing the device compliance status. Administrators can evaluate this information and decide if conditional access is then needed or if you can continue to use Azure without any conditional access policies.

Azure Classic Portal vs. Azure Portal

In January 2018, Microsoft discontinued the Azure classic portal. When it comes to using device compliance policies, the version of the Azure portal that you used would help determine how you could set up your policies. The difference between the two portals is how compliances function.

- If an administrator uses the classic Azure portal, only one device compliance policy is used for all of your different devices.

- In the new Azure portal, compliances can be created for each different type of device platform that connects to an Azure subscription.

When an administrator created a device compliance policy using the classic Azure portal, the policy would not have shown up in the current Azure portal. The policy would still be in effect and the policy would have had to be managed using the classic Azure portal.

If a Device Compliance Policy was created in the classic Azure portal and then one is created in the current Azure portal, the current Azure portal policy will take precedence over the policy created in the classic portal. If an Azure administrator wants their devices to use all of the new compliance policy features, the administrator must create the policy in the current Azure portal.

Creating a Compliance Policy

To create a compliance policy, the Azure administrator needs to ensure that a few requirements and steps are completed before creating the policies. The following requirements are needed to set up compliance policies:

- Subscriptions

- Microsoft Intune

- To use Conditional Access, your organization needs an Azure Active Directory (AD) Premium edition. If using Microsoft Intune compliance only, your organization doesn't require an Azure AD subscription.

- Supported platforms
  - Android
  - Android Enterprise
  - iOS
  - MacOS
  - Windows 10
  - Windows 8.1
  - Windows Phone 8.1

The administrator must also enroll devices in Intune (required to see the compliance status). It is also necessary to enroll the devices to one user or enroll the device without a primary user assigned. Enrolling devices to multiple users is not supported.

Once you have ensured that your organization has met the minimum requirements to set up compliance policies, then the next step is to actually create the policy. The following steps will walk you through the process of creating a policy:

1. Sign in to the Intune portal.

2. Select Device Compliance. Administrators can choose from the following options:

- **Overview:** This will show you a summary of devices along with the number of devices that are compliant or not evaluated. This screen will also show the list of policies and individual settings in those policies.

- **Manage:** This screen allows an administrator to create new device policies, send notifications to non-compliant devices, and it will also allow an administrator to enable network fencing. Network fencing allows an administrator to create a compliance policy based on a network location.

- **Monitor:** This section allows an administrator to check the compliance status of their devices along with checking the status at the setting and policy levels.

- **Setup:** This option allows an administrator to use built-in compliance policies, use Jamf Pro software to manage your end-users' Macs, add a mobile threat defense connector, and enable Microsoft Defender advanced threat protection (ATP).

3. Select Policies ➤ Create Policy. To create a policy, the administrator needs to fill in the following properties:

- **Name:** Administrators need to enter a name for the new policy.

- **Description:** Administrators should enter a description for the policy so that the policy is easy to recognize and maintain in the future. This setting is optional, but highly recommended.

- **Platform:** Here is where the administrator can choose the platform of their devices. Administrators have the following options to choose from:
  - Android
  - Android Enterprise
  - iOS

- MacOS
- Windows Phone 8.1
- Windows 8.1 and later
- Windows 10 and later

- **Settings:** This section allows the administrator to choose which policy settings that they want to implement.

4. Once you have completed filling in all the sections, select OK and then choose **Create** to save your changes.

The policy is now created and the policy will now show up in the policy list. The next step is to assign the policy to your user groups. To assign user groups to your policy, complete the following steps:

1. Choose the policy that you want to assign to a user group. Policies are shown in **Device Compliance ➤ Policies.**

2. Select the policy and then choose **Assignments.** Administrators have the ability to include or exclude Azure Active Directory (AD) security groups.

3. To see your Azure AD security groups, choose the **Selected Groups** option. Select the user groups that you want this policy to apply to and then choose **Save** to deploy the policy to the users.

Migrating Policies to MDM

Once an organization decides to move to Microsoft Azure, one of the tasks that an administrator will need to consider is moving on-site Group Policy Object settings (GPOs) to MDM. The first thing that the administrator needs to do before migrating their GPOs to MDM is to analyze their current GPOs and figure out what needs to be moved to the MDM management tool in Azure.

Microsoft understands that GPO analysis needs to be done and that's why they developed the MDM Migration Analysis Tool (MMAT) to help administrators complete this task.

MMAT looks at your organization's GPOs to see which ones have been created for a user or computer. MMAT then generates a report that an administrator can use to see which equivalent MDM policies will need to be set. The report that MMAT will generate can be in both XML and HTML formats.

To ensure that your administrators get all of the current features of MMAT, make sure that you download the current version. If you would like to get more information about the MDM Migration Analysis tool or download the most current version of the tool, please visit https://github.com/WindowsDeviceManagement/MMAT.

If your Azure administrator decides that they want to use the MMAT, they will need to complete the following steps:

1. Install the Remote Server Administration Tools.

2. Install the zipped folder for MMAT to your computer and unzip the folder.

3. Open Windows PowerShell as an administrator.

4. In PowerShell, change the directory location to where you installed the MMAT files (these files include PowerShell scripts).

5. Run the following PowerShell script:

```
Set-ExecutionPolicy -ExecutionPolicy Unrestricted -Scope Process
$VerbosePreference="Continue" ./Invoke-MdmMigrationAnalysisTool.ps1
-collectGPOReports -runAnalysisTool
```

After the `Invoke-MdmMigrationAnalysisTool.ps1`script is completed, the Azure administrator will have three reports that they can look at:

MDMMigrationAnalysis.xml   This file is the XML version of the MMAT report and it contains information about the policies that are set for the targeted user and computer. It will also show you how these policies map to MDM.

MDMMigrationAnalysis.html   This file is the HTML version of the same XML report.

MdmMigrationAnalysisTool.log   This file is a log file that will give Azure administrators more information about how the MMAT tool ran.

Device Configuration Profiles

Another way to set up Intune rules as an administrator is a Device Configuration Profile. Profiles work like policies since they are also another way to put rules onto your Intune devices.

Microsoft Intune, along with device configuration profiles, allows an administrator to configure settings and features that can be enabled or disabled on the different devices that your users will connect with.

Device Configuration Profile Options

Device configuration profile settings and features are added to your configuration profiles. Administrators can build these profiles for devices and platforms, including iOS, Android, and Windows. After these profiles are built, then an Intune administrator can apply or assign these profiles to their devices. These device configuration settings and features can include some of the following:

Administrative Templates   Administrative templates have hundreds of Windows 10 (and above) settings that an administrator can set for programs and features including Internet Explorer, OneDrive, Office, and other programs. These settings are very similar to setting up GPOs but they are all cloud based settings.

Certificates   Certificate settings allow an Intune administrator to configure certificates for applications like WiFi, VPN, and email profiles. These settings can be configured for many different devices including Android and Android Enterprise, iOS and MacOS, Windows Phone 8.1, Windows 8.1, and Windows 10 and later.

Custom Profile   Custom profile settings allow an Intune Administrator to configure options that are not automatically included with Intune. For example, an administrator can set a custom profile that allows you to create ADMX-backed policy or even enable self-service password resets. Custom profile allows you to set options for Android and Android Enterprise, iOS and MacOS, and Windows Phone 8.1 devices.

Delivery Optimization   Delivery optimization allows Intune administrators to set up and configure updates to Windows 10 (and above) devices that connect to the cloud.

Device Features   Device features make it easy for administrators to configure iOS and MacOS devices. These settings allow administrators to configure things like AirPrint, notifications, and lock screen messages. Administrators can set these configurations on iOS and MacOS devices.

Device Restrictions   Device restrictions allow an Intune administrator to configure settings for things like hardware, data, and security settings on your devices. Device restrictions can be created to prevent iOS device users from using their device's camera. Device restrictions can be used on Android and Android Enterprise, iOS and MacOS, Windows 10 Team, and Windows 10 and later devices.

Edition Upgrade   Edition upgrade allows you to upgrade Windows 10 (and later) devices to a newer version of Windows.

Email   Email options allow you to create, monitor, and assign Email Exchange ActiveSync email settings for your devices. For example, email profiles allow your users to have access to your organization's email while using their own personal devices. Email options can be set for Android and Android Enterprise, iOS, Windows Phone 8.1, and Windows 10 and later devices.

Endpoint Protection   Endpoint protection allows you to set Windows 10 (and above) options for BitLocker and Windows Defender settings. For example, you can set Windows Defender for a threat score setting. If a user with a high threat score rating attempts to access cloud-based resources, you can stop this device from accessing your resources.

Identity Protection   Identity protection allows an Intune administrator to control the Windows Hello for Business experience on Windows 10 and Windows 10 Mobile devices. Identity protection settings allow you to configure options for devices such as PINs and gestures for Windows Hello for Business.

Kiosk   Kiosk settings allow an administrator to configure a Windows 10 (and later) device to run a single application or run many applications. Kiosk systems are normally designed for use in a location where many people can use the same device and that device will only run limited applications. Administrators have the ability to also customize other features, including a start menu and a web browser. Kiosk settings are also available for Android and Android Enterprise and iOS devices, but you need to configure these devices as device restrictions. So it can still function as a Kiosk device but it's configured differently.

Shared Multi-User Device   Shared multi-user devices are devices where multiple users will use the device to do day to day activities. This is different than a Kiosk based machine. Kiosk based machines are machines used by many users but they run limited programs. Shared multi-user devices are devices that users use to do their job while at work but other users will use the same device. These devices normally run all of the organization's software so people can do their jobs. For example, if you are in an environment where you have shift workers. You may have multiple shifts and different people will use a machine when they are working during their shift.

Shared multi-user device settings allow an administrator to control many of the device features and manage these shared devices through Intune.

 To see a complete or updated list of device configuration profile settings, please visit Microsoft's website at https://docs.microsoft.com/en-us/intune/device-profiles.

Building Device Configuration Profiles

One nice advantage that you will notice is that building device configuration profiles work a lot like building device compliances. Many of the same settings are available as you build the device configuration profile. To build a device configuration profile, you would complete the following steps:

1. Sign in to the Intune portal.

2. Select **Device Configuration**. Administrators can choose from the following options:

   - **Overview:** This will show you the status of your profiles and it also provides additional details on the different profiles that you have assigned to your users and devices.

   - **Manage:** This screen allows an administrator to create device profiles, upload PowerShell scripts that can run within the profile, and add data plans to eSIM devices.

   - **Monitor:** This section allows an administrator to view the status of a device configuration profile and see if that profile was a success or failure. This screen also allows you to view logs about your profiles.

   - **Setup:** This option allows an administrator to add a certificate authority or enable Telecom Expense Management in the profile.

3. Select **Profiles ➤ Create Profile** to create a profile. The Intune administrator needs to fill in the following properties:

   - **Name:** Administrators need to enter a name for the new profile.

   - **Description:** Administrators should enter a description for the profile so that the profile is easy to recognize and maintain in the future. This setting is optional, but highly recommended.

- **Platform:** Here is where the administrator can choose the platform of their devices. Administrators have the following options to choose from:
  - Android
  - Android Enterprise
  - iOS
  - MacOS
  - Windows Phone 8.1
  - Windows 8.1 and later
  - Windows 10 and later
- **Profile type:** Select the type of settings you want to create. The list that will be shown will depend on the platform you choose.
- **Settings:** This section allows the administrator to choose which profile settings that they want to implement.

4. Once you have completed filling in all the sections, select **OK** and then choose **Create** to save your changes.

Once you have completed building the device configuration profile, the next step would be to add a scope tag to the profile. Scope tags allow an administrator to assign and filter policies to a specific group (for example HR or Sales) of employees. To add a scope tag, complete the following steps.

1. Select **Scope (Tags)**.

2. Select **Add** to create a new scope tag. Or, select an existing scope tag from the list.

3. Select **OK** to save your changes.

Summary

There are two different ways that you can format your hard disk in a Windows 10 operating system: FAT32 and NTFS. NTFS has many advantages over FAT32, including security, disk quotas, and compression, just to name a few. If you format a FAT32 partition using Windows 10, then encryption will be available. But on any older Windows clients, FAT32 will not include encryption.

In addition to the way you format your hard disk, you can configure your hard disk as a basic disk or a dynamic disk and must choose to either leave your disk partition system as the default MBR or choose to convert it to a GPT disk. You can use the Disk Management MMC snap-in to configure your hard disks and file system.

In this chapter, I explained how compliance polices, along with Conditional Access, ensures that administrators can stop users and devices that don't follow the rules that your organization has determined as necessary for access.

I also talked about converting onsite GPOs to MDM using the MMAT tool. The MMAT tool allows an administrator to analyze GPOs and determine which MDM policies will be the equivalent setting.

Finally, you learned about using device configuration profiles. Device configuration profiles work like GPO policies but they are policies that are designed strictly for cloud-based rules.

Exam Essentials

Understand the different hard-disk storage types.   Windows 10 supports three types of disk storage: basic, dynamic, and GUID partition table (GPT). Basic storage is backward compatible with other operating systems and can be configured to support up to four partitions. Dynamic storage is supported by all Windows operating systems above Windows 2000 and allows storage to be configured as volumes. GPT storage allows you to configure volume sizes larger than 2 TB and up to 128 primary partitions.

Know Compliance Policies   Make sure you understand how compliance policies, along with Conditional Access, ensures that administrators can stop users and devices that don't follow the rules that your organization has determined as necessary for access.

Understand the MMAT Tool   Understand that GPO analysis needs to be done and how the MDM Migration Analysis Tool (MMAT) helps administrators complete this task.

Know Device Configuration Profiles   Device configuration profile settings and features are added to your configuration profiles. Administrators can build these profiles for devices and platforms, including iOS, Android, and Windows and these settings are for cloud based Intune devices.

Review Questions

1. You are the administrator for an organization that has 100 devices that run Windows 10 Pro. The devices are joined to Azure AD and enrolled in Microsoft Intune. You need to upgrade the computers to Windows 10 Enterprise. What should you configure in Intune?

   A. A device enrollment policy

   B. A device cleanup rule

   C. A device compliance policy

   D. A device configuration profile

2. You are creating a device configuration profile in Microsoft Intune. You need to implement an ADMX-backed policy. Which profile type should you use?

   A. Identity protection

   B. Custom

   C. Device restrictions

   D. Device restrictions (Windows 10 Team)

3. You are the network administrator for a large training organization. Your organization plans to deploy Windows 10 tablets to 50 meeting rooms. These tablets will be managed by using Microsoft Intune. The tablets have an application named Storm1 that many users will use. You need to configure the Windows 10 tablets so that any user can use Storm1 without having to sign in. Users must not be able to use other applications on the tablets. Which device configuration profile type should you use?

   A. Kiosk

   B. Endpoint protection

   C. Identity protection

   D. Device restrictions

4. You have 175 computers that run Windows 10. The computers are joined to Microsoft Azure Active Directory (AD) and enrolled in Microsoft Intune. You have been asked to enable self-service password reset on the sign-in screen. Which settings should you configure in Microsoft Intune?

   A. Device configuration

   B. Device compliance

   C. Device enrollment

   D. Conditional access

5. Will has installed Windows 10 on his Windows XP computer. The machine is now a dual-boot computer. He has FAT32 for Windows XP and NTFS for Windows 10. In addition, he boots his computer to Windows XP Professional for testing an application's compatibility with both operating systems. Which of the following file systems will be seen by both operating systems?

   A. Only the FAT32 partition will be seen by both operating systems.

   B. Only the NTFS partition will be seen by both operating systems.

   C. Neither the FAT32 partition nor the NTFS partition will be seen by both operating systems.

   D. Both the FAT32 partition and the NTFS partition will be seen by both operating systems.

6. Paige is considering upgrading her basic disk to a dynamic disk on her Windows 10 computer. She asks you to help her understand the function of dynamic disks. Which of the following statements is true of dynamic disks in Windows 10?

   A. Dynamic disks can be recognized by older operating systems such as Windows NT 4 in addition to new operating systems such as Windows 10.

   B. Dynamic disks are supported only by Windows 2000 Server and Windows Server 2003.

   C. Dynamic disks support features such as simple partitions, extended partitions, spanned partitions, and striped partitions.

   D. Dynamic disks support features such as simple volumes, extended volumes, spanned volumes, mirrored volumes, and striped volumes.

7. Bruce frequently works with a large number of files. He is noticing that the larger the files get, the longer it takes to access them. He suspects that the problem is related to the files being spread over the disk. What utility can be used to store the files contiguously on the disk?

   A. Disk Defragmenter

   B. Disk Manager

   C. Disk Administrator

   D. Disk Cleanup

8. You have a Microsoft 365 subscription. All computers are enrolled in Microsoft Intune. You have business requirements for securing your Windows 10 devices. You need to lock any device that has a high Windows Defender Advanced Threat Protection (Windows Defender ATP) risk score. Which device configuration profile type should you use?

   A. Kiosk

   B. Endpoint protection

   C. Identity protection

   D. Device restrictions

9. You have been asked by your boss to set up a device configuration profile in Intune to allow your users to be able to reset their own passwords. Which device configuration profile option should you configure in Microsoft Intune?

   A. Kiosk

   B. Endpoint protection

   C. Identity protection

   D. Custom

10. Your company uses Microsoft Intune to manage all devices. The company uses conditional access to restrict access to Microsoft 365 services for devices that do not comply with the company's security policies. You want to view which devices will be prevented from accessing Microsoft 365 services. What should you use?

   A. The Device Health solution in Windows Analytics

   B. The Windows Defender Security Center

   C. Device compliance in the Intune admin center

   D. The Conditional access blade in the Azure Active Directory admin center

Chapter

11

Planning and Managing Microsoft Intune

In this chapter, I am going to talk about Microsoft Intune and how you can use it to manage devices and software. I will show you how to set up and configure an Intune subscription and how you can use that subscription to help your network users get the most out of the network resources and software.

I will start the chapter by talking about managing devices using Intune. I will show you how to provision user accounts and enroll devices. I will also discuss how to manage and configure devices using the Microsoft Intune subscription.

I will continue the discussion by showing you how to deploy and configure updates using Intune. I will show you how to use the in-Console monitoring tools and how to approve and decline updates.

I will then talk about working with mobile devices, including Windows tablets, broadband metering and tethering, and how to wipe mobile devices for employees who leave the company.

Finally I will show you how to use Intune to help deploy and maintain your company's software packages. I will also talk to you about SideLoading applications into your users' devices. We will then talk about the different type of reports that you can run to check on the different hardware and software in your environment.

So let's get started with the ability to use Microsoft Intune to help manage and maintain your corporate devices.

It looks like Microsoft is rebranding Microsoft Intune. The new name seems to be Intune Microsoft Enterprise Mobility + Security. This issue is that the exam objectives still are showing the name as Intune. Since the exam objectives still use the name Intune, I will refer to it that way in this chapter. But even if the name does change, the information is still the same.

Managing Devices with Microsoft Intune

I think that the first thing we need to discuss in this chapter is exactly what Microsoft Intune is. Microsoft Intune is a device management system (see Figure 11.1). Microsoft Intune allows administrators to manage mobile devices, mobile applications, and PC management capabilities all from the cloud.

FIGURE 11.1   Microsoft Intune Dashboard

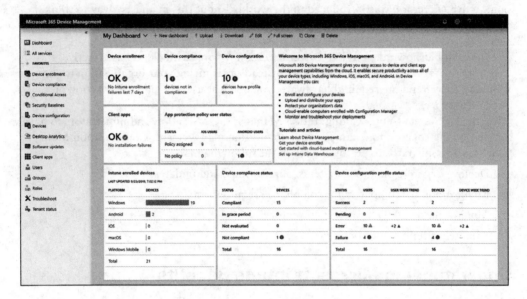

Administrators using Intune can provide their users with access to corporate applications, data, and resources from almost anywhere and on almost any device while also keeping your corporate information secure.

Microsoft Intune also helps you save money because Intune allows you to license users instead of licensing devices. So if you have a user that works from multiple devices (laptop, tablet, and Windows phone) you only pay once for the user license instead of multiple times for all of the user's devices.

Administrators can use Microsoft Intune to support and manage Windows 10. Administrators can use Intune on a Windows 10 device for the following tasks:

- Enrollment

- Organization resource access

- Application management

- Policies

- Inventory

- Reporting

- Remote wipe

Microsoft Intune is built on Microsoft Azure Active Directory and System Center. Active Directory is a Directory Services database created by Microsoft. Directory Services was originally designed by Novell and starting in Windows Server 2000, Microsoft's version, Active Directory, was introduced to the world. To put this in an easy way to think about, Active Directory is just a database that allows administrators to control access to the network.

Microsoft has now taken Active Directory to a new level with cloud based Active Directory or Azure Active Directory. Now instead of requiring your organization to buy Windows Server and the required hardware, you can just use a cloud based version of Active Directory.

Microsoft System Center Configuration Manager (SCCM) allows administrators to have a wide-ranging solution for change and configuration management. Configuration Manager allows an administrator to perform some of the following tasks:

- Deploy corporate operating systems, applications, and updates.

- Monitor and fix computers for compliance requirements.

- Monitor hardware and software inventory.

- Remotely administer devices.

Understanding Microsoft Intune Benefits

Microsoft Intune provides many different benefits to help an IT department be more productive and keep systems running all on the same software. Intune allows an IT department the ability to keep corporate data secure while allowing users to access the same company software from any device that they want to work from. Let's take a look at some other Intune benefits:

- Multiple device enrollments for users. Licenses are per user and not per device. So users can work from multiple devices.

- Corporate data security for users and applications like Microsoft Exchange, Outlook, and Office.

- The ability to use Office 365 from any approved device.

- Since Microsoft Intune is a cloud based system, the IT department is not required to build an infrastructure. This saves the additional cost of buying and maintaining hardware and software.

- Microsoft Intune extends your System Center Configuration Manager through both the cloud and on premise versions by connecting the two systems together through the use of an application connector.

- Microsoft 24/7 support is available through worldwide phone support or online support. Also administrators have access to Microsoft.com for Intune FAQs and knowledge base.

- Corporations have multiple licensing options available to them to choose from. Intune is also part of the Enterprise Mobility Suite by default.

Configuring Intune Subscriptions

When you are considering using Microsoft Intune, you must think about the subscription type you want. You can start with a free 30-day trial or move directly into a full paid subscription. Either choice allows you to start managing mobile devices and corporate computers immediately.

One of the nice advantages of Intune subscriptions is available if you decide to add at least 150 user licenses. If you reach 150 licenses, you get to use Microsoft's FastTrack Benefits Center. This benefit also allows a Microsoft specialist to work with your organization as part of the FastTrack benefits. The Microsoft specialist then helps you get the most out of using Intune and all of its benefits.

The process to start using Microsoft Intune is very easy and free. You go to Microsoft's website and sign up for a free 30-day trial of Intune. Then you start adding your users, groups, and devices. If you decide that Microsoft Intune is right for your organization, you can then sign up for one of the monthly rates.

Once you have decided to take that next step, you need to start redesigning your company's infrastructure to include the cloud-based subscription. This can be as easy as setting up your DNS servers to include the cloud-based services or as complex as adding all of your devices to the cloud and phasing out many of the infrastructure servers that you currently have running in house.

Whatever you decide, one of the most important phases of moving to a cloud-based system is planning. Once you have made the decision to move to the cloud, that's when the real work and planning comes into play:

- Will you be moving all users to Azure Active Directory?

- Will you be using the cloud just for device and software deployment?

- Will you be phasing out in-house equipment?

- Will you allow users to use their own devices (Bring Your Own Device [BYOD])?

- If users use their personal devices, will you supply them with corporate software applications?

- Will you be using Office 2019 or Office 365?

When you sign up for a Microsoft Intune account, you will choose a domain for your Intune subscription. After you sign up for your Intune subscription, Microsoft will send you an email that will contain your Intune information. Figure 11.2 shows you an example of the information contained within the Microsoft Intune email.

FIGURE 11.2   Microsoft Intune email

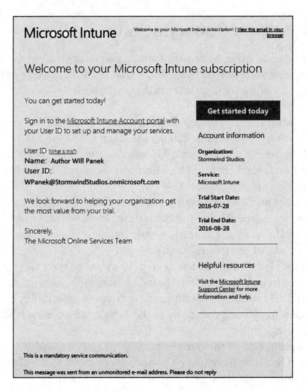

In Exercise 11.1, I will show you how to set up a free Microsoft Intune 30-day trial account. You will need to complete this exercise to do some of the other exercises during this chapter.

EXERCISE 11.1

Setting Up a Microsoft Intune Account

1. Go to the Microsoft Intune website (https://www.microsoft.com/en-us/ microsoft-365/enterprise-mobility-security/compare-plans-and-pricing).

2. Click the Try Now button.

3. At the Welcome to Microsoft Intune page, fill out the required information (Country, First Name, Last Name, etc.) and then click Next (shown in Figure 11.3).

FIGURE 11.3   Microsoft Intune Signup

4. At the Create Username screen, create a username and password. Click Next.

5. You will need to prove you're not an Internet robot by verifying your account. Enter in a cell phone number so that a verification code can be texted to you. Enter the code and click Verify. Then click the Create My Account link.

6. You will see a screen showing you a link to your portal and your username. Print this page out for later use.

7. Type the portal link into your web browser and put in your username and password.

8. In the lower-left corner of the Menu window, click the Intune link to bring up the Intune Enterprise Mobility + Security dashboard.

Provisioning User Accounts

Once you have decided to sign up for the Microsoft Intune subscription, you next need to start assigning your corporate users and groups to Intune. By assigning users and groups, you are choosing which individuals get to access the cloud based services of Intune and the IT Departments get to start using all of the Intune benefits.

As stated previously, once you sign up for the Microsoft Intune subscription, you will receive an email with your user information along with a link to the Microsoft Intune Enterprise Mobility + Security Portal. Click on that link and then sign in. Once you sign in, you will automatically be redirected to the Intune Enterprise Mobility + Security Dashboard. This is where you can start creating your users and groups.

During the Microsoft Intune subscription process, you create a domain name and that domain is added to a Microsoft extension by default. So for example, if I choose a domain named Stormwind, then the default Microsoft subscription will look like; `Stormwind .onmicrosoft.com`. If your company already owns its own domain name, then you can use that domain instead of the default Microsoft option.

Setting Administrator Accounts

Be sure to decide which way you want to set up your cloud based domain because if you decide to just use Microsoft's default, all of your users will end up with an onmicrosoft. com extension for their User Principal Names (UPN). Using a pre-owned domain name can make your life in IT much easier because your users will log in using the same domain name that they are used to using now on a daily basis.

When setting up your cloud based Azure Active Directory, you can have the cloud based version of Active Directory (Azure Active Directory) work with the on-premise server based version of Active Directory by using the Azure Active Directory (AD) Connect tool (formerly known as the Directory Synchronization tool, Directory Sync tool, or the DirSync.exe tool).

You can download the Azure Active Directory (AD) Connect tool on Microsoft's Azure website. After logging into your Azure dashboard, choose Azure AD and then choose the Azure AD Connect link.

The Azure Active Directory (AD) Connect tool is a server-based application that can be installed onto a server that is currently joined to your local domain. The connect tool allows your corporate on-site users to synchronize to your cloud based services.

When you decide to connect your cloud based Azure Active Directory to your on-site server based Active Directory, user administration becomes much easier for your IT department members. It allows your users to use a single sign-on to access both the local resources and the cloud based resources. When users have to log in using different accounts, it puts mores stress on an IT Department and / or help desk.

The first users that you should add to Microsoft Intune are your administrators. By adding the administrators first, then they can start to help also build other user accounts. When you are choosing administrative privileges, you can choose from three choices; Tenant Administrator, Service Administrator, or Device Enrollment Manager. So let's go ahead and take a look at each of the following administrator's permissions.

Tenant Administrator

Organizations have the ability to set an administrator up as Tenant Administrators. Tenant Administrators are used for very specific tasks. Normally, Tenant Administrators are assigned only one administrator role. This one administrative role determines the administrative scope for the user and the tasks they can manage. Tenant Administrators can be any of the following roles:

Billing Administrator   The Billing Administrator is allowed to make purchases, handle company subscriptions, manage support items, and handle service health issues.

Global Administrator   The Global Administrator has the ability to access all administrative features. By default, the administrator who signs up for the Intune subscription is the Global Administrator for your organization.

- Global Administrators are the only administrators that can assign other administrators their rights.

- Organizations have the ability to have more than one Global Administrator within your organization.

Password Administrator   Password Administrators have the ability to deal with user password issues like resetting passwords, managing requests, and monitors service health. Password Administrators are allowed to reset passwords for users and other Password Administrators.

Service Support Administrator   The Service Support Administrators can manage service requests and they can handle service health requests.

User Management Administrator   User Management Administrators can deal with user issues like resetting passwords, handling service health requests, and managing user accounts and groups.

Service Administrator

This is a tough role to truly understand because Intune really doesn't assign a Service Administrator role. Actually the Service Administrator role is just a Tenant Administrator role with the Global Administrator permission assigned to the individual who signed up for the Microsoft Intune subscription. Service Administrators use the administrative console to handle the daily tasks for Intune.

Device Enrollment Manager

One of the great benefits of using Microsoft Intune is the ability of users to enroll multiple devices. By default, each user can enroll five devices if they want. If you want a user to help other users enroll devices, then you can also make a user a Device Enrollment Manager. This role allows an administrator or user the ability to enroll devices for other users. This is also useful for companies that have Kiosk type machines. Your Device Enrollment Manager can enroll these types of systems.

Creating a User in Intune

Once you have decided to use Microsoft Intune, you must start setting up user accounts within Intune so that your users can start accessing the benefits of using Intune.

For users to access Intune, they must have a valid license. When a user has a valid user license, they can then enroll up to five of their devices. This way they can use different devices to do different tasks from both work and home.

When adding users into the Intune portal, you can do it either one user at a time or by bulk import from a CSV file. When adding users, you must assign licenses to each of these users. No matter how you add a user, adding a license to that user is not needed at the time that the user is created. But a license must be associated to that user before that user can access Intune.

If you decide to import your users from your on-site Active Directory to the cloud, the users will NOT have a license. You will be required to assign licenses to your users after the Active Directory merger to Intune.

So let's take a look at how easy it is to create a new user. In Exercise 11.2, I will walk you through the process of creating a new user in the Intune Management Console.

EXERCISE 11.2

Adding Users into Microsoft Intune

1. Open the Microsoft Intune Portal by clicking the link in the email that you received from creating your subscription in Exercise 11.1.

2. Once in the Intune Dashboard, under Management, click the Users link.

3. In the center console under Users, you will see a New with a down arrow. Click on New and choose User (shown in Figure 11.4).

FIGURE 11.4 Intune New User

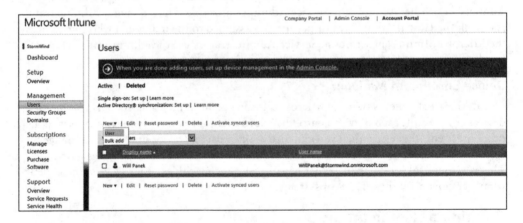

4. If you are asked to log back in, put in your Intune username and password.

5. At the New User Details screen, enter the User's Name and Username in the form of a user principal name (UPN) (see Figure 11.5).

FIGURE 11.5   Intune New User Details

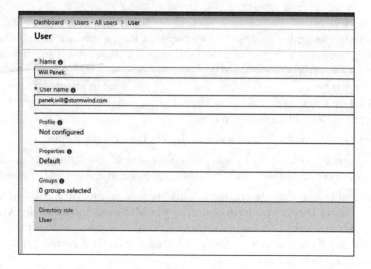

6. At the Assign Role field, you must decide if this new user should have administrative rights and which type.

7. At the Group field, don't choose any groups. We will add users to a group in another exercise.

8. At the Send Results In An Email screen, make sure there is an email address for this user and click Create.

9. At the Results screen, print out the user's temporary password (see Figure 11.6). Click Finish.

FIGURE 11.6   Intune New User Results Page

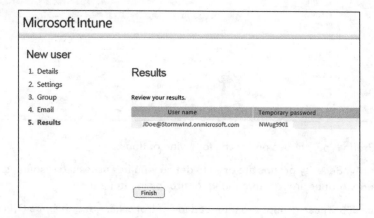

10. Close the Portal.

Now that we have looked at creating a user in the Intune Management Console, let's take a look at how to create groups.

To manage devices and users, Intune uses Azure Active Directory (Azure AD) groups. An administrator can utilize groups to fit an organization's needs. Creating groups in Intune helps administrators have more flexibility when it comes to Intune management. Administrators can setup groups based on devices, users, geographic locations, departments, or even hardware types. Creating the groups are done in about the same way, but deciding which groups to create is where the planning and decision making takes place.

Administrators can add these group types:

- Assigned groups: Manually add users or devices into a static group.

- Dynamic groups: Automatically add users or devices to user groups or device groups based upon a created expression. Dynamic groups require Azure AD Premium.

Any users and groups that are created can also be seen in the Microsoft 365 admin center, the Azure Active Directory admin center, and in Microsoft Intune in the Azure portal. Microsoft recommends that if an administrator's primary role is device management, that they utilize the Microsoft Endpoint Manager Admin Center. In Exercise 11.3, I will show you how to create a new group.

EXERCISE 11.3

Create a New Group

1. Open the Microsoft Endpoint Manager Admin Center and sign in.

2. Select Groups ➢ New Group as shown in Figure 11.7.

FIGURE 11.7 Choosing the New Group Link

3. In the Group type, choose one of the following options:

   - Security: Security groups are used to define who has access to resources. Security groups are recommended for groups in Intune.

   - Office 365: These groups are intended to control access and to share Office 365 resources.

4. Enter a specific Group name and Group description for the new group so others will know what the group is used for.

5. Enter the Membership type. There are several options available for Membership types as shown in Figure 11.8. These include:

   - Assigned: an administrator manually assigns users or devices to this group, and can remove users or devices.

   - Dynamic User: an administrator creates membership rules to add and remove members automatically.

   - Dynamic Device: an administrator creates dynamic group rules to add and remove devices automatically.

FIGURE 11.8   Choosing the Membership Type

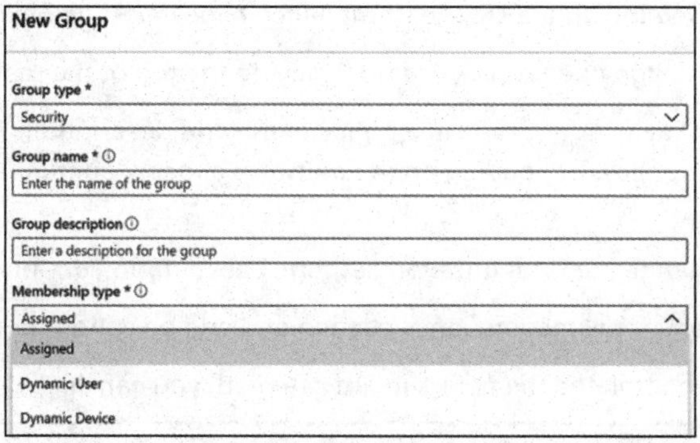

6. To add the new group, select Create. The new group is now shown in the list.

After you create the new group, you can manage that group from the administrative console. Administrators have the ability to change the group membership at any time. Managing and maintaining groups is easily accomplished from the administrative console.

Now that we have seen how to create users and groups, let's take a look at how to set up Intune Policies.

Creating Intune Policies

Administrators have the ability to place rules on security settings, firewall settings, and Endpoint Protection settings on your Intune mobile devices and applications. Think of Intune Policies as network Group Policies. These are rules that you can put on devices or users.

Once you decide to move to Microsoft Intune for your devices, it's important to use Intune policies to help manage the devices on your network and setup Endpoint protection. Microsoft Intune helps your IT staff deploy devices and applications and Intune policies allow the IT team to manage the settings on these deployments. When you build a policy, you can deploy that policy to the user groups that you setup in the previous section. Then when the users log into Intune, the policy then becomes their baseline policy.

You can create policies for the different types of devices available for Microsoft Intune. You can create policies for Androids, iOS, Mac OS X, Windows, Software, Computer Manager, and Common Mobile Device Settings.

In Exercise 11.4, I will walk you through the steps required to setup a Microsoft Intune policy. Administrators have the option to change the policy at any time.

EXERCISE 11.4

Creating an Intune Policy

1. Open the Intune administration portal.

2. In the left pane, click Device Compliance.

3. In the Manage section on the Device Compliance page, click the Policies link.

4. When the result page opens, click Create Policy on the top of the results pane.

5. In the Create Policy window, type in a policy name and description. Then choose the platform for the policy. Depending on the platform chosen, configuration settings will populate.

6. You can now change the Configuration settings based upon your platform choice.

7. Select the Actions for Noncompliance section and add an action for noncompliance.

8. Once you have completed the field and are satisfied, you can click Create.

Now that we have looked at how to setup Intune, users and groups, and policies, it's time to look at how an administrator enrolls devices in Intune.

Enrolling Devices Using Intune

To take advantage of using Intune, you must enroll devices into the Intune system. To enroll clients into this system, you must download the Intune client software onto the devices that need to be enrolled.

Now for some of the different devices on the market today, you may need to take additional steps in order for them to work with your Intune network. For example, to use the Apple iOS, an Apple Push Notification service (APNs) certificate must be imported from Apple so that you can manage iOS devices. This certificate allows Intune administrators to manage iOS.

When an administrator goes to enroll the many different devices on the Intune network, as stated, some of the different devices require different installation options.

Apple iOS   Administrators need to import an Apple Push Notification service (APNs) certificate from Apple so that you can manage iOS devices. Administrators need to open the Microsoft Intune administration portal and then go to Administration ➢ Mobile Device Management ➢ iOS and Mac OS X ➢ Download the APNs Certificate Requests (see Figure 11.9). Administrators then must save the certificate signing request (.csr) file locally. The .csr file is then used to request a trust relationship certificate from the Apple Push Certificates Portal. The administrator then needs to click the Upload the APNs certificate.

FIGURE 11.9   Upload an APNs Certificate Screen

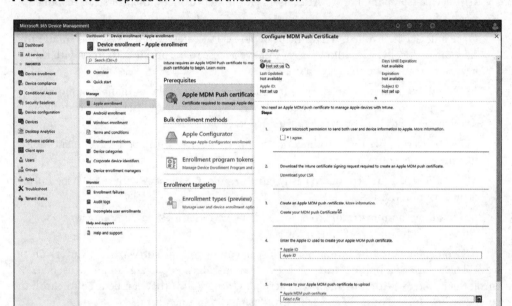

Android Devices   No additional configurations in the Intune console are needed to enable Android mobile device enrollment.

Windows Phone   Administrators must set up some management requirements before Windows Phones will work with your Intune network. DNS Administrators need to create CNAME records in order for users to connect to the Intune network resources. Windows Phones also require a certificate to establish encrypted communications between the client device and the Intune cloud based system.

Windows Devices   Windows devices get connected basically the same way as Windows Phones. The DNS Administrators have to create a CNAME record and then applications can be SideLoaded into the Windows computer. Users can also connect to Intune by using the Intune Management portal.

Sideloading applications using Intune will be explained in greater detail later in this chapter. Sideloading basically means loading pre-bought or company applications using the Windows Store, Intune, or images.

Administrators can use the Mobile Device Management (MDM) tools to help your company users enroll different devices and manage their Intune accounts. MDM has some of the following benefits:

- MDM gives users the capabilities of enrolling their own devices through the use of the self-service Company Portal. After users enroll their devices, the users can install corporate applications.

- Once a device is enrolled, MDM helps deploy certificates, WiFi, VPN, and email profiles automatically. This allows users to have access to corporate resources with the necessary security configuration options.

- MTM allows administrators to use broad management tools for managing mobile devices, passcode resets, device lockouts, data encryption, and the ability to fully wipe a stolen device to help protect against corporate data loss.

- MTM helps simplify the enrollment of corporate devices using bulk enrollment tools like the Apple Configurator.

- MTM allows administrators to easily enroll Apple iOS devices with the Device Enrollment Program (DEP).

- MTM allows administrators to enforce a much stricter lock down policy for iOS, Android, and Windows Phone devices.

To enroll clients into the Intune network, you can install the software in a variety of ways. The company administrator can provide an installation package to allow users to enroll their systems. Administrators can setup a Group Policy that can be used to enroll the computer into Intune or users can self-enroll using the Intune portal.

If you decide to use MDM, you must first set up the mobile device management authority. This enables management of device platforms, and allows your devices to be enrolled with the company portal app.

Before enrolling your Windows 10 Desktop, you must confirm which version of Windows that you have installed. In Exercise 11.5, I will walk through how to verify which version of Windows you have.

EXERCISE 11.5

Confirm the Version of Windows

1. To display Windows Settings options, right-click the Windows Start icon and select Settings (see Figure 11.10).

FIGURE 11.10   Windows Settings Screen

2.   Select System ➤ About (see Figure 11.11).

FIGURE 11.11   Windows About Screen

3. In the Settings window you will see a list of Windows specifications for your computer. Within this list, locate the version.

4. Confirm that the Windows 10 version is 1607 or higher.

The steps presented in this book are for Windows 10 version 1607 or higher; if the version you are using is 1511 or lower, follow the steps located on Microsoft's website: https://docs.microsoft.com/en-us/intune-user-help/enroll-windows-10-device#enroll-windows-10-version-1511-and-earlier-device. In Exercise 11.6, I will show you how to enroll a Windows 10 desktop version 1607 or higher device.

EXERCISE 11.6

Enroll Windows 10 Desktop Version 1607 or Higher

1. Return to Windows Settings and select Accounts (see Figure 11.12).

FIGURE 11.12 Windows Settings Screen

2. Select Access work or school ➤ Connect (see Figure 11.13).

FIGURE 11.13   Access Work or School Screen

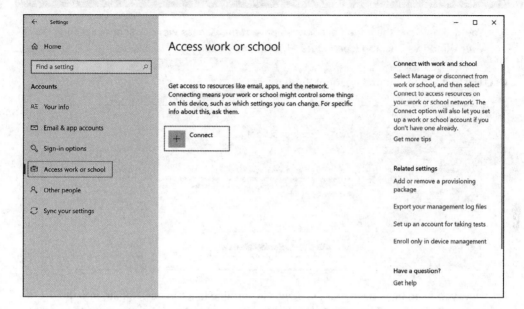

3.   Sign in to Intune with your work or school account (see Figure 11.14) and then select Next.

FIGURE 11.14   Setup a Work or School Account Screen

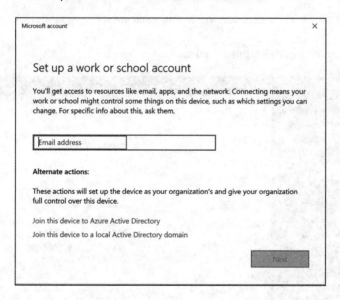

You will see a message showing that the device is registering with your company or school.

4.   When you see the "You're all set!" screen, select Done.

EXERCISE 11.6 *(continued)*

5. You will now see the added account as part of the Access work or school settings on your Windows Desktop (see Figure 11.15).

FIGURE 11.15 Added Account Screen

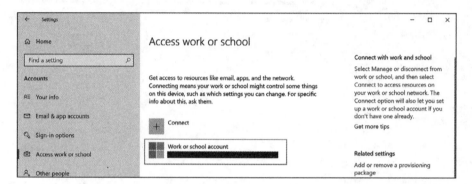

6. Now you need to confirm that the device is enrolled in Intune by signing into the Microsoft Endpoint Manager Admin Center as a Global Administrator or an Intune Service Administrator.

7. To view the enrolled devices in Intune, select Devices ➢ All devices.

8. Verify that the device is enrolled within Intune as shown in Figure 11.16.

FIGURE 11.16 Intune Enrolled Devices Screen

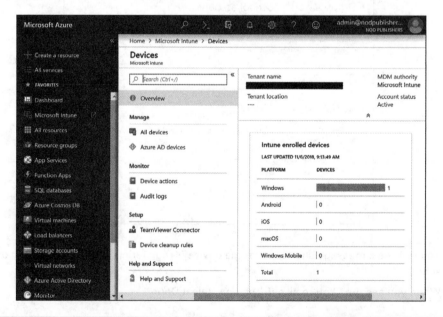

Configuring the Intune Connector Site

To understand how connectors work, we must first understand what a connector does and why we use them in the computer industry. Connectors allow different types of devices to communicate with each other. So for example, let's say we had a Microsoft Exchange server and a UNIX based mail server. You would add a connector in to the Exchange server so that it could communicate and understand the UNIX mail server. That's how Intune Connectors work also.

Intune connectors allow Microsoft Intune to communicate and understand other types of devices and software. So if we decide to use Azure Active Directory and Azure Exchange, we can install a connector so that the Azure Exchange can work with the corporate Exchange mail server.

Exchange devices have the ability to be managed through both the on premise Exchange servers and the hosted Exchange Servers in the cloud. The Exchange connector connects your users with your Exchange deployments and the connector lets you manage your mobile devices through the Intune console.

Administrators who have been using System Center Configuration Manager to manage their computers, Macs, and UNIX based devices can add the Intune connector so that they can manage all of these devices from one console.

To configure connectors, in the Intune Management Console, click on the Admin link. Then expand the Mobile Device Management section. You would then click on the device or software package and then setup the connector.

Configuring Intune Alerts

One of the nice advantages of using Intune is the ability to monitor and see alerts within Intune. When looking at these Intune alerts, there are different levels of severity within the alerts. Table 11.1 shows you the different alert types and what each type means.

TABLE 11.1   Intune Alert Types

Alert	Description
(!) Critical	This alert shows you that you have a serious issue that needs to be investigated and fixed.
(⚠) Warning	This alert shows you that there may be an issue but that issue is not very serious at this time. These alerts need to be investigated to make sure that they do not become a problem in the future.
(i) Informational	This alert shows you that there is some information about a product but it's not a problem. For example, an informational alert may tell you that there is an upgrade to a connector that you have installed.

When dealing with Intune monitoring and alerts, there are a few settings that you can setup to help configure how alerts work. For example, under the Alerts section in the Azure portal, you can setup recipients who will receive emails when alerts happen.

So if you get a critical error, an email can be sent to an administrator so that the IT department can work on resolving the issue as fast as possible. If you don't setup email alerts, someone will need to monitor the Intune system daily to watch for issues. Intune Administrators have the ability to set different email recipients for different alert types. So Critical alerts can go to one IT person and warnings can go to another.

Administrators also have the ability to enable or disable certain alert types. So if you are getting a warning that you know is not going to affect your Intune system, you can disable the warning to remove it completely. This way it's not a message your Intune Administrators need to see on a daily basis.

To configure your Alerts and Notifications, in the Intune Management Console, click on the Admin link. Then expand Alerts and Notifications. You can then create new alert rules and notifications.

Supporting Applications

Microsoft Intune gives an organization the ability to deploy and maintain software from the cloud. The advantage to this is that the software issued through Intune is licensed to the user and not the hardware. So what this means is that you can deploy a copy of Office to a user using multiple devices and when that user works on corporate data, that data is secure. That's the real advantage to Intune. This allows your users to work securely from their iPhone, Windows laptops, or tablet.

Microsoft Intune also allows an organization to use their current business apps by using the Intune App Wrapping tool. The Intune App Wrapping tool is a command line application that builds a package around the in-house application. Then the business application can be managed by the Intune mobile application management policies.

The Intune App Wrapping tool also gives you secure data viewing through the Intune Managed Browser, AV Player, Image viewer, and the PDF viewer. Administrators also have the ability to deny specific applications or web addresses from being accessed from specific types of mobile devices. Finally, when dealing with corporate data and security, Administrators have the ability to wipe out a device in the event that the device is stolen, lost, or the employee leaves the company.

Deploying Applications Using Intune

The way that we do business in the corporate world continues to change on a daily basis. Today, many of our users bring in their own devices (BYOD: Bring Your Own Device). Because of BYOD, it is getting harder for IT departments to deploy software.

As stated earlier in this chapter, Microsoft Intune (Figure 11.17) is a cloud-based desktop and mobile device management tool. Intune helps IT departments provide their users with access to company applications, data, and resources. The users have the ability to access these resources from any type of device (i.e., Apple, Android, or Windows devices).

FIGURE 11.17   Microsoft Intune

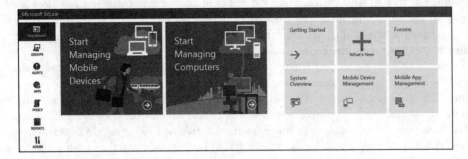

One of the issues that we face as IT administrators is that we have multiple copies of software throughout a company and multiple version types (Apple versions of Office compared to Windows versions). Let's take a look at Office as our example. Many times we have older versions of Office (Office 2010/2016) and newer versions of Office (Office 2019 / Office 365).

This is where Microsoft Intune can help out an IT department. You can upload software packages to Intune and your users can get current copies of the software from the web. Also, Intune helps your organization protect its software by giving you extra security and features. Intune also allows you to setup application management policies that allow an IT department to manage applications on different devices.

As long as a device is compatible with Microsoft Intune, you can deploy the applications to that device. Depending on the device and the application, deployment options may vary. Administrators have the ability to upload their applications to Microsoft Intune or link a Windows Store application to Microsoft Intune storage.

To deploy applications using Intune, you must use the proper software installation type based on the different devices that your users may be using. Microsoft gives you a trial subscription of 2 GB of cloud storage. You can purchase more storage depending on how much money you want to spend.

Intune Software Publisher

To make an application available for your users to deploy, you must upload the installation package and then publish the package. As soon as you add or modify an application in Microsoft Intune, the Microsoft Intune Software Publisher starts. Then from the publisher, you can choose and configure the software installation type.

To use the Microsoft Intune Software Publisher, you must have Microsoft .NET 4.0 installed onto the Windows system. After you install .NET, restart the system and you should be able to use the Microsoft Intune Software Publisher.

Sideload Apps by Using Microsoft Intune

Sideloading an application means that you are loading an application that you already own or one that your company created into a delivery system (i.e. Intune, Microsoft Store, or images).

You may be familiar with Sideloading apps into the Windows Store. This is the process of building or buying your own application and then adding it to the Windows Store so that all of your users can download and use that app. Sideloading an application into Microsoft Intune means the same thing. We are taking an application that we built or bought and adding it into Microsoft Intune for user downloads.

Think about how you deploy software today. You buy a package and either manually install the software to your users or use some type of deployment package like System Center Configuration Manager. The only difference now is that the application gets loaded into the cloud and can be deployed to any device that is compatible with the application.

On Windows 10 devices, Intune supports many different app types and deployment scenarios. After an administrator has added an app to Intune, they can then then assign that app to users and devices.

The app types supported on Windows 10 devices are Line-of-business (LOB) apps and Microsoft Store for Business apps.

An LOB app is one that is added from an app installation file. The following steps will help you to add a Windows LOB app to Microsoft Intune.

Adding a Windows LOB App to Microsoft Intune

Step 1: Specify the software setup file:

1. Sign in to the Microsoft Endpoint Manager Admin Center.

2. Select Apps ➤ All Apps ➤ Add.

3. Select Line-of-Business app as the App type in the Add App pane.

Step 2: Configure the app package file:

1. Select App Package File in the Add App pane.

2. Select the Browse button in the App Package File pane. Then select a Windows installation file with the extension .msi, .appx, or .appxbundle.

3. Select OK when done.

Step 3: Configure app information:

1. Select App Information in the Add App pane.

2. In the App Information pane, configure the information such as name, description, publisher, etc.

3. Select OK when done.

Step 4: Finish up:

1. Verify that the app information is correct in the Add App pane.

2. To upload the app to Intune, select Add.

Step 5: Update a line-of-business app:

1. Sign in to the Azure portal.

2. Select All Services ➤ Intune. Intune is in the Monitoring + Management section.

3. Select Client Apps ➤ Apps.

4. Find and select the desired app in the list of apps.

5. In the Overview blade, select Properties.

6. Select App package file.

7. Select the folder icon and browse to the location of the updated app file. Select Open. The app information is updated with the package information.

8. Confirm that the App version reflects the updated app package.

An administrator can install apps on a Windows 10 device in one of two ways depending on the app type. The app types are:

- User Context: The app is installed for that user on the device when the user signs in to the device.

- Device Context: The app is installed directly to the device by Intune.

After an app is added to Intune, the app can then be assigned to users and devices. An administrator can assign an app to a device whether or not the device is managed by Intune.

Once an application has been uploaded to Intune you'll want to deploy the app to your users. To do this, you'll need to assign the app to an Intune group. You need to click on the Apps link and then choose the app for deployment in the Windows Intune portal. The following steps show how to assign an app:

1. Sign in to the Microsoft Endpoint Manager Admin Center.

2. Select Apps ➤ All Apps.

3. Select the app you want to assign in the Apps pane.

4. Select Assignments in the Manage section of the menu.

5. Select Add Group to open the Add Group pane.

6. Next, you will want to select the assignment type. There are several options available:

   - Available for enrolled devices: Assigns the app to groups of users who can install the app from the Company Portal app or website.

   - Available with or without enrollment: Assigns the app to groups of users whose devices are not enrolled with Intune.

- ▪ Required: The app is installed on devices in the selected groups.
- ▪ Uninstall: The app is uninstalled from devices in the selected groups.

7. Select Included Groups to select the groups of users.

8. After you have selected one or more groups, select Select.

9. Select OK in the Assign pane.

10. Select Exclude Groups if you want to exclude any groups.

11. Select Select if you have chosen to exclude any groups.

12. Click OK in the Add Group pane.

13. Select Save in the app Assignments pane.

To monitor the properties of apps, you can:

1. Sign in to the Microsoft Endpoint Manager Admin Center.

2. Select Apps ➢ All Apps.

3. Select an app to monitor in the list of the apps. This will open the app pane, which shows an overview of the device status and the user status.

Deep-Link Applications by Using Microsoft Intune

One of the nice advantages of using Windows 10 is that you can purchase Windows Store applications. After you purchase the applications, you can deploy the Windows Store application (deep-link) to all of your users.

Supporting Broadband Connectivity

Administrators have a few weapons in their broadband arsenal. Two different options that we can setup as Administrators is the ability to see how much network or software bandwidth is being used (metering) and how we can setup our Windows 10 devices to use your cellular Internet connections (tethering).

Understanding Metering

Administrators have the ability to limit and monitor network usage by configuring the network as a metered network. Network metering allows network downloading to be watched or metered and then administrators can charge users or departments for the network usage.

This is becoming something that many IT departments have started doing due to budgeting. Many IT departments are non-revenue-generating departments and because of this, it can be difficult for an IT administrator to get a budget passed. But with network metering, you can charge other departments for the amount of bandwidth and network that is being used.

When setting up your company's Internet connection, your ISP has the ability to charge by the amount of data used. That's called a metered Internet connection. If you have a metered Internet connection, setting your network connection to metered in Windows can help you reduce the amount of data you send and receive. To set this up in Windows, you would take the following steps;

1. Click Start ➤ Settings, and then tap Network & Internet.

2. Tap or click on the Wi-Fi link and then, under Metered Connection, turn Set As A Metered Connection on or off.

Administrators also have the ability to limit how much bandwidth a user or department gets to use when downloading applications. This is referred to as Software metering.

To setup software metering, an Administrator must use a combination of Microsoft Windows Intune and System Center Configuration Monitor.

Understanding Broadband Tethering

Tethering allows a user to use their Windows 10 mobile device through their cellular phone. If you have a Windows 10 mobile device and want it to access the Internet, you can go through your cell coverage to get online.

Tethering can also be connecting one mobile device to another mobile device for Internet access. So let's say I have an iPad with a cellular Internet connection. I can connect another Windows 10 tablet to that iPad to gain Internet access. So tethering is the ability to connect one device to another for Internet access. Before you set up tethering, there are a few things that you should know:

- There may be extra charges when connecting your data connection with another device.

- Applications and updates may not be downloaded over a metered connection and by default, tethered and mobile broadband connections are metered.

- Many cellular carriers require that you pay an extra fee for allowing your phone to be a hotspot for tethering. To enable tethering on most devices, you setup your mobile device as an Internet hotspot.

Understanding Data Synchronization

Data Synchronization allows you to synchronize your devices with your servers. These servers can be network based or cloud based. Administrators have the ability to synchronize work folders and they can also use the Sync Center to use one application for all of their synchronization needs.

To enable synchronization on the Windows 10 device, click on the Start button and choose Settings. When you are in the Settings window, click on the Accounts link to setup your user accounts and synchronization (see Figure 11.18).

FIGURE 11.18   Data Synchronization

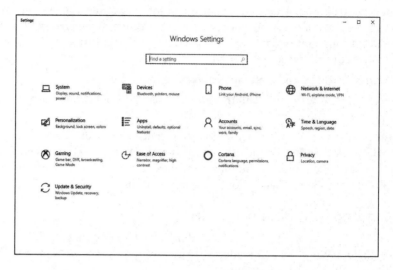

Once you enter into the Account link, you can choose the bottom option (Sync your settings) to setup all of your synchronization settings (see Figure 11.19).

FIGURE 11.19   Sync your settings

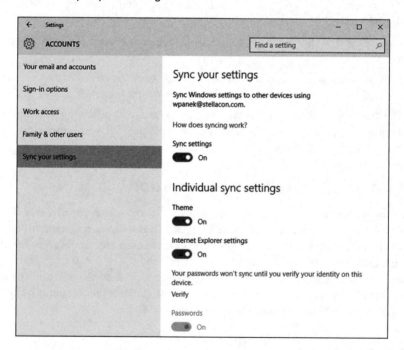

One of the final things that you want to look at in the Accounts link is the Work access link. The Work access link allows you to connect your device to your work or school, sign into Azure, and enroll in to device management (see Figure 11.20).

FIGURE 11.20   Sync your settings

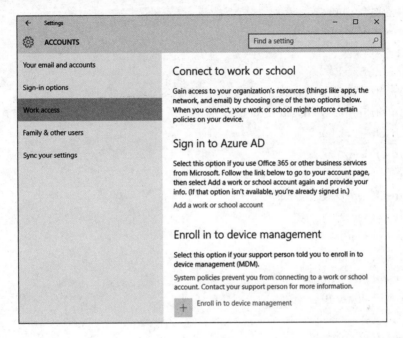

Using Mobile Application Management

One of the advantages to using Intune is the ability to download applications to many different platforms. One concern that IT departments may have is that their users will download corporate applications on personal devices. Since many companies now allow BYOD, there needs to be tools that allow a company to control company data on personal devices. This is where *Mobile Application Management (MAM)* can help your organization.

Mobile application management is part of Intune and it is a suite of administrator management tools that allow you to manage, configure, publish, update, and monitor applications for your mobile devices.

The advantage to using MAM is that an administrator has the ability to manage and protect the company's data from within the application that the user is using. For example, an administrator can manage a work related application that has confidential information on it and that application can be on almost any type of device (including personal devices).

Mobile application management will work with many of the Microsoft productivity applications including:

- Microsoft Azure Information Protection Viewer
- Microsoft Bookings
- Microsoft Cortana
- Microsoft Dynamics CRM
- Microsoft Edge
- Microsoft Excel
- Microsoft Flow
- Microsoft Intune Managed Browser
- Microsoft Invoicing
- Microsoft Kaizala
- Microsoft Launcher
- Microsoft OneDrive for Business
- Microsoft OneNote
- Microsoft Outlook
- Microsoft Planner
- Microsoft PowerApps
- Microsoft Power BI
- Microsoft PowerPoint
- Microsoft SharePoint
- Microsoft To-Do
- Microsoft Skype for Business
- Microsoft StaffHub
- Microsoft Stream
- Microsoft Teams
- Microsoft Visio Viewer
- Microsoft Word

> For a complete list of applications that Intune and MAM will support, please visit Microsoft's website https://docs.microsoft.com/en-us/intune/apps-supported-intune-apps.

There are two configurations that are supported by Intune MAM. These are:

- Intune MDM + MAM
- MAM without device enrollment (MAM-WE)

With Intune MDM + MAM, administrators can manage apps only by using MAM and using app protection policies only on devices that are enrolled with Intune MDM. To manage, you need to log into the Azure portal at https://portal.azure.com and use the Intune console.

With MAM-WE, administrators can manage apps using MAM and using app protection policies on devices that are not enrolled with Intune MDM. Apps can be managed by using Intune on devices that are registered with third-party Enterprise Mobility Management (EMM) providers. To do so, you can to log into the Azure portal at https://portal.azure.com and use the Intune console or use Intune on devices that are registered with the third-party providers or on devices that are not enrolled with MDM at all.

Windows Information Protection

Since corporations are allowing personnel to bring their own devices into the corporate network, there is an ever-mounting risk of possible data leaks from users using apps and services that are not controlled by the corporate network.

To help protect against the possible data leaks, Microsoft created, Windows Information Protection (WIP), which was formerly known as Enterprise Data Protection (EDP). WIP is a built-in Windows 10 feature that allows an administrator to maintain and monitor company data separate from any personal data that is on a user's device.

WIP aids in protecting against possible data leaks and protects enterprise apps and data on both enterprise-owned and personal devices without interfering with the user's experience while on the corporate network. Users do not need to open any special apps or enter into any specific modes in order for WIP to work. Users just use apps that they are used to and WIP will provide the data protection.

Besides separating corporate and personal data, WIP can also determine which users and apps have access to particular data and can determine what users are allowed to do with that corporate data. For example, an administrator has the ability to stop a user from copying corporate data from an approved app and pasting that data into another unapproved app.

The WIP Intune policy maintains a list of protected apps, corporate network locations, the levels of protection granted and the encryption settings.

WIP provides the following:

- Allows an administrator to track issues and find corrective actions by using audit reports.

- Integrates with existing management systems to deploy, configure and manage WIPs. Management systems can include Microsoft Intune, System Center Configuration Manager (SCCM), or an MDM.

- Provides added protection for present line-of-business apps without needing to update any apps.

- Provides the capability to remove corporate data from Intune MDM enrolled devices while, at the same time, not touching the personal data on a device.

- Separates personal data from corporate data, without the need for the user to change apps or settings.

An administrator can set a WIP policy with a different level of protection and management modes. There are four protection and management modes. They are as follows (see Figure 11.21):

- Block: Prevents users from engaging in unauthorized actions, such as copying and pasting corporate data. WIP searches for unacceptable data sharing and will stop the user from performing any further.

- Allow Overrides: Alerts users whenever they try to execute an unauthorized action. The user can ignore the warning and proceed with the unauthorized action; however, WIP will log the event in its audit log where an administrator can review it later.

- Silent: Will run in the background, tracking the user's actions with no indicator of an unauthorized action and logging any inappropriate data sharing. However, if an action is blocked, the action will be prevented as usual.

- Off: WIP is disabled and provides no protection or auditing.

FIGURE 11.21   Configure Windows Information Protection Settings

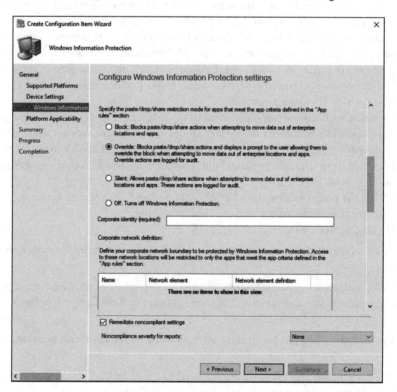

It's not recommended, but an administrator can turn off WIP. This can be done without data loss to the devices that were managed by WIP. WIP can be turned back on, but the previously applied decryption and policy information will not be automatically reapplied.

WIP uses System Center Configuration Manager (SCCM) to design and implement WIP policies. Once an administrator has set up SCCM they must create a configuration item for WIP; this is the WIP policy.

Creating a Configuration Item for WIP

To create a configuration item for WIP, follow the following steps:

1. Open the SCCM console, click the Assets And Compliance node, expand the Overview node, expand the Compliance Settings node, and then expand the Configuration Items node (see Figure 11.22).

FIGURE 11.22   System Center Configuration Manager console

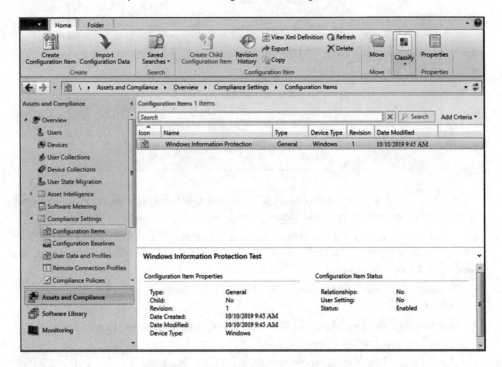

2. Click the Create Configuration Item button. The Create Configuration Item Wizard will start (see Figure 11.23).

FIGURE 11.23   Create Configuration Item Wizard

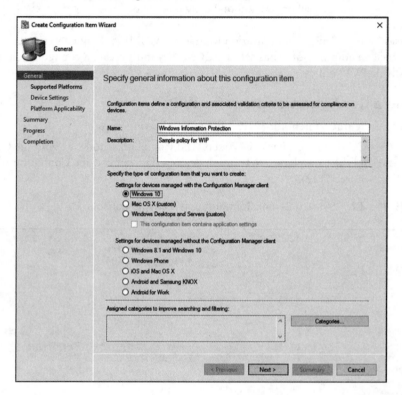

3. On the General Information screen, type a name (required) and a description (optional) for the policy into the Name and Description boxes.

4. In the Specify The Type Of Configuration Item That You Want To Create area, pick the option that represents whether you'd like to use SCCM for device management, and then click Next. The options are as follows:

   - Settings For Devices Managed With The Configuration Manager Client: Windows 10

   - Settings For Devices Managed Without The Configuration Manager Client: Windows 8.1 and Windows 10

5. On the Supported Platforms screen (see Figure 11.24), click the Windows 10 box, and then click Next.

FIGURE 11.24 Create Configuration Item Wizard - Supported Platforms

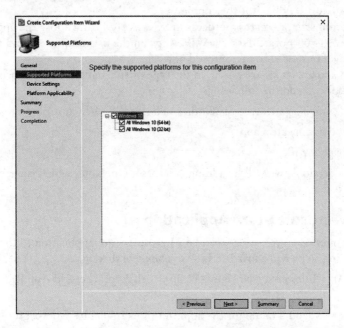

6. On the Device Settings screen (see Figure 11.25), click Windows Information Protection, and then click Next.

FIGURE 11.25 Create Configuration Item Wizard - Device Settings

The Configure Windows Information Protection settings page appears, where an administrator can configure a policy for the company.

When an administrator creates a process in SCCM, they can choose the apps that will be granted access to corporate data via WIP. Apps on the list can protect and restrict data from being copied or moved to unapproved apps.

The steps to add app rules are based on the type of rule template that is being applied. An administrator can add the following:

- Store app (known as a Universal Windows Platform (UWP) app
- Signed Windows desktop app
- AppLocker policy file

In the follow sections, we will be adding Microsoft OneNote, which is a store app, to the App Rules list.

Adding a Microsoft Store Application

There may be times when you need to add a Microsoft Store application to the App Rules list. The following steps will show you how to complete this task:

1. From the App Rules area (see Figure 11.26), click Add. The Add App Rule box appears.
2. In the Title box, add a name for the app. In this example, it's Microsoft OneNote.
3. In the Windows Information Protection Mode drop-down list, click Allow. Clicking Allow turns WIP on to help protect that app's company data.
4. Pick Store App from the Rule Template drop-down list. The box will change to show the store app rule options.
5. Type the name of the app and the name of its publisher, and then click OK. For this UWP app example, the Publisher is CN=Microsoft Corporation, O=Microsoft Corporation, L=Redmond, S=Washington, C=US and the Product name is Microsoft .Office.OneNote.

FIGURE 11.26 Create Configuration Item Wizard - Add App Rule

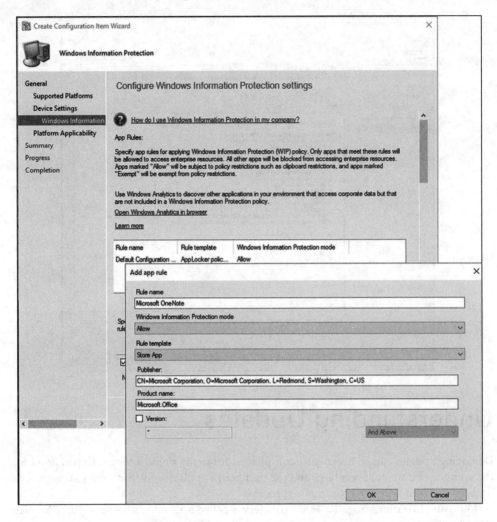

After configuring the policy, an administrator can review all of the settings by looking at the Summary screen. Click on Summary to review the policy choices (see Figure 11.27) and then click Next to finish and save the policy.

FIGURE 11.27   Create Configuration Item Wizard - Summary Screen

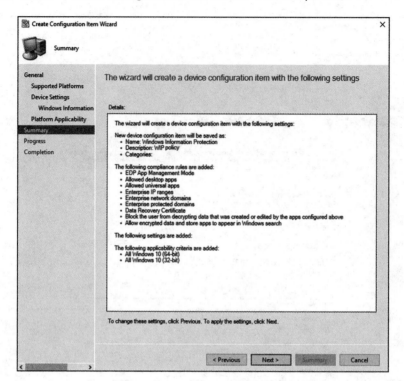

Understanding Updates

Deploying updates can be a very difficult process for many organizations. Depending on the number of users that you have and the number of applications that each user uses, updates can be a very time consuming process.

Many organizations install a Microsoft server called a Windows Server Update Services (WSUS). WSUS servers allow administrators to deploy Microsoft product updates to computers that are running the Windows operating system. Administrators can manage all of their organization's Microsoft updates from one application.

The downside to WSUS is that it is used for Microsoft updates. So you can deploy updates to all of your applications, Microsoft and Non-Microsoft, by using the Intune management portal.

Deploying Software Updates Using Intune

When you decide to use Intune to deploy your updates, you get a lot of options that you get to consider and setup. For example, do you want to approve all of your updates or do you want the updates to automatically deploy? Many administrators like to approve all of their updates so that they have a chance to test them first before deploying.

Intune stores only the update policy assignments, not the actual updates. The devices still need to access Windows Update to obtain the updates.

Intune provides the following policy types to manage updates:

- Windows 10 update ring—a collection of settings that configures when Windows 10 updates get installed.

- Windows 10 feature updates (public preview)—brings devices to the Windows version that you specify and freezes the feature set on those devices until you choose to update them. Figure 11.28 shows the Windows 10 update ring.

FIGURE 11.28 Overview of Update Types

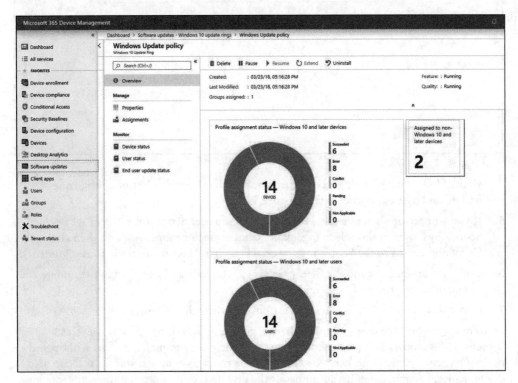

To create and assign update rings follow these steps:

1. Sign in to the Microsoft Endpoint Manager Admin Center.

2. Select Devices ➢ Windows ➢ Windows 10 Update Rings ➢ Create.

3. Under Basics, specify a name, a description (optional), and then select Next (as shown in Figure 11.29).

FIGURE 11.29 Create Windows 10 Update Ring

4. Under Update Ring Settings, configure your required settings. After configuring update and user experience settings, click Next.

5. If you want to apply scope tags, you can do that under Scope Tags. Select + Select Scope Tags to open the Select Tags pane. Choose one or more tags, and then click Select and return to the Scope Tags page. Then click Next to continue to Assignments.

6. Under Assignments, choose + Select Groups To Include and then assign the update ring to one or more groups. Click Next to continue.

7. Under Review + Create, review the settings and then click Create.

To manage your Windows 10 update rings, go to the portal, navigate to Devices ➤ Windows ➤ Windows 10 Update Rings and select the policy to manage. This will open the policy Overview page. From here you can view the rings' assignment status. You can also delete, pause, resume, extend, and uninstall the update ring by selecting the actions from the top of the Overview pane (see Figure 11.30).

FIGURE 11.30 Overview Pane Actions

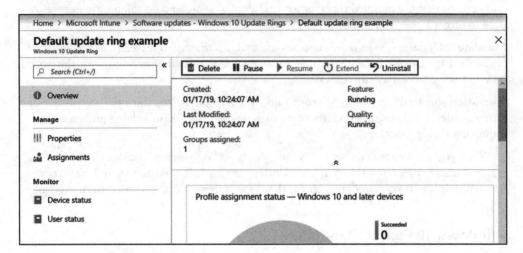

Identifying Required Updates

When you decide to use Intune for updates, you need to decide which type of updates that you want to install. Administrators have the ability to choose what type of updates they want to install.

All Updates   All updates section means just that, all updates. Every possible update that can be deployed will be shown under the All updates Section.

Critical Updates   Critical updates are updates that are released to fix a specific issue that is for a critical bug that is not security related.

Security Updates   Security updates are updates that need to be applied to fix a security issue. These security issues are used by hackers to either hack into a device or software.

Definition Updates   Definition updates are normally software updates that contain additions to a product's definition database. Definition databases get used to identify objects that have very specific attributes. These attributes look for malicious code, phishing websites, or junk mail.

Service Packs   Service packs are a collective set of all current hotfixes, security updates, critical updates, and updates. Normally service packs also contain additional fixes for known issues that are found since the release of the product. Service packs may also contain customer requested design changes or features.

Update Rollups   Update rollups are current hotfixes, security updates, critical updates, and updates that are bundled together for easy deployment. Update rollups are normally used to target a specific component or software package.

Mandatory Updates   Mandatory updates are updates that are released to either fix or replace a software or hardware issue. Mandatory updates are required to run or the device or Windows system may stop functioning properly.

Non-Microsoft Updates   Non-Microsoft updates are updates for third party software and hardware devices. These are updates that other vendors release for solving problems or improving their product.

When you configure settings for Windows 10 update rings in Intune, the administrator is also configuring the Windows Update settings. If a Windows update setting has a Windows 10 version dependency, the version dependency is noted in the settings details.

Windows 10 Feature Updates

With Windows 10 feature updates, the administrator selects the Windows feature version that they want devices to stay at. When a device receives a Windows 10 feature updates policy, the device will update to the version of Windows specified. If a device already runs a later version of Windows, then it will remain at its current version.

Until you modify or remove the Windows 10 feature updates policy, devices won't install a new Windows version. If the policy is edited to specify a newer version, devices can then install the features from that Windows version.

To create and assign Windows 10 feature updates, follow these steps:

1. Sign in to the Microsoft Endpoint Manager Admin Center.

2. Select Devices ➤ Windows ➤ Windows 10 Feature updates ➤ Create.

3. Under Basics, specify a name, a description (optional), and for Feature Update To Deploy, select which version of Windows you want, and then select Next.

4. Under Assignments, choose + Select Groups and then assign the update ring to one or more groups. Click Next.

5. Under Review + Create, review the settings and click Create to save.

To manage the Windows 10 feature updates, follow these steps:

1. In the admin center, go to Devices ➤ Windows ➤ Windows 10 Feature Updates and select the policy to manage. The policy opens to its Overview pane.

2. From the Overview pane, the administrator can configure the following options:

   ▪ Select Delete to delete the policy from Intune and remove it from devices.

   ▪ Select Properties to modify the deployment. On the Properties pane, select Edit to open the deployment settings or assignments to modify the deployment.

   ▪ Select End User Update Status to view information about the policy.

Using Intune Compliance Reports

An administrator can use Intune to deploy Windows updates to Windows 10 devices. The administrator will want to review a policy report on the deployment status for the configured Windows 10 update rings. To do so, follow these steps:

1. Sign in to the Microsoft Endpoint Manager Admin Center.

2. Select Devices ➤ Overview ➤ Software Update Status.

3. To view additional details, select Monitor. Then below Software Updates, select Per Update Ring Deployment State and choose the deployment ring to review.

In the Monitor section, the administrator can choose one of the following reports to view more detailed information about the update ring:

- Device status: Shows the device configuration status.

- User status: Shows the username, status, and last report date.

- End user update status: Shows the Windows device update state.

Using Intune Reports

One of the best tools that Microsoft Intune offers is the ability to obtain all of the different types of reports. The Intune Reports help an Administrator monitor the status of your enrolled devices and see if there are any issues that need to be addressed. The reports also allow an Administrator to examine both the hardware and software inventory.

Microsoft Intune reports allow an administrator to monitor the health and activity of endpoints, and provides other reporting data across Intune. Examples include being able to see report regarding device compliance, device health, and device trends. An administrator is also able to build custom reports.

Intune reports are categorized into the following areas of focus:

- Operational: Provides targeted data that helps an administrator focus and take action.

- Organizational: Provides a wider summary of an overall view, such as device management state.

- Historical: Provides patterns and trends over a period of time.

- Specialist: Allows an administrator to use raw data to create their own custom reports.

Using Intune reports allows an administrator to search and sort, perform data paging, review performance, and export data.

- Search and sort: Search and sort across every column.

- Data paging: Scan data based on paging, either page by page or by jumping to a specific page.

- Performance: Quickly generate and view reports created from large tenants.

- Export: Export reporting data generated from large tenants.

PowerShell Commands

Table 11.2 is a list of just some of the PowerShell commands that administrators can use to manage, configure, and view applications in Azure.

TABLE 11.2   PowerShell commands

Command	Description
Add-AzureADApplicationOwner	This command is used to add an owner to an application.
Add-AzureADApplicationPolicy	Administrators can use this command to add a policy to an application.
Get-AzureADApplication	This command allows an administrator to view an application.
Get-AzureADApplicationExtensionProperty	This command allows you to view the extension properties of an application.
Get-AzureADApplicationOwner	This command allows an administrator to view who is the owner of an application.
Get-AzureADApplicationPasswordCredential	Administrators can use this command to view an application password.
Get-AzureADApplicationPolicy	This command allows an administrator to view an application policy.
New-AzureADApplication	This command allows an administrator to create a new application in Azure.
New-AzureADApplicationExtensionProperty	Administrators can use this command to create extension properties of an application.
New-AzureADApplicationPasswordCredential	This command creates password credentials for an application.
Remove-AzureADApplication	Administrators can use this command to delete an application.

Command	Description
`Remove-AzureADApplicationExtensionProperty`	This command allows an administrator to remove an extension property of an application.
`Remove-AzureADApplicationOwner`	Administrators can use this command to remove an owner from an application.
`Remove-AzureADApplicationPasswordCredential`	This command allows an administrator to remove the password credentials from an application.
`Set-AzureADApplication`	Administrators can use this command to update an application.

Summary

In this chapter, we talked about the cloud and Microsoft Intune. I showed you how Microsoft Intune can help you manage devices and software. I showed you how to set up and configure an Intune subscription and how you can use that subscription to help your network users get the most out of their network resources and software.

I also talked about managing devices using Intune. I showed you how to provision user accounts and enroll devices. I also discussed how to manage and configure devices using the Microsoft Intune subscription.

I then continued the chapter by discussing how to deploy and configure software and updates using Intune.

I then talked about how to work with mobile devices including Windows tablets, broadband metering and tethering and I also showed you how to wipe mobile devices for employees who leave the company. I spoke about using MAM and WIP and how you can set policies to help control how applications are deployed to your users. I then showed you how to use Intune to help deploy and maintain your company's software packages and updates.

I showed you the different types of reports that an Administrator can run using Intune. These reports can help an Administrator see what devices still need updates and also what hardware may need to be installed or replaced.

Exam Essentials

Understand Microsoft Intune.   Understand what Microsoft Intune can do to help your network. Make sure you understand how users and devices get connected to Intune.

Know how to configure a Microsoft Intune Subscription.   Understand how to setup and manage a Microsoft Intune Subscription. Understand how to configure a device to use Microsoft Intune.

Understand the Microsoft Intune Benefits.   Understand what Microsoft Intune benefits can be used in a corporate environment. Understand how these benefits, like remote wipe, can help you protect corporate data.

Understand Intune Connectors.   Understand Microsoft Intune Connectors allow Microsoft Intune to work with software within a network. The connector allows the cloud based software to communicate properly with the infrastructure based software.

Know how to setup Intune Alerts.   Understand each type of Intune alerts and which alerts are important to fix immediately or which alerts just are giving you information. Understand how to setup notifications for each alert type.

Understand Intune MAM and WIP.   Understand Microsoft Intune Mobile Application Management (MAM) and Windows Information Protection (WIP) and how these tools can help you manage and protect applications.

Know how to work with Intune Reports.   Understand that the different Reports help an administrator monitor the status of Intune managed devices. These Reports give you information on the status of software updates, software installed, and certificate compliance. Understand how reports also let you examine the inventory of your network's hardware and software.

Review Questions

1. You are the network administrator for your organization. Your users use both desktops and tablets to access the network. Your tablet users use a 4G mobile broadband Wi-Fi connection. You need to watch how much data your users are using on this connection. How do you do that?

    A. Configure the broadband connection as a metered network.

    B. Turn on network resource monitoring.

    C. Enable performance monitoring.

    D. Enable tablet metering in the tablets settings.

2. You manage 1,000 Windows 10 computers. All of the computers are enrolled in Microsoft Intune. You manage the servicing channel settings by using Intune. What should you do if you want to review the servicing status of a computer?

    A. From Device configuration-Profiles, view the device status.

    B. From Device compliance, view the device compliance.

    C. From Software updates, view the audit logs.

    D. From Software updates, view the Per update ring deployment state.

3. You are the IT Manager of a large manufacturing company. Sales personnel are allowed to bring their own personal Windows 10 devices to the office. The company allows the sales people to install company software and use their devices to retrieve company mail by using the management infrastructure agent. One of your sales people reports that their Windows 10 laptop was stolen while at the airport. You need to make sure that no one can steal any of the corporate data or access any corporate emails. Which two actions should you perform? Each correct answer presents part of the solution. (Choose two.)

    A. Prevent the computer from connecting to the corporate wireless network.

    B. Remove the computer from the management infrastructure.

    C. Reset the user's password.

    D. Do a remote wipe on the user's laptop.

4. You are the IT Director for a large school system. The school has decided that students can bring in their own devices to do school work with. Your organization uses Microsoft Azure Active Directory and Intune for all of the student's applications and network authentication. You need to be sure that students that are using iPads as well as Windows 10 devices have full access. What do you need to do to be sure that all iOS devices can get access?

    A. Add a Student Portal app from the Apple App Store.

    B. Create a device enrollment manager account.

    C. Configure an Intune Service Connector for Exchange.

    D. Import an Apple Push Notification service (APNs) certificate.

5. You have 200 Windows 10 computers that are joined to Microsoft Azure Active Directory (AD) and enrolled in Microsoft Intune. You want to enable self-service password reset on the sign-in screen. Which settings should you configure from the Microsoft Intune blade?

    A. Device configuration

    B. Device compliance

    C. Device enrollment

    D. Conditional access

6. You are the IT Manager for WillPanek.com. The company has an Active Directory domain and a cloud based Azure Active Directory. The two are synchronized together by using the Azure Active Directory Synchronization Tool. The company also uses System Center Configuration Manager. You need to use Configuration Manager to manage devices registered with Intune. What do you need to do to accomplish this? (Choose two.)

    A. Create a new device enrollment manager account in Microsoft Intune.

    B. In Microsoft Intune, configure an Active Directory Connector.

    C. Configure the Microsoft Intune Connector role in Configuration Manager.

    D. Create the Microsoft Intune subscription in Configuration Manager.

7. Your company has a Microsoft Azure subscription. All the users in the marketing department use their own personal devices that run either iOS or Android based systems. All the devices are enrolled in Microsoft Intune. The company has developed a new mobile application named App1 for the Marketing department. You need to ensure that only the Marketing department users can download App1. What should you do first?

    A. Add App1 to Intune.

    B. Add App1 to a local server for users to use.

    C. Add App1 to Microsoft Store.

    D. Configure the iOS and Android systems to use the new application.

8. You are the IT director for a large company that has decided to move to the cloud. The company wants to use Azure Active Directory and Microsoft Intune. The company has been looking into this because users have been using multiple devices to get their job done. When your users get added to Intune and get licensed, how many devices can each user add by default?

    A. 4

    B. 10

    C. 15

    D. None. Device Administrators are the only person who can add devices to Intune.

9. You are the administrator of a company that builds its own applications. You have decided that you want to install a company application to all employees by using the Windows Store. Which term is used to refer to installing corporate apps through the Windows Store?

    A. WS Installations

    B. BranchCache

    C. Image Installation

    D. Sideloading

10. You are the IT Director for Stormwind training studios. Your company has decided to start using Microsoft Intune for all of their software deployments. You want to set up a notification system so that you see all alerts and your IT Manager only gets notified for Critical alerts. How do you accomplish this? Choose all that apply.

A. Setup all event notifications for the IT Manager in Intune.

B. Setup all event notifications for the IT Director in Intune.

C. Setup Critical event notifications for the IT Manager in Intune.

D. Setup Critical event notifications for the IT Director in Intune.

Chapter

12

Managing Security

MICROSOFT EXAM OBJECTIVES COVERED IN THIS CHAPTER:

✓ **Manage Windows Defender**

- Implement and manage Windows Defender Application Guard; implement and manage Windows Defender Credential Guard; implement and manage Windows Defender Exploit Guard; implement Windows Defender Advanced Threat Protection; integrate Windows Defender Application Control; manage Windows Defender Antivirus, Deploy and update applications

In this chapter, I am going to talk about defending your Windows 10 system directly by using the built-in security features of Windows Defender Security Center. I will show you the different ways that you can protect your system using the Defender Security Center options.

I will show you how to protect your Windows 10 devices by using the Windows 10 Firewall. The Windows 10 Firewall can help protect your client systems from being illegally breached, but when you're building a network, your Windows Firewall should NOT be your only firewall. Your network connection to the Internet should also be protected by some type of firewall, but that is an entirely different course (depending on your firewall type).

I am also going to dive into protecting Windows 10 and also using Azure to help protect your network. Windows 10 offers protection like Windows Firewall and Azure offers organizations multiple ways to protect devices and data by using Azure tools like Windows Defender Application Guard, Windows Defender Advanced Threat Protection, and Windows Defender Antivirus.

So let's get started by looking at protecting your Windows 10 devices by using Windows Firewall.

Managing Windows Security

Windows 10 includes built-in Windows Security (see Figure 12.1), which includes antivirus protection. Windows 10 devices are automatically protected from the very moment that your users start using Windows 10. Windows 10 Security is always scanning the system for viruses, malware (malicious software), and security dangers. Not only does Windows 10 provide real-time protection, Microsoft continually does updates to make sure that your corporate devices stay safe and that the devices are protected from any new threats.

FIGURE 12.1   Windows 10 Security dialog box

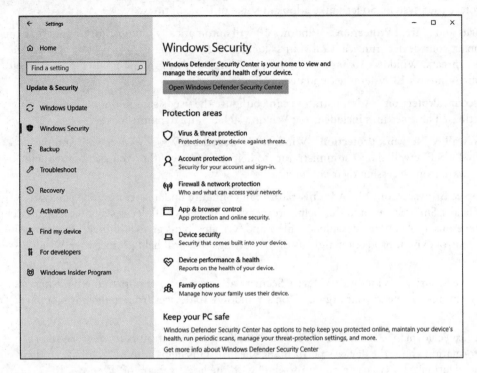

Windows Defender Security Center

Windows 10 includes the Windows Defender Security Center (see Figure 12.2). The Windows Defender Security Center is a built-in Windows 10 application that protects your system from viruses and spyware. It is included free with the operating system, and once you turn your operating system on, Windows Defender starts automatically protecting your system.

FIGURE 12.2   Windows Defender Security Center

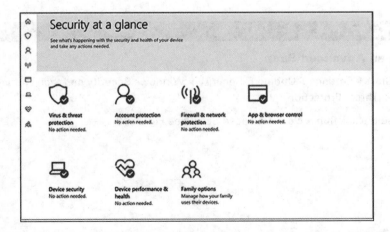

The Windows Defender Security Center has multiple options that you can set to help protect your system. So let's take a look at some of these options.

Virus and Threat Protection   Windows 10 will automatically monitor for threats that can impact your device, run scans on your system, and get updates to help protect against any new threats. Windows 10 has an antivirus built in and it will get automatic updates when your Windows 10 systems get updated.

Account Protection   Administrators can configure the user's sign-in options and account settings. These settings include using Windows Hello and dynamic lock.

Firewall & Network Protection   Windows 10 includes a Windows Firewall, and the Windows Firewall allows administrators to help prevent unauthorized users or malicious software from accessing their computer.

App & Browser Control   Administrators can configure update settings for Windows Defender SmartScreen and this helps protect your Windows 10 devices against potentially dangerous applications, downloads, files, and websites. This gives administrators the ability to control exploit protection and customize settings that will help protect your Windows 10 devices.

Device Security   Windows 10 Device Security allows administrators to use built-in security options to defend your organization's Windows 10 devices from malicious software attacks.

Device Performance & Health   Windows 10 allows administrators to view the status information about the device's performance health. This helps administrators keep their organization's devices clean and up-to-date with the latest version of Windows 10.

Family Options   The Family Options feature in Windows Security is not a feature that most administrators will configure in a corporate environment. These options provide tools to help manage children's computer access. Parents can use Family Options to help keep their children's devices clean and up-to-date with the latest version of Windows 10 and to protect their children when they are on the Internet.

In Exercise 12.1, I will show you how to run an advanced virus and threat scan on your Windows 10 device.

EXERCISE 12.1

Running an Advanced Scan

1. Click Start ➢ Settings ➢ Update & Security ➢ Windows Security and then choose Virus & Threat Protection.

2. Choose the link Run A New Advanced Scan (see Figure 12.3).

FIGURE 12.3   Run A New Advanced Scan link

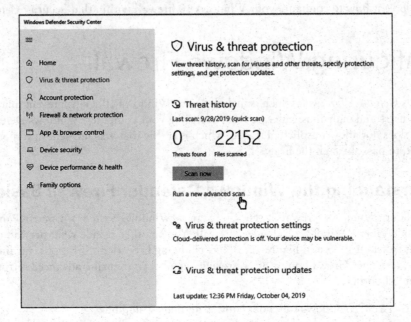

3.   Make sure the radio button is on Full Scan and click the Scan Now button (see Figure 12.4).

FIGURE 12.4   Advanced scan options

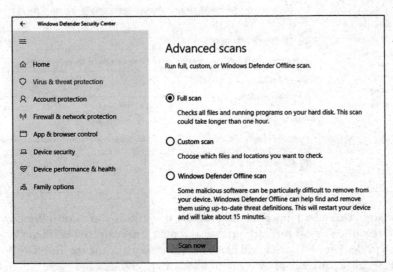

4.   The scan will take a while. After the scan finishes, close the Defender Security Center.

Now that you understand how to work with the Windows 10 Security Center, let's take a closer look at how to configure your Windows 10 firewall within that Security Center.

Configuring Windows Firewall

Windows Defender Firewall, which is included with Windows 10, helps prevent unauthorized users and malicious software from accessing your computer. Windows Defender Firewall does not allow unsolicited traffic, which is traffic that was not sent in response to a request, to pass through the firewall.

Understanding the Windows Defender Firewall Basics

You configure Windows Firewall by clicking Start ➤ Windows System ➤ Control Panel ➤ Large Icons View ➤ Windows Defender Firewall. You can then decide what firewall options you want to set (as shown in Figure 12.5), like changing firewall notifications, turning the Windows Defender Firewall on or off, restoring defaults, configuring advanced settings, and troubleshooting.

FIGURE 12.5 Windows Defender Firewall settings dialog box

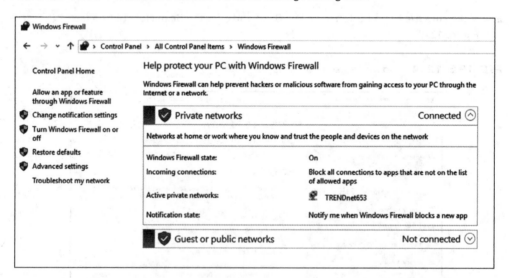

The Windows Defender Firewall settings dialog box allows you to turn Windows Defender Firewall on or off for both private and public networks. The Turn On Windows Defender Firewall setting will block incoming sources, and the Turn Off Windows Defender Firewall setting will allow incoming sources to connect.

There is also a check box for Block All Incoming Connections, Including Those In The List Of Allowed Apps. This feature allows you to connect to networks that are not secure. When Block All Incoming Connections is enabled, all incoming connections (even ones allowed in the allowed apps list) will be blocked by Windows Defender Firewall.

Windows Firewall with Advanced Security

You can configure more-advanced settings by configuring Windows Defender Firewall with Advanced Security. To do so, right-click Start and choose Windows System ➤ Control Panel ➤ Large Icons View ➤ Windows Defender Firewall ➤ Advanced Settings. The Windows Defender Firewall With Advanced Security dialog box appears, as shown in Figure 12.6.

FIGURE 12.6   Windows Defender Firewall With Advanced Security

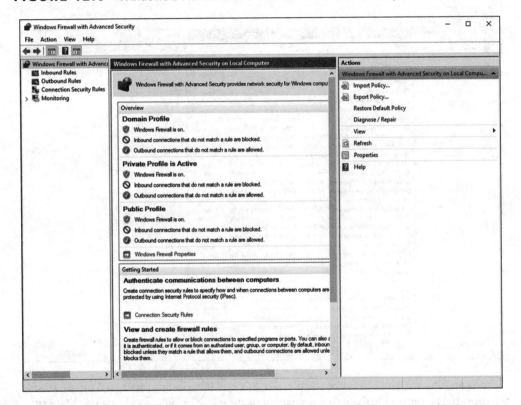

The scope pane to the left shows that you can set up specific inbound and outbound rules, connection security rules, and monitoring rules. The central area shows an overview of the firewall's status when no rule is selected in the left pane. When a rule is selected, the

central area shows the rule's settings. The right pane shows the same actions as the Action menu on the top. These are just shortcuts to the different actions that can be performed in Windows Firewall. Let's take a more detailed look at some of the elements in Windows Defender Firewall.

Inbound and Outbound Rules

Inbound and outbound rules consist of many preconfigured rules that can be enabled or disabled. Obviously, inbound rules (see Figure 12.7) monitor inbound traffic and outbound rules monitor outbound traffic. By default, many are disabled. Double-clicking a rule will bring up its Properties dialog box (Figure 12.8).

FIGURE 12.7 Inbound rules

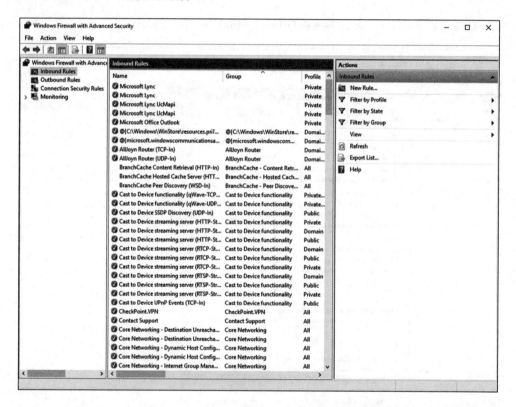

You can filter the rules to make them easier to view. Filtering can be based on the profile the rule affects, on whether the rule is enabled or disabled, or on the rule group. You can filter a rule by clicking which filter type you want to use in the right pane or by clicking the Actions menu on the top of the screen.

FIGURE 12.8   An inbound rule's Properties dialog box

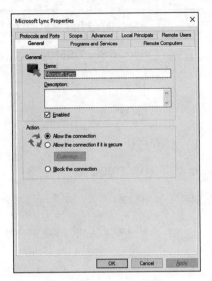

If you can't find a rule that is appropriate for your needs, you can create a new rule by right-clicking Inbound Rules or Outbound Rules in the scope pane and then selecting New Rule. The New Inbound (or Outbound) Rule Wizard will launch, and you will be asked whether you want to create a rule based on a particular program, protocol or port, pre-defined category, or custom settings.

As you are setting up the firewall rules, you have the ability to configure authenticated exceptions. No matter how well your system security is set up, there are almost always times when computers on your network can't use IPsec. This is when you set up authenticated exceptions. It's important to understand that when you set up these authenticated exceptions, you are reducing the security of the network because it allows computers to send unprotected IPsec network traffic. So make sure that the computers that are added to the authenticated exceptions list are managed and trusted computers only. Table 12.1 shows you some of the most common port numbers and what those port numbers are used for.

TABLE 12.1   Common Port Numbers

Port Number	Associated Application or Service
20	FTP Data
21	FTP Control

TABLE 12.1 Common Port Numbers *(continued)*

Port Number	Associated Application or Service
22	Secure Shell (SSH)
23	Telnet
25	SMTP
53	DNS
67/68	DHCP/BOOTP
80	HTTP
102	Microsoft Exchange Server
110	POP3
443	HHTPS (HTTP with SSL)

Complete Exercise 12.2 to create a new inbound rule that will allow only encrypted TCP traffic.

EXERCISE 12.2

Creating a New Inbound Rule

1. Right-click Start ➤ Windows System ➤ Control Panel ➤ Large Icon View ➤ Windows Defender Firewall.

2. Click Advanced Settings on the left side.

3. Right-click Inbound Rules and select New Rule.

4. Choose a rule type. For this exercise, choose Custom so you can see all the options available to you. Then click Next.

5. At the Program screen, choose All Programs. Then click Next.

6. Choose the protocol type as well as the local and remote port numbers that are affected by this rule. For this exercise, choose TCP, and ensure that All Ports is selected for both Local Port and Remote Port. Click Next to continue.

7. At the Scope screen, choose Any IP Address for both local and remote. Then click Next.

8. At the Action screen, choose Allow The Connection Only If It Is Secure. Click Next.

9. At the Users screen, you can experiment with these options if you want by entering users to both sections. Once you click one of the check boxes, the Add and Remove buttons become available. Click Next to continue.

10. At the Computers screen, you can choose what computers you will authorize or allow through this rule (exceptions). Again, you can experiment with these options if you want. Click Next to continue.

11. At the Profiles screen, choose which profiles will be affected by this rule. Select one or more profiles and click Next.

12. Give your profile a name and description, and then click Finish. Your custom rule will appear in the list of inbound rules, and the rule will be enabled.

13. Double-click your newly created rule. Notice that you can change the options that you previously configured.

14. Delete the rule by right-clicking the new rule and choosing Delete. A dialog box will appear asking you if you are sure. Click Yes.

15. Close the Windows Defender Firewall.

Connection Security Rules

Connection security rules are used to configure how and when authentication occurs. These rules do not specifically allow connections; that's the job of inbound and outbound rules. You can configure the following connection security rules:

- Isolation: To restrict a connection based on authentication criteria
- Authentication Exemption: To specify computers that are exempt from authentication requirements
- Server-to-Server: To authenticate connections between computers
- Tunnel: To authenticate connections between gateway computers
- Custom

Monitoring

The Monitoring section shows detailed information about the firewall configurations for the Domain Profile, Private Profile, and Public Profile settings. These network location profiles determine what settings are enforced for private networks, public networks, and networks connected to a domain.

Real World Scenario

Use More Than Just Windows Defender Firewall

When doing consulting, it always makes me laugh when I see small to midsize companies using Microsoft Windows Defender Firewall and no other protection. Microsoft Windows Defender Firewall should be your *last* line of defense. You need to make sure that you have good hardware firewalls that separate your network from the world.

Also watch Windows Defender Firewall when it comes to printing. I have run into many situations where a printer that needs to communicate with the operating system has issues when Windows Defender Firewall is enabled. If this happens, make sure that the printer is allowed in the Allowed Programs section of the Windows Defender Firewall.

Datacenter Firewall

Firewalls allow an administrator to set up policies on who or what can be allowed past the firewall. For example, if you want to allow DNS traffic to pass through the firewall, you would enable port 53. If you want the traffic to leave the firewall, you would configure port 53 outbound. If you want to have the traffic enter into the company, you would configure inbound.

Datacenter Firewalls were introduced with Windows Server 2016 network layer, Stateful, multitenant firewalls. Network administrators that work with virtual network tenants can install and then configure firewall policies. These firewall policies can help protect their virtual networks from unwanted traffic from Internet and intranet networks.

The Datacenter Firewall allows you to set up granular access control lists (ACLs) and this allows you to apply firewall policies at the VM interface level or at the subnet level. To create ACLs on the Datacenter Firewall, an administrator can use Windows PowerShell.

The following is an example of the PowerShell command that is used to assign the ACL to the AccessControlList property of the network interface.

```
$nic.properties.ipconfigurations[0].properties.AccessControlList = $acl
```

Windows Server 2016/2019 Datacenter Firewall gives you the following tenant benefits.

- Administrators have the ability to define firewall rules that help protect Internet-facing workloads on virtual networks.

- Administrators have the ability to define firewall rules to protect data between virtual machines on the same Layer 2 or different Layer 2 virtual subnets.

- Administrators have the ability to define firewall rules to protect and isolate network traffic between tenants on a virtual network from a service provider.

So now that we have taken a look at Windows Defender Firewall, let's now look at protecting your Windows 10 devices by using Azure.

Managing Security

Another way that you can help defend your corporate devices is by using Microsoft Azure. Azure has many different tools that allow an administrator to control and protect the company's Windows 10 devices.

Earlier in the chapter, I talked about using the Windows Defender Security Center. Now we are going to look at using Windows Defender in Azure.

Implementing Azure Windows Defender Advanced Threat Protection

When talking about Windows Defender, it can be a little confusing to people. The reason for this is that Windows 10 has come with Windows Defender and Azure also now comes with Windows Defender. So when IT people are discussing Defender, it's important that they specify which version they are talking about. I am going to talk about Azure's version of Windows Defender and the benefits that it provides to organizations.

Your organization's IT department can have even better threat protection when they combine Azure Windows Defender Advanced Threat Protection (Windows Defender ATP) with Azure Advanced Threat Protection (Azure ATP), as shown in Figure 12.9. Figure 12.9 was taken directly from Microsoft's website and it shows all of the different ways Azure ATP and Windows Defender ATP can work together.

FIGURE 12.9 Inbound rules

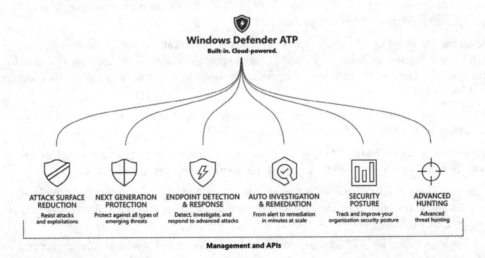

Azure ATP allows organizations to monitor domain controller traffic while Windows Defender ATP allows organizations to monitor endpoints (for example, user's devices).

Organizations can use both of these defenses together for the best possible protection and both of can be managed by using a single Azure interface.

When deciding to integrate Azure ATP and Windows Defender ATP together, you get the benefits of both systems working together. Some of these benefits include:

Endpoint Behavioral Sensors   Endpoint behavioral sensors are sensors that are built into the Windows 10 operating system and these sensors gather and process behavioral data for things like the registry, files, processors, and communications. This data is then sent to the Windows Defender ATP.

Azure ATP Sensors and Stand-Alone Sensors   These sensors can be placed directly onto your domain controllers or they can be set up to port mirror directly from your domain controller to Azure ATP. These sensors have the ability to collect and parse traffic for multiple protocols that work with authentication, or authorization or just for informational gathering.

Threat Intelligence   Threat intelligence is comprised of multiple Microsoft tools, security groups, and third party threat defending partners. Threat intelligence allows Windows Defender ATP to properly recognize tools and activities that hackers use and then report alerts when those tools or activities are observed.

Cloud Security Analytics   Cloud security analytics uses multiple detection signals and Microsoft insights to detect and recommend protection against advanced threats.

Azure ATP uses multiple technologies to detect suspicious behavior during all phases of a cyber based attack. These phases include:

The Investigation Phase (Reconnaissance)   This is the phase where hackers gather information on a target organization. This phase can include information gathering by using Internet investigation, dumpster diving, etc.

Scanning Phase   This phase is when an attacker tries to scan for vulnerabilities. These can be port scanners (looking for open ports to access), vulnerability scanning (looking for known vulnerabilities), and network scanning (looking at network components like routers and firewalls).

Access Phase   This is the phase when hackers try to gain access to your network based on the investigation phase and scanning phase.

Maintaining Access Phase   This is the phase when hackers try to put back doors or software in place so that the hackers can continue to gain access to your network.

Clearing Their Tracks Phase   Hackers that are any good will try to clear their tracks so that no one knows that they were there. This is when hackers will try to delete logs and any evidence that the hack even took place.

Windows Defender ATP uses Microsoft technologies and expertise to help detect and stop the different phases of a hacker. By using their experience, Microsoft has put in advanced methods to detect hacking before the hacks take place.

Understanding Windows Defender Application Guard

One of the biggest issues that we have in IT is the Internet. It's a world game changer and a company game changer. But that also means it's an IT game changer. We in IT have to rethink how we protect our networks and that's because of the Internet.

Years ago, hackers had to use phone lines, and that helped prevent a lot of hacker wannabes. Phone lines were easy to track, and it could be expensive for a young hacker to spend a lot of money on phone calls. Especially, if they were unsuccessful with their hacks.

Today, anyone can hack from anywhere because of the World Wide Web and they pay only a monthly fee for Internet access. So we must rethink how we protect our data and our companies. This is where Application Guard can help us.

Application Guard was specifically designed for Windows 10 and Microsoft Internet browsers (Edge & Internet Explorer). Application Guard works with Windows Edge to isolate untrusted web sites, thus protecting your organizations network and data while users are working on the Internet.

As an Enterprise Administrator, you can pick and choose which websites are defined as trusted sites. These sites can be internal websites, external websites, company websites, and cloud based organizations. If a site is not on the trusted list, it is then considered untrusted and automatically isolated when a user visits the site.

When a user accesses a website (using Edge or IE) that is not on the trusted list, Microsoft Edge will be automatically opened in an isolated Hyper-V enabled container. This container will be a separate environment from the host operating system and this will help protect untrusted websites from causing damage to the Windows 10 system. Also since the website will be isolated, any type of attack will not affect the corporate network or its data.

Windows Defender Application Guard is disabled by default. Windows Defender Application Guard works in two modes: Standalone or Enterprise. Standalone mode allows a non-corporate user to use Windows Defender Application Guard without any administrator configured policies. Enterprise mode is used in an enterprise environment and can be configured automatically by the Enterprise Administrator.

Windows Defender Application Guard Standalone Mode

If a user wants to use Standalone mode, they need to be using either Windows 10 Enterprise edition (version 1709 or higher) or Windows 10 Pro edition (version 1803). The user must install Application Guard manually on their Windows 10 device and then they need to manually start Microsoft Edge in Application Guard while they are browsing untrusted sites.

Exercise 12.3 will show you how to install Windows Defender Application Guard using the Windows 10 Control Panel.

EXERCISE 12.3

Installing Windows Defender Application Guard

1. Right-click Start ➢ Windows System ➢ Control Panel ➢ Large Icon View ➢ Programs And Features.

2. Click the link Turn Windows Features On Or Off.

3. Scroll down and check the box for Windows Defender Application Guard (shown in Figure 12.10) and then click the OK button.

FIGURE 12.10 Installing Windows Defender Application Guard

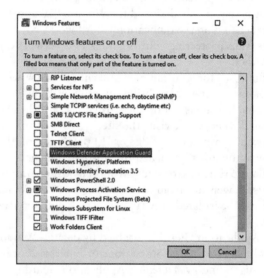

4. After Windows Defender Application Guard installs, close Control Panel.

Users can also install Windows Defender Application Guard by using PowerShell. To do this, you need to right-click on PowerShell and choose the top option, Run As Administrator (see Figure 12.11).

FIGURE 12.11 Opening PowerShell as an administrator

Once you are in the PowerShell window, you want to run the following PowerShell command and then you need to restart the Windows 10 device:

```
Enable-WindowsOptionalFeature -online -FeatureName Windows-Defender-
ApplicationGuard
```

In Exercise 12.4, I will show you how to use Windows Defender Application Guard in Standalone mode. I will be using Windows 10 and Microsoft Edge for this exercise. To complete this exercise, you must complete Exercise 12.3 and install Windows Defender Application Guard on your Windows 10 device.

EXERCISE 12.4

Using Windows Defender Application Guard

1. Open Microsoft Edge.

2. From the options menu, choose New Application Guard Window (see Figure 12.12).

FIGURE 12.12 New Application Guard Window option

3. You will need to wait for Application Guard to set up the isolated environment (see Figure 12.13). This may take a few moments.

FIGURE 12.13   Application Guard starting screen

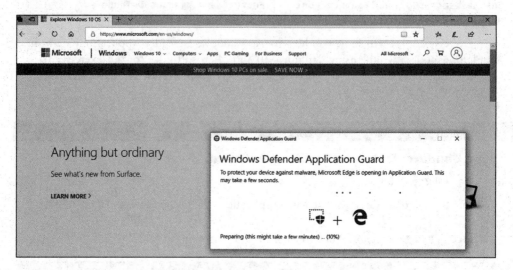

4.   As you can see in Figure 12.14, I opened Microsoft's website in Application Guard mode and you can see that in the upper left hand corner of the window. Close Edge.

FIGURE 12.14   Microsoft's website in Application Guard mode

Windows Defender Application Guard Enterprise Mode

Windows Defender Application Guard in the enterprise environment is not much different for the user as in Standalone mode. The main difference is that the Enterprise Administrator configures the Windows Defender Application Guard application. The Enterprise Administrator sets up and configures the application. When a user accesses an untrusted website, Windows Defender Application Guard automatically starts.

So let's take a look at some of the enterprise based systems will benefit from Windows Defender Application Guard:

Enterprise Desktops and Laptops   Enterprise desktops are machines that are joined to your domain and they are managed by your company's administrators. Enterprise Administrators can configure Windows Defender Application Guard through System Center Configuration Manager or Microsoft Intune with Enterprise Mobility + Security (EMS).

Microsoft Intune is now called Microsoft Intune with Enterprise Mobility + Security (EMS). For the rest of the chapter, I will refer to it as just Intune. There is no reason to add the "with Enterprise Mobility + Security (EMS)" every time we mention Intune.

Bring Your Own Device (BYOD) Laptops   Normally organizations that allow users to use their own devices for company business need to follow company rules. So these devices are normally managed by the Enterprise Administrators through Intune. If a user wants to use a personal device but they don't want to follow corporate rules, most companies won't allow the use of the personal device.

In Exercise 12.5, I will show you how to use Windows Defender Application Guard in Enterprise mode. Before your organization can use Application Guard in Enterprise mode, administrators must install Windows 10 Enterprise edition (version 1709 or higher) on their corporate network or the needed functionality will not work.

EXERCISE 12.5

Windows Defender Application Guard Enterprise

1. Install Application Guard using either a Group Policy Object, System Center, or Mobile Device Management (MDM).

2. In a Group Policy, set the Network Isolation settings that you want followed (see Figure 12.15). To set this option, in your GPO editor go to Administrative Templates\ Network\Network Isolation\Enterprise Resource Domains Hosted In The Cloud setting.

FIGURE 12.15 Network Isolation GPO

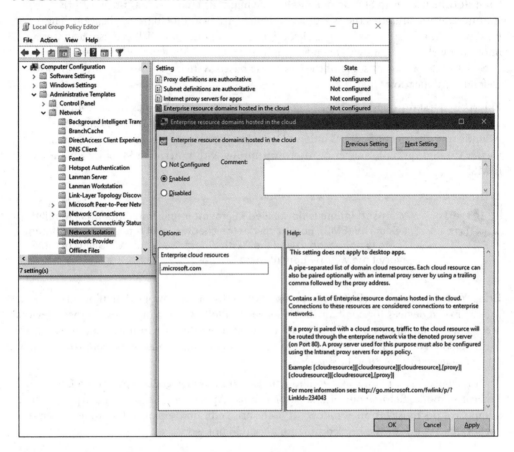

3. Next, go to Administrative Templates\Network\Network Isolation\Domains Categorized As Both Work And Personal setting. Enter in the websites that you trust.

4. Next, go to Computer Configuration\Administrative Templates\Windows Components\Windows Defender Application Guard\Turn On Windows Defender Application Guard In Enterprise Mode setting.

5. Click the Enabled radio button, choose Option 1 (see Figure 12.16), and click OK.

FIGURE 12.16   Turn On Windows Defender Application Guard In Enterprise Mode setting

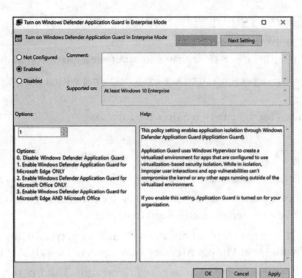

6. Close the GPO editor.

Understanding Windows Defender Credential Guard

Windows Server 2016 and Windows 10 Enterprise introduced a new security measure called Windows Defender Credential Guard. Windows Defender Credential Guard is a virtualization-based security to help isolate critical files so that only system software that is privileged can access those critical files.

Once it's enabled, a Windows 10 machine that is part of Active Directory or Azure Active Directory will have the system's credentials protected by Windows Defender Credential Guard.

After an administrator enables Windows Defender Credential Guard, the Local Security Authority (LSA) process in the operating system works with a new component named the isolated LSA. The isolated process stores and protects the system's critical data.

Once data is stored by the isolated LSA process, the system then uses the virtualization-based security to protect the data and that data is no longer accessible to the rest of the operating system.

To enable Windows Defender Credential Guard, the following requirements should be met:

- Machine must support virtualization-based security (required)
- Secure boot (required)
- TPM 1.2 or 2.0, either discrete or firmware (preferred, provides binding to hardware)
- UEFI lock (preferred, prevents attacker from disabling with a simple registry key change)

The virtualization-based security requires the following:

- 64-bit CPU
- CPU virtualization extensions plus extended page tables
- Windows hypervisor (does not require Hyper-V Windows Feature to be installed)

If an administrator wants to use Windows Defender Credential Guard in a Hyper-V virtual machine, the following requirements need to be met:

- The Windows 10 (version 1607 or higher) or Windows Server 2016/2019 system must have Hyper-V with Input Output Memory Management Unit (IOMMU).
- The Hyper-V virtual machine must be set as Generation 2 and virtual TPM needs to be enabled.

Once administrators have met the minimum requirements for setting up Windows Defender Credential Guard, they can enable it by either using the Windows Defender Device Guard hardware readiness tool or Group Policy Objects or directly in the Registry.

In Exercise 12.6, I will show you how to enable Windows Defender Credential Guard using a Group Policy Object.

EXERCISE 12.6

Windows Defender Credential Guard

1. Open the Group Policy Management editor on Windows Server 2016.

2. Create a new GPO and click the GPO and choose Edit.

3. Go to Computer Configuration ➢ Administrative Templates ➢ System ➢ Device Guard.

4. Double click the option Turn On Virtualization Based Security and then choose the Enabled option (see Figure 12.17).

5. In the Turn On Virtualization Based Security option, select Platform Security Level box, choose either Secure Boot or Secure Boot and DMA Protection.

FIGURE 12.17   Turn On Virtualization Based Security setting

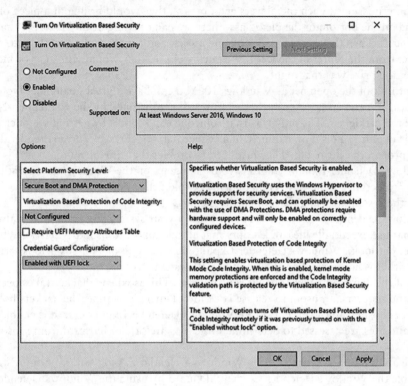

6. In the Credential Guard Configuration box, click Enabled with UEFI lock, and then click the OK button.

7. Close the Group Policy Management Console.

Implementing and Managing Windows Defender Exploit Guard

Another way that Microsoft has started protecting systems is by using Windows Defender Exploit Guard. Windows Defender Exploit Guard helps protect your Windows 10 system against malware, ransomware, and other types of attacks. It does this by reducing the attack surface of a device.

So does it mean when someone says that they are reducing the attack surface of a system? The way I always explain it is in this way. I am a huge hockey fan. When I lived in NJ, I used to go to dozens of hockey games.

Now think of a hockey net (or soccer net) as the Windows system. During one of the hockey intermissions (when the players get a break), they would bring out a piece of plexiglass and on the bottom of the plexiglass, there was an opening just a bit bigger than a hockey puck. Then they would give someone a stick and a puck and allow them to shoot at the net from the center of the ice. If the puck went in, they would win a car or money or whatever the prize was that night.

Now think of the open net as Windows 10. You can have a great goaltender (your firewall) but if someone is good enough, they can still get the puck by the goaltender. Now think of the plexiglass. The only way that someone can score is by getting the puck in that tiny little opening. This is an example of a reduced attack surface. The goaltender doesn't need to protect the entire net. They just need to protect that tiny opening.

Windows Defender Exploit Guard is your plexiglass on the Windows 10 operating system. By protecting common ways that hackers exploit the system, the hackers now have to get into the system by using that tiny little opening.

Windows Defender Exploit Guard helps protect your system from common malware hacks that use executable files and scripts that attack applications like Microsoft Office (for example, Outlook). Windows Defender Exploit Guard also looks for suspicious scripts or behavior that is not normal on the Windows 10 system.

One of the common hacks today is ransomware. This is when a hacker takes over your system and requests a ransom to release your files. During this time, the hackers hold your documents hostage until you pay. Once Windows Defender Exploit Guard is enabled, folders and files are assessed to determine if the files are safe or harmful from ransomware threats.

There are multiple ways to turn on Windows Defender Exploit Guard. Administrators can enable the Windows Defender Credential Guard by using the Windows Defender Security Center, a Group Policy Object, System Center Configuration Manager (SCCM), or Mobile Device Management (MDM) using Microsoft Intune with EMS.

In Exercise 12.7, I will show you how to enable Windows Defender Exploit Guard using the Windows Defender Security Center.

EXERCISE 12.7

Windows Defender Exploit Guard

1. Open the Settings center by clicking on the Start button and clicking on the Settings (the spoke) icon.

2. Choose Update and Security.

3. Click on Windows Security and choose Virus and threat protection.

4. Choose Ransomware Protection and make sure the setting is turned on (see Figure 12.18).

FIGURE 12.18   Turn On Ransomware setting

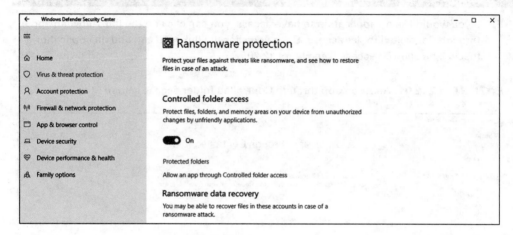

5. Click on Protected folders (see Figure 12.19) to see what folders are currently protected. You can click on the + Add a protected folder to add additional folders.

FIGURE 12.19   Protected Folders screen

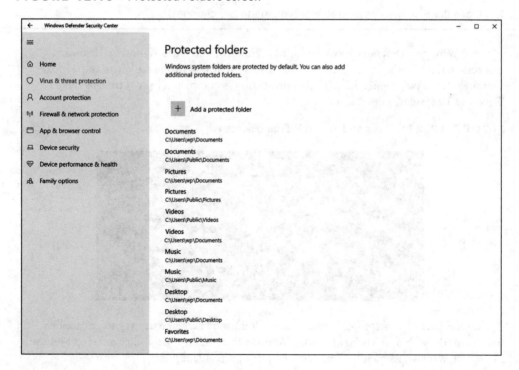

6. If you would like an application to have access, you can click on the link Allow an app through Controlled folder access. Once you click the link, you can add an application that will be allowed access (see Figure 12.20).

FIGURE 12.20 Allow an app through Controlled folder access screen

7. Close the Security Center (reboot if you made any changes).

Once Windows Defender Exploit Guard is enabled, when the Windows 10 system suspects that a file is a danger, the Windows 10 system will display a Virus and Threat Warning screen (see Figure 12.21). This protection is completed in real time as the Windows 10 system is operating.

FIGURE 12.21 Virus and Threat Warning screen

Another part of controlling application exploitation is when users try to get applications from the web and Microsoft Store. Administrators have the ability to setup and use Microsoft Windows Defender SmartScreen (see Figure 12.22).

FIGURE 12.22   Windows Defender Smart Screen

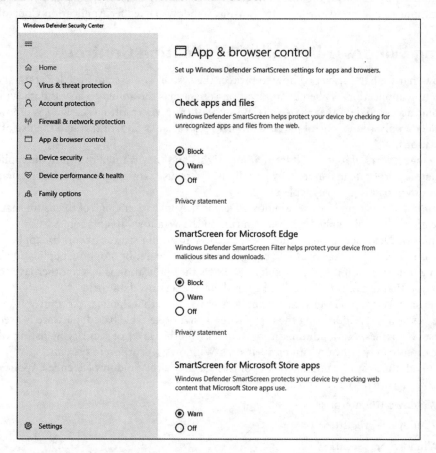

Windows Defender SmartScreen helps administrators protect their employees when they try to visit websites that have previously been reported as phishing or malware websites. Windows Defender SmartScreen also helps Windows 10 if an employee tries to download potentially malicious files.

SmartScreen allows Windows 10 to determine if a downloaded application or an application installer that may be potentially malicious. It does this by:

- Looking at downloaded files and seeing if those files are on a list of known malicious software sites or if programs that are being downloaded are known to be unsafe. If any file or program is on these lists, SmartScreen will prompt the user with a warning to let that user know that the data or site might be malicious.

- When a user downloads a file or program that isn't on the list, SmartScreen will show the user a warning prompt, to just advise caution.

Another way that your organization can help protect their users against downloading applications that are possibly harmful is using Windows Defender Application Control.

Using Windows Defender Application Control

So now that we have discussed how to protect the system and system files, let's talk about protecting applications. When an application runs, it has the ability to access data with the same access to data that a user has. Because of this, Microsoft has created Windows Defender Application Control (WDAC) to help stop attacks of data through the use of applications.

For many years, if a user had local admin rights and they wanted to install an application onto a corporate machine, they just did it. Users just assume that applications that they buy or download is just trustworthy.

Administrators can now use Windows Defender Application Control to ensure that only applications that you explicitly allow can run on the Windows 10 computers.

Windows Defender Application Control allows an administrator to control applications and this is a big advantage over just using antivirus software. By stopping applications from running unless an administrator explicitly allows the application is just another layer of protection that organizations can utilize in their war against data theft.

For many years, top level security analysts have stated that application control is one of the best ways for addressing the many threats that executable based malware is used against companies. Now, administrators can add another layer of security by listing what applications can specifically run on their own Windows 10 corporate systems.

If an administrator wants to create policies for use with Windows Defender Application Control, they need to meet the following system requirements:

- Windows 10 Enterprise

- Windows Server 2016

- Windows Server 2019

Administrators can configure Windows Defender Application Control through the use of a Group Policy Object or by using Mobile Device Management (MDM) and Microsoft Intune with EMS. After Windows Defender Application Control is set up, administrators can create and configure policies by using GPOs or Intune.

Summary

In this chapter, I discussed using Windows Defender Firewall with Advanced Security. Windows Defender Firewall helps prevent unauthorized users from connecting to the Windows 10 operating system. Windows Defender Firewall is an extra line of defense, but it should not replace a perimeter firewall for your network.

I also talked about protecting devices using Windows Defender Security. I talked about how your Organization's IT department can have even better threat protection when they combine Azure Windows Defender Advanced Threat Protection (Windows Defender ATP) with Azure Advanced Threat Protection (Azure ATP).

I then talked about using Windows Defender Application Guard. Application Guard was specifically designed for Windows 10 and Microsoft Internet browsers (Edge & Internet Explorer). Application Guard works with Windows Edge to isolate untrusted websites, thus protecting your organization's network and data while users are working on the Internet.

I spoke about using Windows Defender Exploit Guard and how it helps protect your Windows 10 system against malware, ransomware, and other types of attacks. It does this by reducing the attack surface of a device.

I then talked about using Windows Defender Credential Guard. Windows Defender Credential Guard is a virtualization based security to help isolate critical files so that only system software that is privileged can access those critical files.

Finally, I explained how Windows Defender Application Control allows an administrator to control applications and how administrators can stop applications from running unless an administrator explicitly allows the application.

Exam Essentials

Know how to configure Windows Defender Firewall.   Know how to set up and maintain Windows Defender Firewall with Advanced Security. Know that you can set up inbound and outbound rules by using Windows Defender Firewall. Know how to allow or deny applications by using Windows Defender Firewall.

Understand Windows Defender Application Guard.   Understand how Application Guard works with Windows Edge and Internet Explorer to isolate untrusted websites.

Know Windows Defender Credential Guard.   Know how Windows Defender Credential Guard uses virtualization-based security to help isolate critical files so that only system software with privileges can access those critical files.

Understand Windows Defender Exploit Guard.   Understand how Windows Defender Exploit Guard helps protect your Windows 10 system against malware, ransomware, and other types of attacks.

Know Windows Defender ATP.   Know and understand how to combine Azure Windows Defender Advanced Threat Protection (Windows Defender ATP) with Azure Advanced Threat Protection (Azure ATP).

Understand Windows Defender Application Control.   Understand how Windows Defender Application Control allows an administrator to control which applications are allowed on a Windows 10 system.

Review Questions

1. You are the administrator for an organization with 275 computers that all run Windows 10. These computers are all joined to Microsoft Azure Active and all computers are enrolled in Microsoft Intune with EMS. You need to make sure that only approved applications are allowed to run on all of these computers. What should you implement to ensure this?

   A. Windows Defender Credential Guard

   B. Windows Defender Exploit Guard

   C. Windows Defender Application Control

   D. Windows Defender Antivirus

2. You are the administrator of a large training company. All of your machines run Windows 10. You have a Windows 10 machine that has a virus that was caused by a malicious font. You need to stop this type of threat from affecting your corporate computers in the future. What should you use?

   A. Windows Defender Exploit Guard

   B. Windows Defender Application Guard

   C. Windows Defender Credential Guard

   D. Windows Defender System Guard

3. You are the administrator for an organization where all computers run Windows 10. You need to make sure that critical files are isolated so that only system software with privileges can access those critical files. What should you implement to ensure this?

   A. Windows Defender Credential Guard

   B. Windows Defender Exploit Guard

   C. Windows Defender Application Control

   D. Windows Defender Antivirus

4. You are the IT Director for a large school system. You need to set up inbound and outbound rules on the Windows 10 machines. What do you need to do to accomplish this?

   A. Windows Defender Credential Guard

   B. Windows Defender Exploit Guard

   C. Windows Defender Application Control

   D. Windows Defender Firewall with Advanced Security

5. You are the administrator for StormWind Studios. You are trying to set up your Windows Defender Firewall to allow DNS inbound and outbound rules. Which port number would you set up?

   A. Port 20

   B. Port 25

   C. Port 53

   D. Port 80

6. You are the IT Manager for WillPanek.com. The company has an Active Directory domain and a cloud-based Azure Active Directory. You need to protect your systems from common malware hacks that use executable files and scripts that attack applications like Microsoft Office (for example, Outlook). What do you need to do to accomplish this?

    A. Windows Defender Credential Guard

    B. Windows Defender Exploit Guard

    C. Windows Defender Application Control

    D. Windows Defender Firewall with Advanced Security

7. You are the administrator for StormWind Studios. You are trying to set up your Windows Defender Firewall to allow SMTP inbound and outbound rules. Which port number would you setup?

    A. Port 20

    B. Port 25

    C. Port 53

    D. Port 80

8. You are the administrator for a large organization and all computers run Windows 10. These computers are all joined to Microsoft Azure Active and all computers are enrolled in Microsoft Intune with EMS. You need to ensure that all applications installed on the Windows 10 systems are only applications that are approved by the IT department. What should you implement to ensure this?

    A. Windows Defender Application Control

    B. Windows Defender Credential Guard

    C. Windows Defender Exploit Guard

    D. Windows Defender Antivirus

9. You are the administrator of a large publishing company. All of your corporate machines run Windows 10. You need to ensure that no software will affect the Windows 10 machines from common malware hacks that use executable files and scripts to attack applications. What should you use?

    A. Windows Defender Application Guard

    B. Windows Defender Credential Guard

    C. Windows Defender System Guard

    D. Windows Defender Exploit Guard

10. You are the administrator for StormWind Studios. You are trying to set up your Windows Defender Firewall to allow FTP traffic. Which two port numbers would you setup?

    A. Port 20 and 21

    B. Port 25 and 53

    C. Port 53 and 80

    D. Port 80 and 443

Chapter

13

Configuring Auditing

MICROSOFT EXAM OBJECTIVES COVERED IN THIS CHAPTER:

✓ **Monitor devices**

- Monitor device health (e.g., log analytics, Windows Analytics, or other cloud-based tools); monitor device security

One of the tasks that administrators will need to do on a daily basis is fixing Windows 10 systems that are having issues.

There are many ways to determine what issues a Windows 10 system may be having, and there are many tools to help you solve the issues.

The best way to protect any Windows 10 system is to make sure the users' files are stored on a network server and backed up daily. But there may be times when you need to back up the Windows 10 system.

Windows 10 includes a full backup and restore application (Backup and Restore [Windows 7]) that allows a user or an administrator to maintain a backup copy of any of the Windows 10 component files and data files that are considered critical to the operation of their day-to-day business. In this chapter we will discuss using the Microsoft Azure Backup utility and how easy it is for your users and IT administrators to quickly and easily back up their documents to the cloud.

Finally, there will be times when an administrator needs to monitor the Windows 10 system. Sometimes, performance optimization can feel like a luxury, but it can be very important, especially if you can't get your Windows 10 system to run applications the way they are intended to run. The Windows 10 operating system has been specifically designed to keep your mission-critical applications and data accessible even in times of failures.

The most common cause of such problems is a hardware configuration issue. Poorly written device drivers and unsupported hardware can cause problems with system stability. Failed hardware components (such as system memory) may do so as well. Memory chips can be faulty, electrostatic discharge can ruin them, and other hardware issues can occur. No matter what, a problem with your memory chip spells disaster for your Windows 10 system.

Usually, third-party hardware vendors provide utility programs with their computers that can be used for performing hardware diagnostics on machines to help you find problems. These utilities are a good first step to resolving intermittent problems, but Windows 10 comes with many utilities that can help you diagnose and fix your issues.

In this chapter, I'll cover the tools and methods used for measuring performance and troubleshooting failures in Windows 10. Before you dive into the technical details, however, you should thoroughly understand what you're trying to accomplish and how you'll meet this goal.

Monitoring Windows

Because performance monitoring and optimization are vital functions in network environments of any size, Windows 10 includes several monitoring and performance tools.

Introducing Performance Monitor

The first and most useful tool is the Windows 10 *Performance Monitor*, which was designed to allow users and system administrators to monitor performance statistics for various operating system parameters. Specifically, you can collect, store, and analyze information about CPU, memory, disk, and network resources using this tool, and these are only a handful of the things you can monitor. By collecting and analyzing performance values, system administrators can identify many potential problems.

You can use Performance Monitor in the following ways:

Performance Monitor ActiveX Control   Windows 10 Performance Monitor is an ActiveX control that you can place within other applications. Examples of applications that can host the Performance Monitor control include web browsers and client programs such as Microsoft Word and Microsoft Excel. This functionality can make it easy for application developers and system administrators to incorporate Performance Monitor into their own tools and applications.

Performance Monitor MMC   For more common performance monitoring functions, you'll want to use the built-in Microsoft Management Console (MMC) version of Performance Monitor.

Data Collector Sets   Windows 10 Performance Monitor includes Data Collector Sets. This tool works with performance logs, telling Performance Monitor where the logs are stored and when a log needs to run. The Data Collector Sets also define the credentials used to run the set.

To access the Performance Monitor MMC, you open Administrative Tools and then choose Performance Monitor. This launches the Performance MMC and loads and initializes Performance Monitor with a handful of default counters.

You can choose from many different methods of monitoring performance when you are using Performance Monitor. A couple of examples are listed here:

- You can look at a snapshot of current activity for a few of the most important counters. This allows you to find areas of potential bottlenecks and monitor the load on your servers at a certain point in time.

- You can save information to a log file for historical reporting and later analysis. This type of information is useful, for example, if you want to compare the load on your servers from three months ago to the current load.

You'll get to take a closer look at this method and many others as you examine Performance Monitor in more detail.

In the following sections, you'll learn about the basics of working with the Windows 10 Performance Monitor and other performance tools. Then you'll apply these tools and techniques when you monitor the performance of your network.

> Your Performance Monitor grows as your system grows, and whenever you add services to Windows 10, you also add to what you can monitor. You should make sure that, as you install services, you take a look at what it is you can monitor.

Deciding What to Monitor

The first step in monitoring performance is to decide *what* you want to monitor. In Windows 10, the operating system and related services include hundreds of performance statistics that you can track easily. For example, you may want to monitor the processor. This is just one of many items that can be monitored. All performance statistics fall into three main categories that you can choose to measure:

Performance Objects   A *performance object* within Performance Monitor is a collection of various performance statistics that you can monitor. Performance objects are based on various areas of system resources. For example, there are performance objects for the processor and memory as well as for specific services.

Counters   *Counters* are the actual parameters measured by Performance Monitor. They are specific items that are grouped within performance objects. For example, within the Processor performance object, there is a counter for % Processor Time. This counter displays one type of detailed information about the Processor performance object (specifically, the amount of total CPU time all of the processes on the system are using). Another set of counters you can use will allow you to monitor print servers.

Instances   Some counters will have *instances*. An instance further identifies which performance parameter the counter is measuring. A simple example is a server with two CPUs. If you decide you want to monitor processor usage (using the Processor performance object)—specifically, utilization (the % Total Utilization counter)—you must still specify *which* CPU(s) you want to measure. In this example, you would have the choice of monitoring either of the two CPUs or a total value for both (using the Total instance).

To specify which performance objects, counters, and instances you want to monitor, you add them to Performance Monitor using the Add Counters dialog box. Figure 13.1 shows the various options that are available when you add new counters to monitor using Performance Monitor.

FIGURE 13.1   Adding a new Performance Monitor counter

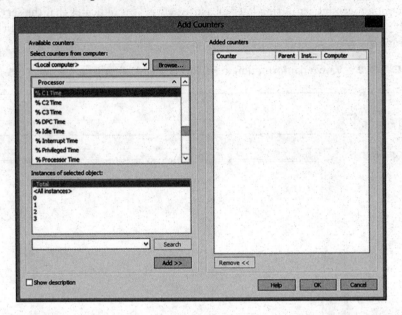

The items that you will be able to monitor will be based on your hardware and software configuration. For example, if you have not installed and configured Hyper-V, the options available within the Hyper-V Server performance object will not be available. Or, if you have multiple network adapters or CPUs on the Windows 10 system, you will have the option of viewing each instance separately or as part of the total value.

Viewing Performance Information

The Windows 10 Performance Monitor was designed to show information in a clear and easy-to-understand format. Performance objects, counters, and instances may be displayed in each of three views. This flexibility allows system administrators to quickly and easily define the information they want to see once and then choose how it will be displayed based on specific needs. Most likely, you will use only one view, but it's helpful to know what other views are available depending on what it is you are trying to assess.

You can use the following main views to review statistics and information on performance:

Graph View   The *Graph view* (sometimes referred to as the Line view) is the default display that is presented when you first access the Windows 10 Performance Monitor. The chart displays values using the vertical axis and time using the horizontal axis. This view is useful if you want to display values over a period of time or see the changes in these values over that time period. Each point that is plotted on the graph is based on an average value calculated during the sample interval for the measurement being made. For example, you may notice overall CPU utilization starting at a low value at the beginning of the chart and then becoming much higher during later measurements. This indicates that the server has become busier (specifically, with CPU-intensive processes). Figure 13.2 provides an example of the Graph view.

FIGURE 13.2   Viewing information in Performance Monitor Graph view

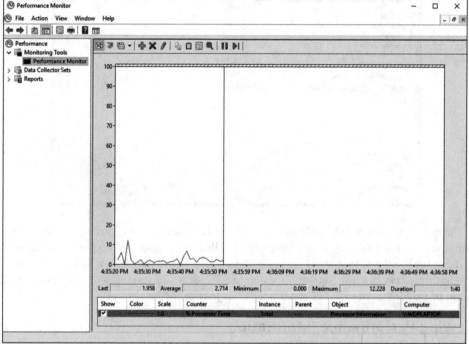

Histogram View   The *Histogram view* shows performance statistics and information using a set of relative bar charts. This view is useful if you want to see a snapshot of the latest value for a given counter. For example, if you were interested in viewing a snapshot of current system performance statistics during each refresh interval, the length of each of the bars in the display would give you a visual representation of each value. It would also allow you to compare measurements visually relative to each other. You can set the histogram to display an average measurement as well as minimum and maximum thresholds. Figure 13.3 shows a typical Histogram view.

Report View   Like the Histogram view, the *Report view* shows performance statistics based on the latest measurement. You can see an average measurement as well as minimum and maximum thresholds. This view is most useful for determining exact values because it provides information in numeric terms, whereas the Graph and Histogram views provide information graphically. Figure 13.4 provides an example of the type of information you'll see in the Report view.

FIGURE 13.3   Viewing information in Performance Monitor Histogram view

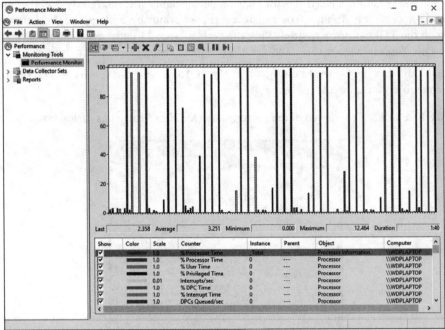

FIGURE 13.4   Viewing information in Performance Monitor Report view

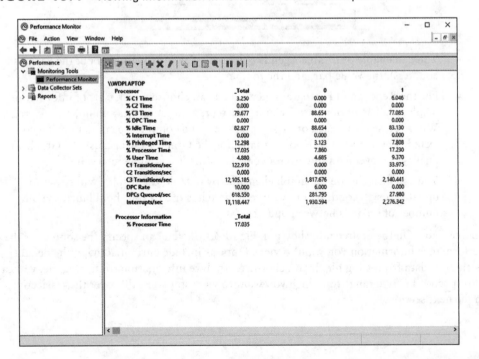

Managing Performance Monitor Properties

You can specify additional settings for viewing performance information within the properties of Performance Monitor. You can access these options by clicking the Properties button in the Taskbar or by right-clicking the Performance Monitor display and selecting Properties. You can change these additional settings by using the following tabs:

General Tab On the General tab (shown in Figure 13.5), you can specify several options that relate to Performance Monitor views:

FIGURE 13.5 General tab of the Performance Monitor Properties dialog box

- You can enable or disable legends (which display information about the various counters), the value bar, and the toolbar.
- For the Report and Histogram views, you can choose which type of information is displayed. The options are Default, Current, Minimum, Maximum, and Average. What you see with each of these options depends on the type of data being collected. These options are not available for the Graph view because the Graph view displays an average value over a period of time (the sample interval).
- You can also choose the graph elements. By default, the display will be set to update every second. If you want to update less often, you should increase the number of seconds between updates.

Source Tab On the Source tab (shown in Figure 13.6), you can specify the source for the performance information you want to view. Options include current activity (the default setting) or data from a log file. If you choose to analyze information from a log file, you can also specify the time range for which you want to view statistics. I'll cover these selections in the next section.

FIGURE 13.6   Source tab of the Performance Monitor Properties dialog box

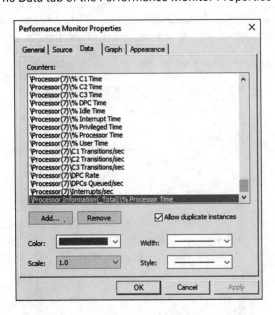

Data Tab   The Data tab (shown in Figure 13.7) lists the counters that have been added to the Performance Monitor display. These counters apply to the Chart, Histogram, and Report views. Using this interface, you can also add or remove any of the counters and change the properties, such as the width, style, and color of the line and the scale used for display.

FIGURE 13.7   The Data tab of the Performance Monitor Properties dialog box

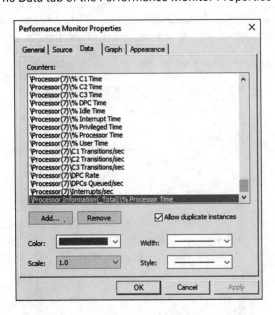

Graph Tab   On the Graph tab (shown in Figure 13.8), you can specify certain options that will allow you to customize the display of Performance Monitor views. First you can specify what type of view you want to see (Line, Histogram, or Report). Then you can add a title for the graph, specify a label for the vertical axis, choose to display grids, and specify the vertical scale range.

FIGURE 13.8   The Graph tab of the Performance Monitor Properties dialog box

Appearance Tab   Using the Appearance tab (see Figure 13.9), you can specify the colors for the areas of the display, such as the background and foreground. You can also specify the fonts that are used to display counter values in Performance Monitor views. You can change settings to find a suitable balance between readability and the amount of information shown on one screen. Finally, you can set up the properties for a border.

FIGURE 13.9   The Appearance tab of the Performance Monitor Properties dialog box

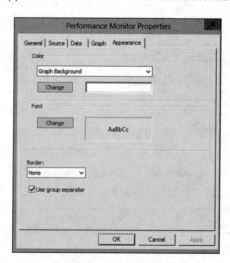

Now that you have an idea of the types of information Performance Monitor tracks and how this data is displayed, we'll take a look at another feature—saving and analyzing performance data.

Saving and Analyzing Data with Performance Logs and Alerts

One of the most important aspects of monitoring performance is that it should be done over a given period of time (referred to as a *baseline*). So far, I have shown you how you can use Performance Monitor to view statistics in real time. I have, however, also alluded to using Performance Monitor to save data for later analysis. Now let's take a look at how you can do this.

When viewing information in Performance Monitor, you have two main options with respect to the data on display:

View Current Activity   When you first open the Performance icon from the Administrative Tools folder, the default option is to view data obtained from current system information. This method of viewing measures and displays various real-time statistics on the system's performance.

View Log File Data   This option allows you to view information that was previously saved to a log file. Although the performance objects, counters, and instances may appear to be the same as those viewed using the View Current Activity option, the information itself was actually captured at a previous point in time and stored into a log file.

Log files for the View Log File Data option are created in the Performance Logs And Alerts section of the Windows 10 Performance tool.

Three items allow you to customize how the data is collected in the log files:

Counter Logs   *Counter logs* record performance statistics based on the various performance objects, counters, and instances available in Performance Monitor. The values are updated based on a time interval setting and are saved to a file for later analysis.

Circular Logging   In *circular logging*, the data that is stored within a file is overwritten as new data is entered into the log. This is a useful method of logging if you want to record information only for a certain time frame (for example, the past four hours). Circular logging also conserves disk space by ensuring that the performance log file will not continue to grow over certain limits.

Linear Logging   In *linear logging*, data is never deleted from the log files, and new information is added to the end of the log file. The result is a log file that continually grows. The benefit is that all historical information is retained.

Now that you have an idea of the types of functions that are supported by the Windows 10 Performance tools, you can learn how you can apply this information to the task at hand—monitoring and troubleshooting your Windows network.

Real World Scenario

Real-World Performance Monitoring

In our daily jobs as system engineers and administrators, we come across systems that are in need of our help. . .and may even ask for it. You, of course, check your Event Viewer and Performance Monitor and perform other tasks that help you troubleshoot. But what is really the most common problem that occurs? From my experience, I'd say that you suffer performance problems many times if your Windows 10 operating system is installed on a subpar system. Either the system's hardware minimum requirements weren't addressed or the operating system is not configured properly.

Using Other Performance-Monitoring Tools

Performance Monitor allows you to monitor different parameters of the Windows 10 operating system and associated services and applications. However, you can also use three other tools to monitor performance in Windows 10. They are Reliability Monitor, Task Manager, and Event Viewer. All three of these tools are useful for monitoring different areas of overall system performance and for examining details related to specific system events. In the following sections, you'll take a quick look at these tools and how you can best use them.

Reliability Monitor

Windows 10 Reliability Monitor is part of the Windows Reliability and Performance Monitor snap-in for Microsoft Management Console (MMC). The easiest way to access the Reliability Monitor is to type **perfmon /rel** in the Start Search box and press Enter.

The Reliability Monitor provides a system stability overview and allows an administrator to get details about events that may be impacting the Windows 10 reliability. Reliability Monitor calculates a stability index based on a certain period of time and it then shows that stability index in the System Stability Chart.

The Reliability Monitor shows information, all on their own separate lines, about application failures, Windows failures, miscellaneous failures, warnings, and information.

The Reliability Monitor shows an administrator a period of time on the Windows 10 system and the administrator can click on any of the events during that specific period of time and see what Information, Warnings, or Errors that may have happened during that time period.

Administrators can then use the information gathered by the Reliability Monitor to help diagnose the issues that the Windows 10 system may be having.

Task Manager

Performance Monitor is designed to allow you to keep track of specific aspects of system performance over time. But what do you do if you want to get a quick snapshot of what the local system is doing? Creating a System Monitor chart, adding counters, and choosing a view is overkill. Fortunately, the Windows 10 Task Manager has been designed to provide a quick overview of important system performance statistics without requiring any configuration. Better yet, it's always readily available.

You can easily access Task Manager in several ways:

- Right-click the Windows Taskbar, and then click Task Manager.
- Press Ctrl+Alt+Del, and then select Task Manager.
- Press Ctrl+Shift+Esc.
- Type **Taskman** in the Windows Search box.

Each of these methods allows you to access a snapshot of the current system performance quickly.

Once you access Task Manager, you will see the following seven tabs:

These tabs can be different on Windows client machines. For example, Windows 10 Home can vary from Windows 10 Enterprise.

Processes Tab   The Processes tab shows you all the processes that are currently running on the local computer. By default, you'll be able to view how much CPU time and memory a particular process is using. By clicking any of the columns, you can quickly sort by the data values in that particular column. This is useful, for example, if you want to find out which processes are using the most memory on your server.

By accessing the performance objects in the View menu, you can add columns to the Processes tab. Figure 13.10 shows a list of the current processes running on a Windows 10 computer.

FIGURE 13.10   Viewing process statistics and information using Task Manager

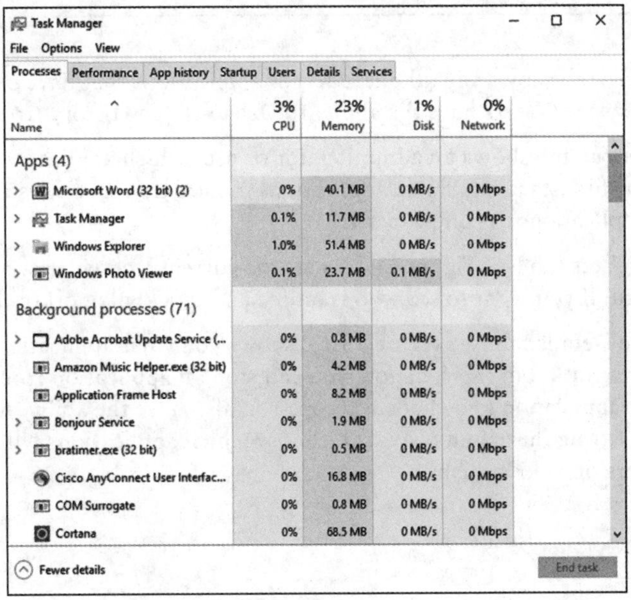

Task Manager				
File Options View				
Processes Performance App history Startup Users Details Services				
Name	**3%** CPU	**23%** Memory	**1%** Disk	**0%** Network
Apps (4)				
> ⬛ Microsoft Word (32 bit) (2)	0%	40.1 MB	0 MB/s	0 Mbps
> 🗔 Task Manager	0.1%	11.7 MB	0 MB/s	0 Mbps
> 🗔 Windows Explorer	1.0%	51.4 MB	0 MB/s	0 Mbps
> 🖼 Windows Photo Viewer	0.1%	23.7 MB	0.1 MB/s	0 Mbps
Background processes (71)				
> ⬜ Adobe Acrobat Update Service (...	0%	0.8 MB	0 MB/s	0 Mbps
🗔 Amazon Music Helper.exe (32 bit)	0%	4.2 MB	0 MB/s	0 Mbps
🗔 Application Frame Host	0%	8.2 MB	0 MB/s	0 Mbps
> 🗔 Bonjour Service	0%	1.9 MB	0 MB/s	0 Mbps
> 🗔 bratimer.exe (32 bit)	0%	0.5 MB	0 MB/s	0 Mbps
🌐 Cisco AnyConnect User Interfac...	0%	16.8 MB	0 MB/s	0 Mbps
🗔 COM Surrogate	0%	0.8 MB	0 MB/s	0 Mbps
⭕ Cortana	0%	68.5 MB	0 MB/s	0 Mbps
⌄ Fewer details				End task

Performance Tab One of the problems with using Performance Monitor to get a quick snapshot of system performance is that you have to add counters to a chart. Most system administrators are too busy to take the time to do this when all they need is basic CPU and memory information. That's where the Performance tab of Task Manager comes in. Using the Performance tab, you can view details about how memory is allocated on the computer and how much of the CPU is utilized (see Figure 13.11).

FIGURE 13.11 Viewing CPU and memory performance information using Task Manager

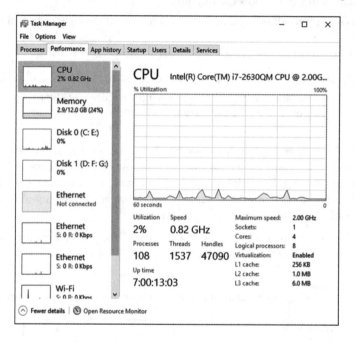

App History This tab shows you all of the recent applications that have been running on the Windows 10 system. Users have the ability to Delete Usage History from this tab.

Startup The Startup tab shows an administrator or user which applications get started when the machine first starts up. Some applications require that services start at system startup for the applications to run properly.

Users Tab The Users tab (see Figure 13.12) lists the currently active user accounts. This is particularly helpful if you want to see who is online and quickly log off or disconnect users.

Details Tab The Details tab (see Figure 13.13) shows you what applications are currently running on the system. From this location, you can stop an application from running by right-clicking the application and choosing Stop. You also have the ability to set your affinity level here. By setting the affinity, you can choose which applications will use which physical processors on your system.

FIGURE 13.12   Viewing user information using Task Manager

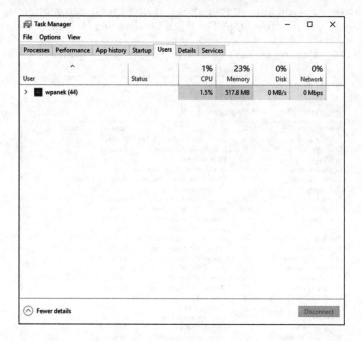

FIGURE 13.13   Viewing currently running applications using Task Manager

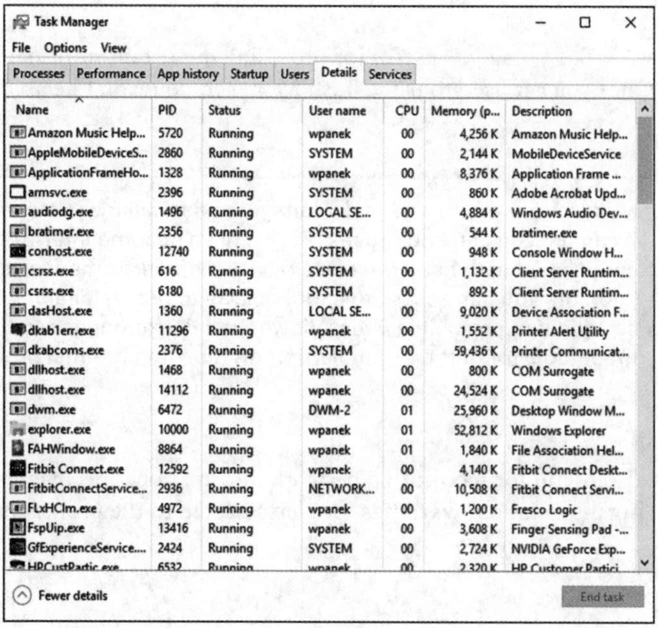

Services Tab The Services tab (see Figure 13.14) shows you what services are currently running on the system. From this location, you can stop a service from running by right-clicking the service and choosing Stop. The Open Services link launches the Services MMC.

FIGURE 13.14 Viewing services information using Task Manager

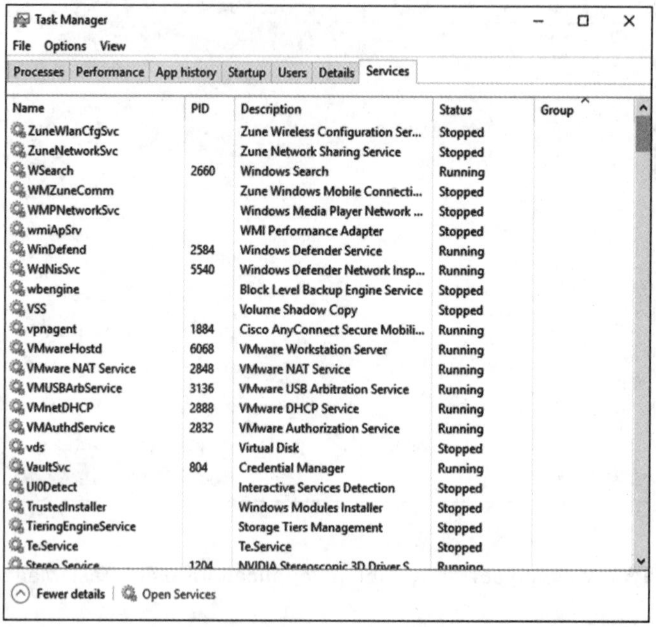

Name	PID	Description	Status	Group
ZuneWlanCfgSvc		Zune Wireless Configuration Ser...	Stopped	
ZuneNetworkSvc		Zune Network Sharing Service	Stopped	
WSearch	2660	Windows Search	Running	
WMZuneComm		Zune Windows Mobile Connecti...	Stopped	
WMPNetworkSvc		Windows Media Player Network ...	Stopped	
wmiApSrv		WMI Performance Adapter	Stopped	
WinDefend	2584	Windows Defender Service	Running	
WdNisSvc	5540	Windows Defender Network Insp...	Running	
wbengine		Block Level Backup Engine Service	Stopped	
VSS		Volume Shadow Copy	Stopped	
vpnagent	1884	Cisco AnyConnect Secure Mobili...	Running	
VMwareHostd	6068	VMware Workstation Server	Running	
VMware NAT Service	2848	VMware NAT Service	Running	
VMUSBArbService	3136	VMware USB Arbitration Service	Running	
VMnetDHCP	2888	VMware DHCP Service	Running	
VMAuthdService	2832	VMware Authorization Service	Running	
vds		Virtual Disk	Stopped	
VaultSvc	804	Credential Manager	Running	
UI0Detect		Interactive Services Detection	Stopped	
TrustedInstaller		Windows Modules Installer	Stopped	
TieringEngineService		Storage Tiers Management	Stopped	
Te.Service		Te.Service	Stopped	
Stereo Service	1204	NVIDIA Stereoscopic 3D Driver S...	Running	

Fewer details | Open Services

As you can see, Task Manager is useful for providing important information about the system quickly. Once you get used to using Task Manager, you won't be able to get by without it!

Make sure that you use Task Manager and familiarize yourself with all that it can do; you can end processes that have become intermittent, kill applications that may hang the system, view NIC performance, and so on. In addition, you can access this tool quickly to get an idea of what could be causing you problems. Event Viewer and Performance Monitor are both great tools for getting granular information on potential problems.

Event Viewer

Event Viewer is also useful for monitoring network information. Specifically, you can use the logs to view any information, warnings, or alerts related to the proper functioning of the network (see Figure 13.15). You can access Event Viewer by clicking the Start button, then selecting Windows Administrative Tools ➤ Event Viewer or by right-clicking the Start button and choosing Event Viewer. Clicking any of the items in the left pane displays the various events that have been logged for each item.

FIGURE 13.15   Event Viewer

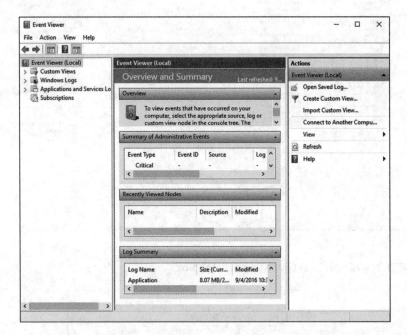

Each event that is preceded by a blue "i" icon designates that these events are informational and do not indicate problems with the network. Rather, they record benign events such as Microsoft Office startup or a service starting.

Problematic or potentially problematic events are indicated by a yellow warning icon or a red error icon (see Figure 13.16). Warnings usually indicate a problem that wouldn't prevent a service from running but might cause undesired effects with the service in question.

Error events almost always indicate a failed service, application, or function. For instance, if the dynamic registration of a DNS client fails, Event Viewer will generate an error. As you can see, errors are more severe than warnings because, in the case of DNS, the DNS client cannot participate in DNS at all.

Double-clicking any event opens its Event Properties dialog box, shown in Figure 13.17, which displays a detailed description of the event.

FIGURE 13.16 Information, errors, and warnings in Event Viewer

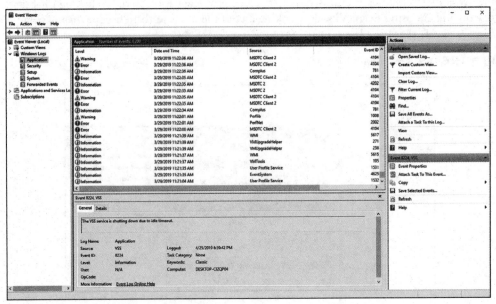

FIGURE 13.17 An Event Properties dialog box

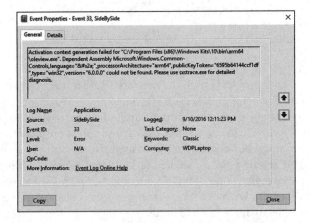

Event Viewer can display thousands of different events, so it would be impossible to list them all here. The important points of which you should be aware are the following:

- Information events are always benign.
- Warnings indicate noncritical problems.
- Errors indicate show-stopping events.

Let's discuss some of the logs and the ways that you can view data:

Applications and Services   The *applications and services logs* are part of Event Viewer where applications (for example, Hardware events) and services log their events. Internet Explorer events would be logged in this part of Event Viewer. An important log in this section is the Key Management Service log (see Figure 13.18). This is where all of your Key Management Service events get stored.

FIGURE 13.18   The applications and services logs

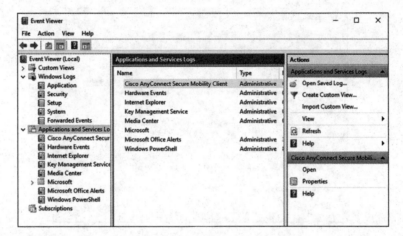

Custom Views   *Custom views* allow you to filter events (see Figure 13.19) to create your own customized look. You can filter events by event level (critical, error, warning, and so on), by logs, and by source. You also have the ability to view events occurring within a specific time frame. This allows you to look only at the events that are important to you.

FIGURE 13.19   Create Custom View dialog box

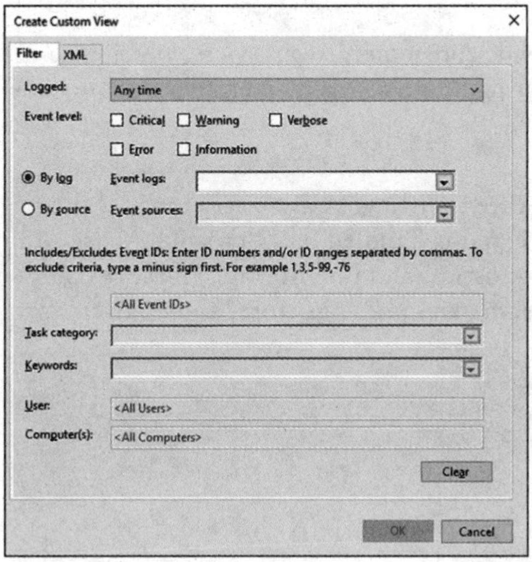

Subscriptions   *Subscriptions* allow a user to receive alerts about events that you predefine. In the Subscription Properties dialog box (see Figure 13.20), you can define what type of events you want notifications about and the notification method. The Subscriptions section is an advanced alerting service to help you watch for events.

FIGURE 13.20   Subscription Properties dialog box

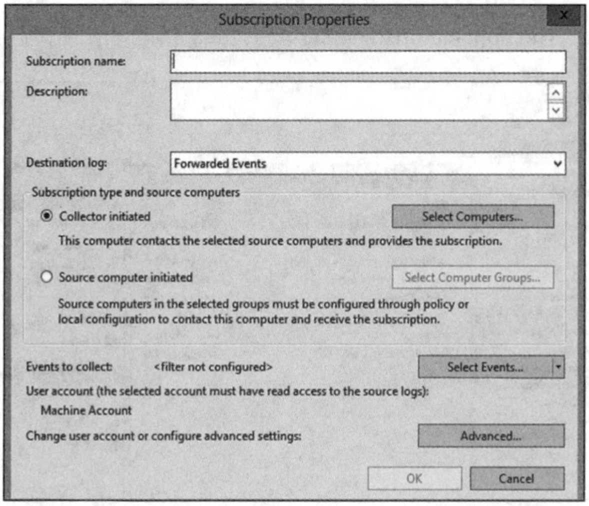

Monitor Cloud-Based Tools

Microsoft offers a couple different cloud-based tools for monitoring services. These include:

- Azure Monitor, which is designed for the cloud but can also be used to monitor on-premises systems.
- System Center Operations Manager (SCOM), which is designed for on-premises and for the cloud.

These two tools provide core monitoring services, which include alerts, service uptime tracking, health monitoring for application and infrastructure, diagnostics, and analytics.

Azure Monitor

Azure Monitor is software that runs as a service (SaaS). All of the supporting infrastructure runs in Azure and is handled by Microsoft. Azure Monitor was created to perform analytics, diagnostics, and monitoring. The core components of the infrastructure, such as collectors, metrics and logs store, and analytics are run by Microsoft (see Figure 13.21).

Many of the following figures were taken directly from Microsoft's website. Since many of the figures point out specific issues, most of the following figures were taken from Microsoft's website to demonstrate those points.

FIGURE 13.21   Azure Monitor Dashboard

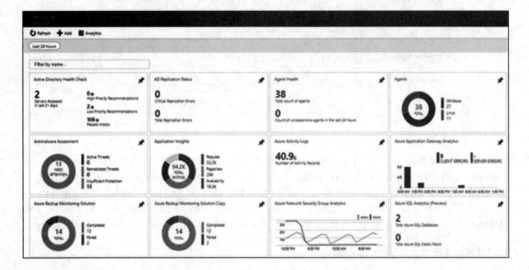

Here are a few things that you can do with Azure Monitor:

- With Application Insights you can detect and diagnose issues across applications and dependencies.

- For VMs and Azure Monitor for Containers you can compare infrastructure issues.

- Using Log Analytics for troubleshooting and deep diagnostics you can monitor data.

- Using smart alerts and automated actions you can support operations at scale.

- Using Azure dashboards and workbooks you can create visualizations

The following figure provides a view on how Azure Monitor works, shown in Figure 13.22. In the middle are the two fundamental types of data used by Azure Monitor, these are the data stores for metrics and logs. On the left side are the sources that populate the data stores. On the right side are the various functions that Azure Monitor can perform with this collected data.

As I mentioned earlier, all the data that is collected by Azure Monitor fits into one of two fundamental types, metrics and logs.

- Metrics are numerical values that express a piece of the system at a specific point in time. They are capable of supporting real-time scenarios.

- Logs contain other kinds of data, which is arranged into records with different sets of properties for each type.

FIGURE 13.22   How Azure Monitor Works

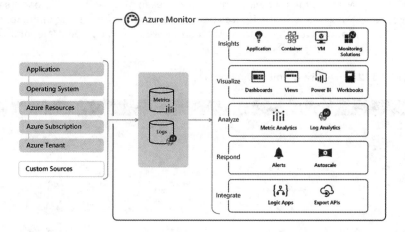

Data collected by Azure Monitor will appear on the right-hand side on the Overview page in the Azure portal. You may notice several charts that display the performance metrics. If you click on any of the graphs, it will open the data in Metrics Explorer, shown in Figure 13.23, so you can chart the values of various metrics over a given period of time. You can also view the charts or pin them to a dashboard to view them with other visualizations.

FIGURE 13.23   Metrics Explorer

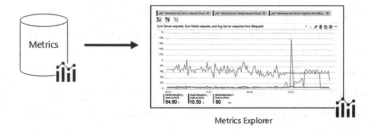

Metrics Explorer

Log data that is accumulated with Azure Monitor can be analyzed by using queries. You can create and test queries by using Log Analytics in the Azure portal (see Figure 13.24).

FIGURE 13.24   Log Analytics

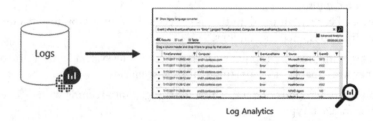

Log Analytics

Azure Monitor collects data from a wide variety of sources, including data collected from the following tiers:

- Application monitoring data is about the performance and functionality of the code written, regardless of its platform.

- Guest OS monitoring data is about the operating system on which the application is running.

- Azure resource monitoring data is about the operation of an Azure resource.

- Azure subscription monitoring data is about the operation and management of an Azure subscription, including the data on the health and operation of Azure itself.

- Azure tenant monitoring data is about the operation of tenant-level Azure services, such as Azure Active Directory.

Azure Monitor starts collecting data as soon as you create an Azure subscription and start adding resources. The Activity log records when resources were created or modified and the Metrics will show how the resources are performing.

Using the Data Collector API, Azure Monitor can collect log data from any REST client which will allow you to create custom monitoring scenarios.

Azure Monitor includes several features and tools that can provide helpful insights into your applications and other resources. These features include; Application Insights, Azure Monitor for containers, and Azure Monitor for VMs.

Application Insights

Application Insights monitors the availability, performance, and usage of web applications that are either hosted in the cloud or on-premises. It uses Azure Monitor to provide insight into an application's operations and to diagnose problems without waiting for a user to report it. Application Insights includes connection points to several different development tools and can integrate with Visual Studio to support DevOps processes (see Figure 13.25).

FIGURE 13.25   Application Insights

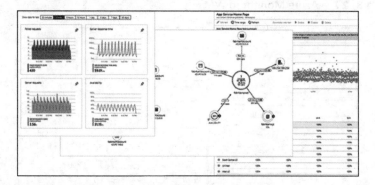

Azure Monitor for Containers

Azure Monitor for Containers is a feature intended to monitor the performance of container workloads. It shows performance visibility by collecting memory and processor metrics from controllers, nodes, and containers. Container logs are also collected (see Figure 13.26).

FIGURE 13.26 Azure Monitor for Containers

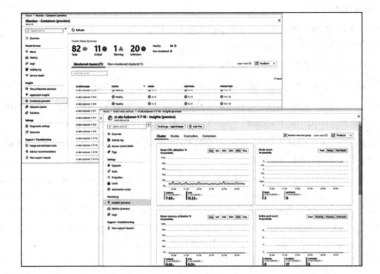

Azure Monitor for Containers monitors the performance and health of Azure Kubernetes Services or Azure Container Instances. It also collects container logs and inventory data about containers and their images.

Azure Monitor for VMs

Azure Monitor for VMs monitors the Azure virtual machines (VMs) by analyzing the performance and health of the Windows and Linux VMs. This includes support for monitoring performance and application dependencies for VMs hosted on-premises or on another cloud provider (see Figure 13.27).

FIGURE 13.27 Azure Monitor for VMs

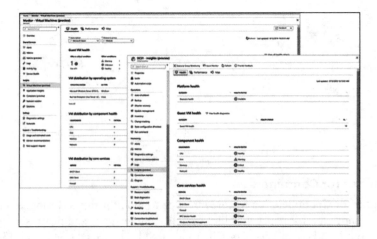

Azure Monitor for VMs delivers health monitoring for the guest Azure VMs when you're monitoring Windows and Linux virtual machines. It evaluates the health of major operating system components to determine the current health state. When it determines the guest VM is experiencing an issue, it will generate an alert.

In addition to monitoring data, Azure Monitor allows you to perform other functions to meet your needs. You can perform the following:

- Alerts inform you of critical conditions and can attempt to take corrective action. Alert rules (see Figure 13.28) provide near real-time alerting based on metric numeric values, while rules based on logs allow for complex logic across data from numerous sources. Alert rules use action groups, which contain unique sets of recipients and actions that can be shared across multiple rules.

FIGURE 13.28   Alerts

* Subscription ❶	Resource group ❶	Time Range ❶
Contoso IT - demo ⌄	mms-eus ⌄	Past Hour ⌄

Contoso IT - demo > mms-eus

Total Alerts	Smart Groups ❶	Total Alert Rules		Learn More
29	**1**	**15**		About Alerts ⧉
Since 8/1/2018, 4:38:39 PM	96.55% Reduction	Enabled 13		

SEVERITY	TOTAL ALERTS		NEW	ACKNOWLEDGED	CLOSED
Sev 0	26	▬▬▬▬▬▬	26	0	0
Sev 1	0		0	0	0
Sev 2	3	▬	3	0	0
Sev 3	0		0	0	0
Sev 4	0		0	0	0

- Autoscale allows just the amount of resources needed in order to handle application workload. Azure Monitor allows you to create rules that use metrics collected to determine when resources will be added automatically to handle increases in workload and can save money by removing idle resources. You can specify a minimum and maximum number of instances and the logic for when to increase or decrease resources (see Figure 13.29).

FIGURE 13.29   Autoscale

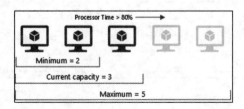

- Azure dashboards allow you to join different kinds of data, including metrics and logs, into a single pane in the Azure portal (see Figure 13.30).

FIGURE 13.30 Azure Monitor Dashboard

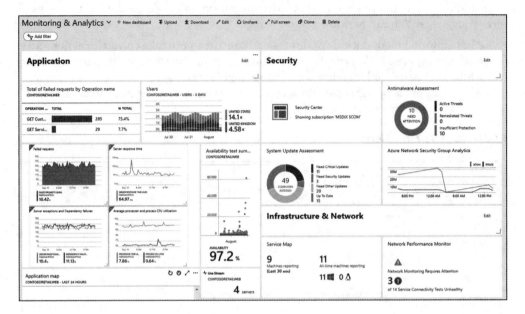

- Views show log data in Azure Monitor. Each view includes a single tile that can be depicted as bar and line charts and lists summarizing critical data (see Figure 13.31).

FIGURE 13.31 Views

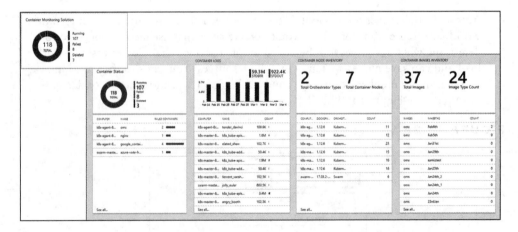

- Power BI is a business analytics service that provides interactive visualizations across a wide variety of data sources and makes data available to others either within or outside the organization. You can configure Power BI to import log data automatically from Azure Monitor (see Figure 13.32).

FIGURE 13.32   Power BI

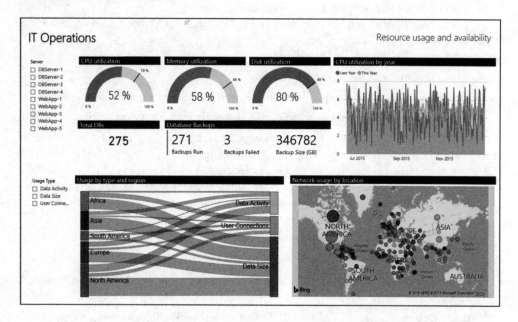

- Azure Event Hubs are a streaming platform and event breakdown service that transforms and stores data using any real-time analytics provider. Use Event Hubs to stream Azure Monitor data to partner SIEM and monitoring tools.

- Logic Apps is a service that allows the automation of tasks and processes using workflows that combine different systems and services. Activities are available that read and write metrics and logs in Azure Monitor, which allows you to build workflows integrating with a variety of other systems.

- Multiple APIs are available to read and write metrics and logs to and from Azure Monitor, as well as accessing generated alerts. You can also use them to configure and retrieve alerts.

System Center Operations Manager

From 2015 until April 2018, Operations Management Suite (OMS) was a bundle of the following Azure management services:

- Azure Automation
- Azure Backup

- Application Insights
- Operational Insights (later called Log Analytics)
- Site Recovery

The functionality of the services that were part of OMS did not change when discontinued; they were realigned under Azure Monitor.

In March 2019, Microsoft released System Center 2019.

System Center 2019 enables deployment and management of Windows Server 2019 at a larger scale to meet data center needs.

System Center 2019 provides the following:

- Tools to monitor and manage data centers.
- Support and management capabilities in the most current versions of Windows Server.
- Enables hybrid management and monitoring capabilities with Azure.

System Center 2019 is a Long Term Servicing Channel (LTSC) release and provides five years of standard support and five years of extended support.

Service Map integration with System Center Operations Manager (SCOM) allows you to automatically create distributed application diagrams in Operations Manager (OM) that are based on the dynamic dependency maps in Service Map.

Azure Management Pack allows you to perform the following tasks:

- View performance and alert metrics in SCOM
- Integrate with web application monitoring in Application Insights
- Monitor additional platform as a service (PaaS) services, such as Azure Blob Storage, Azure Data Factory, etc.

Virtual Machine Manager (VMM) 2019 (see Figure 13.33) enables simplified patching of VMs by integrating with Azure Update Management.

FIGURE 13.33   Virtual Machine Manager (VMM) 2019

Monitor Azure Device Security

Azure IoT Central Applications is an Internet of Things (IoT) application platform that lessens the load and cost of developing, managing, and maintaining enterprise-grade IoT solutions. Azure IoT Central Applications provides you with the ability to focus energy, money, and time working with a business with IoT data rather than simply maintaining and updating an intricate and continually changing IoT infrastructure. Use Microsoft Azure IoT Central Applications to monitor devices and change settings.

Azure IoT Central Applications are hosted by Microsoft, which reduces the administration overhead of managing applications.

The web user intake allows you to monitor device conditions, create rules, and manage devices and their data through their life cycle. It also enables you to act on device insights by extending IoT intelligence into line-of-business applications.

Azure IoT Central allows for the following:

- Reducing management burden
- Reducing operational costs and overheads
- Easily customizing applications while working with the following:
    - Industry-leading technologies such as Azure IoT Hub and Azure Time Series Insights
    - Enterprise-grade security features such as end-to-end encryption

Azure IoT Central Applications has four personas who interact with an Azure IoT Central Application. They are the builder, operator, administrator, and device developer. Each is described below:

- A builder is responsible for defining the types of devices that connect to the application and customizing the application for the operator.
- An operator manages the devices connected to the application.
- An administrator is responsible for administrative tasks such as managing users and roles within the application.
- A device developer creates the code that runs on a device connected to your application.

After the builder defines the types of devices that can connect to the application, a device developer creates the code to run on the devices. The device developer utilizes Microsoft's open-source Azure IoT SDKs to create the device code. These SDKs have broad language, platform, and protocol support to meet your needs to connect the devices to the Azure IoT Central Application. The SDKs can help you implement the following device capabilities:

- Create a secure connection.
- Send telemetry.
- Report status.
- Receive configuration updates.

An operator uses Azure IoT Central Applications to manage the devices. Operators perform tasks such as:

- Monitoring the devices connected to the application.
- Troubleshooting and remediating issues with devices.
- Provisioning new devices.

As a builder, you create custom rules and actions that operate over data streaming from connected devices. An operator can enable or disable these rules at the device level.

An operator can:

- Use the Device Explorer page to view, add, and delete devices connected to the Azure IoT Central Applications.
- Maintain an up-to-date inventory of devices.
- Keep device metadata up-to-date by changing the values stored in the device properties.
- Control the behavior of devices by updating a setting on a specific device from the Settings page.

To View an Individual Device

1. On the left navigation menu, choose Device Explorer.
2. Choose a device template from the Templates list.
3. In the right-hand pane of the Device Explorer page, you will see a list of devices created from that device template. Choose an individual device to see the device details page for that device (see Figure 13.34):

FIGURE 13.34   Templates

Another way an administrator can view the events collected from a specific computer in Azure is to run a query in Logs Analytics. Administrators can run the following query:

```
Event | where Computer = = "ComputerName"
```

To Add a Device to an Azure IoT Central Application

1. On the left navigation menu, choose Device Explorer.

2. Choose the device template to create a device.

3. Choose + New.

4. Choose Real or Simulated. A real device is for a physical device that you connect to your Azure IoT Central Application. A simulated device has sample data generated for you by an Azure IoT Central Application.

To connect a large number of devices to an application, you can bulk import devices using a CSV file. The CSV file should have the following columns and headers:

- IOTC_DeviceID (The device ID name should be all lowercase.)
- IOTC_DeviceName (This column is optional.)

To Bulk Register Devices in an Application

1. On the left navigation menu, choose Device Explorer.

2. On the left panel, choose the device template to bulk create the devices.

3. Select Import (see Figure 13.35).

FIGURE 13.35 Select Import

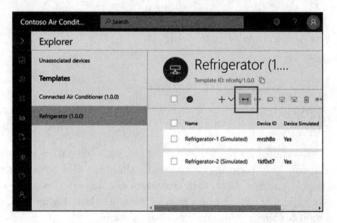

4. Select the CSV file that has the list of device IDs to be imported.

5. Device import starts once the file has been uploaded. You can track the import status at the top of the device grid.

6. Once the import completes, a success message is shown on the device grid (see Figure 13.36).

FIGURE 13.36   Import Complete Success Message

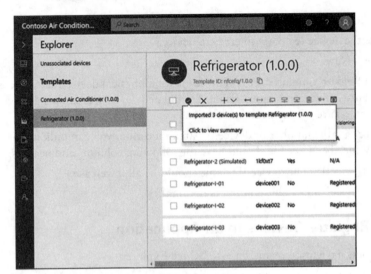

To Delete a Device (Either Real or Simulated) from an Azure IoT Central Application

1. On the navigation menu, choose Device Explorer.
2. Choose the device template of the device to delete.
3. Check the box next to the device to delete.
4. Choose Delete.

Summary

The chapter covered monitoring the Windows 10 system. Monitoring performance on Windows 10 is imperative to rooting out any issues that may affect your network. If your systems are not running at their best, your end users may experience issues such as latency, or worse, you may experience corruption in your network data. Either way, it's important to know how to monitor the performance of your systems.

We also examined how to use the various performance-related tools that are included with Windows 10. Tools such as Performance Monitor, Task Manager, and Event Viewer can help you diagnose and troubleshoot system performance issues. These tools will help you find typical problems related to memory, disk space, and any other hardware-related issues you may experience.

Knowing how to use tools to troubleshoot and test your systems is imperative, not only to passing the exam, but also to performing your duties at work. To have a smoothly running network environment, it is vital that you understand the issues related to the reliability and performance of your Windows 10 systems.

I next discussed using Monitor Cloud-Based Tools. Microsoft offers a couple different cloud-based tools for monitoring services and these include Azure Monitor and System Center Operations Manager (SCOM). These two tools provide core monitoring services, which include alerts, service uptime tracking, health monitoring for application and infrastructure, diagnostics, and analytics.

Finally, I talked about Monitor Azure Device Security. Azure IoT Central is an Internet of Things (IoT) application platform that lessens the load and cost of developing, managing, and maintaining enterprise-grade IoT solutions. Azure IoT Central provides you the ability to focus energy, money, and time working with a business with IoT data, rather than simply maintaining and updating an intricate and continually changing IoT infrastructure.

Use Microsoft Azure IoT Central Applications to monitor devices and change settings. Azure IoT Central Applications are hosted by Microsoft, which reduces the administration overhead of managing applications.

Exam Essentials

Know the importance of common performance counters.   Several important performance-related counters deal with general system performance. Know the importance of monitoring memory, print server, CPU, and network usage on a busy server.

Understand the role of other troubleshooting tools.   Windows Task Manager and Event Viewer can both be used to diagnose and troubleshoot configuration- and performance-related issues.

Understand how to troubleshoot common sources of server reliability problems.   Windows 10 has been designed to be a stable, robust, and reliable operating system. Should you experience intermittent failures, you should know how to troubleshoot device drivers and buggy system-level software.

Know Monitor Cloud-Based Tools   Microsoft offers a couple different cloud-based tools for monitoring services and these include Azure Monitor and System Center Operations Manager (SCOM).

Understand Monitor Azure Device Security   Azure IoT Central is an Internet of Things (IoT) application platform that lessens the load and cost of developing, managing, and maintaining enterprise-grade IoT solutions.

Review Questions

1. You are the administrator for an organization that uses a hybrid onsite and Azure network. You use Microsoft Azure Log Analytics workplace to collect all of the event logs from the computers at your organization. You have a computer named Laptop1. Laptop1 has Windows 10 loaded on the system. You need to view the events collected from Laptop1. Which query would an administrator run in Log Analytics?

   A. Eventview | where SourceSystem = = "laptop1"

   B. Eventview | where Computer = = "laptop1"

   C. Event | where SourceSystem = = "laptop1"

   D. Event | where Computer = = "laptop1"

2. You need to stop an application from running in Task Manager. Which tab would you use to stop an application from running?

   A. Performance

   B. Users

   C. Options

   D. Details

3. You are the network administrator for Stellacon Corporation. Users in the sales department have been complaining that the Sales application is slow to load. Using Performance Monitor, you create a baseline report for one of the computers, monitoring memory, the processor, the disk subsystem, and the network subsystem. You notice that the disk subsystem has a high load of activity. What other subsystem should you monitor before you can know for sure whether you have a disk subsystem bottleneck?

   A. Memory

   B. Processor

   C. Network

   D. Application

4. You are the network administrator for an organization that has decided to migrate to Windows 10. Part of your job requires that you are able to complete the following:

   ▪ Collect data from the local or remote Windows 10 computers on the network. You can collect data from a single computer or multiple computers concurrently.

   ▪ View data as it is being collected in real time, or historically from collected data.

   Which Window 10 application can you use to achieve your task?

   A. Event Viewer

   B. Computer Monitor

   C. Windows 7 Monitor

   D. Performance Monitor

5. You are the network administrator for a large organization. You are running Windows 10 machines throughout your network along with Windows Server 2019. You need to use Event Viewer to review event logs for Critical and Error events only. You need to see ALL of these events from the logs. What do you do to achieve this?

    A. Use the Administrative Events view.

    B. Create a custom view and choose Administrative Events.

    C. Do a search on the system log for all of these events.

    D. Create a custom view and select Critical, Error, and Verbose for all logs.

6. You are the network administrator for an organization that runs Windows Server 2019 and Windows 10. On a Windows 10 machine, you are asked by your IT manager to collect performance data for a period of three weeks. The IT manager wants CPU utilization, disk utilization, and memory utilization all included in the data collected. How should you accomplish this?

    A. Create a User Defined Data Collector set.

    B. Create a custom performance set.

    C. Create a Trace event.

    D. Create a session Data Collector set.

7. While using Performance Monitor, you use the following output mode. Which output mode are you using?

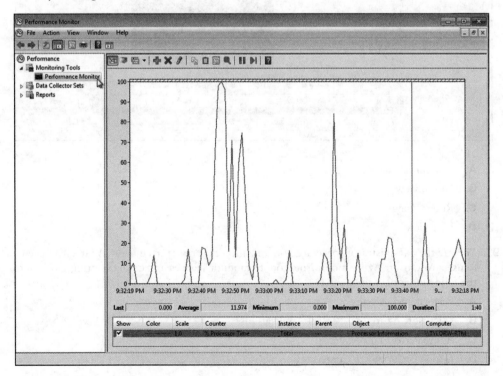

  A. Histogram Bar view

  B. Graph view

  C. Report view

  D. Line view

8. While using Performance Monitor, you use the following output mode. Which output mode are you using?

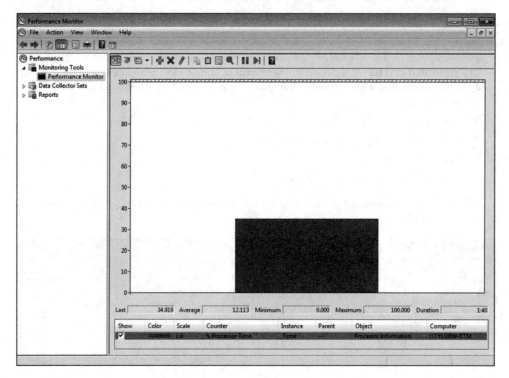

  A. Histogram Bar view

  B. Graph view

  C. Report view

  D. Line view

9. You are the administrator for a large organization that has started using Azure. You need to use a Microsoft Azure monitoring tool to monitor devices and change settings. Which of the following tools can you use?

  A. Performance Monitor

  B. Microsoft Azure IoT Central Applications

  C. Azure Performance Center

  D. Intune Performance Center

10. You are the administrator for a large training organization that uses an Azure network. You have decided to use Microsoft Azure Log Analytics workplace to collect event logs from all of the different Azure connected machines. You have a computer named AzureSystem1 and AzureSystem1 uses Windows 10. An administrator wants you to view the events collected from AzureSystem1. Which query would an administrator run in Log Analytics?

    A. Eventview | where SourceSystem = = "AzureSystem1"

    B. Event | where Computer = = "AzureSystem1"

    C. Eventview | where Computer = = "AzureSystem1"

    D. Event | where SourceSystem = = "AzureSystem1"

Appendix

Answer to Review Questions

Chapter 1: Windows 10 Installation

1. A. The Boot Configuration Data (BCD) store contains boot information parameters that were previously found in Boot.ini in older versions of Windows. To edit the boot options in the BCD store, use the bcdedit utility, which can be launched only from a command prompt.

2. B. By modifying the changes on the local Group Policy, you can manually configure your Windows Update settings. You can automatically configure the Windows Update settings by creating a server-issued Group Policy Object (GPO).

3. A. The /unattend option can be used with the Setup.exe command to initiate an unattended installation of Windows 10. You should also specify the location of the answer file to use when using the Setup.exe utility.

4. D. You would use the Sysprep utility. The /generalize option prevents system-specific information from being included in the image.

5. A. The DISM utility with the /get-drivers switch allows you to find out which drivers are installed on the .wim.

6. D. DISM is a command-line utility that can be used to create and manage Windows 10 image (.wim) files. You can configure a reference installation as desired and then use DISM to create an image of the installation that can then be deployed to the remaining computers.

7. B. WDSUTIL is a command-line utility that can be used to configure the WDS server. Several other configuration options need to be specified on the WDS server, and you can set them using WDSUTIL.

8. C. Windows System Image Manager (SIM) is used to create unattended answer files in Windows 10. It uses a GUI-based interface to set up and configure the most common options that are used within an answer file.

9. C. You enable WDS servers to respond to client requests through the Windows Deployment Services (WDS) Microsoft Management Console (MMC) Snap-in. In the PXE Properties dialog box, enable the option Respond To Client Computers.

10. B. The /generalize option prevents system-specific information from being included in the image. The Sysprep.exe command can be used with a variety of options. You can see a complete list by typing **sysprep/?** at a command-line prompt.

Chapter 2: Configuring Users

1. A. The Group Policy Result Tool is accessed through the GPResult command-line utility. The gpresult command displays the resulting set of policies that were enforced on the computer and the specified user during the logon process.

2. A. Audit Account Logon Events is used to track when a user logs on, logs off, or makes a network connection. You can configure auditing for success or failure, and audited events can be tracked through Event Viewer.

3. B, C. The password Abcde! meets complexity requirements because it is at least six characters long and contains an uppercase letter, lowercase letters, and a symbol. The password 1247445Np meets complexity requirements because it is at least six characters long and contains an uppercase letter, a lowercase letter, and numbers. Complex passwords must be at least six characters long and contain three of the four types of characters—uppercase letters, lowercase letters, numbers, and symbols.

4. B. Windows 10 LGPOs allow you to configure all of the above except for folder redirection. Folder redirection needs to be done through a server based Group Policy Object (GPO).

5. D. Account Lockout Policy, a subset of Account Policies, is used to specify options that prevent a user from attempting multiple failed logon attempts. If the Account Lockout Threshold value is exceeded, the account will be locked. The account can be reset based on a specified amount of time or through administrator intervention.

6. D. The Restore Files and Directories user right allows a user to restore files and directories regardless of file and directory permissions. Assigning this user right is an alternative to making a user a member of the Backup Operators group.

7. B. The Enforce Password History policy allows the system to keep track of a user's password history for up to 24 passwords. This prevents a user from using the same password over and over again.

8. B. Account Lockout Policy, a subset of Account Policies, is used to specify options that prevent a user from attempting multiple failed logon attempts. If the Account Lockout Threshold value is exceeded, the account will be locked. The account can be reset based on a specified amount of time or through administrator intervention.

9. C. The New-LocalUser command allows you to create a new local user on a Windows 10 machine.

10. A. You do not want this user to have any administrator rights. To allow this user to change Windows Update manually, you must set this in an LGPO.

Chapter 3: Managing Data

1. A, B. The Sales group needs Modify on the NTFS security and Change shared permission settings in order to do their job.

2. D. Windows 10 comes with a feature called BitLocker Drive Encryption. BitLocker encrypts the drive so if it's removed or stolen, the data can't be accessed. To configure BitLocker, you must either use a Local Group Policy or use the BitLocker icon in Control Panel.

3. A, C, D. BitLocker Drive Encryption is a data protection feature available in Windows Education, Enterprise, and Professional editions of Windows 10.

4. D. When both NTFS and share permissions have been applied, the system looks at the effective rights for NTFS and share permissions and then applies the most restrictive of the cumulative permissions. If a resource has been shared and you access it from the local computer where the resource resides, then you will be governed only by the NTFS permissions.

5. A. The easiest way to manage this transition is to simply rename Rick's account to John. It is very important to remember that rights and permissions get associated to a user's SID number and not a username. By renaming Rick's account to John, John will automatically have all of the rights and permissions to any resource that Rick had access to.

6. E. By giving Tom Modify on the NTFS security setting, you're giving him just enough to do his job. You could also give Sales or Finance the Modify permission, but then everyone in those groups would be able to delete, change, and do more than they all need. Also, Tom does not need Full Control to change or delete files.

7. C, E. The Admin group needs Full Control on the NTFS security and shared permission settings in order to do their job. To be able to give other users permissions, you must have the Full Control permission.

8. D. Smart cards are plastic cards (the size of a credit card) that can be used in combination with other methods of authentication. This process of using a smart card along with another authentication method is called two-factor authentication or multi-factor Authentication.

9. A. Filename extensions for known files are hidden by default. If you want to be able to see the filename extension for all files, you must uncheck the box Hide Extensions For Known File Types.

10. B. Microsoft BitLocker Administration and Monitoring (MBAM) will allow the IT department to use enterprise-based utilities for managing and maintaining BitLocker and BitLocker To Go.

Chapter 4: Managing the Windows 10 Environment

1. A. In Windows 10, you can edit the Registry with REGEDIT or REGEDT32. You should always use extreme caution when editing the Registry because improper configurations can cause the computer to fail to boot.

2. D. When the computer enters sleep mode, the data will be saved to memory, and the computer will be put into a power-saving state. Sleep mode combines the features of standby and hibernation so that all data is saved, but the computer restores faster than if the computer was put into hibernation mode.

3. A. You should use the Windows ReadyDrive technology to help speed the resume time of your computer after it has been put into hibernation mode. ReadyDrive is a new technology that is used in conjunction with hybrid hard disk drives, which combine flash memory with standard hard disk technology. This allows data to be stored in flash memory, which enables the hard disk to remain spun down longer and also improves the time required for the computer to resume after being put into hibernation mode.

4.   C. When a Windows 10 computer is configured with the Power Saver power plan, the computer's display and hard disk will be turned off after 20 minutes of inactivity in order to conserve energy. The computer will be put into sleep mode after one hour of inactivity when using the Power Saver power plan.

5.   A. The easiest way to configure the Desktop is by right-clicking an open area of the Desktop and choosing Personalize.

6.   C. The easiest way to recover a deleted file is to restore it from the Recycle Bin. The Recycle Bin holds all of the files and folders that have been deleted as long as there is space on the disk. From this utility, you can retrieve or permanently delete files.

7.   C. You can configure what actions will occur if the service fails to start on the Recovery tab of the service's Properties dialog box. For example, you can configure the service to attempt to restart, or you can configure the computer to reboot.

8.   A, C. In Windows 10, you can edit the Registry with REGEDIT or REGEDT32. You should always use extreme caution when editing the Registry because improper configurations can cause the computer to fail to boot.

9.   A. You configure keyboard and mouse properties in Control Panel.

10. C. On a laptop computer, Denise can use the battery meter to view the amount of battery power available and to change the power plan configured for the computer.

Chapter 5: Configuring Security and Devices

1.   C. Running the Sigverif.exe program will run a check against all the drivers installed on your machine and then notify you of any drivers that are unsigned.

2.   A. The Print Management tool has a utility called Migrate Printers. This utility allows an administrator to migrate the print server queues from one machine and transfer those print settings to another machine.

3.   C. If you need to get a stalled computer up and running as quickly as possible, you should start with the Driver Rollback option. This option is used when you've made changes to your computer's hardware drivers and now you have issues.

4.   B. The Roll Back Driver option is the easiest way to roll back to a known good driver. You could also use the System Restore utility to roll back your computer to a known restore point if you make harmful changes to your computer, but Driver Rollback is easier and faster.

5. D. The `Printbrm.exe` command should be run from a command prompt with administrative permission. This command is the command-line version of the Print Management tool.

6. B. When you disable the drivers, the drivers are still installed on the Windows 10 system but they are not active. Administrators like to use the disable option so the user can always re-enable the drivers later for use.

7. C. Windows Defender Firewall, which is included with Windows 10, helps to prevent unauthorized users or malicious software from accessing your computer. Windows Defender Firewall does not allow unsolicited traffic (traffic that was not sent in response to a request) to pass through the firewall.

8. C. Device Manager is the utility included with Windows 10 that allows you to configure and manage your devices and hardware. You can also configure your drivers within Device Manager.

9. A. Driver rollback allows you to replace a newly installed driver with the previous driver. You can do the driver rollback using the Device Manager utility.

10. B. To get the latest drivers for any piece of hardware, you need to use the Upgrade Drivers button in Device Manager. After the upgrade button is chosen, you can use downloaded drivers or drivers from a new DVD.

Chapter 6: Configuring Network Connectivity

1. A, C. The `ipconfig /release` and the `ipconfig /renew` commands will allow your machine to receive a new IP address from the DHCP server.

2. C. Because the first octet starts with 192, it's a Class C. If the first octet starts with 1–126, it's a Class A. 128–191 is a Class B, and 192–223 is a Class C.

3. C. The default gateway is the router's IP address. The default gateway allows you to get from your subnet to another subnet.

4. D. The DNS server turns a hostname into an IP address so you can connect to a machine by the machine name. If you can connect to a machine by using the TCP/IP address but not the name, DNS is the issue.

5. D. Ipconfig /registerdns will automatically register the Windows 10 machine with the DNS server. The registration will include the Windows 10 machine name and the IP address.

6. A, B. You have to use either a Class A or Class B. Class C addresses can only handle 254 users. 10.x.x.x and 172.16.x.x are both able to handle the 675 users and they are both internal private address schemes that anyone can use.

7. A. Create a new Workgroup and add all the employees to the Workgroup. You don't want to use a HomeGroup because even though it's five users, you need to make sure that permissions are setup properly so that users can't look at data of other users. Because they are never going to get any larger, there is no reason to have them use any version of Active Directory or Windows Server.

8. C, D. Class A addresses go from 1–126 (127 is used for the loopback address). Class B addresses go from 128–191, and Class C addresses are from 192–223.

9. A, B. Class A addresses go from 1–126 (127 is used for the loopback address). Class B addresses go from 128–191, and Class C addresses are from 192–223.

10. A. Azure is Microsoft's cloud-based Active Directory subscription. Azure is great if you don't want to deal with the worries of managing and maintaining a server room and all of the hardware and it's also great for accessing Active Directory from anywhere in the world.

Chapter 7: Configuring Recovery

1. D. All of the applications that are running on the Windows 10 machine will show up under the Details tab. Right-click the application and end the process.

2. A. The Roll Back Driver option is the fastest way to return the driver to the previous version. You could also use System Restore, but rolling a Driver back is easier and faster.

3. C. The Back Up Now button allows you to start a backup and configure a Windows 10 backup.

4. D. If you need to back up and restore your Windows 10 machine, you need to use the Windows 10 Backup and Restore Center.

5. C. Using images allows you to back up and restore your entire Windows 10 machine instead of just certain parts of data.

6. A. If you need to disable previous versions on the D: volume, this needs to be done from the System Protection settings in the computer system properties.

7. A. You have to manually copy all the encrypted files because the backup software will not work with the encrypted files in Windows 10.

8. C, D. There are two ways to repair system files on Windows 10. You can do it by using the installation disc and choosing Repair during the installation, or you can boot to the advanced options and select Repair Your Computer.

9. A, B, C, D. Restore points allow you to bring your system back to a previous point in time, and they should be created at all of the times listed.

10. A. Starting the computer in Safe Mode loads the basic VGA drivers and allows you to fix any video issues, including using the Driver Rollback utility.

Chapter 8: Installing and Updating Windows 10

1. **A, E.** If you are going to implement the Secure Boot feature of Windows 10, then make sure the system firmware is set up as Unified Extensible Firmware Interface (UEFI) and not BIOS. You also need to make sure the disks are converted from Master Boot Record (MBR) disks to a GUID Partition Table (GPT) disk.

2. **B.** Windows Autopilot profiles allow an administrator to choose how the Windows 10 system will be set up and configured on Azure AD and Intune.

3. **B.** When installing or upgrading Windows 10, the version of Windows 10 that is installed must match the CPU version. For example, if your system is a 32-bit system, you must use a 32-bit version of Windows 10. If your system is a 64-bit system, you can install either the 32-bit or 64-bit version of Windows 10.

4. **D.** You would use the Sysprep utility. The /generalize option prevents system-specific information from being included in the image.

5. **A.** The DISM utility with the /get-drivers switch allows you to find out which drivers are installed on the WIM.

6. **D.** Windows Autopilot profiles allow an administrator to choose how the Windows 10 system will be setup and configured on Azure AD and Intune.

7. **B.** wdsutil is a command-line utility that can be used to configure the WDS server. Several other configuration options need to be specified on the WDS server, and you can set them using wdsutil.

8. **C.** Windows System Image Manager (SIM) is used to create unattended answer files in Windows 10. It uses a GUI-based interface to set up and configure the most common options that are used within an answer file.

9. **C.** You enable WDS servers to respond to client requests through the Windows Deployment Services (WDS) Microsoft Management Console (MMC) snap-in. In the PXE Properties dialog box, enable the option Respond To Client Computers.

10. **B.** The /generalize option prevents system-specific information from being included in the image. The sysprep.exe command can be used with a variety of options. You can see a complete list by typing sysprep/? at a command-line prompt.

Chapter 9: Managing Authentication

1. **B.** Azure AD Identity Protection allows an Azure administrator to use the same type of protection that Microsoft uses to protect and secure users' identities.

2. D. Administrators can use the New-AzureADPolicy command to create a new Azure AD policy.

3. A. The Get-AzureADPolicy command allows an Azure admin to view an Azure AD policy.

4. C. The Password Reset section of Azure AD allows an administrator to determine if they want to enable Self-service password resets (SSPR). If an organization decides to enable this feature, users will be able to reset their own passwords or unlock their accounts.

5. B. Azure AD Connect is a Microsoft utility that allows you to set up a hybrid design between Azure AD and your on-site AD. Azure AD Connect allows both versions of AD to connect to each other.

6. B. Administrators can use the Add-AzureADApplicationPolicy command to add an application policy.

7. D. Administrators can use the Set-AzureADPolicy command to update an Azure AD policy.

8. D. Administrators can't change or delete the initial domain name that is created but Azure administrators do have the ability to add their organization's new or existing domain names to the list of supported names.

9. A. Administrators can use the Custom Domain Names section of Azure AD to create your organization's new or existing domain names to the list of supported names.

10. B. Administrators can use the Get-AzureADDirectorySetting command to view their directory settings.

Chapter 10: Managing Devices

1. D. You can upgrade your devices by using a device configuration profile. The option that you want to configure is Edition Upgrade. Edition Upgrade allows you to upgrade Windows 10 (and later) devices to a newer version of Windows.

2. B. One of the options you have in device configuration profiles is the ability to set up custom profiles. Custom profile settings allow an Intune administrator to configure options that are not automatically included with Intune. For example, as an administrator, you can set a custom profile that allows you to create ADMX-backed policy or even enable self-service password resets.

3. A. Kiosk settings allow an administrator to configure a Windows 10 (and later) device to run a single application or run many applications. Kiosk systems are normally designed in a location where many people can use the same device and that device will only run limited applications.

4. A. One of the options that you can set in device configuration profiles is the ability to setup custom profiles. Custom profile settings allow an Intune Administrator to configure options that are not automatically included with Intune. For example, an administrator can set a custom profile that allows you to create ADMX-backed policy or even enable self-service password resets.

5. D. Both Windows 10 and Windows XP Professional support FAT32 and NTFS, so both file systems will be viewable on both operating systems.

6. D. Dynamic disks are supported by all Windows operating systems above Windows Server 2000. Windows 10 supports mirrored volumes.

7. A. The Disk Defragmenter utility is used to rearrange files so that they are stored contiguously on the disk. This optimizes access to those files. You can also defragment disks through the command-line utility Defrag.

8. B. Endpoint protection allows you to set Windows 10 (and above) options for BitLocker and Windows Defender settings. For example, you can set Windows Defender for a threat score setting. If a user with a high threat score rating attempts to access cloud-based resources, you can stop this device from accessing your resources.

9. D. One of the options that you can set in device configuration profiles is the ability to setup custom profiles. Custom profile settings allow an Intune Administrator to configure options that are not automatically included with Intune. For example, an administrator can set a custom profile that allows you to create ADMX-backed policy or even enable self-service password resets.

10. C. One of the advantages to using Azure is the ability to protect corporate data by ensuring that users and devices meet certain requirements. When using Intune, this is referred to as compliance policies. Compliance policies are rules and settings that your users and their devices must follow in order to connect and access Intune.

Chapter 11: Planning and Managing Microsoft Intune

1. A. Administrators have the ability to limit and monitor network usage by configuring the network as a metered network. Network metering allows network downloading to be watched or metered and then administrators can charge users or departments for the network usage.

2. D. To review a policy report on the deployment status for the Windows 10 update ring, sign in to the Microsoft Endpoint Manager Admin Center. Then, select Devices ➤ Overview ➤ Software Update Status. To review software updates, select Monitor, and then below Software Updates, select Per Update Ring Deployment State and choose the deployment ring to review.

3. C, D. As long as the salesperson's personally owned Windows 10 laptop is being managed by the management infrastructure agent, administrators can use the remote wipe feature. When you do a remote wipe, all of the company's data gets wiped from the device.

4. D. An Apple Push Notification service (APNs) certificate must be imported from Apple so that the school can manage iOS devices. This certificate allows Intune administrators to manage iOS.

5. A. You will want to go to device configuration. To do this sign in to the Azure portal and click on Intune. Create a new device configuration profile by going to Device Configuration ➢ Profiles ➢ Create Profile. Configure any needed settings. Click OK and then click Create.

6. C, D. If using Configuration Manager, Administrators must configure Configuration Manager to manage mobile devices. To do this, it requires administrators to create a Windows Intune subscription and use a connector to synchronize user accounts.

7. A. Before you can setup any Intune policies regarding applications, you must first add that application to Intune.

8. C. By default, licensed users can add up to 15 devices to their accounts. Device Administrators have the ability to add devices to Intune but users do have the ability to enroll 15 devices on their own. The limit was changed from 5 to 15 for a user. So, a single Intune user can now enroll up to 15 devices using a single Intune license.

9. D. Sideloading an application means that you are loading an application that you already own or one that your company created into a delivery system (i.e. Intune, Microsoft Store, or images).

10. B, C. Intune Administrators have the ability to setup different notifications to different emails based on alert type. So you can send all alerts, critical alerts, warnings, and informational alerts to different IT members.

Chapter 12: Managing Security

1. C. Administrators can use Windows Defender Application Control to ensure that only applications that you explicitly allow can run on Windows 10 computers.

2. A. Windows Defender Exploit Guard helps protect your system from common malware hacks that use executable files and scripts to attack applications like Microsoft Office (for example, Outlook). Windows Defender Exploit Guard also looks for suspicious scripts or behavior that is not normal on the Windows 10 system.

3. A. Administrators can use Windows Defender Credential Guard to help isolate critical files so that only system software with proper privileges can access those critical files.

4. D. Windows Defender Firewall with Advanced Security allows you to set up inbound and outbound rules by using Windows Firewall.

5. C. To configure your Windows Firewall to allow DNS inbound and outbound traffic, you would set up port 53. Port 20 is for FTP data, port 25 is for SMTP (mail), and port 80 is HTTP.

6. B. Windows Defender Exploit Guard helps protect your system from common malware hacks that use executable files and scripts that attack applications like Microsoft Office (for example, Outlook). Windows Defender Exploit Guard also looks for suspicious scripts or behavior that is not normal on the Windows 10 system.

7. B. To configure your Windows Defender Firewall to allow SMTP inbound and outbound traffic, you would set up port 25. Port 20 is for FTP data, Port 53 is for DNS, and Port 80 is HTTP.

8. A. Administrators can use Windows Defender Application Control to ensure that only applications that you explicitly allow can run on Windows 10 computers.

9. D. Windows Defender Exploit Guard helps protect your system from common malware hacks that use executable files and scripts to attack applications like Microsoft Office (for example, Outlook). Windows Defender Exploit Guard also looks for suspicious scripts or behavior that is not normal on the Windows 10 system.

10. A. To configure your Windows Defender Firewall to allow FTP traffic, you would set up ports 20 and 21. Port 25 is for mail and Port 53 is for DNS. Port 80 is HTTP, and Port 443 is for HTTPS.

Chapter 13: Configuring Auditing

1. D. Administrator can view the events collected from a specific computer in Azure is to run a query in the Logs Analytics.

2. D. All of the applications that are running on the Windows 10 machine will show up under the Details tab. Right-click the application and end the process.

3. A. You should check the memory counters. If your computer does not have enough memory, it can cause excessive paging, which may be perceived as a disk subsystem bottleneck.

4. D. Performance Monitor allows you to collect data from your local computer or remote Windows 10 machine from a single computer or multiple computers concurrently, view data as it is being collected in real time, or historically from collected data, have full control over the selection of what data will be collected, by selecting which specific objects and counters will be collected, choose the sampling parameters that will be used, meaning the time interval that you want to use for collecting data points and the time period that will be used for data collection.

5. D. You would have to create a custom view to achieve this task. You could not use the Administrative Events view (default custom view) because it also includes all warnings.

6. A. Data collector sets are used to collect data into a log so that the data can be reviewed. You can view the log files with Performance Monitor.

7. D. The graphic is an example of a Line view output. The three options are Line view, Histogram Bar view, and Report view.

8. A. The graphic is an example of a Histogram Bar view output. The three options are Line view, Histogram Bar view, and Report view.

9. B. Use Microsoft Azure IoT Central Applications to monitor devices and change settings. Azure IoT Central Applications are hosted by Microsoft, which reduces the administration overhead of managing applications.

10. B. Administrator can view the events collected from a specific computer in Azure is to run a query in the Logs Analytics.

Index

M

X–Y–Z

Online Test Bank

Register to gain one year of FREE access after activation to the online test bank to help you study for your MCA Modern Desktop Administrator certification exams—included with your purchase of this book! All of the chapter review questions and the practice tests in this book are included in the online test bank so you can practice in a timed and graded setting.

Register and Access the Online Test Bank

To register your book and get access to the online test bank, follow these steps:

1. Go to bit.ly/SybexTest (this address is case sensitive)!
2. Select your book from the list.
3. Complete the required registration information, including answering the security verification to prove book ownership. You will be emailed a pin code.
4. Follow the directions in the email or go to www.wiley.com/go/sybextestprep.
5. Find your book on that page and click the "Register or Login" link with it. Then enter the pin code you received and click the "Activate PIN" button.
6. On the Create an Account or Login page, enter your username and password, and click Login or, if you don't have an account already, create a new account.
7. At this point, you should be in the test bank site with your new test bank listed at the top of the page. If you do not see it there, please refresh the page or log out and log back in.